Legal Restraints on the Use of Military Force

Legal Restraints on the Use of Military Force

Collected Essays by Michael Bothe

Edited by

Thilo Marauhn and Barry de Vries

BRILL
NIJHOFF

LEIDEN | BOSTON

Library of Congress Cataloging-in-Publication Data

Names: Marauhn, Thilo, editor. | Vries, Barry de, editor.
Title: Legal restraints on the use of military force : collected essays by
    Michael Bothe / edited by Thilo Marauhn and Barry de Vries.
Description: Leiden, The Netherlands : Koninklijke Brill NV, [2021] |
    Includes bibliographical references. | In English, with some
    chapters in French.
Identifiers: LCCN 2020047502 (print) | LCCN 2020047503 (ebook) |
    ISBN 9789004380585 (hardback) | ISBN 9789004380592 (e-book)
Subjects: LCSH: War (International law) | Intervention (International law) |
    Terrorism (International law) | Nuclear nonproliferation. | United Nations.
    Security Council. | Humanitarian law. | Combatants and non-combatants
    (International law) | War--Protection of civilians. | War victims--Legal
    status, laws, etc.
Classification: LCC KZ6385 .L445 2021 (print) | LCC KZ6385 (ebook) |
    DDC 341.6/3--dc23
LC record available at https://lccn.loc.gov/2020047502
LC ebook record available at https://lccn.loc.gov/2020047503

Typeface for the Latin, Greek, and Cyrillic scripts: "Brill". See and download: brill.com/brill-typeface.

ISBN 978-90-04-38058-5 (hardback)
ISBN 978-90-04-38059-2 (e-book)

Copyright 2021 by Koninklijke Brill NV, Leiden, The Netherlands.
Koninklijke Brill NV incorporates the imprints Brill, Brill Hes & De Graaf, Brill Nijhoff, Brill Rodopi,
Brill Sense, Hotei Publishing, mentis Verlag, Verlag Ferdinand Schöningh and Wilhelm Fink Verlag.
All rights reserved. No part of this publication may be reproduced, translated, stored in a retrieval system,
or transmitted in any form or by any means, electronic, mechanical, photocopying, recording or otherwise,
without prior written permission from the publisher.
Requests for re-use and/or translations must be addressed to Koninklijke Brill NV via brill.com or copyright.com.

This book is printed on acid-free paper and produced in a sustainable manner.

Contents

lic Information on the Selected Essays of Michael
Bibl
Bo

uction to Michael Bothe's Writings on "Legal Restraints on
Military Force"   1

1
;

nd Non-Legal Norms
ıingful Distinction in International Relations?   15

mites des Pouvoirs du Conseil de Sécurité   49

rity Council's Targeted Sanctions against Presumed Terrorists
Need to Comply with Human Rights Standards   63

.mits to the Use of Force Imposed by International Law
Current Problems   81

5   Will Current International Crises Result in Structural Shifts in
International Law?   147

PART 2
International Security

6   Terrorism and the Legality of Pre-emptive Force   165

7   Peacekeeping and International Humanitarian Law
Friends or Foes?   181

PART 3
Arms Control

8   Obligations and Protection of Individuals   193

9   Verification of Disarmament Treaties   205

10   Non-Proliferation of Weapons of Mass Destruction
Treaty Regimes between Efficiency and Discrimination   216

PART 4
The Law of Armed Conflict: General Questions

11   Le Droit de la Guerre Et les Nations Unies
A Propos des Incidents Armés au Congo   237

12   The Historical Evolution of International Humanitarian Law, International Human Rights Law, Refugee Law and International Criminal Law   334

13   Multiculturalism and the Development of International Humanitarian Law   343

14   Setting the Scene
New Technologies – New Challenges for IHL?   353

15   De Facto Control of Land or Sea Areas
Its Relevance under the Law of Armed Conflict, in Particular Air and Missile Warfare   359

16   The International Committee of the Red Cross and the Additional Protocols of 1977   373

PART 5
Conduct of Hostilities: Protecting the Environment

17   Protection of the Environment in Times of Armed Conflict   399

Contents

Bibliographic Information on the Selected Essays of Michael Bothe IX

An Introduction to Michael Bothe's Writings on "Legal Restraints on the Use of Military Force" 1

PART 1
Basic Issues

1 Legal and Non-Legal Norms
A Meaningful Distinction in International Relations? 15

2 Les Limites des Pouvoirs du Conseil de Sécurité 49

3 Security Council's Targeted Sanctions against Presumed Terrorists
The Need to Comply with Human Rights Standards 63

4 Limits to the Use of Force Imposed by International Law
Current Problems 81

5 Will Current International Crises Result in Structural Shifts in International Law? 147

PART 2
International Security

6 Terrorism and the Legality of Pre-emptive Force 165

7 Peacekeeping and International Humanitarian Law
Friends or Foes? 181

PART 3
Arms Control

8 Obligations and Protection of Individuals 193

9 Verification of Disarmament Treaties 205

10 Non-Proliferation of Weapons of Mass Destruction
Treaty Regimes between Efficiency and Discrimination 216

PART 4
The Law of Armed Conflict: General Questions

11 Le Droit de la Guerre Et les Nations Unies
A Propos des Incidents Armés au Congo 237

12 The Historical Evolution of International Humanitarian Law,
International Human Rights Law, Refugee Law and International
Criminal Law 334

13 Multiculturalism and the Development of International
Humanitarian Law 343

14 Setting the Scene
New Technologies – New Challenges for IHL? 353

15 De Facto Control of Land or Sea Areas
*Its Relevance under the Law of Armed Conflict, in Particular Air and
Missile Warfare* 359

16 The International Committee of the Red Cross and the Additional
Protocols of 1977 373

PART 5
Conduct of Hostilities: Protecting the Environment

17 Protection of the Environment in Times of Armed Conflict 399

CONTENTS VII

18 Legal Restraints on Targeting
Protection of Civilian Population and the Changing Faces of Modern Conflict 407

19 The Ethics, Principles and Objectives of Protection of the Environment in Times of Armed Conflict 421

20 The ILC Special Rapporteur's Preliminary Report on the Protection of the Environment in Relation to Armed Conflicts
An Important Step in the Right Direction 440

21 Protection of the Environment in Relation to Armed Conflicts
A Preliminary Comment on the Work of the International Law Commission 452

PART 6
Protected Persons and Human Rights, Relief

22 Le Sort des Blessés et Malades
Un but Fondamental de la Croix-Rouge 473

23 Relief Actions
The Position of the Recipient State 493

24 Human Rights Law and International Humanitarian Law as Limits of Security Council Action 501

PART 7
Occupation

25 Beginning and End of Occupation 529

26 Limits of the Right of Expropriation (Requisition) and of Movement Restrictions in Occupied Territory 536

27 Cutting off Electricity and Water Supply for the Gaza Strip
Limits under International Law 546

VIII CONTENTS

28 The Right to Provide and Receive Humanitarian Assistance in
Occupied Territories 551

PART 8
Other Issues Concerning the Law of Armed Conflict

29 Neutrality in Naval Warfare
What is Left of Traditional International Law? 573

30 Conflits Armés Internes et Droit International Humanitaire 591

PART 9
Implementation and Enforcement of IHL

31 Fact-finding as a Means of Ensuring Respect for International
Humanitarian Law 611

32 Remedies of Victims of War Crimes and Crimes against Humanities
*Some Critical Remarks on the ICJ's Judgment on the Jurisdictional
Immunity of States* 632

33 Prevention and Repression of Breaches of International
Humanitarian Law 648

34 Complementarity
*Ensuring Compliance with International Law through Criminal
Prosecutions – Whose Responsibility?* 662

35 The Role of National Law in the Implementation of International
Humanitarian Law 676

Bibliographic Information on the Selected Essays of Michael Bothe

1   "Legal and Non-Legal Norms: A Meaningful Distinction in International Relations?" *Netherlands Yearbook of International Law* 11 (1980): 65–95.

2   "Les Limites des Pouvoirs du Conseil de Sécurité," in René-Jean Dupuy (ed.), *Le développement du rôle du Conseil de Sécurité, Colloque, La Haye, 21–23 juillet 1992*. Martinus Nijhoff Publishers, 1993: 67–81.

3   "Security Council's Targeted Sanctions against Presumed Terrorists: The Need to Comply with Human Rights Standards." *Journal of International Criminal Justice* 6 (2008): 541–555.

4   "Limits to the Use of Force Imposed by International Law: Current Problems," in Jorge Cardona Llorens (ed.), *Cursos Euromediterráneos de Derecho Internacional* 11/12. Tirant lo Blanch, 2007/2008: 307–368.

5   "Will Current International Crises Result in Structural Shifts in International Law?" *Recueils de la Société Internationale de Droit Penal Militaire et de Droit de la Guerre* 20 (2015): 231–248.

6   "Terrorism and the Legality of Pre-emptive Force." *European Journal of International Law* 14 (2003): 227–240.

7   "Peacekeeping and International Humanitarian Law: Friends or Foes?" *International Peacekeeping* 3 (1996): 91–95.

8   "Obligations and Protection of Individuals," in Daniel Bardonnet (ed.), *The Convention on the Protection and Elimination of Chemical Weapons: A Breakthrough in Multilateral Disarmament*. Brill/Nijhoff, 1995: 419–431.

9   "Verification of Disarmament Treaties," in Giovanni Gasparini and Natalino Ronzitti (eds.), *The Tenth Anniversary of the CWC's Entry into Force: Achievements and Problems*. Istituto Affari Internazionali, 2007: pp. 45–56.

10   "Non-Proliferation of Weapons of Mass Destruction: Treaty Regimes between Efficiency and Discrimination," in *The Challenges of Disarmament and Non-Proliferation*. Instituto per gli Studi di Politica Internazionale, 2007: pp. 55–78.

11   "Le Droit de la Guerre et les Nations Unies: a Propos Des Incidents Armés au Congo." *Etudes et travaux de l'Institut universitaire de hautes études internationales* 5 (1967): 135–242.

12   "The Historical Evolution of International Humanitarian Law, International Human Rights Law, Refugee Law and International Criminal Law," in Horst Fischer, Ulrike Froissart, Wolff Heintschel von Heineff and

Christian Raap (eds.), *Krisensicherung und Humanitärer Schutz – Crisis Management and Humanitarian Protection. Festschrift für Dieter Fleck.* Berliner Wissenschaftsverlag, 2004: 37–45.

13   "Multiculturalism and the Development of International Humanitarian Law," in Sienho Yee and Jacques-Yvan Morin (eds.), *Multiculturalism and International Law.* Martinus Nijhoff Publishers, 2009: 617–628.

14   "Setting the Scene: New Technologies – New Challenges for IHL?" in Wolff Heintschel von Heinegg (ed.), *International Humanitarian Law and New Weapons Technology.* International Institute of Humanitarian Law, 2012: 51–56.

15   "De Facto Control of Land or Sea Areas: Its Relevance under the Law of Armed Conflict, in Particular Air and Missile Warfare." *Israel Yearbook on Human Rights* 45 (2015): 51–66.

16   "The International Committee of the Red Cross and the Additional Protocols of 1977," in Robin Geiß, Andreas Zimmermann and Stefanie Haumer (eds.), *Humanizing the Laws of War. The Red Cross and the Development of International Humanitarian Law.* Cambridge University Press, 2017: 57–80.

17   "Protection of the Environment in Times of Armed Conflict," in Najeeb Al-Nauimi and Richard Meese (eds.), *International Legal Issues Arising under the United Nations Decade of International Law.* Brill/Nijhoff, 1995: 95–104.

18   "Legal Restraints on Targeting: Protection of Civilian Population and the Changing Faces of Modern Conflict." *Israel Yearbook of Human Rights* 31 (2001): 35–49.

19   "The Ethics, Principles and Objectives of Protection of the Environment in Times of Armed Conflict," in Rosemary Rayfuse (ed.), *War and the Environment: New Approaches to Protecting the Environment in Relation to Armed Conflict.* Brill/Nijhoff, 2014: 91–108.

20   "The ILC Special Rapporteur's Preliminary Report on the Protection of the Environment in Relation to Armed Conflicts: An Important Step in the Right Direction," in Pia Acconci et al. (eds.), *International Law and the Protection of Humanity. Essays in Honour of Flavia Lattanzi.* Brill/Nijhoff, 2016: 213–224.

21   "Protection of the Environment in Relation to Armed Conflicts: a Preliminary Comment on the Work of the International Law Commission," in James Crawford, Abdul Koroma, Said Mahmoudi and Alain Pellet (eds.), *The International Legal Order: Current Needs and Possible Responses. Essays in Honour of Djamchid Momtaz.* (Brill/Nijhoff, 2017: 641–659.

22   "Le Sort des Blessés et Malades: Un but Fondamental de la Croix-Rouge." *Annales d'études internationales* 8 (1977): 93–110

23 "Relief Actions: The Position of the Recipient State," in Frits Kalshoven (ed.), *Assisting the Victims of Armed Conflict and Other Disasters*. Martinus Nijhoff Publishers, 1989: 91–97.

24 "Human Rights Law and International Humanitarian Law as Limits of Security Council Action," in Robert Kolb and Gloria Gaggioli (eds.), *Research Handbook on Human Rights and Humanitarian Law*. Edward Elgar Publishing, 2013: 371–390.

25 "Beginning and End of Occupation." *Collegium* 34 (2006): 26–33.

26 *Limits of the Right of Expropriation (Requisition) and of Movement Restrictions in Occupied Territory*. Expert Opinion (2012).

27 *Cutting off Electricity and Water Supply for the Gaza Strip: Limits under International Law*. Expert Opinion (2014).

28 *The Right to Provide and Receive Humanitarian Assistance in Occupied Territories*. Expert Opinion (2015).

29 "Neutrality in Naval Warfare: What is Left of Traditional International Law?" in Astrid J.M. Delissen and Tanja J. Gerard (eds.), *Humanitarian Law of Armed Conflict - Challenges Ahead. Essays in Honour of Frits Kalshoven*. Martinus Nijhoff Publishers, 1991: 387–405.

30 "Conflits armés internes et droit international humanitaire." *Revue générale de droit international public* 82 (1978): 82–102.

31 "Fact-finding as a Means of Ensuring Respect for International Humanitarian Law," in Wolff Heintschel von Heinegg and Volker Epping (eds.), *International Humanitarian Law Facing New Challenges. Symposium in Honour of Knut Ipsen*. Springer, 2007: 249–268.

32 "Remedies of Victims of War Crimes and Crimes against Humanities: Some Critical Remarks on the ICJ's Judgment on the Jurisdictional Immunity of States," in Anne Peters, Evelyn Lagrange, Stefan Oeter and Christian Tomuschat (eds.), *Immunities in the Age of Global Constitutionalism*. Brill/Nijhoff, 2014: 99–115.

33 "Prevention and Repression of Breaches of International Humanitarian Law." *International Institute of Humanitarian Law Yearbook* 1986–87: 115–128.

34 "Complementarity: Ensuring Compliance with International Law through Criminal Prosecutions – Whose Responsibility?" *Friedenswarte* 83 (2008): 59–72.

35 'The Role of National Law in the Implementation of International Humanitarian Law," in Christophe Swinarsky (ed.), *Etudes et essais sur le droit international humanitaire et sur les principes de la Croix-Rouge en l'honneur de Jean Pictet*. Martinus Nijhoff Publishers, 1984: 301–312.

An Introduction to Michael Bothe's Writings on "Legal Restraints on the Use of Military Force"

Thilo Marauhn

1

"Legal restraints on the use of military force" – this is a lifetime topic of *Michael Bothe.*

It is not the only field of law he has extensively addressed in his writings. Federalism as power sharing and the protection of the environment have likewise been drivers of his authorship. But this volume's focus has been the strongest and the most enduring.

Michael's contributions to the field are extraordinarily strong academic pieces, likewise strong in political (idealist rather than cynic) and personal terms (an extraordinary teacher, engaged and empathic). His longing for peace and his eagerness to avoid or at least reduce human suffering in times of armed conflict have driven his manifold interventions. As this volume demonstrates, political ideals coupled with a sense of human responsibility can benefit from solid doctrinal underpinnings in international law. *Michael* has brought together idealism, pragmatism and the law in a unique fashion that does not only provide insights into important matters of every day politics of his lifetime but that can serve as a stimulus for future contributions to the field. This forward looking potential of many contributions authored by *Michael* invites current and future researchers of public international law to move ahead.

It will be no surprise that the majority of the chapters included in this volume focus on the law of armed conflict. The International Red Cross and Red Crescent Movement, in 2017, honoured *Michael* by granting to him the Movement's highest award, the Henry Dunant Medal. His commitment and contribution to the development and promotion of international humanitarian law, beginning with his pivotal role in the Diplomatic Conference on the Reaffirmation and Development of International Humanitarian Law Applicable in Armed Conflicts from 1974 to 1977 and extending to his current promotion of humanitarian protection, as academically mirrored in this volume may provide guidance to generations to come.

This introduction will provide an overview of *Michael's* contributions included herein and aims at guiding readers through the various chapters of the book.

© KONINKLIJKE BRILL NV, LEIDEN, 2021 | DOI:10.1163/9789004380592_002

2

The particular characteristics of international law, its horizontal character, the relative importance of states (as authors, addressees and guardians of international law) and the absence of compulsory judicial dispute settlement are particular obvious when it comes to the use of military force in international relations, notwithstanding its long history in international law. As of today, uncertainties and indeterminacies are stronger in respect of *ius ad bellum* than in the context of *ius in bello*. This is largely due to the fact that the law of armed conflict and in particular international humanitarian law has gone through a major process of codification since the mid-19th century. The sharpening of *ius ad bellum* rules from the Porter Convention, across the League of Nation's Covenant, the Kellogg-Briand Pact, and the UN Charter must be considered impressive, but it has not erased the indeterminacies and political trends which have led *Thomas Franck* to raise the question of "Who Killed Article 2 (4)?" in the 1970s.[1] *Michael Bothe* has had a particular interest and a sensitivity for some of the very basic issues that called for academic debate and discourse in this context. His 1980 contribution on "Legal and Non-Legal Norms – a Meaningful Distinction in International Relations?"[2] raises the important question on the role of what is often labelled "soft law". The indeterminacy of international law includes at the same time its flexibility. International law is less static than municipal law and includes a sense of dynamics that emerges not only from state practice (as well as the practice of international organizations and other non-state actors) but also from political processes and the particular normativity of pertinent documents. *Michael's* discussion of "legal and non-legal norms" takes note of the mere multitude of non-legal norms ("The foregoing analysis has demonstrated that there is an important body of rules which regulate state behaviour in international relations, and which do not fall within the category of legal rules".[3]). It is practice-driven but benefits from contextualization and politico-doctrinal sensitivity. Focusing on non-law sheds light on some of the basic challenges of public international law, its normativity and its binding character. On the one hand, *Michael* points out that "[a] legal agreement is distinguished from a non-legal one by the different intention of the parties",[4] and

---

1   Thomas M. Franck, 'Who Killed Article 2(4)? Or: Changing Norms Governing the Use of Force by States' (1970) 64 AJIL 809.
2   Michael Bothe, 'Legal and Non-Legal Norms – A Meaningful Distinction in International Relations?' (1980) 11 Netherlands Yearbook of International Law 65.
3   *Ibid.,* 93.
4   *Ibid.,* 94.

INTRODUCTION

he warns against "letting law come in by the back door".[5] On the other hand, he highlights "two basic notions in social rule-making: promise and authority", "the basis of the various types of non-legal obligation described" in his article.[6] This leads him to call for a terminological change: replacing the notion of "non-legal norms" by "political norms", taking note of "the idea of *polis,* of the civic community".[7]

Community entails not only the civic community. One of the advances of international law in the 20th century was the spread of international organizations. As important as they are, there are limits to their powers. These are not only political limits arising from the power of states setting up these organizations. But such limits likewise arise from international law. *Michael* has addressed these limits in his paper "Les limites de pouvoirs du Conseil de Sécurité",[8] published in 1992, and in his analysis of targeted sanctions and their human rights implications in 2008.[9] He shares the general perception voiced by *Antonia Handler Chayes* and *Abram Chayes* in their 1995 "The New Sovereignty", arguing that "the only way most states can realize and express their sovereignty is through participation in the various regimes that regulate and order the international system".[10] But he likewise points out that international law, the international legal system, is in itself a system of checks and balances with limitations imposed upon the entities emerging from international law itself, including the very notion of sovereignty: "La souveraineté étatique est assez souvent considérée, comme un mal, mais elle n'est certainement pas un mal en soi. Elle est toujours un fondement, principe de base de l'ordre international. Elle est l'expression de l'intérêt de chaque organisation étatique de ne pas être dominée par d'autres puissances, que ce soit par la voie d'une action unilatérale ou par le truchement d'une organisation multilatérale".[11] Checks and balances include "a legal duty to seek to make UN listing and de-listing decisions consistent with due process requirements".[12]

---

5   *Ibid.,* 95.
6   *Ibid.,* 95.
7   *Ibid.,* 95.
8   Michael Bothe, 'Les limites de pouvoirs du Conseil de Sécurité' in René-Jean Dupuy (ed), *Le développement du rôle du Conseil de Sécurité, Colloque, La Haye, 21–23 juillet 1992* (Martinus Nijhoff Publishers 1993) 67.
9   Michael Bothe, 'Security Council's Targeted Sanctions against Presumed Terrorists. The Need to Comply with Human Rights Standards' (2008) 6 Journal of International Criminal Justice 541.
10   Abram Chayes and Antonia Handler Chayes, *The New Sovereignty* (Harvard University Press 1998), 27.
11   Bothe (n 10) 81.
12   Bothe (n 11) 555.

International law in itself is a process. Thus, many prominent lawyers have addressed changing norms in international, including "Changing Norms Governing the Use of Force by States".[13] *Michael* has not only addressed "Limits to the Use of Force Imposed by International Law. Current Problems"[14] but he also raised the question whether "[...] Current International Crises Result in Structural Shifts in International Law?".[15] While focusing on a critique of the "old intergovernmental character"[16] of the international legal order he raised the question of whether this "traditional model" has come under pressure. In a way, *Michael* de-constructs the sovereignty-centred system by pointing towards civil society and to new networks, but he wisely refrains from presenting a new model possibly replacing the old one.

His down-to-earth approach is among the particularly impressive features of *Michael Bothe*'s writings. While being aware and explicitly taking up theories of international law he largely avoids the heavenly space of meta-analyses with its many pitfalls and draws the attention of readers, both academics and practitioners, to the application of the law in highly sensitive contexts. In the context of post-9/11 counter-terrorist operations he brilliantly addressed the issue of anticipatory self-defence in his critical assessment of the U.S. National Security Strategy submitted to Congress by President Bush on 17 September 2002.[17] Going carefully through the various criteria of self-defence and, in particular, of the so-called Caroline formula in respect of anticipatory self-defence, *Michael* states: "Any expansion of the right of pre-emptive self-defence beyond the *Caroline* formula is just not workable".[18] This does not mean to ignore the practical problems arising from new security challenges as they became manifest with the 9/11 attacks, including the difficulty to determine the attacker, to discuss the victim, and related issues. According to *Michael* multilateralism provides perspectives for solution.[19] Multilateralism is, however, not without problems as he illustrates in his short contribution on "Peacekeeping and International

---

13   Franck (n 3).

14   Michael Bothe, 'Limits of Force Imposed by International Law. Current Problems' in Jorge Cardona Llorens (ed), *Cursos Euromediterráneos de Derecho Internacional 11/12* (Tirant lo Blanch 2007/2008) 307.

15   Michael Bothe, 'Will Current International Crises Result in Structural Shifts in International Law' (2015) 20 Recueils de la Societe Internationale de Droit Penal Militaire et de Droit de la Guerre 231.

16   *Ibid.*, 247.

17   Michael Bothe, 'Terrorism and the Legality of Pre-emptive Force' (2003) 14 European Journal of International Law 227.

18   *Ibid.*, 237.

19   *Ibid.*, 239–240.

INTRODUCTION

Humanitarian Law",[20] arguing, however, clearly that "[w]here there is a situation in which international humanitarian law applies (...), it applies also in relation to the UN".[21]

Up until today, one branch of public international law, which is of ultimate importance for international security, has been neglected by many scholars, not, however, by *Michael Bothe* who – together with *Wolfgang Graf Viththum* – was rapporteur on "Legal Questions of Arms Control in Contemporary International Treaty Law"[22] in 1989 on the occasion of the bi-annual meeting of the German Society of International Law. In his careful and in-depth analysis of the approaches to, the instruments of, the objectives, and the implementation of the law of arms control, *Michael* has set high standards, which are reflected in the three papers selected for this volume. The first thereof celebrates a breakthrough, namely the signing in 1993 of the Convention on the Protection and Elimination of Chemical Weapons.[23] *Michael's* paper is part of an edited volume emerging from a unique workshop held by The Hague Academy of International Law. Roughly ten years later *Michael* was happy to celebrate the tenth anniversary of the CWC's entry into force and provided insights into the "Verification of Disarmament Treaties".[24] Among the challenges still on the table, and re-surfacing currently more than all of us had hoped for, is the topic of another 2007 contribution: "Non-Proliferation of Weapons of Mass Destruction".[25] *Michael's* contributions to the law of arms control have not only been unique; they benefited from his close scrutiny of weapons law as part of international humanitarian law, which he had addressed pretty early in his career with a 1973 monograph on the prohibition of chemical and bacteriological weapons.[26] Indeed, his

---

20 Michael Bothe, 'Peacekeeping and International Humanitarian Law: Friends or Foes?' (1996) 3 International Peacekeeping 91.

21 *Ibid.,* 94.

22 Michael Bothe and Wolfgang Graf Vitzthum, *Rechtsfragen der Rüstungskontrolle im Vertragsvölkerrecht der Gegenwart* (C.F. Müller 1990).

23 Michael Bothe, 'Obligation and Protection of Individuals' in Daniel Bardonnet (ed), *The Convention on the Protection and Eliminitation of Chemical Weapons: A Breakthrough in Multilateral Disarmament* (Brill/Nijhoff 1995) 419.

24 Michael Bothe, 'Verification of Disarmament Treaties' in Giovanni Gasparini and Natalino Ronzitti (eds), *The Tenth Anniversary of the CWC's Entry into Force: Achievements and Problems* (Istituto Affari Internazionali 2007) 45.

25 Michael Bothe, 'Non-Proliferation of Weapons of Mass Destruction. Treaty Regimes between Efficiency and Discrimination' in Instituto per gli Studi di Politica Internazionale, *The Challenges of Disarmament and Non-Proliferation* (2007) 55.

26 Michael Bothe, *Das völkerrechtliche Verbot des Einsatzes chemischer und bakteriologischer Waffen* (Carl Heymanns Verlag 1973).

unique expertise – mirrored in many pertinent publications– on chemical weapons, their control, and eventually their disarmament, coupled with his meta-perspective on arms control law as a whole have often been made use of and referred to by political decision-makers. He even was the key lawyer representing the complainant before the Federal Constitutional Court in a case concerning the stationing of chemical weapons in the Federal Republic of Germany[27] by the United States, and a group of Tahitians in their effort to challenge, before the European Commission on Human Rights, the legality of French Nuclear testing in the Pacific.[28]

3

The law of armed conflict has been predominant in *Michael Bothe*'s international law writings. This is the branch of international law, which also saw his most prestigious international office, when he served as President of the International Humanitarian Fact-Finding Commission from 2007 until 2012.

In this volume we have included six contributions addressing general questions of the law of armed conflict. They extend from the history of international humanitarian law[29] to current challenges thereof,[30] they cover the multiculturalism in the development of this branch of international law,[31] the role of the United Nations[32] and of the International Committee of the Red

---

27   Bundesverfassungsgericht 29 October 1987, 2 BvR 624/83.

28   European Commission of Human Rights, *Noël Narvii Tauira and Eighteen Others v. France*, Application No. 28204/95 4 December 1995.

29   Michael Bothe, 'The Historical Evolution of International Humanitarian Law, International Human Rights Law and International Criminal Law' in Horst Fischer, Ulrike Froissart, Wolff Heintschel von Heineff and Christian Raap (eds), *Krisensicherung und Humanitärer Schutz – Crisis Management and Humanitarian Protection. Festschrift für Dieter Fleck* (Berliner Wissenschaftsverlag 2004) 37.

30   Michael Bothe, 'Setting the Scene: New Technologies – New Challenges for IHL?' in Wolff Heintschel von Heinegg (ed) *International Humanitarian Law and New Weapons Technology* (International Institute of Humanitarian Law 2012) 51.

31   Michael Bothe, 'Multiculturalism and the Development of International Humanitarian Law' in Sienho Yee and Jacques-Yvan Morin (eds) *Multiculturalism and International Law* (Martinus Nijhoff Publishers 2009) 617.

32   Michael Bothe, 'Le droit de la guerre et les Nations Unies. A propos des incidents armés au Congo' (1967) 5 Etudes et travaux de l'Institut universitaire de hautes études internationales 135.

INTRODUCTION

Cross,[33] and they address the difficult issue of *de facto* control of land or sea areas.[34]

There are some commonalities which we find when reading Michael's contributions on the law of armed conflict in general:

First, he always includes a careful doctrinal analysis of the law as it stands. In thus far, one might argue that this mirrors his education and training in a rather positivist German academic environment at the time. His excellent doctrinal skills have not only lent his broader analysis recognition and acceptance. But they have also contributed to facilitating a contextualization of the law based upon common ground between academia and practice, and thereby opening perspectives for the development of the law in light of perceived deficiencies. His analysis of the ICRC provides a brilliant example thereof, leading to the conclusion that – over time – improvements in the law of armed conflict have always benefitted from "the conceptual work of the ICRC".[35]

Second, *Michael* has often managed to historically embed his legal argument, be it for the sake of a broader perspective when discussing the historical evolution of international humanitarian law ("It is a history of making and breaking the law, of applying or not applying the law".[36]), be it to uphold core principles thereof ("The principle of distinction is not old-fashioned, it must not be modified, it can and must be applied in an appropriate way".[37]). *Michael's* perspective on public international in general, and on IHL more specifically, reflects a delicate sense for the balance of continuity and change in the making, implementation, and enforcement of this fragile body of law.

Third, and I believe most important, is his ambition to move international humanitarian law out of the narrow space of academic and bureaucratic expertise. This has led *Michael* to refer to international human rights law in an effort to strengthen international humanitarian law (while avoiding the weakening of both branches of law by depriving them of their specialties) and to include civil society more often than many other authors of his generation

---

33 Michael Bothe, 'The International Committee of the Red Cross and the Additional Protocols of 1977' in Robin Geiß, Andreas Zimmermann and Stefanie Haumer (eds), *Humanizing the Laws of War. The Red Cross and the Development of International Humanitarian Law* (Cambridge University Press 2017) 57.

34 Michael Bothe, 'De Facto Control of Land or Sea Areas: Its Relevance under the Law of Armed Conflict, in Particular Air and Missile Warfare' (2015) 45 Israel Yearbook on Human Rights 51.

35 Bothe (n 36) 79.

36 Bothe (n 32) 37.

37 Bothe (n 33) 56.

have done. Arguing for a "sharper focus on the individual",[38] pointing out that "the fact that an individual has a remedy under human rights law gives additional strength to the rules of international humanitarian law corresponding to the human rights norm alleged to be violated",[39] underlying the "primordial importance" of the rule of reason "for the protection of the human person",[40] and writing in support of "a major improvement for the protection of civilians in international and non-international conflicts"[41] – this all mirrors *Michael's* personal engagement, sometimes close to activist, based on his ability to go beyond positive law in his writings.

The three characteristic features of his publications on international humanitarian law can also be traced in three contributions included in this volume focusing on protected persons,[42] relief, [43] and human rights.[44] Occasionally, *Michael* selected topics to pursue a humanitarian agenda full of empathy. "Philia", if I may refer to Aristotle's Nicomachean Ethics, friendship or affection, have not only characterized *Michael's* writings but also his personality, throughout his academic career, throughout his life. There are many witnesses to this.

Nevertheless, he also was very political, not merely humanitarian. This ability to fight for what he perceived and experienced as convincing is, among others, reflected in some of his contributions on the law of occupation. Michael has not shied away from controversies if need be, just as he has not shied away from difficult questions necessitating practical answers. His contribution on the "Beginning and end of occupation"[45] may serve as an initial example here. In this contribution *Michael* discusses how to apply the law of occupation to new manifestations of a similar nature. He identifies two features of belligerent occupation, which he subjects to a closer analysis: "a foreign military presence and the lack of consent of the occupied State".[46] His kind of disillusioning

---

38 Bothe (n 32) 39.

39 *Ibid.,* 45.

40 Bothe (n 33) 56.

41 Bothe (n 36) 80.

42 Michael Bothe, 'Le sort des blessés et malades: un but fondamental de la Croix-Rouge' (1977) 8 Annales d'études internationales 93.

43 Michael Bothe, 'Relief Actions: The Position of the Recipient State' in Frits Kalshoven (ed), *Assisting the Victims of Armed Conflict and Other Disasters* (Martinus Nijhoff Publishers 1989) 91.

44 Michael Bothe, 'Human rights law and international humanitarian law as limits of Security Council action' in Robert Kolb and Gloria Gaggioli (eds), *Research Handbook on Human Rights and Humanitarian Law* (Edward Elgar Publishing 2013) 371.

45 Michael Bothe, 'Beginning and end of occupation' (2006) 34 Collegium 26.

46 *Ibid.,* 27.

INTRODUCTION

conclusion when discussing the Israeli withdrawal from the Gaza strip points out that it is "not clear, whether one can consider that the occupation of the Palestinian territory has been terminated".[47] At the end of his analysis *Michael* does not succeed in developing a broader approach but underlines the need for a case-by-case assessment, which "remains a difficult task". But he considers the relevance of the above criteria proven.

We have decided to include three expert opinions drafted by *Michael* on the law of occupation. They mirror his ability to provide consultancy in clear terms, and to do this is a politically sensitive manner. The first of these expert opinions, submitted in 2012, discusses expropriations and movement restrictions in occupied Palestinian territories. *Michael* establishes violations of Articles 46 and 52 of the Hague Regulations as well as of Articles 27, 49 (1), 53 and 55 Geneva Convention IV in the context of the establishment of the so-called Fire Zone 918 for training purposes of the Israeli Defence Forces.[48] The second of these expert opinions, submitted in 2014, discusses the international law limits to the cutting of electricity and water supply for the Gaza Strip. Based upon a careful analysis of Geneva Convention IV and Additional Protocol I, *Michael* concludes that "[u]nder international humanitarian law, Israel is obliged, in the current conditions of armed conflict, to maintain water supplies from Israel to the Gaza Strip at current level and of an electricity supply sufficient to meet the basic needs of the civilian population".[49] Submitted in 2015, the third expert opinion included in this volume is probably the most exciting and the most forward looking in terms of the law of occupation. It concerns the right to provide and receive humanitarian assistance in occupied territories. *Michael* was asked to draft this piece against the background of Israel "in various ways impedes humanitarian assistance given by various organizations to the population of the OPT".[50] The argument presented brings together international humanitarian law and international human rights law. In light of the fact that humanitarian assistance is an under-researched topic from the perspective of international humanitarian law, we believe that *Michael* has broken some new ground while at the same time addressing very specific details such as the withholding of consent by the occupying power, demolitions related to

---

47 *Ibid.,* 29.

48 Michael Bothe, *Limits of the right of expropriation (requisition) and of movement restrictions in occupied territory,* Expert Opinion 2012.

49 Michael Bothe, *Cutting off electricity and water supply for the Gaza Strip: Limits under international law,* Expert opinion 2014, 5.

50 Michael Bothe, *The right to provide and receive humanitarian assistance in occupied territories,* Expert Opinion 2015.

humanitarian assistance, relief actions without consent and the treatment of relief workers.[51] We hope that the publication of this expert opinion in this volume will contribute to enhance debates about current challenges related to the law of occupation.

After pointing to two other publications included in this volume, one focusing on neutrality[52] and the other one on non-international armed conflict,[53] the five concluding chapters focus on a topic that has always been at the center of *Michael*'s interest in international law more generally and in international humanitarian law more specifically, namely its implementation. Implementation presents a challenging issue: How can we make treaties work? How can we ensure compliance with them? Can they possibly be enforced, even if there is only optional judicial dispute settlement in international law? *Michael* has researched into these questions extensively, with a particular focus on international humanitarian law. He has understood that in the absence of judicial means to ensure compliance with international law, relatively soft means are equally important, including "fact-finding as a means of ensuring respect for international humanitarian law".[54] Having conducted a major research project on fact-finding in international law, *Michael* has continuously demonstrated an ability to combine soft and hard elements in this process. Last not least, his membership and eventual presidency of the International Humanitarian Fact-Finding Commission provided him with the requisite practical insights. Individuals can, however, seek remedies also at the national level by referring to international humanitarian law, provided that jurisdictional immunity of states does not go too far. It is in this light that he has criticized the ICJ's judgment on the jurisdictional immunity of states.[55] The further development and strengthening of national and international criminal law have become a fascinating topic, which

---

51   *Ibid.*

52   Michael Bothe, 'Neutrality in naval warfare: What is left of traditional international law?' in Astrid J.M. Delissen and Tanja J. Gerard (eds), *Humanitarian Law of Armed Conflict – Challenges Ahead, Essays in Honour of Frits Kalshoven* (Martinus Nijhoff Publishers 1991) 387.

53   Michael Bothe, 'Conflits armés internes et droit international humanitaire' (1978) 82 Revue générale de droit international public 82.

54   Michael Bothe, 'Fact-finding as a means of Ensuring Respect for International Humanitarian Law' in Wolff Heintschel von Heinegg and Volker Epping (ed), *International Humanitarian Law Facing New Challenges. Symposium in Honour of Knut Ipsen* (Springer 2007) 249.

55   Michael Bothe, 'Remedies of Victims of War Crimes and Crimes Against Humanities: Some Critical Remarks on the ICJ's Judgment on the Jurisdictional Immunity of States' in Anne Peters, Evelyn Lagrange, Stefan Oeter and Christian Tomuschat (eds), *Immunities in the Age of Global Constitutionalism* (Brill/Nijhoff2014) 99.

INTRODUCTION

Michael never got too euphoric about. His publications on these issues mirror a realistic assess of the (limited, but important) role of criminal in the context of international humanitarian law, its implementation and enforcement.[56]

For many years, the main focus of implementation-related research by international law scholars has focused on national implementation. The issue has been interesting for a number of reasons: First, it concerns the relationship between (public) international law and national / municipal law – an issue area that allows for broad, albeit sometimes pseudo-theoretical discussions. *Michael* would not have invested too much energy into such a topic. Second, national implementation has attracted the attention of lawyers because it bridges the national and the international perspective, and allows for participation of constitutional (national) law experts in international legal discourse. Even though *Michael* combined both levels of the law, national and international, he can easily be described as a genuine international lawyer, hence, not being in need of the bridge from the national to the international. Third, national implementation has always been perceived as very much a doctrinal area of the law. With his desire to contextualize, *Michael* would not focus on research questions just because of their doctrinal character. There was something more basic, and one might say: more important to his interest in implementation, including national implementation. For *Michael*, international law has always been meaningful when having an impact on society, on real life. While it would probably go too far to argue that he has perceived the law, among others, through its ability to effectuate social change, he, nevertheless has always been interested in making it effective, in other words: meaningful for the human being. In this sense, national implementation is part of making international law work, and the last chapter in this volume precisely focuses on "the role of national law in the implementation of international humanitarian law".[57]

4

Michael Bothe is one of the most prominent and influential scholars of international humanitarian law. His publications on legal restraints on the use of

---

56   Michael Bothe, 'Complementarity: Ensuring compliance with international law through criminal prosecutions – whose responsibility?' (2008) 83 Friedenswarte 59.

57   Michael Bothe, 'The role of national law in the implementation of international humanitarian law' in Christophe Swinarsky (ed) *Etudes et essais sur le droit international humanitaire et sur les principes de la Croix-Rouge en l'honneur de Jean Pictet* (Martinus Nijhoff Publishers1984) 301.

military force not only been important at the time of their publication. They continue to be relevant for the interpretation and further development of this highly important area of international law. The publication of this volume is meant to provide guidance, food for thought and incentives for controversies not only for his friends and colleagues but for the international legal community, practitioners and academics alike, senior and junior, old and young. We believe that *Michael's* highly appreciated doctrinal skills, combined with his contextualized assessment of the law, and his deep empathy for the needs of human being in most difficult situations, with a particular view to the victims of armed conflict, will provide a stimulus to address these issues in the future.

It is a big "Thank you" to *Michael* which concludes this introduction.

PART 1

Basic Issues

1

Legal and Non-Legal Norms
A Meaningful Distinction in International Relations?

1 Introduction*

In his final speech at the Helsinki Conference (CSCE) in 1975, Prime Minister Wilson called the Final Act of the Conference a "moral commitment", not an international treaty.[1] Thus, the Act is not binding as a matter of international law, though it is quite clear from the historical context, and from the wording of the Final Act[2] itself, that the participating states have some sort of obligation ("commitment") to base their future conduct on the provisions of the Final Act. The Act formulates norms, rules intended to determine state behaviour, but these rules are not of a legal character. This is, apparently, the assumption underlying the Wilson statement, to which many similar statements could be added. As will be shown, a considerable body of state practice based on the same concept has developed, and points to the existence of non-legal (pre-legal, para-legal, moral, political) obligations as distinguished from legal ones.[3] Is it a valid distinction, can a distinction really be made between legal and non-legal norms?[4] If so, what constitutes the difference? What is the basis of obligation in both cases?

The fact that law is not the only system of social rules determining human behaviour is well known to legal theory.[5] The functioning of a society needs

---

* The author wishes to express his gratitude to Dr. Karin Oellers-Frahm and Lothar Gundling for their most valuable help in preparing this article.
1 30 *Europa-Archiv* (1975) D 543.
2 14 ILM (1975) p. 1292. For details see below.
3 Cf., Virally, "La deuxième décennie des Nations Unies pour le développement, Essai d'interpretation para-juridique", 16 AFDI (1970) pp. 9–33, at p. 28 et seq.; Schweisfurth, "Zur Frage der Rechtsnatur, Verbindlichkeit und völkerrechtlichen Relevanz der KSZE-Schlussakte", 36 ZaoRV (1976) pp. 681–726.
4 McDougal, for example, criticizes the distinction between law and policy as being "unreal" ("International Law, Power and Policy: A Contemporary Conception", 82 Hague Recueil (1953 I) pp. 137–259 at p. 144). On the other hand, Wengler seems to regret the possible erosion of the concept of *legal* obligation, see Wengler, "Rechtsvertrag, Konsensus und Absichtserklärung im Völkerrecht", 31 Juristenzeitung (1976) pp. 193–197 at p. 197.
5 Hart, *Der Begriff des Rechts* (1961/1973) p. 17 et seq.; Radbruch, *Einführung in die Rechtswissenschaft,* 9th ed. (1952) p. 12 et seq.; Kelsen, *Reine Rechtslehre* 2nd ed. (1960) p. 60 et seq.; Geiger, *Vorstudien zu einer Soziologie des Rechts,* 2nd ed. (1970) p. 125 et seq.

© KONINKLIJKE BRILL NV, LEIDEN, 2021 | DOI:10.1163/9789004380592_003

rules which make behaviour predictable to a certain extent. To use the terminology of the New Haven School, rules or norms formulate shared or community expectations[6] as to how those to whom a norm is addressed will behave.

These rules, however, vary greatly in nature. There is a long tradition in social science (understood in a broad sense) of distinguishing various categories of social rules. But while there is considerable agreement that there are differences, there is considerable disagreement as to their precise character. It can be said, however, that legal rules are but one of the means of formulating community expectations. There have been few, if any, social systems where legal norms were the only means of doing so. Betting and gambling do not give rise to legal obligations, but in many social systems there is a strong expectation that what is lost will be paid. Gentlemen's agreements may not be enforced by courts of law, but it is nevertheless expected that they will be honoured. In countries where abortion is legal, there still exists an expectation, at least in certain parts of the community, that abortion will not be resorted to, it being forbidden by a non-legal, a moral norm. Some of these non-legal norms are considered to be of divine origin, others are based on social usage.

The determination of the dividing line between legal and other kinds of norms has given rise to a considerable amount of theoretical debate,[7] and many answers have been provided to the question of what constitutes the essence of law, as distinguished from other sets of rules determining human behaviour. This question has presented particular difficulties in relation to norms determining state behaviour in international relations.[8] For those who consider centralized enforcement as the essential characteristic of law, it has been difficult to define international law as law at all. It is not the purpose of this article to join sides with any of the parties to the academic dispute as to why and to what extent the rules concerning state behaviour in international relations fall within the, or a, definition of law. Rather, an empirical approach is

---

6 Cf., on this terminology, Schreuer, "New Haven Approach und Völkerrecht", in Schreuer, ed., *Autorität und internationale Ordnung* (1979) pp. 63–85 at p. 68; Schachter, "Towards a Theory of International Obligation", in Schwebel, ed., *The Effectiveness of International Decisions* (1971) pp. 9–31 at p. 22 et seq.

7 See, in particular, the literature quoted in n. 5.

8 Kunz, "Völkerrecht, allgemein", in Strupp and Schlochauer, eds., *Wörterbuch des Völkerrechts*, (1960 et seq.) vol. 3 pp. 611–631 at p. 614; Mössner, *Einführung in das Völkerrecht* (1977) p. 6 et seq.; Menzel and Ipsen, *Völkerrecht*, 2nd ed. (1979) p. 38 et seq.; Brierly, *The Law of Nations*, 6th ed. (1963) p. 68 et seq., Berber, *Lehrbuch des Völkerrechts*, vol. 1, 2nd ed (1975) p. 9 et seq.; Hart, op.cit., n. 5 p. 293 et seq.; Blenk-Knocke, *Zu den soziologischen Bedingungen völkerrechtlicher Normenbefolgung* (1979) p. 41 et seq.

proposed. In international practice, we can observe that community or shared expectations are formulated by means of rules which the relevant actors consider to be legal ones. There are other cases, such as the CSCE Final Act, where it is quite clear that the rules are not supposed to be legal ones. In still other cases, this issue is disputed. It is hoped that a careful analysis of the practice can shed some light on, and provide a deeper understanding of, the difference, if any, between legal and non-legal norms in international relations. To this end, it is proposed to proceed in three steps: a brief survey of the legal theory which is the basis of the relevant international practice; a review of international practice; conclusions to be drawn from this practice.

2 Non-Legal Norms in International Relations – Some Preliminary Remarks

Usage (an important kind of non-legal norm in many societies) has played a significant role not only in the domestic sphere, but also in international relations, and still does so to a certain extent. Usages were formerly very important for the conduct of war, but the development of customary law and the Hague codifications of 1899 and 1907, including the famous Martens clause, have brought them into the ambit of law.[9] Usages still are the basis for the rules of international courtesy.[10] The question whether a rule of courtesy has become accepted as law, has changed its character from being a non-legal rule into being a rule of (customary) law has always been, and still is, difficult to answer.

This article will deal mainly with two other modes of formulating expectations by way of non-legal rules, namely non-legal agreements and resolutions of international organizations, because both are of considerable practical significance in current international relations.

An agreement binding in law is created by the corresponding declarations of the parties expressing their consent to be so bound. There are, however, cases of agreements where there is no consent to be bound *as a matter of law* – where the parties do not intend to create legal obligations. In such cases, the

---

9 Berber, *Lehrbuch des Völkerrecht,* vol. 2, 2nd ed. (1969) p. 67 et seq.; Guggenheim, *Traite de Droit international public,* vol. 2 (1954) p. 305 et seq.; Kalshoven, *The Law of Warfare* (1973) p. 24 et seq. In the treatises of the last century, a certain number of rules which are now part of the customary law of war were called usages (*Kriegssitte*), see Heffter, *Das Europäische Völkerrecht der Gegenwart* (1844) p. 201 et seq.; Bluntschli, *Das modern Völkerrecht der civilisirten Staaten,* 2nd ed. (1872) p. 304 et seq.

10 Blomeyer, "Courtoisie", in Strupp and Schlochauer, eds., op.cit., in n. 8, vol. 1 p. 301 et seq.

PART 1: BASIC ISSUES

agreement does not create legal obligations.[11] However, to the extent that the parties, even in the absence of a legal obligation, want to do something reasonable and sensible, they do intend, as a rule, to comply with the agreement, and expect the same from the other side. There are, thus, shared expectations formulated in a non-legal form – non-legal obligations. Such non-legal agreements are often called gentlemen's agreements. There exists, as will be shown, a wide variety of such non-legal agreements in international relations,[12] the CSCE Final Act being an example.

One of the controversies in this area concerns terminology. These agreements are often referred to as "non-binding" ones,[13] but this is a *contradictio in adiecto*. These agreements seriously formulate expectations, and are meant to be binding, but not as a matter of law.[14] Another terminological proposal has been *"de facto* agreements".[15] This does not duly take into account the normative character of the agreement; the relevant distinction is not that between law and fact, it is that between an obligation under the law and an obligation outside the ambit of law. Therefore, the terms "extralegal" or "non-legal" are to be preferred.

A related problem is that of the binding force of unilateral declarations. Such declarations can be legally binding under certain circumstances, but even if they are not legally binding, they may constitute a political commitment.[16]

The question of obligations deriving from resolutions of international organizations is a highly complex one. There are resolutions which are clearly

---

11   See on this interpretation of Art. 2 (1) of the Vienna Convention on the law of Treaties, Rotter, "Die Abgrenzung zwischen völkerrechtlichem Vertrag und ausserrechtlicher zwischenstaatlicher Abmachung", in Marcic et al., eds., *Internationale Festschrift für Alfred Verdross* (1971) pp. 413–433; Schweisfurth, loc.cit., in n. 3 p. 685 et seq. See also, the literature quoted in n. 13 and 14.

12   Wengler, "Die Abgrenzung zwischen völkerrechtlichen und nichtvölkerrechtlichen Normen im internationalen Verkehr", in *Legal Essays, A Tribute to Frede Castberg* (1963) pp. 332–352; Munch, "Unverbindliche Abmachungen im zwischenstaatlichen Bereich", in *Mélanges offerts à Juraj Andrassy* (1968) pp. 214–224; Fawcett, "The Legal Character of International Agreements", 30 BYIL (1953) pp. 381–400.

13   See Schachter, "The Twilight Existence of Non-binding International Agreements", 71 AJIL (1977) pp. 296–304; Münch, "Non-binding Agreements", 29 ZaöRV (1969) pp. 1–11.

14   Roessler, "Law, De Facto Agreements and Declaration of Principle in International Economic Relations", 21 GYIL (1978) pp. 27–59 at p. 41; Delbriick, "Die völkerrechtliche Bedeutung der Schlussakte der Konferenz über Sicherheit und Zusammenarbeit in Europa", in Bernhardt, von Munch and Rudolf, eds., *Drittes deutsch-polnisches Juristen-Kolloquium* vol. 1, (1977) pp. 31–50 at p. 42; Schweisfurth, loc.cit., in n. 3 p. 684 et seq.

15   Roessler, loc.cit.

16   Wengler, loc.cit., in n. 15 p. 346 et seq.; Fiedler, "Zur Verbindlichkeit einseitiger Versprechen im Völkerrecht", 19 GYIL (1976) pp. 35–72, in particular at p. 68 et seq.

LEGAL AND NON-LEGAL NORMS

legally binding, such as Security Council decisions under Article 25 of the UN Charter. The legal effect of resolutions which are not binding by virtue of a provision of the constituent treaty of an organization is one of the most controversial problems of international law today.[17] The heat of debate, however, often obscures the recognition of a very simple fact: that the possible *legal* effect of resolutions is only a part, a single aspect of their overall *political* effect.[18] The fact that a resolution is not legally binding does not make it a *quantite negligeable* in international relations. In many cases, resolutions of international organizations are taken very seriously by states; there is a strong expectation that states will comply with them.[19] In such cases, it is quite appropriate to say that these resolutions contain non-legal rules.

Theoretically, a resolution and an agreement appear to be quite different, the former being a unilateral (collective) act, the latter a bi- or multilateral one.[20] In fact, however, resolutions, whether adopted by majority vote, unanimously or by consensus, are also the result of a negotiating process, they are generally based on some kind of understanding between the states voting in favour or, at least, not objecting to them. The notion of "consensus", which has become very important in the practice of international organizations, has especially blurred the line between resolution and agreement.[21] Finally, international practice has invented the "agreement-resolution", this being a resolution of particular political (and legal?) significance.[22]

---

17   Asamoah, *The Legal Significance of Declarations of the General Assembly of the United Nations* (1966); Castafieda, *Legal Effects of United Nations Resolutions* (1969); Suy, "Innovations in International Law-Making Processes", in Macdonald, Johnston and Morris, eds., *The International Law and Policy of Human Welfare* (1978) pp. 187–200; R.-J. Dupuy, "Droit déclaratoire et droit programmatoire: de la coutume sauvage à la 'soft law' ", in *L'élaboration du droit international public, Société française pour le droit international, Colloque de Toulouse* (1975) pp. 132–148; "Das Problem der Rechtssetzung durch internationale Organisationen", in *Berichte der Deutschen Gesellschaft für Völkerrecht*, vol. 10, Report by Golsong, pp. 1–50, Report by Ermacora, pp. 51–95; Miehsler, "Zür Autorität von Beschlüssen internationaler Organisationen", in Schreuer, ed., *Autorität und internationale Ordnung* (1979) pp. 35–61.

18   This is rightly pointed out by Lagoni in "Resolution, Erklärung, Beschlüss", in Wolfrum, Prill and Bruckner, eds., *Handbuch Vereinte Nationen* (1977) pp. 358–364 at p. 363. See also, Heidensticker, "Zur Rechtsverbindlichkeit von Willensakten der Generalversammlung", *Vereinte Nationen* (1979) pp. 205–210 at p. 209;Constas, "The Capacity of International Organizations to Exercise Political 'Pressure' ", 25 *Revue hellenique* (1972) pp. 338–360.

19   For details see below, section 3.2.

20   Virally, loc.cit., in n. 3 at p. 25.

21   Suy, loc.cit., in n. 17 at p. 194.

22   Castañeda, op.cit., in n. 17 at p. 160 et seq.; Dupuy, loc.cit., in n. 17 at p. 140 et seq.; Ruge, *Der Beitrag von UNCTAD zur Herausbildung des Entwicklungsvölkerrechts* (1976) p. 1ll et seq.

Legally speaking, there is, however, a difference between a declaration by a state that it will be bound by a text – a declaration which must directly or indirectly be addressed to the other party or parties – and participation in a voting process with regard to a text. Thus, a vote for a resolution is not equivalent to a declaration to be bound under the law of treaties.[23] On the other hand, it is not legally impossible, depending on the circumstances, for a state, when voting on a resolution, to declare its consent to be bound by the terms thereof at the same time.[24] This is basically a question of interpretation of the state's conduct, for which both the text of the resolution and "explanations of vote" may be particularly relevant. When it comes to political undertakings, this distinction between casting a vote and expressing consent to be bound appears to be still less certain.

3 Non-Legal Norms – a Review of International Practice

These preliminary observations form the basis for a survey of international practice where the technique of non-legal norms has been used to regulate state behaviour, including some controversial or borderline cases.

3.1 *Concerting Political Attitudes through Non-Legal Agreements*

In international relations, there is a considerable need for states to concert their activities. The most spectacular example of this phenomenon is so-called "summit diplomacy"-meetings of leaders of state which generally conclude with some kind of declaration on the future activity and attitude of the participating states. With varying degrees of precision, states give assurances, or declare how they intend to behave. This is a practice in all parts of the world, important for East-West relations,[25] for economic co-ordination among the Western industrialized countries,[26] North-South relations[27] and for many other fields. The declared policies may range from general assurances of co-operation to specific details, such as future co-ordination of monetary policies,[28]

---

23   Tomuschat, "Die Charta der wirtschaftlichen Rechte und Pflichten der Staaten", 36 ZaöRV (1976) pp. 444–491 at p. 472 et seq.

24   See Virally, loc.cit., in n. 3 at p. 26; J.P. Miiller, *Vertrauensschutz im Völkerrecht* (1971) p. 251 et seq.

25   For some examples see below, text accompanying n. 36.

26   The so-called economic summits, which have become a regular practice.

27   Conference on International Economic Co-operation, Final Document, 2 June 1977, *Archiv der Gegenwart* (1977), 21053 B.

28   See, for example, Bonn Summit, Final Declaration, 17 July 1978, para. 28 et seq., 33 *Europa-Archiv* (1978) D 462 et seq.

LEGAL AND NON-LEGAL NORMS

limitation of energy consumption (including actual figures),[29] or measures to be taken in cases of aircraft hijacking.[30] It is generally agreed that these joint statements do not create legal obligations, yet they do play an important role in international relations as a factor of stabilization, by making state behaviour more predictable.[31] In other words, such joint statements are, at least in many cases, not just propaganda which is not be taken seriously. There is at least a certain degree of expectation that states will indeed do what they have declared to be their intention. This explains why the wording of such declarations is often negotiated with considerable care, and debated with great heat. It thus appears appropriate to state that, depending on their wording, such joint statements do create obligations, but obligations of a political, non-legal character.

It is not possible, in the framework of this article, to give a complete survey of this concerting of political attitudes by states. Only a few examples will be given. In some of these cases the nature of the obligations deriving from an agreement or joint statement are not very clear, and their qualification as legal or non-legal is problematical.

An early example of an agreement which appears to be of a non-legal character is the tripartite declaration by France, Great-Britain and Spain of 1907 on the *status quo* in the Mediterranean and North Africa. It took the form of two exchanges of notes which stated that it was the general policy of the parties to maintain their territorial possessions. The published negotiating history suggests that this arrangement was not a "treaty" in the formal sense.[32] A controversial example is the so-called Lansing-Ishii agreement of 1917 on policies to be pursued in relation to China. H. Lauterpacht claims that a true treaty relationship was not intended, while E. Lauterpacht contends that such a view cannot necessarily be inferred from the relative generality of the agreement's content.[33]

---

29   Declaration of the Tokyo Summit, 29 June 1979, 34 *Europa-Archiv* (1979) D 354.

30   Bonn Declaration on Hijacking, adopted 17 July 1978, by the heads of government of Canada, France, the Federal Republic of Germany, Italy, Japan, the UK and the US. The Declaration provides for certain measures to be taken against states which refuse to extradite or prosecute aerial hijackers and/or fail to return hijacked aircraft. Text: 73 AJIL (1979) p. 133 et seq.

31   Rotter, loc.cit., in n. 11 at p. 420 et seq.

32   Münch,-loc.cit., in n. 13 at p. 4.

33   Münch, loc.cit., in n. 13 at p. 5; E. Lauterpacht, "Gentleman's Agreements", in Flume et al., eds., *Internationales Recht und Wirtschaftsordnung, Festschrift für F.A. Mann zum 70. Geburtstag* (1977) pp. 381–398 at p. 381 et seq.

The legal character of the Allied understandings on the future post-war settlements is also controversial.[34] Especially on the British side, there were statements that the Atlantic Charter, and the final documents of the Cairo, London, Yalta and Potsdam conferences were not legally binding. On the other hand, the Soviet Union has always insisted on the fact that the Potsdam "agreement" was a legally binding one. With respect to Yalta and Potsdam in particular, it is probably correct to distinguish between the various parts of the agreements reached. Some parts are of such a nature as to produce specific legal obligations for the participating states, while others determine lines of policy, and their qualification as legally binding would not appear to be justified.

The conclusion of the "State Treaty" between Austria and the Allied Powers was preceded by the so-called Moscow Memorandum of April 1955, which constituted an agreement between Austria and the Soviet Union and disposed of a number of Soviet objections to the restoration of Austrian sovereignty. Although the status of the agreement is somewhat controversial, the better view seems to be that it is a non-legal, "political" agreement. Austrian literature on the subject stresses the fact that the Austrian Government delegation which negotiated the Moscow agreement did not possess the necessary constitutional authority to enter into a legally binding agreement of this kind.[35]

Another field where non-legal norms have played a significant role in post-war practice is that of disarmament.[36] First, disarmament is a field where the UN General Assembly has passed numerous resolutions, a matter we shall deal with in the next section. As to the use of non-legal agreements, the negotiating process of SALT is quite illustrative. SALT I was preceded by a US-Soviet common declaration of 5 May 1971, which defined the subjects upon which agreement was envisaged. After SALT I, Nixon and Brezhnev agreed on "Basic Principles of Negotiation on the Further Limitation of Strategic Offensive Arms", a document adopted on 21 June 1973 in solemn form, and containing a preamble and using a formula which is typical of treaties ("Have agreed as follows").

---

34   Münch, loc.cit., in n. 13 at p. 5; Schachter, loc.cit., in n. 13 at p. 297 et seq.; Schlochauer, "Atlantik-Chaiter" in Strupp and Schlochauer, op.cit., in n. 8, vol. 1 p. 95; Schlochauer, "Jalta-Konferenz von 1945", ibid., vol. 2 pp. 162–165; von der Heydte, "Potsdamer Abkommen von 1945", ibid., vol. 2 pp. 786–790; Rotter, loc.cit., in n. 11 at p. 414 et seq.

35   Rotter, loc.cit., in n. 11 at p. 416 et seq.; Verdross, *Die immerwährende Neutralität Osterreichs* (1978) p. 31.

36   Bothe, "Zur Dogmatik eines völkerrechtlichen Kriegsverhütungsrechts, Verfahren und Inhalt des Recht der Rüstungskontrolle und Abrüstung", in Delbrück, ed., *Völkerrecht und Kriegsverhütung* (1979) pp. 213–233 at p. 227 et seq. See also Schachter, loc.cit., in n. 6 at p. 14 et seq.

LEGAL AND NON-LEGAL NORMS

There was a mutual undertaking by the "two Sides" to "continue active negotiations in order to work out a permanent agreement on more complete measures on the limitation of strategic offensive arms ... Over the course of the next year the two Sides will make serious efforts to work out the provisions of the permanent agreement on more complete measures on the limitation of strategic offensive arms with the objective of signing it in 1974". Some details of the agreement already reached were spelled out (inclusion of both quantitative and qualitative aspects, verification, modernization and replacement). Further details of the future treaty were given in a US-Soviet Communique dated 3 July 1974, and the Joint Statement on Strategic Offensive Arms, issued at Vladivostok on 24 November 1974 (duration, ceiling for delivering vehicles and MIRVs). The concrete ceiling was, however, announced by President Ford. The SALT II Treaty was finally signed by Brezhnev and Carter in 1979, but has so far (Summer 1980) not been ratified.

Meanwhile, the SALT I Interim Agreement had, in accordance with its terms, expired in October 1978. Its application was extended, however, by agreed unilateral declarations. US-Soviet relations were also made the object of a more comprehensive statement, namely the "Declaration of Basic Principles of Relations Between the United States of America and the Union of Soviet Socialist Republics" of 29 May 1972, also a document in solemn form, using the formula "Have agreed as follows". Nevertheless, even if one applies very liberal standards to the definition of treaties binding as a matter of law, it would not be appropriate to include the statements concerning the SALT negotiations, the extension of SALT I and the Declaration of Principles in such a definition. Even documents which appear to be international treaties may not always be construed in this sense. This seems to have been the view of Secretary of State Kissinger when he stated, with reference to both the Declaration of Principles and the 1973 Agreement on the Prevention, of Nuclear War:[37]

> These statements of principle are not an American concession; indeed, we have been affirming them unilaterally for two decades. Nor are they a legal contract; rather, they are an aspiration and a yard-stick by which we assess Soviet behaviour ...

What, if anything, becomes clear in this statement is the concept of an expectation formulated in political rather than legal terms.

---

37   71 Department of State Bulletin (1974) p. 510.

This also characterizes the CSCE Final Act. There, any intent of the Parties to enter into an agreement binding as a matter of international law was conspicuously absent. As this question has been dealt with extensively in legal writings,[38] it may suffice to recall some basic facts. The document did not use the term "Have agreed", but "Have adopted the following". The document was not considered as capable of being registered as a "treaty" or an "international agreement" under Article 102 of the UN Charter. The declarations of many participating governments clearly stated that the document was not intended to be binding as such under international law, and there are no declarations to the contrary. On the other hand, it appears clearly that the Parties are determined to base their conduct on the provisions of the document, and expect the same behaviour from the other Parties. The character and content of these obligations, however, are by no means uniform: there are general programmes, norms which lay down directly applicable standards of state behaviour, and recommendations and guidelines for practical measures of co-operation. In summary, we are again confronted with shared expectation formulated in political, and not in legal terms.

This is probably also (at least partly) the correct interpretation of another important set of documents containing a political settlement, viz., the Camp David agreements between Israel and Egypt.[39] These agreements consist essentially of two agreed "frameworks": one for peace in the Middle East, and one for the conclusion of a peace treaty between Egypt and Israel. The first contains a number of policy guidelines, some of them rather specific. If this were a treaty, it would probably be a treaty *in favorem tertii,* which would, in the light of the existing tension in the area, be rather far-reaching. It is hard to conceive that Israel and Egypt would bind themselves under international law as to the content of separate peace treaties to be negotiated between, on the one hand, Israel, and on the other Jordan, Syria, and Lebanon. Therefore, it is hardly surprising that the word "should" was quite often used instead of "shall". In the light of the whole context, it is thus more appropriate to see this

---

38 See Schweisfurth, loc.cit., in n. 3; Delbruck, loc. cit., in n. 14; Skubiszewski, "Der Rechtscharakter der KSZE-Schlussakte", in Bernhardt, von Munch and Rudolf, eds., op.cit., in n. 14 at pp. 13–30; Kühne, "Die Schlussakte der KSZE: Zur Bedeutung, Auslegung und Anwendung von Verhaltensregeln in den Ost-West-Beziehungen", in Delbruck, Ropers and Zellentin, eds., *Grünbuch zu den Folgewirkungen der KSZE* (1977) pp. 137–154; Schütz, "Probleme der Anwendung der KSZE-Schlussakte aus völkerrechtlicher Sicht", ibid. pp. 155–175; Fawcett, "The Helsinki Act and International Law", 13 *Revue beige* (1977) pp. 5–9; Blech, "Die KSZE im Entspannungsprozess", 30 *Europa-Archiv* (1975) pp. 681–692 at p. 686 et seq.

39 For the text, see 17 ILM (1978) p. 1466 et seq.

LEGAL AND NON-LEGAL NORMS

general framework as a political agreement, at least as far as those questions are concerned which are not strictly confined to relations between Israel and Egypt. The preamble to the Peace Treaty,[40] in which the Parties reaffirm their "adherence" to the "Framework", does not add additional legal value to the latter document.

As far as the relations between Egypt and Israel are concerned, it is, on the other hand, quite possible to interpret the agreement as a legal *pactum de negotiando*.[41] The text of the second framework points in that direction:

> In order to achieve peace between them, Israel and Egypt agree to negotiate in good faith with a goal of concluding within three months of the signing of this framework a peace treaty between them.

There then follow a number of items on which agreement has been reached. A difficult problem remains: did the Egyptian President and the Israeli Prime Minister have the constitutional authority to legally bind their respective states as to the content of the treaty to be negotiated? This rather militates against the assumption of a *legal* obligation.

The concerting of attitudes between governments through non-legal agreements in stages, preceding formal legal agreement, does not only happen in politically sensitive areas such as those hitherto described. Non-legal agreements can also be found on such matters as the regulation of shared resources in the field of international water law.[42]

Another case where the dividing line between concerted political action and legal agreement has become controversial is the Brussels Communique of 31 May 1975, issued by the Prime Ministers of Greece and Turkey, which stated that the dispute between the two countries over the continental shelf in the Aegean Sea should be resolved by the International Court of Justice.[43] Greece considered the document to constitute an agreement under international law, which Turkey denied. The Court left this question open, and simply looked at the content of the document; even if it were a legal agreement, it could not,

---

40 For the text, see 18 ILM (1979) p. 382.

41 On the difficulty in distinguishing between a political agreement to conclude a treaty and a legal *pactum de contrahendo,* see also Wengler, loc.cit., in n. 12 at p. 334.

42 See, *Management of international water resources: institutional and legal aspect,* UN Doc. ST/ESA/5, p. 30 et seq.

43 See, Oellers-Frahm, "Die Entscheidung des Internationalen Gerichtshofes im griechisch-türkischen Streit um den Festlandsockel in der Aegaeis", 18 ArchVR (1978/80) pp. 375–392 at p. 385 et seq.

26 PART I: BASIC ISSUES

according to its terms, be a basis for the jurisdiction of the Court.[44] Judge Lachs considered the agreement as a legal *pactum de negotiando*.[45]

3.2 Resolutions of International Organizations as a Non-Legal Means of International Regulation

The creation of international obligations by resolutions of international organizations constitutes a problem where generalizations are dangerous. Distinctions must be made in many areas, the main ones being the *circumstances of adoption* (adoption by majority vote, unanimous vote, consensus, reservations expressed by particular states), and the *content and language* of a resolution. As to the latter aspect, one can distinguish, *inter alia,* between declarations purporting to state existing principles of international law, declarations purporting to create new principles of international law, and declarations promoting specific programmes.[46]

As examples of the first category, one can mention the Declaration on Principles of International Law concerning Friendly Relations and Co-operation among States,[47] the Declaration on the Strengthening of International Security,[48] and the Resolution on the Question of Chemical and Biological Weapons.[49] These and similar resolutions constitute evidence of existing international law, though such evidence is not necessarily conclusive.[50] To the extent that their claim to formulate existing legal rules holds true, there is a legal obligation to comply with their provisions. Insofar as this claim does not correspond to the true state of the law, such resolutions may still formulate shared expectations in non-legal form. Thus, the Declaration on the Prohibition of the Use of Nuclear and Thermo-nuclear Weapons[51] was said to express "the universal aspiration on a high moral plane",[52] although, on its face, it purports to formulate *legal* principles.

A case of a General Assembly resolution purporting to create a new rule of international law is the Declaration of Legal Principles Governing the Activities of States in the Exploration and Use of Outer Space.[53] There is a considerable

---

44   ICJ Reports 1978, p. 39 et seq., para. 94 et seq. of the Judgment.
45   Ibid., p. 51.
46   Asamoah, op.cit., in n. 17 *passim;* Castaneda, op.cit., in n. 17 *passim.*
47   Resolution 2625 (XXV).
48   Resolution 2734 (XXV).
49   Resolution 2603 (XXIV)A.
50   Asamoah, op.cit., in n. 17, at p. 46 et seq., p. 116 et seq., and p. 124 et seq.
51   Resolution 1653 (XVI).
52   Asamoah, op.cit., in n. 17, at p. 116.
53   Resolution 1962 (XVIII).

LEGAL AND NON-LEGAL NORMS

tendency among legal writers to accept the thesis that this resolution has indeed achieved what it purported to do: it has created a new norm of international law.[54] This is somewhat difficult to explain on the basis of the traditional rules on sources of international law. In the view of the present writer, the most convincing explanation is to regard the instant general consensus of the international community, as expressed in the resolution, as a source of international law which is not mentioned in Article 38 of the ICJ Statute.[55]

Two other resolutions purporting to create a new rule of international law have remained much more controversial: the Declaration of Principles Governing the Sea-Bed and the Ocean Floor, and the Subsoil thereof, beyond the Limits of National Jurisdiction,[56] which declared that area and its resources to be the common heritage of mankind, not subject to national appropriation; and the so-called Moratorium Resolution regarding the exploitation of the sea-bed beyond the limits of national jurisdiction,[57] which stated that, pending the establishment of an international sea-bed regime, "States and persons, physical or juridical, are bound to refrain from all activities of exploitation of the resources of the area of the sea-bed and ocean floor, and the subsoil thereof, beyond the limits of national jurisdiction". There are voices which claim that the former resolution does indeed constitute a source of legal obligations,[58] and that the moratorium would appear to be a logical consequence of these obligations. This, however, has never been admitted by the technologically advanced countries. In reply to the question whether the German Federal Government considered itself bound by the moratorium resolution, the Minister of State for Foreign Affairs stated in the German *Bundestag* that the resolution was not obligatory under international law, but that one had to admit that the resolution had acquired a high political importance.[59]

---

54   Asamoah, op.cit., in n. 17 at p. 157 et seq.

55   Simma, "Methodik und Bedeutung der Arbeit der Vereinten Nationen für die Fortentwicklung des Völkerrechts", in Kewenig, ed., *Die Vereinten Nationen im Wandel* (1975) pp. 79–102 at p. 97 et seq. Frowein, "Der Beitrag der internationalen Organisational zur Entwicklung des Völkerrechts", 36 ZaöRV (1976) pp. 147–167 at p. 152.

56   Resolution 2749 (XXV).

57   Resolution 2574 (XXIV).

58   Anand, *Legal Regime of the Sea-Bed and the Developing Countries* (1976) p. 193 et seq.

59   Gündling, "Völkerrechtliche Praxis der Bundesrepublik Deutschland im Jahre 1977", 39 ZaöRV (1979) pp. 555–624 at p. 570; Saffo, "The Common Heritage of Mankind: Has the General Assembly Created a Law to Govern Seabed Mining?" 53 Tulane Law Review (1979) pp. 492–520 at p. 512; Skubiszewski, "La nature juridique de la 'Declaration des principes' sur les fonds marins", 4 *Annales d'études internationales* (1973) pp. 237–248. See also, Graf Vitzthum, "Die Bemühungen um ein Regime des Tiefseebodens", 38 ZaöRV (1978) pp. 745–800 at p. 787 et seq.; idem, *Der Rechtsstatus des Meeresbodens* (1972) p. 277.

Resolutions intended to promote specific programmes are, for example, the Universal Declaration of Human Rights[60] and the Declaration on the Granting of Independence to Colonial Countries and Peoples.[61]

The Universal Declaration of Human Rights proclaims the rights contained therein rather as a goal than as rights already guaranteed under international law. Many of the rights have been enshrined in subsequent treaties, and at least some of them have become part of customary international law.[62] Nevertheless, in the view of many writers, the resolution as such is "only of moral authority",[63] and constitutes a non-legal programme of action.[64] The legal status of the Declaration on the Granting of Independence to Colonial Countries and Peoples is highly controversial.[65] While writers and officials from the Third World maintain that it embodies legal obligations, there are other views to the effect that this is only partly so, that the resolution goes beyond existing international law, and that, to that extent, it only formulates political principles, a political programme of action. The political weight of the resolution, however, is undisputed; it has set out one of the most effective programmes of the United Nations.

The foregoing examples illustrate a general phenomenon: the political importance of General Assembly resolutions, their "moral force"[66] – a moral or political obligation deriving from these resolutions.[67] This political weight of General Assembly resolutions was used in the 1950s by the United States (then in a position to master the required majorities) against the Soviet Union, and it is now used by the Third World against the Western industrialized states, and quite effectively so.

For the purposes of the problem under review, two elements of this political effect of General Assembly resolutions must be distinguished: the pressure exerted by a resolution even on objecting states, and the formulation of shared expectations. Resolutions mobilize public opinion. In the long run, it is politically difficult for a state to violate principles consistently reiterated by the General Assembly, even if the state concerned vehemently objects to them, but, in the short run, there is a low expectation that an objecting state will comply.

---

60   Resolution 217 (III).

61   Resolution 1514 (XV).

62   Verdross and Simma, *Universelles Völkerrecht* (1976), p. 599 et seq.

63   Asamoah, op.cit., in n. 17 at p. 191.

64   On this notion of "programme", see R.-J. Dupuy, loc.cit., in n. 17 at p. 144 et seq.

65   Asamoah, op.cit., in n. 17 at p. 177 et seq.

66   Sloan, "The Binding Force of a 'Recommendation' of the General Assembly of the United Nations", 25 BYIL (1948) pp. 1–33 at p. 30.

67   Virally, loc.cit., in n. 3 at p. 24.

LEGAL AND NON-LEGAL NORMS

On the other hand, it is quite reasonable to expect that states which accept a resolution without reservation are prepared to comply with its terms. This expectation of compliance is, as an astute observer of United Nations practice has pointed out, only marginally dependent on the existence of a legal obligation to comply.[68] States do find it somewhat easier not to comply with resolutions which are not legally binding, but this is only one factor among many in determining actual compliance, and not necessarily the decisive one. A number of other matters serve as indicators of the authority of a resolution, and its potential to generate obligations[69]: the circumstances which have led to its adoption, the degree of agreement on which it is based, form (e.g., "declaration"), content of a document, the political rank of the organ adopting the resolution, and implementation procedures.

Implementation procedures, in particular, illustrate the fact that compliance with resolutions is indeed expected. There are a considerable number of cases where implementation procedures have been established with a view to monitoring (and finally securing?) compliance with resolutions having no formally binding force. A few well known examples may be recalled.

The development probably started with ECOSOC Resolution 624 B (XXII),[70] dated 1 August 1956, which required states and Specialized Agencies to submit reports on progress achieved in the field of human rights, dealing with all the rights contained in the Universal Declaration of Human Rights. This has prompted a certain number of reports, the procedure having been refined over the years. The procedure will, however, probably be replaced by that under the Covenant on Civil and Political Rights.

To monitor the implementation of Resolution 1514 (XV) on decolonization, the General Assembly, by Resolution 1654 (XVI), created the Committee which has become known as the "Committee of 24".[71]

These implementation procedures, mainly making use of periodic reports, have become a common feature in the United Nations system. They

---

68   Higgins, "Compliance with United Nations Decisions on Peace and Security and Human Rights Questions", in Schwebel, ed., op.cit., in n. 6 pp. 32–50 at p. 37 et seq.

69   Higgins, loc.cit.; Miehsler, loc.cit., in n. 17 p. 44 et seq.; see also, Golsong, loc.cit., in n. 17 at p. 35 et seq.

70   See, Khol, "Berichtssystem", in Wolfram, Prill and Bruckner, eds., op.cit., in n. 18pp. 48–58 at p. 53 et seq.; *United Nations Action in the Field of Human Rights,* UN Doc. ST/HR/2, p. 169 et seq.

71   Virally, *"Droit international et décolonisation devant les Nations Unies",* AFDI (1963) pp. 508–541 at p. 528 et seq.

30   PART 1: BASIC ISSUES

are applied by the UN General Assembly, by other UN organs and by the Specialized Agencies with respect both to binding international treaties and to recommendations.[72]

Implementation procedures are not only a proof that compliance is expected, they are also a means of exerting pressure to secure compliance, even where a state objects. The flood of resolutions concerning South Africa and Namibia, which have also provided for implementation procedures, is an example of this.[73]

The practical effects which resolutions of international organizations, and General Assembly resolutions in particular, have had on state practice have led some authors to speak of quasi-legal obligations,[74] or a *"droit programmatoire".*[75] Others insist on the non-legal, "political", or "moral" character of the obligations arising from resolutions, but it is clear that these resolutions do shape international practice, and practice, as in the cases of usages,[76] shapes law.[77] Thus, political obligations deriving from resolutions may finally grow into legal obligations. In this sense, resolutions are an important factor of the law-creating process in international relations[78]; their "moral force ... is in fact a nascent legal force".[79]

3.3   *International Economic Relations and Non-Legal Regulations*

The field of international economic relations is particularly suitable for a demonstration of the use of the non-legal approach in international rulemaking. A broad spectrum of non-legal regulations have been used to cope with international economic problems. The following survey cannot be comprehensive, and is limited to some significant examples.

---

72   Sohn, "Procedures Developed by International Organizations for Checking Compliance", in Schwebel, ed., op.cit., in n. 6 pp. 51–56; *United Nations Action in the Field of Human Rights,* op.cit, in n. 70, at p. 169 et seq.

73   See Cadoux, *"L'organisation des Nations Unies et le problème de l'Afrique australe, L'evolution de la strategie des pressions Internationales",* 23 AFDI (1977) pp. 127–174.

74   Castañeda, op.cit., in n. 17 at p. 176.

75   Dupuy, loc.cit., in n. 17 at p. 144 et seq. See also, Virally, *"La notion de programme, Un instrument de la coopération technique multilatérale",* AFDI (1968) pp. 530–553 at p. 532 et seq.

76   See above, text accompanying n. 9 and 10.

77   Sir Kenneth Bailey, *"Making International Law at the United Nations",* ASIL Proceedings (1967) pp. 233–239 at p. 239; see also, Golsong, loc.cit., in n. 17 at p. 12 et seq.

78   Schachter, *"The Evolving Law of International Development",* 15 Columbia Journal of Transnational Law (1976) pp. 1–16 at p. 3 et seq.; Virally, loc.cit., in n. 74 at p. 531; see also, Ruge, op.cit., in n. 22 at p. 116 et seq.

79   Sloan, loc.cit., in n. 17 at p. 32.

LEGAL AND NON-LEGAL NORMS

3.3.1 General Principles – Resolutions

The whole arsenal of pressure available in the United Nations has been mobilized in order to promote changes in the existing international economic system in favour of the underdeveloped countries. For this purpose, resolutions of a programmatic character, e.g., the International Development Strategy for the Second United Nations Development Decade,[80] and resolutions purporting to state existing law, e.g., those concerning permanent sovereignty over natural resources,[81] have both been adopted. Two resolutions are of particular importance in this struggle for a New International Economic Order: the Declaration and Programme of Action on the Establishment of a New International Economic Order,[82] adopted without a vote (but with serious reservations on the part of the Western industrialized states)[83] by the Sixth Special Session of the General Assembly on 1 May 1974, and the Charter of

Economic Rights and Duties of States,[84] adopted on 12 December 1974 by a roll-call vote of 120 in favour to 6 against, with 10 abstentions. It was the Western industrialized states which voted against the resolution or abstained. As the record shows, these resolutions have not been accepted in their entirety, either as reflecting existing law or as political guidelines.[85] Nevertheless, certain parts of them may well be considered as stating existing law, and, at least to the extent that agreement concerning their content existed, they have not merely formulated the wishes of the Third World, but the expectations of the wider community. They have, to a considerable degree, shaped the ensuing debate on changes in the existing international economic system. A number of issues raised by these resolutions have been made the object of North- South negotiations; agreement, or at least significant progress, has been reached on many of them,[86] e.g., multinational corporations, commodity trade, transfer of technology, trade preferences for developing countries,

---

80   Resolution 2626 (xxv).

81   In particular, Resolutions 1803 (xvii), 2158 (xxi), 3171 (xxviii).

82   See Tomuschat, loc.cit., in n. 23; Petersmann, "The New International Economic Order: Principles, Politics and International Law", in Macdonald, Johnston and Morris, eds., op.cit., in n. 17 pp. 449–469.

83   For a summary of the views expressed, see 1974 UN Monthly Chronicle no. 5 p. 45 et seq.

84   Resolution 3281 (xxix).

85   See the detailed analysis by Petersmann, *"Internationales Recht und Neue Internationale Wirtschaftsordnung"*, 18 ArchVR (1978/80) pp. 17–44 at p. 34 et seq., who rightly points out that a distinction has to be made between the various provisions of the Charter. See also Tomuschat, loc.cit., in n. 23.

86   See, *inter alia,* Petersmann, loc.cit., in n. 85; Prill, "Weltwirtschaftsordnung", in Wolfram, Prill and Bruckner, eds., op.cit., in n. 18 pp. 524–536, in particular, p. 526 et seq.

32   PART 1: BASIC ISSUES

and reform of the international monetary system taking into account the interests of developing countries. The associations of producer-countries of raw materials have become a fact of international life, at least with regard to some materials. The question of compensation for nationalization has remained controversial, but it seems that the position of the Western industrial states is also softening in this respect.[87] This brings us to some more specific issues of international economic regulations, where the non-legal approach has also been widely used.

3.3.2   Trade

It is quite obvious that matters requiring an important organizational framework, like the Integrated Programme for Commodities, can only be dealt with by a legally binding document. In a considerable number of cases, however, regulations concerning international trade have been adopted which are not of a legally binding character.

For instance, the Generalized System of Preferences adopted by UNCTAD in 1970 does not constitute a legally binding commitment.[88] As far as GATT is concerned, there are such general policy statements as the Tokyo Declaration on Multilateral Trade Negotiations of 1973, fixing a programme and certain (procedural as well as substantive) Principles for negotiation.[89] This is a typical example of a political programme indicating some basic elements of agreement, but not yet constituting legally binding obligations. This programme has now been fulfilled by the 1979 agreements reached by the Tokyo-Round, which have taken the form of binding treaties.[90]

Within the framework of GATT, there has often been a discrepancy between the requirements of law and those of the economic circumstances of the day.[91] Thus, measures of doubtful legality and also measures of a nonbinding

---

87   See the different formulations used in this context in Resolutions 1803 (XVII) and 3171 (XXVIII). See also, Meessen, "Völkerrechtliches Enteignungsrecht im Nord-Sud-Konflikt", in Kewenig, ed., *Völkerrecht und international wirtschaftliche Zusammenarbeit* (1978) pp. 11–34.

88   Roessler, loc.cit., in n. 14 at p. 29; Graham, "The US Generalized System of Preferences for Developing Countries: International Innovation and the Art of Possible", 72 AJIL (1978) pp. 513–541 at p. 519.

89   12 ILM (1973) p. 1533.

90   Swiss Federal Council, Botschaft über die in den Multilateralen Handelsvereinbarungen unter der Ägide des GATT (Tokio-Runde) erzielten Ergebnisse, 24 September 1979, BB1. 1979 III pp. 1–581, in particular, at p. 90. See also, Graham, "Results of the Tokyo Round", 9 *Georgia Journal of International and Comparative Law* (1979) pp. 153–175.

91   John H. Jackson, *World Trade and the Law of GATT* (1969) p. 755 et seq.

LEGAL AND NON-LEGAL NORMS

character have been used quite frequently.[92] As an example, one may quote the provisional *de facto* application of GATT by newly independent states.[93]

3.3.3 Codes of Conduct

In other important areas of international economic relations, non-legal methods of regulation have also been adopted, or are being discussed. The most prominent examples are the issues of multinational corporations,[94] transfer of technology[95] and restrictive business practices.[96]

In 1976, the OECD Council adopted the "Guidelines for Multinational Enterprises", which are not legally binding, and a decision "on Intergovernmental Consultation Procedures" concerning these Guidelines, which is binding.[97] This is a somewhat surprising mixture of a substantive regulation which is not legally binding and a binding implementation procedure.[98]

In the United Nations, the fight about the legal character of the UN Code on Transnational Corporations, and the UNCTAD Codes on Transfer of Technology is still undecided, as is the struggle about implementation procedures.[99] While the developing countries want a code in the form of a multilateral treaty

---

92   Roessler, loc.cit., in n. 14 pp. 46, 54, with further references at p. 52 n. 90. See also, Roessler, "GATT and Access to Supplies", 9 *Journal of World Trade Law* (1975) pp. 25–40 at p. 39 et seq.

93   *Basic Documents,* suppl. 15 p. 64.

94   Francioni, "International Codes of Conduct for Multinational Enterprises: an Alternative Approach", 3 IYIL (1977) pp. 143–170; Studier, "Verhaltenskodizes für multinationale Konzerne und die Interessenposition der Entwicklungsländer", 11 VRU (1978) pp. 411–431; Nelli Feroci, "Società multinazionali: verso un codice di condotta", 33 *La Comunità Internazionale* (1978) pp. 356–374; UN Docs. E/5655 paras. 41 et seq., E/C. 10/9, paras. 3744, 57–61, 71–88, E/C. 10/17, paras. 152–170. See also, R. Schwartz, "Are the OECD and UNCTAD Codes Legally Binding?", 11 International Lawyer (1977) pp. 529–536.

95   Kewenig, "Technologietransfer aus völkerrechtlicher Sicht", in Kewenig, ed., *Völkerrecht und Internationale wirtschaftliche Zusammenarbeit* (1978) pp. 71–96, in particular, p. 78 et seq.; Rubin, "International Code of Conduct on the Transfer of Technology", 73 AJIL (1979) pp. 519–520; Cousin, "Le Project de la C.N.U.C.E.D. de Code international de Conduite pour le Transfert de techniques", 19 GYIL (1976) pp. 199–222 at p. 204 et seq. Draft International Code of Conduct on the Transfer of Technology, UN DOC. TD/CODE TOT/25 = 19 ILM (1980) pp. 773 etseq.

96   Davidow and Chiles, "The United States and the Issue of the Binding or Voluntary Nature of International Codes of Conduct Regarding Restrictive Business Practices", 72 AJIL (1978) pp. 247–276.

97   15 ILM (1976) p. 967 et seq. The Decision was revised in 1979, 18 ILM (1979) p. 1171.

98   On the legal effect and practical effectivity of the OECD Guidelines, see Baade, "The Legal Effects of Codes of Conduct for Multinational Enterprises", 22 GYIL (1979) pp. 11–52, at 29 et seq.

99   See Kewenig, loc.cit., in n. 95.

34 PART 1: BASIC ISSUES

(like the Code of Conduct on Liner Conferences),[100] the Western industrialized states insist on a "voluntary" code, which is not legally binding.[101] The "Multi-laterally Agreed Equitable Principles and Rules for the Control of Restrictive Business Practices"[101a] take the form of recommendations. It is remarkable, however, that a code which is not legally binding and an elaborate implementation procedure are not considered as being mutually exclusive. Thus, even a code which is not obligatory as a matter of law, can constitute a formulation of serious expectations.

3.3.4   International Monetary Relations

International monetary relations are also a field where the non-legal approach to regulation has been widely used.[102]

The "par value" system of Bretton Woods was only in part based on legal obligations. A deviation from this system was not a violation of a legal obligation, though it did make a state ineligible to use the resources of the International Monetary Fund. In 1971, the system broke down. The new regime of central rates with wider margins of fluctuation was based on the "Smithsonian Agreement", implemented by a decision of the Fund's Executive Directors, both of which were clearly not meant to be legally binding. When this regime also collapsed, and the common practice of floating developed, the Fund issued, in 1974, "Guidelines for the Management of Floating Exchange Rates" of a "tentative and experimental character". All this was clearly at variance with the IMF Articles of Agreement, which technically speaking still constituted the applicable law. Amendment of the IMF Articles of Agreement has legalized the situation, giving states considerable freedom. The Fund may, with a majority of 85% of the votes, recommend exchange arrangements.[103] Although not legally binding, such recommendations would command a considerable degree of acceptance, and thus have a good chance of being applied. They thus constitute a non-legal means of formulating expectations.

---

100   See Grewlich, "Die UN-Konvention über einen Verhaltenskodex fur Linienkonferenzen", 35 ZaöRV (1975) pp. 742–758.

101   A similar split can be seen between observations submitted by employers' organizations and those made by trades unions, see UN Doc. E/C. 10/20 para. 29 et seq.

101a   UN Doc. TD/RBP/CONF/10 = 19 ILM (1980) pp. 813 et seq.

102   Roessler, loc.cit., in n. 14 at p. 42 et seq.; Petersmann, "Völkerrechtliche Fragen der Weltwährungsreform", 34 ZaoRV (1974) pp. 452–502; Pohl, "Von Bretton Woods nach Jamaika, Bilanz der Reformarbeiten für die künftige Weltwährungsordnung", 31 Europa-Archiv (1976) pp. 139–146; Hahn, "Elemente einer neuen Weltwährungsordnung", in Kewenig, ed., op.cit., in n. 87 pp. 215–242.

103   Art. IV, as amended.

LEGAL AND NON-LEGAL NORMS

Another type of regulation which may also be discussed under the heading of non-legal obligations is the so-called "stand-by arrangement" of the Fund.[104] When a member wants to obtain liquidity from the Fund, the latter may, under certain conditions, raise objections, but it may agree not to do so if the state gives assurances on its economic policy. This stand-by arrangement does not legally bind the state to pursue the stated economic policy, but if it does not do so it loses its rights to use the Fund's resources without challenge. To discuss this kind of agreement under the heading of non-legal obligations is, however, to a certain extent misleading. This becomes clear if one puts the question the other way around: could the Fund, without violating a *legal* commitment, challenge an application made by the state if the state indeed pursued the economic policy provided for in the stand-by agreement? It is submitted that the answer is negative. The stand-by agreement is, it seems, an example of a legal rule which does not impose a specific obligation to do something, but provides for certain negative consequences if certain behaviour is not followed. Thus, non-compliance is not illegal, but risky. The law of war contains a number of such rules. No state is obliged to mark its medical units with the distinctive emblem of the red cross. But if they are not so marked, they are not protected![105]

3.3.5 Concerted Action by Developed Countries in International Economic Questions

There is an intense network of concerted action in the international economic field, to a large extent in non-legal form, among the Western industrialized countries. The so-called economic summits have already been mentioned.[106]

An example of an international trade regulation in non-legal form is the OECD Trade Pledge of 1974.[107] When it was feared that the financial consequences of the oil crisis would lead to the creation of new protective trade barriers, OECD members entered into an informal "joint undertaking", declaring their determination not to restrict imports or to artificially stimulate exports for a period of one year. The agreement worked quite well and was renewed four times.

---

104   Roessler, loc.cit. in n. 14 at p. 44; E. Lauterpacht, loc.cit., in n. 33 at p. 382.

105   An example of a provision, where this distinction is clearly made is Art. 67 para.l of Protocol I Additional to the Geneva Conventions (text in 38 ZaöRV (1978) p. 86 et seq.), which defines the protection of military elements of civil defence. While non-compliance with the conditions of protection normally only results in loss of protection, without being unlawful, one particular case of non-compliance is expressly stated to be an unlawful act.

106   See above, section 3.1.

107   Roessler, loc.cit., in n. 14 at p. 52 et seq.; for the text of the 1978 version, see 33 *Europa-Archiv* (1978) D 455.

Another important – and politically sensitive – area of trade policy is the export of nuclear technology.[108] Because such export could lead to the acquisition of the know-how and technology necessary for the construction of atomic bombs, there has been considerable pressure from both the United States and the Soviet Union for the use of such technology by the receiving countries to be subject to effective controls. Other exporting countries tended to be less meticulous about this question. Thus, the receiving countries showed an understandable inclination to consider the matter of control when deciding between competing offers from exporting countries. In 1976, the main countries exporting nuclear technology (USA, USSR, UK, France, Czechoslovakia, Federal Republic of Germany, German Democratic Republic, Italy, Japan, Sweden and Switzerland) agreed on a common policy on this question of control. This was laid down in the London Guidelines for the export of nuclear material, equipment or technology.[109]

According to what apparently constitutes the common view of the participating states, these guidelines do not constitute a legally binding treaty, but a moral and political commitment.[110] This is also confirmed by legal writings.[111] The guidelines seem to have a considerable impact on state behaviour, and states make strenuous efforts to justify their actions under the guidelines. Thus, the Federal Republic of Germany publicly insisted on the fact that its nuclear dealings with Brazil were not in violation of the guidelines.[112]

4   Differences and Similarities between Legal and Nonlegal Obligations

The debate on the distinction between agreements which are legally binding and those which are not, as well as the discussion on the legal significance

---

108   Courteix, "Les accords de Londres entre pays exportateurs d'équipements et de matières nucléaires", 22 AFDI (1976) pp. 27–50.

109   17 ILM (1978) p. 220.

110   Statement of the Government of the Federal Republic of Germany, see Gündling, loc.cit., in n. 59 at p. 609.

111   Meyer-Wöbse, *Rechtsfragen des Exports von Kernanlagen in Nichtkernwaffenstaaten* (1979) p. 61 et seq.; Courteix, *Exportations nucléaires et non-proliferation* (1978) p. 63 (in spite of characterizing the guidelines as a gentlemen's agreement, she appears to construe them as a bundle of unilateral (legally?) binding declarations).

112   Franko, "US Regulation of the Spread of Nuclear Technology Through Suppliers Power: Lever or Boomerang", 10 *Law and Policy in International Business* (1978) pp. 1181, 1194. See also Goldschmidt and Kratzer, *Peaceful Nuclear Relations* (1978) p. 43.

LEGAL AND NON-LEGAL NORMS

of resolutions of international organizations, often take one thing for granted, viz., that it makes a difference whether an obligation is a legal or a non-legal one. On the basis of the practice reported, a closer examination of this assumption should be undertaken.

4.1 The Certainty of Expectations

It appears from the international practice that obligations which are clearly non-legal are still taken seriously by states. Documents which do not create legal obligations nevertheless formulate community or shared expectations of state behaviour.

It may be that policy declarations or joint statements of intent are, in certain cases, propaganda, but a certain *favor seriositatis* should be granted to states. It should not lightly be presumed that states did not mean what they said. It is hard to assume that the European States would have adopted the CSCE Final Act in the solemn form which they did if they had had no intention to do what the Act required. It has also been shown that the implementation record of binding resolutions is only marginally better than that of non-binding ones.[113] The practice of providing implementation procedures for resolutions which are not formally binding lends additional weight to the submission that there is a serious expectation of compliance. Does this actually mean that there is no difference in the certainty of expectations created by legal and non-legal obligations? It is a commonplace that a careful analysis of a document and its surrounding circumstances has to be made in order to determine the exact scope of the expectations created by it, and this is the case with documents containing legal or non-legal obligations.

As to the surrounding circumstances, an important difference exists between non-binding resolutions and legally binding agreements.

If a state which accepts a treaty obligation states, before acceptance, that it does not particularly like the treaty, this is irrelevant to the legal effect. If, however, a state votes against a resolution, or expresses reservations, there is a lesser degree of expectation, if any at all, that the state will comply with such a resolution than in the case of adoption without objection. This is an important political function of explanations of vote, beyond their possible effect in preserving a legal position.

As to the content of the obligation formulated in a particular document, the certainty of expectation depends on the precision of the wording. Both non-legal and legal obligations may be put in vague or precise terms, and that

---

113 See above, n. 62.

influences the certainty of expectations in both cases.[114] If an agreement is expressly called "tentative", the expectation of compliance is rather low, and it hardly appears conceivable that such an agreement would be put in legal form. This shows one of the advantages of non-legal obligations: greater flexibility.[115] It will be shown that one of the reasons for states choosing the non-legal approach to international obligations is that they want to preserve a certain amount of freedom, that they shy away from the rigidity of legal obligations. The practice of placing considerable emphasis on the non-legal character of a document (e.g., CSCE Final Act) could not be explained if the certainty of expectations created by a non-legal document were the same as that resulting from a legal document. All this suggests that, depending on the wording of a particular norm, there is indeed a difference in degree of certainty of expectation between legal and non-legal obligations. To put it in the words of Virally[116]:

> L'engagement morale est moins contraignant ... Cet élément de souplesse s'oppose à la rigidité du droit, mais ne suffit pas à réduire l'obligation morale a une obligation purement potestative, c'est-à-dire a une non-obligation, qui ne lie pas. Le lien de l'engagement moral est plus lâche que celui de l'engagement juridique, mais il lie celuit qui l'a pris.

4.2 *Measures to Secure Compliance*

Another area where legal and non-legal obligations could be distinguished concerns the measures to secure their performance. It has already been pointed out, however, that implementation procedures, essentially monitoring devices, are used without significant distinction for observing compliance with both legal and non-legal obligations. Some of the procedures relating to compliance with non-legal obligations are quite elaborate (e.g., OECD procedures concerning multinational enterprises[117]), others are very flexible.[118]

For the settlement of disputes, however, a difference is to be seen. As a matter of principle, a non-legal obligation cannot be the basis of a decision of a court of law. Non-legal obligations may become legally relevant by virtue of

---

114 Dupuy, loc.cit., in n. 17 at p. 140; Virally, loc.cit., in n. 31 at p. 21 et seq.; UN Doc. E/C. 10/17 para. 159.
115 Rotter, loc.cit., in n. 11 at p. 421.
116 Loc.cit., in n. 31 and 29.
117 See above, text accompanying n. 97 and 98.
118 See the implementation procedures for the *Generalized System of Preferences,* UN Doc. TD/B/331, no. VIII. As to the reasons for the relative lack of precision of these provision, see ibid. p. 12.

legal principles, in particular the principle of estoppel, or because they are referred to in a treaty. Documents which are not legally binding as such may be used as proof of customary law, but they cannot directly be made the basis of a court judgment. The present state of the judicial settlement of international disputes, however, does not permit this distinction between legal and non-legal obligations to be considered as practically important since few disputes are settled by international courts.[119]

A further consideration also makes the distinction appear less rigid than it seems at first glance. Under international law, the parties to a dispute before a court, and especially an arbitral tribunal, have considerable freedom to determine the law to be applied by the judges. If a court is permitted to decide *ex aequo et bono,* non-legal obligations may well become particularly relevant. A remarkable document in this connection is the agreement between Tunisia and Libya submitting the question of the delimitation of the continental shelf between them to the ICJ for adjudication.[120] The Court was asked, *inter alia,* to take into account equitable principles as well as "the recent trends admitted at the Third Conference on the Law of the Sea" (Art. 1 of the Special Agreement). Thus, the Court was asked to apply rules which were not necessarily rules of law, because it is rather controversial which, if any, of the rules on which a consensus seems to be developing at the Law of the Sea Conference have already become part of customary law.[121] Thus, one traditional and fundamental difference between legal and non-legal rules appears to have vanished.

Another area where a distinction between legal and non-legal obligations may have to be made is that of permissible reaction to a violation. It is evident that the violation of non-legal obligations may not trigger reprisals in a technical sense. They may not give rise to acts which would be unlawful if they were not a (proportional) reaction to an illegal act.[122] There is, however, a similarity between a treaty and a non-legal agreement: if one party does not fulfill its obligations, the other party may also refuse to perform its duties under the agreement. Technically, this is not a reprisal, as the non-performance of a non-legal duty is not an unlawful act. However, for practical purposes such a reaction is,

---

119   Schweisfutth, loc.cit., in n. 3 at p. 711 et seq.

120   18 ILM (1979) p. 49.

121   On the question of extended coastal state jurisdiction, national practice seems to be *grosso modo* in conformity with the Negotiating Texts of the Law of the Sea Conference, see Moore, "National Legislation for the Management of Fisheries Under Extended Coastal State Jurisdiction", 11 *Journal of Maritime Law and Commerce* (1980) pp. 153–182.

122   Delbrück, loc.cit., in n. 14 at p. 45; Wengler, loc.cit., in n. 12 at p. 335.

of course, similar to a reprisal, or to a suspension of the operation of a treaty under Article 60 of the Convention on the Law of Treaties.

With respect to non-binding resolutions, it would also seem at first glance that non-compliance, not being a violation of law, could not give rise to formal sanctions, such as the deprivation of certain membership rights. The accuracy of this assertion depends on the provisions of the constituent treaties relating to the sanctions. It is, however, argued that a persistent violation even of non-binding resolutions could amount to a disregard of fundamental *legal* principles of the organization,[123] and thus give rise to formal sanctions. Again, the line between legal and non-legal obligations becomes blurred.

Furthermore, the practical relevance of "formal" sanctions is rather questionable. International practice encompasses a wide variety of methods of inflicting harm on states ("value deprivations") and these can be used against a state as a reaction to breaches of international obligations, by the "victim" state, by other states, by international organizations or by non-governmental actors, e.g., cutting economic and cultural contacts (where such contacts do not exist as a matter of law), discontinuing negotiations, halting the ratification of an important treaty, alerting public opinion against a state (which will, as a rule, show a great sensibility to a loss of international prestige and credibility).[124] These "value deprivations" may be applied in the case of violation of both legal and non-legal obligations,[125] and may even be used to deter a state from exercising its rights. There is, however, still a difference between violations of legal and non-legal obligations, in particular as far as public opinion is concerned. It may be that in some cases this difference will be ignored by world public opinion, but, probably more often, the blame attached to a state breaching a legal obligation will be more severe than that attaching to one which does not honour a political commitment.[126] In this sphere, there is of course no sharp dividing line between legal and non-legal obligations; much depends on political circumstances.

---

123 Wenglei, loc.cit., in n. 12 at p. 343 et seq.; Castaneda, op.cit., in n. 17 at p. 176 et seq.; ICJ Advisory Opinion, *Voting Procedure on Questions Relating to Reports and Petitions Concerning the Territory of South-West Africa,* Seperate Opinion of Judge Lauterpacht, ICJ Reports (1955) p. 120.

124 Virally, loc.cit., in n. 3 at p. 30.

125 To choose a non-legal form of obligation in order to avoid adverse effects in case of non-performance is, thus, not very realistic. See, however, the American attitude with respect to the Generalized System of Preferences, as quoted by Graham, loc.cit., in n. 88 at p. 519.

126 See Delbrück, loc.cit., in n. 14 at p. 46.

LEGAL AND NON-LEGAL NORMS

4.3 *Termination of Obligations*

For some authors, an important difference between legal and non-legal obligations lies in the fact that termination of the latter is much easier.[127] This follows from the fact that the certainty of expectation is lower in the case of non-legal obligations. However, generalizations are impossible, and there are legal agreements which may be denounced at any time. Equally, there are non-legal agreements where there is a clear expectation that they will not be declared politically irrelevant overnight.[128] It would be hard to conceive that a European State could declare, just out of caprice, that it no longer considered the CSCE Final Act to be a political commitment. On the other hand, there are other cases of non-legal agreements where there is no such expectation of duration. If a non-legal commitment is made by the executive branch of government, there is no expectation that such a commitment will survive a legislative act to the contrary.

In some cases, the formulation of the agreement itself provides for only a reduced or limited expectation. Thus, the "Agreed Conclusions of the Special Committee on Preferences" not only stressed their non-binding character, but expressly stated that the preferences could subsequently be withdrawn.[129] On the other hand, the system as a whole was set up for a duration of ten years. Furthermore, the existence of an implementation procedure suggested that there was some expectation of duration. It was expected as a minimum that the withdrawal clause would not be used capriciously.[130]

4.4 *Questions of National Law*

The question of the relationship between national and international law involves two main questions: first, the authority, under national law, to bind the state internationally, and second, the implementation of international law in the national sphere.

As a rule, the conduct of foreign relations falls within the powers of the executive branch of government, though in many constitutions the authority of the executive to legally commit the state vis-a-vis other subjects of international law is limited by the requirement of previous parliamentary consent. This limitation usually applies to legal commitments. This is an important difference between legal and non-legal obligations. Entering into non-legal commitments

---

127   Virally, loc.cit., in n. 3 at p. 29.
128   Schweisfurth, loc.cit., in n. 3 at p. 710 et seq.
129   UN Doc. TD/B 331, p. 6.
130   On the history of implementation by the United States, see Graham, loc.cit., in n. 88 at p. 526 et seq.

is a question of the political responsibility of the executive vis-a-vis the legislative branch (where such responsibility exists), and is a matter for the political control exercized by parliament over the executive branch; in general, there is no obligatory submission of such commitments for parliamentary approval. It was, therefore, a matter of policy, not of constitutional law, when the CSCE Final Act was formally reported to national parliaments.[131]

As to the second question, application of international law in the national sphere, the solutions provided by national constitutions vary. Many constitutions provide for the incorporation of rules of international law into the domestic legal system. Some of them grant international obligations precedence over national *lex posterior*. The rules providing for the incorporation of international law into national law are, as a rule, limited to the international *legal* obligations of the state. Thus, non-legal international obligations need some act of the competent national organ in order to become relevant in the national sphere. They never take precedence over a *lex posterior*. These differences in national legal systems also explain why there are differences with respect to publication in official gazettes and the like. Non-legal agreements are not usually published in the same way as international treaties or other documents containing legal obligations.[132]

It is, therefore, within the field of national law that the distinction between legal and non-legal international obligations remains most clearly established. Since the possibility of a judicial pronouncement is much greater in the national sphere than at the international level, the distinction still has its practical relevance, at least in cases where the national question may become an issue.

5 The Reasons for Adopting a Non-Legal Approach

On the basis of the differences which have been discussed above it is now possible to summarize some of the reasons which induce states to choose the non-legal approach to international regulation, and thereafter to shed some

---

131 Schweisfurth, loc.cit., in n. 3 at p. 691.

132 This is often used as an argument for or against the legal character of a specific obligation. See Rotter, loc.cit., in n. 11 at p. 415; Schweisfurth, loc.cit., in n. 3 at p. 691. A rare example of a non-legal agreement published in the same way as an international treaty is the "Statement of Intent" between the US Department of Energy and the Ministry for Research and Technology of the Federal Republic of Germany on co-operation in coal technology, dated 7 October 1977, published *Bundesgesetzblatt* (1977) II, 1239. This statement is clearly not legally binding. Both parties intended to participate in a certain project: "Such intent ... is signified by the signatures ... " (final paragraph of the Statement).

LEGAL AND NON-LEGAL NORMS

light on the functions of non-legal norms in international relations.[133] Non-legal regulations often serve as a compromise between sovereignty and order.[134] Since there may be a difference in degree as to the certainty of the expectation of compliance between a legal and a non-legal obligation, and since there is a good chance that the condemnation will be less in the case of a violation of a non-legal obligation, states often choose this approach when they wish to create a *modus vivendi,* but feel the necessity of preserving some way out.

The need to formulate an agreement, thus circumscribing certain expectations, while at the same time retaining some possibility of a way out is particularly apparent where a situation is still fluid. As a rule, states are prepared to accept a legal commitment only if they can reasonably foresee that they will be in a position to comply with it. If, in the view of the relevant decision-makers, the prognosis of an ability to comply is not safe enough, a state will refrain from entering into a legal obligation. The same holds true for the prognosis of the willingness or ability of the other party or parties to honour their engagement. Nevertheless, it can still be useful to formulate an agreement, even at that level of limited predictability, since it may to some extent enhance the certainty of mutual expectations; it serves a useful purpose to give some form and shape to the elements of agreement upon which an understanding has been reached. In this situation, the non-legal approach is appropriate. This is the gist of the non-legal character of the CSCE Final Act. The process of political *detente* between Eastern and Western Europe had not developed to an extent which would have allowed the states to make a prognosis of correct behaviour vis-a-vis one another sufficient to have prompted them to enter into a stable legal relationship.[135]

The same kind of rationale explains the use of non-legal forms of regulation in the field of international economic relations, especially in the monetary field.[136] Where the predictability of economic requirements is as low as it is in the field of the development of exchange rates, it is not possible for states to make firm legal commitments. However, in this situation too, it is still useful to formulate shared expectations, be they only of a lower degree of certainty. A non-legal commitment seems to be an appropriate means of doing this, and the various phases of the regulation of the exchange rate system and the Generalized System of Preferences may be recalled as examples.

---

133   Schweisfurth, loc.cit., in n. 3 at p. 713 et seq.
134   Roessler, loc.cit., in n. 14 at p. 41.
135   Delbrück, loc.cit., in n. 14 at p. 36 et seq.; Schweisfurth, loc.cit, in n. 3 at p. 713 et seq.
136   See above, section 3.3.4.

A non-legal commitment is, thus, often much easier for a state to accept than a legal one. In all probability, here lies the reason why states do not reject resolutions the terms of which they would by no means accept as a treaty. This presents both an opportunity and a danger. As resolutions also give rise to expectations, they trigger a certain pressure for compliance which is often, as has been shown, effective in the long run. They influence practice, and practice influences law. Thus, these resolutions are a non-legal step on the way to legal change; whether this is seen as a positive or a negative aspect of the matter depends, of course, on whether one likes the content of the change thus effected.

Another reason why a non-legal form may be used involves questions of status and prestige. States are often willing to face the facts and live with a situation which they do not like, but they will not formally recognize it. Thus, they may be prepared to accept a situation in a non-legal *modus vivendi* which they would be loath to recognize in a treaty.[137] A similar line of thought might be the reason for the non-legal character of the nuclear suppliers' guidelines. If this were a legal agreement, the Federal Republic of Germany would have to insist, as a matter of policy and constitutional law, on a clause relating to application to Berlin. This would have raised considerable political difficulties with many of the participating states, difficulties which were avoided as the document took a non-legal form.

This leads to a more general reason for adopting the non-legal approach: avoiding the difficulties involved in the process of the creation of legal norms.

The process of negotiation and entry into force of international treaties is a rather slow one. Seventeen years elapsed from the date of adoption of the Universal Declaration of Human Rights until the adoption of the text of the two UN Human Rights Covenants by the General Assembly, and it took ten years more before the Covenants entered into force. Such agreements as the OECD Trade Pledge of 1974 would not have been possible in a legal form, for reasons of time.

One of the reasons why the process of entry into force is so time-consuming is the length of the decision-making process "at home". This leads to one of the most important (and problematic) reasons for the non-legal approach: avoidance of problems in the sphere of national procedures, especially from the legislative branch. This is one of the reasons why, in the field of international trade regulations and GATT in particular, a non-legal approach has been used; the American administration was willing to enter into these agreements, but

---

137 Roessler, loc.cit., in n. 14.

LEGAL AND NON-LEGAL NORMS

the US Senate, pursuing a different policy, could not have been expected to give its advice and consent.[138]

The non-legal approach might also be helpful where the powers of a government agency or of a lower level of government to represent or bind the state (or themselves) internationally are doubtful. Thus, trans-frontier co-operation between municipalities is often described as "informal".[139]

6   The Pros and Cons of the Non-Legal Approach

It still appears from international practice that the "normal" method of formulating expectations is constituted by the legal norm, but, it has been shown above that there are a number of cases where states have had recourse to non-legal forms of regulation, partly because there were insurmountable obstacles to the creation of a legal norm, partly because a legal commitment, with its special status, formality and stability would not have appeared to be appropriate under the circumstances. One could thus say that non-legal norms play a useful role in international relations. There are, however, a certain number of doubtful points. If the non-legal norm is hailed because it circumvents the obstacles involved in the creation of a legal norm, one must not forget that a number of these obstacles, unpleasant as they may appear to a particular decision-maker, have a justification of their own. This is, in particular, true for domestic checks relating to international commitments of the state. It is, after all, a democratic principle that fundamental policy decisions should be taken by those directly elected by the people.[140] On the other hand, it is a legitimate question whether systems of checks and balances having their origin in times when international intercourse was less intense, and required less international regulation, are still appropriate when a state must cope with a highly complex international order. When the principle of "regulation" of international monetary exchanges was the gold standard, there was no need for states to agree quickly on measures to stop international currency speculation. Once the net of international regulation becomes tighter, as it has done, weaving

---

138   Roessler, loc.cit.., in n. 14 at p. 47 et seq. On "the relations between US Senate and President in the field of disarmament, see Bothe, loc.cit., in n. 36 at p. 232.

139   See Bothe, "Rechtsprobleme grenzüberschreitender Planung"; 102 *Archiv des öffentlichen Rechts* (1977) pp. 68–89 at p. 72 et seq.

140   See Tomuschat, "Der Verfassungsstaat im Geflecht der internationalen Beziehungen", 36 *Veröffentlichungen der Vereinigung der Deutschen Staatsrechtslehrer* (1977) pp. 7–63 at pp. 26–37.

46 PART 1: BASIC ISSUES

and reweaving this net must be accomplished more quickly. Re-shaping national procedures with regard to the international representation of the state might, to a certain extent, be an alternative approach to that of adopting non-legal international regulations..

7 Legal and Non-Legal Obligations – Some Conclusions

The foregoing analysis has demonstrated that there is an important body of rules which regulate state behaviour in international relations, and which do not fall within the category of legal rules. Being social rules, they have many features in common with legal rules, but there are also important differences. Both kinds of rules formulate community expectations. They provide some stability in international relations by making state behaviour more predictable,[141] but non-legal rules do so to a lesser extent. The advantage of non-legal rules is that they provide some stability in cases where a legal rule, with all its rigidity, would not be acceptable to states, would serve no useful purpose or would be too difficult to create. Their danger lies in the fact that they enable the salutary difficulties involved in the *law*-making process to be circumvented, and that law is thereby not created where it could and should be.

State practice is aware of the differences between the two kinds of norms. It is because of these differences that state practice often insists upon the distinction being made,[142] and that states argue about this. Thus, a definition of the dividing line is necessary. It does not correspond to the realities of international life, in the light of state practice, to treat the distinction as being a matter of degree.[143] A certain rule is a legal or a non-legal one; one cannot say that one rule is more legal than another.

On facing the issue of an exact definition of the dividing line between the two kinds of norms, one is confronted with the basic structural weakness of international law, viz., its decentralized system of application and interpretation. In principle, each state decides for itself what the law is – binding and effective third party settlement being the exception. Thus, there is often doubt about the "true" legal solution. This also applies to the definition of the dividing line between legal and non-legal norms, but it is not a problem specific to this distinction.

---

141 Rotter, loc.cit., in n. 11 at p. 420 et seq.

142 Baum, "Die soziologische Begründung des Völkerrechts als Problem der Rechtssoziologie", 1 *Jahrbuch für Rechtssoziologie und Rechtstheorie* (1970) pp. 257–274 at p. 259.

143 *Contra*, Schachter, loc.cit., in n. 6 at p. 30 et seq.

LEGAL AND NON-LEGAL NORMS

The main matter dealt with has been the different effects of legal and non-legal obligations, and attention has also been devoted to the reasons for adopting the legal or non-legal approach. These considerations are also important for the question dealt with rather briefly at the beginning of this article: when is a given obligation a legal one?[144] A legal agreement is distinguished from a non-legal one by the different intention of the parties. In the case of a legal agreement, the legal obligation results from the declaration of a party that it consents to be bound *as a matter of law.* Where there is no explicit declaration to this effect, the intent of the parties has to be inferred from the circumstances. There, the elements of our analysis become important. A state, for example, cannot be said to have consented to a legal obligation where the situation is too fluid or too unstable to warrant the state's assuming a rigid duty. The same holds true, *mutatis mutandis,* for the proof of an *opinio juris* as an element of customary law.[145] A state cannot be said to have accepted a practice as a matter of law (even where it acts in conformity with this practice) if the whole context suggests that its attitude is rather tentative.

The differences between legal and non-legal norms should also caution against doctrinal approaches which bring them into too close proximity. It has been said that non-legal obligations are obligations of good faith.[146] The principle of good faith, upon which the doctrine of estoppel is based,[147] often legally obliges a state to behave as others expect it to, even where this expectation is not itself based on a legal rule, thus protecting reliance and confidence in certain cases.[148] It is not the purpose of this article to analyze the cases in which the principle of estoppel has this effect, but it would be going too far if, because compliance with non-legal rules can be expected, states were, as a general rule, estopped, i.e., legally prevented, from violating non-legal rules. This would amount to letting law come in by the back door. In the view of the present writer, this suggests that the qualification of non-legal obligations as obligations of good faith is somewhat dangerous. "Good faith" is a legal concept, and basing respect for non-legal obligations on a legal concept would not seem to be appropriate.

This leads to the more fundamental question of the basis of an obligation. There are two basic notions in social rule-making: promise and authority.

---

144 See above.

145 Cf., Schachter, loc.cit., in a 6 at p. 11.

146 Virally, loc.cit., in n. 3 at p. 29.

147 Menzel, "Estoppel-Prinzip", in Strupp and Schlochauer, eds., op.cit., in n. 8, vol. 1, p. 441 et seq.

148 Müller, op.cit., in n. 24 at p. 5 et seq.

These are also relevant for law-making. Rules are created by a legislature which has the formal authority to do this, or by promises recognized by law as legally binding. But the concepts of promise and authority are valid as sources of obligation beyond the domain of law. They are also the basis of the various types of non-legal obligation described in this article. These non-legal obligations are important enough to raise a question of terminology. It appears somewhat unsatisfactory to designate these obligations in an essentially negative way, by saying what they are *not*. Thus, the term "non-legal" should probably be replaced by another which positively conveys the idea of the character of the obligation. Two terms are in current use in this respect: "moral" and "political".

The difficulty with the former term is that it is often used to designate obligations pertaining to the *forum internum*[149]: it is illegal to kill, it is immoral to think of killing. *If* this is the difference between law and morality, the obligations dealt with in this article would be inadequately described by the term "moral". If, however, moral norms are simply defined as social norms other than legal ones,[150] then the term is appropriate in our context.

The term political conveys the idea of *polis,* of the civic community. As the obligations described find their final *raison d'être* in the requirements of the life of the international community, "political" would seem to be an appropriate term, which does not raise the same problems as the word "moral".

---

149 Radbruch, op.cit., in n. 5 at p. 16; cf., on the other hand, Kelsen, op.cit., in n. 5 at p. 61 et seq.; see also Geiger, op.cit., in n. 5 at p. 293 et seq.; Green, "Law and Morality in a Changing Society", in Green, *Law and Society* (1975) pp. 1–60.

150 Kelsen, op.cit., at p. 60.

2

Les Limites des Pouvoirs du Conseil de Sécurité

1 Introduction

Ce n'est qu'à partir de certain événements récents que la question des limites des pouvoirs du Conseil de sécurité a gagné une certaine actualité. Pendant longtemps, la question ne s'est pas vraiment posée, tout au contraire. Le Conseil de sécurité était inactif, bloqué par le veto. Des limitations de caractère procédural l'ont empêché d'agir. Le Conseil n'a pris des mesures que dans les cas assez rares où il existait un consensus des grandes puissances, au moins dans une certaine mesure. Ce fut d'abord les opérations pour le maintien de la paix (*peace-keeping operations*) rendues possibles par le fait que les grandes puissances ont eu l'intérêt commun de contenir certains conflits et d'en empêcher la dégénération en conflits qui risquaient de faire s'affronter ces puissances de façon directe et immédiate.[1] Il y eut aussi certaines mesures liées à la décolonisation auxquelles les grandes puissances de l'Ouest ne s'opposaient pas, notamment celles concernant la Rhodésie du Sud,[2] l'Afrique du Sud[3] et la Namibie.[4] Toutes ces décisions du Conseil de sécurité étaient peu controversées, sauf pour certains aspects des opérations pour le maintien de la paix. Mais, dans ces derniers cas, les conflits politiques ne concernaient pas vraiment les pouvoirs du Conseil de sécurité, mais plutôt l'usage que le Secrétaire général avait fait du mandat que le Conseil lui avait confié.[5]

La disparition du conflit entre les deux superpuissances a également fait disparaître le veto quasi automatique quand le Conseil de sécurité voulait trancher des conflits internationaux. De ce fait, il y a une renaissance des activités du Conseil de sécurité et dès le début de cette relance des questions sérieuses ont été posées quant à la légalité ou au moins les bases juridiques

---

1 Bothe, «Friedenserhaltende Maßnahmen», dans Simma (dir. publ.), *Charta der Vereinten Nationen*, pp. 535 ss.

2 Résolution 217 (1965): embargo concernant des armements et du pétrole ; résolution 221 (1966) : emploi de la force pour mettre en œuvre l'embargo ; résolution 232 (1966), 277 (1970), 288 (1970), 314 (1972), 409 (1977) : embargo plus général.

3 Un embargo de livraisons d'armes a été décidé contre L'Afrique du Sud, résolution 418 (1977).

4 Notamment les résolutions constatant l'illégalité de la présence continue de l'Afrique du Sud en Namibie : 276 (1970), 283 (1970), 301 (1971).

5 B. Nolte et T. Fitschen, « Konflikte, Kongo", dans R. Wolfrum (dir. publ.), *Handbuch der Vereinten Nationen*, 2e éd. 1991, pp. 456 ss.

© KONINKLIJKE BRILL NV, LEIDEN, 2021 | DOI:10.1163/9789004380592_004

précises de l'exercice des pouvoirs du Conseil de sécurité. Un premier type de problèmes s'est posé lors du conflit du Golfe, à savoir celui de la délégation des fonctions du Conseil de sécurité à un groupe d'Etats (c'est de cette façon que l'on peut en effet envisager les résolutions autorisant le recours à la force),[6] ainsi que, plus tard, celui de la portée des résolutions d'armistice qui imposent à l'Iraq un certain nombre d'obligations assez étendues.[7] Un deuxième type de problèmes est celui du sort des populations opprimées ou menacées, ce qui inclut la question de savoir si le Conseil peut entreprendre ou autoriser une intervention humanitaire.[8] Le dernier de ces problèmes est en effet posé par l'affaire libyenne, dans laquelle le chapitre VII de la Charte a été invoqué dans des circonstances un peu surprenantes pour les juristes, ce qui a soulevé des critiques notamment du côté arabe.[9]

2 La Portée des Pouvoirs du Conseil de Sécurité

On ne peut pas parler des limites des pouvoirs du Conseil de sécurité sans parler de leur fondement juridique. La manière de définir ces pouvoirs implique aussi leurs limites. C'est donc par voie d'interprétation des dispositions qui confèrent au Conseil certains pouvoirs qu'il faut aussi dégager leurs limites.

Cela nous amène à diviser la réflexion en trois parties :

- considérations générales concernant les pouvoirs du Conseil, notamment la question des pouvoirs généraux/spécifiques et celle des pouvoirs implicites ;
- l'interprétation de certaines dispositions fondamentales pour les fonctions du Conseil de sécurité, notamment l'article 39 et la notion de menace à paix ;
- le principe de la proportionnalité en tant que limitation générale des pouvoirs du Conseil.

---

6 Au sujet des questions juridiques soulevées par l'« autorisation » donnée par le Conseil de sécurité, voir O. Schachter, « United Nations Law in the Gulf Conflict », *American Journal of International Law*, vol. 85, 1992, pp. 452 ss., 461 s.

7 Résolution 687 du 3 avril 1991. Voir à cet égard B. Graefrath et M. Mohr, « Legal Consequences of an Act of Aggression : The Case of the Iraqi Invasion and Occupation of Kuwait», *Austrian Journal of Public and International Law*, vol. 43, 1992, pp. 109 ss., 120 ss.

8 Bothe, «The Legitimacy of the Use of Force to Protect the Rights of Peoples and Minorities», dans *Peoples and Minorities in International Law. The Second Amsterdam International Law Conference* (à paraître).

9 *Questions d'interprétation et d'application de la Conventions de Montréal de 1971, ordonnance du 14 avril 1992, CIJ Recueil 1992*, p. 114.

3 Les Pouvoirs du Conseil de Sécurité : Questions Générales

3.1 *Pouvoirs Discrétionnaires ou Limités Par le Droit*

La première question que se pose à l'égard de notre sujet est celle de savoir, si les dispositions du chapitre VII, à l'article 39, constituent de véritables termes juridiques, qui accordent par conséquent au Conseil un pouvoir de constatation et de prendre des mesures qui est un pouvoir fondé sur et limité par le droit. Ou est-ce que la Charte accorde au Conseil de sécurité un pouvoir discrétionnaire (absolu ou limité mais en tout cas incontrôlable) de constater l'existence d'une situation où il peut (ou faut-il plutôt dire : où il veut) intervenir? Ni en théorie ni dans la pratique la dernière solution ne serait acceptable. Les Nations Unies sont basées sur le respect du droit, et il serait inconcevable d'exclure le droit comme facteur déterminant d'un élément clé de leurs activités. Le Conseil de sécurité n'est pas une sorte de pape du droit international: « Roma locuta, causa finita.» En pratique, l'étendue des pouvoirs du Conseil de sécurité est en effet discutée et l'argument juridique est utilisé pour en déterminer des limites. Le Cour, dans son ordonnance sur les mesures provisoires dans l'affaire libyenne, paraît avoir laissé ouvert son jugement final sur l'effet juridique des résolutions pertinentes du Conseil de sécurité, se réservant ainsi un contrôle judiciaire et reconnaissant de façon implicite qu'il existe des limites juridiques des pouvoirs du Conseil.[10]

Mais, d'autre part, les notions clés de l'article 39 de la Charte ont un caractère général et vague et peuvent donner lieu à des interprétations diverses. En plus, on ne peut que reconnaître qu'au moins fait le Conseil est maître de leur interprétation. Il a, pour continuer un peu en latin, une sorte de *jus primae noctis* en ce qui concerne l'interprétation de ses pouvoirs. Une fois la question décidée par le Conseil, il devient extrêmement difficile d'en contester le bien-fondé.[11]

La meilleure formule juridique pour exprimer cette situation est de reconnaître au Conseil de sécurité non pas un pouvoir discrétionnaire, mais une *marge d'appréciation* en ce qui concerne les situations visées à l'article 39. Ce terme est, par exemple, utilisé par la Cour européenne des droits de

---

10   Voir notamment les paragraphes 42 et 43 de l'ordonnance, *CIJ Recueil 1992*, pp. 126 s.

11   Dans son avis consultatif du 20 juillet 1962 concernant *Certaines dépenses des Nations Unies,* la Cour exprime cette idée de manière suivante : « chaque organe doit ... , tout au moins en premier lieu, déterminer sa propre compétence» (*CIJ Recueil 1962*, p. 168) ; mais voir également les remarques critiques concernant ces passages contenues dans l'opinion individuelle de Fitzmaurice, *ibid.*, p. 203. Cf. à cet égard également A. Verdross et B. Simma, *Universelles Völkerrecht,* 3e éd., pp. 166 s.

52 PART 1: BASIC ISSUES

l'homme[12] et aussi, quant au fond, par la Cour de justice des Communautés européennes.[13] Il est implicite dans le concept même de marge d'appréciation qu'il ne s'agit pas d'un pouvoir illimité.

Il est vrai qu'il n'existe aucun contrôle judiciaire direct. Mais il existe des contrôles indirects, décentralisés et subtils qui sont caractéristiques pour le droit international en général: la protestation par le refus d'obéissance, le contrôle juridictionnel indirect quand la question se pose comme question incidente devant des tribunaux nationaux ou internationaux et finalement l'acceptation par la communauté internationale.

C'est sur la base de cette conception que nous aimerions analyser quelques limitations juridiques des pouvoirs du Conseil de sécurité.

3.2 *Pouvoirs Généraux ou Pouvoirs Spécifiques*

L'article 24, paragraphe 1, semble accorder au Conseil des pouvoirs de caractère général. La Charte confère au Conseil de sécurité « la responsabilité principale du maintien de la paix et de la sécurité internationales ». Mais, à vrai dire, il faut distinguer la responsabilité, ou plutôt la fonction du Conseil de sécurité et les pouvoirs dont il peut disposer. A cet égard, l'article 24, paragraphe 2, deuxième phrase, paraît plutôt restrictif : «Les pouvoirs spécifiques accordés au Conseil de sécurité pour lui permettre d'accomplir lesdits devoirs sont définis aux chapitres VI, VII, VIII et XII.» La question décisive est celle de savoir si ces pouvoirs spécifiques sont les seuls dont dispose le Conseil ou si l'on doit ajouter à ces pouvoirs spécifiques des pouvoirs généraux. Dans son avis consultatif concernant la présence continue de l'Afrique du Sud en Namibie, la Cour a retenu la seconde possibilité. On y lit :

> Au paragraphe de [l'article 24], la mention des pouvoirs spécifiques accordés au Conseil de sécurité en vertu de certain chapitres de la Charte n'exclut pas l'existence de pouvoirs généraux destinés à luis permettre de s'acquitter des responsabilités conférées par le paragraphe 1 [14]

Pour fonder et motiver sa conclusion, la Cour se réfère notamment à une déclaration faite par le Secrétaire générale devant le Conseil en 1947.

---

12   J.A. Frowein, «European Convention on Human Rights (1950)», dans Bernhardt (dir. publ.), *Encyclopedia of Public International Law,* Inst. 8, pp. 184 ss., 188.

13   Cf. notamment la jurisprudence concernant les restrictions de la liberté de mouvement basées sur l'ordre public, CJCE, *Re., 1994,* 1337 (*Van Duyn*) ; 1975, 1219 (*Rutili*) ; 1977, 1999 (*Bouchereau*) ; 1982, 1665 (*Adoui et Cornuaille*).

14   *CIJ Recueil 1971,* p. 52.

LES LIMITES DE POUVOIRS DU CONSEIL DE SÉCURITÉ

Mais cette interprétation reste contestable. Il faut se souvenir du fait que la Charte, elle aussi, constitue un compromis. Dans l'intérêt de la majorité des Etats qui est constituée par les Etats moins puissants, la prédominance des grandes puissances dans le système du maintien de la paix est de quelque façon compensée par le fait que les pouvoirs du Conseil de sécurité sont définis de façon assez stricte. En plus, la pratique récente du Conseil de sécurité va plutôt à l'encontre de l'acceptation de pouvoirs généraux. Dans la plupart des cas, quand le Conseil veut imposer des obligations aux Etats membres, il se réfère de façon expresse au chapitre VII. Cela a été fait dans les affaires de la Rhodésie, de l'Afrique du Sud, de l'Iraq, de la Yougoslavie et de la Libye. Nous nous demandons s'il ne serait pas préférable de fonder le résultat auquel la Cour est arrivée dans l'affaire de la Namibie plutôt sur la notion des pouvoirs implicites que sur celle des pouvoirs généraux.

3.3 *Le fondement des Décisions Obligatoires du Conseil : L'article 39*

Dans la mesure où on limite les pouvoirs du Conseil à ceux qui lui sont conférés de façon spécifique, le champ d'application du chapitre VII, en vertu duquel le Conseil put prendre des décisions obligatoires (ce qu'il ne peut pas faire en vertu du chapitre VI), devient une question primordiale et fondamentale. Les situations dans lesquelles le chapitre VII s'applique sont définies à l'article 39: une menace contre la paix, une rupture de la paix ou un acte d'agression.

C'est vraiment la notion de la menace contre la paix qui offre les espaces les plus vastes pour une interprétation généreuse et pour une conception large des pouvoirs du Conseil. Evidemment, la notion clé est celle de la paix. Est-ce que « paix »ne signifie qu'absence de violence militaire entre les Etats? Où est-ce que la violation de certaines valeurs fondamentales de l'ordre international peut également constituer une menace contre la paix?[15] Cette question s'est posée en particulier quant au respect des droits de l'homme. Est-ce qu'une violation constante et massive des droits de l'homme au sein d'un Etat constitue une menace contre la paix? La Conseil jusqu'alors n'a jamais répondu à cette question par l'affirmative. Dans les situations où il y avait, au sein d'un Etat, de graves violations des droits de l'homme, le Conseil s'est toujours fondé sur un élément additionnel à cette violation pour arriver à la conclusion qu'il y avait une situation visée par l'article 39. Cela est notamment le cas dans les

---

15 En ce qui concerne la paix « négative » ou « positive », cf. H. Neuhold, « Peace, Threat to », dans Bernhardt (dir. publ.), *Encyclopedia of Public International Law,* Inst. 4, pp. 100 ss., 102.

résolutions concernant la Rhodésie du Sud,[16] l'embargo contre l'Afrique du Sud[17] et la question des populations opprimées en Iraq,[18] il faut dire qu'on peut donner de bonnes raisons pour cette position très prudente et réticente du Conseil. La définition de la paix comme une notion essentiellement négative a au moins l'avantage de la clarté. Toutes autres conceptions présupposent une nouvelle définition de la paix qui est difficile à faire et pour laquelle, en l'absence du contrôle judiciaire, il est difficile de trouver des limites.

Une autre notion qui est significative pour l'étendue des pouvoirs du Conseil est celle de la « menace ». Selon la terminologie de la Charte, un danger encore un peu éloigné pour la paix ne déclenche que les pouvoirs accordés au Conseil en vertu du chapitre VI (un « différend dont la prolongation est susceptible de menacer le maintien de la paix ... »), tandis que la menace comporte un danger direct et immédiat. Mais où est la ligne de partage entre le direct et l'indirect ?

3.4 *Les Pouvoirs Spécifiques en Vertu du Chapitre VII*

Les pouvoirs dont dispose le Conseil en vertu du chapitre VII sont les suivants: les recommandations en vertu de l'article 39 (cela inclut toutes sortes d'actions non obligatoires, y compris des opérations pour le maintien de la paix basées sur le consentement des parties), des mesures provisoires selon l'article 40, des mesures de coercition non militaires en vertu de l'article 41 et des mesures de coercition militaires en vertu du l'article 42. Un sujet controversé est la question de savoir si l'article 48 peut servir comme une base indépendante pour un mandat donné par le Conseil de sécurité à certains Etats de prendre des mesures militaires ou autres. L'économie générale du chapitre VII suggère plutôt que l'article 48 ne se réfère qu'aux modalités des mesures que nous venons d'énumérer et ne constitue pas une base de compétence indépendante.[19]

---

16   Dans les résolutions 217 (1965) et 221 (1966), le Conseil reconnaît que les violations des droits de l'homme qui ont lieu en Rhodésie du Sud constituaient une menace à la paix. Mais l'élément justificatif fondamental de l'action du Conseil était le danger d'un conflit en Afrique australe et la violation du droit d'autodétermination.

17   Tout en condamnant les violations des droits de l'homme en Afrique du Sud, le Conseil ne voit une menace à la paix et à la sécurité internationales que dans l'acquisition d'armes par ce pays (résolution 418(1977)).

18   Dans la résolution 688 (1991) concernant des populations menacées en Iraq, le Conseil, apparemment, ne regarde pas la répression même comme une menace à la paix, mais seulement ses « conséquences ». Il est à supposer que ce choix de terminologie est intentionnel.

19   Cf. B.-O. Bryde, dans Simma *et al.* (dir. publ.), *Charta der Vereinten Nationen, Kommentar,* 1991, art. 48 n. 4.

Cette question est de quelque façon liée à celle plus générale de savoir si le Conseil peut déléguer ses pouvoirs à certains Etats. Il est vrai, une sorte de délégation est prévue au chapitre VIII, selon lequel le Conseil de sécurité peut donner son consentement à une action coercitive entreprise par une organisation régionale sous la responsabilité et l'égide propre de cette dernière. Cependant, le pouvoir de délégation doit s'arrêter là. Les membres des Nations Unies on conféré, en vertu de l'article 24, la responsabilité pour le maintien de la paix au Conseil de sécurité et non pas à une autre entité que le Conseil peut imaginer. Toutes les règles de procédure auxquelles l'exercice de cette responsabilité est soumise pourraient être contournées si l'on admettait un tel pouvoir délégation.

Si l'on conçoit donc la résolution de 29 novembre 1990 qui « autorise » l'emploi de la force contre l'Iraq comme une délégation (parce que ce n'est pas le Conseil de sécurité qui décidera finalement sur cet emploi, mais des gouvernements coopérant avec le gouvernement du Koweït), la résolution est mal fondée sur la Charte. Mais elle peut être considérée comme légale en tant que réglementation concernant un droit que ces Etats possèdent de toute façon, à savoir le droit de légitime défense collective.

Pour des raisons semblables à celles évoquées en ce qui concerne la délégation, des actions de coercition visée par l'article 42 doivent être des actions conduites sous la direction effective du Conseil de sécurité et non pas des actions entreprises par certains Etats membres pour leur propre compte sur la base de leur propre décision, jouissant d'une sorte de bénédiction globale du Conseil de sécurité.[20] Pour cette raison, il est difficile de caractériser l'action militaire des alliés contre l'Iraq comme une mesure coercitive en vertu de l'article 42.[21]

Certains vont critiquer le raisonnement que nous venons de développer comme trop systématique et restrictif. Mais nous croyons que cette approche précise et systématique est en effet nécessaire pour empêcher, tout au moins pour essayer d'empêcher, un usage illimité de pouvoirs mal définis. Cependant, il faut modifier et nuancer un peu cette approche par la conception des pouvoirs implicites.[22] A ne pas en douter, le Conseil de sécurité dispose de pouvoirs implicites. Cependant, la notion des pouvoirs implicites est étroitement

---

20   Cf. Urquhart, « The Role of the United Nations in the Iraq-Kuwait Conflict in 1990 », *SIPRI Yearbook 1992*, pp. 617 ss., 619; Bothe, «Die Golfkrise und die Vereinten Nationen », *Demokratie und Recht*, 1991, pp. 2 ss.

21   Cf. le rapport du Secrétaire général soumis à la quarante-sixième Assemblée générale (doc. A/46/1, chap. IV), qui reconnaît que les dispositions des articles 42 et suivants n'étaient pas appliquées de façon stricte.

22   Verdross/Simma, *op. cit. Supra* note 11, p. 495.

liée à celle de pouvoirs spécifiques. On ne peut pas et on ne doit pas déduire des pouvoirs implicites des buts de la Charte. Cela rendrait l'ensemble de l'équilibre des compétences établi par la Charte illusoire. Comme dans le droit constitutionnel américain, d'où vient la notion de « implied powers »,[23] ainsi que dans le droit d'autres Etats fédéraux,[24] la notion de pouvoirs implicites est liée à celle des pouvoirs énumérés. Les pouvoirs implicites sont ceux qui sont nécessaires pour l'accomplissement effectif des pouvoirs énumérés. Mais on peut également déduire certains pouvoirs implicites d'une pluralité, d'un ensemble de pouvoirs explicites, « resulting powers »[25] dans la terminologie du droit constitutionnel des Etats-Unis d'Amérique.

Si l'on conçoit les pouvoirs implicites du Conseil de sécurité de cette façon, on peut constater un ensemble de compétences quand même considérable. Donnons quelques exemples: si le Conseil de sécurité a le pouvoir de prendre des mesures coercitives, il doit nécessairement avoir la compétence de définir le comportement que l'Etat destinataire de ces mesures devra observer pour rétablir une situation conforme à la Charte. Cet Etat doit par exemple retirer ses troupes derrière une ligne déterminée ou à déterminer, il doit s'abstenir de certains actes d'assistance à une rébellion en cours sur le territoire de l'Etat victime, etc. Notamment la question du trace d'une frontière peut jouer un rôle dans ce contexte.[26]

Notamment, la résolution du Conseil de sécurité concernant le règlement de l'armistice à la fin de la guerre du Golfe pose de façon très sérieuse la question de savoir jusqu'où vont ces pouvoirs implicites.[27] Est-ce que le pouvoir de

---

23   M. Bothe, *Die Kompetenzstruktur des modernen Bundesstaates in rechtsvergleichender Sicht,* 1977, pp. 144 ss.

24   Bothe, *op. cit.,* pp. 194 ss. (Australie), 207 (Suisse), 215 ss, (République fédérale d'Allemagne).

25   Bothe, *op. cit.,* p. 145.

26   Cette question était un des éléments des conditions de l'armistice entre les alliés et l'Iraq arrêtées par le Conseil de sécurité dans sa résolution 687 du 3 avril 1991.

27   La résolution concernant l'armistice entre les alliés et l'Iraq contient essentiellement trois sortes de devoirs :
     a) Devoir concernant le règlement du conflit original :
       – démarcation de la frontière
     b) Devoirs concernant une attitude « paisible » à l'avenir :
       – établissement d'une zone démilitarisée.
       – désarmement chimique contrôle,
       – désarmement nucléaire contrôle
       – prohibition de tout recours ou assistance au terrorisme.
     c) Devoirs de compenser les dommages et de redresser certaines souffrances causées par la guerre :
       – réparation des dommages,
       – rapatriement de certaines personnes.

prendre des mesures coercitives implique le pouvoir d'imposer à un agresseur des obligations spécifiques visant à empêcher toute répétition de l'acte d'agression? Une réponse affirmative à cette question fournirait un fondement juridique pour les mesures de contrôle des armements et des activités nucléaires imposées à l'Iraq par le Conseil de sécurité. Un tel pouvoir du Conseil de sécurité est certainement utile, mais il est moins évident qu'il est nécessaire et approprié pour prendre des mesures coercitives de façon efficace. Dans la même ligne de raisonnement, il faut se demander si le pouvoir de prendre des mesures coercitives en relation avec un acte d'agression implique aussi le pouvoir de prendre des mesures pour liquider des conséquences de l'agression. Une réponse affirmative à cette question fournirait le fondement juridique pour le règlement des dommages adopté par le Conseil sécurité dans la résolution déjà citée. Le moindre qu'on puisse dire à cet égard est que la façon dans laquelle le Conseil interprète ses pouvoirs implicites est un peu hardie.

En résumé, on peut constater que les limites des pouvoirs du Conseil de sécurité dépendent en grande mesure de la manière de définir le lien qui doit exister entre le pouvoir de prendre des mesures coercitives (pouvoir explicite) et certaines mesures supplémentaires (pouvoirs implicites).

4   Le Principe de la Proportionnalité

La dernière réflexion que nous venons de développer s'approche déjà d'une notion générale utilisée souvent quand il s'agit de tracer des limites pour l'exercice de certains pouvoirs, à savoir le principe de proportionnalité. Selon ce principe, d'une manière générale, tout exercice d'un pouvoir public doit être nécessaire, apte et approprié pour atteindre un but public et les restrictions que cet exercice impose à d'autres biens et intérêts ne doivent pas être excessives en relation avec l'avantage obtenu ou anticipé pour l'intérêt favorisé. La question décisive est celle de savoir si le principe, ainsi formulé, constitue un principe général de droit aux termes de l'article 38, paragraphe 1, lettre c), du Statut de la Cour internationale de Justice.

Ce principe se trouve dans le droit constitutionnel et administratif de certains pays européens.[28] En droit allemand, par exemple, il est reconnu comme un principe constitutionnel qui détermine des limites auxquelles sont soumis

---

28   L. Wildhaber, «Limitations on Human Rights in Times of Peace, War and Emergence: A Report on Swiss Law», dans A. de Mestral *et al.* (dir. publ.), *La limitation des droits de l'homme en droit constitutionnel comparé,* 1986, p. 54 ; C.-A. Colliard, *Libertés publiques,* 6e éd., 1982, p. 179.

certains pouvoirs de restreindre la liberté des sujets de droit.[29] A partir du droit administratif et constitutionnel des pays européens, le principe a trouvé sa place bien établie dans la jurisprudence de la Cour de justice des Communautés européennes.[30]

Dans le domaine de la protection internationale des droits de l'homme, les clauses limitatives des pactes et des conventions, notamment la formule « des mesures nécessaires, dans une société démocratique », reflètent également l'idée de la proportionnalité. C'est dans ce sens que les clauses limitatives ont été appliquées par la Cour européenne des droits de l'homme.[31]

La discussion européenne ayant eu une grande influence sur les débats constitutionnels canadiens, le principe de la proportionnalité se retrouve quant au fond aussi dans la clause limitative de la nouvelle Charte canadienne des droits et libertés. Là aussi, on est bien d'accord que cette clause (« dans des limites qui sont raisonnables et dont la justification puisse se démontrer dans le cadre d'une société libre et démocratique ») reflète l'idée de la proportionnalité.[32] Cela est, paraît-il, reconnu non seulement dans la doctrine mais également dans la jurisprudence de la Cour suprême canadienne.

D'une certaine façon, la discussion canadienne sert de pont entre la doctrine européenne et celle américaine. L'idée de fond qui est derrière le principe de la proportionnalité te qu'il a été développé dans la doctrine européenne est plutôt exprimée dans les termes de la « rule of reason » dans la doctrine américaine.[33] On retrouve cette règle dans des contextes biens différents et aussi dans des termes variés. Le droit constitutionnel américain reconnaît aussi le principe que toute limitation de droits individuels doit être justifiée par le besoin de protéger un autre intérêt étatique. A cet égard, la doctrine connaît une différenciation : La limitation d'une liberté « ordinaire » se justifie quand elle est « reasonable related to a state interest » (*rational relation test*).[34] D'autre part, la limitation de certains droits fondamentaux n'est admise que dans le cas où elle est nécessaire pour poursuivre un « compelling state interest » (*strict*

---

29   Cf. K. Stern, *Das Staatsrecht der Bundesrepublik Deutschland,* vol. 1, 2ᵉ éd., 1984, pp. 861 ss.

30   Pour la réglementation des marchés agricoles, CJCE, *Rec.,* 1977, 1211 (*Bela-Mühle*), et 1979, 2137 (*Atlanta Amsterdam*) ; pour les restrictions de la libre circulation des marchandises, *Rec.,* 1979, 649 (*Rewe,* mieux connu sous « *Cassis de Dijon* ») ; pour la liberté de mouvement, *Rec.* 1989, 1263 (*Commission c. Allemagne*).

31   Affaire *Sunday Time, Rec. a30* (1970), p. 42; Affaire *Dudgeon, Rec. A45* (1981), pp. 23 s.

32   P. Hogg, «Section One of the Canadian Charter of Rights and Freedoms», dans A. de Mestral *et al* (dir. publ.), *op cit. supra* note 28, pp. 3 ss., 14ss.

33   Cf. Hogg, *loc. cit.*.

34   L. Tribe, *American Constitutional Law,* 2ᵉ éd., 1988, pp. 1306, 1451.

LES LIMITES DE POUVOIRS DU CONSEIL DE SÉCURITÉ

scrutiny test).[35] Ce sont, au fond, deux variations de l'idée de la proportionnalité qui se distinguent par le poids relatif qui est donné à la liberté limitée dans l'une ou l'autre hypothèse.[36]

Une autre notion de droit constitutionnel américain liée à la proportionnalité est celle du « undue burden ». La Constitution interdit aux Etats, selon l'interprétation développée par la Cour suprême, d'adopter des mesures affectant le commerce entre les divers Etats qui constituent un « undue burden on interstate commerce ».[37] Récemment, la notion de « undue burden » a également été introduite dans la théorie des limitations des droits fondamentaux, notamment dans la décision récente relative à l'avortement.[38]

Nous retrouvons également la notion de la proportionnalité dans certains domaines de droit international public. Dans le domaine du droit de la guerre, ce concept régit l'admissibilité des dommages « collatéraux ». Il interdit toute attaque, dirigée contre un objectif militaire, qui cause des dommages à la population civile ou aux objets civils et qui sont excessifs comparés à l'avantage militaire anticipé.[39] Dans le domaine de la liberté du commerce international, les règles du GATT interdisent des entraves au commerce qui ne sont pas nécessaires pour protéger certains biens nationaux.[40] Finalement, et c'est l'exemple peut-être le plus significatif, dans le domaine des contrôles exercés par l'Agence internationale de l'énergie atomique, on constate également dans certains détails des règlements de procédure l'idée de la proportionnalité.[41]

Il est donc possible de conclure que le principe de la proportionnalité constitue en effet un principe général qui limite l'exercice de certains pouvoirs de l'autorité publique. D'autre part, il s'agit d'un principe dont l'application pratique est très difficile. Car le principe présuppose une comparaison de choses qui sont en vérité incomparables.[42] Si par exemple une limitation de la souveraineté d'une Etat est exigée dans l'intérêt général, comment peut-on dire que le dommage causé pour cet intérêt à la souveraineté est ou n'est pas excessif en

---

35 Tribe, *op. cit.,* pp. 1451 ss.

36 Bothe/Bleckmann, dans A. de Mestral (dir. publ.), *op. cit. supre* note 28, pp. 155 ss., 108 s.

37 M. Bothe, «Völkerrecht und Bundesstaat, Gedanken zu einem juristischen Gegenverkehr», dans Bernhardt *et al.* (dir. publ.), *Völkerrecht als Rechtsordnung – Internationale Gerichtsbarkeit – Menschenrechte. Festschrift für Hermann Mosler,* 1983, pp. 111 ss., 124 ss.

38 *Planned Parenthood of Southeastern Pennsylvania* v. *Casey,* 1992 US Lexis 4751.

39 Article 51 du Protocole I additionnel aux Conventions de Genève.

40 Voir par exemple les articles XX et XXI du Gatt, Bothe, *loc. cit. supre* note 37, p. 127.

41 Cf. T. Lohmann, *Die rechtliche Struktur der Sicherungsmaßnen der Internationalen Atomenergie-Organisation,* thèse Francfort, 1992, p. 117.

42 Baxter, «Criteria of the Prohibition of Weapons in International Law», dans Ehmke *et al., Festschrift für Ulrich Scheuner,* 1973.

relation avec l'avantage pour le maintien de la paix? Dans le domaine du droit interne des Etats, ce sont les tribunaux qui sont en mesure de résoudre ces incertitudes. La comparaison de l'incomparable est toujours possible quand le résultat de la comparaison est obligatoire en vertu des pouvoirs juridictionnels dont disposent les tribunaux. Il est donc certain que l'existence d'une juridiction obligatoire facilite largement l'application pratique du principe de proportionnalité. Mais est-ce que l'application de ce principe présuppose nécessairement l'existence d'un tel pouvoir judiciaire? Le fait que nous trouvons en effet et sans doute aussi au sein du droit international positif où ce pouvoir n'existe pas des cas d'application du principe de la proportionnalité, nous paraît suggérer que l'application de ce principe est en effet possible même à défaut d'un pouvoir judiciaire compétent pour trancher de différends relatifs à la proportionnalité. Cette question nous ramène, cependant, à celle évoquée au début de nos réflexions, à savoir aux limitations procédurales auxquelles les pouvoirs du Conseil de sécurité sont soumis.

5   Les Limitations Procédurales

Comme nous l'avons vu, les règles de fond qui sont la base des pouvoirs du Conseil de sécurité et qui en fixent en même temps les limites offrent une considérable latitude d'interprétation. Il y a donc une possibilité réelle de ce que des préférences politiques diverses se reflètent dans l'interprétation et l'application ou la non-application de ces dispositions. La même difficulté existe en ce qui concerne le principe de la proportionnalité en tant que limite générale des pouvoirs du Conseil. Cet état du droit prouve et souligne l'importance continue des limitations procédurales.

Parmi ces limitations procédurales, le droit de veto joue toujours un rôle primordial. Son importance est évidemment en fonction de la situation politique globale. Actuellement, il n'y a que la Chine qui de quelque façon sert de gardien aux intérêts de la souveraineté établi. C'est la Chine qui reste un contrepoids significatif contre le pouvoir politique des Etats-Unis. Un amendement à la Charte qui changerait la composition du Conseil de sécurité et notamment les membres permanents aurait évidemment un grand impact sur le mécanisme politique en ce qui concerne la façon dans laquelle les décisions du Conseil de sécurité sont prises. La question des limitations procédurales se poserait alors de façon différente.

Un autre genre de limitation procédurale serait évidemment le contrôle judiciaire. L'introduction d'un tel contrôle pourrait paraître utopique. Cependant, nous sommes actuellement en présence d'une affaire où la Cour internationale de Justice est appelée à se prononcer sur la validité et/ou la légalité de certaines résolutions adoptées par le Conseil de sécurité, à savoir le différend entre la Libye d'une part et les Etats-Unis et la Grande-Bretagne de l'autre.[43] Malgré le fait que la Cour, dans sa décision sur les mesures provisoires, ait accepté (dans le cadre de cette procédure, il faut le souligner) les résolutions du Conseil de sécurité comme facteur déterminant, elle a certainement laissée ouverte, et cela de façon assez claire, la possibilité qu'elle se prononce dans la procédure normale sur la validité et l'effet des décisions du Conseil de sécurité. On est ainsi en présence d'une compétence indirecte de la Cour d'exercer un contrôle judiciaire sur une action du Conseil de sécurité. Car la base de la juridiction de la Cour est la Convention de Montréal et non pas la Charte des Nations Unies. S'il existe de cette façon des voies indirectes d'arriver à un contrôle judiciaire des actions du Conseil de sécurité, on peut se demander s'il ne serait pas préférable de créer des voies directes et d'éviter de cette façon que le hasard détermine les actions soumises au scrutine judiciaire de celles qui ne le sont pas.

6   Conclusions

Cette communication a été rédigée dans le but de promouvoir l'idée de *rule of law* dans les relations internationales. Dans cet esprit, elle souligne certaines techniques juridiques visant à limiter le pouvoir du Conseil de sécurité. Leur but est de restreindre le champ d'action discrétionnaire et non contrôlable. En le faisant, nous avons adopté une approche optimiste que certains vont peut-être qualifier d'idéaliste. Mais, à notre avis, cette approche se justifie. A quoi sert-elle? A l'intérêt de la souveraineté étatique? Oui, pourquoi pas! La souveraineté étatique est assez souvent considérée, comme un mal, mais elle n'est certainement pas un mal en soi. Elle est toujours un fondement, principe de base de l'ordre international. Elle est l'expression de l'intérêt de chaque organisation étatique de ne pas être dominée par d'autres puissances, que ce soit par la voie d'une action unilatérale ou par le truchement d'une organisation multilatérale. Il est vrai qu'il est toujours possible de protéger et de couvrir l'erreur, l'inhumanité, même le crime derrière le manteau de la souveraineté. Mais qui nous assure que les grandes puissances et les organisations internationales dominées par elles sont toujours inspirées par le bien commun, agissent toujours de façon juste et humaine? Si la souveraineté sert de prétexte

---

43   *Questions d'interprétation et d'application de la Convention de Montréal de 1971, ordonnance du 14 avril 1992, CIJ Recueil 1992,* p. 126.

pour couvrir des attentats contre les valeurs communes de l'humanité, il doit y avoir d'autres possibilités de l'empêcher que la puissance de certains Etats peu nombreux qui exercent leur pouvoir prédominant soit unilatéralement soit par l'intermédiaire d'un organe des Nations Unies. La puissance exercée par ces organes doit être légitimée par le droit et non pas par le pouvoir. C'est dans le sens de ses autres possibilités qu'il faut rechercher les solutions futures. Cela permettre de maintenir et de renforcer les limitations juridiques du pouvoir des Nations Unies et servira de cette façon à les rendre plus acceptables et plus acceptées.

3

Security Council's Targeted Sanctions against Presumed Terrorists

The Need to Comply with Human Rights Standards

1   Introductory Remarks: The Need for Individual Remedies

International organizations developed as elements of the interstate system of international law, as tools to regulate the relations between states and to organize their cooperation. Therefore, conceptually, they were not held to address individuals, at least not directly. As a consequence, procedural rules for the relationship between international organizations and individuals, including legal remedies for individuals against acts of international organizations, could be considered as being a non-issue.

There was an early recognition of an obvious exception to this assumption: this was and is the relationship between the organization and its employees. Since the creation of international organizations after the First World War, administrative tribunals or at least independent commissions or appeal boards have been established by these organizations to deal with formal complaints of the employees against the organizations.[1] Apart from this exception, international organizations are sealed off from legal challenges put forward by individuals: no remedy is provided by the organizations, and they are immune from legal process in the courts of states.[2] This, it is submitted, has for a long time constituted a major flaw in the law of international organizations, a serious lacuna in the guaranty of the rule of law in international relations.[3]

There have always been three different approaches in solving this problem where it was recognized as such. One possibility is the waiver of immunity (very rare)[4] or also some kind of reduction of that immunity, which, however,

---

1   G. Vandersanden, Administrative Tribunals, Boards and Commissions in International Organizations', in *Encyclopaedia of Public International Law* (EPIL), vol. 1 (Elsevier: Amsterdam, 1992) 27–31.

2   P.C. Szasz, 'International Organizations, Privileges and Immunities, in EPIL, vol. II (Elsevier: Amsterdam, 1995) 1325–1333.

3   M. Bothe, 'Internationale Organisationen und das Rechtsstaatsprinzip, in J. Jekewitz et al. (eds), *Des Menschen Recht zwischen Freiheit und Verantwortung. Festschriftfilr Karl Josef Partsch zum 75. Geburtstag* (Berlin: Duncker and Humblot, 1989) 493–514.

4   Bothe, *supra* note 3, at 512.

© KONINKLIJKE BRILL NV, LEIDEN, 2021 | DOI:10.1163/9789004380592_005

has so far not been accepted.[5] A second possibility is arbitration. This is a common feature in the contractual practice of international organizations and also provided for in some international agreements.[6] The third option is the provision for judicial or at least equivalent institutions in the law of the organization itself. The pioneer of this approach was the European Coal and Steel Community (ECSC) Treaty of 1951, which did not only establish a Court of Justice, but also provided for the judicial review of decisions directed against, or directly affecting, enterprises or associations.[7] This set the precedent for the law of the European Communities created thereafter, and now for the European Union.

On the universal level, an approach similar to that of the ECSC was adopted for acts or omissions of the Seabed Authority created by the United Nations Convention on the Law of the Sea (UNCLOS) of 1982. Article 187 of the Convention provides for a number of disputes between the Authority and certain natural or legal persons related to seabed mining activities to be adjudicated by the Sea-Bed Dispute Chamber of the Law of the Sea Tribunal.

Another example for a review process is the World Bank Inspection Panel. In giving credits for different projects, the Bank indeed affects individual rights of natural or legal persons affected by a project. The Panel, however, is not a judicial institution. In contradistinction to permanent courts or arbitration tribunals, its decisions are not binding. However, the members of the panel enjoy a high degree of independence, and their reports have a considerable weight.[8]

In other situations where operations of international organizations directly affect individuals the solution has rather been one of muddling through. This is in particular the case of UN peacekeeping operations where the problem is obvious due to the immediate contact between the personnel of the operations and the population of the country where an operation is taking place. There have been cases where states espoused claims of the victims of peacekeeping operations and exercised a right of diplomatic protection against the

---

5   Szasz, *supra* note 2, at 1332.

6   Bothe, *supra* note 3, at 511 et seq.

7   Art. 33 ECSCT.

8   IBRD Resolution 93-10 and IDA Resolution 93–6, 22 September 1993. For an analysis of essential elements of this procedure, see L. Boisson de Chazournes, 'The World Bank Inspection Panel: About Public Participation and Dispute Settlement, in T. Treves et al. (eds), *Civil Society, International Courts and Compliance Bodies* (The Hague: T.M.C. Asser Press, 2005), 187 et seq. See also *infra* note 39.

UN.[9] In other cases, the organization set up claims commissions to deal with these issues.

The problem of legal remedies for individuals affected by acts or omissions of international organizations has often been seen as a matter of expediency, of political advisability. But it is more than that. The right to a remedy is a fundamental human right. It applies, first of all, to the protection of the individual against the state. In this perspective, it forms part of human rights treaties: Articles 8 and 10 of the Universal Declaration of Human Rights, 6 and 13 European Convention of Human Rights (ECHR), and 14 International Covenant on Civil and Political Rights (ICCPR). The recognition that equivalent restraints must apply to international organizations if and to the extent that they affect individuals in a way similar to states has been slow. It took about 20 years from the creation of the ECSC before a first judgement of the European Court of Justice (ECJ) accepted that the European Economic Community (EEC) was indeed bound by human rights in its relationship to individuals.[10]

In relation to universal organizations, that recognition has been even slower. This may also be due to the fact that it is only recently that the UN has been in a practical situation to violate individual human rights. However, in the international discourse on the accountability of international organization,[11] it is generally recognized that international organizations are indeed bound by the customary law of human rights. As the Report of the International Law Association (ILA) Committee puts it:

> As part of the process of humanisation of international law, human rights guarantees are increasingly becoming an expression of the common constitutional traditions of States and can become binding upon IO-s as general principles of law. The consistent practice of the UN General Assembly and of the Security Council points to the emergence of a customary rule to this effect.[12]

---

9 As to the practice concerning UN Operations in the Congo (ONUC), see R. Higgins, *United Nations Peacekeeping 1946–1967: Documents and Commentary* vol. III: Africa (Oxford: Oxford University Press, 1980), at 272 et seq.

10 The first case where the ECJ recognized this human rights obligation was the judgment of 12 November 1969 in the case of *Stauder v. Stadt Ulm,* case 29/69, ECJ Reports 1969, 419.

11 See Committee on Accountability of International Organizations of the International Law Association, Report of the Seventieth Conference, New Delhi, 2002, at 772–806.

12 *Ibid.,* at 789.

In the Recommended Rules and Practices elaborated by the ILA Committee, the situation of temporary territorial administration by an international organization, the imposition of coercive economic measures, peacekeeping and peace enforcement measures are singled out as situations where the said principle is relevant.

A major case in point is the system of 'targeted sanctions'.

2   Remedies against Security Council Decisions – What Need?

Traditional non-military enforcement measures pursuant to Article 41 of the Charter are value deprivations imposed upon states as collectivities. The measures expressly mentioned are the interruption of economic relations, i.e. embargoes, and of other communications (of which the interruption of air traffic has had a major significance in recent times). This type of measure has rightly been criticized as both ineffective and unjust. It is unjust because it mainly hits the innocent population. It is ineffective because it does not or only rarely reaches those who are personally responsible for a threat to the peace or a breach of the peace. In the light of this experience, a system of 'targeted' sanctions has been developed which is directed specifically against these persons.

There are in particular three types of restrictions or deprivations on such persons:

(i)   travel restrictions;
(ii)   financial restrictions;
(iii)   criminal responsibility.

These targeted sanctions have been used in a number of situations characterized by the Security Council as constituting a threat to the peace: Liberia, Sierra Leone, the Taliban in Afghanistan.[13] They are now used in particular as

---

13   Travel restrictions and/or freezing of financial assets concerning persons designated ('listed') by a Committee of the Security Council have been imposed by a number of UNSC resolutions in the following cases: Sierra Leone, resolutions 1132 of 8 October 1997 and 1171 of 5 June 1998: Afghanistan, Taliban, Al-Qaida, resolutions 1267 of 15 October 1999, 1333 of 19 December 2000, 1390 of 16 January 2002, 1455 of 17 January 2003, 1526 of 30 January 2004, 1617 of 29 July 2005, 1735 of 22 December 2006; Iraq, resolution 1483 of 22 May 2003; Liberia, resolutions 1521 of 22 December 2003, 1532 of 12 March 2004; Côte d'Ivoire, resolutions 1572 of 15 November 2004, 1584 of 1 February 2005, 1643 of 15 December 2005; Sudan (Darfur), resolution 1591 of 29 March 2005; DRC, resolutions 1596 of 18 April 2005, 1649 of 21 December 2005, 1698 of 31 July 2006; Lebanon, resolution 1636 of 31 October 2005; North Korea, resolution 1718 of 14 October 2006; Iran, resolutions 1737 of 23 December 2006, 1747 of 24 March 2007.

SANCTIONS AGAINST PRESUMED TERRORISTS

measures imposed *by* the Security Council in the fight against terrorism and against the proliferation of weapons of mass destruction.[14]

The implementation of these resolutions requires a two or even three level system: The basic decisions are taken by the Security Council, but they must be implemented on the level of the various states. It is states which freeze assets, deny entry, etc. In the case of the European Union, the Union is a level between the Security Council and the states which has become a major point of legal controversy.

This multilevel system works in two different ways. In some cases, the Sanctions Committee, i.e. the Security Council itself places the individual or entity concerned on a list (listing decision). It is then the function and duty of the lower levels (states, European Community/Union) to make sure that the measures in question are indeed implemented in relation to all individuals or entities so listed. This can be called automatic listing at the lower level(s). The other option is that the Security Council defines the group of persons or entities which are subject to sanctions in a general way. It is then the function and duty of the lower level(s) to make sure that all persons falling into that definition are indeed so listed and the corresponding measures are taken against them. This can be called autonomous listing at the lower level.[15] In the latter case, there are reporting duties and a monitoring mechanism. As far as the need for a remedy is concerned, in the former case, all essential decisions concerning the individual are taken by the Security Council. If the binding character of Security Council resolutions is to be taken seriously, the lower level(s) have no choice but to take the measures against the listed individual. This is why the Security Council directly affects the legal position of the individual. The Security Council decision constitutes an exercise of public authority vis-à-vis the individual. Therefore, according to customary human rights standards, there must be a remedy against the Security Council's decisions.

In the case of autonomous listing decisions, no individual is named by the Security Council. The names on the list are determined by states or by the European Community/Union. The human rights standards applying to these listing decisions are those binding the state in question or the EC. Those standards may, however, be affected, and the human rights protection limited, by the fact that there is, according to Article 25 of the UN Charter, an international legal duty of the state in question and/or the EC to adopt certain measures.

---

14   Resolutions 1373 of 28 September 2001 on the fight against terrorism, 1540 of 28 April 2004 on the non-proliferation of weapons of mass destruction.

15   This is the situation under UN resolutions 1373 and 1540.

Both types of targeted sanctions have encountered serious criticism. Allegations were made that there were persons on the lists who, according to the applicable standards, should not be there because those persons or entities did not fulfil the criteria for being listed. At both levels, the listing decisions have not been transparent. The individuals in question practically had no way of finding out why they were listed. While in the case of autonomous listing decisions, there is a possibility of judicial review which cannot be excluded, the situation of individuals listed by the Security Council was rather desperate. Theoretically, states could sponsor an individual's claim and request a delisting. That proved to be difficult. The individual in question had no access to the decision making process of the Sanctions Committee.

These criticisms were uttered in various forums. Doubts have been formulated in academic writings,[16] NGO position papers[17] and, in particular, court decisions.[18] The UN General Assembly dealt with them, and the Security Council reacted to them, albeit in a rather lukewarm manner. The Council of the European Union has also addressed the issue.[19] So did the Parliamentary Assembly of the Council of Europe, criticizing the current practice in no uncertain terms.[20]

Three studies which dealt with the problem were brought to the attention of the Security Council and the General Assembly:

---

16   D. Frank, 'UN-Sanktionen gegen Terrorismus und europdische Menschenrechtskonvention, in S. Breitenmoser et al. (eds), *Human Rights, Democracy and the Rule of Law, Liber Amicorum Luzius Wildhaber* (Zurich: Dike, 2007) 237; C. Warbrick, 'The European Response to Terrorism in an Age of Human Rights', 15 *E]IL* (2004) 989–1018; I. Cameron, 'UN Targeted Sanctions, Legal Safeguards and the European Convention on Human Rights', 72 *Nordic Journal of International Law* (2003) 159–214; P. Fitzgerald, 'Managing Smart Sanctions Against Terrorism Wisely', 36 *New England Law Review* (2002) 957–983; St. Schmahl, 'Effektiver Rechtsschutz gegen "targeted sanctions" des UN-Sicherheitsrats?, *Europarecht* (2006) 566; H. Aust and N. Naske, 'Rechtsschutz gegen den UN-Sicherheitsrat durch europaische Gerichte?, 61 *Zeitschrift fur Öffentliches Recht* (zor) (2006) 587.

17   Human Rights Watch, U.N.: Sanctions Rules Must Protect Due Process, 4 March 2002, available at http://hrw.org/english/docs/2002/03/04/global5839.htm (visited 31 May 2008).

18   See below Part 3.

19   Council of the European Union, *Basic Principles on the Use of Restrictive Measures (Sanctions)*, 7 June 2004, Doc. 10198/1/04 PESC 450 REV1; cf. also Council of the European Union, *Guidelines on implementation and evaluation of restrictive measures (sanctions) in the framework of the EU Common Foreign and Security Policy* 2 December 2005, Doc. 15114/05 PESC 1084 Fin 475.

20   Council of Europe, Parliamentary Assembly, Resolution 1597 (2008) and Recommendation 1824 (2008), both adopted 23 January 2008 and based on the Report (Doc. 11454) of the Committee on Legal Affairs and Human Rights (Rapporteur D. Marty, Switzerland) entitled 'United Nations Security Council and European Union blacklists'.

SANCTIONS AGAINST PRESUMED TERRORISTS

(i)   The European Convention on Human Rights, Due Process and UN Security Council Counter-Terrorism Sanctions. Report prepared by Iain Cameron; Council of Europe, Restricted Document, 6 February 2006;

(ii)   Targeted Sanctions and Due Process. The responsibility of the UN Security Council to ensure that fair and clear procedures are made available to individuals and entities targeted with sanctions under Chapter VII of the UN Charter. Report by Bardo Fassbender, Institute of Public International Law at the Humboldt University, Berlin. Study commissionedby the United Nations Office of Legal Affairs, 20 March 2006; and

(iii)   Strengthening Targeted Sanctions through Fair and Clear Procedures. White Paper prepared by the Watson Institute Targeted Sanctions Project, Brown University, 30 March 2006.[21]

Both the UN General Assembly and the Security Council have reacted to these concerns. In its resolution on the 2005 World Summit Outcome,[22] the General Assembly declared:

> We also call upon the Security Council, with the support of the Secretary-General, to ensure that fair and clear procedures exist for placing individual and entities on sanctions lists and for removing them, as well as for granting humanitarian exemptions.

This is reflected in a statement issued on 22 June 2006 by the President of the Security Council:[23]

> The Council is committed to ensuring that fair and clear procedures exist for placing individuals and entities on sanctions lists and for removing them, as well as for granting humanitarian exemptions. The Council reiterates its request to the 1267 Committee to continue its work on the Committee's guidelines, including on listing and de-listing procedures. ...

In addition, the Security Council adopted a number of resolutions providing for a review of listing decisions and for a de-listing procedure, in particular: Resolutions 1617 (2005); 1730 (2006); 1735 (2006).

---

21   Annex to the letter dated 19 May 2006 from the Permanent Representatives of Germany, Sweden and Switzerland to the United Nations addressed to the President of the Security Council, UN Doc. A/60/887-S/2006/331.

22   UN Doc. A/RES/60/1, 24 October 2005.

23   UN Doc. S/PRST/2006/28, 22 June 2006.

PART 1: BASIC ISSUES

Implementing these resolutions, the Sanctions Committees have elaborated guidelines for the review of listing decisions and for de-listing:

(i)   Guidelines of the Security Council Committee Established Pursuant to Resolution 1267 (1999) Concerning Al-Qaida and the Taliban, adopted on 7 November 2002, as amended;

(ii) Guidelines of the Committee Established Pursuant to Resolution 1636 (2005).

Resolution 1730 (2006) is of particular interest as it requests the Secretary-General to establish within the Secretariat the so-called Focal Point, a kind of revamped letter box where a listed individual can indeed submit a request for delisting. This triggers a consultation process with the 'designating government(s)', i.e. governments which had taken the initiative to have the individual placed on the list, and the government(s) of citizenship and residence. If none of those governments recommends a de-listing, the person remains on the list. If one of those governments recommends a de-listing, the Sanctions Committee will take the request on its agenda. The individual requesting de-listing will be informed of the result. To call this procedure a 'remedy' for the individual would really be an exaggeration.

3   Litigation

Not surprisingly, the issue of listing and de-listing has given rise to litigation in national jurisdictions and before the courts of the European Community. Of particular relevance are two judgments of the Court of First Instance, one[24] concerning an automatic listing, the other[25] autonomous listings.

In the first case, the Court held that the Community was indeed bound by the decisions of the Security Council and that it had no authority to review their international legality except where the decision violated a rule of *ius cogens*. The Court held that this was not the case, at least not after the Security Council had provided to the individual, through the establishment of the Focal Point, some possibility of triggering a review process.

---

24   *Ahmed All Yusuf& Al Barakaat International Foundation v. Council and Commission,* Court of First Instance, case 306/01; *Yassin Abdullah Kadi v. Council of the European Union and Commission of the European Communities,* Court of First Instance, case T-315/01, both relating to UN Doc. S/RES/1267 of 15 October 1999); Judgment of 21 September 2005.

25   *Organisation des ModJahedines du people dIran v. Council of the European Union,* Court of First Instance, case T-228/02, judgement of 12 December 2006; *Sison v. Council of the European Union,* Court of First Instance, case T-47/03, judgement of 11 July 2007; *Stichting Al-Aqsa v. Council of the European Union,* Court of First Instance, case T-327/03, judgement of 11 July 2007; all three relating to UN Doc. S/RES/1373 of 28 September 2001.

This judgement was widely criticized. An appeal was lodged against it. The Advocate General, Poiares Maduro, in his conclusions of 16 January 2008, requested the Court of Justice to reverse it.[26] At the time of writing, the Court has not yet rendered its decision.

The Opinion of Advocate General Maduro makes a very strong case for an effective protection of fundamental rights in the framework of listing and de-listing decisions of a Sanctions Committee and the implementation of such decisions in the Community legal order. That implementation is fully subject to the constitutional guarantees of Community law. A decision of the Security Council does not enjoy a 'supra-constitutional' status.[27] The Court does no review a decision of the Security Council, but it must make sure that the implementation of this decision at the Community level does not violate fundamental rights. These constitutional guarantees apply also where the measure in question serves the purpose of effectively fighting international terrorism:[28]

> The fact that the measures at issue are intended to suppress international terrorism should not inhibit the Court from fulfilling its duty to preserve the rule of law.
>
> ...
>
> (T)he indefinite freezing of someone's assets constitutes a far-reaching interference with the peaceful enjoyment of property. The consequences for the person concerned are potentially devastating ... Of course, this explains why the measure has such a strong coercive effect and why 'smart sanctions' of this type might be considered a suitable of even necessary means to prevent terrorist acts. However, it also underscores the *need for procedural safeguards* which require the authorities *to justify such measures and demonstrate their proportionality* not merely in the abstract, but in the concrete circumstances of the given case.

The procedural safeguards which are required are twofold:

> Both the right to *be* heard and the right to effective judicial review constitute fundamental rights that form part of the general principles of Community law.

---

26   Opinion of Advocate General Poiares Maduro delivered on 16 January 2008 (henceforth 'Opinion'), *Yadi v. Council and Commission,* Court of First Instance, case C-402/05 P.

27   § 25 of the Opinion.

28   §§ 45 et seq. of the Opinion, emphasis added.

According to the Advocate General, both rights have been severely infringed. As to the right to be heard,

> the Community institutions have not afforded any opportunity to the appellant to make known his views on whether the sanctions against him are justified and whether they should be kept in force.[29]

As the Court of First Instance had relied on the UN de-listing procedure in order to save the Security Council decision from further judicial scrutiny, the view of the Advocate General on the fundamental rights significance of that procedure is of particular importance:[30]

> The existence of a de-listing procedure at the level of the United Nations offers no consolation in that regard. That procedure allows petitioners to submit a request to the Sanctions Committee or to their government for removal from the list. Yet, the processing of that request is purely a matter of intergovernmental consultation. There is no obligation on the Sanctions Committee actually to take the views of the petitioner into account. Moreover, the de-listing procedure does not provide even minimal access to the information on which the decision was based to include the petitioner in the list.[31]

As to the right to a judicial remedy, the Advocate General demands that there is

> an independent tribunal assessing the fairness of these allegations and the reasonableness of these sanctions.[32]

As has already been pointed out, the other cases brought before the Court of First Instance related to autonomous listing decisions of the European Community in this situation, the question whether a decision of the Security Council relating to a particular person had to be implemented in all circumstances did not arise. In these cases, the Court indeed applied the requirement of procedural safeguards, found them to be lacking and annulled the Community Regulation to the extent it applied to the petitioners. In the PMOI case, the Council then granted the petitioner a hearing – and kept it on the list. Whether

---

29   § 51 of the Opinion.

30   See *supra* Part 2 *in fine.*

31   § 51 of the Opinion.

32   § 53 of the Opinion.

SANCTIONS AGAINST PRESUMED TERRORISTS

this decision will stand remains to be seen,[33] in particular in light of the fact that in the meantime, the competent British administrative tribunal has enjoined the UK government to remove the petitioner from the list.[34]

The type of judicial review of measures implementing a Security Council listing decision which is proposed by the EC Advocate General involves a serious risk for the effectiveness of targeted sanctions: where a request for judicial review is successful, the uniform application of a sanction throughout the World is in danger. However, the answer to this problem cannot be the denial of the protection of fundamental rights. It has to be the establishment of procedural safeguards deserving that name at the level of the UN. The concluding remarks of the Advocate General point in this direction:

> Had there been a genuine and effective mechanism of judicial control by an independent tribunal at the level of the United Nations, then this might have released the Community from the obligation to provide for judicial control of implementing measures that apply within the Community legal order. However, no such mechanism currently exists.[35]

4   The Way out – a Soft System of Remedies

So far, the procedure of the Security Council does not live up to the fundamental rights requirements just described. This involves the risk that the listing decisions will not be implemented and judicial remedies at the implementation level have a fair chance of success. The question has, thus, to be asked what reforms of the Security Council procedure are needed, along the lines alluded to by the Advocate General, which would make that procedure safe against such challenges. Similar demands have been formulated by the Parliamentary Assembly of the Council of Europe.[36] Although no formal proposals are on the table at the UN, there are initiatives and debates in this direction.[37] As pointed

---

33   It is reported that a new application is about to be brought before the Court of First Instance.

34   Judgement of the Proscribed Organizations Appeal Commission dated 30 November 2007. *Lord Alton of Liverpool & others (In the matter of The People's Mojahadeen Organisation of Iran) v. Secretary of State for the Home Department,* available at www.siac.tribunals.gov.uk/ poac/Documents/outcomes/PC022006%20PMOI%20FINAL% (visted 31 May 2008).

35   § 54 of the Opinion.

36   Resolution 1597 (2008) of 23 January 2008, see *supra* note 20.

37   On 8 November 2007, the Governments of Denmark, Liechtenstein, Sweden and Switzerland sponsored a Workshop in New York where an exchange of views took place

74   PART 1: BASIC ISSUES

out by the Advocate General, there should be standards for the listing decisions themselves and an effective remedy against such decisions.

4.1   *Procedural Standards for Security Council Decisions*

The standards to which the decisions of the Security Council should live up
are classical requirements of due process, formulated in many national constitutions, in the Universal Declaration of Human Rights, in the ICCPR and
in regional human rights treaties. They constitute a solid body of customary
human rights law.

The relevant standards can be summarized as follows:

(i)   There must be a general normative standard for any measure affecting
       individual rights;
(ii)   such measures must be based on reliable evidence;
(iii) the individual must have an effective remedy against such measure,
       which implies:
       (a)   The measure must be notified in an understandable way;
       (b)   The individual must have an opportunity to appeal;
       (c)   In the last resort, an independent and impartial body must be able
              to review the measure;
       (d)   The body must play a really decisive, not merely advisory role.

The first one of these standards derives from the rule that any limitation of a
fundamental right must be based on law. As formulated in Article 29 paragraph
2 of the Universal Declaration:

> In the exercise of his rights and freedoms, everyone shall be subject only
> to such limitations as are determined by law solely for the purpose of se-
> curing due recognition and respect for the rights and freedoms of others
> and of meeting the just requirements of morality, public order and the
> general welfare in a democratic society.

A limitation is 'determined by law' only if the relevant legal rule is clear and
precise enough.

---

on a discussion paper regarding the establishment of a review panel to deal with petitions for de-listing, see the statement of Ambassador Wenaweser of Liechtenstein before
the Security Council on 14 November 2007, UN Doc. S/PV.5779, at 28. The documents of
the workshop are available at the website of the Permanent Mission of Liechtenstein to
the United Nations: http://www.liechtenstein.li/en/fl-ausssenstelle-newyork/ (visited 31
May 2008).

The second and the third of these standards are derived from the principles of procedural due process as they are formulated in Article 10 of the Universal Declaration:

> Everyone is entitled in full equality to a fair and public hearing by an independent and impartial tribunal, in the determination of his rights and obligations and of any criminal charge against him.

The right to a judicial remedy is explicitly enshrined in Article 8 of the Universal Declaration:

> Everyone has the right to an effective remedy by the competent national tribunals for acts violating the fundamental rights granted him by the constitution or by law.

In a number of human rights treaties, these rules have been formulated as applying to states. The wordings used in the Universal Declaration, too, rather protect the individual against infringements perpetrated by state authorities. The development of the powers of international organizations which enables them to affect, by their activities, individual rights, is, as already pointed out,[38] of relatively recent origin. As the structure of international organizations is different from that of states, the rules applying to states cannot be applied to organizations in an identical way. It is however essential that the rules applying to organizations provide an equivalent protection to individuals. As the rights enshrined in the Universal Declaration are nowadays considered to constitute a core of customary law guarantees, these norms are particularly relevant for international organizations which are not bound by any of the human rights treaties, but 'only' by customary law.

In the case of states, there is always a balance between the rights of the individual and the public interest. Individual freedoms are not unlimited, but a core of individual freedom must always be observed. Where similar rules protecting individual freedom apply to organizations, the functions and tasks of the organization concerned must also be taken into account in striking the said balance.

The essential procedural standard is that of procedural fairness, implying transparency and 'equality of arms'. Transparency is usually assured by a requirement that the person affected must have a hearing before the

---

38   See *supra* Part 1.

measure is taken. This is not always possible without endangering the purpose of the measure. In that case, the necessary transparency must be ensured afterwards.

The first necessary element of transparency is notification. The affected individual must be in a position to know what measure has been taken against him/her. For that purpose, some kind of public announcement by the Security Council is not enough. Therefore, a formal notification will have to be done either by the Sanctions Committee or by the state where the individual resides or has his/her usual abode, or where the affected enterprise has its place of business. That notification provides legal certainty and would constitute a reasonable basis for any review procedure. Therefore, a regulation for Security Council listing decisions must contain rules on notification.

The individual must be able to understand the notification. This means, first, that the notification must be made in a language which the individual understands. It also means that the affected individual must be able to understand the reasons for the decision, that is the evidence on which it is based and the factual and legal evaluation. This procedural requirement is essential. Therefore, listing decisions of the Security Council must state reasons.

There is one fundamental balancing problem involved in this requirement, namely the treatment of information which is confidential for legitimate reasons of public interest. The basic rule should be that the person affected or his/her attorney must have access to any information which is essential for the decision. He/she must be able to evaluate or refute that evidence. If this is not possible, the information must at least have been scrutinized by an impartial and independent third party, e.g. a judge. Therefore, a regulation for Security Council listing decisions must contain appropriate rules on the treatment of confidential information. Evidence which cannot be scrutinized by the affected individual (or in another reliable way?) may not be used against him/her.

4.2 *Judicial or Equivalent Review*

The core of the right to an effective remedy is the judicial review of the decisions taken by an executive (or as the case may be: legislative) authority. As already pointed out above, in the case of international organizations, this is a difficult matter. It is somewhat difficult to imagine the Security Council establishing an independent tribunal to review its decisions. Thus, a search for equivalent options is necessary However, if one takes the admonition expressed by the EC Advocate General seriously, these other options must not be too lenient – otherwise the judicial institutions of the EC will not renounce to their right and duty to review implementing measures in the light of EC fundamental rights standards.

SANCTIONS AGAINST PRESUMED TERRORISTS

This search for other equivalent procedures has to take into account some basic requirements for this equivalence:

(i) The purpose of the procedure is to safeguard individual rights. Therefore, the aggrieved individual must be entitled to trigger the procedure.

(ii) It must at least provide some elements which make it comparable to a judicial procedure. Therefore, the members of the reviewing body must provide adequate guarantees of independence and impartiality.

(iii) It must provide the necessary guarantees of a fair trial.

(iv) It must provide adequate assurances of actual implementation.

An example of such a procedure can be found in the 'inspection panels' established by the World Bank:[39]

(i) Aggrieved organizations may seize the panel where they claim to be directly and adversely affected by a failure of the Bank to respect certain relevant rules in designing, appraising or implementing a loan project.

(ii) The members are appointed for a fixed term by the Executive Directors. They may not be associated with the Bank immediately before, during or immediately after their membership in the panel. This is a certain guarantee for independence. Only the provision on removal by decision of the Executive Directors is somewhat lax.

(iii) The procedure is split in two phases. The Panel first decides whether the requesting party fulfils the eligibility criteria and makes a recommendation to the Executive Directors whether there should be an investigation. It is then up to the Executive Directors to decide whether there is an investigation. This gives the Executive Directors the possibility of preventing an investigation.

(iv) The procedure must lead to a report which contains the findings of the Panel as to whether the relevant rules have been violated. It is then up to the Executive Directors to decide which consequences are drawn from the findings. This provides no strict guarantee that the findings of the Panel will be respected. An incentive to respect the findings of the Panel would be to make the recommendations and findings of the Panel and the corresponding reactions of the Executive Directors public.

From the point of view of the equivalence criteria described above, that procedure is not an ideal solution. It provides, however, some sort of hints as to possibility of an independent non-judicial review procedure. The essential point is that it constitutes a fruitful compromise. The procedure was designed to improve the quality of the World Bank's operation. It does not constitute

---

39 See supra note 8.

an outside judicial review, it is administrative in nature. On the other hand, it provides a guarantee for an independent control of decisions and an effective remedy for those actors which are affected by the Bank's decisions. That independence and the ensuing impartiality provide a certain equivalence to a procedure of judicial review.

Therefore, a review procedure for Security Council action affecting individuals by targeted sanctions could be inspired by the example of the World Bank inspection panels. The procedure of the WTO Dispute Settlement Understanding provides an additional indication as to how a procedure like that of the Inspection Panel could be brought closer to a binding judicial decision: the recommendations of the reviewing body should become binding if the Council does not reject them within a certain period of time.

The essential characteristics of such a procedure can, thus, be summarized as follows:

(i)   the transparency of the listing procedure;
(ii) a review of the listing decisions providing essential guarantees of fairness, namely:
      independence of the reviewing body;
      appropriate screening of review requests;
      effective and fair taking of evidence;
      speedy procedure;
      publicity of the results of the procedure;
      high probability of implementation of the reviewing decision.

Let it be it noted that the Parliamentary Assembly of the Council of Europe, in its catalogue of requirements for a listing and de-listing procedure respecting the rule of law, adds a right of compensation for victims of wrong listing decisions.[40] Legal logic militates for this proposal, but it would involve difficult questions of non-contractual liability of the UN which might be used as a pretext for blocking any reform. There remains, on the other hand, the responsibility of any government proposing the inclusion of a person or entity in a relevant list according to the norms of the respective state concerning its liability for the illegal conduct of its organs.

In the course of political debates in the framework of the UN, proposals of the kind presented in this article have been criticized as undermining the binding force of Security Council decisions. It is no surprise that such arguments can be heard in particular from representatives of the Permanent Members of the Security Council, the P5. Such a critique is unfounded. A better transparency

---

40   Resolution 1597 (2008), §5.1.4.

of Security Council decisions and a possibility to challenge such decisions in a procedurally organized way does not put into question the binding force of the decisions. It only elaborates the limitations of the powers of the Security Council which are inherent in the Charter and which follow from a very basic principle underlying the Charter, which is the respect due to the rule of law. It is true that there is a real possibility of unilateral action by states and by the European Community which might not implement a Security Council decision. However, the principles which inspire such a refusal are the very same ones which also apply at the level of the UN, at least according to a modern interpretation of the obligations deriving from UN provisions and rules.

According to the Parliamentary Assembly of the Council of Europe,[41] there is a special responsibility of those Members of the organization, who are also members of the Security Council:

> to use their influence (in this body) in favour of upholding the values embodied in the European Convention of Human Rights, both by ensuring the necessary improvements in procedural and substantive rules and through the positions they take on individual cases.

In the light of the legal situation of the EC, there is a particular responsibility incumbent on the EC Members who are also members of the Security Council, in particular on the two Permanent Members of the Security Council. According to the Opinion of the EC Advocate General,[42] those EC Members have a particular duty to see to it that there is no incompatibility between UN obligations and the obligations as EC members. This duty is derived from Article 307 EC, which is a variation of the principle of EU loyalty (Article 10 EC):

> (The) duty (pursuant to Article 307 paragraph 2) requires Member States to exercise their powers and responsibilities in an international organization such as the United Nations in a manner that is compatible with the conditions set by the primary rules and the general principles of Community law. As Members of the United Nations, the Member States, and particularly – in the context of the present case – those belonging to the Security Council, have to act in such a way as to prevent, as far as possible, the adoption of decisions by organs of the United Nations that are liable to enter into conflict with the core principles of the Community legal

---

41 Resolution 1597 (2008), § 7.2.
42 § 32 of the Opinion.

order. The Member States themselves, therefore, carry a responsibility to minimize the risk of conflicts between the Community legal order and international law.

It is, thus, not only a matter of expediency for the European Members of the Security Council, but also a legal duty to seek to make UN listing and de-listing decisions consistent with due process requirements. It is submitted that the creation of an appropriate review process is the best way to achieve this goal.

4

Limits to the Use of Force Imposed by International Law

Current Problems

1 Legal Restraints on the Use of Military Force – Introduction

To restrain the use of force is an important function of any legal order. This applies to the international legal order, too. In contradistinction to most other legal orders, however, there are two types of international legal restraint on the use of military force: the prohibition to use military force (*ius contra bellum*)[1] and rules of behavior if force is used despite that prohibition (*ius in bello*). This can be imagined as a system of two dams, the first one primary and the second one a fall back position. Once the first dam (the prohibition of the use of force) is broken, the second one still prevents the worst excesses of violence.

Both types of rules are constantly violated. It is the very weakness of the first type of restraint which renders the second type necessary. There were times when it was thought (in particular after the Second World War) that war was outlawed and that the *ius in bello* was no longer necessary. This proved to be an illusion. Armed conflicts continued and require an appropriate regulation of their conduct. The end of the so-called Cold War has not brought general peace, quite to the contrary. But also the *ius in bello* is very often not respected as it should be. There is practically no current conflict where there are no allegations of violations of that law.

There is, thus, a fundamental question: Are these legal restraints possible and meaningful? Are the really valid norms? Or have they become obsolete through their constant violation? Are they an illusion? This is a crucial question which we will try to answer at the end of these lectures.

A frequent explanation of what is said to be the insignificance or limited significance of these legal restraints is the claim that what matters in high politics

---

1 In legal doctrine, the term frequently used is *ius ad bellum*. But that terminology is not correct, because the essence of the relevant norm is not the right to use force, but the duty not to use force. This meaning is better conveyed by the term *ius contra bellum*.

© KONINKLIJKE BRILL NV, LEIDEN, 2021 | DOI:10.1163/9789004380592_006

82 PART 1: BASIC ISSUES

(and we are dealing with sensitive security issues, thus with high politics) is power and not law.[2] The relationship between law and power has always been a difficult question. Law needs power, and power needs law. One has to look at the reality: in the political reality of the international order, there is a real impact of law on the exercise of power. This impact most often becomes reality through a legal discourse which accompanies and influences decisions relating to the use of force.

Why is this so and how does it work? The sense of any legal norm is to influence human behaviour. But the fact that law in a given case does not achieve this result is no proof that the norm does not exist, is not a valid norm. Law creates contrafactual expectations.[3] It is constantly challenged, but it nevertheless creates a security of expectations. In the words of the ICJ[4]:

> It is not to be expected that in the practice of States the application of the rules in question should have been perfect, in the sense that States should have refrained, with complete consistency, from the use of force or from intervention in each other's internal affairs. The Court does not consider that, for a rule to be established as customary, the corresponding practice must be in absolutely rigorous conformity with the rule. In order to deduce the existence of customary rules, the Court deems it sufficient that the conduct of States should, in general, be consistent with such rules, and that instances of State conduct inconsistent with a given rule should generally have been treated as breaches of that rule, not as indications of the recognition of a new rule. If a State acts in a way prima facie incompatible with a recognized rule, but defends its conduct by appealing to exceptions or justifications contained within the rule itself, then whether or not the State's conduct is in fact justifiable on that basis, the significance of that attitude is to confirm rather than to weaken the rule.

The quote clearly shows that the essential point concerning the validity and effectiveness of legal norm relating to the use of force is a discourse. There are actors who use force, as a rule claiming it is lawful, and there are others who contradict, claiming that the acts in question are unlawful. This is the essence of a legal discourse. It is used to legitimize or to delegitimize the use of military

---

2   E. BLENK-KNOCKE, "Sociology of International Law", in: R. Bernhardt (ed.), *Encyclopedia of Public International Law (EPIL)* vol. IV, 2000, 449–452, at 450.

3   A. FISCHER-LESCANO, *Globalverfassung,* Weilerswist 2005, 85 et seq.

4   *Military and Paramilitary Activities in and against Nicaragua* (*Nicaragua v. United States of America*), ICJ Reports 2986, para. 186.

LIMITS OF FORCE IMPOSED BY INTERNATIONAL LAW

force, both on the level of the *ius contra bellum* and on that of the *ius in bello*. This is not just a legal matter, it is also a political one, at least in questions of high politics.

Examples are the debates about the intervention in Iraq and that on the use of cluster ammunitions. The US-British intervention in Iraq 2003 was accompanied by an extensive legal debate around the world, both in academic and in political circles. The interveners built up legal justifications,[5] which were contradicted by others.[6] In particular in the United Kingdom, there was an extensive political debate about the legality of the action before the decision was formally taken, and this played a major role for the political acceptance, grudging as it was, of the intervention in that country.[7]

The use of cluster ammunitions is a current legal and political debate which has recently given rise to a new international treaty, the Convention on Cluster Munitions adopted in Dublin on May 30, 2008 and signed in Oslo on 3 December 2008,[8] very controversial as major military powers did not join. It is claimed (and this was the starting point of the legal discourse) that the use of these ammunitions constitutes as a rule a violation of the principle of proportionality, which is a fundamental element of the law of armed conflict.[9] This is controversial,[10] but this claim has been the basis of attempts to ban these weapons through a new treaty provision or to make at least sure that these weapons are construed in a way that there actual use does not violate that principle.[11] Despite the new Convention, that legal discourse continues and is

---

5   C. GREENWOOD, "The Legality of the Use of Force: Iraq 2003", in: M. Bother/ M.E. O'Connell/ N/ Ronzitti (eds.), *Redefining Sovereignty: The Use of Force after the Cold War,* Ardsley Park 2005, pp. 387–416.

6   M. BOTHE, "Has Article 2 (4) Survived the Iraq War?", in: Bothe/O'Connell/Ronzitti, op. cit. note 5, pp. 417–431; R. FALK, "What future for the UN Charter System of War Prevention?" 97 *AJIL* 590 (2003), at 596; T. FRANCK, "What Happens Now?" 97 *AJIL* 607 (2003), at 614; C. SCHALLER, "Massenvernichtungswaffen and Präventivkrieg", 62 *ZaöRV* 641 (2002), at 649 et seq.

7   O. EBERL/ A. FISCHER-LESCANO, *Grenzen demokratischen Rechts?. Die Entsendeentscheidungen zum Irakkrieg in Großbritannien, den USA und Spanien,* HSFK (Hessische Stiftung Friedens- und Konfliktforschung, Frankfurt) Report 8/2005.

8   See BLACK-BRANCH, "The Legal Stats of Cluster Munitions", 22 *Humanitäres Völkerrecht-Informationsschriften* 186 et seq. (2009).

9   See below 3.3.

10   On the US position, see J. R. Crook, "Contemporary Practice of the United States Relating to International Law", 101 *AJIL* 478–508 (2007), at 501 et seq.

11   Currently, the issue of cluster munitions has been pursued through two different for a, namely the Convention on Certain Conventional Weapons (CCW), preferred inter alia by the United States, and a human rights oriented process, promoted in particular by Norway, the so-called Oslo Process. See W. BOESE, Cluster Munitions Control Efforts Make Gains,

part of a political process where, simply formulated, one side tries to improve the legal protection of the civilian population in times of armed conflict and the other side wants to maintain the possibility to use a weapon considered to be militarily effective.

What is the basis for the effectiveness of the legal argument? It is the fact that there is a political public for that argument. A public which constitutes an important force for the decision maker in question is responsive to the legal argument. This implies a number of problems. Not the least of these problems is the role of the media. Critical media can play a salutary role, but there is also a potential of distorting manipulation of news. In addition, the role of law changes with the political context and the political culture. Furthermore, the law and the lawyers are often used to legitimize the use of force, even where this should not happen. The legal argument can be abused. Lawyers might find comfort in the fact that a legal discourse is effectively part of the political discourse, but this is a delicate social and ethical question.

There is, thus, a need and a quest for the "objective" law. How is it possible to find out what this is? This is a procedural question to which we will revert.[12]

The critics of the validity of law as a restraint on the use of military force have to face a fundamental question: why was this law created to begin with? This law was not imposed on the States from somewhere above, it was created by the States themselves. They must have had reasons for doing so. A clarification of the question of whether and how the law works can be obtained by finding out why and how the law is created. How have legal restraints on the use of force been created, so to say invented? We will find out that it is through a delicate mixture of sometimes contradictory factors. These norms were created as a response to real political, social and human problems. In respect of these problems, different actors have tried to pursue different interests, those in power often trying to maintain a *status quo*, those disadvantaged by a given situation trying to change the law. In this context, it is not only economic or security interests which have shaped the attitude of relevant decision-makers. Moral and religious motives also play an important role. This is why the historic survey shows that scandalisation, that is the moral rejection of things that happen, can make law.[13] We will show how important this is, also today.

     Arms Control Today, http://www.armscontrol.org/act/2007_07_07-08/Cluster.asp. It is the latter process which has resulted in the Convention of 2008, the former one is still open.

12   See below under 5 on the possibilities of judicial clarification of the law.

13   N. LUHMANN, *Das Recht der Gesellschaft*, 1995, 581; A. FISCHER LESCANO, op. Cit. Note 3, 67 et seq.

LIMITS OF FORCE IMPOSED BY INTERNATIONAL LAW

With these general considerations in mind, let us, first, analyse the development of the prohibition of the use of force, the *ius contra bellum*. Killing is evil. This is a moral principle which all humankind has in common. Therefore, where military force is used, there seems to exist a genuine moral, social or political need to justify the use of military force as not being evil in certain circumstances. Against this backdrop, in particular the monotheistic religions have developed different theories of justifying wars, the *"djihad"* in Islam, the *"bellum iustum"* in Christian theology. It is the latter doctrine which has had a considerable impact on the early development of international law in Europe relating to the use of force. *Bellum iustum* is an armed conflict conducted by legitimate actors with a just cause, right intentions and just means,[14] the latter being a *iustus modus bellandi*. Be it noted that in this concept, the idea of two levels of restraint is already implied in this definition.

In the 18th century, it became more and more apparent that it was impossible, due to the decentralised character of the international legal order, to find out in a legally binding way whose cause was "just". That question had to be left open, which meant that the law became indifferent as to the question whether starting a particular war was lawful or not. That indifference of the law did not mean that there was a "right" to resort to war. If there is a right, resistance against the exercise of this right is itself unlawful. But this was not the legal situation in relation to war. War was lawful for both sides.[15] Such legal construction presupposes a certain socio-political context, it cannot develop outside such context. There were time in Europe when a positive attitude towards war and the military was prevailing. War was indeed an accepted continuation of politics by other means. It was in this spirit that all sides went into the First World War with great enthusiasm.

But the great sufferings caused by that war fundamentally changed that public attitude to war. There was a public outcry. There was a *"colère publique"* in front of these horrors,[16] there was a public scandalisation. Its first "official" result were those procedural provisions in the Covenant of the League of Nations which establish procedures for the settlement of disputes. They were

---

14 W. GREWE, *The Epochs of International Law*, English translation by M. Byers, Berlin/ New York 2000, pp. 105 et seq.

15 See *inter alia* Grewe, op. cit. note 14, pp. 203 et seq. W.E. HALL, *A Treatise on International Law*, 2nd ed. Oxford 1884, pp. 60 et seq.; for further references see B. FASSBENDER, "Die Gegenwartskrise des völkerrechtlichen Gewaltverbots vor dem Hintergrund der geschichtlichen Entwicklung", 31 *Europäische Grundrechte-Zeitschrift* 241–256 (2004), at 243.

16 FASSBENDER, loc. Cit. note 15, at pp. 242 et seq.; on the phenomenon of *colère publique* see A. FISCHER-LESCANO, op. cit. note 3, pp. 67 et seq with further references.

meant to prevent that such horrors might happen again. They were, however, only relative prohibitions to resort to war, kind of standstill obligations not to use force while these mechanisms were working.[17] But the scandalisation went on and had a further impact on the political elites. It is fully reflected in the Briand-Kellog Treaty of 1928, by which States renounce to war as an instrument of politics. It is remarkable that this treaty was very soon ratified by next to all States.[18] This did not prevent the 2nd World War, but it had the consequence that triggering this war was considered as a crime (crime against peace, crime of aggression). This consequence was formulated in the Statutes of the international military tribunals established at the end of the Second World War, the tribunals of Nuremberg and Tokyo. The Nuremberg Tribunal explicitly argued that the Briand-Kellog Pact had not only outlawed war, but had made it a crime. The major perpetrators were punished accordingly by the International Military Tribunals of Nuremberg and Tokyo.

This scandalisation was also the basis of the purpose of the United Nations Charter to protect future generations from the "scourge of war", and it was the rational of its provisions prohibiting the use of force and establishing a system of collective security.[19] That public perception of war as a horror remained the same in the years after the war, despite (or perhaps because) the huge development of armaments, including the atomic bomb. This has been the political and social basis for the continued validity of the prohibition. It has been upheld by the ICJ in a number of judgments and advisory opinions, starting with the *Nicaragua case* already quoted.

Is the world, thus, in order, at least as to the existence of the prohibition of the use of force? No, it is not. Recently, there have been serious attempts to undermine these perceptions of war, the scandalisation in the face of war.[20] The clearest example was the politics of the intervention in Iraq. They were based on the concept that war can be morally justified if there are good reasons for it (which include the assumption that one's own losses will be bearable). Whatever the legal technicalities used to justify the intervention – this is a resurgence of the old *bellum iustum* theories. It is this concept (and, as we already

---

17   Art. 12 para. 1, 13 para. 4, 15 para. 6 of the League of Nations Covenant.

18   When the Pact entered into force on July 24, 1929, the 15 signatories and 32 other States had ratified. Until the end of 1929, 8 more States ratified.

19   See below 2.1. M. E. O'CONNELL, "Defending the Law against Preemptive Force", in A. Fischer-Lescano et al. (eds.), *Peace in liberty. Festschrift für Michael Bothe zum 70. Geburtstag*, 2008, 237–248, at 239 et seq.

20   M. BOTHE, "Terrorism and the Legality of Pre-emptive Force", 14 *EJIL* pp. 227–240 (2003), at 237 et seq.

know, illusion) which underlies the so-called "revolution in military affairs" (RMA) – a strategic concept which through the use of modern technology, in particular information technology, claims to gain quick and therefore rather unbloody victory over a less sophisticated adversary.[21] That concept worked tremendously well in the first weeks of the Iraq intervention, until the mission was "accomplished" – and the real problems began.

The same (flawed) concept of war underlies the pre-emptive strike philosophy put forward by the Bush administration in its National Security Strategy of 2002[22]:

> The greater the threat, the greater the threat of inaction – and the more compelling the case for taking anticipatory action to defend ourselves, even if uncertainty remains as to the time and place of the enemy's attack. To forestall and prevent such hostile acts by our adversaries, the United States will, if necessary, act pre-emptively.
>
> ... [I]n an age where the enemies of civilization openly and actively seek the world's most destructive technologies, the United States cannot remain idle while dangers gather.[23]

This approach means that attempts to solve problems by peaceful means should be abandoned at an early stage and resort to force is preferred because, that is the assumption or rather illusion, it would be more effective.

Although this old new approach to war has been discredited by the developments in Iraq, Afghanistan and the Middle East, it is still with us and there is a real danger that public attitudes, at least in some relevant countries, turn back to regarding war as something positive, at least under certain conditions. That would be the end of the prohibition of the use of force.[24] It is necessary for conscientious international lawyers to be vigilant.

Let me now turn to the discourse on the *ius in bello*. In early modern times, the rules concerning the conduct of war were still rather rough. The question whether prisoners could be killed or held for ransom was still discussed. Grotius, the father of modern international law, was not the father of modern humanitarian law.[25] It was a philosopher of the age of enlightenment,

---

21 T. GONGORA/ H. V. RIEKHOFF (eds.), *Towards a Revolution in Military Affairs?. Defense and Security at the Dawn of the Twenty-First Century,* Westport 2000.

22 Available at www.whitehouse.gov/nsc/nss.html.

23 Op. cit. note 22, at p. 15.

24 BOTHE, loc. cit. note 20.

25 F. MÜNCH, "War, Laws of, History", in R. Bernhardt, *EPIL* vol. IV (2000), pp. 1386–1388.

Jean-Jacques Rousseau, who, in his *Contrat Social* of 1762[26] formulated the basic idea on which the restraints of the modern law of armed conflict are based: War is a relationship between sovereigns which fight by military means against the military effort of the other. Basic principles which are still valid flow from this concept: the principle of distinction between the civilian population and combatants, the prohibition of unnecessary suffering (which is unreasonable because not necessary for the military victory), the decent treatment of prisoners (which is reasonable because they no longer contribute to the military effort of the adversary).

These were not only philosophical concepts, they also corresponded to the reality of the "cabinet wars" of those times.[27] They were reflected in the first treaty on the modern law of armed conflict, namely a treaty on friendship and commerce between the United States and Prussia of 1785, concluded by two spirits of the enlightenment, King Frederick II of Prussia and Benjamin Franklin. It contains a chapter on the decent treatment of prisoners in wartime. This was a case where the development of the law was triggered by the enlightened interest of the rulers themselves. Nevertheless, it took some time to abolish certain remains of the old times: The prohibition of privateering was only achieved by the Treaty of Paris of 1856 which ended the Crimean War, also the first multilateral treaty on the law of armed conflict.

Yet in the further development of the law of armed conflict, scandalisation as already explained showed its importance. Henry Dunant was shocked to see the suffering of the wounded soldiers in the field during the battle of Solferino of 1859, left without the medical care which the medical science would already have made possible at that time. He published his famous book "A Memory of Solferino"[28] and started what we would today call an initiative from civil society which soon reached the diplomats. It resulted in the Geneva conference of 1864 which adopted the first Geneva Convention, the "Convention for the amelioration of the treatment of the wounded of the armies in the field". Since then, the law of armed conflict has been continuously developed through treaty law. There were two lines of development: a kind of stocktaking of the existing law in the Hague Peace Conferences of 1899 and 1907 which contained only a limited response to "the latest" developments,[29]

26　J.-J. ROUSSEAU, *Du Contrat Social*, 1762 ; English translation : *The Social Contract*, Penguin Books 1968.

27　W. G. GREWE, op. cit. note 14, pp. 367 et seq.

28　H. DUNANT, *Un Mémoire de Solférino*, 1862 ; English versions 1939, 1959 an 1986.

29　There are only four Declarations which respond to newer development in weapons technology: on launching of projectiles from balloons (1899, 1907), projectiles the only object of which is the diffusion of asphyxiating or deleterious gases (1899), bullets which flatten

and the continuous adaptation of the Geneva law to the experiences of changing conflicts: the Geneva Conventions of 1906, 1929, 1949 and their Additional Protocols of 1977 and 2006. These various steps of amending the Geneva
Conventions are based on the wish to fill gaps in the law which had appeared
in the armed conflicts preceding them.[30] They have been, in a way, the result
of a scandalisation concerning the fate of the victims in the spirit of Henry
Dunant, but more and more institutionalized in the form of a specialized body,
the International Committee of the Red Cross which has the recognized task
to promote this development. During the time after the 2nd World War, this development received a strong impetus from the human rights movement, a key
document being the resolution of the Teheran Human Rights Conference 1968
entitled "Human Rights in Armed Conflict",[31] followed by a resolution of the
General Assembly which invited the Secretary-General to study the need of
further treaty making.[32] This triggered or at least accelerated the development
towards the Additional Protocols of 1977. Yet the scandalisation prompted by
what large parts of civil society considered as violations of fundamental values
was not the only force present in the process which lead to the negotiations on
the two Protocols and which shaped the course of these negotiations. There
was a strong political interest in legitimizing anticolonial "liberation" wars and
to delegitimize certain American practices used in Vietnam as well as the Israeli settlement policy. And there were obviously, countervailing interests. On
the other hand, scandalisation has so far not lead to a definite breakthrough in
one important element of the legal restraint on military force, and that is the
explicit prohibition of nuclear weapons.[33]

These examples show that the basic accommodation of various interest involved in this historic discourse has never been simple. There is a continuing
tension between the interests of those forces who want to see no restraints on

---

easily in the human body (1899). In addition, the Convention VIII of 1907 relative to the
laying of automatic submarine contact mines also belongs to this category.

30   For a short summary of the development, see M. BOTHE in M. BOTHE/K.J. PARTSCH/
W. A. SOLF, *New rules for Victims of Armed Conflicts. Commentary on the Two 1977 Protocols
Additional to the Geneva Conventions of 1949*, The Hague/Boston/London 1982, pp. 1 et seq.

31   Resolution XXIII adopted by the International Conference on Human Rights, Teheran, 12
May 1968, reproduced in D. Schindler/ J. Toman (eds.), *The Laws of Armed Conflict*, 4th ed.
2004, o. 347.

32   Respect for Human Rights in Armed Conflicts, UNGA resolutions 2444 (XXIII) of 19
December 1968.

33   See below 3.3. The Advisory Opinion of the ICJ of 8 July 1996 *Legality of the Threat or
use of Nuclear Weapons* can only be considered a partial victory of the civil society move
based on this scandalisation.

their strategic concepts, and those whose primary interest is the protection of victims. Nevertheless, the principle of distinction and the principle of humanity have been established, maintained and concretised in this long discourse.

For various reasons, however, the principle of distinction is currently being questioned from various sides. It is claimed that there is a new phenomenon of war, "new wars" where this principle has no proper place anymore.[34] Certain fighting groups which do not possess well organised armies in uniform and sophisticated weaponry claim that the principle of distinction inappropriately favours regular and powerful armies. They maintain that they depend on hiding in a civilian surrounding and that, in order to be effective, they cannot refrain from attacking also "soft" civilian targets and civilians. But also those States who have and use strong regular armies rather have a tendency to see in the principle of distinction, at least if strictly interpreted, an unwelcome, even unacceptable restraint on effective fighting, namely on the choice of targets and the use of high yield weaponry. They insistence of some States on nuclear capabilities is a case in point. In addition, the non-respect of the principle of distinction by certain fighting groups provides a reason or at least a pretext for violating this principle as well. In modern "asymmetrical conflict", the reciprocal interest of the parties in limiting damage no longer functions in the same way as in the case of traditional "symmetrical" conflict. This is a crucial challenge for the effectiveness of the law of armed conflict as it has developed over more than two hundred years. This is an ongoing discourse. Below, it will be shown that this phenomenon of new wars has so far not lead to a change in the traditional principles.[35]

2 The Prohibition or Justification of the Use of Force (*Ius Contra Bellum*)

2.1 *The Prohibition*

The prohibition of the use of force was first formulated as a prohibition of "war" in the Briand-Kellog Treaty of 1928. The early formulations of the prohibition, already mentioned above, in terms of a prohibition of "war" led to a futile debate about the definition of war and attempts to evade the prohibition by claiming that a certain use of force did not amount to war in the sense of the prohibition.[36] Therefore, the UN Charter now formulates the prohibition

---

34 H. MÜNCKLER, *Die "neuen" Kriege,* Hamburg 2002.
35 See below 3.2. and 3.
36 For example the Japanese intervention in China in the 1930ies.

LIMITS OF FORCE IMPOSED BY INTERNATIONAL LAW

as a prohibition of the use of force in international relations (Art. 2 (4)) of the Charter:

> All members shall refrain in their international relations from the threat or use of force against the territorial integrity or political independence of any State, or in any other manner inconsistent with the Purposes of the United Nations.

There are a number of problems involved in the interpretation of this provision (which in its essential content also constitutes customary law)[37]:

- What means "force" in the sense of this provision? Only military force?
- Do the words "against the political independence of any State, or in any other manner inconsistent with the Purposes of the United Nations" limit the scope of the prohibition? In other words: are there uses of force which, due to the said addition, are outside the scope of prohibition?
- In particular, are there low intensity transborder uses of force which are below the threshold of the prohibition?
- Does the prohibition also apply to the use of force by non-state actors (e.g. terrorists) and, if so, under which conditions?

The current practical significance of these questions is, however, limited because, as we will show, the bulk of the controversy lies elsewhere.

It is now generally accepted that force in the meaning of this article is only military or paramilitary force. Other forms of pressure, in particular economic pressure, are not covered. They may constitute a forbidden intervention, but not a use of force.

Secondly, the words quoted cannot be understood as a restriction of the prohibition, in the sense that there are types of the use of force which do not fall under the prohibition of article 2 (4). This results in particular from the negotiating history, and claims for such a reduction of the content of the prohibition have always been rejected.

Thirdly, there are certain low level transborder uses of forces which are below the threshold of the prohibition, but it is by no means certain where the threshold lies. The really practical question is not the definition of the prohibited use of force, but rather the definition of the armed attack which triggers the right of self-defence and the threshold problems this implies.

---

37   See the judgment of the ICJ in the *Nicaragua case*, loc. cit. note 4, paras. 187 et seq.

The same is true, *mutatis mutandis*, for the problem of private actors. Whether an armed operation conducted by private actors constitutes a forbidden use of force is really relevant only for the question of permissible reactions by the victim State. But for this purpose, what matters is not the definition of forbidden force, but the definition of the armed attack which triggers the right of self defence. We will revert to the problem below.

2.2   *The Exceptions*

The exceptions to the prohibition are probably of greater importance then the prohibition itself. It is these exceptions that play the major role in the legal discourse described above, it is these exceptions on which most attempts to justify a use of force are based. There are two generally recognised exceptions: self-defence and an authorization by the Security Council.

2.2.1   Self-defence

Self-defence is action by a State defending itself against an "armed attack" (Art. 51 UNCh). As "self-defence" is the most frequently used justification for the use of force, it has to be very carefully considered. It is in this question that misrepresentations of fact and misinterpretations of law play a major role.

Lawful self-defence presupposes that there is an armed attack. The definition of the armed attack is crucial for the right of self-defence. Where there is no armed attack, there can be no self-defence. Both the text and the very purpose of Art. 51 do not permit to renounce to this requirement.[38] This has been an issue in all three major cases before the International Court of Justice which dealt with the use of force in particular cases. In the *Nicaragua case,*[39] the United States claimed to have acted in the exercise of the right to collective self-defence for El Salvador. The Court denied the existence of an armed attack for reasons of fact and law. In the *Oil Platforms case* between Iran and the United States,[40] the Court held that for the two incidents which the United States claimed to have constituted an armed attack, the United States could not prove that the first use of force could be attributed to Iran. In the *Congo case*, the Court took this requirement as a legal *acquis* and carefully analysed which of

---

38   In particular, the use of the word "inherent" in Art. 31 does not support an interpretation which would regard the actual existence of an armed attack as not absolutely necessary for triggering a right of self-defence, O'CONNELL, loc. cit. note 19, 240.

39   *Military and Paramilitary Activities in and against Nicaragua (Nicaragua v. USA)*, supra note 4, paragraph 195 of the judgment.

40   *Case concerning Oil Platforms (Iran v. USA)*, ICJ, Judgment of 6 November 2003, ICJ Reports p. 161, paragraphs 61, 64, 71.

LIMITS OF FORCE IMPOSED BY INTERNATIONAL LAW

the behavior of the parties involved constituted an armed attack triggering a right of self-defense.[41]

It is generally recognised that the notion of armed attack is narrower than that of "use of force" in Art. 2 para. 4.[42] This means: not all forms of unlawful use of force automatically constitute an armed attack which triggers a right of self-defence. But where the threshold between an armed attack and a "simple" use of force lies is difficult to determine. An additional threshold question is posed by the definition of aggression. It is by no means clear whether all armed attacks automatically fall within the definition of aggression, despite of the fact that the French text of Art. 51 of the Charter uses the words "agression armée" where the English text says "armed attack". The practice of the Security Council in evaluating certain situations in the light of the UN Charter rarely determines that there is an "act of aggression". The only two cases of such a determination are the condemnation of South Africa's "aggression" against Angola in 1976 and 1980[43] and two Israeli air attacks against Tunisia.[44] Otherwise, the Council prefers the term "breach of the peace" (e.g. the North Korean attack against South Korea 1950[45] or the Iraqi invasion of Kuwait 1990[46]).

A further important question is that of the use of force by non-state actors. Recent examples are the attacks against the United States perpetrated 11 september 2001, and, at least according to one possible interpretation, Hizbollah attacks against Israel in 2006. The ICJ, in its Advisory Opinion on the construction of the wall in Palestine, has explicitly rejected the concept that an attack by non-state actors could be an armed attack within the meaning of Art. 51,[47] a holding which has become the subject of some controversy. According to the jurisprudence of the Court, in the case of transborder force used by non-state actors, the right of self-defence only exists where another State is substantially involved in that use of force. In its *Nicaragua* Judgement, the Court deduced this requirement from an interpretation of the General Assembly Declaration on the Definition of Aggression[48] which it considered, at least in this respect,

---

41 *Case concerning Armed Activities on the Territory of the Congo (DRC v. Uganda)*, paragraphs 130 *et seq* of the Judgment.

42 A. RANDELZHOFER, "Article 51", in B. Simma (ed.), *The Charter of the United Nations. A Commentary*, 2nd ed. 2002, mag. note 4.

43 Security Council Resolution 387 of 31 March 1976 and 474 of 27 June 1980.

44 Security Council Resolutions 573 of 4 October 1985 and 611 of 25 April 1988.

45 Security Council Resolution 82 of 25 June 1950.

46 Security Council Resolution 660 of 2 August 1988.

47 ICJ, *Legal Consequences of the Construction of a Wall in the Occupied Palestinian Territory*, Advisory Opinion dated 9 July 2004, para. 139.

48 Resolution 3314 (XXIX) of 14 December 1974.

to be a formulation of the rule of customary law.[49] Whether the threshold of "substantial involvement" was reached in the case of the support given to Al Qaeda by the then effective government of Afghanistan, the Taliban, is somewhat controversial.[50] There are very good reasons to answer this question in the affirmative,[51] an essential condition for the lawfulness of the "Operation Enduring Freedom" in Afghanistan. Indeed, the case of Afghanistan shows that it could not be otherwise: If it were only the attack by Al Qaeda which triggered a right of the self-defence for the United States and a right of collective self-defence for its allies, that right would not provide any title to intervene in Afghanistan. Art. 51 grants a right of military action only against the attacking State, not against any other State.[52]

Another controversial question is the beginning and the end of the right of self-defence. The text of Art. 51 would suggest that the right of self-defence only exists where there already is an armed attack, and where this attack is still going on. The prevailing view, however, holds that self-defence is also permissible where there is an *immediate* threat of an armed attack (anticipatory self-defence). This is deduced from the *Caroline* case, a case between the United States and Great Britain which happened in 1841. This is its famous definition of the right of anticipatory self-defence, as it is formulated by the United States State Secretary Webster: there must be a

> necessity of self-defence, instant overwhelming, leaving no choice of means, and no moment for deliberation.[53]

It is somewhat puzzling how this case survived the new formulation of the right of self-defence in the UN Charter. Be that as it may, military action against a perceived longer term threat (e.g. the possession of weapons of mass destruction by a State considered to be hostile) cannot be justified as self-defence (illegality or preventive of pre-emptive self-defence). That expanded notion of self-defence which is put forward in particular by the National Security Strategy

---

49 ICJ, loc. cit. note 4, para. 195.

50 C. STAHN, " 'Nicaragua is dead, long live Nicaragua" – the Right to Self-defence under Art. 51 UN Charter and International Terrorism", in C. Walter et al. (eds.), *Terrorism as a Challenge for National and International Law: Security versus Liberty?*, Berlin et al. 2004, 827–877, in particular at 838 et seq.

51 Y. DINSTEIN, "Humanitarian Law on the Conflict in Afghanistan", 96 *AJIL Proc* 23–25 (2002), at 25.

52 Stahn, loc. cit. note 50, at 867.

53 29 *British and Foreign State Papers* 1129 (1840–1841), at 1138; see also W. MENG, "The Caroline", in Bernhardt, *EPIL*, vol. I, 1992, 538.

LIMITS OF FORCE IMPOSED BY INTERNATIONAL LAW

(NSS) of the United States of 2002[54] has not received the kind of general recognition which would be necessary for a modification of a Charter norm through specific customary law. It is significant to note that the United States and the United Kingdom did not use that concept in order to justify their intervention in Iraq[55] and the doctrine of pre-emptive self-defence is not repeated in the NSS of 2006.

Another related question, which also plays some role in evaluating the legality of the Operation Enduring Freedom in Afghanistan, is this: when does the right of self-defence end? It is too simple to answer this question by saying that it ends when the armed attack triggering the right of self-defence is over. Is it really over when the actual fighting has calmed down? In the case of 9/11 (if that was an armed attack in which Afghanistan was substantially involved), was it over once the airplanes had hit their targets? Is it essential whether new attacks are threatening? Is there such a notion as an ongoing situation of an armed attack even though there are times of relative calm? The answer to all these questions is far from settled. Two points, however, can be made: There is a difference between lawful self-defence and unlawful "retaliation" which only occurs after the fact.[56] Secondly, the Security Council has never accepted the Israeli claim that there was a situation of permanent hostility, as equivalent to an armed attack, which would have justified its several military incursions into Arab territories as being self-defence,[57] nor has the ICJ accepted a similar line of argument put forward by the United States in the *Platforms case*.[58]

Self-defence is lawful only if it is not excessive in relation to the actual armed attack (principle of proportionality). This principle has repeatedly been violated. In the *Platforms case*,[59] the ICJ held that indeed the United States reaction to the alleged Iranian attack was, at least in one of the two attacks, disproportionate, even assuming that there had been a previous attack by Iran. The attack by Israel against Lebanon in 2006 is another case in point. The essential armed attack against Israel which would have triggered an Israeli right

---

54   See above the text accompanying note 23.

55   M. BOTHE, loc. cit. note 6.

56   R. HIGGINS, "International Law and the Avoidance, Containment and Resolution of Disputes". 230 *RdC* (1991 V), at 308 et seq; O. SCHACHTER, *International Law in Theory and Practice*, 154.

57   S. A. ALEXANDROV, *Self-Defence Against the Use of Force in International Law*, 1996, p. 167; see also the analysis provided by the UN Secretariat in *Repertory of Practice of UN Organs*, Suppl. 5, vol. II, p. 177.

58   *Case Concerning Oil Platforms (Iran v. USA)*, loc. cit. note, 40, para. 51.

59   *Ibidem*, para. 77.

of self-defence was the kidnapping of two Israeli soldiers. It is by all reasonable standards disproportionate to destroy entire towns and villages as a reaction.[60]

2.2.2 Security Council Authorisation

Authorisation of the use of force by the Security Council is part of the system of enforcement measures under Chapter VII of the UN Charter. The cases in which such authorisation is legally possible, thus, depend on the definition of the situations to which Ch. VII applies (Art. 39 UNCh, in particular the notion of "threat to the peace"). In recent years, the Security Council has considerably expanded that notion to include also gross and systematic violations of human rights,[61] support for, and acts of, terrorism,[62] as well as the proliferation of weapons of mass destruction.[63]

Since the case of the Iraqi invasion of Kuwait (resolution 678 of 29 November 1990), the Security Council interprets its powers under Art. 42 in the sense that it must not necessarily itself conduct a military enforcement action, but may authorise the use of force by (particular) States. Generally, this authorisation is expressed in a phrase like "use all means at their disposal". That has become a current and uncontroversial practice of the Security Council so that it cannot anymore be doubted that this practice is lawful.[64]

---

60   S. Weber, Die israelischen Militäraktionen im Libanon und in den bestzten palästinensische Gebieten"44 *AVR* 460–480 (2006), at 468 et seq.

61   A number of resolutions rather rely on the external effects of violations of human rights and in particular the suppression of certain population groups. There are however, a number of resolutions where it is the mere violation of human rights which is the constitutive element of a "threat to the peace", see Security Council resolutions 827 of 25 May 1993 (Yugoslavia), 929 of 22 June 1994 (Rwanda), 940 of 31 July 1994 (Haiti), 1203 of 24 October 1998 (Kosovo),, 1264 of 15 September 1999 (East Timor), 1556 of 30 July 2004 (Darfur).

62   Security Council resolutions 748 of 31 March 1992 (Libya), 1214 of 8 December 1998, 1267 of 15 October 1999, 1333 of 19 December 2000 (Afghanistan), 1368 of 12 september 2001, 1373 of 28 september 2001 ("9/11"); 1277 of 12 November 2001, 1566 of 8 October 2004 (general declarations). The resolutions adopted as a reaction to the assassination of the Lebanese Prime-Minister in 2005 are also related to this series of resolutions on terrorism, Presidential Statement 2005/4 of 15 February 2005, resolutions 1595 of 7 April 2005, 1757 of 30 May 2007.

63   Security Council resolution 1540 of 28 April 2004. In order to prevent a supposed Iranian nuclear armament program, the Security Council also acted on the basis of Art. 41: see resolutions 1737 of 23 December 2006 and 1747 of 24 March 2007.

64   Resolutions 678 of 29 November 1990 (Iraq); 794 of 3 December 1992 (Somalia, UNITAF); 816 of 31 March 1993, 836 of 4 June 1993 (Bosnia-Herzegovina); 929 of 22 June 1994 (Rwanda, Operation Turquoise); 940 of 31 July 1994 (Haiti); 1244 of 10 June 1999 (Kosovo); 1886 of 20 December 2001 (Afghanistan, ISAF); 1484 of 30 May 2003 (DRC); 1511 of 16 October 2003, 1536 of 8 June 2004 (Iraq).

LIMITS OF FORCE IMPOSED BY INTERNATIONAL LAW

The essential question in particular cases has been whether a certain resolution of the Security Council could be interpreted as containing such an authorisation, and whether this authorisation is still valid. Both questions were relevant in the case of Iraq 2003. The legal justification for the intervention put forward by the United States was that in light of the continuous violations of the armistice conditions of Resolution 687 of 3 April 1991, the old authorisation of the use of force was kind of revived, a very doubtful construction. By its armistice resolution, the Security Council created a new legal regime for the situation in Iraq. It was up to the Council to decide what followed from the violation of this regime, not for self appointed agents of the Council.[65]

Can an authorisation given *ex post facto* have a justifying effect? This is somewhat controversial. If one accepts this possibility it becomes a matter of the interpretation of the resolution in question. In the case of certain interventions in West Africa, there are Security Council resolutions which can indeed be interpreted as an *ex post facto* authorization.[66] On the other hand, the Security Council resolutions relating to the foreign military presence in the Kosovo[67] and in Iraq[68] cannot be interpreted in this sense.[69] There is so far no such resolution concerning the "Operation Enduring Freedom" in Afghanistan (which was characterized by the intervening States as an action of [collective] self-defence); the Security Council has only authorized ISAF.[70]

2.2.3 Other Exceptions

Other justifications of the use of force are sometimes based on a restrictive interpretation of Art. 2 (4) or of a customary law addition to the exceptions. The major cases are the protection of a country's own nationals abroad (very controversial)[71] and the so-called humanitarian intervention (not lawful

---

65   M. WELLER, "Enforced Negotiations: The Threat and Use of Force to Obtain an International Settlement for Kosovo", 5 *International Peacekeeping* 4–27 (1999), in particular relating to the US-British intervention in Iraq BOTHE, loc. cit. note 6, at 517; O. CORTEN, "Opération Iraqi Freedom", 36 *RBDI* 206-?? (2003).

66   Resolutions 788 of 19 November 1992 (Liberia); 1162 of 17 April 1998 (Sierra Leone).

67   Resolution 1244 of 10 June 1999.

68   Resolutions 1472 of 28 March 2003, 1483 of 22 May 2003, 1511 of 16 October 2003.

69   N. KRISCH, "Unilateral Enforcement of the Collective Will: Kosovo, Iraq, and the Security Council", 3 *MPYUNL* 59 (1999).

70   Resolution 1386 of 20 December 2001.

71   T. SCHWEISFURTH, "Operations to Rescue National in Third States Involving the Use of Foreign Relation to the Protection of Human Rights", 23 *GYIL* 159–180 (1980), R. LILLICH, "Forcible Self-Help by States to protect Human Rights", 53 *Iowa LR* 325 et seq. (1967/68).

according to the prevailing view).[72] A special case is the intervention "by invitation", i.e. with the consent of the "receiving" State – probably the current states of the "Operation Enduring Freedom" in Afghanistan[73] and of the foreign military presence in Iraq (although the latter is also covered by a Security Council resolution[74]).

2.2.3.1 *Operations to Protect a Country's Nationals Abroad*

As to the protection of a country's own nationals the life of which is threatened in a foreign territory, there are four legal constructions which are used to justify such military action. The first is reading down the definition of the unlawful use of force contained in Art. 2 (4).[75] The second one is the construction of a customary law of self-defence which has in a somewhat puzzling way survived.[76] The third one is to construe the threat to the life of the citizens as an armed attack within the meaning of Art. 51. The fourth one, finally is the development of a new customary justification which would derogate from the exclusive or exhaustive character of the justifications provided by the Charter. Although there is a considerable practice of States rescuing their nationals from a threat to their life without the consent of the State where the threat occurs, none of the major cases is uncontroversial.[77] A major problem of this justification is the possibility of its abuse. The history of the last decades is full of examples of interventions where it used as a pretext of interference in the national affairs of a country.[78]

---

72   S. CHESTERMAN, *Just War or Just Peace. Humanitarian Intervention and International Law,* 2001.

73   L. DOSWALD-BECK, "The Legal Validity of Military Intervention by Invitation of the Government:, 56 *BYIL* 189–252 (1985); G. NOLTE, *Eingreifen auf Einladung,* 1999.

74   Resolution 1511 of 16 October 2003.

75   See above 2.1.

76   This is often linked to the adjective "inherent" in Art. 51, see above 38.

77   One of the clearest cases of a non-abusive action to save a States own nationals was the Israeli action in Entebbe. It triggered an intensive doctrinal debate and a discussion in the Security Council. In the latter, a majority of the States intervening in the debate denied the legality of the operation. See BEYERLIN, "Die israelische Befreiungsaktion von Entebbe in völkerrechtlicher Sicht", 37 *Zeitschrift für ausländisches öffentliches Recht und Völkerrecht* 213 et seq. (1977).

78   One of the most evident cases of abuse was the intervention in Grenada led by the United States in 1983. The political reason for it was the fact that the United States and also some of the neighbouring Caribbean States disliked the policies of the then new government. One of the legal justifications put forward was an alleged need to save the lives of American present in the country. It soon became apparent that those American were not at all in danger, see DOSWALD-BECK, "The Legality of United States Intervention in Grenada", 31 *NILR* 355 et seq. (1984).

2.2.3.2 *Humanitarian Intervention*

It is very peculiar that the justification of the use of force as humanitarian intervention is more academic then practical. The idea to fight for the purpose of defending human rights seems to be intellectually attractive. Thus, it is philosophers and political scientist dealing with international relations who defend this idea. But also in legal doctrine, there is a considerable number of voices claiming that justification as being positive customary law. If one looks at the views expressed by States, there is much less enthusiasm for this idea.

There are, essentially, two lines of argument, similar to the ones discussed for the protection of national abroad. The first one consists of constructions which equate the suppression of the human rights of a population to an armed attack. It is relatively easy to derive a right of collective self-defence from that construction.[79] The other possibility is, also as in the previous case, the recognition of some kind of customary legal development. The essential reason to reject either construction is the fact that they have no basis in actual practice.[80] Three cases are usually mentioned a possible precedents for the recognition of a right to humanitarian intervention. The first one is the Indian intervention in what was then East Pakistan in 1971 which led to the independence of that part of Pakistan and the creation of the State of Bangladesh. The second one is the Tanzanian intervention in Uganda 1979 which ousted the regime of the dictator Idi Amin. The third one is the Vietnamese intervention in Cambodia which terminated the Pol Pot-regime. In all three cases indeed, the human rights situation in the target countries of the intervention was abominable. But in no case did the intervening countries rely on a right of humanitarian intervention. They justified their operation by variations of self-defence. In the Cambodia case, the legality of the Vietnamese intervention was rejected in the practice of the UN.[81]

In contradistinction to the later American and British intervention in Iraq, not much effort went into the legal justification of the Kosovo bombing by NATO. It appears that even in NATO countries, there was a widespread reluctance among politicians to recognize a right of humanitarian intervention. The German Foreign Minister at the time said before the UNGA that the Kosovo intervention should not be considered as a precedent[82] (which is the contrary of a claim of customary legal entitlement). On the other hand, many States

---

79 Cfr. J. DELBRÜCK, "Effektivität des Gewaltsverbots", 74 *Friedenswarte* 139 et seq (1999), 152.

80 For a comprehensive analysis of that practice, see CHESTERMAN, op. cit. note 72.

81 WARBRICK, "Kampuchea: Representation and Recognition". 30 *ICLQ* 234 et seq (1981).

82 S. VÖNEKY/ M. RAU, "Völkerrechtliche Praxis der Bundesrepublik Deutschland im Jahre 1999", 61 *ZaöRV* 877 et seq. (2001), at 1094.

expressed their strong opposition to the very idea of a right of humanitarian intervention.[83]

The question of humanitarian intervention also plays a major role in the current debate about a responsibility to protect. That concept was developed by the International Commission on Intervention and State Sovereignty, established by the Government of Canada[84] and was then taken over in documents of the United Nations, in particular the World Summit Outcome Document 2005.[85] The International Commission proposed military action mandated by the Security Council as an *ultima ratio* where no other way to end massive and systematic violations of human rights was possible, but it did not go as far as declaring lawful unilateral action by States in case the Security Council failed to act, and the UN documents dealing with the "R2P" certainly do not go further, quite to the contrary.

2.2.3.3   *Intervention by Invitation*

Intervention by invitation[86] is a widely used practice, and in many cases uncontroversial. But on the other hand, a number of these cases have been highly problematic and controversial indeed. The reason why intervention by invitation is lawful is that it does not constitute a "use of force" if it occurs with the will, even at the request of the government in power. Thus, the essential point is whether there is a situation which corresponds to the definition of "force" in Art. 2 (4) or not. It is clear that consent of the target State must be effective at the time of the intervention. Any permission given beforehand, but no longer in existence at the time of the intervention, does not have a justifying effect. The prohibition of the use of force being a norm of *ius cogens*, it cannot be validly be waived by an agreement.[87] Another crucial point for determining whether the intervention actually constitutes a use of force is whether the request or consent comes from a government which is entitled to speak for the target country. Most of the Soviet intervention were

---

83   See in particular the positions taken by Russia, China and India in the debate of the Security Council on 26 March 1999, Security Council Press Release SC/6659.

84   International Commission on Intervention and State Sovereignty, *Responsibility to Protect*, 2001.

85   A/RES/60/1 of 16 september 2005.

86   G. NOLTE, op. cit. note 73.

87   See S. KADELBACH, *Zwingendes Völkerrecht*, 1992, 226 et seq. This was for example a problem in relation to the intervention right granted to the guarantee powers in the agreements related to Cyprus in 1959, T. OPPERMANN, "Cyprus" in Bernhardt, *EPIL* vol. I, 1992, 924 et seq.

based on a consent of a local actor, but for instance in the case of Hungary (1956) and Afghanistan (1980), a new government was instituted by the Soviet Union, in the case of Afghanistan even after the previous government had been overthrown and killed. In these cases, it is not really possible to consider that intervention as lawful. At present, the foreign presence in Iraq and Afghanistan is based on the consent of a new government created as a consequence of the foreign intervention. Whether and to what extent this consent changes the characterization of the foreign military presence as constituting a use of force is debatable. But in addition to the consent of the new government, ISAF in Afghanistan and the foreign military presence in Iraq are not based on a Security Council resolution.[88] Thus their lawfulness is established as from the adoption of these resolutions but not with retroactive effect.[89]

3   The *Ius in Bello*

The *ius in bello* as it is today is the result of a complex development of treaty law over more than a century.[90] To a large extent (controversial in detail) it is also customary law.[91]

Being, as already explained, a second line of defence to restrain violence in a situation where the *ius contra bellum* has been unable to prevent the use of force, it appears quite logical that this body of law, the *ius in bello* applies without distinction based on the *ius contra bellum*. This is indeed the positive law, the principle of the equality of parties under the law of armed conflict, at least as far as international armed conflicts are concerned. As is clearly reflected in the preamble of AP I[92] this remains the law[93] despite of attempts to revive just war ideas.

---

88   For Afghanistan see above note 70; for Iraq note 68.

89   See above notes 67, 68 and 69 and accompanying text.

90   See above text accompanying notes 28 et seq.

91   ICRC/ J. M. HENCKAERTS/ L. DOSWALD-BECK (eds.), *Customary International Humanitarian Law*, 2004.

92   "The High Contracting Parties ... Reaffirming ... of the Geneva Convention ... and of this Protocol must be applied ... without any adverse distinction based on the nature of origin of the armed conflict or on the causes espoused by or attributed to the Parties to the conflict".

93   R. KOLB, *Ius in bello. Le droit international des conflits armés*, 2nd ed. 2009, at 16 et seq.

3.1 The Scope of Application of the *Ius in Bello*

3.1.1 The International Armed Conflict

Traditionally, the *ius in bello* was the "law of war, which applied in times of war "in the legal sense". This lead to all kinds of artificial legal constructions to argue for or against the application of the law of war in particular cases, similar to the question of definition of was in relation to its prohibition in the 1920ies and 1930ies.[94] In modern practice, the notion of "war" has been replaced by that of "armed conflict", term used in treaty language for the first time in the Geneva Conventions of 1949.[95] The same terminology has since been applied by the Hague Convention for the Protection of Cultural Property in the Event of Armed Conflict 1954[96] and its additional protocols,[97] the Protocols Additional to the Geneva Conventions 1977[98] and the United Nations Convention regarding certain conventional weapons 1980.[99] That expansion or clarification of the scope of application of the law of armed conflict has one major consequential problem, namely the threshold between armed conflict and violence or use of force which remains below that level.[100] There are two conflicting approaches to this problem: On the one hand, it is considered that a simple minor border incident, a shot across the border, would not trigger the application of the law of armed conflict. Accordingly, it is held that the application of the law of armed conflict requires hostilities of a certain intensity. In this sense, the United Kingdom declared on the occasion of the signature of AP I[101]:

> 1... the government ... declare that they have signed on the basis of the following understanding:
>
> (a) In relation to Article 1, that the term "armed conflict" of itself and in its context implies a certain level of intensity of military operations

---

94   F. GROB, *The Relativity of War and Peace,* 1949.

95   Common articles 2 and 3 of the Conventions; another term used for the same reason in the debate in the 1950ies was "war in the material sense", see L. KOTZSCH, *The Concept of War in Contemporary History and International Law,* 1956.

96   Schindler/ Toman, op. cit. note 31, p. 999.

97   1st Protocol 1954, 2nd Protocol 1999, Schindler/ Toman, op. cit. p. 1037.

98   Schindler/ Toman, op. cit. pp. 711 et seq.

99   Convention of Prohibitions or Restrictions on the Use of Certain Conventional Weapons Which May Be Deemed to be Excessively Injurious or to Have Indiscriminate Effects, 10 October 1980, Schindler/ Toman, op. cit. pp. 181 et seq, with six additional protocols; its provision on the scope of application refers to the Geneva Conventions and their Additional Protocols.

100   K. J. PARTSCH, in BOTHE/PARTSCH/SOLF, op. cit. note 30, at pp. 623 et seq.

101   SCHINDLER/ TOMAN, op. cit. note 31, p. 814.

LIMITS OF FORCE IMPOSED BY INTERNATIONAL LAW

which must be present before the Conventions of the Protocol are to
apply in a given situation ...

On the other hand, it is necessary that where an armed conflict breaks out,
the Conventions and AP I should apply right from the beginning, i.e. when the
first shot is fired. In this sense, Pictet argues in his Commentary to common
Article 1[102]:

> Any difference between two States and leading to the intervention of
> armed forces is an armed conflict within the meaning of Article 2 ... It
> makes no difference how long the conflict lasts, or how much slaugh-
> ter takes place. The respect due to human personality is not measured
> by the number of victims. Nor, incidentally, does the application of the
> Convention necessarily involve the intervention of cumbrous machinery.
> It all depends on the circumstances. If there is only one single wounded
> person as a result of the conflict, the Convention will have been applied
> as soon as he has been collected and tended, the provisions of Article 12
> observed in his case, and his identity notified to the power on which he
> depends.

The two approaches are not easily reconciled. In the case of an international
armed conflict, the better argument is that of Pictet. In a non-international
armed conflict, the threshold question, as will be explained, is different.[103]

3.1.2 The Non-International Armed Conflict

The idea that some or all of the law of war should also apply in the case of civil
war has a long tradition, and it was put into practice in the American Civil
War.[104] The technical way of achieving this result was the so-called recognition
of belligerency: The government in place would recognise the rebel entity as
a party to the armed conflict, and through this (constitutive!) recognition the
rebels would acquire the status of a subject of international law being able to

---

102   J. S. PICTET, *The Geneva Conventions of 12 August 1949, Commentary*, vol. I, 1952, p. 32.

103   This may explain the wording of the United Kingdom declaration which is really formu-
      lated with a view to the problem of wars of national liberation within the meaning of
      Article 1 para. 4 AP I.

104   This practice has two aspects: first, the famous Lieber Code, General Order no. 100 pro-
      claimed by President Lincoln, is a restatement of the law of "war" in the traditional legal
      sense, but it was meant to apply in a "civil war", see S. VÖNEKY, "Der Lieber Code und
      die Wurzelndes modernen Kriegsvölkerrecht", 62 *ZAöRV* 424 et seq (2002). Secondly, the
      attitude of the Federal Government was interpreted as a recognition of belligerency., see
      E. RIEDEL, "Recognition of Belligerence", in Bernhardt, *EPIL* vol. IV, 2000, 47 et seq.

be the addressee of the norms of the law of international armed conflict. This was not a very practical construction, and even in the American Civil War, it was not the result of an explicit recognition, but of an interpretation of certain acts of the Federal Government in relation to that conflict. It took several decades until the idea of applying the law of armed conflict to non-international armed conflicts became a generally accepted reality in the Geneva Conventions of 1949. Despite the horrible experiences of the Spanish Civil War (where there was no recognition of belligerency), it was still in 1949 not acceptable to the majority of States to apply the entire bulk of the law of armed conflict to "non-international armed conflicts", using the new terminology. Thus, the Conventions of 1949 only establish in the form of a "mini-convention[105] some basic rules for these conflicts. And when in the Diplomatic Conference of 1974–1977 another attempt was made to expand the protection of the victims of non-international armed conflicts, that was only a limited success. As a result of this resistance, the threshold of application of AP II relating to the protection of the victims of non-international armed conflict is higher than that of common Article 3, and the scope of protection reached during the negotiations of four years was seriously watered down in the very final phase of the conference, although it still goes further than that provided by common article 3.[106] Thus, up to this day, a distinction has to be made between international and non-international armed conflicts. A special case are in this respect wars of national liberation,[107] which AP I counts as international armed conflicts. The relevance of this special status has no longer any significant practical relevance.

However, despite the difficulties which the attempt to expand the protection of the victims of non-international armed conflicts encountered in the Geneva Diplomatic Conference 1974–1977, it can be shown that in recent years, a certain convergence between the legal regimes of the international and the non-international armed conflict has occurred.[108] Nevertheless, the distinction remains relevant. The crucial point is the distinction between combatants and civilians. In an international armed conflict, a combatant may lawfully take part in hostilities, and he/she may therefore be individually targeted (may

---

105   Art. 3 common to the Conventions.

106   AP II is more elaborate in its human rights provisions (Arts. 4–6), the provisions on the wounded, sick and shipwrecked (Arts. 7–12) and even in the provisions on the protection of the civilian population (Arts. 13–18).

107   Art. 1 (4) AP I.

108   This is the well documented result of the ICRC's customary law study, ICRC/ Doswald Bekc/ Henckaerts (eds.), op. cit. note 91, vol. I, p. xxix.

LIMITS OF FORCE IMPOSED BY INTERNATIONAL LAW

kill and be killed). A civilian may not be targeted, but may not take part in hostilities (may not kill and may not be killed). If he/she does it nevertheless he/she loses his/her protection, but only as long as he/she takes part in the hostilities, i.e. may not be killed after having ceased to take part in hostilities. As will be shown, governments are loath to concede this status of combatants, with the ensuing rights, to rebels in a non-international armed conflict. This remains the basic flaw of the relating to non-international armed conflict. The principle of equality of the parties, which has been explained above as a major factor of the effectiveness of the *ius in bello*, is not accepted to a full extent in the case of a non-international armed conflict. The reciprocity or equality only exist to a limited extent, namely concerning the set of basic rules which are indeed applicable in non-international armed conflict.

The existence of a special regime for non-international armed conflicts leads to further problems of thresholds. There is, first, the threshold between the international and the non-international armed conflict. It depends on the status of the parties. An international armed conflict is a conflict between States or parties having a status which is equivalent to that of a State, at least for the purpose of applying the law of armed conflict. A non-international armed conflict is a conflict within a State. This means that at least one of the parties to the conflict is not a State, but an entity existing within a State. It can be a conflict between a State/government and a dissident entity or a conflict between such entities. This is certainly plausible as a matter of theoretical principle – but the concrete cases are difficult to decide. In the process of the dissolution of States, for example, a conflict will start as a non-international armed conflict, between the State and a secessionist entity, but once the secessionist entity has a degree of success, it may gain the status of a State. For example, the conflict between the Kuomintang and the Communists led by Mao Tse Tung was a non-international armed conflict, which was then, in the course of the events, transformed into the conflict between the government of the PRC and the government which had fled to Taiwan. Neither side recognises the other as a State, both sides claim that it still is a non-international conflict – the Taiwan position being slowly modified. Yet for the purposes of the application of the law of armed conflict, both sides would, in the case of a military encounter, probably be considered to be States or at least (in the case of the Government of Taiwan) as being a *de facto* regime and having, thus, a status equivalent to a State[109] – with the consequence that the law relating to international armed conflict were to apply.

---

109 FROWEIN, *Das de facto-Regime im Völkerrecht,* 1968, pp. 45, 58 et seq.

The other threshold is that between the armed conflict and violence below the level of an armed conflict. The distinction is of considerable practical relevance. The law of armed conflict applies between the "parties". There is a relationship of a certain reciprocity, or, as has been pointed out, of equality among the parties. Both sides are bound by the same rules. In the case of violence below that level, it is a relationship between, on the one hand, a government enforcing the law, subject to human rights limitations while doing so, and on the other hand, a group involved in criminal activities. The borderline between the two situations is difficult to draw, but it has to be drawn.

The provision on the scope of application of AP II clearly indicates this necessity (Article 1 para. 2):

> This protocol shall not apply to situations of internal disturbances and tensions, such as riots, isolated and sporadic acts of violence and other acts of a similar nature, as not being armed conflicts.

Wherever that line might be drawn, it is certainly different from the "first shot" theory which, at least according to one view, applies in international armed conflict.[110] The first shot will be a "sporadic act of violence". It will as a rule take some time of fighting until the riots mutate, legally speaking, into an "armed conflict".

The situation is further complicated by the question whether there is only one such threshold or several ones, i.e. there are different regimes for different types of non-international armed conflicts. A look at the provisions defining the scope of application of different rules shows that there are at least two different thresholds, that between an ordinary non-international armed conflict (Common Article 3) and internal armed disturbances etc., and that between the qualified, i.e. higher intensity non-international armed conflict and the ordinary armed conflict as well as internal disturbances. While common Article 3 applies to all non-international armed conflicts, AP II applies only to some of them. According to Article 1 para. 1 AP II, these are conflicts

> which take place in the territory of a High Contracting Party between its armed forces and dissident armed forces or other organized armed groups which, under responsible command, exercise such control over a part of its territory as to enable them to carry out sustained and concerted military operations and to implement this Protocol.

---

110   See above text accompanying note 102.

LIMITS OF FORCE IMPOSED BY INTERNATIONAL LAW

This describes a conflict of a certain intensity. A major flaw of this provision is that it excludes (based on a drafting oversight) conflicts between dissident groups.

The Statute of the ICC follows the same concept of two types of non-international armed conflicts, one of a higher, one of a lower level of intensity. Its provision defining war crimes (Article 8) contains two lists of such crimes, one[111] applying to all types of non-international armed conflicts, the other[112] applying only to higher intensity ones. The definitions are clearly inspired by AP II:

> (d) Paragraph 2 (c) applies to armed conflicts not of an international character and thus does not apply to situations of internal disturbances and tensions, such as riots, isolated and sporadic acts of violence or other acts of a similar nature.

Paragraph (f), the definition of the higher level armed conflict, adds to this phrase the following:

> It applies to armed conflict that take place in the territory of a State when there is a protracted armed conflict between governmental authorities and organized armed groups or between such groups.

The latter definition is wider and more flexible than that of Article 1 para. 1 AP II. It avoids the error of excluding conflicts between non-state groups, it leaves out the requirement of controlling territory, but replaces this by the requirement that fighting be "protracted" and the group be "organised".

3.1.3   Mixed Conflicts

The problem of thresholds is further complicated by the phenomenon of mixed conflicts. Recent history is full of examples of such internationalised internal conflicts: Afghanistan, Iraq, Darfur, Georgia. Where there is an external intervention into an internal conflict, three relationships have to be distinguished: that between the government and the dissident group or between dissident groups (internal), (if the intervention is on the side of the government) that between the intervenor and the dissident group(s) (arguably an international one) and (if the intervention is on the side of the

---

111   Article 8 para. 2 (c).
112   Article 8 para. 2 (e).

108 PART 1: BASIC ISSUES

dissident group) that between the intervenor and the government (certainly an international one).

As in the case of the threshold between international and non-international armed conflicts, much depends on the qualification of the status of parties in concrete cases. In the Vietnam conflict, for instance, there were four parties: the United States, the DRV (North Vietnam), the South Vietnamese Government and the Vietcong. Clearly, the relationship between the United States and North Vietnam was that of an international armed conflict, the relationship between the South Vietnamese government and the "rebel movement" of the Vietcong that of a non-international conflict. As North Vietnam had not recognised the South Vietnamese Government, the qualification of that relationship was uncertain.

In the current situation in Iraq and Afghanistan, the first question which arises as to the relationship between the government and dissident groups or between foreign intervenors and dissident groups is whether there is an armed conflict or whether there is just a question of law enforcement. Apparently, this situation changes according to different localities. There have been and still are places where the situation is one of law enforcement only. Before the establishment of the new government, this was a question of the duty of the occupying power to maintain law and order in the occupied territory.[113] After the establishment of the new government and the agreements between this government and the intervenors, it is a question of the intervenors assisting the government in fulfilling this same task. Yet, both in Iraq and in Afghanistan, there have been and there continue to be situations of protracted fighting. They constitute armed conflicts. The question is whether these armed conflicts are subject to the regime of an international or to that of a non-international armed conflict. There are three possible solutions to this question: (a) the entire conflict (i.e. both the relationships between the government and the dissidents and that between the intervenors and the dissidents) is international, (b) the entire conflict is non-international, and (c) the conflict is split into two different regime, non-international in the relationship between government and dissidents, international in the relationship between the intervenors and the dissidents.

The variant (a) would provide the highest level of protection for the victims. But there is no indication that this is accepted in State practice.[114] Variant

---

113 See below 3.5.2.

114 See for a critical review of the situation J. G. Stewart, "Towards a single definition of armed conflict in international humanitarian law: A critique of internationalized armed conflict", 85 *IRRC* 313 (2003).

LIMITS OF FORCE IMPOSED BY INTERNATIONAL LAW

(c) entails serious problems of implementation. It means two different legal regimes on one and the same battlefield. Variant (b) provides a lower level of protection, but it is relatively simple to implement. As to the practical result, the United States Supreme Court has adopted the variant (b). The Court reserves the legal regime of international armed conflict to conflict between States.[115] It then interprets Art. 3 common to the Geneva Conventions as a kind of residual provision which is applicable in all cases where the more elaborate system of the law of international armed conflict applies. Thus, according to the US Supreme Court, article 3 common to the Geneva Convention provides the legal yardstick for the behavior of United States troops in Afghanistan. These means that the prisoners made in this conflict do not enjoy prisoner of war status, but the Court interprets protection which article 3 provides to detainees rather strictly.[116] It seems that there is a growing international support for this position.

3.2 *The Principle of Distinction – Combatants and Civilians*

The principle of distinction, as has already been pointed out above,[117] is a fundamental rule of the *ius in bello* which considerably restrains permissible violence in times or armed conflict. It has two aspects: one relating to persons, the other relating to objects. As far as the first aspect is concerned, the fundamental distinction is that between civilians and combatants. Only combatants have, in times of armed conflict, the "licence to kill"[118]:

> Members of the armed forces of a Party to the conflict ... are combatants, that is to say they have the right to participate directly in hostilities.

On the other hand, they may lawfully be killed, they are lawful individual targets of deadly force. Civilians may not take part in hostilities, at least not directly. On the other hand, they may not be individually targeted, unless and for such time as they take directly part in hostilities.

If a combatant is taken prisoner, he/she is entitled to prisoner of war status. This does not only guarantee a decent treatment in captivity, it also implies the so-called combatant privilege, namely that he/she may not be punished for the

---

115 *Hamdan v. Rumsfeld,* 45 ILM 1130 (2006), at 1154; 126 S.Ct. 2749 (2006).
116 The Court emphasizes that Mr. Hamdan must be judged by a "regularly constituted court". The Military Commissions established to judge the detainees at Guantanamo Bay, according to the Court do not live up to this requirement.
117 See text accompanying notes 26 and 27.
118 Art. 43 para. 2 AP I.

lawful participation in hostilities, i.e. participation which respects the law of armed conflict. This is the corollary of the licence to kill. The combatant has not done anything unlawful when he/she performed acts of hostility within the framework of applicable international legal standards. On the other hand, a civilian who is captured by an adversary after having taken part in hostilities is entitled to a treatment according to human rights standards, but not to the combatant privilege.[119]

It is thus clear that this distinction is fundamental both for the protection of civilians and for the protection of combatants in case of capture. The immunity of civilians from attack will only be respected if the adversary can be sure that those who look like civilians are civilians, i.e. are harmless. This is why a combatant which hides behind a civilian appearance foregoes his/her combatant privilege. This is a fundamental issue in asymmetrical conflicts. The current problem is that this distinction is undermined by different actors for different reasons. Certain modern "guerilla" and suicide bombing practices systematically violate the duty of distinction. On the other hand, the practice of "targeted killings"[120] often denies to civilians, guilty as they may be in a concrete case, the legal protection they are entitled to. Such constructions as "unlawful combatants", designed to deny to those persons the protections they enjoy as civilians as well as those provided to combatants under international humanitarian law, removes any incentive for those persons to distinguish themselves and to behave in accordance with international humanitarian law. Furthermore, whether and to what extent the same distinction applies in all or some non-international armed conflicts is a very controversial question. As a matter of principle, there is no combatant privilege in non-international armed conflicts.[121]

To explain this problem in more detail, it is, however, necessary to start with the situation in international armed conflicts: Combatants are the members of the armed forces of a party to an armed conflict,[122] i.e. persons belonging to the military organisations of a State or an entity having, in this respect, the same rights and duties as a State:

> The armed forces of a Party to the conflict consist of all organized armed forces, groups and units which are under a command responsible to

---

119   W. SOLF, in BOTHE/PARTSCH/SOLF, op. cit. note 30, at p. 255.

120   See above text accompanying note 108, see below text accompanying note 133.

121   M. BOTHE, "Töten und getötet warden – Kombattanten, Kämpfer und Zivilisten im bewaffneten Konflikt", in K. Dicke et al. (eds.), *Weltinnenrecht. Liber Amicorum Jost Delbrück,* Berlin 2005, 67–84, at 72 et seq.

122   Art. 43 para. 2 AP I, already quoted.

LIMITS OF FORCE IMPOSED BY INTERNATIONAL LAW

that Party for the conduct of its subordinates, even if that Party is represented by a government or an authority not recognized by an adverse Party.[123]

This definition involves, at a closer look, two questions, namely the status of an entity as "party to the conflict" and that of the military organisation which belongs to a party to the conflict.

As to the first question, it involves a question of status which is clear – but only at a first glance AP I binds the States parties thereto. In addition, it binds, as a matter of treaty law, too, liberation movements which have made a declaration which is equivalent to ratification as provided in Art. 96 para. 3 AP I. But as Art. 43 para. 1, just quoted, also constituted customary international law, there are other entities which may become parties to a conflict and be bound by the corresponding customary rule. These are, first of all, international organisations, in particular the United Nations, if and to the extent that forces which are an organ of the United Nations are engaged in hostilities which amount to an armed conflict. One the other hand, States which are not parties to AP I are also bound by the same customary rule. Entities which are not recognized as States, but which *de facto* posses powers like a State, are also bound. It is in this connection that the threshold between the international and the non-international armed conflict, already discussed above,[124] which also depends on the status of the parties becomes particularly relevant.

Two more examples of status questions may be added in this connection. The first one is Palestine. In 1989, the PLO tried to ratify the Geneva Conventions and AP I. whether that attempt was successful, is open to debate – the PLO is not in the official list of parties.[125] But at the latest since the partially

---

123   Art. 43 para. 1 AP I.

124   3.1.

125   The official list of parties in http://www.icrc.org/ihl.nsf/ contains the following footnote: "On 21 June 1989, the Swiss Federal Department of Foreign Affairs received a letter from the Permanent Observer of Palestine to the United Nations Office at Geneva informing the Swiss Federal Council "that the Executive Committee of the Palestine Liberations Organization, entrusted with the functions of the Government of the State of Palestine by decision of the Palestine National Council, decided, on 4 May 1989, to adhere to the Four Geneva Conventions of 12 August 1949 and the two Protocols additional thereto".

    On 13 september 1989, the Swiss Federal Council informed the States that it was not in a position to decide whether the letter constituted an instrument of accession, "due to the uncertainty within the international community as to the existence or non-existence of a State of Palestine".

successful Oslo agreements in 1993, the Palestinian people, represented by the PLO (now by the Palestinian Authority) is a subject of international law which can be, and is(!), a party to the conflict with Israel. There are, however, repeated acts of violence perpetrated by Palestinians which cannot be attributed to the PA, but to entities which are not parties to the conflict.

The second example is Afghanistan. When the forces of the Operation Enduring Freedom intervened in Afghanistan in 2001, the effective government of Afghanistan were the Taliban – despite the fact that they were not recognised as such by most States. This government effectively controlled most of the territory of Afghanistan. There was, thus, an armed conflict between the States participating in the OEF and Afghanistan. That situation changed with the defeat of the Taliban (which apparently was not as complete as it first appeared). A new government was installed which gave its consent to the further operation of the OEF in the country (in addition to that of a newly created UN mandated force, ISAF). Whether the Taliban organisation can still be considered as a party to the conflict, is another question.

A word on the armed conflict between Lebanon and/or Hizbollah on the one side, and Israel on the other must also be added. One party to the conflict is Lebanon, at least because Israel attacked targets on Lebanese territory. The fighters against Israel, however, did not belong to the Lebanese army, they belonged to the organisation of the Hizbollah. There are three different possibilities to legally explain this situation: As there were Hizbollah ministers in the Lebanese government, one can consider the military organisation of the Hizbollah as armed forces of the State of Lebanon, however organisationally distinct from the regular army. One can also consider Hizbollah as an entity separate from the Lebanese State. In that case, one has to ask whether it possesses a sufficient degree of organisation which makes it equivalent to a State, in which case it can be considered a party to the conflict in its own right. As the Hizbollah has often been descrived, with a considerable degree of plausibility, as a "State in the State", this is an explanation which is better than the third one which would treat Hizbollah as a group of non-State actors, simply criminals.

Once there is clarity about the parties to the conflict, the ensuing question is whether the persons actually engaged in hostile acts are member of the military apparatus of one of those parties. In the case of Palestine, the acts perpetrated by persons which cannot be attributed to the PA are not performed by members of the military organisation belonging to a party to the conflict, thus not by combatants. In the case of the Lebanese conflict, according to the better explanation (variant 1 or 2), the Hizbollah fighters were combatants. In the case of Afghanistan, the Taliban fighters were combatants, entitled to

LIMITS OF FORCE IMPOSED BY INTERNATIONAL LAW

prisoner of war status (!) at least during the first phase of the conflict, i.e. until the instauration of a new government after the initial success of the OEF. The current situation is far from being clear.

All[126] persons which are not combatants are civilians. We have thus a negative definition of the civilian population: civilians are all those who are not combatants. In the case of non-international armed conflicts, where there is no combatant status recognised for the rebel fighters, that approach suffers from legal difficulties. From a logical point of view, one might think that there cannot be any protected civilians because there are no combatants. Of course, this cannot be true as such conclusions would be highly detrimental to the protection of the victims of armed conflicts.

In addition, one has to ask what happens if the principle of distinction is not respected either by the combatants (because he/she fails to distinguish him/herself) or by the civilian (who takes part in hostilities).

As to the combatant, there are certain minimum requirements of distinction: According to Art. 44 AP I:

> all combatants are obliged to distinguish themselves while they are engaged in an attack of in a military operation preparatory to an attack.

The provision does not say how the combatant has to distinguish him/herself. Generally, it is expected that the combatant wears some kind of a uniform. Of course, a combatant cannot, and is not obliged to, distinguish himself/or herself at all times. Nevertheless, he/she may be individually targeted at all times.

However, the provision contains a further concession to guerrilla practices which is the major reason for the fact that the United States has not ratified Protocol I, claiming that it lowers the duty of distinction to an unacceptable extent[127]:

> Recognizing, however that there are situations in an armed conflict where, owing to the nature of the hostilities an armed combatant cannot so distinguish himself, he shall retain the status of a combatant provided that, in such situation, he carries his arms openly

---

126 With a minor exception: there are also non-combatant members of the armed forces, namely medical and religious personnel. They have a special status.

127 For references and a critical discussion see G. ALDRICH, "Prospects for United States Ratification of Additional Protocol I to the 1949 Geneva Conventions", 84 *AJIL* 1–20 (1991) at 7 et seq.

(a) during each military engagement
(b) during such time as he is visible to the adversary while he is engaged in a military deployment preceding the launching of an attack in which he is to participate.

The background of this provision is the "young man on a motor scooter before a street café" scenario: a young man clothed in the usual wide Vietnamese civilian dress (which in Western eyes looks like a pyjama) drives through the street of Saigon. He stops in front of a street café full of American soldiers, takes a hand grenade from underneath his "pyjama", throws it into the crowd and drives away.

The young man on the motor scooter, when captured, is not entitled to prisoner of war status even if he is otherwise a combatant, i.e. belongs to the armed forces of a party to the conflict. But he is entitled to "protections equivalent to" those provided by the Third Convention, which means POW treatment without combatant privilege.[128]

The question is whether these rules are reasonable ones. It is suggested that they are. It appears that they correspond to an American practice during the Vietnam War.[129] It is true that it waters down the duty of distinction to a bare minimum. But at least where a soldier really has to face a danger, i.e. where he/she sees persons in front of him/her and has to decide whether to shoot or not to shoot, the potential attack has to distinguish himself/herself. And this reduction of the duty of distinction only applies under special conditions, in hostilities of a special nature. The provision does not say what these hostilities of a special nature are. It is generally recognised that there are wars of national liberation and also situations of occupation. To avoid any confusion, it must also be emphasised that Art. 44 (3) AP I does not grant a combatant status, it presupposes this status, and determines the conditions when a persons which is a combatant loses the advantages which go with that status. No civilian carrying arms openly becomes a combatant by doing so.

As to the civilian who takes part in hostilities: this is a widespread practice. Most of the suicide bombers, freedom fighters, terrorists etc. are civilians as they do not belong to a military or at least paramilitary organisation of a party to an international armed conflict as required by Art. 43 AP I and the corresponding rule of customary international law. He/she loses his/her immunity

---

128   Solf, loc. cit. note 119.

129   It is quite significant in this respect that the delegates of the United States and of Vietnam to the Diplomatic Conference in Geneva 1974–1977 agreed very early the negotiations on a text of what was to become Art. 44 AP I, SOLF in BOTHE/PARTSCH/SOLF, op., cit. note 30, 248. The American resistance to that provision is a later development.

LIMITS OF FORCE IMPOSED BY INTERNATIONAL LAW

while he/she is taking a direct part in hostilities. During that time, but only during that time, he/she may be individually targeted. When he or she is at home and back to his/her civilian occupation, for example ploughing the field during the day, he/she may not be individually targeted. This gives rise to the so called "revolving door phenomenon": a person goes into the door as fighter and comes out as a protected civilian and back. But this revolving door is positive law. This clearly flows from the text of Article 51 AP I and is also a rule of customary law.[130] It entails the question from what moment on a civilian can be considered to take a direct part in hostilities. When he/she leaves the house at night, when he/she joins the group which is about to take some action, when a bomb is actually placed on the bridge? And when does he/she cease to take a direct part in hostilities? When he/she leaves the place of the hostile action, on only when he/she arrives at home?

Furthermore, it is very difficult to determine the position of those who do not go out to actually engage in hostile action, but who are the masterminds behind such action. Probably, one has to accept that there is some kind of operations control of civilian hostile action which is equivalent to direct participation.[131] This is one of the problems involved in the practice of targeted killings. If the masterminds of suicide attacks are considered to continuously participate in hostilities, the soldiers of the other side are entitled to kill them at any time.[132] It is to be noted that the Supreme Court of Israel in a recent case dealing with the Israeli practice of targeted killings in a general way, applies the same line of argument.[133]

3.3 The Principle of Distinction – Military Objectives and Civilian Objects

Another consequence of the principle of distinction is that between "military objectives" (objects which may be attacked) and "civilian objects" (objects which may not be attacked). That distinction, fundamental as it is, is also sometimes blurred.

---

130 ICRC/ Henckaerts/ Doswald-Beck, op. cit. note 91, vol. 1, p. 20; S. OETER, "Das militärische Vorgehen gegenüber bewaffneten Widerstandskämpfern in besetzten Gebieten un internen Konflikten", in Fischer-Lescano et al. (eds.), op. Cit. Note 19, 503–522, at 509.

131 See on these questions the study by the ICRC, "Interpretive Guidance on the Notion of Direct Participation in Hostilities", 90 IRRC 991 et seq (2008).

132 As a rule, however, they will not be combatants because they do not belong to the military organisation of a party to the conflict.

133 *Public Committee against Torture in Israel v. Israel,* Israel Supreme Court, Judgment of 16 December 2006, 46 *ILM* 375 (2007). As the case was brought by a human rights organisation in the form of a general challenge of the practice, the interesting question of the concrete application of these legal considerations was not addressed.

116 PART 1: BASIC ISSUES

Military objectives are defined as objects

> which may by their nature, location, purpose of use make an effective
> contribution to military action and whose total or partial destruction,
> capture or neutralization, in the circumstances ruling at the time, offers
> a definite military advantage.[134]

This is a broad definition, but it implies serious limitations as to permissible targets. It plays a major role in modern air warfare. In this respect, the central problem is what is called dual use objects. These are, in particular, traffic, energy and telecommunication infrastructure which are indeed capable of military use, but are not necessarily used for military purposes.

A first practical problem is bridges. Bridges have traditionally been regarded as military objectives because of their importance for military logistics. Because they facilitate the movements of troops and supplies to the front, they provide a meaningful contribution to the military effort. But they constitute military objective only if they provide such contribution in the concrete circumstances. The military advantage which is the criterion of the military objective is a contextual notion. Normally civilian objects may become military objectives if they are used for military purposes, and objects which are normally so used may not be considered military objectives if they are not.[135] In particular during the Kosovo bombing campaign, a number of bridges were bombed which had no military significance whatsoever. The purpose of the bombing was political (to induce the political elite of Serbia to negotiate with NATO), not military, a practice which is unacceptable under the current law of armed conflict.[136]

A second practical problem has been the telecommunication infrastructure. It cannot not be assumed that all telecommunication facilities are used for military purposes. That is an important question of fact. In assessing the legality of an attack against the television station in Belgrade in 1999, a committee set up by the Prosecutor of the ICTY in order to consider whether war crimes falling into the jurisdiction of that court had been committed by the NATO forces, concluded that the entire technical telecommunication system

---

134   Art. 52 para. 2 AP I.

135   See the debate between Y. DINSTEIN, Legitimate Military Objectives Under the Current *Jus in Bello*, in A. E. Wall (ed.), *Legal and Ethical Lessons of NATO's Kosovo Campaign*, US Naval War College International Law Studies vol. 78, Newport 2002, pp. 139–172, at 150 et seq. and M. BOTHE, Targeting, *ibidem* pp. 173–187, at 177 et seq.

136   BOTHE, loc. cit. note 135, at 180 et seq.

LIMITS OF FORCE IMPOSED BY INTERNATIONAL LAW

of Yugoslavia was inseparably linked to the military system. This also applied to the technical communication infrastructure of the television station which was, thus, rendered a military objective. This conclusion, it is submitted, is somewhat doubtful.[137]

These definitions presuppose in a way that the military objectives are clearly distinguishable. But what happens if this is not the case? If civilians and civilian objects are intermingled with military objectives? That problem is addressed by the prohibition of indiscriminate attacks in the form of area bombardment:

> an attack by bombardment or any other methods or means which treats as a single military objective a number of clearly separated and distinct military objectives located in a city, town, village or other area containing a similar concentration of civilians or civilian objects,[138]

This provision, which has to be read with all its conditions, was a problem in the recent armed conflict in Lebanon. Israel attacked a number of villages and towns in Southern Lebanon causing considerable civilian losses. The military objectives alleged to be in these areas were Hizbollah positions, in particular launching sites for Kassim missiles. It was apparently impossible, at least very difficult, to exactly locate them. Quite to the contrary, the confusion about their location was, it appears, deliberately used by Hizbollah as a kind of cover. In this situation, there were no "clearly separated and distinct" military objectives and it was thus not unlawful to consider an entire area as a military objective.[139] Whether the current situation in Afghanistan, where it is alleged that there have been civilian casualties as a consequence against Taliban positions in Southern Afghanistan remains to be ascertained.

Even where attacks are correctly directed against military objectives, it can realistically not be excluded that civilian damage nevertheless occurs as an unavoidable side effects of those attacks. This is what is called, in technical terms, "collateral damage". The permissibility of collateral damage is limited by the principle of proportionality according to which an attack is prohibited

> which may be expected to cause incidental loss of civilian life, injury to civilians, damage to civilian objects, or a combination thereof, which

---

137   BOTHE, loc. cit. note 135, at 179 et seq.
138   Art. 51 (5)(a) AP I, emphasis added.
139   Whether the principle of proportionality (see below) was respected in these cases is a different question.

would be excessive in relation to the concrete and direct military advantage anticipated.[140]

This principle is both reasonable and difficult. It is reasonable because it balances the military interest of using force effectively and the civilian interest of not being drawn into a conflict which, it must be repeated, is to be limited to a confrontation between the military efforts of the parties to the conflict. Therefore, the principle of proportionality is basic for the principle of distinction. It is, on the other hand, difficult because it implies a comparison between two things for which there is no real yardstick of comparison, military advantage on the one hand and civilian loss on the other: How many civilian lives for how many meters of advance of a tank battalion?

Despite these imperfections of the so-called "proportionality equation", it is still the best available solution for the problem of how to restrict collateral damage. This means, however, that the application of the proportionality principle by necessity gives rise to uncertainties and controversies of interpretation.

The classical issue is the physical damage caused in the vicinity of the military objective which is attacked. This is an old problem of the law of armed conflict. An examples is the "Christmas bombing" of Hanoi 1972 (operations "Linebacker II") where in particular bridges and the railroad yard was targeted. It was claimed that this was done with great circumspection in order to avoid civilian losses in the vicinity.[141]

Beyond the question of damages caused in the vicinity of military objectives, indirect damages have also to be assessed according to the yardstick of proportionality. This has been a very important practical problem during recent armed conflicts. For example during the bombing campaign against Iraq in 1991, a considerable part of the traffic and energy infrastructure of Baghdad was destroyed.[142] This had disastrous consequences for the living conditions, in particular the health services in Baghdad. *Inter alia*, a rise in infant mortality resulted.[143] It has to be emphasised that this type of indirect damage has to go into the proportionality equation.

---

140 Art. 51 (5)(b) AP I.

141 B. M. CARNAHAN, "Linebacker II" and Protocol I: The Convergence of Law and Professionalism, 31 *American University LR* 861–868 (1982).

142 Human Rights Watch, *Needless Deaths in the Gulf War: Civilian Casualties During the Air Campaign and Violations of the Laws of War*, New York, 1991, http://www.hirw.org/reports/1991/gulfwar.

143 A. ASCHERIO et al, "Effects of the Gulf War in infant and child mortality in Iraq", 1992 *New England Journal of Medicine* 931–936, http://www.ncbi.nlm.nih.gov/pubmed/1513350?dopt=Abstract.

LIMITS OF FORCE IMPOSED BY INTERNATIONAL LAW

The practical application of these rules based on the principle of distinction presupposes a two-pronged evaluation on the part of those who decide upon an attack: They must evaluate whether a target is a military objective and, secondly, what will be the amount of incidental civilian damage. The principle of proportionality the requires the decision-maker to relate that damage to the direct military advantage anticipated and, if he has several means to achieve that advantage at his disposal, to choose the one which implies less civilian damage.[144] The first evaluation raises the question of sources of information and of error. It must, first of all, be stressed that this evaluation is a legal duty the violation of which entails the responsibility of the State violating it. Thus, when the United States during the Kosovo campaign attacked the Chinese embassy in Belgrade, which by factual error had been taken for a military objective, the United States apologised and paid compensation. But what is the yardstick of the duty of diligence which makes the error a violation of the rule? It might well be that an error occurs even if all possible diligence is used in making the evaluation. The drafters of AP I solved this problem by the word "feasible". Feasible measures must be taken in performing that evaluation.[145] What this means was further clarified by a number of interpretative declarations made by States on the occasion of signature or ratification. According to the declaration made by the government of Canada,[146]

> The word "feasible" means that which is practicable or practically possible, taking into account all circumstances ruling at the time, including humanitarian and military considerations;"

To this, the declaration by the Federal Republic of Germany adds:

> On the basis of all information available to him at the relevant time, and not on the basis of hindsight;

This boils down to the old Roman adage: *Nemo ultra posse tenetur.* But what this means in concrete circumstances may be difficult to determine. Much depends on the concrete situation. In the case of targeting in air warfare, there is a longer and sophisticated planning process, where relevant information can be carefully weighed and checked. These decisions are not taken "in the heat

---

144   Art. 57 AP I.
145   Art. 57 para. 2 (a)(i) and (ii) AP I.
146   Reproduced in Schindler/Toman, op. cit. note 31, p. 797; see also the declarations by Belgium, France, Ireland, Italy, the Netherlands, Spain, UK.

of the battle". The information concerning the site of the Chinese embassy in Belgrade, just mentioned, for example, could be easily checked by looking on a map of Belgrade – wherever the targeting information came from. Thus, there are good reasons to believe that indeed the necessary diligence was not applied.[147] On the other hand, during an advance in land warfare, targeting decisions for artillery, for example, may have to be taken on very short notice. Even though the decisions may have to be taken on an unclear basis of information, waiting for certainty may involve an unacceptable risk of losses. These differences may account for the result of a study by Human Rights Watch on the respect of international humanitarian law during the Iraq war in 2003[148] which found out that targeting by coalition forces in air warfare was in much better conformity with the rules than that in land warfare.

The extent of the diligence in ascertaining the nature of a target may also be influenced by the behavior of the sire which is to be attacked. For the sake of reducing civilian losses, the parties to a conflict are under a duty to take precautions against attacks, in particular to avoid placing military objectives "within of in the vicinity of military objectives".[149] More specifically, it is prohibited to use

> the presence or movements of the civilian population ... to render certain points or areas immune from military operations, in particular in attempts to shield military objectives from attacks ...

these obligations have been and continue to be violated in a number of recent or current conflicts the use of "human shields", in some cases voluntary ones, is a heinous practice and a war crime.[150] Yet any careless or reckless attitude of the side to be attacked does not absolve the attacking side from its duties to take precautionary measures.[151] But nevertheless, such attitude is bound to have certain objective consequences. Where a party deliberately and systematically

---

147 Whether this error excludes the criminal intent which is the prerequisite of a war crime is another question, see Articles 30 and 32 ICC Statute.

148 Human Rights Watch, *Off Target: The Conduct of War and Civilian Casualties in Iraq*, 2003, http://www.hrw.org/reports/2003/usa1203.

149 Art. 58 AP I.

150 Art. 8 (2)(xxiii) ICC Statute; cfr. M. M. SCHMITT, "Asymmetrical Warfare and International Humanitarian Law", in W. Heintschel von Heinegg/ V. Epping (eds.), *International Humanitarian Law Facing New Challenges. Symposium in Honour of Knut Ipsen*, 2007, 11–48 at 29; M. SASSÒLI, "Human Shields and International Humanitarian Law", in Fischer-Lescano et al. op. cit. note 19, 567–578, at 568 et seq.

151 Art. 51 para. 8 AP I.

places concealed firing positions of rockets in the middle of towns and villages it creates a situation where the prohibition of indiscriminate attacks no longer protects those populations as already indicated above.[152] In addition, a policy of hiding firing positions in a concentration of civilians affects the ability of the attacker to ascertain the character of his/her objectives. Nevertheless, the attacker will have to take those civilians being a "shield" into account when establishing a proportionality equation.

The duty to reduce civilian damages to the extent possible in a given situation requires targeting which is as accurate as possible under the circumstances. This poses particular problems where a party to conflict has weapons with different accuracy at its disposal. As precision guided missiles, even in the most sophisticated armies, are not in unlimited supply, a responsible commander cannot be expected not to have recourse to other, less sophisticated weapons and to use up all precision weapons as long as they are available. Nevertheless, the availability of precision ammunition is an element in the duty to minimize civilian losses. The argument that one side simply should not have to use those weapons because the other side did not have them is a flawed consideration of reciprocity.[153]

All these considerations are a major issue in the application of the proportionality principle to nuclear weapons. As formulated in AP I, these rules make it difficult to imagine, to say the least, a use of nuclear weapons which does not cause excessive damages, taking into account, in particular, the long term effect of these weapons. Therefore, during the negotiations of AP I and thereafter, a number of nuclear weapon States and some of their allies maintained that AP I did not apply to nuclear weapons. This was apparently argued on the basis of an assumption that applicable customary law was somewhat more generous with respect to permissible uses of nuclear weapons.

When the UN General Assembly submitted to the ICJ the question of the legality of the use of nuclear weapons, the Court, in its advisory opinion,[154] laid this debate to rest. It held that at least essentially similar rules of customary international law applied anyway. It was argued before the Court that one could not imagine any use of nuclear weapons which respected the principle of proportionality. But on the other hand, nuclear powers argued that this can very well be imagined. The Court notes that none of those powers had come forward with any scenario where this would be the case.[155] Therefore, the Court came to the result that indeed the use of nuclear weapons violated a

---

152   See text accompanying note 138.
153   SCHMITT, loc. cit. note 150, at 42.
154   *Legality of the Threat or Use of Nuclear Weapons,* Advisory Opinion of 8 July 1996.
155   Loc. cit. para. 94.

122 PART 1: BASIC ISSUES

number of principles of international law, including the proportionality principle. This, it must be stressed, is the unanimous view of the Court. What divided the Court was the possibility of exceptions to this rule. Only two judges can be quotes as envisaging the possibility of a lawful, i.e. not disproportionate use of such weapons.[156] On the other hand, three judges categorically denied this possibility.[157] The majority (which only constituted the majority due to the casting vote of the President), however, left the question whether in extreme circumstances the use of nuclear weapons could be lawful open.[158] This was a *non liquet*; the Court did not positively state that this use was lawful. This lack of authority of the exception is often overlooked, however. The avowed policy of nuclear powers had settled comfortably in the niche thus left by the Court.[159]

These rules, based on the principle of distinction, are general rules concerning the methods of combat. They apply to attacks by any kind of weapon, primitive or highly sophisticated. But it has been shown that they pose a number of difficult problems of interpretation. Thus, there has been, for about a century, a series of attempts to ban particular weapons regardless of the fact whether their use in a concrete case violates the principle of distinction. This attempt has been successful in relation to biological and chemical weapons, but not in relation to nuclear weapons.

3.4 *Prohibited Weapons – the Principles of Distinction and Unnecessary Suffering*

The move to ban particular weapons because of their typical effects which were undesirable even in times of war started with the Declaration of St. Petersburg of 1868. These bans, or attempts to achieve such bans, have been and continue to be inspired by two considerations which are deeply rooted in the concept of legally limited military violence as it was developed in the age of enlightenment.[160] It is the concept that war is a conflict between the military organisation of one State against the military effort of the other. Any force not reasonably related to the purpose of subduing the military effort of the other

---

156 See the dissenting opinions by GUILLAUME, *ICJ Reports* 1996, 287 et seq; SCHWEBEL, *ibid.* 311, at 320 et seq.

157 See the dissenting opinions by SHABUDDEEN, *ibid.* 375, at 381 et seq, 402; WEERAMANTRY, 429, at 514 et seq; KOROMA, 556 et seq.

158 Loc. cit., para. 97.

159 See M. BOTHE, "Nuklearstrategie nach dem IGH-Gutachten?", 71 *Friedenswarte* 249–259 (1996); H. Müller, "Das Gutachten des IGH – ein Beitrag zum nuklearen Abrüstungsdiskurs", *ibidem* 261–272.

160 See above sec. 1.

LIMITS OF FORCE IMPOSED BY INTERNATIONAL LAW 123

side is unreasonable – and unlawful.[161] It has been shown that the principle of distinction is an offspring of that approach, and it is also the basis for the prohibition of particular weapons which in their typical conditions of use violate this principle. The other basic consideration is that even as applied against combatants, certain types of weapons may cause suffering which goes beyond what is needed to achieve the legitimate effect, namely to kill or incapacitate those who fight. These are weapons which cause, in this sense, "superfluous injury"[162] or "unnecessary suffering".[163] The latter principle was already the basis for the St. Petersburg Declaration of 1868 and of the Hague Declaration of 1899 on Expanding Bullets (so-called dum-dum bullets)

These two different but related considerations have remained relevant for the prohibition of certain weapons until the present time. In this respect, one has to distinguish between what is now called weapons of mass destruction (WMD) and "conventional" weapons.

As to WMD, the development started with the prohibition of chemical weapons through the Hague Declaration of 1899 concerning Asphyxiating Gases. The more important instrument in this respect is, however, the Geneva Protocol of 1925 "for the Prohibition of the Use in War of Asphyxiating, Poisonous or other Gases, and of Bacteriological Methods of Warfare". It was inspired by the horrors which the use of these weapons had caused among combatants during the 1st World War, but the essential rationale of the prohibition remains the uncontrollable effect of these weapons on the civilian population. After the 2nd World War and after long negotiations, this treaty has been buttressed by two treaties prohibiting not only the use, but also the possession of these weapons, a rule which renders the prohibition of use more effective. These are the Biological Weapons Convention of 1972[164] and the Chemical Weapons Convention of 1993.[165] The ICJ, in its advisory opinion on the use of nuclear weapons already mentioned, has held that none of the

---

161 D. FLECK, "Völkerrechtliche Gesichtspunkte für ein Verbot der Anwendung bestimmter Kriegswaffen", in D. Fleck (ed.), *Beitrage zur Weiterentwicklung des humanitären Völkerrechts für bewaffnete Konflikte,* 1973, 1–23.

162 Art. 23 (e) Hague Regulations 1899 version.

163 Art. 23 (e) Hague Regulations 1907 version. The difference of the two versions stems from the different unofficial English versions. The official French versions both use the term *maux superflus.*

164 Convention on the Prohibition of Development, Productions and Stockpiling of Bacteriological (Biological) and Toxin Weapons and on Their Destruction, Schindler/ Toman, op. cit. note 31, p. 135.

165 Convention on the Prohibition of the Development, Production, Stockpiling and Use of Chemical Weapons and on Their Destruction, Schindler/ Toman, op. cit., p. 239.

existing treaties on the prohibition of specific weapons could be interpreted as covering nuclear weapons. There is, thus, no treaty provision specifically banning the use of nuclear weapons. There is, however, the non-proliferation treaty[166] banning the possession of nuclear weapons for all member States – except the "official" nuclear powers. Thus, for nuclear weapons, the only norms restraining their use are the general norms on the methods of warfare which have been presented above.

As to conventional weapons, a controversial debate in the 1970ies finally led to the conclusion, in 1980, of the United Nations Convention of Prohibitions and Restrictions on the Use of Certain Conventional Weapons which May be Deemed to be Excessively Injurious or to Have Indiscriminate Effects.[167] The title shows that both considerations just explained have inspired the convention. It is a framework convention, the specific prohibitions of certain weapons being contained in (until now) five additional protocols:

- non-detectable fragments,
- mines, booby-traps and other devices,
- incendiary weapons
- blinding laser weapons.
- explosive remnants of war

The most controversial issue has been that of anti-personnel mines. They are very effective and unexpensive weapons, hence popular with the military of many a country. But their effect on the civilian population, when they are left unexploded in the ground during and after the conflict, is devastating. Removal of the mins and treatment of the victims is very costly. Hence, they are the object of general condemnation from civil society. However, the Protocol on Mines does not prohibit the use of mines, not even that of anti-personnel mines in a general way. It only prohibits it under certain circumstances which brings that prohibition of a weapon rather close to the prohibition of certain means and methods of warfare discussed above. Thus, the progress achieved by the mines protocol as compared to the pre-existing legal prohibition is minimal. That is why the critical movement to ban those mines put further pressure on international decision-makers. The result of this pressure was a convention negotiated outside the framework of the UN Weapons Convention, namely the so-called Ottawa Convention on the Prohibition of the Use, Stockpiling, Production and Transfer of Anti-personnel Mines and on their Destruction of

---

166   Treaty on the Non-Proliferation of Nuclear Weapons of July 1, 1968.
167   Schindler/ Toman, op. cit., p. 181.

LIMITS OF FORCE IMPOSED BY INTERNATIONAL LAW

1997.[168] This treaty finally contains a comprehensive prohibition of possession and use, but at the price that very important States have refused to participate: among others China, Russia, United States, but also certain conflict prone regions (Israel, the entire Arab World [with the laudable exception of Algeria, Tunisia, Jordan and Qatar], Iran; India and Pakistan), but also a group which is not so conflict probe, namely a large part of Central and Eastern Europe (Ukraine, Belarus, Poland and the Baltic States). Seen in this light, this important restraint on a highly indiscriminate weapons certainly leaves to be desired.

The latest issue in the field of weapons prohibitions is that of cluster ammunitions, already mentioned.[169] The humanitarian issue is very similar to that of mines. Cluster ammunitions are bombs or similar devices which split into a great number of sub-ammunitions, or bomblets which then affect a larger area. The first problem is the possible indiscriminate effect on a large area, discussed above. But the problem which is more serious for the civilian population is the fact that not all the sub-ammunition explode (so-called duds). They then lie on or in the ground with the risk of exploding when being stepped upon or touched – an effect which is the same as that of anti-personnel mines. Despite the fact that, as in the case of landmines, an international treaty containing a far reaching prohibition has been achieved, but without the participation of major military powers, the question is still pursued within the framework of the UN Weapons Convention with a hope to bring the objector countries aboard.

3.5   *Persons in the Hands of an Adverse Party*

Persons which are in the hands of the enemy are particularly exposed to being badly treated as a result of the conflict. There are essentially two categories of such persons: detainees and the population of occupied territories. International humanitarian has particular rules for the protection of such persons.

3.5.1   Regimes of Detention

There are two very elaborate protective regimes of detention for two categories of persons in international armed conflicts: prisoner of war status for combatants according to the IIIrd Convention and internees according to the IVth Convention. These two regimes are supplemented by certain other protective provisions such as article 11 AP 1. For persons which do not benefit from these

---

168   Schindler/ Toman, p. 285.

169   See above text accompanying notes 8 et seq.

specific protections, AP I now provides a residual protective regime in the form of a lengthy article (article 75 AP I) which is inspired by human rights provisions, but enhances the protection provided by human rights as it excludes the possibility of derogation to which certain human rights provisions are subject.

In the case of non-international conflicts, article 3 common to the Geneva Conventions also provides a certain protection for detainees, and so does article 6 AP II.

In the case of detention, human rights law provides, as a matter of principle, protection parallel to that of the said rules of international humanitarian law.[170]

3.5.2 The Law of Occupation

"Belligerent occupation" is a form of military presence in a foreign country which occurs during an armed conflict. The regime of belligerent occupation is regulated by certain provisions of the Hague Regulations and the Fourth Geneva Convention. It applies where the authority over a certain territory has in fact passed into the hands of the other belligerent.

Belligerent occupation has to be distinguished from other forms of military presence which are based on the consent of the territorial State. In the latter caser, the rights and duties of the foreign military forces flow frim that consent. The dividing line may not always be as clear as one would thing. Where the consent is given by an authority which is under the influence of the occupying power, doubts are possible as to whether this consent can really set aside the protective regime of belligerent occupation. One would not conclude that the cooperation conceded during the 2nd World War to the German occupant by such governments as that of Quisling in Norway would exclude the application of the law of occupation.[171]

Belligerent occupation beings once a certain authority is *de facto* established by the foreign forces.[172] It is in this moment that the responsibility of the occupying powers to secure law and order in the occupied territory begins. This was an issue during the rapid advance of the United States forces towards Baghdad in 2003. Looting started very soon after the collapse of the defences of the old system. It was questionable whether at the relevant time enough

---

170 For details see below 3.6.

171 E. CASTRÉN, *The Present Law of War and Neutrality,* 1954, p. 217.

172 Art. 43 of the Hague Regulations: "The authority of the legitimate power having in fact passes into the hands of the occupant, the latter shall take all the measures in his power to restore, and ensure, public order and safety, while respecting, unless absolutely prevented, the laws in force in the country".

LIMITS OF FORCE IMPOSED BY INTERNATIONAL LAW

de facto control had already been established by the United States so that the situation could be characterised as occupation.

The status of the occupying power is that of a *de facto* authority which has powers which are similar to that of a government. This includes the maintenance of law and order, but also the general welfare of the population.[173] The means to fulfil this responsibility are thus those which are typical for a government, i.e. law enforcement. The international legal standards limiting the powers of law enforcement are, as a consequence, applicable human rights standards, in addition to specific norms of the law of occupation. This is a somewhat controversial issue to which we will revert in the next section.

The authority of the occupying power is often challenged by force. There situations where the occupying power is no longer in a position to maintain its authority in a law enforcement mode. The status of the ensuing conflict, however, is not necessarily that of an international armed conflict. The answer to the question of applicable rules depends in particular on the status of the groups or organisations challenging the occupant's authority.[174]

As a matter of principle, occupation ends when the occupying power leaves the occupied territory. Whether and to what extent the regime of occupation also ends when a government of the occupied territory agreed to the foreign presence (cases of Iraq and Afghanistan) is a difficult question. One can argue that, certainly in the case of Iraq, these are situations where the consent of a government would not set aside the regime of belligerent occupation.

3.6 Overlapping Regulatory Regimes – Human Rights and International Humanitarian Law

The analysis of the question of the protection of persons in the hand of the enemy has already shown that human rights law may also be relevant in times of armed conflict. Thus, the relationship between the two bodies of law has to be clarified. This is an issue of great current practical importance. Historically, the development of guarantees of human rights and of the law of armed conflict are different, although both stem from the philosophical heritage of the age of enlightenment.[175] The law of human rights is concerned with the relationship between the individual and a State (the individual's own State or a foreign one), while the international law of armed conflict is concerned with striking a balance between various interests of belligerent States which, however, is in the interest of the individuals which are the victims of armed

---

173 Hague Regulations, Art. 43, 55; IVth Geneva Convention, art. 55, 56, 59; AP I, art. 69.
174 See already above, sec. 3.1.3.
175 See already above text accompanying notes 25 et seq.

conflict, a fact which finds it expression in the term "international humanitarian law". Human rights, since the American and French revolutions, developed as a matter of State constitutional law. It is only since the massive violations of human rights which occurred during the first half of the 20th century that human rights became the object of international guarantees. On the other hand, the law of armed conflict has always been a matter of international law. It is only since the middle of the 20th century that the internal dimension of its implementation[176] attracts more attention. In the second half of the 20th century, the development of international humanitarian law owes much to the international guarantee of human rights. Resolutions entitled "Human Rights in Armed Conflict"[177] were decisive for the successful development of the protections of international humanitarian law in the second half of the 20th century. Without going in any way into the question of the relationship between human rights and international humanitarian law, these resolutions simply see international humanitarian law as a necessary means to protect human rights and demand, therefore the adoption of new instruments of international humanitarian law.

Nevertheless, the relationship between the two bodies of law has remained doubtful and controversial. That relationship is a special case of the problem generally posed by the phenomenon of fragmentation of international law. There can be no doubt that the scopes of application of human rights and international humanitarian law are not mutually exclusive. The major human rights treaties contain specific provisions for their application (or, as the case may be, suspension) in times of crises, including armed conflict. On the other hand, certain norms of international humanitarian law, e.g. article 75 AP I, Art. 4–6 AP II, are in part textually identical with human rights norms, and they are designed to perpetuate the application of certain human rights during the time of armed conflict by excluding the possibility to suspend those norms during armed conflict.

Logically speaking, an overlap between the two bodies of law is possible only where both apply according to their own rules on their respective scope of application. The application of international humanitarian law requires the existence of an armed conflict.[178] Human rights law applies in a situation where a person is subject to the "jurisdiction" of a State. This jurisdiction is not

---

176   See below 4.1.

177   Human Rights in Armed Conflict, Resolution XXIII adopted by the International Conference on Human Rights, Teheran, 12 May 1968; Respect for Human Rights in Armed Conflict, UNGA Res 2444 (XXIII), 10 December 1968.

178   See above 3.1.

limited to territorial jurisdiction – a highly controversial issue, but by now an established practice of UN human rights bodies, of the ICJ and it is as to the result confirmed by certain decisions of the European Court of Human Rights.[179] On the other hand, certain countries contest this type of extraterritorial application of human rights. This question is particularly relevant for the application of the European Convention of Human Rights by European countries having armed forces in Iraq. This would be an extraterritorial application of the ECHR. This possibility had been recognised, as a matter of principle, by the European Court of Human Rights in a case concerning the Turkish occupation of Northern Cyprus.[180] However, in a more recent *obiter dictum* concerning a case in Serbia,[181] the Court added some puzzling geographic strings to that possibility – which, however, have not been consistently by the Court itself.[182] In that later case (concerning Turkish operations in Northern Iraq) the Court just asked the decisive question it had asked in the Northern Cyprus and in the Serbian case, namely whether an exercise of jurisdiction was involved in the measures complained of – which the Court had affirmed in the Northern Cyprus case and denied in the Serbian and Turkish case. However, on the basis of the said *obiter dictum*, the English High Court denied the application of the European Convention in respect of British operations in Iraq, except in the case of detention.[183]

As a result of the case law of the ECtHR, one has to conclude that fighting in an international armed conflict is not an excise of jurisdiction. There are, however, typically four situations where indeed a victim of armed conflict is subject to the jurisdiction of a party to the conflict: belligerent occupation, the situation of a belligerent national in the territory of the other belligerent, detention and the non-international armed conflict. On the other hand, combat operations are not an exercise of jurisdiction over the enemy[184]; thus, the question of overlapping protective regimes does not arise, at least not in international armed conflicts.

---

179 The ECtHR has never really argued the question of parallel application. It has simply applied the ECHR to situations of armed conflict without mentioning the question of the application of international humanitarian law to the same situation.

180 European Court of Human Rights, *Loizidou v. Turkey*, Merits, App. 15318/89, 18 December 1996 [1996] ECHR 70.

181 European Court of Human Rights, *Banković case*, App. 52207/99, 12 December 2001.

182 European Court of Human Rights, *Issa v. Turkey*, App. 31821/96, 16 November 2004.

183 English High Court, *Al Skeini and others v. Secretary of State for Defence*, 14 December 2004 [2004] EWCH 2911 (Admin), paras. 287 et seq. of the judgement.

184 *Banković case*, note 181, paragraph 82 of the Judgement.

It is in those four situations that the question of overlapping regimes does arise in armed conflict and their relationship has, thus, to be determined. At a closer look, that relationship is different in those different situations.

The two most obvious situations where human rights law applies are the non-international armed conflict and the treatment of nationals of one belligerent party in the territory of the other party. In both situations, event which mays constitute violations of human rights occur on the territory of the State in question, there is thus no problem as to the scope of application of the relevant human rights treaty.

In the case of detention, the treatment of prisoners of war and of interned persons is regulated by the sophisticated protective regime of the IIIrd and IVth Geneva Convention.[185] In respect of the persons falling under these regimes, there is no room for the concurrent application of human rights rules. The two regimes constitute indeed a *lex specialis* in relation to the general rules of human rights protection. This is important both for the ground and for the length of detention. On the other hand, persons not benefiting from the protection of the IIIrd or IVth Convention are entitled to the protection provided by the relevant norm of human rights. Where these rules are subject to a derogation, Article 75 AP I or Articles 4–6 AP II provide a safety net.

In the case of belligerent occupation, the relationship is that of cumulative application. Contradictions where that cumulative application might present problems are difficult to imagine. In some cases, the rules of international humanitarian law may justify a limitation of fundamental rights. A case in point is the protection of private property (to the extent that private property is protected as a human right which is controversial). The destruction of property is admissible where it is in conformity with Art. 53 of the IVth Convention, i.e. where it "is rendered absolutely necessary by military operations". This norm constitutes a limitation of the right to property as it is, for instance, guaranteed by the Protocol to the ECHR.[186]

The case of nationals of a belligerent in the territory of the other belligerent has been of great practical relevance in the conflict between Ethiopia and Eritrea.[187] The situation is regulated by Art. 38 of the IVth Convention. The protection of those person "shall continue to be regulated, in principle, by the

---

185 See already above 3.5.

186 Where Art. 1 of the Protocol refers to "general principles of international law" this can be interpreted as covering this conclusion – although this was probably not exactly what the drafters of the Protocol meant.

187 Eritrea Ethiopia Claims Commission (EECC), Partial Award, Civilian Claims, Eritrea's Claims 15, 16, 23 & 27–32, 17 December 2004, paragraphs 123 et seq.

LIMITS OF FORCE IMPOSED BY INTERNATIONAL LAW

provisions concerning aliens in time of peace". This general reference to peace-time law includes the application of the relevant human rights norms. The exceptions to these rules are also clearly stated by art. 38: "special measures authorized by the present Convention, in particular by Articles 27 and 41 thereof". These exceptions constitute valid limitations to the respective fundamental rights. Article 41 relates to assigned residence and the case of internment, already mentioned. Article 27 *in fine* facilitates in a general way "measures of control and security in regard to protected persons as may be necessary as a result of the war".

4 Implementation and Enforcement

Having explained the major characteristics of both the *ius contra bellum* and of the *ius in bello*, it is not necessary to come back to the question asked in the beginning: Are these norms really meaningful despite their constant violation?

First, a general *caveat*: There is no denying the fact of these violations. But the quantified relationship between the cases where the law is violated and those where it is observed has not really been made the object of reliable research. One thing can, however, be safely stated: alleged violations have not been acquiesced in by the political and legal discourse mentioned in the beginning which has accompanied the use of military force. This is not just reflected in a political debate, but also in the development of specific tools and procedures designed to ensure the respect of the rules of international law relating to the use of military force. It is to these rules and procedures we must now turn our attention.[188]

4.1 *Ius in Bello*

The armed conflict is an extreme situation. In times of peace, international law is most often applied as a routine on the basis of legal expert advice. That process of ensuring compliance with the law is not easily available for the law of armed conflict.[189]

---

188 For an overview see M. BOTHE, "Rechtliche Hegung von Gewalt zwischen Theorie und Praxis", in: Buffard/ Crawford/ Pellet/ Wittich (eds.), *International Law Between Universalism and Fragmentation, Festschrift in Honour of Gerhard Harfner,* 2008, 141 et seq.

189 For an overview see R. WOLFRUM/ D. FLECK, Enforcement of International Humanitarian Law in D. Fleck (ed.), *The Handbook of International Humanitarian Law,* 2nd ed., Oxford 2008, pp. 675 et seq.

132 PART 1: BASIC ISSUES

4.1.1   Internalisation of Norms

In this situation, the internalisation of the relevant norms is essential, i.e. that the relevant actors (including the simple soldier) know the law and have a positive attitude towards it. The drafters of the Conventions and the Additional Protocols have seen this need and have provided for a number of measures to this effect. The first and probably most important one is the duty to disseminate the content of the Conventions and the Additional Protocols.[190] Rules of application have to be adopted by the States parties.[191] All this should ensure that the actors within a State which have to apply this law know it and understand it.

The most important actors are the armed forces. In this respect, certain practices have developed which are capable of ensuring that the law has the appropriate impact on the actual behaviour of the soldier. The first is so-called military manuals and guidelines. This is a venerable tool by which military commanders ensure that their troops behave in conformity with international law. The first example was the General Order no. 100 issued by President Lincoln during the American Civil War, better known as the Lieber Code.[192] In the recent two decades, there has been a growing practice of States adopting similar documents, which most often are called "manuals".[193] These manuals translate the relevant international law into internal military rules; therefore, they are an important means to ensure that the national armies indeed behave as they should. It is interesting to note in addition, that these manuals are not only a means to ensure respect of international humanitarian law, but also a way of shaping it.[194] They are public record, are read by other States and, thus, form part of the legal discourse which, as pointed out in the introduction, is essential for the development and implementation of that part of international law.

While these manuals contain general rules, it is a current practice to issue rules of behaviour for specific military missions. These are called "rules of engagement". They are documents of military expediency, but it is important that legal considerations go into the drafting of these documents. As these documents are usually secret, this is not known, but one can assume that it is the case.

Another procedure is confidential. But it is at least known from publications that legal considerations go into the decision making process. This is the

---

190   Geneva Conventions, Art. 47/48/127/144; AP I, Art. 83; AP II, Art. 20.

191   AP I, Art. 80.

192   Reproduced in D. SCHINDLER/ J. TOMAN (eds.), *The Law of Armed Conflict*, 4th ed. 2004, p. 3.

193   M. BOTHE, "Customary International Humanitarian Law: Some Reflections on the ICRC Study", 8 *YIHL* 143–178 (2004), at 156 et seq.

194   BOTHE, *loc. cit.* note 193, at pp. 176 et seq.

LIMITS OF FORCE IMPOSED BY INTERNATIONAL LAW

targeting process in modern air and missile warfare.[195] It is a highly formalised process where targets are identified, chosen, proposed to higher command echelons, and then authorised, most often at a relatively high military level. In this process, military lawyers have indeed a word to say.

4.1.2 Guardians of the Public Interest

A second type of procedures designed to ensure compliance with the law of armed conflict are institutions which can be called advocates or attorneys of the public interest, watchdogs of the application of the law of armed conflict.

The first institution which must be mentioned in this connection is the United Nations, in particular the Security Council. Since the Council considers grave violations of international humanitarian law to constitute a threat to the peace,[196] the Security Council becomes a major actor in enforcing international humanitarian law. It has established international or "hybrid" criminal tribunals[197] and in a general way confirmed its willingness to intervene in cases of grave violations of international humanitarian law.[198]

A completely different, but probably the most important international agent for ensuring respect of international humanitarian law is the International Committee of the Red Cross. Based on its "right of initiative,[199] it regularly observes the behaviour of States or groups which are parties to an armed conflict and reminds them of their corresponding duties. Concrete violations are as a rule not denounced publicly, but through confidential demarches. Only where States do not properly react to these confidential calls, the ICRC goes public. In addition to this general mission, the ICRC has specific functions in relation to the correct treatment of prisoners of war.

While the major tool of the ICRC is its presence at all hotspots and its confidential diplomatic initiatives, other watchdogs depend entirely on publicity to influence the behaviour of parties to armed conflicts. This is in particular the weapon of the big human rights organisations like Amnesty International and Human Rights Watch.[200] These organisations have indeed repeatedly inquired

---

195   See T. MONTGOMERY, "Legal Perspectives from the EUCOM Targeting Cell", in A. E. Wall (ed.), *Legal and Ethical Lessons of NATO's Kosovo Campaign,* US Naval War College International Law Studies, vol. 78, 2002, pp. 189–197.

196   Resolutions 808 of 22 February 1993 (Yugoslavia) and 955 of 8 November 1994 (Rwanda).

197   See below note 205.

198   See resolution 1838 of 23 December 2006 on the protection of the civilian population in times of armed conflict.

199   Y. SANDOZ, "Le droit d'initiative du Comité international de la Croix-Rouge ", 22 *GYIL* 352–373 (1979).

200   Both organisations have, for instance, issued reports on violations of international humanitarian law during the armed conflict between Israel and Lebanon in 2006: AI,

134 PART 1: BASIC ISSUES

into alleged violation of the law of armed conflict and through their reports drawn the attention of the public to these violations. These organisations of civil society have indeed become a major factor in the initiatives to ensure respect of the law of armed conflict. Their work has become an important element in this legal discourse, referred to in the introduction, which is crucial for the development, implementation and respect of the law of armed conflict.

4.1.3 Interstate Dispute Settlement

Traditional means of interstate dispute settlement also play a role as procedures to ensure the respect of the law of armed conflict. The Conventions only provide for a non-intrusive type of settlement procedure, namely enquiry. That has been further developed by AP I in the form of a permanent fact-finding commission (Art. 90 AP I), whose obligatory competence is based on a specific recognition which has to be declared in addition to ratification, the so-called optional clause of the ICJ Statute serving as a model). So far, more than a third of the parties to AP I have made that declaration. At the time when the Protocols were drafted (1974–1977), in the high days of the East-West and North-South conflict, it was impossible to agree on any obligatory third party dispute settlement, even less on judicial settlement.

That overall political situation has changed. The ICJ has repeatedly dealt with alleged violations of international humanitarian law (Nicaragua case,[201] DRC v. Uganda[202]). In recent times, international arbitration also was resorted to, namely in the conflict between Ethiopia and Eritrea.[203] The Claims Commission established by the two States has developed an interesting case law. What is the practical impact of those judicial decisions? In the current international order, there is a high probability that they will indeed be implemented. In addition, the case law is another important component of the legal discourse already mentioned.

Israel/Lebanon: Hizbullah's Attacks on Northern Israel, Report published 14 September 2006; AI, Lebanon: Deliberate Destruction or "collateral damage"? Israel attacks civilian infrastructure, Report published 23 August 2006 (available at http://www.amnesty.org/); HRW, Civilians under Assault. Hezbollah's Rocket Attacks on Israel in the 2006 War, available at http://hrw.org/reports/2007/iopt0807/; HRW, Why They Died. Civilian Casualties in Lebanon during the 2006 War, available at http://hrw.org/reports/2007/lebanon0907/.

201 See above note 4.

202 *Armed Activities on the Territory of the Congo* (*DRC v. Uganda*), Judgement of 19 December 2005.

203 The legal basis is the Algiers Agreement dated 12 December 2004. The decisions are available at the website of the Permanent Court of Arbitration, http://www.pca-cpa.org/. For an analysis see the contribution in De Guttry/ Post/ Venturini (eds.), The 1998–2000 War between Eritrea and Ethiopia, 2009.

LIMITS OF FORCE IMPOSED BY INTERNATIONAL LAW

4.1.4 International and National Criminal Law

After some not very successful attempts at the end of the 1st World War,[204] it is since the end of the 2nd World War that criminal law plays a major role as a means to enforce the respect of the law of armed conflict. Criminal prosecutions have been instituted before international tribunals. This development started at the end of the 2nd World War with the international military tribunals of Nuremberg and Tokyo. They have set important precedents. For a number of decades, however, during the time of the East-West conflict, there was no follow-up to this innovative approach. But in the 1990ies, based on a new scandalisation in the face of the human tragedies caused by war, the ICTY and the ICTR were created by Security Council decisions[205] and finally the ICC by a treaty. Despite the resistance which the latter has met by certain States (not only the United States), the start of the Court has been better than one might have expected. States have referred cases to the Court, and also the Security Council referred the case of Darfur to the Court, the United States and China limiting themselves to a few critical remarks, but not casting a veto.[206]

In addition, national criminal tribunals play an increasing role in sanctioning violations of the law of armed conflict. States are under a duty to prosecute grave breaches of the Geneva Conventions applying the principle of universal jurisdiction,[207] a rule which for a long time had fallen into oblivion but which more and more plays a practical role. In addition to this treaty obligation, there is also a customary right to establish universal jurisdiction relating to war crimes beyond the scope of "grave breaches".[208] Certain human rights treaties provide for the same obligation, and the right to exercise universal jurisdiction also applied to genocide and crimes against humanity. While this is generally accepted as a matter of principle, there are three controversial issues.

---

204 Art. 227 of the Treaty of Versailles.

205 In addition, there are so-called hybrid courts set up in cooperation between the United Nations and the countries concerned (Sierra Leone, Cambodia, Timor Leste), see L. A. DICKINSON, The Promise of Hybrid Courts, 97 *AJIL* 295 (2003); C. P. R. ROMANO/ A. NOLLKAEMPER/ J. KLEFFNER (eds.) *International Criminal Courts, Sierra Leone, East Timor, Kosovo and Cambodia,* Oxford 2004.

206 M. BOTHE, "International Legal Aspects of the Darfur Conflict", in A. Reinisch/ U. Kriebaum (eds.), *The Law of International Relations – Liber amicorum Hanspeter Neuhold,* 2007, pp. 1–18, at 16.

207 Geneva Conventions, Article 49, 50/50, 51/129, 130/146, 147. A similar, but more precisely circumscribed obligation applies pursuant to Protocol II to the Hague Convention for the Protection of Cultural Property in the Event of Armed Conflict, articles 15 and 16.

208 ICRC, op. cit. note 91, vol. I, pp. 604 et seq.

First, what is the relationship between the principle of universal jurisdiction and the traditional rules on the immunity of State organs? Secondly, does the right/obligation to establish universal jurisdiction also apply where the alleged perpetrator is not a national of the prosecuting State and not (yet?) present in its territory? Thirdly, in the case of foreign offenders, does the principle of universal jurisdiction only apply if the home State is unable or unwilling to exercise its jurisdiction (so-called principle of subsidiarity)? These questions have played a major role in a number of cases where indeed alleged perpetrators of war crimes and crimes against humanity have been brought before the courts of countries other than their own.[209]

What is the practical impact of criminal law for ensuring respect of the law of armed conflict. "Deterrence" is often invoked, but this is a myth, even in national criminal law. Most of the war criminals are part of a more or less official system. They do not receive any signals inducing a different behaviour from outside their system. As a practical matter, war criminals are not deterred. The real effect of international criminal law is different, and it is twofold. First and foremost, it corresponds to a fundamental societal need that such gross violations, which very often have caused unspeakable suffering, do not remain unpunished. "No impunity" is a political and social postulate, and it is often a necessary tool for bringing peace to conflict torn societies, hence the bitter debate about amnesties in some countries. In addition, the case law of criminal tribunals contributes to the development of a legal culture, also to a greater certainty of the law. It is thus another important component of the legal discourse already referred to.[210]

4.1.5   Individual Remedies

Individual remedies before national or international courts also play a practical role in two ways. Where there is a parallel application of human rights law and international humanitarian law, remedies provided for the protection of human rights can be used and are used. Cases of this type have been brought before the Interamerican Court of Human Rights[211] and the European Court of Human Rights,[212] with varying success.

---

209   S. MACEDO (ed.), *Universal Jurisdiction: National Courts and the Prosecution of Serious Crimes under International Law,* Philadelphia 2004.

210   See above 1.

211   *Las Palmeras, Preliminary Objections,* Judgment of 4 February 2000, Series C, no. 66; *Bámaca Velásquez v. Guatamala,* Judgment of 25 November 2000, Series C, no. 70, 22 *HRLJ* 367 (2001).

212   See already above notes 180–814.

LIMITS OF FORCE IMPOSED BY INTERNATIONAL LAW

The second case of individual remedies is claiming compensation for damages suffered from violations of international humanitarian law. Whether the law of armed conflict which applies between the States can give rise to individual rights under the national law of various countries still is hotly debated. The United States, under the Alien Tort Claims Act, has been rather generous in opening their courts for claims against foreign persons, including the agents of foreign governments.[213] There is a considerable, though controversial practice of the courts of a number of States relating to violations of the laws of war during the 2nd World War.[214] Several cases were brought before the courts of European States in relation to the Kosovo campaign.[215] They have so far not being very successful, but this is not necessarily the last word. One of the cases is now pending before the German Federal Constitutional Court.[216] There is a clear trend to recognise such individual claims, including a resolution of the Human Rights Commission of the United Nations requiring States to provide for such a remedy in their national laws.[217]

4.1.6   Conclusions

All this shows that it is through a complex mixture of various procedures that respect for the law of armed conflict is ensured. Different actors are at work: the States involved in a conflict (i.e. their governments, their military, their courts), this States, organisations acting in the general interest, international and national courts or similar institutions, and not least the victims of violations. The procedures may be formal and informal. The system has a multilevel character: It consists of national and international procedures, bot preventive and repressive. That complex system does not prevent all violations, but it certainly

---

213   28 USC § 1350; for a recent analysis see A. FISCHER LESCANO, "Subjektivierung völkerrechtlicher Sekundärregeln", 2007 *AVR*, pp. 39 *et seq.*

214   For the recent court practice, see R. HOFMANN, "Victims of Violations of International Humanitarian Law: Do They Have an Individual Right to Reparation against States under International Law", in P.-M. Dupuy/ B. Fassbender/ M. N. Shaw/ K. P. Sommermann (eds.) *Common Values in International Law. Essays in honour of Christian Tomuschat*, Kehl 2006, pp. 341–359, at 352 et seq. S. PERRAKIS, "De la reparation des victims du droit international humanitaire et l'affaire des "réparation de guerre allemandes" en Grèce", in Fischer-Lescano et al. (eds.) op. cit. supra note 19. Pp. 523–550.

215   For the Netherlands : Civil Court of Amsterdam, *Dedovi v. Kok et al.*, Judgment of 6 July 2000, 759/99 SKG.

216   Constitutional complaint against a judgment of the German Federal Court (Bundesgerichtshof) of 2 November 2006, available at http://lexetius.com/2006,2924. As of 2010, the case is still pending before the Federal Constitutional Court.

217   Resolution 2005/35 of 19 April 2005, confirmed by UNGA Resolution 60/147 of 21 March 2006.

138 PART I: BASIC ISSUES

has the potential to reduce them, not only but also by increasing the political costs of violations.

4.2 *Ius Contra Bellum*
4.2.1 Multilevel and Divers Instruments and Procedures
The means to ensure compliance with the prohibition of the use of force are different from those relating to the *ius in bello* just described. But in this field, too, there is a complex and multilevel mix of tools and procedures designed or used to ensure respect for the *ius contra bellum*.

A very important role is played by the political processes preceding the use of military force and having the potential to prevent it. These processes are both international and national. The legal discourses accompanying the decision-making processes relating to the use of force are of particular importance. They can increase or reduce the political cost of resorting to force.

At the international level, there is a hosts of mechanisms having this potential. It is important that there are ways for States to claim respect for their interests without resorting to force. International dispute settlement, where we not can observe a proliferation of procedures, is important in this respect. There are also measures which can reduce threats to security interests of State. This is in particular the case of arms control and disarmament. Be it noted that these mechanisms from time to time do not function and fall into crisis. Cases in point are the doubts about the respect of, or even clear violations of, the Non-proliferations Treaty in the case of Iraq,[218] North Korea[219] and Iran[220] or the suspension of the CFE Treaty[221] by Russia.

---

218   On the confused development of the arms control regime imposed upon Iraq by the Security Council in the armistice resolution 687 of 21 April 1991 see S. Ritter, "The Case for Iraq's Qualitative Disarmament", http://www.armscontrol.org/act/2000_06/iraqjun.asp?print.

219   On the somewhat erratic history of North Korea's accession to, violation of, rejection of and finally renewed adherence to, the NPT see http://www.armscontrol.org/factsheet/northkoreaprofile.aps.

220   At the time of writing (February 2008) the question of the purpose of the Iranian uranium enrichment program, which the Security Council wants Iran to abandon, is still a matter of controversy. The latest relevant Security Council resolution are 1696 of 31 July 2006, 1737 of 23 December 2006 and 1747 of 24 March 2007. See also the Report of the Director General of the IAEA on the Board of Governors, dated 15 November 2007, Doc. GOV/2007/58.

221   Effective 12 December 2007, the President of the Russian Federation suspended the 1990 Conventional Armed Forces in Europe (CFE) Treaty as a reaction to US plans to establish a missile defence system in Eastern and Central Europe.

4.2.2 Internalisation of Norms and the Role of National Checks and Balances

At the national level, the question is whether and to what extent there are political checks and balances which make it more difficult for a government to resort to the use of military force. As a rule, such checks and balances only exist in functioning democracies, and not to the same extent in all of them.[222] A major element of these checks and balances is the parliamentary control of governmental decisions to resort to force. A general trend can be ascertained in Western countries to increase the influence of parliaments on governmental decisions to use military force. This is highly developed in a number of continental European States,[223] it is a matter of attempts of political reform in the United Kingdom, and a matter of constitutional debate in the United States in particular since the Vietnam War and the controversial "War Powers Resolution".[224]

The courts also play a role in the national systems of checks and balances concerning governmental decisions to resort to force. There are not only procedural checks, such as the requirement of a parliamentary consent already mentioned, but also substantive constitutional rules which restrain the resort to military force and might therefore be enforced by the Courts. The best known of these substantive constitutional restraints is the article of the Japanese constitution which, if taken literally, would prevent Japan from having an army at all.[225] There is also a prohibition to resort to a war of aggression in a number of European constitutions. Although attempts have been made to use such provisions to enjoin governments not to engage in certain armed conflicts, the courts have rather shied away from using the powers they might have in this respect.[226]

---

[222] This consideration is the basis for the theory of democratic peace, B. RUSSETT, *Grasping the Democratic Peace: Principles of a Post-Cold War World,* Princeton 1993. For a recent critical analysis of the theory, see H. PATOMÄKI, "Global Security: Learning from Possible Futures", in H. G. Brauch et al. (eds.), *Globalization and Environmental Challenges. Reconceptualizing Security in the 21ˢᵗ Century,* Heidelberg 2008, 915, at 917 et seq.

[223] The most recent step in this direction is the 2008 constitutional revision in France, see Art. 35 of the French constitution as amended by the *Loi constitutionnelle* no. 2008–724 of 23 July 2008.

[224] 50 USC §§ 1541–1548; see M. BOTHE/ A. FISCHER-LESCANO, "The Dimension of Domestic Constitutional and Statutory Limits on the Use of Military Force", in Bothe/ O'Connell/ Ronzitti (eds.), op. cit. note, 195, at 203.

[225] M. BOTHE/ A. FISCHER-LESCANO, loc. cit. note 224, at 198.

[226] M. BOTHE/ A. FISCHER-LESCANO, loc. cit. note 224, at 207.

140   PART 1: BASIC ISSUES

Despite these checks and balances, a prominent means of "law enforcement" in respect of the *ius contra bellum* remains unilateral (self-defence). In this situation, the public discourse, public opinion is a necessary and also practically important means to ensure the respect of the prohibition to use force. The cases show, however, that there is a clear danger of abuse of the legal argument.[227]

4.2.3   Collective Security – the Role of the Security Council

The powers of the Security Council under the UN Charter are the major means of the international community to prevent and render unnecessary the unilateral resort to military force. Since the end of the East-West conflict, the Security Council seems to be in a better position to fulfil this responsibility. To maintain or restore peace is not the same as enforcing the law prohibiting resort to force, but the two should in most cases coincide. It is hard to imagine that under the Charter of the United Nations, peace can be maintained without upholding the rule of law. In this connection, the selectivity of the Council's approach is a major problem. There is no convincing rational criterion in the selection of cases where the Security Council acts and where it does not act. This is political horse trading where the veto power of the P5 plays an important, though not exclusive rule. Nevertheless, the fact that the Security Council since 1990 can play an active role as peace-maker constitutes an important progress. Be it noted that also in relation to the powers of the Security Council, as pointed out above, there is the danger of abuse of the legal argument.[228]

4.2.4   Judicial Procedures – International Dispute Settlement

This means that there is a genuine need for an objective clarification of the legal situation, i.e. for the use of judicial and quasi-judicial procedures. They play a practical role, albeit until now a marginal one. In the case of the *ius contra bellum*, too, there is the phenomenon of multilevel mechanisms. Both the national and international courts play a role. In addition, one has to distinguish between a preventive and a repressive role of courts.

As to prevention, this has so far been a matter of national procedures only, and not very successfully.[229]

---

227   See above 2.2.

228   See above notes 67 to 69 and accompanying text, for the case of Iraq; *cfr.* Also J. A. FROWEIN, "Uni-lateral Interpretation of Security Council Resolutions". In V. Götz/ P. Selmer/ R. Wolfrum (eds.), *Liber amicorum Günther Jaenicke – Zum 85. Geburtstag*, Berlin et al. 1998, pp. 97–112.

229   See above text accompanying note 226.

LIMITS OF FORCE IMPOSED BY INTERNATIONAL LAW

As to the legal evaluation of uses of force after they happened, the first relevant case before the ICJ was the Nicaragua case against the United States, a very bitter battle.[230] The United States refrained from participating in the proceedings on the merits. Nicaragua won, but later, after a change of government, withdrew the action before damages were awarded. Nevertheless, the case has been fundamental in shaping and clarifying the law on such matters as the definition of "armed attack" and collective self-defence. In the later case of Iran v. United States concerning the destruction of oil platforms in the Persian Gulf,[231] both sides pleaded on the basis of the holdings of the Court in the *Nicaragua case* – although the United States had rejected the earlier judgement. Once more on the basis of the holdings of Nicaragua, certain issues were clarified in the judgement in *DRC v. Uganda*.[232] There can be no doubt that the Nicaragua case has fundamentally shaped the law in question of the prohibition of the use of force.

But one must not be too optimistic. The role of the ICJ in enforcing the respect for the *ius contra bellum* remains limited. In the cases relating to the use of force, the major basis for the jurisdiction of the Court is the optional clause of Art. 36 (2) of the ICJ Statute. The network of jurisdictional links created by the declarations of States made under that provision still is too thinly woven. Only about a third of the States Parties to the Statute have made this declaration, and a number of them has made a reservation excluding defence or security matters.[233] Yugoslavia, alleging the illegality of the NATO bombing campaign during the Kosovo crisis 1999, has unsuccessfully tried an action on the basis of Art. 36 (2).[234]

In recent years, other forms of judicial dispute settlement also play a role. The recent example is the case law of the Ethiopia-Eritrea Claims Commission[235] which has also addressed the question of the *"ius ad bellum"* –although its competence to do so is not uncontroversial.[236]

---

230   *Military and Paramilitary Activities in and against Nicaragua (Nicaragua v. United States) (Merits)*, 27 June 1986.

231   *Oil Platforms (Iran v. United States) (Merits)*, 6 November 2003.

232   *Armed Activities on the Territory of the Congo (DRC v. Uganda)*, 19 December 2005.

233   For an analysis see BOTHE, loc. cit. note 188, at 147 et seq.

234   Legality of the Use of Force, cases of *Yugoslavia v. Belgium* and other States, Decisions of 2 June 1999, essentially confirmed by the Judgments of 15 December 2004, *Serbia-Montenegro v. Belgium* and other States.

235   See above note 203.

236   C. GRAY, "The Eritrea/Ethiopia Claims Commission Oversteps its Boundaries", 17 *EJIL* 699 (2006).

The latter case as well as the case of *DRC v. Uganda* at least give some hope for a greater role of international judicial dispute settlement in the enforcement of the *ius contra bellum*.

4.2.5 National and International Criminal Law

As to criminal law, the tribunals of Nuremberg and Tokyo also had jurisdiction over, and tried cases of, the violation of the prohibition of war as it existed at that time. The relevant provision of the Statutes of the Tribunals of Nuremberg and Tokyo is formulated as

> Crimes against the peace: namely, planning, preparation, initiation or waging of a war of aggression, or a war in violation of international treaties, agreements or assurances, or participation in a common plan or conspiracy for the accomplishment of any of the foregoing,[237]

A number of the leaders of Germany and Japan were sentenced on that account.

In contradistinction to war crimes, the crime of aggression did not play a role in the ensuing national prosecutions of crimes committed during the 2nd World War. Nor was the question of the violation of the *ius contra bellum* placed within the jurisdiction of the special tribunals created by the Security Council for the form Yugoslavia and for Rwanda. However, the "crime of aggression" falls within the jurisdiction of the ICC, but the entry into force of this provision is conditional upon the adoption of a definition of aggression in the form of a treaty amendment.[238] That competence of the ICC could effectively exclude the abuse of the legal argument justifying the use of force which has been pointed out above. But it is for that very reason that this extension of the Court's powers has met with considerable resistance. A number of States which otherwise support the Court (United Kingdom, France, Germany) have their own agenda of resorting to the use of force, shown by the fact that they participated in military action which were not mandated by the Security Council. The legality of these actions is controversial: Kosovo 1999, Afghanistan 2001, Iraq 2003. As long as this agenda exists, it is in the interest of these States to exercise some kind of political control over the possibility prosecutions for the crime of aggression. The technical way of achieving this control is to make any prosecution of the crime of aggression

---

237 Agreement for the Prosecution and Punishment of the Major War Criminals of the European Axis, 8 August 1945, Art. 6 (a).
238 Art. 5 (1)(d), (2) ICC Statute.

LIMITS OF FORCE IMPOSED BY INTERNATIONAL LAW

depend on a determination by the Security Council, i.e. some kind of political filter which could prevent prosecutions which are undesirable in the opinion of powerful States. The is the major problem encountered in the process of drafting the definition of the crime of aggression required by the Statute.[239]

There are also cases in which the obligation of an aggressor (or more generally of a State having violated the *ius contra bellum*) to pay compensation for the damages caused by that illegal act has been applied in practice: The first one is the United Nations Compensation Commission established by the Security Council after the defeat of Iraq in 1991.[240] The awards made by the Commission relate to the responsibility of Iraq for violations of the *ius contra bellum*, (with a minor exception) not to violations of the *ius in bello*.[241] This Compensation Commission has developed an extensive case law which sheds light on a number of issues of responsibility for war damages. As already mentioned the Ethiopia-Eritrea Claims Commission has also dealt with the question of damages for the violation of the *ius ad bellum*.

Thus, the web of measures designed to ensure the respect of the *ius contra bellum* is not as tight as it is for the *ius in bello*. But it exists. In this respect, it is important to note that there are both preventive and repressive mechanisms. The former ones are, in particular, the checks and balances to which national decision decisions to resort to force are subject (parliamentary control, judicial review). In addition, there are procedures within international organisations, in particular the United Nations which serve the purpose of preventing the use of force. The powers of the Security Council to take measures for the maintenance of peace and security are triggered by situations that may lead, but have not yet led to the use of force. It is important that such situations are systematically brought before, and dealt with by, the Security Council – a demand the fulfilment of which leaves to be desired.

---

239 As to the course of the negotiations, see the Report of the Special Working Group on the Crime of Aggression, Doc. ICC-ASP/5/35; Discussion Paper proposed by the Chairman, 16 January 2007, Doc. ICC-ASP/5/SWGCA/2; and the Report on the informal intersessional meeting of 25 July 2007, Doc. ICC-ASP/6/SWGCA/INF.1. In Julio 2010, the Review Conference of the Rome State adopted a treaty amendment on the crime of aggression which, however, will not be activated before the year 2017, Resolution RC/Res.b of 11 June 2010.

240 Resolution 687 of 3 April 1991, paras. 16–19; for a review see D. CARON/B. MORRIS, "The UN Compensation Commission: Practical Justice, not Retribution", 13 *EJIL*, pp. 183–199 (2002).

241 Cfr. M. BOTHE, " 'Other Relevant Rules of International Law' under Art. 31 of the Provisional rules for Claims Procedure", in A. Timoshenko (ed.), *Liability and Compensation for Environmental Damage, Compilation of Documents*, UNEP 1998, pp. 63–64.

PART 1: BASIC ISSUES

4.3   *The Relationship between the Ius Contra Bellum and the Ius in Bello*

It is in particular the question of compensation for damages which raises the problem of the relationship between the *ius in bello* and the *ius contra bellum*.

As it has been said in the beginning, both areas of international law constitute two levels of legal restraint on the use of military force. But how do they co-exist, legally speaking? It is only recently, with the development of enforcement mechanisms for both areas of the law, that the issue has gained practical relevance. This is in particular true for the conflict between Ethiopia and Eritrea where the International Claims Commission dealing with the conflict has addressed both areas of the law – although its competence to do so has been somewhat doubtful.[242]

In this respect, distinctions are necessary. As to criminal law sanctions, the coexistence between the two legal regimes is relatively easy. The respect for the *ius contra bellum* does not justify any violations of the *ius in bello*. Thus, the soldiers or other officials of a victim of aggression are criminally liable for any violation of the *ius in bello* they may have committed, and they cannot derive any justification from the fact that their State acted in self-defence. Thus, criminal responsibility for violations of both areas of the law can be applied in parallel.

In the case of claims for damages, however, there is the question of compensation of reciprocal claims. Violations of both legal regimes entail State responsibility and thus the duty to pay compensation for damages caused by such violations. Where the victim of an act of aggression, however, violates the *ius in bello*, it will as a rule be entitled to a reverse claim to damages caused by the entire war. But it can also be argued that the claim of the victim of a violation of the prohibition of the use of force is reduced to the extent that it has itself caused a damage in violation of the *ius in bello*.

5   Final Remark

International legal restraints on the use of military force are valid and not unrealistic. But they are not as effective as they should be. Thus, they continue to be a challenge for the international order and for the legal profession.

A few conclusions as to where we stand:

A political and cultural background for the respect of both areas of the law remains essential. In the field of the *ius in bello*, this is promoted by the dissemination of international humanitarian law and by a number of internal

---

242   GRAY, loc. cit. note 236.

LIMITS OF FORCE IMPOSED BY INTERNATIONAL LAW

measures such as military manuals and guidelines. In shaping a legal conscience, the role of criminal courts, both national and international, is essential. In the case of the *ius contra bellum* that role is rather played by international and national political processes, in particular parliamentary debate. The role of judicial procedures is less prominent, at least not as prominent as it should be.

The tremendous development of the international dispute settlement system has also had an influence on the law law relating to the use of military force, in both respects. The jurisprudence of the ICJ has greatly enriched the legal discourses accompanying and restraining the use of military force. International dispute settlement can also be a means to ensure that victims can really get a compensation for the losses they suffer as a result of armed conflict, a fundamental requirement of justice which makes itself felt in the international community.

Justice for the victims is also a fundamental concern of criminal law. It is in this sense that the rejection of "impunity" has to be understood. Both international and national criminal courts have engaged in this fight. That development is not without problems and obstacles. States are both too lenient and overactive in relation to criminal prosecutions, concerning their own or foreign nationals. The practical role of criminal law has been more important in the field of the *ius in bello* than in that of the *ius contra bellum*.

Bibliography

Arnold, R./Hildbrand, P. A. (ed.), *International Humanitarian Law and the 21st Century's Conflicts,* 2005.

Bothe, M., Partsch, K. J., Solf, W. A., *New Rules for Victims of Armed Conflicts. Commentary on the Two 1977 Additional Protocols to the Geneva Conventions of 1949,* 1982.

Bothe M./O'Connell, M.E. / Ronzitti, N. (eds.), *Redefining Sovereignty: The Use of Force After the Cold War,* 2005.

Brownlie, I., *International Law and the Use of Force by States,* 1963.

Byers, M., *War Law. Understanding International Law and Armed Conflict,* 2005.

Cassese, A. (ed.), *The Current Regulation of the Use of Force,* 1986.

David, E., *Principles de droit des conflits armés,* 4th ed. 2005.

Dinstein, Y., *The conduct of hostilities under the law of international armed conflict,* 2004.

Dinstein, Y., *war, Aggression and Self-Defence,* 4th ed. 2005.

Durham, H./ McCormack, T. L. H. (ed.), *The Changing Face of Conflict and the Efficacy of International Humanitarian Law,* 1999.

Fisler Damrosch, L./ Scheffer, D. J. (ed.), *Law and Force in the New International Order,* 1991.

Fleck, D. (ed.) *Handbook of International Humanitarian Law,* 2nd ed. 2008.

Franck, T.M., *Recourse to Force. State Action Against Threats and Armed Attacks,* 2002.

Gasser, H. P., *Humanitäres Völkerrecht,* 2007.

Gray, C., *International Law and the Use of Force,* 3rd ed. 2008.

Green, L. C., *The Contemporary Law of Armed Conflict,* 3rd ed. 2008.

Heintschel von Heinegg, W./ Epping, V. (Hrsg), *International Humanitarian Law Facing New Challenged, Symposium in Honour of Knut Ipsen,* 2007.

Henckaerts, J. M. / Doswald-Beck, Louise (ed.), *Customary International Humanitarian Law,* 2 vols., 2004.

Kolb, R., *Ius in bello. Le droit international des conflits armés,* 2nd ed. 2009.

Krisch, N., *Selbstvereidigung und kollektive Sicherheit,* 2001.

Pictet, J. S., *The Geneva Conventions of 12 August 1949, vol. I,* 1952; *vol. II,* 1960; *vol. III,* 1960; *vol. IV,* 1958.

Rogers, A. P. V., *Law on the Battlefield,* 2nd ed. 2004.

Ronzitti, N., *Diritto internazionale dei conflitti armati,* 3rd ed. 2006.

Sandoz, Y./ Swinarski, C./ Zimmermann, B. (Hrsg), *Commentary on the Additional Protocols of 8 June 1977 to the Geneva Conventions of 12 August 1949,* 1987.

Sassòli, M./Bouvier, A., *How Does Law Protect in War? Cases, Documents and Teaching on Contemporary Practice in International Humanitarian Law,* 2nd ed. 2006.

Schindler, D./ Toman, J. (eds.), *The Laws of Armed Conflicts,* 4th ed. 2004.

UK Ministry of Defence (Hrsg), *The Manual of the Law of Armed Conflict,* 2004.

Will Current International Crises Result in Structural Shifts in International Law?

The organizers of the conference formulated the subject as a question requiring prognosis.[1] Yet projections are, by definition, uncertain. Throughout the past three decades, the development of the international order has largely been characterized by surprises and therefore wrong predictions. One of the most blatant, yet fashionable errors during the early 1990s was the "end of history". Yet history has unfolded, taking a few unexpected turns. Thus, this contribution' must approach the subject with great modesty, trying to extrapolate a few expectations from what we have more or less recently observed.

1 A Chicken-and-Egg Problem

When trying to answer the above question, one encounters a chicken-and-egg problem: what are the causal links affecting the changing character of crises, in particular armed conflicts, and the changes to the international legal order? Is the international legal order in flux because crises reveal fluctuating characteristics? Or has the character of crises changed because the international legal order has changed? This question should be approached in a pragmatic way. Some characteristics of the traditional international legal order will be highlighted and then some challenges to those characteristics, which occurred over the last few decades, will be analyzed. The contribution will then try to evaluate the possible impact of these challenges on the functioning of the international legal system.

---

1 For a slightly modified German version, see Michael Bothe, 'Neue Formen bewaffneter Konflikte – neue Strukturen der internationalen Ordnung?' in G. Biaggini/O. Diggelmann/C. Kaufmann (eds.), *Polis und Kosmopolis. Festschrift für Daniel Thürer*, Dike/Nomos: Zürich/St. Gallen/Baden-Baden 2015, pp. 4 3 -54.

2 The Starting Point: The Traditional Structure of International Law and Its Relevance for Crisis Management

The traditional model of the international legal order is that of a system composed of sovereign territorial States. In principle, the whole terrestrial surface of the Earth has been divided among them. It is a decentralized legal system. In a formal sense, these States are equal on account of the principle of sovereign equality. States are the only – and in more recent times the primary – subjects of international law. International law mainly deals with the interactions between States in times of peace and war. They deal with each other via their central bureaucracies whose representatives in theory derive their full powers from the head of State. These bureaucracies have monopolized international relations. International law only regulates individuals, who are subject to States' jurisdiction, indirectly, e.g. where international law protects the interests of aliens. In this sense, the sovereign State is impermeable. Historical wisdom has it that this system was firmly established in 1648 by the Peace Treaties negotiated and concluded in Münster and Osnabrück (both situated in Westphalia) after the Thirty Years' War, which is why it is called the Westphalian system.[2]

Whether this is historically accurate is another matter. In any event, this model is often used for describing the overall structure of the international system. Reality has never fully corresponded to the model. In general, however, the model has been applied, and this has had a number of concrete implications for the present topic, how crises are dealt with.

2.1 *Law-making in the Westphalian System*

States are the masters of the international legal order. Their organs participate in the formation of customary international law. Their competent organs create legal rights and obligations for States by concluding treaties with one another. A particular aspect of this law-making is the negotiation and conclusion of international treaties through multilateral "diplomatic" conferences, i.e. conferences where State bureaucracies meet. A first major example of this development were the Hague Peace Conferences of 1899 and 1907. That approach was continued under the League of Nations and reached its peak in the codification conferences after the Second World War. Current international law

---

2 See Claus Kreß, 'Major Post-Westphalian Shifts and Some Important Neo-Westphalian Hesitations in the State Practice on the International Law on the Use of Force', vol. 1 *Journal on the Use of Force and International Law* 2014, pp. 11–54, a very inspiring text dealing with a number of issues discussed in the present contribution.

CRISES AND STRUCTURAL SHIFTS IN INTERNATIONAL LAW 149

was to a large extent shaped by these conferences. The Vienna Conventions on the law of treaties, on diplomatic and consular relations, but also the Geneva Conventions of 1949 (GC) and their Additional Protocols (AP) are key examples of that approach.

2.2   *The Law of Armed Conflict*

In that system, the State not only has the monopoly of the use of force in the internal sphere, it also has the monopoly of legitimizing military force in the external sphere. Traditional international law is indifferent as to the use of force in the internal sphere. It follows the inherent logic of the system to regard war as a State-to-State relationship, and the fundamental rule of the laws of war, the decisive basis for legal restraints on military force, namely the principle of distinction, conforms to that same reasoning. States exercise that monopoly only through a State organ specifically designated for that purpose, the armed forces. This is the only State organ with a "license to kill": if killing by members of the armed forces occurs within an armed conflict and respects the limits imposed by the laws of war, the act of killing will be lawful under international law. Members of the armed forces therefore enjoy "combatant privilege": no other State may punish them for such killing. Only the members of the armed forces enjoy this privilege. Members of the secret services, for example, do not. Military force may only be directed against the military effort of the opposing belligerent State. The principle of distinction has been refined and has been given effect. However, the various multilateral treaties ranging from the Paris Declaration of 1856 to the recent conventions on certain conventional weapons as well as B and C weapons have not altered this principle.

Nonetheless, the Westphalian system is only a model. Reality has never fully conformed to it. Yet the typical reaction of the actors involved in the system has been to create legal constructions designed to make the exceptions fit the model. International regulation of internal armed conflicts does not fit into the system. "Recognition of belligerency" did the trick, as it brought the non-State entity into the system. That proved impossible after the Spanish Civil War, during which there had been no recognition of belligerency. The time was ripe to modify the system, which was achieved through the adoption of Art. 3 common to the GC and, 25 years later, AP II. But that change did not really fit into the system. The question why this provision should be binding upon both sides was left to legal theory – which developed different yet difficult constructions to that end. There is only one serious treaty attempt to deal with this issue, namely Art. 96 para. 3 AP I, which provides for a special procedure to ensure the application of the Protocol in the case of a war of national liberation, a kind of modern recognition of belligerency.

A second problem is that of State organs with the license to kill. There have always been armed groups outside the armed forces. If certain conditions are met, they are equated with the armed forces. In this regard, special criteria (with significant variations) can be found in the Hague Regulations, the Geneva Conventions and AP I. Thus, the Westphalian model is preserved.

2.3 The Prohibition of the Use of Force – *Ius Contra Bellum*

When the freedom of States to resort to war was gradually restricted from the Paris Peace Treaties of 1919 onwards, the rules followed the logic of the Westphalian system. "War" was a specific kind of relationship between sovereign States. The prohibition to resort to "war" contained in the League of Nations Covenant was addressed to Member States and in the Briand-Kellogg Treaty, States Parties renounced war.

In the UN Charter, the prohibition of the threat or use of force applies to "all Members" "in their international relations", i.e. in inter-State relations. The right of self-defence, although the text does not say so explicitly, is interpreted as justifying the use of force by a State against an armed attack perpetrated by another State. This is the interpretation given by the ICJ in 2004 (*Wall* case).[3] The system of collective security is interpreted accordingly. During the first 55 years of its existence, the Security Council usually interpreted the "threat to or breach of the peace" in Article 39 of the UN Charter as a situation of inter-State use of force or threat thereof.

2.4 *International Dispute Settlement and Compliance*

The Westphalian model has also developed typical forms of conflict management. They are enumerated in Article 33 of the UN Charter. "Negotiation" is inter-State as are "arbitration" and "judicial settlement".

In the decentralized legal order, the typical unilateral means to ensure compliance with international law is reprisal, an injurious act which would be unlawful were it not used as a means to ensure compliance. In the law of armed conflict, belligerent reprisals did play a major practical, often unfortunate role. In this context, respect for the law essentially is a matter of reciprocity, at least from a practical point of view.

---

3 ICJ, *Legal Consequences of the Construction of a Wall in the Occupied Palestinian Territory,* Advisory Opinion, 9 July 2004, § 139.

3 The Challenges to the Westphalian System

After this review of relevant characteristics of the Westphalian system, it is now possible to analyze the challenges to that system as they have appeared in the last few decades. Some of them are really new, some appeared much earlier.

3.1 *The First System Change: International Organizations*

It must be briefly recalled that the first change to the decentralized Westphalian system was the establishment of international organizations since the end of the First World War. The United Nations and regional organizations account for many of the changes that must be addressed in the present context. But these organizations, at least in the beginning, did not modify the essentially intergovernmental character of the system.

3.2 *Further Steps: Civil War, Individual Criminal Responsibility and Human Rights*

At the end of the Second World War, three developments took place, which do not fit into the Westphalian model but were of great relevance to the future evolution of the international legal order. The introduction of these post-Westphalian norms, however, has been a difficult process.

As already indicated, an important type of non-state player is integrated into the international legal order by the Geneva Conventions of 1949, namely the parties to non-international armed conflicts (NIAC). This development has encountered serious difficulties. Article 3 common to the GC does not place civil war on the same footing as war between States, it is only a mini-convention. Nor does AP II of 1977 go as far as humanitarians would have liked in bringing the level of restraint on violence to that of international conflicts. The far-reaching approximation of the law applying to NIACs to the law applying to international armed conflicts happened more recently through the development of customary international law.[4] Yet it remains incomplete. States may still punish fighters in a NIAC for their participation in the conflict and there is no combatant privilege in NIACs. This is, so to say, the remaining resistance of the Westphalian system.

Another important step taken at the end of World War II was the recognition of individual criminal responsibility for war crimes, crimes against

---

4 Jean-Marie Henckaerts and Louise Doswald-Beck, *Customary International Humanitarian Law,* ICRC/CUP: Cambridge 2005, vol. 1, p. xxix.

humanity and crimes against peace, even if committed by State organs.[5] This is at odds with the idea of the impermeability of the sovereign State, one of the pillars of the Westphalian system. Despite the fact that the new rule was put into practice by the International Military Tribunals of Nuremberg and Tokyo and also by national courts, its general application remained, after these first cases, a utopian agenda for some decades to come. It finally gained widespread application in the 1990s, culminating in the establishment of the ICC.

The most fundamental innovation, however, was the international protection of human rights. It gives the individual a place in international law which runs counter to the very basis of the Westphalian system. The international protection of human rights has over the last seven decades changed the nature of the international order in a most fundamental way. It has led to a value orientation of the international order, a process called constitutionalization. This is relevant also for the way in which the system deals with conflicts.

3.3 *Current Challenges*

The State is the cornerstone of the Westphalian system. Therefore, one has to look at forms of discourse that cast doubt on the continued validity of the formal equality of States (sovereign equality). If a UN Secretary-General talks about the need to "redefine sovereignty",[6] we should contemplate what that could entail.

First, is sovereign equality on the demise? Different qualifications currently in use invite the question. There are "rogue States", "failed States", there is the phenomenon of "State terrorism". While the qualification of a State being "rogue" is devoid of any legal meaning, the concept "failed State" poses the serious legal problem of whether it enjoys the same protection of its borders against the use of force by other States as do non-failed States. Some authors maintain that it does not.[7] If this were true, one would have to develop a legal criterion of differentiation between the failed and other States. Any such attempt should be strongly discouraged. The real problem, namely the fact that so-called failed States often serve as a base of operations for terrorist organizations, has to be addressed through other legal considerations.

---

5   Art. 7 Charter of the International Military Tribunal, annexed to the London Agreement dated August 8th, 1945.

6   Among the abundant literature, see e.g. Michael Bothe/Mary Ellen O'Connell/ Natalino Ronzitti (eds.), *Redefining Sovereignty. The Use of Force after the Cold War,* Transnational Publishers: Ardsley 2005.

7   Matthias Herdegen, 'Der Wegfall effektiver Staatsgewalt', vol. 34 *Berichte der Deutschen Gesellschaft für Völkerrecht,* pp. 49–85 (1996), at p. 61.

The definition of the State is relevant for dealing with situations where certain changes in governmental structures result in the creation of a new State. True, this is an old question, and the traditional answer lies in effectivity. Yet, in formulating a response to the dissolution of former Yugoslavia, the Badinter Commission[8] developed additional criteria, namely respect for human rights and minorities as a precondition of recognition. It seems that the new value orientation of the international order creates a counterweight to, or at least supplements, the traditional importance of effectivity. Yet the latter still matters. Although the value orientation of international law certainly prohibits considering the IS as a State, that entity possesses effective governmental powers, despite its criminal character. It therefore makes sense to treat it as the equivalent of a State at least for the purpose of applying the rules of *ius ad bellum* and *ius in bello*. Thus, U.S. air strikes against IS positions can qualify as collective self-defense of Iraq.

This leads to a general discussion on the rise of non-State actors. The essential question is how these actors fit into the regulatory system of the international legal order, and in particular into the international law of armed conflict. In order to give an adequate answer to this question, different types of non-State actors have to be distinguished. There are, first, territorial units which have not attained statehood, e.g. parties to internal armed conflicts. It is sometimes difficult to determine who they are, e.g. in the case of the multiplicity of parties to the conflict in Syria. There are fighting groups that have no such territorial infrastructure, e.g. al-Qaeda. There are private fighters related to governments, although they do not form part of the armies, e.g. mercenaries, or private organizations performing functions otherwise fulfilled by the military, so-called PMC s. There are on the other hand organizations from civil society that assist victims of armed conflict, relief organizations. There are, last but not least, intergovernmental organizations. All these types of organizations or entities are part of an international reality that can be somewhat chaotic. Criteria are needed to determine how different entities are to be integrated into, or repressed by, the international legal system. In this sense, a new theory of the subjects of international law is needed. Developing such a theory poses both political and legal challenges. The current debate on a new compliance mechanism for international humanitarian law illustrates the point. There is general agreement that non-State actors

---

8   Malgosia Fitzmaurice, 'Badinter Commission (for the Former Yugoslavia)', in Rüdiger Wolfrum (ed.), *Max Planck Encyclopedia of Public International Law*, available at www.mpepil. com.

154 PART 1: BASIC ISSUES

have to be included, but proposals are lacking as to how this could or should be done.[9]

3.4 Current Procedures of Law-making in Quest of Efficiency and Legitimacy

The Westphalian approach to law-making is to leave it in the hands of "States", that means governmental bureaucracies. It is apparent that this traditional intergovernmental law-making system is too slow and inefficient. In particular, there is now a widespread reluctance of States to engage in treaty-making. The current slow and cumbersome process of designing a new mechanism for better implementation of IHL is a case in point. After years of debate, some modest achievements appear to be possible, but the procedures and institutions to be created are strictly voluntary, not based on a legally binding treaty.

In view of the difficulties of treaty-making, some procedures have been designed and applied to overcome the problem of the slowness or inefficiency of the traditional law-making processes.

One approach is the attempt of law-making by expert groups. Nongovernmental institutions establish expert groups to elaborate rules where the current state of the law seems to be unclear or insufficient, apparently in the hope to contribute in this way to the clarification and development of the law. This approach is not only used in the field of the law of armed conflict, but it has become particularly visible in this area. Examples are the San Remo Manual on International Law Applicable to Armed Conflicts at Sea and the San Remo Manual on the Law of Non-International Armed Conflicts, both established by the San Remo Institute of International Humanitarian Law, the Manual on International Law Applicable to Air and Missile Warfare elaborated by an expert group convened by HPCR at Harvard, and the Interpretive Guidance on the Notion of Direct Participation in Hostilities published by the ICRC, elaborated with the help of an expert group.

This expert work cannot replace treaties. However, to the extent that this work is accepted by relevant actors, i.e. by State organs applying the law, in particular national and international courts, and more generally in international discourse on crises and conflicts, it has the potential of becoming an agreed interpretation of treaties or customary international law. The Manuals mentioned above are quoted as evidence of customary international law; they are used in drafting national military manuals. This too is a slow process. But there

---

9   Michael Bothe, 'Warum wird humanitäres Völkerrecht eingehalten oder verletzt?' vol. 28 *Humanitäres Völkerrecht. Informationsschriften,* pp. 55–67 (2015), at p. 65.

CRISES AND STRUCTURAL SHIFTS IN INTERNATIONAL LAW

is a lower risk of it being blocked. It is therefore an important supplement to intergovernmental treaty-making. What matters is acceptance by relevant actors, which must be carefully analyzed. In this respect, the State bureaucracies retain a crucial role. The Westphalian system of law-making is modified, but not really replaced by something else.

Another phenomenon which has to be discussed in this context is what can be called enhanced intergovernmental law-making. There are in particular treaty-making procedures with essential input from civil society. There is no major international conference on treatymaking or treaty application (conferences of States Parties to a treaty) without intensive civil society participation. Their lobbying is a great treaty facilitator. The recent treaties on the ban of antipersonnel mines and on cluster munitions are good examples of efforts by civil society. They would not have been possible without that input. The movement, however, is not always successful, as is shown by the failure of U.S. NGOs to overcome the resistance of the U.S. Government to the Rome Statute of the ICC. As a reaction to the leading role in the development of IL claimed by the ICRC, the governments insisted at the 31st International Red Cross and Red Crescent Conference that the process of establishing or strengthening means for better compliance with that law had to be "State-driven", i.e. the State bureaucracies had to be in the driver's seat.'[10] The Westphalian system resists challenges, with all the negative consequences that has for the problem solving capacity of the system.

3.5   *The Prohibition of the Use of Force – Just Wars?*

One of the current challenges to the Westphalian system relates to the prohibition of the use of force. We can observe, in international discourse, an attempt to expand the license to use force through legal constructions. There are actually two such attempts. The first one fits well into the traditional Westphalian system, namely the debate about imminence, i.e. the permission to use force against an attack that is expected sooner or later, but has not yet taken place. That debate still centres on the meaning or continued validity of the so-called Webster formula ("necessity of self-defence, instant, overwhelming, leaving no choice of means and no moment for deliberation"),[11] formulated in 1841, in the heyday of the Westphalian system.

---

10   31st International Conference of the Red Cross and Red Crescent, Resolution 1: "Strengthening Legal Protection for Victims of Armed Conflicts", OP 6: "recognizing the primary role of States in the development of international humanitarian law".

11   Christopher Greenwood, 'Caroline, The, in *MPEPIL, supra* note 8.

The second one is closely related to the emergence of non-State actors. Traditionally, self-defence is allowed as a reaction to an armed attack perpetrated by a State against another State. Currently, the argument is made that self-defence is also justified against an armed attack coming from a non-State actor. Legal practice during the first decades of the United Nations solved the problem of non- State cross-border use of force via a rule of attribution. An attack by a non-State actor constitutes aggression and triggers a right of self-defence against the State where the attack originated if the latter State is "substantially involved" in the attack. This is the definition used in the GA Resolution on the Definition of Aggression and quoted as a rule of customary international law by the ICJ in the *Nicaragua* case.'[12] This rule of attribution has its own difficulties regarding the degree of control that triggers attribution. This has led to an often mentioned controversy between the ICJ and the ICTY. The post-Westphalian approach holds that the detour via the rule of attribution is unnecessary. The attacks committed by al-Qaeda on 9/11 are said to trigger a right of self-defence of the U.S. against al-Qaeda in Afghanistan (or anywhere else al-Qaeda is found), regardless of whether the Afghan government of the time (the Taliban government), or any other government, was substantially involved. Although it has been argued that this is the correct, so to say post-Westphalian legal construction of the right to self-defence, it remains problematic. Military force against al-Qaeda strongholds situated on the territory of a given State constitutes an armed attack against the territorial integrity of that State. What can be the justification for self-defence against the territory of a State except the fact that the targeted State is somehow involved in the non-State entity's use of force? On the basis of said post-Westphalian construction, the U.S. has conducted vast campaigns of targeted killings, mainly by drones, in a number of countries. It would certainly be an exaggeration to state that this practice is accepted by the international community at large as being the new law. I submit that the Westphalian construction still makes sense and is upheld by a number of States sufficient to disallow any conclusion that the post-Westphalian approach constitutes the new law.

3.6 *The Law of Armed Conflict - Whither the Principle of Distinction?*

Another important challenge to an essential element of the Westphalian system, namely the principle of distinction, is the constructive expansion of the

---

12   ICJ, *Military and Paramilitary Activities in and against Nicaragua* (*Merits*) (*Nicaragua v. U.S.*), Judgment, 27 June 1986, § 195.

CRISES AND STRUCTURAL SHIFTS IN INTERNATIONAL LAW 157

"license to kill", which can be observed in international discourse. Based on the rule that in armed conflicts combatants and civilians directly taking part in hostilities may be targeted by deadly force, the post-Westphalian legal construction put forward by the U.S. has it that there is an international armed conflict between the U.S. and international terror, and that therefore those fighting for international terror constitute legitimate military objectives even if they are not fighting at the time they are killed. They are branded "unlawful combatants". That construction, too, is not accepted as law by the international community at large. Combatants are only persons who derive their license to kill from the fact that they belong to the armed forces or an equivalent armed unit belonging to a State. Only these persons can be targeted any time anywhere. When caught, they enjoy combatant privilege unless they have lost it for a particular reason, e.g. because they have failed to distinguish themselves while fighting. Other persons using force are just criminals and may be treated as such. Yet the use of deadly force against criminals is lawful only as a means of last resort in order to protect persons against an imminent threat or as a means to stop a fleeing criminal. It is worth noting that the German Advocate General, in a recent case involving a drone attack killing an alleged terrorist fighter in Pakistan, has expressly refrained from applying the U.S. doctrine of there being an international armed conflict with international terror.[13] He instead declared the attack to be lawful because it was directed by the agents of one party to a non-international conflict, namely the U.S., against the fighters of another party. He construed two interconnected non-international armed conflicts, one in Afghanistan and one in Pakistan, the U.S. being an intervening party in both of them. That deserves further discussion. Doubt as to the correctness of that decision may be raised for other reasons. It grants the "license to kill", i.e. combatant status, to the agents of the CIA who conducted the operation. This is problematic as another element of the principle of distinction has been undermined. Be that as it may, the post-Westphalian construction expanding the license to kill by making persons lawful military targets who according to a traditional legal understanding would just be civilian criminals has not been accepted as law by the international community at large.

Another current challenge to the principle of distinction is the so-called asymmetrical conflict. This is a conflict where one (State or non-State) party

---

13   Generalbundesanwalt (Federal Chief Prosecutor), Decision dated 20 June 2013, available at www.generalbundesanwalt.de/docs/drohneneinsatz-vom_04oktober2010_mir_ali_pakistan.pdf.

systematically uses means of attack in violation of the law of armed conflict because it would be in a situation of inferiority if it only used lawful means.[14] This is a fundamental challenge to reciprocity as a means to ensure compliance with the laws of war as the superior party is tempted to violate the law as well. But reciprocity is only an incentive for compliance, not its legal precondition. Value-free reliance on reciprocity is incompatible with the current value orientation of the international legal system. Reciprocity has no place where fundamental values of the system are at stake.

A final challenge is the emergence of cyber warfare. It is a challenge for the role of the State. Traditional *ius in bello* and *ius ad bellum* address the State as actor and target, and relate acts of individuals to the State through rules of attribution. Cyber warfare is characterized by the difficulty, even impossibility, of clearly attributing an act of hostility to a State. The Tallinn Manual on the International Law Applicable to Cyber Warfare[15] has great merit in showing how to apply the traditional law of armed conflict to cyber warfare, and it has addressed, but not really solved this problem of attribution. This is a challenge to the Westphalian system, but the solution can only be found in a neo-Westphalian approach. There must be new rules enjoining States to adopt measures of control that can overcome the attribution problem. Non-governmental netiquette alone cannot be a solution in situations of armed conflict, or where causation of damage equivalent to armed conflict is at stake. This is easier said than done.

3.7 *International Dispute Settlement and Compliance*

Perhaps the most important changes to the Westphalian system are those affecting the means designed to ensure compliance with international obligations and corresponding dispute settlement procedures.

The traditional means to induce States to comply with their obligations, reprisals, have fallen into disrepute. In the decentralized international order, there is always a risk of allegations and counterallegations of unlawful acts which may lead to a mutual escalation of claims of unlawful behaviour and thus of reprisals. In the ILC Articles on State Responsibility, what used to be reprisals are now called "countermeasures", which are carefully circumscribed.

---

14   Michael N. Schmitt, 'Asymmetrical Warfare and International Humanitarian Law', in Wolff Heintschel von Heinegg/Volker Epping (eds.), *International Humanitarian Law Facing New Challenges. Symposium in Honour of Knut Ipsen,* Springer: Heidelberg/ Berlin 2007, pp. 11–48.

15   Michael N. Schmitt (ed.), *Talinn Manual on the International Law Applicable to Cyber Warfare,* CUP: Cambridge 2013.

CRISES AND STRUCTURAL SHIFTS IN INTERNATIONAL LAW

In IIL, there are now many cases of explicitly prohibited reprisals, namely reprisals against most categories of victims of armed conflict.

Another possible approach to the problem of countermeasures is that adopted by the WTO, where States' responses to alleged violations of trade rules are subject to a highly sophisticated dispute settlement procedure. Countermeasures are lawful only if they have passed the test of dispute settlement. In other fields of the law, institutionalized dispute settlement has not reached the same degree of refinement, but it is faring quite well. Both the ICJ and international arbitration are indeed used, even with a certain degree of success, to settle disputes involving the use of force.

The emergence of non-State actors and the perspective of individuals affected by the armed conflict, however, pose a problem for the traditional dispute settlement system. International adjudication still is strictly intergovernmental. This means that interests not sponsored by governments are strongly disadvantaged. The case between Germany and Italy concerning jurisdictional immunities illustrates the problem. It related to proceedings before Italian courts brought by victims of German war crimes claiming compensation. The Italian courts had rejected Germany's claim of jurisdictional immunity, and Germany brought the case before the ICJ claiming that the Italian courts had violated German rights. The governments of Germany and Italy were in agreement that immunity had to be granted, but Italy was sued by Germany because of the alleged violation committed by the Italian courts. Although the Italian agents did an admirable job defending the position of the Italian courts (and the interests of the victims by the same token) as distinguished from the position of the Italian Government which had to hire them, the situation would have been completely different if the true parties in interest, namely the victims, had been given their day in court.[16]

It should be noted that international arbitration has become more open to participation of non-State parties. The rules of the PCA now allow for cases to be brought by or against non-State parties, a possibility that still has not been used in any case involving the use of force.

Yet the most fundamental change in litigation concerning international crises and the use of force is the role of individual remedies, i.e. procedures granting the victim of an international wrong direct access to a court capable of rendering a binding decision. This change has effects at two levels: cases

---

16   Michael Bothe, 'Remedies of Victims of War Crimes and Crimes against Humanity: Some Critical Remarks on the ICJ's Judgement on the Jurisdictional Immunity of States', in Anne Peters/Evelyne Lagrange/Stefan Oeter/Christian Tomuschat (eds.), *Immunities in the Age of Global Constitutionalism*, Brill/Nijhoff: Leiden/Boston 2015, pp. 99–115, at p. 101.

before international human rights courts (or other human rights treaty bodies) and remedies before national courts.

Although the ECtHR has had some difficulties in dealing with cases involving armed conflicts, it had to (and did) deal with important cases brought by victims of military force: cases concerning non-international armed conflicts (the Chechnya cases),[17] cases of detention (*Al-Skeini*[18] and more recently *Hassan*[19]) or other cases where the State bound by the European Convention exercises *de facto* control (the Cyprus cases[20]). This truly is a post-Westphalian improvement of formal procedures to ensure compliance with relevant international law and to protect victims of armed violence.

Individual remedies before national courts are more difficult, but their role is increasing. They are needed and useful to close a "justice gap" left by governmental and intergovernmental handling of victim compensation. Actions brought by persons subjected to forced labor by Germany during the Second World War before U.S. courts finally led to the establishment of the Foundation "Remembrance, Responsibility and Future" which provided for several billion USD in compensation paid to victims of that particular type of war crime. The plaintiffs in some of the Italian cases still have a chance despite the ICJ's judgment as the Italian Constitutional Court enjoined Italian courts for constitutional reasons not to implement the decision of the World Court.[21] The fight goes on.

Non-judicial dispute settlement has become open to the participation of non-State parties – albeit with certain difficulties. The inclusion of non-State parties has been achieved with great legal ingenuity. An early example can be found in the Paris Peace Talks between the U.S. and North Vietnam in the 1970s, where both States had to bring along their respective ally considered to be non-State by the other side: North Vietnam with the Vietcong and the U.S. with the government of South Vietnam. The problem was solved by the particular shape of the negotiating table, French carpenters providing good offices. A recent problem is the Minsk process concerning Ukraine, where one side refuses to speak to the rebels, while the other insists that these very rebels have to be involved. A sophisticated system of nightly parallel negotiations was established. It worked, at least to a certain extent. The problem was also faced

---

17   ECt.HR, *Isayeva, Yusupova and Bazayeva v. Russia,* Grand Chamber, 24 February 2005, App. 57947/00, 57948/00, 57949/00.

18   ECt.HR, *Al Skeini v. UK,* Grand Chamber, 7 July 2011, App. 55721/07.

19   ECt.HR, *Hassan v. UK,* Grand Chamber, 16 September 2014, App. 29750/09.

20   ECt.HR, *Loizidou v. Turkey (Preliminary Objections),* Judgment, 23 March 1995, 15318/89.

21   Italian Constitutional Court, Judgment of 23 October 2014, no. 238.

by earlier peace talks concerning Syria, and if that conflict is to be solved, the issue will again have to be addressed.

Dispute settlement has become post-Westphalian. It is open to the representation of a variety of interests (including non-governmental interests, or interests not sponsored by governments) yet still not sufficiently so. The value orientation of the international order, or the constitutionalization of this order has a greater chance.

4 The Current and Future International Legal Order

Have international crises, or the ways in which these crises are managed, fundamentally changed the character of the international legal order? We have somewhat reformulated the question: has the international legal order become post-Westphalian in the sense that its old intergovernmental character has been undone? There are certainly some important and salutary post-Westphalian elements. The system is more open to the different interests at stake, and therefore, it is submitted, it has become more humane. The system includes procedures for defending basic values. A major factor of this change is globalization. The centralization of the system brought about by the development of international organizations is now supplemented by a global civil society. Different strands of opinion form part of a global discourse on conflicts and conflict settlement.

But there are more fundamental changes, continuous challenges and unsolved problems. The modern State has lost a good deal of its monopolies, but in a globalized world, where the economy, civil society, public opinion and (yes!) crime have shaped global networks, the State and its governing elites have increased responsibilities. The requirements flowing from a global system cannot be fulfilled without some order. It is the task of governing and bureaucratic elites working together to ensure that order: fighting injustices that happen anywhere or on a global scale, protecting human beings against all kinds of infringements. This is of course a responsibility that goes well beyond the subject of this paper, which is how the system deals with crises. But crisis management is part of this challenge, and international law has to be developed in a way that gives law its appropriate role in meeting the challenge.

PART 2

International Security

6

Terrorism and the Legality of Pre-emptive Force

1   Introduction: Current Scenarios

The title of this article is formulated in general and abstract terms. It is not intended to provide a legal opinion on a particular event or contingency. Nevertheless, if legal science is to make a meaningful contributions to the ongoing debate on the legitimate use of force in international relations, it must consider specific scenarios. As will be shown, certain variations regarding facts trigger different legal arguments. If these differences are brought to bear, the paper has indeed to refer to current policy debate and actual policy planning, as is documented, for instance, in the 'National Security Strategy' submitted to Congress by President Bush on 17 September 2002. This is also the approach taken by Abraham Sofaer in his contribution to this symposium.

The Strategy can be seen in the tradition of an older debate which received new impetus after the end of the East-West conflict: the perception of 'new threats'[1] and the discussion about effective and legitimate responses to these threats. The Strategy brings specific threats into sharp focus and pinpoints specific means of dealing with them, including but not limited to the use of military force.

The scenario of the threats is twofold. The first scenario is non-state violence, i.e. terrorism – whatever the exact definition of that phenomenon might be. The second is the existence of 'rogue' states, which may harbour or at least support terrorists and/or which possess or acquire weapons of mass destruction (WMD) and are willing to use them without restraint.

2   The Point of Departure: The Illegality of Anticipatory Self-defence

The point of departure of the legal debate is uncontroversial: the prohibition of the use of force is a valid norm of customary international law and is enshrined in the Charter of the United Nations. Thus, any specific use of force can be lawful only if it can be based on an exception to this rule which is valid

---

1   Weller, 'The Changing Environment for Forcible Responses to Non-Traditional Threats', 92 *ASIL Proceedings* (1988) 177.

© KONINKLIJKE BRILL NV, LEIDEN, 2021 | DOI:10.1163/9789004380592_008

as a matter of law. Leaving aside the question of intervention by invitation, there are two such exceptions: self-defence and authorization by a competent international organization.

Furthermore, it is uncontroversial that lawful self-defence requires the existence of an armed attack. It is on the interpretation of that principle that there is indeed disagreement. For this principle is only the starting-point of the legal debate when it comes to the assessment of particular situations. There are at least three questions:

– What exactly is an armed attack? Could it be understood as including threats to use force? Are there, in addition, situation which, as a matter of law are to be considered as equivalent to an armed attack?
– Who, in addition to the immediate victim, is entitled to use the right to self-defence?
– What is the point of reference for determining what is attack and what is self-defence? This is a question which arises where acts of violence occur in the context of an existing larger framework of tension or reciprocal use of force.

We shall now examine these questions in order.

3   The Definition of Armed Attack

According to the rule of customary international law, which is formulated in Article 31 of the Vienna Convention on the Law of Treaties, the interpretation of the Charter must start with the 'ordinary meaning to be given to the terms of the treaty'. It is by this means that one must ascertain whether and to what extent an attack may include an action which is threatened, but which has not yet occurred. The usual method of ascertaining this 'ordinary meaning' is by recourse to dictionaries. Thus, Webster's Encyclopedic Dictionary states: 'an offensive military operation with the aim of overcoming the enemy ...', or: 'an offensive move in a performance or contest', and: 'Attack ... applies to the beginning of hostilities'. The Oxford Dictionary defines attack as: 'violent attempt to hurt, overcome, defeat'. All of these definitions imply that attack is an actual action in the sense of a move forward. A threat of action does not yet constitute an attack in the ordinary meaning of the term.

But Article 31 also refers to the ordinary meaning of the terms 'in their context'. This means that other parts of the text have to be analysed as to whether they shed some light on the meaning of a certain term. As to the meaning of the term 'armed attack' in Article 51, one has first to take into account the text immediately connected to the term. The relevant sentence reads: '... an armed attack occurs'. It does not add 'or threatens'. This also suggests that what is means is an attack which actually happens, not one which is merely likely to happen.

The next element of the context which needs to be considered is the formulation of the rule to which Article 51 constitutes the exception: Article 2(4) prohibits both the threat and the use of force. Thus, the Charter framers clearly were aware of the problem of the threat of force. It is hard to conceive that it was merely due to a drafting oversight that the notion of threat was only mentioned in the rule and not in the exception.

Furthermore, it is appropriate to refer to Article 39, which defines those situation where the Security Council may take action under Chapter VII of the Charter, while Article 51 defines the situations where a state may unilaterally decide to use military force. In Article 39, three terms are used: 'threat to the peace, breach of the peace, or act of aggression'. These notions together, quite obviously, cover a field which is broader than that of an armed attack within the meaning of Article 51. In this provision, too, the framers of the Charter did indeed consider the situation of a 'threat', but the text clearly suggests that the power to authorize the use of force in the case of a mere threat lies with the Security Council alone. Such case remains below the threshold at which a state may decide to use force unilaterally.

Finally, according to Article 31 of the Vienna Convention again, the meaning of the term of a treaty must be ascertained 'in the light of its object and purpose'. It is the object and purpose of the Charter of the United Nations to restrain the unilateral use of force. An interpretation which excludes the threat of an attack from the notion of armed attack that triggers the right to self-defence is certainly compatible with, if not required by, this object and purpose.

The conclusion is thus clear: 'armed attack' in the sense of Article 51 is an actual armed attack, which happens ('occurs'), not one which is only threatened. This conclusions is shared by the overwhelming majority of legal doctrine, which clearly holds 'anticipatory self-defence' to be unlawful.[2]

This being so, the use of force in response to a perceived threat of an attack con be considered as lawful only if it is possible to show that, for some

---

2 Y. Dinstein, *War, Aggression, and Self-Defence* (1988), at 184; Randelzhofer, 'Article 51', in B. Simma (ed.), *The Charter of the United Nations. A Commentary* (2nd ed., 2002) 803 (with many references, but citing no position to the contrary): O'Connell, 'The Myth of Pre-emptive Self-Defence', Paper prepared in conjunction with the ASIL Presidential Task Force on Terrorism, at 8 *et seq* (also containing further references).

reason, the interpretation of the term 'armed attack' must be construed more broadly, using a broader notion of context, founding itself on more general consideration. If one considers strategies of legal reasoning which are used, in practice, to justify the use of force in particular cases, the approach based on an expansive interpretation of 'armed attack' is very common. Two examples may be given before we turn to the question of anticipatory or pre-emptive self-defence.

The first example is that of indirect attacks. The rule prohibiting the use of force applies to situations involving states; it is not, as a matter of principle, concerned with actors which are not subject of international law. However, in situation whereby a state is actually involved, to a sufficient degree, in non-state violence, it is indeed accepted that this involvement is equivalent to an armed attack and may thus entail the same consequences as an armed attack, namely it can trigger the right of self-defence. To quote the definition of aggression adopted by the General Assembly in 1974:[3]

> Any of the following acts qualify as an act of aggression:
>
> ...
>
> (g) The sending by or on behalf of a State of armed bands, groups, irregulars or mercenaries, which carry out acts of armed force against another State of such gravity as to amount to the acts listed above (i.e. acts of transborder military force by state organs), or its substantial involvement therein.

In its *Nicaragua* judgment, the ICJ accepted this text as being an expression of customary law and took it as a point of departure for the legal assessment in that particular case.[4] On the basis of this construction, the intervention of the United States and its allies in Afghanistan after September 11 was, controversial details apart, justified as self-defence. This is an approach to legal reasoning which can be called a constructive armed attack, or a situation equivalent to an armed attack.

The second example of this constructive armed attack approach is the so-called 'blue water theory'. It has remained controversial and is now legal history. According to this theory, to quote the 'Friendly Relations' Declaration of the General Assembly,[5]

---

3 GA Res. A/3315 of 14 December 1974.
4 *Military and Paramilitary Activities in and against Nicaragua,* ICJ Reports (1986) 14, at 103.
5 Annex to Resolution 2625 (XXV).

> [t]he territory of a colony or other non-self-governing territory has, under the Charter, a status separate and distinct from the territory of the State administering it ...

The consequence of this construction is, then, drawn in the elaboration of the prohibition of the use of force:

> Every State has the duty to refrain from any forcible action which deprives peoples referred to in the elaboration of the principle of equal rights and self-determination of their right to self-determination and freedom and independence.

The background of these formulation is the attempt, be it achieved or not, to construe the suppression of fights for decolonization as armed attacks which thereby trigger a right of (individual and collective) self-defence.

These examples may suffice to show that the concept of constructive armed attack, or a situation equivalent to an armed attack, is not foreign to the arsenal of international legal reasoning. But whether such constructions have really become positive international law is another question. In this respect, one has to note that the use of the consequence of the 'blue water theory' to serve as a legal justification of counterforce was not really accepted by the Western powers at the relevant time. This International Court of Justice, in its *Nicaragua* judgment, which accepting the construction of an armed attack by involvement in non-state transborder violence, gave it a somewhat restrictive interpretation which, according to some authors, sheds some doubts on the legality of the US intervention in Afghanistan, a view which I do not share.

Having these general consideration concerning the interpretation of the notion of armed attack in mind, we can now turn to the question of anticipatory or pre-emptive self-defence. Many authors acknowledge that a threat may be so direct and overwhelming that it is just not feasible to require the victim to wait to act in self-defence until the attack has actually started. In this case, a situation equivalent to an armed attack prevails. A formula expressing this idea and its limits, which is not uncontroversial,[6] but still quoted with considerable agreement, is that pleaded by the United States in the *Caroline* case in 1841: There must be 'a necessity of self-defence, instant overwhelming, leaving no choice of means, and no moment for deliberation'.[7] It is thus at least

---

6   Randelzhofer, *supra* note 2; O'Connell, *supra* note 2.

7   State Secretary Webster, *British and Foreign State Papers* 29 (1840–1841), at 1129, 1138.

170 PART 2: INTERNATIONAL SECURITY

defensible that the principle of necessity and immediacy, as expressed in the *Caroline* formula, be considered as part of customary international law, even under the United Nations Charter.[8] I submit that this is as far as pre-emptive self-defence possibly goes under current international law.

It is interesting to note that President Bush's National Security Strategy seems to recognize this as being the law, as the same time distancing itself from it:[9]

> Legal scholars and international jurists often conditioned the legitimacy of pre-emption on the existence of an imminent threat – most often a visible mobilization of armies, navies and air forces preparing an attack.

This is a point of departure based on the *Caroline* formula. But the text continues:

> We must adapt the concept of imminent threat to the capabilities and objective of today's adversaries ... The greater the threat, the greater the risk of inaction – and the more compelling the case for taking anticipatory action to defend ourselves, even if uncertainty remains as to the time and place of the enemy's attack.

It is hard to tell whether this is meant as an argument *de legal lata* or *de lege ferenda*. There is nothing in current state practice, case law or legal writing which would suggest this broad, even overly broad construction of a situation equivalent to an armed attack is part of positive customary law today. The marriage between the precautionary principle, known from the field of national and international environmental law, and the right to self-defence is, to say the least, a novelty. In the field of environmental law, the precautionary principle means that action to protect the environment may or must be taken, even in the case of uncertainty about the danger. If transferred to the field of legitimization of the use of force, that rule would the read: in case of uncertainty, strike – a somewhat weird conclusion.

Whether or not the argument of the gravity of the threat is valid as a matter of fact, a good factual argument does not make new law. The *lex ferenda* aspect of the argument will analysed below. *De legal lata,* however, the expansion of

---

8 Dinstein, *supra* note 2, at 182, 244; Meng, 'The Caroline', in R. Bernhardt (ed.), *Encyclopedia of Public International Law*, vol. 1 (2000), at 537 *et seq.*

9 'National Security Strategy', at 15, available at www.whitehouse.giv/nsc/nss.html.

TERRORISM AND THE LEGALITY OF PRE-EMPTIVE FORCE

the right of anticipatory self-defence proposed in the National Security Strategy is not acceptable.

There are voices that contradict this assertion. They maintain that a broader interpretation of admissible self-defence is still the law, that older conceptions of permissible self-defence have somehow survived the entry into force of the Charter of the United Nations. The argument takes as a point of departure an argument which constitutes a recourse to context, as already mentioned above. The particular context used for the interpretation is a further element in the text of Article 51, namely that it recognizes self-defence as an 'inherent' right. They understand this word as a referral to previous concepts of self-defence predating the Charter. As a matter of textual interpretation, one can engage in a kind of intellectual game: Does the notion of an inherent right allow or even require a broader interpretation of the term 'armed attack'? Or does the narrow notion of an armed attack, used without qualification or addition, limit the concept of an inherent right? Both constructions are logically possible. But it is certainly not possible, without betraying the basic professional rules of interpretation, to re-interpret the notion of self-defence, understood, according to the ordinary meaning as developed above, as a proportionate response to an actual attack, as meaning any use of force reasonable under the (threatening) circumstances. Whether or not the *Caroline* formula was too restrictive as far as the law of the nineteenth century is concerned, whether or not a broader concept of the use of pre-emptive force is based on natural law concepts was positive law in the nineteenth century, nothing in state practice suggest that such concept could have survived the entry into force of the Charter or has been revived since that date. Any other conclusion would treat both the Kellog-Briand Pact and the Charter of the United Nations incorrectly as being irrelevant.

This is true, although, admittedly, the concept of necessity as expressed in the *Caroline* formula is not static.[10] It is a concept which allows for some flexibility and adaptation to the circumstances of each particular case. But it certainly cannot be extended to a situation where there is uncertainty – and time for many months to debate in national and international fora, including serious negotiations on ways of handling the dispute other than by the use of military force.[11]

---

10   See Kirgis, 'Pre-emptive Action to Forestall Terrorism', *ASIL Newsletter*, July/September 2002, at 5.

11   In this respect, it is useful to note the analysis of the threat posed by Iraq contained in a recent paper published by the UK Government, a paper designed to justify the US approach: whether there are any remaining stock of BW or CW substances is uncertain, and it is probable that there are some production facilities that could be used ('Iraq's

4 The 'Attacker': The Failed State and Non-state Force

Another scenario related to that of 'indirect' force, already mentioned above, has also to be analysed in this context, namely situations where armed force is used by non-state groups from a territory which is not effectively controlled by the (or a) government of the state in question. The question arises whether this could be considered a situation equivalent to an armed attack by that state according to the 'substantial involvement' formula reported above, this would probably not be the case. In the case of a failed state, there is no government to be 'involved'.

Or can an omission constitute an involvement? This appears somewhat doubtful. On the other hand, it is possible to argue that indeed an omission is equivalent to an action where there is a legal duty to act that is violated by the omission. On the basis of the assumption that there is a legal duty of every state to prevent transborder activities of terrorism originating from its territory, that construction may be considered valid. It is to be recognized that this may be the only way in which a state is able to protect itself against transborder force in a case where a right to self-defence would exist if that force were used by organs of the neighbouring state.[12] This construction is in any event preferable to a thesis, which can sometimes be found in legal doctrine, to the effect that a 'failed state' is not protected by the principle of the prohibition of the use of force.

5 The Victim and Others: Collective Self-defence

The current debate about a pre-emptive strike against Iraq raises an additional problem as to who is entitled to exercise a right of self-defence. Self-defence is the right of the victim of an attack. Although the prohibition of the use of force may be considered as an obligation valid *erga omnes*, the right of individual

---

Weapons of Mass Destruction. The Assessment of the British Government', at 19 *et seq*, available at www.official-documents.co.uk/document/reps/Iraq/cover.htm). No nuclear weaponry is currently available, but Iraq might acquire the ability to produce such weapons under certain conditions which may or may not be fulfilled in the future (*ibid.*, at 26 *et seq*). All this is not the type of immediate threat which leaves 'no moment for deliberation'.

12 It may be argued that this was the true justification for the British attack on the *Caroline*, which gave rise to the diplomatic correspondence from which the famous formula used by Webster stems.

TERRORISM AND THE LEGALITY OF PRE-EMPTIVE FORCE

self-defence accrues only to the victim of the attack. In other words: no self-defence without a victim.[13]

Assuming pre-emptive self-defence were lawful, it would be the supposed or anticipated victim that possessed this right. Where the *Caraline* formula is applied, there can be no doubt about the identity of the victim. But in the case of the threat posed by Iraq, there is a serious problem. The danger that Iraq might attack the territory of the United States if far-fetched.[14] Is, then, a right of anticipatory self-defence also claimed where the danger is that of an attack against a military presence abroad, e.g. the United States forces stationed in Saudi Arabia or Qatar? That would really overstrain the notion of a situation equivalent to an armed attack.

In this situation, there remains the right of collective self-defence. If one assumes that Israel, Saudi Arabia, Turkey or Iran are threatened by the weapons of mass destruction in the possession of Iraq, a scenario which is not far-fetched, and that this threat constitutes a situation equivalent to an armed attack, a right of collective self-defence would also exist for the United States, if and to the extent that requirements of this right are fulfilled. According to the *Nicaragua* judgment of the ICJ, the right of collective self-defence requires a request by the victim possessing the right of individual self-defence.[15] Thus, a pre-emptive strike by the United States against Iraq would require a request made by a state of the region which could be considered to be directly threatened by missiles in the possession of Iraq.

6 Self-defence within an Existing Armed Conflict

The last question *de lege lata* which has to be examined in considering the legality of pre-emptive strikes is that of the point of reference for the determination of what constitutes an armed attack and what is defence. This problem is quite clear in the case of an armed conflict. Where an international armed conflict between two States exists, that point of reference is the beginning of the armed conflict. Once that conflict exists the only question to be asked under the rules of the *ius ad bellum*, the prohibition of the use of force, is: who

---

13   A. de Hoogh, *Obligations* erga omnes *and International Crimes* (1996), at 327.

14   Missiles currently available could reach parts of Turkey and Saudi Arabia as well as Israel, Bahrain, Qatar, Georgia, Azerbaijan and Armenia. Missiles which might become available would also be able to reach larger parts of Turkey, Southern Russia and even some small Greek Islands ('Iraq's Weapons of Mass Destruction', *supra* note 11, at 31).

15   *Supra* note 4, at 105.

started the whole conflict? The individual military action undertaken within the framework of the conflict can only be judged in the light of the *ius in bello*, but not by the yardstick of the *ius ad bellum* independently from the question which party violated the *ius ad bellum* by starting the conflict. The consequences of this legal situation for the legality of military action which might be called pre-emptive are obvious. The question of the legality of anticipatory self-defence is simply irrelevant for assessing the legality of individual operations undertaken in the framework of an ongoing armed conflict.[16]

Israeli writers have quite often used the argument of the existence of an armed conflict between Israel and the Arab States to justify certain military actions undertaken by Israel. Examples are the destruction of an Iraqi nuclear reactor by Israel in 1981, otherwise unlawful pre-emptive self-defence,[17] and the Beirut raid in 1968, otherwise an unlawful armed reprisal.[18] In principle, an individual military action undertaken within the framework of an armed conflict cannot be singled out to be judged according to the yardstick of the *ius ad bellum*. But then the question arises whether there exists an ongoing armed conflict which covers the individual action. In relation to Israel, the Security Council has never accepted that argument and always judged individual Israeli actions in relation to each particular incident which did or did not trigger a right of self-defence for Israel.[19]

In relation to a preventive strike by the United States against Iraq, the question thus arises as to how their current relationship is to be characterized. The first question to be asked is whether the armed conflict which started with the invasion of Kuwait by Iraq still exists, meaning that the United States are still entitled to a right of collective self-defence for the victim Kuwait (and/or that the authorization to use force given by the Security Council in Resolution 678 of 29 November 1990 is still open as a basis for military action, a related but different question). It is submitted that the success of the alliance and the armistice resolution fundamentally changed the situation. The actual armed attack committed by Iraq was repelled, the sovereignty of the Kuwaiti authorities over their territory reinstalled. The armed conflict ended. A situation of

---

16   The question may be asked whether in certain cases a conflict is limited to a certain theatre of war, or in a similar way, the expansion of the conflict beyond these bounds might constitute an action which should be judged on its own merits in the light of the prohibition of the use of force.

17   Dinstein, *supra* note 2, at 186.

18   Blum, 'The Beirut Raid and the International Double Standard', 64 *AJIL* (1970) 73.

19   O'Brien, 'Reprisals, Deterrence and Self-defence in Counterterror Operations', 30 *Va.J. of International Law* (1990) 421, at 426.

self-defence no longer existed. It is true that the Security Council still considered the situation came under Article 39 of the Charter and that the Council thus continued to act under Chapter VII of the Charter.[20] But that does not mean that the armed conflict continued. The measures taken by the Security Council were typical for a post-conflict situation. Iraq repeatedly violated the provisions of the armistice resolution. But this does not mean that the armed conflict was reactivated. When the United States, and later the United Kingdom, indeed attacked Iraq to enforce the no-flight zones, the question whether they were justified arose anew.

The question which arises as a consequence is whether there has been a continuous armed conflict since that resumption of military activities, meaning that the legality, under the *ius ad bellum*, of a new attack would not constitute a question separate from that of the legality of the earlier bombing, I submit that the various bombing periods constituted separate periods of armed conflict, each of which ahs to be assessed separately in the light of the *ius ad bellum*. The notion of continuous armed conflict is a dangerous one, open to abuse.

It was argued that the authorization given earlier by the Security Council was still open as a basis for the military action. This is a different question. Here we switch to the second type of legal justification of the use of force mentioned in the Introduction above. It would have been for the Security Council, not for individual states, to determine the consequences to be drawn from the breach of its resolutions. Such breach could not automatically re-establish the situation as it was before the resolutions. Thus, the resolution of April 1991 does not constitute a valid basis for strikes against Iraq taking place in 2002 or 2003.

Another possibility might be to argue that an armed conflict broke out between Iraq and the United States because Iraq supported some of the terrorist activities of Al Qaeda. Whatever Iraq did to train or otherwise support Al Qaeda fighters, no evidence has been submitted to date that indicates Iraq's involvement in the September 11 attacks was in any way comparable to that of the Taliban, which, as pointed out above, was the basis for the fact that the United States possessed a right of self-defence against Afghanistan. Thus, the construction of an armed conflict between the United States and Iraq cannot justify any pre-emptive strike by the former against the latter.

---

20   SC Res. 687 of 3 April 1991: 'The Security Council ... Conscious of the need to take the following measures acting under Chapter VII. ...'

7   Lex Ferenda

As has been pointed out above, the legal reasoning developed in the National Security Strategy may also be understood as an advocacy *de lege ferenda*. The question which has to be asked is how this change in the law could be achieved, and what type of modification of the law might be desirable. As an amendment to the UN Charter to modify Article 2(4) is out of the question, a change in customary law might be a way. A usual procedure to modify customary law is to break it and to accompany the breach by a new legal claim. This is, for instance, how the development was triggered which finally led to the recognition, also under customary law, of the concept of the exclusive economic zone in the Law of the Sea. Does President Bush's National Security Strategy constitute a step in this direction?

This leads us to the further question of whether such development would be desirable. We have, thus, to ponder the pros and cons of changing the restrictive concept of anticipatory self-defence presented above.

The case for a change of this restrictive concept of pre-emptive self-defence is made by the National Security Strategy:

> Given the goals of rogue states and terrorist, the United States can no longer solely rely on a reactive posture. The inability to deter a potential attack, the immediacy of today's threats, the magnitude of potential harm that could be caused by our adversaries' choice of weapons, do not permit that option. We cannot let out enemies strike first.[21]

To put it simply, the argument is: we cannot wait. Indeed, the traditional approach has always had the drawback of depriving a potential victim of the possibility to choose the most advantageous moment to fight a danger which may be extreme.[22] The argument, thus, is not new. It has been used by Israel to justify a number of incursions into the territory of its neighbours, and has been rejected by the Security Council.[23] The prohibition of the use of force, including the prohibition of anticipatory self-defence, has developed in international practice and doctrine despite the awareness of this

---

21   *Supra* note 9, at 15.

22   Hailbronner, in D. Schindler and K. Kailbronner, 'Die Grenzen des völkerrechtlichen Gewaltsverbots', 26 *Beriche der Deutschen Gesellschaft für Völkerrecht* 49, at p. 80 *et seq* (1986).

23   See, for instance, SC Res. 487 of 19 June 1981 relating to the Israeli attack against the nuclear reactor in Baghdad.

TERRORISM AND THE LEGALITY OF PRE-EMPTIVE FORCE

drawback. This should make us think twice before arguing for a change of the law.

An essential argument for maintaining the restrictive concept is the problem of vagueness and the possibility of abuse. Any new rule to be created would have to give an adequate answer to the following questions: How to define and limit a possibly expanded right of self-defence? How serious must the threat be? Is possession of weapons of mass destruction enough? Who is threatened and who may attack? What about the possession of nuclear arms by India, Pakistan, North Korea and Israel? What precisely distinguishes them (if there is a difference), in legal terms, from Iraq? What does 'harbouring' terrorists mean? There must be knowledge. But if there is, what kind of effort is a state required to make in order not to be considered as harbouring terrorists? Satisfactory answers to these questions are not at hand. All to easily, a standard of reasonableness boils down to subjectivity and speculation.

The National Security Strategy seems to recognize the dilemma, in particular the risk of abuse:

> ... nor should nations use pre-emption as a pretext for aggression.

This sentence is followed, however, by a somewhat enigmatic postulate:

> Yet in an age where the enemies of civilization openly and actively seek the world's most destructive technologies, the United States cannot remain idle while dangers gather.

Does this sequence imply a differentiation between (other) 'nations' and the United States? Is the demand, thus, a special law for the hegemon? Does the strategy, in its attempt to change the law of self-defence, also want to abolish the principle of sovereign equality?

If one looks seriously at the problems caused by the argument *de lege ferenda*, more question than answers appear. Any expansion of the right of pre-emptive self-defence beyond the *Caroline* formula is just not workable.

That being so, an additional problem of legal policy arises, namely the vulnerability of the prohibition of the use of force. The impossibility of placing any legal limit on the exception means that the validity of the prohibition of the use of force itself will be in jeopardy. A look back into history can clarify the problem. In the early times of modern international law, in the era of Grotius, the theory of 'just war', of *bellum iusum* applied: a war was lawful when fought for a just purpose and by just means. International practice of the eighteenth and nineteenth centuries had to accept that this rule was not viable.

It was impossible to determine in any particular case whose cause was just and whose not. As a result, the rule of *bellum iustum,* which at the outset was understood as legal restraint on war, turned into the opposite: international law became indifferent as to resort to war. Until the end of the First World War, resort to war was not forbidden, except in the case of a specific treaty (for instance, in the case of Belgian neutrality). Thus, the attempt to create a rule which is unable to give a workable definition of permissible force might end in the abolition of the prohibition of the use of force altogether, as previously occurred. This would mean destroying one of the most important and salutary cultural and political achievements of the twentieth century.

That danger is all the more real as the rule prohibiting the use of force is particularly vulnerable for another reason as well. This rule was not really developed by state practice. There has never been a consistent practice of abstention from the use of force. What changed after the First World War was the reaction of relevant actors against the use of force. An *opinio iuris* slowly emerged that war was unlawful, and official reactions to the use of force changed accordingly. This change was brought about by a more fundamental societal change, a change of social value judgments. Shocked by the immense human suffering caused by the First World War, society was no longer ready to accept war as a positive phenomenon as it had done before, when pacifism that existed was rather ridiculed by the societal establishment of the day. Briefly: the rule prohibiting war, and later the use of military force in general, is the product of a change in social value judgments. It lies in the very nature of such process that it is reversible. True, we are a long away from a re-militarization of the value system of our civil society. But if we want to maintain international law as a restraint on the use of military force, we should very carefully watch any attempt on the part of opinion leaders to argue that military force is anything other than an evil that has to be avoided. The lessons of history are telling. If we revert to such broad concepts, such as the just war concept, to justify military force we are stepping on a slippery slope, one which would make us slide back into the nineteenth century when war was not illegal.

It was exactly this concern about the slippery slope which prompted the Kennedy administration during the Cuban missile crisis not to rely on the self-defence argument in order to legally justify the pre-emptive action it took, namely the so-called 'quarantine'. Abram Chayes, then Legal Adviser to the State Department, explains this choice in the following words:

> In retrospect ... I think the central difficulty with the Article 51 argument was that it seemed to trivialize the whole effort at legal justification. No doubt the phrase 'armed attack' must be construed broadly enough to

permit some anticipatory response. But it is a very different manner to expand it to include threatening deployments or demonstrations that do not have imminent attack as their purpose of probably outcome. To accept that reading is to make the occasion for forceful response essentially a question for unilateral national decision that would not only be formally unreviewable, but not subject to intelligent criticism, either ... Whenever a nation believed that interests, which in the hear and pressure of a crisis it is prepared to characterize as vital, were threatened, its use of force in response would become permissible ... In this sense, I believe that an Article 51 defence would have signaled that the United States did not take the legal issues involved very seriously, that in its view the situation was to be governed by national discretion, not international law.[24]

The conclusion, thus, should be clear: a change in the law to the effect of opening up broader possibilities for anticipatory self-defence is not desirable.

The objection which can be raised against the restrictive approach (*de lege lata* or *de lege ferenda*) on the use of military force is that it is 'unrealistic', that in order to be meaningful it should authorize the use of force which is 'reasonable' under the circumstances – and outlaw only 'unreasonable' use of force. But reasonableness and proportionality are concepts which are difficult to operationalize in the context of a decentralized system. They open the door to arbitrariness and subjectivity. It may be that the risk of violation is higher if the rule is very restrictive. Much will then depend on the reaction of other actors in individual cases. It may well be that the international community, reshaping the *opinio iuris*, will one day accept some instances of pre-emptive use of force. But this, it is submitted, is a much safer approach to the interpretation and development of the *ius ad bellum* than loosening any real restraint by boiling it down to a rule of reason – a self-destructive mechanism for the prohibition of the use of force.

8 The Solution of the Dilemma: The Multilateral Option

It is traditional wisdom of legal theory that where substantive law cannot bring about a sufficient degree of legal certainty, procedural rules must be used to obtain results which are socially or politically acceptable. This wisdom can and should be applied to the problem under discussion. We are facing a situation

---

24   A. Chayes, *The Cuban Missile Crisis* (1974), at 63 *et seq.*

where an established rule, i.e. the prohibition of the use of force, including anticipatory self-defence, is challenged. But it is difficult, if not impossible, to create a new rule which is able to accommodate legitimate concerns without opening the door to unacceptable abuse. Practicable substantive legal restraints on the use of pre-emptive force are not readily available. On the one hand, there are serious doubts about the wisdom of the traditional rule which strictly limits anticipatory self-defence, but on the other hand, loosening these limits is also not acceptable, as no workable limits can be conceived as a substitute for the old ones. It is in this situation that the need for accepted procedures legitimizing the use of force arises. That was the Kennedy approach in the Cuban missile crisis when he sought and obtained OAS approval.[25] The claim of better knowledge, better morals or the like does not create sufficient legitimization in the international system.

This procedure does not need to be invented – it already exists. This is, as rightly pointed out by the UN Secretary-General, the authorization by the Security Council. It is, in my view, one of the essential flaws of the National Security Strategy that the United Nations and its system of collective security are not even mentioned, let alone examined as a viable option of security policy. The argument which is often heard against recourse to the Security Council as a source of legitimization is that it is all too often blockaded. There is, indeed, a certain balance of power in the Council, a system of checks and balances, designed with some degree of political wisdom by the drafters of the Charter. As a consequence, a majority led by one of the permanent members of the Council does not necessarily have its way. This is a leverage which all permanent members of the Council have used to their advantage as they thought appropriate. But this is not what can appropriately be called a blockade. Negotiations leading to a reasonable result are not impossible, as they were during the times of the 'automatic' veto which characterized the era of the Cold War. In this new situation, recourse to a Security Council Mandate is the only acceptable solution, both as a matter of law and policy, where, in the light of threats of terrorism and use of weapons of mass destruction by irresponsible governments, military action cannot be construed as constituting self-defence seems to be required.

---

25   The question whether this was a sufficient justification is a different matter.

Peacekeeping and International Humanitarian Law
Friends or Foes?

Peacekeeping and international humanitarian law should be friends, but as a matter of fact, their relationship seems to be a little problematic. An example is the recent report that SFOR soldiers used a trick involving a red cross in order to come close to a suspected war criminal they wanted to arrest. If the report is true, this would constitute an abuse of the emblem. During the 2nd UN peacekeeping operation, ONUC in the Congo, ICRC personnel wearing the emblem was killed by UN peacekeepers. In the meantime, there has been a lot of debate in theory, but also an actual practice, in particular between the ICRC and the UN, concerning the application of international humanitarian law by UN peacekeeping forces. This practical debate and these cases have been accompanied by many academic attempts to clarify the question. These lines offer yet another one of those.

The first question to be asked is: Why? Why should international humanitarian law be applied and in relation to peacekeeping and similar international forces? What is the use of applying international humanitarian law to peacekeeping and other forces used for the purpose of restoring or maintaining peace in a given crisis area? The basic purpose of international humanitarian law is to limit violence in a situation of armed conflict. The fundamental question which has thus to be asked is whether in the case of peacekeeping and other military operations designed to restore peace situations have arisen or can possibly arise where this function of international humanitarian law is needed. It might thus be useful to start by describing a few scenarios where it is at least debatable that this typical function of international humanitarian law is asked for.

In order to solve the relevant problems, the scenarios will not be limited to what is called additional peacekeeping, but cover a wider scope of possible situations.

There is, first of all, the scenario of a full-fledged war, for example the Gulf War where the use of force was authorized by the UN Security Council. There is no doubt that this is a situation where this function of international humanitarian law to limit violence is needed. On the other end of the spectrum, we have the situation of the UN administering a certain territory in a situation where this helpful means to settle or contain a conflict between two states

© KONINKLIJKE BRILL NV, LEIDEN, 2021 | DOI:10.1163/9789004380592_009

claiming this territory. The case in point was UNTEA. This case, the function of peacekeepers is really the same as that of internal forces of order. The law to be applied to those forces must be similar to the police powers military forces may possess in a state. International humanitarian law is irrelevant in that scenario.

These are the easy cases. The real problem arises where situations of organized violence arise within the framework of an overall peaceful situation. UN peacekeepers are described as soldiers without enemies. Unfortunately, this is an incomplete description. There have been and there will be situations where peacekeepers are confronted with some kind of organized resistance, are engaged in actual fighting, make prisoners or are being made prisoners during such encounters. Examples are cases where peacekeeping operations have been the task of disarming troops or militias engaged in a conflict, of arresting criminals which are protected by organized armed groups and of escorting relief transports where those encounter military resistance. If a relief convoy is ambushed and if the other side uses civilians (whatever that term may mean in the particular context) as a shield we have a situation where the standards of behaviour provided by international humanitarian law are very relevant indeed. Peacekeeping troops have a mandate of dismantling military position of a party to an internal or international conflict, this may well be to a situation of fighting where the rules of international humanitarian law concerning the choice of targets may well become relevant. If UN peacekeepers defend safety zones established for the protection of the civilian population and if these safety zones are not respected by the other side, a similar situation arises. In all these cases, the question of standard of behaviour arises. What kind of orders can be legally given by a commander in this situation? What about criminal liability of those engaged in shooting or those taking prisoners on both sides? And, last not least, what is the standard of illegality when it comes to the question of compensation of damages which are caused by an unlawful act?

Having arrived at the conclusion that there can be situations where international humanitarian law might provide a useful standard of behaviour for and in relation to peacekeeping and similar international forces, we have inquire further where the relevant legal problems are. The true difficulty lies in the fact that there are three different, so interrelated problems involved. The first one concerns the situation as such, the problem already alluded in the description of various scenarios. In other words, is there a situation where international humanitarian law is applicable? The other two problems relate to the status of the military forces involved or rather of the entities to which these military forces belong. This is on the one hand the status of the UN, a reasonable organization or of a group of states to which the behaviour of the forces is to be attributed. On the other side of the conflict, forces may belong to states, but also to affections in a decomposing or failing state. We may have militias or a ravel group. The question what kind of legal relationship exists between the parties and entities involved is by no means an easy one.

The first type of problem can be called incidental violence. It is the case of a presence of a foreign force in a given country which is essentially of a peaceful character and based on the consent of the parties. This is the situation of what is called traditional peacekeeping, but also with operations like IFOR and SFOR which are based on the Dayton Agreement. There is no armed conflict between the receiving state and the sending states and/or the UN. It is not an occupation within the meaning of Article 2, para. 2, of the Geneva Conventions of 1949. The question to be answered is whether and to what extent a situation arises within this generally peaceful context, where international humanitarian law constitutes a proper yardstick of behaviour. Whether and to what extent military force may be used by the foreign military personnel is a matter regulated by the contractual relationship existing between the receiving state and the sending entity (state or international organisation). As a rule, it will be a police-like use of force. The general assumption is that force will not be used against the armed forces of the receiving state, but against individuals violating the law which, on the other hand, are not or even cannot be controlled and retrained by the competent organs (police, armed forces) of the receiving state. This situation, the application of international humanitarian law is not called for. A few questions however, remain to be solved. As a rule, the agreement between the relevant entities is not very explicit as to the modalities of the use of force. The Dayton Agreement, for instance, gives a wide scope of discretion of the force commander whether and to what extent to use military force. In this case, additional questions as to the yardstick of behaviour arise. If weapons are used and people are killed, the question of the legal authorisation to use such weapons is a crucial one. Whether and to what extent the discretionary power is given by an international treaty to a force commander is sufficient justification under the relevant criminal law is a doubtful question. Thus, both the national law of the sending state, internal rules of behaviour of the sending international organisation and for the law of the receiving state may be relevant for the legality of the use of weapons.

International humanitarian law is applicable in the case of an armed conflict. Consequently, it is a proper yardstick of behaviour if, incidental to the situation as it is governed by the agreement between the receiving state and the sending entity/ies, a situation arises which can be probably characterized as armed conflict, be it only a small one. An armed conflict presupposes that there are at least two parties processing some kind of military organization which are fighting each other. In the context described, this is possible where, contrary to the assumptions of the basic agreement, hostilities break out between the forces of the sending entity/entities and claims of the receiving state. More often, there will be parties additional to the organized armed forces of the receiving state which possess some kind of military organisation which enables them to be a party to a non-international armed conflict in the relation to the government or to other similar parties existing on the territory of the receiving state. In this case, there can be an international armed conflict in relation to the foreign force present in the territory. If there is such kind of confrontation between military organisations, it is not necessary that there are really long-lasting and sustain hostilities between them in order to speak of an armed conflict. An armed conflict starts with the first shot. Applicable rules must be known from the very first shot. It is not possible to say: 'Just let us wait and see whatever there will be sustain fighting before we can say what rules are applicable'.

Clear as this concept might be in theory, it involves a number of difficult problems as there is an unavoidable overlap between the contractual regime and international humanitarian law. The solution of that problem is a concept which can be called that of double restraint. As a matter of principle, both the restraints of international humanitarian law and those of the applicable international legal regime must be respected. This concept is not as unusual as it might appear at a first glance. This situation also exists in the case of a 'normal' international armed conflict. In the latter case, we are used to distinguishing between the *ius ad bellum* and the *ius in bello*. The aggressor may not invade a foreign territory. This is unlawful. But once the fighting has broken out, both the aggressor and the victim must respect international humanitarian law. This is, for all practical purposes, a double restraint, which, however, sometimes can be forgotten in the case of war. But norms such as the one quoted above implementing the role that the aggressor has to pay damages for his unlawful act are evidence of this rules.

The principle of double restraint is really not difficult as long as the two sets of rules are not contradictory. As long as the rules in question only limit the freedom of action of the entities in question, there is no such contradiction. The respective greater restriction applies. A contradiction only arises where one set of norms requires a behaviour which is forbidden under the other set. Just to give an example. An agreement may provide for handing over arrested criminals to the authorities of the receiving state. But if the arrest takes place in the context of a fighting where international humanitarian law applies, persons arrested are, if they belong to the organized armed forces of the party to the conflict, prisoners of war which may not be handed over to a power which

PEACEKEEPING AND INTERNATIONAL HUMANITARIAN LAW

is not willing to apply the Third Geneva Convention in respect of those persons. It is not possible within this contribution to analyse all possible scenarios. But these lines should suffice to show the direction which the legal analysis of each of these situations can and has to go.

As pointed out above, the second level of problems relate to the status of the sending entity/entities. In this respect, two questions have to be distinguished. The first one is the identification of the sending entities in other words, the question which subject of international law is responsible for the behaviour of the foreign forces. This can be an international organisation, it can be one of several states. If it is an international organisation, then the second problem arises, namely that of the status of that organisation under general international law, or in other words, the capacity of an international organisation to be a subject of international humanitarian law.

The question to be asked, thus, is whether an international organization (a regional organisation or the UN) is internationally responsible for the force. This is the case where the force is an organ of the organisation. The fact that a military operation is authorized by the UN does not have the consequence that the forces involved in that operation become organs of the UN. The forces involved in repelling the Iraqi invasion of Kuwait were those of the states 'cooperating with the government of Kuwait' not of the UN. UNITAF deployed in Somalia to establish a secure environment for the UN operation, opération turquoise in Rwanda and finally IFOR and SFOR in Bosnia- Herzegovina are clear cases where the operation is authorized by a decision of the Security Council, but the forces involved do not become organs of the UN. They are and remain organs of the respective states to which these troops belong. It should be added that in the case of IFOR and SFOR, the troops are also not organs of NATO, although they are under a NATO command. This partial integration of the command structure does not really interrupt the jurisdiction of link between the state and its troops which is constitutive for their character as state organs.

The situation is different in the case of traditional peacekeeping. The original concept developed on the occasion of creation of the first peacekeeping operation, namely the UN Emergency Force, later called UNEP I, by the then Secretary-General Hammarskjöld was clear and explicit. The troops were under the exclusive command of the UN, which meant that the contributing states relinquished a substantial part of command authority over the troops. The authority which the contributing states retained, namely authorities in criminal and disciplinary matters, had to be exercised with the view to making sure that the troops and their members fulfil their international mandate. In this way, the various contingents, although retaining some kind of national identity, became organs of the UN. The UN were internationally responsible for their behaviour. Where the troops committed illegal acts, it was the UN which paid damages. Where the troops were the subject of illegal attacks, it was the UN which complained. This clear concept, however, has come under attack in recent practice, in particular in Somalia. The political background for this was the fact these operations became more and more dangerous and became politically difficult for the government of the contradicting states to leave the fade of their soldiers entirely to the decision of the Secretary-General and to the force commander. Thus, the principle of exclusive command authority of the Secretary-General over the contingent commander and through him over the contingent was put into question. Whether contingent commanders illegally got instructions from their national governments or whether this principle of limited command authority of the UN and the retention of full command by the national government of the contributing state was recognized in the arrangements made between the UN and contributing states somewhat confused. In the case litigated before the German Constitutional Court concerning the constitutionality of German participation in UNOSOM II, the German Government argued that the UN command structure has become comparable to the NATO command structure, meaning retention of full command for the German Minister of defence. Although the Federal Government submitted documents which can be interpreted in this sense, the representative of the UN who testified before the Constitutional Court did not, at least not explicitly, admit that contention of the German Government.

If and to the extent that the troops remain organs of the respective states, the rules of behaviour which they have to obey are found in the international law binding those states, that means customary international law and the treaties to which these states are parties. This means that different standards may apply in relation to different contingents acting on the same theatre. In the case of SFOR and IFOR, for instance, Protocol I Additional to the Geneva Conventions would be applicable to the German contingent, but not to the French and the U.S. ones. This situation, however, does not present too many difficulties as a great part of norms which may become relevant is also part of customary international law which binds all states.

If the UN (or a regional organisation) is the entity which is internationally responsible for the troops, then, and only then, the question arises whether and to what extent international customary applicable in times of armed conflicts binds and/or protects the UN. It is undisputed that the UN is a subject of international law. But this does not necessarily mean that all rules of international law apply to the UN. It is often argued that the UN cannot be a subject of the laws of war because of their specific structure. It is said that they do not possess the necessary internal organisation which international humanitarian law requires. The answer to that question is, however, quite clear both from a theoretical and from a practical perspective. All new subjects of international law are in a way born to the existing international legal order. This is also true for what is sometimes called functional subjects. If states by common agreement create a new subject of international law, such as an international organisation, they cannot create something which is outside the pre-existing legal order. If they give the organization powers and functions which brings the organisation into a situation where certain rules apply, they must also give the organisation the necessary means to comply with these rules. Otherwise the creation of a new legal person would mean a kind of contracting of customary law obligations, which is not acceptable. From a practical point of view, as already indicated above, the UN has to solve that problem by using the organisational resources of the contributing states in order to make sure that the obligations of the UN under applicable rules of international law are indeed respected. Using the disciplinary powers of the contributing states is a practical solution, but if the need arises, there is no legal obstacle preventing the UN from creating a specific court in order to enforce internal rules of the organisation. The administrative tribunals created by the UN and the International Labour Organisation are cases in point.

To summarise: Where there is a situation in which international humanitarian law applies (see the first level of problems), it applies also in relation to the UN. The third type of problem is that of the status of groups or entities existing in the territory of the receiving state. This was a very serious problem in the case of UNOSOM II and UNPROFOR, it remains a difficult problem in relation to IFOR and SFOR. International law regulates the legal relationship between the sending entity and the receiving state, between the UN and Somalia, between the UN and Bosnia-Herzegovina, between the sending states and Bosnia-Herzegovina in the case of SFOR and IFOR. The basic assumption is that everybody on the territory of this state was subject to the jurisdiction of that state. But as a matter of fact, the receiving states which are in a state of fragmentation, do not have an effective control over persons and groups imprisoned on their territory. In this situation, there are two legal possibilities. The first one is to construe a legal relationship under international law between the foreign entity (state or international organisation) and the group in question. Then, this group possesses a limited international personality, be it only for the application of certain fundamental rules of international humanitarian law, but also for the purposes of establishing a limited local international contractual relationship. If and to the extent that the party to a non-international armed conflict is considered to be bound by Article 3 common to the Geneva Convention or even Protocol II Additional thereto, that party possesses a limited international personality. In this case, there is really no logical obstacle for considering the same parties as a subject of international law also in relation to the entity responsible for the foreign troops. While in the case of Somalia, this construction may have presented some practical difficulties, it seems quite clear that the Republica Srpska, although certainly not a sovereign state under international law, possesses a limited international personality for the purpose of the rules governing the presence of both UNPROFOR and IFOR/ SFOR. This would include, to the extent explained above, the applicability of international humanitarian law.

If violence is used by and against groups which cannot be certain to be parties to an armed conflict, these groups constitute, in terms of international humanitarian law, civilians, but they are not protected civilians as and to the extent that they take part in hostilities. They are not bound by international humanitarian law, but are subject to the criminal law of their own state and, subject to the relevant rules on jurisdiction, to the criminal law of other states. As to the treatment by foreign forces, the international legal rules (treaties or customary law) for the protection of human rights apply. If and to the extent that the UN is the relevant entity, the international customary law of human rights is applicable to the acts and missions of the UN forces.

The reasoning which has been developed is, to say the least, somewhat complicated. But that corresponds to the fact that the situation is complicated. These forces, UN peacekeepers and national forces having some kind of peace enforcing or peace restoration mandate are used in a political context which is in many respects open ended and fluid. It is not possible to find a clear black and white answer to these legal problems caused by a grey situation.

This explains the fade which is haunting several attempts to clarify the situation, the most recent one being the 'Convention on the safety of UN and associated personnel'. The Convention constitutes a step forward in some respect. It has clarified the protective duties of the receiving states and this is important. The receiving state must use its criminal law in order to ensure the safety of the UN and associated personnel. There remains the problem of the state unable or unwilling to do this. In this case, the criminal jurisdiction of third states may help. Under Article 10 para. 4, and 14 of the Convention, member states must either take measures necessary to establish their jurisdiction over such crimes in cases where the offender is present in their territory or to create the possibility that such an offender is extradited to a country which is willing issue such jurisdiction. The choices between establishing jurisdiction and providing for extradition, setting the person free for lack of jurisdiction would be illegal. All this is an important progress.

On the other hand, the question of the application of international humanitarian law is not clarified, it is left open. Article 2, para. 2, of the Convention makes it clear that it is not applicable in the case of an improvement action where there is a full-fledged armed conflict opposing organized armed forces of the UN and the state which is the object of such action. But in addition, Article 20 (a) expressly states that the Convention shall affect the 'applicability of international humanitarian law and universally recognized standards of human rights as contained in international instruments in relation to the protection of UN operations and UN and associated personnel or the responsibility of such personnel to respect such UN standards. Thus, the legal problems discussed in this article remain relevant even in cases where, otherwise the UN Convention applies.

PART 3

Arms Control

8

Obligations and Protection of Individuals

1 Introduction

The obligations and the protection of individuals under the Chemical Weapons Convention (CWC) constitute a problem because the Convention has a certain impact on private persons, both natural persons and private enterprises. Some of those impacts are the object of detailed regulation in the Convention and its Annexes. Others require further regulation both through the elaboration of additional instruments within the new Organization and through implementing measures to be taken by the Member States. This paper tries to summarize some of the legal questions posed by this impact of the Convention on private persons.

The first kind of individual obligation the Convention expressly mentions arises from the fact that the purposes of the Convention could be frustrated if the obligations imposed on States Parties under Article I of the Convention were circumvented by private persons engaged in activities which are prohibited to the States Parties. Thus, Member States are under an obligation to prevent this from taking place and to enact specific legislation for that purpose.[1] This obvious task for national legislation is well recognized, and implementing legislation, to the extent it already exists, indeed contains specific provisions for this purpose. As a rule, national legislation makes it a criminal offence to engage in activities prohibited under the Convention.[2] It is not the intent of this paper to go into the details of formulating such a provision. It will rather concentrate on two problem areas which are somewhat more complex, namely some consequences which the destruction of chemical weapons and chemical weapon production facilities as well as the verification régime may have on the interests of private persons or enterprise.

As to the first problem area, the Convention requires States to undertake a hazardous activity, namely the destruction of chemical weapons and of chemical weapon facilities, a process which, in spite of its otherwise beneficial

---

1 Art. VII, para. 1, CWC.
2 §§ 2, 15, 16, German CWC Implementation Act; Arts. 2, 3, 15, Dutch CWC Implementation Act; Arts. 1, 8, Swiss CWC Implementation Act; Sec. 12, Australian Chemical Weapons (Prohibition) Act 1993.

© KONINKLIJKE BRILL NV, LEIDEN, 2021 | DOI:10.1163/9789004380592_010

consequences,[3] endangers both the safety of persons and the environment. Thus, important private and public interests not related to disarmament are affected *by* activities undertaken pursuant to the Convention.

As to the second aspect, the major problem is verification relating to private industries engaged in "activities not prohibited under the Convention", which are subject to a certain scrutiny pursuant to Article VI. The basis of this verification régime is a system of collecting information concerning the activities covered *by* that provision, information which the Government does not possess and thus must obtain from private industry. This information relates to industrial and commercial activities, the confidentiality of which is of great interest to the private enterprise concerned. The other basic element of the verification régime is a system of on-site inspections. The interest of the international community to obtain information for the sake of arms control may be in conflict with the interest of the private enterprise in the production process being safe and undisturbed and information relating to this process being not accessible to other persons who might use it to the economic disadvantage of the enterprise in question. As the inspectors have to move in an accident prone environment, the question of industrial accidents caused by inspection activities and the compensation of damages arising therefrom also requires attention. There are, thus, three main legal questions involved in the inspection process, namely (*a*) access to the premises of an enterprise, (*b*) obtaining and handling information from the premises and (*c*) the safety of production processes.

2 Safety and Environmental Protection

Concern for safety and environmental protection were late comers in the long lists of negotiations issues. In 1990, Peru presented a paper on this matter[4] which regrettably is only inadequately reflected in the final text of the Convention. The basic provisions are Articles VII (3), IV (10) and V (11). As an example, it may suffice to quote one of these provisions, namely Article IV (10):

> Each State Party, during transportation, sampling, storage and destruction of chemical weapons shall assign the highest priority to ensuring the safety of people and to protecting the environment. Each State Party shall

3 This is rightly pointed out by the United States environmental impact assessment conducted for the ratification of the CWC.

4 CD/1024.

OBLIGATIONS AND PROTECTION OF INDIVIDUALS

195

> transport, sample, store and destroy chemical weapons in accordance with its national standards for safety and emissions.

This provision is rather vague and weak. There is no international safety standard prescribed. It is just an obligation to take the safety and environmental interests into account. In addition, there is a *renvoi* to national standards.

As to the destruction of chemical weapons, a few more details are added in Part IV (A) of Annex 2.[5] During storage of weapons preceding destruction, paragraph 9 of this Part allows "safety monitoring and physical security activities". It is to be noted that these activities are only allowed, not required. Nothing special is said on the issue of safe transportation. The way of destruction is left to the Member States in question, the essential requirement being that the processes used are essentially irreversible. Certain destruction processes, however, are prohibited: "Dumping in any body of water, land burial or open-pit burning".[6] This at least prohibits some destruction processes which are totally unacceptable from an environmental and safety point of view. The destruction has to take place according to a plan which the State is required to submit to the Executive Council. This plan must contain information regarding "the national standards for safety and emissions that the destruction facilities must satisfy".[7] These plans are reviewed by the Executive Council but only "to assess their conformity with the order of destruction (prescribed by the Annex)".[8] Thus, this review is not concerned with the protection of the environment and the safety of persons. This is a matter nearly entirely left to the States in question.

Although the Convention, thus, as a matter of principle refers to national standards, an international legal régime which would be indifferent to the environmental hazards involved in the destruction process would run foul of any modem trend of international environmental law. Modem international environmental law is not just concerned with restraining short-term or direct transborder externalities of activities affecting the environment. Modern international environmental law is based on concepts such as common concern, intergenerational equity and the precautionary principle,[9] concepts which go

---

5   For an analysis of these provisions see U. Beyerlin and T. Marauhn, *Abrüstung und Umweltschutz – eine völkerrechtliche Interessenkollision?*, 1994, p. 45.

6   Ann. 2, Part IV (A), para. 13.

7   Ann. 2, Part IV (A), para. 6 (e).

8   Ann. 2, Part IV (A), para. 20.

9   The concept of "common concern of humankind" is in particular reflected by the Convention on Biological Diversity adopted by the Rio Earth Summit in 1992. The application of the "precautionary principle" is required by Principle 15 of the Rio Declaration on

well beyond a traditional concept of transfrontier pollution which stood at the beginning of international environmental law.

Consequently, it appears to me to be inconceivable, it could indeed be cynical, if the community of States (and OPCW for that purpose) were indifferent to a State destroying chemical weapons, for example by incinerating substances without taking the necessary precautions to protect the surrounding population. International environmental law is based on common values – like human rights protection is. In the same way we do not accept a State torturing its own citizens, we cannot tolerate a State poisoning them, or future generations thereof. Thus, it is one of the tasks of the organs of the OPCW to pay further attention to the question of environmentally safe destruction and to see to it that high environmental standards are indeed applied.

3   Verification – the Régime of Information Gathering

It is the purpose of the verification régime established pursuant to Article VI of the Convention to prevent activities not prohibited under the Contention from being misused for the purpose of diverting chemicals to weapons purposes. For that reason, the activities of private industry are made the object of a specific régime of ascertaining facts. The first part of this régime consists of very elaborate information requirements imposed upon Member States. Through initial and annual declarations, States must provide information concerning certain activities relating to specific chemicals supposed to be suitable candidates for diversion, namely chemicals listed in three Schedules (scheduled chemicals) and a rather broad category of other substances (discrete organic chemicals). The information to be given concerns both data on transactions (such as import, export, production, consumption, processing) and facilities where certain activities (in particular processing and production) take place. There is a decreasing degree of detail required from Schedule 1 chemicals to discrete organic chemicals.

Schedule 1 chemicals are a very special case as there are specific limitations on their possession even for permitted purposes, and they may as a matter of principle only be handled in a single small-scale facility.[10] As to Schedules 2 and 3 chemicals, aggregate national data on transactions concerning those chemicals must be provided. In addition, information on each facility where

---

Environment and Development. The idea of intergovernmental equity is contained in Principle 3 of the same Declaration.

10   Ann. 2, Part VII, para. 13.

OBLIGATIONS AND PROTECTION OF INDIVIDUALS

these chemicals are handled in a quantity above a certain threshold must also be given. This includes information regarding activities of each of these facilities and a kind of balance sheet concerning transactions involving each chemical. In relation to discrete organic chemicals, information must be provided on plants producing quantities above a certain threshold, but the information to be provided is of a summary character.

As already pointed out, most of this information which the State is required to give the OPCW is in private hands. The Government may possess parts of that information for other reasons, in particular for reasons of industrial safety supervision or export controls. But so far, there is no State having a legislation ensuring that all the information required under the CWC is somewhere in the Government's hands. Thus, implementing legislation is required in order to make sure that this information is indeed given to the Government by private industry in order to enable the State to pass it on to the Organization. This is a major point in the national implementation legislation which has so far been enacted in a number of States.[11] These provisions create reporting and notification duties.

On the other hand, there is a legitimate interest of the industry concerned in the protection of this information. Not all this information is necessarily a commercial or industrial secret. But as some of the information to be given is rather specific in relation to the activities of a certain facility and the quantity of chemicals used, processed or produced therein, it may well be that it could be used to the enterprise's economic disadvantage by competitors or other persons having an economic interest in that information. Thus, it has to be made sure that this legitimate interest in confidentiality is protected.

In order to evaluate the rules protecting the confidentiality of this information, it is useful to recall that the information flow envisaged by the Convention is divided into three phases: first, the information is given to a collecting agency and then transferred from the collecting agency to the National Authority designated or established under Article VII, paragraph 4, of the CWC. That Authority passes the information on to the OPCW, where this information is reviewed for the purpose of the Convention (second phase). Then, this information is given to the Member State (third phase).[12]

The first phase is a matter of the national legislation of the State collecting the information from private industry and transferring it to the Organization.

---

11   See for instance § 7, German CWC Implementation Act; Arts. 4–6, Dutch CWC Implementation Act; Art. 2, para. 1, cit. *a*, Swiss CWC Implementation Act; Sec. 31, Australian Chemical Weapons (Prohibition) Act 1993.

12   Ann. 3, para. 2 (b) (i).

The German Implementation Act, for instance, contains specific provisions ensuring that this information flow is only used for the purposes of the Convention.[13] The information is protected by the general rules concerning data protection and official secrets.

As to the second phase, the Annex on Confidentiality contains some basic rules concerning the treatment of this information. As a matter of principle, information is considered confidential if so designated *by* the State Party from which it is obtained.[14] This confidential information has to be treated according to certain safety standards. This includes in particular a classification system. Nevertheless, the régime of protection is open to question, especially as far as the consequences of breaches or alleged breaches are concerned. The Director-General is entitled to take punitive and disciplinary measures against staff members having violated their obligations to protect confidential information.[15] The major question, however, is that no private party which is adversely affected by this violation has direct access to the Organization. According to the text of the CWC as it stands, this violation is a matter of the relation between the State to which that aggrieved party belongs and the Organization. In addition, the Organization, according to an express provision of the Confidentiality Annex, [16]"shall not be held liable for any breach of confidentiality committed by members of the Technical Secretariat". Civil and criminal liability of the official having committed the breach (which is not the object of this paper) may be a useful deterrent, but does not solve the question of compensation for damages as the sums at stake may well be beyond the official's capacity to pay. This could leave a serious damage caused by the Organization to private parties without any compensation. For this reason, the Convention may pose a constitutional problem for those States which, like Germany, have a constitution guaranteeing the right of private property. It is at least arguable that a treaty creating a serious risk for a constitutionally protected property interest and at the same time excluding, as a matter of substantive law, any compensation, and as a matter of procedural law, any remedy indeed constitutes an unconstitutional taking of property. The Implementation Act of Germany does not address the problem, although it covers the question of other damages caused by the Organization.[17] This lacuna is even more serious as the settlement of any dispute between the Organization and the Member State affected

---

13 § 6, German CWC Implementation Act.
14 Ann. 3, para. 2 (a) (i).
15 Ann. 3, para. 20.
16 Para. 22.
17 See below, Sec. 4.2.

OBLIGATIONS AND PROTECTION OF INDIVIDUALS

by the breach is still an open question. The Confidentiality Annex[18] provides for a "Commission for the settlement of disputes related to confidentiality". "Composition" and "operating procedures" are governed by rules to be adopted by the Conference of the States Parties, but nothing is said about its powers. Whether it becomes an effective dispute settlement procedure remains to be seen, but it seems highly improbable, although desirable, that it can be directly seised by an aggrieved private party.

As to the third phase, the Confidentiality Annex makes it clear that the reports and declarations provided by the States Parties under Article VI, which are the ones we are dealing with here, have to be provided to all States Parties regardless of the fact that the information may be considered as being confidential.[19] In this case, however, the obligation contained in Article VII, paragraph 6, applies, namely that "each State Party shall treat as confidential and afford special handling to information and data that it receives in confidence from the Organization in connection with the implementation of this Convention". Thus, the general principle of protection is established by the Convention, but whether this principle will indeed function is another matter. It is first of all a matter of the implementing legislation to be enacted by the States Parties to the Convention. The German Implementation Act[20] expressly addresses the problem and provides legal protection also for that information coming from other States. As a matter of principle, the information is protected by the rules concerning official secrets. Particular problems in this respect may exist in countries where statutes (or even the constitution) grants to everybody access to administrative files (Freedom of Information Act or so-called sunshine laws). In Germany, this poses no particular problems, as there is no Freedom of Information Act, except where this information is relevant for the environment and thus the subject of access obligations to be granted under the relevant EC Directive. But this information would come under the exception provided by the Directive in order to protect the confidentiality of international relations and industrial and commercial secrets.[21] The essential problem remains what remedy the aggrieved States and the aggrieved private party might possess in cases where the relevant national legislation does not provide adequate protection or is not respected in a particular case.

---

18   Para. 23.

19   Ann. 3, para. 2 (b) (i).

20   § 6, para. 3, second sentence, and para. 4; see also Sec. 102 of the Australian Chemical Weapons (Prohibition) Act 1993.

21   Art. 3, para. 2, Directive 90/313/EEC.

4 Verification – the Inspection Régime

The verification régime poses three different problems concerning individual rights and duties, namely the access by inspection teams to private premises, the safe conduct of inspections and the protection of information found on those premises.

4.1 *Access*

Under the general verification provisions of the Convention, each State Party is obliged to grant to the inspectors access to facilities as required by the more detailed provisions of the Verification Annex.[22] These provisions are not self-executing, i.e. the State "shall grant" access, but it is not possible under the relevant national law to invoke this international obligation directly against the private parties concerned. Thus, it is the function of the implementing legislation to be enacted according to Article VIII to make sure that access is indeed possible. Access to private premises, if need be, against the will of the owner or possessor, in many States poses constitutional problems. Thus, the least which is required in terms of national law is a statute facilitating such access. This is true even where, under the relevant provision of the Verification Annex,[23] facility agreements are concluded in order to regulate details of on-site inspections. These agreements are concluded between the State in question and the Organization. It would be advisable if the private parties concerned were included in those negotiations, but this is left to the State in question. There must be a means for that State to force any private party concerned *by* that facility agreement to accept it if the State so wishes. Thus, legislation is still necessary even in cases where there are facility agreements.

On closer examination, the duties of private parties which own or possess premises subject to inspection are twofold. First, they have to tolerate the inspection measures provided for in the Convention or agreed upon between the State and the Organization. Secondly, they also have to assist in specific ways in order to facilitate the inspection. This is, for instance, clearly formulated in Section 8 of the German CWC Implementation Act.

In terms of constitutional law, three questions arise:
– What kind of localities enjoy a constitutional protection against intrusion?
– Which restriction may be imposed on such protection by legislation?

---

22 Art. VI, para. 9, for routine inspections, and Art. IX, paras. 11 (*b*), 24, for challenge inspections, for details see Ann. 2, Parts VII, para. 26, VIII, para. 20, IX, para. 17, and (for challenge inspections) X, paras. 20, 46 *et seq.*

23 Parts VI, para. 25, VII, para. 17.

OBLIGATIONS AND PROTECTION OF INDIVIDUALS

- What kind of intrusion, even if justified by legislation, requires in addition a judicial authorization, for instance a judicial warrant?

The answer given to these three questions is by no means uniform. In Germany for instance, industrial and commercial premises are not necessarily considered as enjoying the special constitutional protection of a "home" (*Wohnung*), but are protected in a less specific way by the guarantee of personal freedom. As to the requirement of a warrant, the German implementation is based on a narrow concept of search (for which a warrant is required) and does not consider most of the inspection activities, especially not inspection activities related to routine inspections, as constituting search. The provision on judicial warrants[24] only concerns specific activities in case of a challenge inspection and the alleged use of chemical weapons. The warrant provisions of both the Australian and the (draft) United States implementation legislation are much broader and cover both kinds of inspections. It is indeed open to question whether all the inspection measures envisaged and carefully restricted by the Verification Annex constitute "search" within the meaning of national constitutional law, but it may well be in the interest of the inspected State to conduct a full-fledged search in order to show its compliance with the Convention.

An application to issue a warrant has as a rule to be filed by the representative of the inspected State accompanying the inspection team, or by the agency to which he or she belongs. The question whether and to what extent the court will consider as binding any determination by that agency as to the question whether the warrant is required under the Convention will also vary among States. All these questions have to be taken into account in drafting implementation legislation. The Convention itself does not prescribe any detail, but it requires States to find the most effective way consistent with their own constitutional systems.

4.2 *The Safe Conduct of Inspections*

The problem of safe conduct of inspections is in explicit terms addressed in the Verification Annex.[25] The inspection team shall "observe safety regulations established at the inspection site including those for the protection of controlled environments within a facility and for personal safety". This means that it is the national standard otherwise applicable at the inspected site which has to be applied. But there is a possibility for an international standard, as, according to the same provision, "appropriate detailed procedures shall be considered

---

24   § 10, para. 2, fourth sentence, German CWC Implementation Act.

25   Ann. 3, Part. II, para. 43.

and approved by the Conference ...". These rules have to be developed by the Preparatory Commission.

The question remains what happens if a damage occurs although these standards are respected or because they are violated. The basic rule concerning this problem is the customary rule that a subject of international law is responsible for illegal acts of its agents. Thus, the OPCW is responsible for any act or omission of the inspectors, which are its agents, in violation of the applicable international rule which requires the respect of national or, as the case may be, international safety standards. In contradistinction to the provisions of the Confidentiality Annex, there is no rule in the Verification Annex exempting the Organization from such customary law responsibility. Where this liability is invoked by the inspected State, it becomes a matter of the procedure, still to be elaborated, for the settlement of disputes.

This international rule, however, may not be very helpful for the aggrieved private party, especially if the inspected State for political or other reasons refrains from invoking the responsibility of the Organization.

If the aggrieved individual then wants to sue the Organization, the question of immunity of the latter arises. The exact scope of the immunity of the Organization remains to be determined,[26] but it can be assumed that the Organization will enjoy a complete jurisdictional immunity. This makes it impossible for private persons or enterprises which suffer a damage as a consequence of the act or omission of a member of an inspection team to sue the Organization directly. This could, thus, lead to the situation where there is no remedy, as a matter of both substantive and procedural law, for the person having suffered this damage. The reaction of national implementation legislation to this problem goes in absolutely opposite directions. While the Australian law expressly states that Australia is not liable "for any act or omission on the part of the organization or of an organization inspector, in implementing the Convention in Australia",[27] the German statute expressly states that in case of a damage caused by a member of an inspection team, the Federal Republic of Germany is liable according to the relevant provisions of German law which would be applicable if the damage were caused by an agent of the Federal Republic. The ordinary courts are designated as the competent jurisdiction.[28] Under German constitutional law, this provision probably is constitutionally required as it would be a violation of both the protection of private property and the guarantee of an effective judicial remedy if Germany concluded a

---

26   Art. VIII, paras. 48 and 50.
27   Sec. 103, Chemical Weapons (Prohibition) Act.
28   Para. 14, CWC Implementation Act.

treaty creating an obvious possibility that damage is caused to persons subject to German jurisdiction without any effective remedy to obtain redress. But as other constitutions and statutes seem to be less generous to their subjects, it may well be advisable for the OPCW to create a claims settlement procedure for private damage claims. This would certainly increase the acceptance which the inspection régime might have (or not have) with the chemical industry.

Beyond the specific question concerning the acceptance of the OPCW verification system, this is a general, important, but alas neglected issue of the law of international organizations. Agents of international organizations, working in many fields as diverse as peacekeeping and development assistance, are in a factual position to cause, by their official activities, damage to individuals.[29] It is a fundamental requirement of the rule of law, thus a basic human right requirement, that the individual has an effective remedy in this case. But due to the jurisdictional immunity of the organization and its agents, this is, as a general rule, excluded. An organization adhering to the rule of law should therefore create its own procedure to do justice to individual claims. Examples for such procedures (except for the rights of the officials of international organizations) are still rare. OPCW could set a good legal precedent by creating its own claims settlement procedures for damages arising out of its verification activities.

4.3 *Protection of Information*

The inspectors of the Organization, when conducting inspections, will have access to industrial and commercial secrets. They are entitled to that access in so far as these secrets are related to the purposes of the Convention. It is the purpose of the provisions concerning managed access, in particular relating to the challenge inspections,[30] that measures can be taken to protect secrets unrelated to the Convention.

If and to the extent that information which is to be protected as confidential is gained through the inspection process, that information is protected under the provisions of the Confidentiality Annex, the content of which has already been discussed in relation to information contained in declarations to be submitted to the Organization by Member States. It is of course more serious in relation to information obtained from on-site inspections.

---

29   On this problem cf. M. Bothe, "Internationale Organisationen und das Rechtsstaatprinzip", in *Des Menschen Recht zwischen Freiheit und Verantwortung, FS Karl Josef Partsch zum 75. Geburtstag*, 1989, pp. 493 *et seq.*

30   Ann. 3, Part X, paras. 46 and 48.

5   Conclusion

Effective implementation of the CWC requires certain duties to be imposed upon private persons or enterprises. On the other hand, this very implementation affects rights of these persons or enterprises which deserve protection. The Convention itself cannot solve this problem in elaborate detail. Much depends on a combined effect of the Convention on the one hand and national constitutional and/or statute law on the other. The legal mixture may be somewhat explosive; it requires at least very careful handling. I think that this Workshop has provided a good forum to spread this message.

9

Verification of Disarmament Treaties

Introduction

On the occasion of the 10th anniversary of the entry into force of the CWC, it is appropriate to ask what distinctive features of this arms control and disarmament regime account for its relative success. The first is that the regime constitutes a non-discriminatory and serious combination of arms control and disarmament measures. This distinguishes the CWC from the NPT, which is highly discriminatory, and from the BWC, which is more symbolic than serious. The second feature is the system of compliance control. Its design compares favourably with that of other regimes.

It is the purpose of this paper to analyse the compliance system in a comparative perspective. The core of this system is made up of various fact-finding procedures, called verification. Any evaluation of the performance of the CWC regime has to address the issue of verification. This paper proposes to do so in a comparative perspective, i.e. analyse CWC verification together with other compliance systems in the field of arms control and disarmament. There is an even broader perspective behind this approach as compliance systems are an important part of other treaty regimes as well nowadays, in particular in the field of international environmental law. Modern procedures to ensure compliance with international law owe their progress mainly to two fields: international environmental law and the law of arms control and disarmament. Although the safeguards system developed under the NPT has in many respects set the example, it is the CWC with its comprehensive verification approach which has established the standards, at least in the field of arms control, but perhaps also in other fields.[1] The arms control verification systems that have been negotiated but not put into practice (the BWC Verification Protocol – not adopted; the Comprehensive Test Ban Treaty [CTBT] – not ratified) clearly owe very much to the CWC system, despite all the differences which will be addressed. This paper tries to analyse the design of this system as a tool to deal with security concerns.

---

1   For a comparison see Michael Bothe, Ensuring compliance with Multilateral Environmental Agreements – Systems of Inspection and External Monitoring, in U. Beyerlin/P.-T. Stoll/R. Wolfrum (eds.), Ensuring Compliance with Multilateral Environmental Agreements, 2006, pp. 247, at 249 et seq.

© KONINKLIJKE BRILL NV, LEIDEN, 2021 | DOI:10.1163/9789004380592_011

The CWC establishes verification systems in relation to four different obligations, namely the obligation to:
- destroy chemical weapons in the possession of a country;
- destroy old or abandoned chemical weapons;
- destroy or convert chemical weapons production facilities;
- ensure that toxic chemicals and their precursors are only used for purposes not prohibited by the Convention, i.e. are not diverted to weapons purposes.

The first three obligations are disarmament obligations. The latter is an arms control obligation, it is designed to prevent new armaments. It is in particular this latter one which invites a comparison with other treaty regimes. The other treaties to be considered are the NPT, the BWC (including its Draft Verification Protocol) and the CTBT. The NPT and the CTBT are arms control, not disarmament treaties. The BWC was originally, like the CWC adopted much later, both a disarmament and arms control treaty, but the negotiated verification system only addresses the arms control aspect.

A basic difference between the four treaty regimes is that the NPT, the CWC and the CTBT establish an elaborate compliance system, while the BWC as it stands provides only for a complaint to the Security Council. While the compliance system of the NPT, the CWC and the CTBT also ends with the Security Council, seizing the Council is a means of last resort. It is preceded by an elaborate fact-finding system which normally would make recourse to the Council unnecessary. As to the BWC, the creation of such a system has been rendered impossible by the adamant opposition of the U.S. to a draft Verification Protocol which was very close to being adopted by the Fifth Review Conference in 2001/2002.[2] The provisions of the draft Protocol will nevertheless be included in the following comparative analysis of the design of arms control mechanisms.

1   The Quest for Efficiency: The Reliability of Measures to Ensure Compliance

In order to evaluate the verification systems in question, it is useful to recall the fundamental conflict of interest which they have to solve. There is a fundamental contradiction between the States' interests. On the one hand, the

---

2   For a statement of the course of events see the Final Document of the Fifth Review Conference, BWC.CONF.V/17; for an analysis of the draft Additional Protocol to the BWC see Onno Kervers, Strengthening Compliance with the Biological Weapons Convention: the Draft Protocol, 8 Journal of Conflict & Security Law 161 (2003).

VERIFICATION OF DISARMAMENT TREATIES

system must be reliable in order to provide security. Thus, it must be possible to ascertain all facts relevant in respect of compliance. This requires a certain intrusiveness of the system. On the other hand, States have an interest in not being exposed to intrusive scrutiny. At least some of that interest is legitimate. It starts with the safety of the processes in which relevant materials are handled and keeping commercial and industrial secrets and ends with military security. These conflicting interests must be balanced in the design of the fact-finding procedures.

The major elements of this balance will be described in the following section.

The legal bases for the fact-finding procedures are somewhat different. The NPT (Art. III) only establishes the duty of the non-nuclear weapons states (NNWS) to conclude an agreement with the IAEA for the purpose of verifying their compliance with the treaty obligations. Although the IAEA had already conducted some supervision of nuclear activities before the conclusion of the NPT based on guidelines published in the Information Circular (INFCIRC) 66/Rev.2, a new system was designed for the safeguards under the NPT in the form of a model agreement (INFCIRC 153).[3] This was then developed in a substantial way through a Model Additional Protocol in 1997.[4] While these model agreements shape the system, the legal basis for each state remains the individual bilateral agreement. In the case of the CWC and the CTBT, on the other hand, the essential content of the verification system is regulated in the multilateral treaty itself and its annexes. The same would apply for the BWC Verification Protocol.

2 The Accommodation of Conflicting Interests in Compliance Regimes: Intrusiveness vs. Secrecy

The balance between the interests just described is reflected in the design, i.e. in a number of details of the inspection regimes. They are all different. It has to be remembered that the content of any verification system depends, first of all, on the content of the relevant obligation. The CTBT relates to a particular activity, namely explosions which may constitute a nuclear weapons test. This has a definite impact on the design of the verification system. The other three

---

3 Torsten Lohmann, Die rechtliche Struktur der Sicherungsmaßnahmen der Internationalen Atomenergie-Organisation, Berlin 1993, p. 103 *et seq* on the background of this change.

4 Draft Model Protocol to Strengthen and Improve the Effectiveness and Efficiency of the IAEA Safeguards System, May 15, 1997, 36 ILM 1232 (1997).

regimes are concerned, instead, with diverting materials or facilities from a legitimate civilian to a prohibited military use. But as the materials and facilities are different, the verification systems most also be different.

For obvious practical reasons, the CTBT can rely to a large extent on a nonintrusive verification method, namely long-distance monitoring, e.g. through the collection of seismic and other data.[5] The other systems essentially rely on on-site verification.

In this respect, one basic distinction is the difference between routine inspections on the one hand and *ad hoc* (challenge) inspections on the other. In respect of the former, the general framework of the inspections is known beforehand. It is thus relatively easy to design a sophisticated system drawing a fine balance. That being so, the basic problem of a system limited to routine inspections is that there can be facilities which are outside the scope of these inspections. The NPT, the CWC and the BWC Verification Protocol use routine inspections, the CTBT does not. It provides only for *ad hoc* on-site inspections.[6]

There are four key elements in the verification regimes which are crucial for the balance of interests:
– scope of access;
– scope and means of fact-finding;
– confidentiality;
– reactions to stated or alleged violations.

As to the first element, controlled access, it is essential that on-site verification activities be possible only in relation to certain defined places. It is only at these places that the State is subject to the intrusive control of on-site inspections. As to the scope of fact-finding, the essential point is that information relevant for the purpose of the verification process is targeted, to the extent that it is really necessary. That information must not become known to persons outside the circle of those who really need to know. This has to be ensured by appropriate guarantees. The fact-finding ends with a statement of facts by the inspecting body. The question of what happens if that statement points to some irregularity is the most delicate part of the system.

2.1 *Routine Inspections*

2.1.1 Controlling Access

Declarations. All four types of routine inspections under the CWC are based on declarations. The locations where chemical weapons are stored as well as

---

5 The International Monitoring System, Article IV (B) CTBT.
6 Article IV (D) CTBT.

the quantities of these weapons, the existence of old or abandoned chemical weapons on the territory of a State, and the location of chemical weapons production facilities have to be declared.[7] These declarations are the starting point of the verification process.[8]

As to the arms control element of the CWC, the routine verification process is designed to ascertain whether certain chemicals which have a potential for being used for weapons purposes (but which also have peaceful applications) are being diverted from civilian to forbidden military uses. For this purpose, the States are obliged to declare all facilities where specific chemicals are handled in specific quantities.[9] It is in relation to these sites that routine verification takes place. This gives the State a certain factual control over what is and what is not subject to the verification process, and makes the sites to be inspected known beforehand.

The draft BWC Verification Protocol also relies on an elaborate system of declarations.[10] But as the scope of the facilities to be declared is quite extensive, the ensuing verification only covers a selected part of the facilities.[11] There are randomly selected transparency visits, voluntary assistance visits and voluntary clarification visits.

In the case of the NPT safeguards according to INFCIRC 153, the inspections take place in certain declared facilities at certain strategic points only.[12] After the experience with Iraq and North Korea which proceeded their weapons' programs outside these declared facilities, the declaration duties and the rights of access were expanded in the Additional Protocol. Under certain conditions, a right of access exists even in relation to undeclared facilities.

The examples show that there are two problems inherent in a "declaratory" system: The first is whether the declarations are complete, the second whether all or only a selection of the declared sites are to be inspected. As to the first problem, the correctness of the declarations made under the CWC are usually monitored, but the only way to ascertain whether all relevant sites are declared is through challenge inspections.[13] The selection process is regulated in various ways: comprehensive inspection of all sites, random selection, risk related selection, selection based on quantitative thresholds.

---

7   Art. III CWC.
8   Verification Annex, Parts IV and V.
9   Verfication Annex, Part VI sec. D, Part VII sec. A, Part. VIII sec. A, Part IX sec. A.
10   Art. 4 BWC Prot.
11   Art. 6 BWC Prot.
12   Lohmann, op. cit. p. 103, 205 et seq.
13   See below 3.2.

Key data. Another element limiting the verification process is its content. The fact-finding is limited to certain key data. In the case of the CWC arms control regime, the point of departure for identifying the key data are lists of chemicals known to possess weapon potential. The routine on-site inspections are designed to assess the balance (input, consumption, output) of these relevant chemical substances handled in a particular facility. This is thought to be the decisive indicator by which any diversion to prohibited purposes can be detected or excluded.

The concept of the NPT safeguards is based on similar considerations: the diversion of materiel used for peaceful purposes to weapons purposes should be excluded by controlling the materiel balances of the nuclear fuel cycle. This is the core element of the INFCIRC 153 verification system.[14] As it became clear that the assumption underlying the system was not quite true, i.e. that the verification of materiel balance sheets was sufficiently reliable as an indicator of compliance, the scope of fact-finding was substantially expanded by the Additional Protocol.

One of the difficult problems of the BWC is that the relevant materials are not really known. Technologically, the field of biological warfare is much more open to new developments. Nevertheless, the draft BWC Protocol defines controlled substances and facilities in a very elaborate way.[15]

2.1.2   Limited Publicity

The process of verification is strictly confidential. Confidentiality is indeed a crucial issue of all verification systems. As a matter of principle, the data remain in the Secretariat which is obliged to guarantee their confidentiality.[16]

2.2   *Challenge Inspections*

The possibility of challenge inspections, i.e. on-site inspections performed on the request of a State which doubts whether another State complies with its obligations, exists in the CWC, the BWC draft Protocol and the CTBT. Under the NPT, their role is to a certain extent fulfilled by special inspections which may, after consultations between the Secretariat and the State concerned, be decided by the Board of Governors.[17]

---

14   Lohmann, pp. 119 et seq.

15   Art. 4 and Annex A as well as Appendices.

16   NPT: Art. 15 Model Additional Protocol; CWC: Annex on the Protection of Confidential Information; BWC Prot.: Art. 11 and Annex C on confidentiality provisions.

17   Lohmann, p. 209; INFCIRC 153, § 18.

VERIFICATION OF DISARMAMENT TREATIES

2.2.1   The Obligation to Submit to Challenge Inspections

Under the CWC and the CTBT, the obligation to submit to challenge inspections is rather strict. Under the CWC, there is only a limited control against abuse exercised by the Executive Council.[18] Under the CTBT, the consideration of the Executive Council in admitting a request is a rather formal one.[19] In the case of the BWC draft Protocol, the screening of a request for an "investigation" is more complex.[20]

2.2.2   Measures of Protection

On the other hand, the State which is subject to these inspections may take certain measures to protect data. The rules concerning access to the inspected sites are very detailed. The inspected State may limit access in certain cases (managed access) (Part X of the Verification Annex, nos. 46 et seq). A similar regime applies to investigations pursuant to the CTBT[21] and the BWC draft Protocol.[22]

2.2.3   Limited Publicity

As in the case of routine inspections, the process is strictly confidential.

2.3   *Reactions*

The CWC and NPT verification systems are somehow based on the idea of a self-fulfilling prophecy: their very existence should induce States to comply and not to cheat. The fact that on-site inspections are indeed carried out considerably increases the political cost of non-compliance as the possibility of passing unnoticed decreases. Nevertheless, the issue of reactions to non-compliance remains a serious one.[23]

The path from verification to reaction to non-compliance is somewhat different under the different treaty regimes.

Under the CWC, inspections are a task of the Technical Secretariat (TS). The results, in the absence of any general reporting duties, thus remain within the ambit of the Secretariat. Where the TS, however, has, as a result of the

---

18   Art. IX para. 17.

19   Art. IV paragraphs 39 et seq. CTBT and Part II para. 41 of the Additional Protocol.

20   Art. 9 para. 23 BWC Prot.

21   Art. IV paragraph 57 (b) CTBT and Part. II, paragraphs 86 et seq. of the Additional Protocol.

22   Art. 9 Para. 23.

23   Alan Rosas, Reactions to non-compliance with the Chemical Weapons Convention, in Michael Bothe/Natalino Ronzitti/Alan Rosas (eds.), The New Chemical Weapons Convention – Implementation and Prospects, The Hague et al. 1998, pp. 415 et seq., at 416.

verification activities, "doubts, ambiguities or uncertainties about compliance",[24] it shall inform the Executive Council (EC). The EC may then, *inter alia*, "request the State Party to take measures to redress the situation".[25] If this request is not met, it may, *inter alia*, bring the matter to the attention of the Conference of the States Parties (CSP). The CSP shall "take the necessary measures to ensure compliance" with the Convention.[26] For that purpose, the CSP has three options:

– it may suspend the State's "rights and privileges under this Convention";
– it may "recommend" "collective measures ... in conformity with international law";
– it may bring the issue "to the attention of" the United Nations General Assembly (UNGA) and the UN Security Council (SC).

What the UNGA and/or the SC can do is a matter of their general powers and is not determined by the CWC. All in all, this system of enforcement is not really, except for the fact that behind everything is the Security Council, entitled to take enforcement action under the Charter. In this respect, the systems established by the CTBT[27] and the BWC draft Protocol are very similar.[28]

In the case of the NPT, the technical evaluation of the information received through the verification process is performed by the Secretariat. If a positive finding of compliance by the Secretariat is not possible, the Director General reports to the Board of Governors.[29] The latter may request the state, by a binding decision,[30] to remedy the situation. In the case of persistent non-compliance, the Board of Governors, according to Art. XIII.C of the IAEA Statute,

> shall report the non-compliance to all members and to the Security Council and General Assembly of the United Nations ...

As in the case of the CWC, these bodies' powers concerning further action depend on the Charter of the United Nations.

---

24   Art. VIII paragraph 40 CWC.
25   Art. VIII paragraph 36 CWC; art. 6 para. 104 draft BWC Prot. is comparable.
26   Art. VIII paragraph 21 (k).
27   Art. IV paragraph 65, V CTBT.
28   Art. 9 (1), 12. BWC Prot.
29   Lohmann, p. 236.
30   Lohmann, p. 244.

VERIFICATION OF DISARMAMENT TREATIES

2.4 The Special Arms Control Measures Decided by the Security Council: Iraq and Resolution 1540

Unlike the treaty regimes just described, the inspection system imposed upon Iraq by the armistice resolution of the Security Council in 1991[31] was unlimited in law, limited in practice only by the lack of co-operation of the "host" State. After many had assumed that it was a failure and that Iraq still had weapons of mass destruction and a nuclear weapons programme, it was found that the system had indeed been effective and had discovered everything there was to discover.

The supervision system was established and modified by a series of UNSC resolutions, beginning with resolution 687 (1991), and then continuing in particular with resolutions 1284 (1999) and 1441 (2002). The legal basis for these resolutions was Art. 41 (non-military enforcement measures), based on the assumption that the suspected presence of WMD in the possession of Iraq constituted a threat to the peace. Security Council resolution 1540 of 28 April 2004, which contains measures to stop the proliferation of WMD s, is different. It expressly reserves concerning existing treaty regimes. Its compliance control system does not include any on-site inspections or the like; rather, it is based on a system of State reports.[32]

2.5 Evaluation

Treaty regimes serve two different functions. The first is verification as a means of confidence building. Both the CTBT[33] and the BWC draft Protocol[34] provide for particular confidence-building measures in connection with verification. Participation in the system instils confidence and gives assurances of security. In this respect, the systems can be considered successful. The CWC system works quietly and smoothly, with problems lying in the details, not in the fundamental issues.[35] The safeguard system of the NPT covers all NNWS. It is significant for the acceptance of the system that Brazil, Argentina and South Africa have joined it after having renounced their nuclear option. The members

---

31 Resolution 687 of 3 April 1991.

32 Paragraph 5 of the resolution.

33 Art. IV paragraphs 57 and 68 CTBT.

34 Art. 15 BWC Prot.

35 According to the annual reports of the OPCW, declarations have been submitted as required, with some delays, as to chemical weapons possessed by States, chemical weapons production facilities, riot control agents, facilities handling specific chemicals. The destruction of chemical weapons and production facilities proceeds (in some cases with delays) and is verified. The routine inspection system is working with certain delays and sometimes subject to budgetary restrictions.

of the former Soviet Union, i.e. of a NWS, also gave up nuclear armament and joined the NPT as NNWS. This would not have been possible had the safeguard system not fulfilled its confidence-building function, at least *grosso modo*. The question mark thus left brings us to the second function.

The second function is the prevention of cheating. In the light of the compromise character of the systems which has been stressed above, one could not expect them to be absolutely fool-proof. There have been two cases of cheating – one can say two too much and conclude that the NPT safeguard system has not been successful enough. North Korea started cheating while it was still a party to the NPT. Iraq cheated, too, and for a while successfully. It is only after the general Security Council verification system was imposed on Iraq that the programme was discontinued. This shows the pros and cons of the current situation: the existing verification systems are not an absolute guarantee against cheating, but the establishment of a system as intrusive as the measures taken against Iraq is completely unacceptable as a general principle.

3   Conclusions

How effective are the legal restraints on unlawful armaments and in particular on the proliferation of weapons of mass destruction? The answer seems to be the usual optimism/pessimism paradigm: Is the glass half full or half empty?

The C-weapons disarmament and arms control system seems to be in a relatively stable condition. The safe destruction of the existing stocks proceeds, not without problems, but it works. The inspection system designed to prevent diversion of chemical substances from peaceful to military purposes has started functioning. No major problems are reported.

The B-weapons system, on the other hand, relies for the time being exclusively on hope. In the absence of anything like a serious system to ensure compliance, the treaty remains symbolic rather than a real factor restraining proliferation.

The NPT is of doubtful design. One may conclude that it has not contained the circle of nuclear powers, but restrained its growth. Even though it is one of the multilateral treaties with the broadest participation, it lacks the necessary universality because of the factual importance of the absentees. Its compliance system has worked reasonably well, but timely discovery of non-compliance has not always been possible. The problem of governments pursuing a nuclear option remains and may even become more acute. And whether the treaty can really prevent nuclear weapons from getting into private hands also remains to be seen. The fact that the NPT Review Conference held in 2005 was unable to take any substantive decision on the various problems of the NPT shows that this treaty regime is in crisis.

Even when and to the extent that verification systems work, reaction to non-compliance or to armament by non-participants remains an open issue. Legally speaking, it is in the hands of the Security Council – with all the problems that entails. The unilateral option has also been used, and remains a threat in the background.[36]

In a way, the CWC still stands alone as a model. It creates a non-discriminatory disarmament regime (a distant and neglected goal of the NPT) strictly controlled by an on-site verification system, as well as arms control measures equally under strict on-site control using both routine and *ad hoc* inspections. Above all, the system works despite the technical difficulties and the transaction costs involved.

---

36 See the "Proliferation Security Initiative" announced by President Bush on 31 May 2003.

Non-Proliferation of Weapons of Mass Destruction

Treaty Regimes between Efficiency and Discrimination

1   Introduction

The security problem caused by the proliferation of weapons of mass destruction has changed in character over the last decades. The perception of the problem started with the negotiations of the Non-Proliferation Treaty (NPT) in the late 60ies. The purpose of this treaty was to ensure the *status quo* of the nuclear balance between the military blocks by preventing third States from becoming nuclear powers as well.[1] The basic concept was, thus, inherently discriminatory (or to put it more nicely: asymmetrical): the world should be divided in lawful nuclear powers (in the beginning US, UK and ussr, now the P5) and non-nuclear powers.

The nuclear option, however, remained attractive for a number of States. Under the impact of the great powers, however, the regime very soon got a widespread, though not universal participation. Yet a number of States pursued the nuclear option for security perceptions of their own, partly by remaining outside the NPT, partly although being a party to it, i.e. by cheating.

The concern for the nuclear balance between the superpowers has gone. Whether it might reappear in another form is a question for the future. Today, the security problem posed by nuclear weapons is rather seen, at least by many relevant actors, in the existence of so-called new threats,[2] i.e. in the fact that these weapons could get into the hands of irresponsible governments ("rogue States") or of irresponsible private actors ("terrorists").

In the field of chemical and biological weapons, the legal and practical situation has been different. They are both subject to a treaty regime (the Biological Weapons Convention [BWC] of 1972 and the Chemical Weapons Convention [CWC] of 1993) which is inherently non-discriminatory, at least in theory. The prevention of proliferation is part and parcel of a prohibition of possession and acquisition of the weapons. As a matter of principle, the great powers

---

1   See Michael Bothe, Friedenssicherung und Kriegsrecht, in Wolfgang Graf Vitzthum (ed.), Völkerrecht, 3rd ed. 2004, p. 625.

2   For an analysis see Marc Weller, The Changing Environment for Forcible Responses to Non-traditional Threats, 92 ASIL Proceedings 177 (1998).

NON-PROLIFERATION OF WEAPONS OF MASS DESTRUCTION

are subject to the same obligations as any other State. But the question of the "new threats" also dominates the security issues which these treaty regimes should solve.

If the three treaty regimes were universally obligatory *and* applied in practice, there would be no problem of proliferation. Both is not the case.

As to the problem of universal participation, there remain significant gaps. The NPT has 189 parties, which means a quasi-universal participation. However, the absentees are Israel, India and Pakistan. The treaty status of North Korea was for a while somewhat unclear,[3] but it was clarified that North Korea finally withdrew, which was regretted by the Security Council. The BWC has only 155 parties, but the gaps do not really have a security significance, except for the non-participation of Israel, Egypt and Syria. The CWC enjoys a wider participation, namely 180 parties, the significant absentees being Israel, Iraq, Egypt and Lebanon. There is also one significant late ratifyer, namely Libya 2004.

As to the second problem, the practical application, the means to ensure compliance with these treaties are essential. This is the question which this paper will address first. It will then ask how theses regimes deal with existing asymmetries, in particular whether they affect (positively or negatively) the functioning of these regimes. It will highlight the role which played by the United Nations, in particular the Security Council. The role of, and effect on, non-State actors will also be discussed. On the one hand, non-State actors are essential ingredients of the so-called new threats, on the other hand private industry is a major factor in the relevant regimes. Finally, the paper will come back to the problem of universal participation in relation to the NPT.

2 The Quest for Efficiency: The Reliability of Measures to Ensure Compliance

The basic difference between the three treaty regimes is that the NPT and the CWC establish an elaborate compliance system, while the BWC just provides for a complaint to the Security Council.[4] While the compliance system of the NPT and the CWC could also end with the Security Council,[5] seizing

---

3   For more details see below 4.4.2; see also Chamundeeswari Kuppuswamy, The Nuclear Non-Proliferation Treaty Shaking at its Foundations? Stocktaking after the 2005 NPT Review Conference, 11 Journal of Conflict & Security Law 141 (2006), at 148 et seq.

4   See below 4.4.

5   See below 4.4.

the Council is only a means of last resort. It is preceded by an elaborate fact-finding system which normally would make recourse to the Council unnecessary. As to the BWC, the creation of such a system has been rendered impossible by the adamant resistance of the U.S. against a draft Protocol which was very close to being adopted by the Fifth Review Conference in 2001/2002.[6]

The problem involved in the creation of such systems for ascertaining facts is a fundamental contradiction between the States' interests. On the one hand, the system must be reliable in order to provide security. Thus, it must be possible to ascertain all facts relevant in respect of compliance. This requires a certain intrusiveness of the system. On the other hand, States have interests in not being exposed to intrusive scrutiny, at least some of which are legitimate. They start with the safety of the processes where relevant materials are handled, the maintenance of commercial and industrial secrets and end with military security interests. These conflicting interests must be balanced in the design of the fact-finding procedures.

The major elements of this balance will be described in the following section.

The legal basis for the fact-finding procedures are somewhat different in the two cases. The NPT (Art. III) only provides for a duty of the non-nuclear weapons states (NNWS) to conclude an agreement with the IAEA for the purpose of verifying their compliance with the treaty obligation. Although the IAEA already conducted some supervision of nuclear activities before the conclusion of the NPT based on guidelines published in the Information Circular (INFCIRC) 66/Rev.2, a new system was designed for the safeguards under the NPT in the form of a model agreement (INFCIRC 153).[7] The latter system was developed in a substantial way through a Model Additional Protocol in 1997.[8] These model agreements do shape the system, the legal basis for each state remains the individual bilateral agreement. In the case of the CWC, on the other hand, the essential content of the verification system is regulated in the multilateral treaty and its annexes.

---

6   For a statement of the course of events see the Final Document of the Fifth Review Conference, BWC.CONF.V/17; for an analysis of the draft Additional Protocol to the BWC see Onno Kervers, Strengthening Compliance with the Biological Weapons Convention: the Draft Protocol, 8 Journal of Conflict & Security Law 161 (2003).

7   Torsten Lohmann, Die rechtliche Struktur der Sicherungsmaßnahmen der Internationalen Atomenergie-Organisation, Berlin 1993, p. 103 *et seq* on the background of this change.

8   Draft Model Protocol to Strengthen and Improve the Effectiveness and Efficiency of the IAEA Safeguards System, May 15, 1997, 36 ILM 1232 (1997).

3 The Accommodation of Conflicting Interests in Compliance Regimes: Intrusiveness v. Secrecy

Modern procedures to ensure compliance with international law owe their progress mainly to two fields: international environmental law and the law of arms control and disarmament. Although the safeguards system developed under the NPT has in many respects set the example, it is the CWC with its comprehensive verification approach which has established the standards.

The balance between the interests just described is reflected in a number of details of the inspection regimes. A basic distinction in this respect is the difference between routine inspections on the one hand and challenge or special inspections on the other. In respect of the former, the general framework of the inspections is known beforehand. It is thus relatively easy to design a sophisticated system drawing a fine balance. That being so, the basic problem of a system limited to routine inspections is what happens in those facilities which are outside the scope of these inspections.

There are four key elements in the verification regimes which are crucial for the balance of interests:
- scope of access;
- scope of fact-finding
- confidentiality;
- reactions to stated or alleged violations.

As to the first element, the controlled access, it is essential that on site verification activities are possible only in relation to certain defined places. It is only at these places that the State is subject to the intrusive control of on site inspections. As to the scope of fact-finding, the essential point is that information relevant for the purpose of the verification process is targeted, but only to the extent that it is really necessary. That information must not become known to persons outside the circle of those who really need to know. This has to be ensured by appropriate guarantees. The fact-finding ends with a statement of facts by the inspecting body. The question what happens if that statement points to some irregularity is the most delicate one in the system.

3.1 *Routine Inspections*
3.1.1 Controlling Access
3.1.1.1 *Declarations*

The routine verification process of the CWC is designed to find out whether certain chemicals which have a potential of being used for weapons purposes (but which also have peaceful applications) are diverted from civilian to forbidden military uses. For this purpose, the States are obliged to declare all facilities where specific chemical are handled in specific quantities. It is in relation to these sites that routine verification takes place. This gives the State a certain factual control over what is subject to the verification process and what not, and it makes the sites to be inspected known beforehand.

In the case of the NPT safeguards according to INFCIRC 153, the inspections also take place in certain declared facilities at certain strategic points only.[9] After the experience with Iraq and North Korea which had promoted their weapons' programs outside these declared facilities, the declaration duties and the rights of access were expanded in the Additional Protocol. Under certain conditions, a right of access exists even in relation to undeclared facilities.

3.1.1.2 *Key Data*

Another element limiting the verification process is its content. The fact-finding is limited to certain key data. In the case of the CWC, the point of departure for determining what are the key data are lists of chemicals which are known to possess a weapons potential. The routine on site inspections are designed to ascertain the balance (input, consumption, output) of these relevant chemical substances handled in a particular facility. This is thought to be the decisive indicator by which any diversion to prohibited purposes can be detected or excluded.

The concept of the NPT safeguards is based on similar considerations: the diversion of materiel used for peaceful purposes to weapons purposes should be excluded by controlling the materiel balances of the nuclear fuel cycle. This is the core element of the INFCIRC 153 verification system.[10] As it became clear that the assumption underlying the system, i.e. that the verification of materiel balance sheets was reliable enough as an indicator of compliance, was not quite true, the scope of fact-finding was substantially expanded by the Additional Protocol.

3.1.2 Limited Publicity

The process of verification is strictly confidential. Confidentiality is indeed a crucial issue of both verification systems. As a matter of principle, the data remain in the Secretariat which is obliged to guarantee their confidentiality.[11]

---

9   Lohmann, op. cit. p. 103, 205 et seq.
10   Lohmann, pp. 119 et seq.
11   NPT: Art. 15 Model Additional Protocol; CWC: Annex on the Protection of Confidential Information.

3.1.3 Reactions

The CWC and NPT verification systems are in a way designed as a self-fulfilling prophecy: their very existence should induce States to comply and not to cheat. The fact that indeed on site inspections are performed considerably increases the political cost of non-compliance as the possibility to pass through unnoticed decreases. Nevertheless, the issue of reactions to non-compliance remains a serious one.[12]

The path from the verification system to reaction to non-compliance is somewhat different under the two treaty regimes.

Under the CWC, the inspections are a task of the Technical Secretariat (TS). The results, in the absence of any general reporting duties, thus remain within the ambit of the Secretariat. Where the TS, however, has, as a result of the verification activities, "doubts, ambiguities or uncertainties about compliance",[13] it shall inform the Executive Council (EC). The EC, then, may *inter alia* "request the State Party to take measures to redress the situation".[14] If this request is not met, it may, *inter alia*, bring the matter to the attention of the Conference of the States Parties (CSP). The CSP shall "take the necessary measure to ensure compliance" with the Convention.[15] For that purpose, the CSP has three options:

- It may suspend the State's "rights and privileges under this Convention";
- It may "recommend" "collective measures ... in conformity with international law";
- It may bring the issue "to the attention of" the UNGA and the UNSC.

What the GA and/or the SC can do is a matter of their general powers, it is not determined by the CWC.[16] This is not really a tough looking system of enforcement, except for the fact that behind all this, there is the Security Council entitled to take enforcement action under the Charter.

In the case of the NPT, the technical evaluation of the information received through the verification process is performed by the Secretariat. If a positive finding of compliance by the Secretariat is not possible, the Director General reports to the Board of Governors.[17] The latter may request the state, by a binding

---

12 Alan Rosas, Reactions to non-compliance with the Chemical Weapons Convention, in Michael Bothe/Natalino Ronzitti/Alan Rosas (eds.), The New Chemical Weapons Convention – Implementation and Prospects, The Hague et al. 1998, pp. 415 et seq., at 416.

13 Art. VIII paragraph 40 CWC.

14 Art. VIII paragraph 36 CWC.

15 Art. VIII paragraph 21 (k).

16 See below/.

17 Lohmann, p. 236.

decision,[18] to remedy the situation. In the case of persistent non-compliance, the Board of Governors, according to Art. XIII.C of the IAEA Statute,

> shall report the non-compliance to all members and to the Security Council and General Assembly of the United Nations ...

As in the case of the CWC, their powers concerning further action depend on the Charter of the United Nations.

3.2   *Challenge Inspections*

The possibility of challenge inspections, i.e. on site inspections performed on the request of a State which doubts whether another State complies with its obligations, only exists in the case of the CWC. Under the NPT, their role is to a certain extent fulfilled by special inspections which may, after consultations between the Secretariat and the State concerned, be decided by the Board of Governors.[19]

3.2.1   The Obligation to Submit to Challenge Inspections

The obligation to submit to challenge inspections is rather strict. There is only a limited control against abuse exercised by the Executive Council (Art. IX para. 17).

3.2.2   Measures of Protection

On the other hand, the State which is subject to these inspections may take certain measure to protect data. The rules concerning access to the inspected sites are very detailed. The inspected State may limit access in certain cases (managed access) (Part X of the Verification Annex, nos. 46 et seq).

3.2.3   Limited Publicity

As in the case of routine inspections, the process is strictly confidential.

3.2.4   Reactions

The challenge inspection under the CWC ends with the final report of the inspection team which goes to the EC. The Convention does not say that the EC has the formal power to state in any binding way whether there is compliance

---

18   Lohmann, p. 244.
19   Lohmann, p. 209; INFCIRC 153, § 18.

NON-PROLIFERATION OF WEAPONS OF MASS DESTRUCTION

or not. Where it "reaches the conclusion ... that further action may be necessary ... it may take the appropriate measures to redress the situation and to ensure compliance with this Convention".[20] The following steps are the same as in the case of routine inspections.

3.3 The Special Case of Iraq

In contradistinction to the treaty regimes just described, the inspection system imposed upon Iraq by the armistice resolution of the Security Council in 1991[21] was unlimited in law, limited in practice only by the lack of co-operation of the "host" State. After many had assumed that it was a failure and that Iraq still had weapons of mass destruction and a nuclear weapons programme, it was found out that the system was indeed effective and had discovered everything there was.

The supervision system was established and modified by a series of UNSC resolutions, beginning with resolution 687 (1991), and then continued in particular by resolutions 1284 (1999) and 1441 (2002). The legal basis for these resolutions is Art. 41 (non-military enforcement measures), based on the assumption that the suspected presence of WMD in the possession of Iraq constituted a threat to the peace.

3.4 Evaluation

As to the treaty regimes, they serve two different functions. The first one is verification as a means of confidence building. Participation in the system instils confidence and gives assurances of security. In this respect, the systems can be considered as successful. The CWC system works quietly and smoothly, the problems being in details, not in fundamental issues.[22] The safeguards system of the NPT covers all NNWS. It is significant for the acceptance of the system that Brazil, Argentina and South Africa have joined it after having renounced to their nuclear option. The members of the former Soviet Union, i.e. of a NWS, also gave up nuclear armament and joined the NPT as NNWS. This would not have been possible had the safeguards system not fulfilled its confidence

---

20 Art. Art. IX (23) CWC.
21 Resolution 687 of 3 April 1991.
22 According to the annual reports of the OPCW, declarations have been submitted as required, with some delays, as to chemical weapons possessed by States, chemical weapons production facilities, riot control agents, facilities handling specific chemicals. The destruction of chemical weapons and production facilities proceeds (in some cases with delays) and is verified. The routine inspection system is working with certain delays and sometimes subject to budgetary restrictions.

building function, at least *grosso modo*. The question mark thus left brings us to the second function.

The second function is the prevention of cheating. In the light of the compromise character of the systems which has been stressed above, one could not expect them to be absolutely fool-proof. There have been two cases of cheating – one can say two too much and conclude that the NPT safeguards system has not been successful enough. North Korea started cheating while it still was a party to the NPT. Iraq cheated, too, and for a while successfully. It is only after the general Security Council verification system was imposed on Iraq that the programme had to be discontinued. This shows the pros and cons of the current situation: the existing verification systems are no absolute guarantee against cheating, but the establishment of a system as intrusive as the measures against Iraq is completely unacceptable as a general principle.

4   Arms Control and Disarmament in an Asymmetrical World – the Crisis of Reciprocity

Reciprocity is a major factor or driving force for international law.[23] In treaty making, reciprocity in the sense of a *quid pro quo* is a major precondition for the conclusion of a treaty. A treaty is generally accepted by one party because there are corresponding obligations of the other. As to the actual respect of international norms, it is also the mutual expectation of, and interest in, treaty observance that induces States to comply. Reciprocity is a stabilising factor in international relations.

This is, as a matter of principle, also true for arms control and disarmament. The core elements of the arms control treaties between the superpowers during the Cold War are essentially based on this idea of a balance between them, i.e. reciprocity. The same holds true for the newer multilateral treaties such as the CWC. The design of that treaty is that it provides the same security for all parties by submitting all parties to the same discipline.

Reciprocity, however, does not necessarily mean identical obligations for all. In *de facto* asymmetrical situations, unequal obligations may be an appropriate means to compensate these asymmetries. But unequal obligations may just reflect unequal power positions – in which case the lack of reciprocity can be a destabilising factor.

---

23   Bruno Simma, Reciprocity, in: Rudolf Bernhardt (ed.), Encyclopedia of Public International Law vol. IV, pp. 29 et seq.

NON-PROLIFERATION OF WEAPONS OF MASS DESTRUCTION

It is in the light of these fundamental reflections that we shall briefly analyse the various treaty regimes.

4.1 Nuclear and Non-nuclear Powers – the *Quid Pro Quo* of the NPT and Its Fallacies

It has already been pointed out that the NPT regime is inherently asymmetrical. The NNWS, and only them, may not be given, and may not acquire, nuclear weapons (Art. I and II). For that purpose, the NNWS, and only them, are subject to the safeguards system. This means that the NNWS have given up a major part of their freedom of decision in matters of armament, or, if one wishes to put it that way, of their sovereignty. What have they received in exchange? The *quid pro quo* of this deal contains three elements, all three of doubtful value.

The first one is the guarantee of the right to the peaceful use of nuclear energy. Recent developments make it necessary to quote Art. IV para. 1 in full:

> Nothing in this treaty shall be interpreted as affecting the inalienable right of all the Parties to the treaty to develop research, production and use of nuclear energy for peaceful purposes without discrimination and in conformity with Articles I and II of this Treaty.

This implies that any development of nuclear technology which is not for peaceful purposes does not fall under the protection of Art. IV. The essential question raised by the Iran case is whether this "inalienable right" already seizes to exist where other States claim, or have serious reason to believe, that a certain development of nuclear technology is not meant to be for "peaceful purposes". What are the powers of the Security Council in this case? What are the procedural safeguards for a State so accused which claims that the development it undertakes is indeed for peaceful purposes only? We will revert to this question below.

The second balancing element consists in the concept that this asymmetrical situation should only be transitional. Therefore, the Treaty recognizes a duty of the Parties to negotiate for a complete nuclear disarmament, i.e. for the complete elimination of nuclear weapons by <u>all</u> States. Art. VI reads:

> Each of the Parties to the Treaty undertakes to pursue negotiations in good faith on effective measures relating to cessation of the nuclear arms race at an early date and to nuclear disarmament, and on a treaty on general and complete disarmament under strict and effective international control.

The ICJ, in its Advisory Opinion on the legality of the threat or use of nuclear weapons, has emphasized and buttressed this obligation.[24] In relation to the said Art. VI, the Court held:

> The legal import of that obligation goes beyond that of a mere obligation of conduct; the obligation involved here is an obligation to achieve a precise result – nuclear disarmament in all its aspects – by adopting a particular course of conduct, namely, the pursuit of negotiations on the matter in good faith.

The third balancing element, finally, is not even found in the treaty itself. Rather vague "positive security" guarantees are given to NNWS by means of unilateral declarations of the nuclear powers[25] which are endorsed by the Security Council.[26] "Negative" guarantees (commitment not to use nuclear weapons) were later given by unilateral declarations of all official NWS, and the Security Council took note of them.[27]

What can be said about the overall effectiveness of the treaty? The safeguards system has worked quite satisfactorily although it has not prevented cheating in the cases of two "unreliable" States. The problem of the lack of universality remains although at least three States have renounced the nuclear option and joined the system after having done so. The elements which should have compensated the discriminatory character of the system have not worked or not worked well: the obligation of complete nuclear disarmament, the assistance in the peaceful use of nuclear energy and security guarantees.

4.2 The Haves and the Have-nots: The Nuclear Suppliers Group

There is yet another element in the non proliferation regime which is asymmetric, and this is the regime of exports controls. The Nuclear Suppliers Group,[28] or "London club", is an informal group of States that possess and thus export nuclear technology through which they coordinate their export controls. The

---

24 International Court of Justice, Legality of the Threat or Use of Nuclear Weapons, Advisory Opinion of 8 July 1996, paragraphs 98 et seq.

25 Declaration of the Depositary States of the NPT, 17 June 1968, Department of State Bulletin vol. 59, no. 1515, p. 57.

26 These declarations were "welcomed" by the Security Council, and the Council recognises that an attack with nuclear weapons against a NNWS would "create a situation in which the Security Council would have to act", Res. 255 of 19 June 1968.

27 Resolution 984 of 11 April 1995.

28 For an updated overview of the activities of the NSG, see the IAEA Doc. INF/CIRC/538/rev.3 of 30 May 2005.

NON-PROLIFERATION OF WEAPONS OF MASS DESTRUCTION

fundamental export condition agreed upon in the club is that any importer of their technology must submit to IAEA safeguards.

4.3   The Haves and the Have-nots: The Australia Group

The Australia Group[29] is in the field of BW and CW similar to the Nuclear Suppliers Group: it coordinates the conditions of export controls. As between parties to the CWC, one can argue that the purpose pursued by these export controls, namely preventing the spread of chemical weapons, is fulfilled by the CWC, so that the export controls are no longer needed. Nevertheless, they are maintained by the Group, officially to enhance the implementation of the Convention. The issue is somewhat controversial.[30]

4.4   The Role of the Security Council in the Field of Arms Control
4.4.1   Treaty Regimes

A number of treaties refer to the Security Council as a kind of enforcement agent in case of non-compliance. This is, in particular, the case of the non-proliferation regimes presented in this paper although the three cases are different.

In the case of the BWC, the complaint alleging non-compliance goes directly to the Security Council (Art. VI).

The CWC, on the other hand, has its own and autonomous non-compliance and dispute settlement procedure. The supreme organ of that system is the Conference of the OPCW (Art. VIII para. 36, IX paras. 23–25, XII). Only in cases of particular gravity will the case be submitted to the UN General Assembly or the Security Council by the Executive Council or by the Conference of the OPCW (Art. VIII para. 36, XII para. 4).

In the case of the NPT, the basis for referring a matter to the Security Council is found in the Statute of IAEA, in the article on safeguards. Art. XII C reads in the relevant part:

> The Board shall report the non-compliance to all members and to the Security Council and General Assembly of the United Nations.

The powers of the Security Council are the same in the three cases. They do not derive from the respective treaties, as those treaties cannot increase nor restrict the powers the Security Council has under the UN Charter. This means

---

29   For information see the website of the group www.australiagroup.net.

30   Natalino Ronzitti, Economic and technological development and trade in chemicals, in: Bothe/Ronzitti/Rosas (eds.) op.cit. note 12, pp. 533 et seq.

that the general Charter powers of the Security Council will determine what the Council may (or may not?) do in a particular instance.

4.4.2 The Powers of the Security Council under the UN Charter

The relevant powers of the Security Council derive from Ch. VI and VII of the Charter. In the case of a dispute "the continuation of which is likely to endanger the maintenance of international peace and security" (Ch. VI, Art. 33), the Council may adopt recommendations (Art. 36). More important are the cases where the Council adopts enforcement measures under Ch. VII. According to Art. 39, this presupposes that the Council "determine(s) the existence of any threat to the peace, breach of the peace, or act of aggression".

There have been three cases where the Security Council has dealt with the issue of the (alleged) nuclear armament of a NNWS, namely Iraq, North Korea and Iran.

In the case of Iraq,[31] the Council acted outside the IAEA system. It had already determined that there was a threat to the peace (even after the withdrawal of Iraq from Kuwait) and had imposed arms control measures on Iraq well before it received the first report from IAEA (resolution 687 of April 1991). These measures followed a double track approach: IAEA was tasked with monitoring concerning nuclear weapons, while a special United Nations organ, namely UNSCOM had to do the monitoring concerning chemical and biological weapons and certain forbidden weapons delivery systems. Access to the relevant information was a difficult issue for both institutions as and to the extent that Iraq did not fully cooperate. It is only after the end of the process that it became clear that both institutions had indeed all information there was – and that nothing hidden was left. Iraq remains a special case in that a State's armament was considered to be an element of a threat to the peace after an armed conflict, which led the Security Council to use all its fact-finding powers and the threat of further enforcement measures in order to make the State comply.

In the case of North Korea, there are different phases of the crisis. North Korean efforts to develop nuclear weapons have a long history. Nevertheless, it became a member of the NPT in 1985. It appears that this was not reason enough for North Korea to give up its nuclear programme, a fact which led to a continued dispute between the country and others, in particular South Korea

---

31 Thilo Marauhn, The Implementaion of Disarmament and Arms Control Obligations Imposed upon Iraq by the Security Council, 52 Zeitschrift für ausländisches öffentliches Recht und Völkerrecht 781 (1992).

and the United States. In 1993, the Security Council dealt for the first time with the nuclear programme of North Korea.

The second phase was the announcement of a nuclear test. The Security Council was immediately seized. In October 2006,[32] the Council declared that the test constituted a threat to the peace and adopted non-military enforcement measures under Article 41 of the Charter. They consist of an arms and technology embargo, and embargo on luxury goods (specially targeting the ruling elite), freezing of relevant financial resources and travel restrictions.

In the case of Iran, action of the Security Council was triggered by the fact that the Board of Governors of the IAEA uttered doubt as to Iran's compliance.[33] On that basis, the Security Council determined that the situation constituted a threat to the peace and, based on Article 40 of the Charter, demanded that Iran discontinue its uranium enrichment programme.[34] The next step was a resolution[35] adopting, based on Article 41, non-military enforcement measures.

While in the case of Iraq, it was not really doubted, at least not in 1991, that there was a threat to the peace, the cases of Iran and North Korea are not so clear. It may well be argued that there is, objectively speaking, no threat to the peace. The leads to the highly controversial question whether the determination made by the Council conclusively disposes of the matter, in other words whether the Council has a discretion in making the determination, or at least a very broad margin of appreciation. This author is of the view that the Security Council has no discretion, only a margin of appreciation. Thus, in contradistinction to the case where there is discretion, the determination may be legally flawed – and especially Iran claims that to be the case. But it is practically very difficult, if not impossible to legally challenge it.

The cases just described relate to the danger of proliferation caused by specific countries. In its efforts to restrain proliferation, the Council has gone a step further. In resolution 1540,[36] it has set up a general scheme of measures designed to prevent the proliferation of WMD s. It determines that

---

32   Resolution 1718 of 14 October 2006.

33   IAEA Board of Governors resolution GOV/2006/14 and various reports of the Director General.

34   Resolution 1696 of 31 July 2006.

35   Resolution 1737 of 23 December 2006.

36   Resolution 1540 of 28 April 2004; see Lars Olberg, Massenvernichtungswaffen kontrollieren. Bilanz nach zwei Jahren UN-Sicherheitsratsresolution 1540, Vereinte Nationen 54 (2006), pp. 189 et seq.

230

PART 3: ARMS CONTROL

> proliferation of nuclear, chemical and biological weapons, as well as their
> means of delivery, constitutes a threat to international peace and security,

and, probably based on Article 41, obliges all member States to adopt a series
of measures designed to prevent that proliferation:

- appropriate legislation prohibiting, and making a criminal offence, proliferation prone activities by non-State actors;
- appropriate control and physical protection measures;
- control measures relating to trade, in particular export and import controls.

This is a new dimension of Security Council activities where the Council acts
as a quasi-legislator, which is somewhat controversial.[37] By resolution 1540, the
Council takes up the precedent by the earlier resolution of combating terrorism which uses a similar approach.[38]

5   Non-State Actors

The treaty regimes mentioned above affect non-State actors in different ways.

5.1   *Private Enterprise*

Private enterprise is in various ways affected by the CWC and NPT regimes and
is a matter of concern for those regimes.

As to the CWC, most of the chemicals which have the potential of serving
for weapons purposes and, thus, present a danger of being diverted to such
purposes are handled by private industry. Thus, it is private industry which is
subject to the verification regime. The functioning of that system is therefore
of vital importance for the private sector, in particular chemical industry. This
explains the very active participation of the chemical industry in the negotiation process of the CWC. It is fair to say that the outcome of these negotiations,
i.e. the CWC has created a system the industry can live with, notwithstanding
the fact that there are occasional assertions to the contrary.

To the extent that peaceful uses of nuclear energy occur in facilities owned
by private enterprise and not in installations run by States, the NPT verification
regime also concerns private industry.

---

37   Markus Wagner, Die wirtschaftlichen Maßnahmen des Sicherheitsrats nach dem
11. September 2001 im völkerrechtlichen Kontext – Von Wirtschaftssanktionen zur
Wirtschaftsgesetzgebung, 63 Zeitschrift für ausländisches öffentliches Recht und
Völkerrecht 879 (2003).

38   Resolution 1373 of 28 September 2001.

5.2 *Terrorism*

Violence by "non-state actors", commonly called terrorism is one of the major security problems of our time. Therefore, the control and prevention of terrorist activities which might use weapons of mass destruction constitutes a major problem. Possession of WMD s by "rogue States" and (whether acquired through rogue States or in any other way) by terrorist organisation is an important, if not the most important issue of non-proliferation. It is addressed by the international community through a kind of double track approach, namely a treaty regime and a control system set up by the Security Council.

As to the first element, the Convention on the prevention of nuclear terrorism[39] largely follows the pattern of the several anti-terrorism treaties. It establishes an obligation to enact criminal legislation, to enforce this legislation, to extradite and to cooperate with other States in the repression of nuclear terrorism.

As to the second element, this is the general proliferation control regime established by the Security Council in resolution 1540 of 28 April 2004, already described.

6   Universality Revisited – or the Problem of Multiple Standards in Matters of Nuclear Armament

The non-universality of participation and the inequality of the treatment of various States having or alleged to have nuclear weapons, or ambitions to acquire such weapons, both within and outside the treaty, remains a serious policy problem. There are five official NWS, namely the P5. They are violating at least one important duty under the NPT, namely the duty to negotiate in good faith a treaty on nuclear disarmament.

There is one State party to the NPT, namely Iran, which pursues a development of its nuclear capabilities and declares this as being for peaceful purposes only – which many other countries do not believe. The objective basis for this suspicion are certain controversial irregularities in the cooperation between Iran and the IAEA. Essentially for that reason, Iran has become the object of Security Council sanctions. A proof of an actual diversion of nuclear material to weapons purposes, or of any concrete measures taken to that effect, remains to be furnished. The Council apparently assumes that there is a threat to the peace, otherwise it could not lawfully take the action it took. But it has not stated what exactly constituted that threat.

---

39   International Convention for the Suppression of Acts of Nuclear Terrorism, adopted by the UN General Assembly, Resolution 59/290, 15 April 2005.

There is another State, North Korea, which has conducted a nuclear weapons programme in violation of the NPT, i.e. while it was a party to the NPT. It has availed itself of the possibility, provided for in the treaty, to denounce it and thus free itself from the obligations imposed by the treaty. That country, too, has become the object of Security Council sanctions. In that case the Council has at least explicitly stated that the nuclear test conducted by North Korea, under the particular circumstances of this case, constituted a threat to the peace.[40]

There are two other countries, India and Pakistan, not members of the NPT, which have openly conducted nuclear tests and officially acquired nuclear weapons. Other countries, in particular the United States, protested against this. By two Presidential Statements, the Security Council "deplored" India's and Pakistan's nuclear tests.[41]

There are certain differences between India and Pakistan. It appears that India has behaved as if it were an official nuclear power in the sense that there have been no claims of proliferation from India to other countries or non-State actors. In relation to Pakistan, there are reasons to believe that nuclear knowhow was leaked in particular to North Korea. In the meantime, the US has concluded a nuclear cooperation agreement, restricted to peaceful uses, with India. The US stance in respect of Pakistan is not that generous, although Pakistan also receives a kind of dividend in form of US silence due to its importance in the fight against Al Qaida and the Taliban.

Finally, there is an unavowed nuclear power not a party to the NPT, namely Israel. This is a constant reason of complaint for other States of the Middle East, but there are no reactions from the P5, nor from the Security Council.

This practice of the international community in respect of the nuclear armament of different States, is, to put it mildly, highly arbitrary. It can be explained as a matter of power politics, but it defies any attempt of legal justification. It threatens the rule of law in international relations and, thus, an essential element of international stability.

7   Conclusions

How effective are the legal restraints on the proliferation of weapons of mass destruction? The answer seems to be the usual optimism/pessimism paradigm: Is the glass half full or half empty?

---

40   Resolution 1718 of 14 October 2006.
41   S/PRST/1998/12 of 14 May 1998 and PRST/1998/17 of 29 May 1998.

The C-weapons disarmament and arms control system seems to be in a relatively stable condition. The safe destruction of the existing stocks proceeds, not without problems, but it works. The inspection system designed to prevent diversion of chemical substances from peaceful to military purposes has started functioning. No major problems are reported.

The B-weapons system, on the other hand, relies exclusively on the principle of hope. In the absence of anything like a serious system to ensure compliance, the treaty remains symbolic rather than a real factor restraining proliferation.

The NPT is a doubtful design. One may conclude that it has not contained the circle of nuclear powers, but restrained its growth. Although it is one of the multilateral treaties enjoying the major participation, it lacks the necessary universality because of the factual importance of the absentees. Its compliance system has worked reasonably well, but timely discovery of non-compliance has not always been possible. The problem of governments pursuing a nuclear option remains and may even become more acute. And whether the treaty can really prevent nuclear weapons from getting into private hands also remains to be seen. The fact that the NPT Review Conference held in 2005 was unable to take any substantive decision on the various problems of the NPR (which have been described) shows that this treaty regime is in crisis.

Even when and to the extent that verification system work, reaction to non-compliance or to armament by non-participants remains an open issue. Legally speaking, it is in the hands of the Security Council – with all the problems that entails. The unilateral option has also been used, and it remains a threat in the background.[42]

---

42   See the "Proliferation Security Initiative" announced by President Bush on 31 May 2003.

PART 4

The Law of Armed Conflict: General Questions

∵

11

Le Droit de la Guerre Et les Nations Unies

A Propos des Incidents Armés au Congo

A la mémoire de mon père

∴

Introduction

1   *Le cadre du Problème*

Pendent leur présence au Congo ex-belge, les troupes des Nations Unies ont, à diverses occasions, recouru à l'emploi de la force, ce qui a provoqué une discussion sur la question de savoir si le droit de la guerre était applicable au cours de ces hostilités.[1] Cette question représente un aspect particulier d'une discussion déjà en cours depuis la fondation des Nations Unies, à savoir si le *jus in bello* est applicable lors d'une action militaire entreprise par les Nations Unies ou sous leur égide.[2] Malgré les travaux de l'Institut de Droit International,[3] cette discussion est encore loin d'avoir abouti à des résultats généralement acceptés.

---

1 Voir, à titre d'example: Bowett, *United Nations Forces*, p. 222 ss., 484 ss. ; Draper, *The Legal Limitation upon the Employment of Weapons by the United Nations Force in the Congo*, ICLQ 12 (1963), p.387 ss.; Seyersted, *United Nations Forces*, BYIL 37 (1961), p. 474; Guérisse-Jaquemin-Kellens, *Les forces armées de l'Organisation des Nations Unies face à leur mission sanitaire et humanitaire*, Annales de droit international medical n° 11 (1964), p. 16 ss. et notamment p. 41 ss.; Militieombudsmannens ämbetsberättelse avgiven vid Riksdagen, ar 1964, p. 283 ss. (rapport du commissaire militaire du parlement suédois).

2 Comme alternative à l'application du droit de la guerre, on a proposé la création d'un « code spécial ». Cf. Yepes, Annuaire 47 I (1957), p. 599 ; Waldock, Annuaire 48 II (1959), p. 203 ; Scelle (Doc. ONU A/CN. 4/SR 6, p. 13) est d'avis « que la réglementation de l'emploi de la police internationale devrait être au premier plan des préoccupations de la Commission (de droit international), qu'il est nécessaire d'établir une réglementation de la fonction exécutive, la plus dangereuse de toutes, et qu'il ne faut plus parler du droit de la guerre ».

3 Session d'Amsterdam 1957 et Session de Bruxelles 1963.

Les divergences au sein de l'Institut[4] en sont la preuve. Les hostilités au Congo sont un bon point de départ pour repenser ces questions.

Notre problème implique deux questions qui doivent être distinguées : le champ d'application du droit de la guerre, I, *ratione personae* et II, *ratione materiae*.

1. L'applicabilité *ratione personae* conduit à se poser deux nouvelles questions :

   a) L'application du *jus in bello* ne doit-elle pas être exclue du fait que les troupes des Nations Unies se trouvent dans une meilleure position en ce qui concerne le droit de recourir à la force (*jus ad bellum*) ? C'est ce qu'on peut appeler le problème de la discrimination ou de l'égalité de l'application du droit de la guerre lors d'un conflit armé.

   b) Pour qu'il y ait application du droit de la guerre, il faut que les personnes qui participent aux hostilités relèvent d'une entité capable d'être destinataire des normes du droit de la guerre. L'ONU est-elle une telle entité ? Et pour le cas d'espèce : est-ce que les soldats qui se battent sous le drapeau de l'ONU relèvent vraiment de l'ONU, ou plutôt de leurs États d'origine ? Lors de la crise congolaise, le même problème s'est également posé d'autre façon : les hommes qui s'opposaient aux troupes onusiennes relevaient-ils d'un sujet du droit international ?

2. L'applicabilité *ratione materiae* concerne le caractère des hostilités : Y a-t-il une situation où le droit de la guerre est applicable ?

Ces questions toucheront des problèmes essentiels du droit de la guerre actuel. Pour avoir néanmoins une base de réflexion, il est utile d'esquisser d'abord les traits généraux de la présence des troupes des Nations Unies au Congo et de donner quelques renseignements de fait sur les hostilités qui ont eu lieu.

2   *Les Traits Généraux de la Présence des Nations Unies au Congo*

Le 30 juin 1960, le Congo belge devint indépendant. Le 5 juillet, des mutineries de la Force Publique congolaise commencèrent à Léopoldville et à Thysville.[5] Les désordres qui en résultaient menèrent à une intervention militaire belge. La République du Congo s'adressa – par deux télégrammes datés des 12

---

4 Voir *infra*, p. 185.

5 Pour la chronique des événements, voir : *La crise congolaise* : janvier 1959-août 1960, *Chronique de politique étrangère* XIII (1960), p. 403 ss. ; *Evolution de la crise congolaise de septembre 1960 à avril 1961, ibid.* CIX (1961), p. 557 ss. ; Gérard-Libois/Verhaegen, *Congo 1960*, 2 tomes ; Gérard-Libois, *Sécession au Katanga* ; Verhaegen, *Congo 1961* : Gérard-Libois/Verhaegen, *Congo 1962*.

LE DROIT DE LA GUERRE ET LES NATIONS UNIES

et 13 juillet[6] – au Secrétaire Général des Nations Unies demandant l'envoi des troupes des Nations Unies. Le 13 juillet, le Conseil de Sécurité adopta la résolution suivante[7] :

> Le Conseil de Sécurité,
>
> *Considérant* le rapport du Secrétaire Général sur la demande pour une action des Nations Unies concernant la République du Congo,
>
> *Considérant* la demande d'assistance militaire adressée au Secrétaire Général par le Président et le Premier Ministre de la République du Congo (S/4382),
>
> 1. *Fait appel* au Gouvernement belge pour qu'il retire ses troupes du territoire de la République du Congo ;
> 2. *Décide* d'autoriser le Secrétaire Général de prendre, en consultation avec le Gouvernement de la République du Congo, les mesures nécessaires en vue de fournir à ce gouvernement l'assistance militaire dont il a besoin et ce, jusqu'au moment où les forces nationales de sécurité, grâce aux efforts du Gouvernement congolais et avec l'assistance technique des Nations Unies, seront à même, de l'opinion de ce gouvernement, de remplis entièrement leur tâche ;
> 3. ...

Un amendement présenté par l'URSS tendant à condamner « l'agression armée de la Belgique » fut rejeté.

Le 22 juillet, le Conseil de Sécurité adopta une deuxième résolution,[8] dans laquelle le Conseil approuva, entre autre, un rapport du Secrétaire Général[9] qui définit le mandat de la force des Nations Unies. Les principes énoncés dans ce rapport et dans les autres déclarations du Secrétaire Général qui ont reçu l'approbation du Conseil de Sécurité sont la base d'interprétation du mandat et des pouvoirs que le Conseil a conférés aux tropes des Nations Unies au Congo et des restrictions qu'il leur a imposées.[10] Dans les résolutions du 8 août 1960,[11] du 21 février 1961[12] et du 24 novembre

---

6   Doc. ONU S/4382.
7   Doc. ONU S/4387.
8   Doc. ONU S/4405.
9   Doc. ONU S/4389.
10 Virally, *Les Nations Unies et l'affaire du Congo en 1960*, AFDI 1960, p. 567 ss. notamment p. 574.
11 Doc. ONU S/4426.
12 Doc. ONU S/4741.

240   PART 4: THE LAW OF ARMED CONFLICT – GENERAL QUESTIONS

1962,[13] le Conseil de Sécurité précisa et élargit encore les tâches et les fonctions de l'ONUC.

La République du Congo a accepté les résolutions du Conseil de Sécurité : les deux premières résolutions furent acceptées dans un accord de base du 27 juillet 1960,[14] la résolution du 8 août dans une lettre du 10 août 1960,[15] la résolution du 21 février 1961 dans un accord de principe du 17 avril 1961,[16] et finalement les résolutions du Conseil de Sécurité dans leur ensemble dans l'accord du 27 novembre 1961.[17]

Selon les résolutions ainsi acceptées et interprétées à la lumière des déclarations du Secrétaire Général, les buts de l'action des Nations Unies au Congo se définissent comme suit :

1. Maintenir l'intégrité territoriale et l'indépendance politique de la République du Congo[18] (un aspect particulier de ce but est la tâche d'assurer le retrait et l'évacuation du Congo de tous les personnels, militaire et paramilitaire, et conseillers d'autres nationalités ne relevant pas du Commandement des Nations Unies ainsi que de tous les mercenaires)[19] ;

2. Maintenir l'ordre public,[20] et notamment :

    a) prévenir le déclenchement d'une guerre civile[21] ;

    b) protéger la vie et la propriété de la population civile.[22]

Les moyens mis à la disposition de l'ONUC pour atteindre ces buts étaient fort restreints. La force des Nations Unies au Congo était conçue selon le modèle de la Force d'Urgence des Nations Unies en Egypte (UNEF),[23] c'est-à-dire qu'elle devait avoir un effet salutaire du fait seul de sa présence. Les troupes des Nations Unies ne devaient donc recourir à la force qu'en cas de légitime défense.[24] Dans les résolutions du 21 février et du 24 novembre 1961, le Conseil de Sécurité élargit cette autorisation. Le recours à la force était alors permis pour prévenir le déclenchement d'une guerre civile[25] et pour appréhender, placer en

---

13   Doc. ONU S/5002.

14   Doc. ONU S/4389/Add. 5.

15   Doc. ONU S/4417/Add. 3.

16   Doc. ONU S/4807/Annexe I.

17   Doc. ONU S/5004.

18   Résolution du 22 juillet 1960, dispositif 2 ; résolution du 8 août 1960, dispositif 3 ; résolution du 24 novembre 1961, considérants.

19   Résolution du 21 février 1961, dispositif 2.

20   Résolution du 22 juillet 1960, considérants; résolution du 24 novembre 1961, considérants.

21   Résolution du 21 février 1961, dispositif 1.

22   Déclaration du Secrétaire Général du 7 décembre 1960, S/PV. 913, p. 5, par. 26.

23   Déclaration du Secrétaire Général, S/PV. 873, p. 5, par. 28.

24   Déclaration du Secrétaire Général, *toc. cit.;* Rapport du Secrétaire Général, S/4389, p. 5.

25   Résolution du 21 février 1961, dispositif 1.

détention ou expulser le personnel étranger ne relevant pas de l'ONUC.[26] Le droit de recourir à la force en cas de légitime défense impliquait, selon l'interprétation du Secrétaire Général, le droit des troupes de « répondre par la force à une attaque armée, notamment aux tentatives de recours à la force qui viseraient à leur faire évacuer les positions qu'elles occupent sur l'ordre du Commandant »[27] ainsi qu'à toute tentative de les empêcher d'exercer leur liberté de mouvement.[28] Cette dernière interprétation était particulièrement importante lors du conflit katangais.

Il résulte de ce mandat restreint que l'action des Nations Unies au Congo ne peut pas être considéré comme mesure coercitive envisagée par l'Art. 42 de la Charte des Nations Unies.[29] Le consentement de l'État-hôte, de la République du Congo, était nécessaire pour la présence des troupes onusiennes au Congo.[30]

3   Les Incidents Armés

Les troupes des Nations Unies ont su, dans une large mesure, remplir leur mandat par leur seule présence, par voie de persuasion et de conciliation. Mais elles ont également fait usage de leurs armes. Le caractère, l'importance et la durée de ces incidents armés varièrent. Mais il s'agissait toujours de conflits

---

26   Résolution du 24 novembre 1961, dispositif 4.

27   Rapport du Secrétaire Général, S/4389, p. 5.

28   Déclaration du Secrétaire Général, S/5053/Add. 14, Annexe XXXI, p. 2, 4; Rapport spécial adressé au Secrétaire Général par M. Bunche, S/5053/Add. 14, Annexe XXXIV, p. 2 ss.; Rapport adressé au Secrétaire Général par le fonctionnaire chargé de l'opération des Nations Unies au Congo, S/5053/Add. 15, p. 1.

29   Cf. Certaines dépenses des Nations Unies (article 17, paragraphe 2, de la Charte), Avis consultatif du 20 juillet 1962 : C.I.J. Recueil 1962, p. 177 ; Miller, *Legal Aspects of the United Nations Action in the Congo*, AJIL 55 (1961), p. 8 ; Abdel Moneim Riad, *The United Nations Action in the Congo and its Legal Basis*, ERIL 17 (1961), p. 19 et ss. ; Schachter, *Legal Issues at the United Nations*, Annual Review of the United Nations Affairs 1960–1961, p. 143 ss. ; idem, *The Relation of Law, Politics and Action in the United Nations,* RdC 109 (1963 II), p. 219 ss.; Seyersted, *United Nations Forces,* BYIL 1961, p. 442 ss.; Wright, *The United Nations and the Congo Crisis,* The Journal of the John Bassett Moore Society of International Law 2 (1962), p. 52; Bowett, *United Nations Forces,* p. 176; Burns-Heathcote, *Peace-keeping by U.N. Forces,* p. 26; Van Langenhove, *Le rôle proéminent du Secrétaire Général dans l'opération des Nations Unies au Congo,* p. 62 ss.; discussion de la résolution du 21 février 1961, p. 121 ss., 218 ss.

30   Cela ne signifie pas que ce consentement, une fois donné, pouvait être retiré librement par la République du Congo (cf. Miller, *loc. cit.,* p. 15). Le consentement n'est pas non plus nécessaire pour chaque action particulière entreprise par les Nations Unies (cf. notamment par. 43 al. a *in fine* de l'accord concernant le statut juridique de l'ONUC, S/5004, p. 12; voir aussi Karabus, *United Nations Activities in the Congo,* ASIL Proceedings, 55th meeting [1961], p. 32; Schachter, *Legal Issues at the United Nations, loc. cit.,* p. 146).

locaux; jamais l'ONUC n'était engagée en des hostilités concertées sur tout le territoire de la République du Congo.[31] Voici quelques exemples typiques:

A Thysville, des soldats marocains tirèrent sur un individu civil armé qui se livrait à des actes de sabotage dans une plantation protégée par l'ONUC. L'individu fut tué.[32]

A Moanda, le 3 mars 1961, un détachement de l'ANC, relevant du Gouvernement central,[33] tâchait d'arrêter un détachement soudanais. Il y eut un échange de six coups de feu. Après cela, deux soldats de l'ANC se rendirent, les autres s'enfuirent. Les soldats capturés furent remis au camp de l'ANC.[34]

A Matadi, au mois de mars 1961, il y eut pendant quelques jours une petite bataille entre des troupes soudanaises et des unités de l'ANC, relevant du Gouvernement central, avec un feu nourri de fusils, de mitrailleuses et de mortiers. Il y eut quelques morts et capturés. Un accord de cessation des hostilités fut signé, de la part de l'ONUC par un capitaine soudanais, de la part de l'ANC par un ministre du Gouvernement central. Les troupes onusiennes se retirèrent alors de Matadi.[35]

A Bukavu, le 16 décembre 1960, il y eut une escarmouche de deux heures et demie entre des éléments de l'ANC, relevant du Gouvernement central mais refusant d'obéir aux ordres de leurs supérieurs, et une unité nigérienne qui tentait de libérer des médecins autrichiens emprisonnés par l'ANC. Il y eut un mort et trois blessés du côté de l'ONUC, dix morts du côté de l'ANC. Les Autrichiens furent libérés.[36]

Les hostilités les plus importantes, on le sait, sont celles qui ont eu lieu au Katanga aux mois de septembre 1961,[37] décembre 1961[38] et décembre 1962/

---

31   I1 y avait, cependant, des menaces dans ce sens; voir Deuxième rapport d'activité présenté au Secrétaire général par son représentant spécial au Congo, S/4557 – A/4557 par. 13 et 23.

32   L'incident eut lieu au début de septembre 1960; voir The New York Times, International Edition, 4-9-1960, p. 1 col. 5 et 5-9-1960, p. 3 col. 7.

33   Cette indication est nécessaire parce qu'il y avait aussi des unités de l'ANC qui relevaient de Gouvernements locaux. Dans ces cas, la situation juridique peut être différente. Voir infra, p. 210 ss.

34   S/4761, par. 12.

35   S/4761, par. 17 ss. et Annexe I1.

36   S/4601 = A/4682, par. 10 s.

37   Rapport du fonctionnaire chargé de l'opération des Nations Unies au Congo au Secrétaire Général, concernant la mise en application du paragraphe A-2 de la Résolution du Conseil de Sécurité du 21 février 1961, S/4940 et Add. 1–12; voir pour une version des événements qui diverge de celle du rapport cité: O'Brien, *Meine Mission in Katanga*, p. 246 ss.; voir également: Gordon, *The United Nations in the Kongo*, p. 124 ss.; Valahu, *The Katanga Circus*, p. 195 ss.; Burns-Heathcote, *Peace-Keeping by U.N. Forces*, p. 100 ss.; Leclerq, *L'ONU et l'affaire du Congo*, p. 275 ss.; Gérard-Libois, *Sécession au Katanga*, p. 237 ss.

38   S/4940 Add. 15–19; voir également: Gordon, *op. cit.*, p. 141 ss.; Valahu, *op. cit.*, p. 220 ss.; Burns-Heathcote, *op. cit.*, p. 132 ss.; Leclerq, *op. cit.*, p. 297 ss.; Gérard-Libois, *op. cit.*, p. 247 ss.

janvier 1963.[39] Les forces de l'ONU et les troupes relevant du Gouvernement du Katanga, qui s'était déclaré Etat indépendant, s'opposèrent, pendant quelques jours, dans des combats assez vifs. Des armes lourdes et des avions furent employés des deux côtés. Il y eut de nombreux morts et prisonniers. Les hostilités de septembre 1961 furent suivies d'un accord de cessez-le-feu,[40] conclu le 20 septembre 1961 entre les Nations Unies et le Gouvernement katangais, et d'un protocole supplémentaire du 13 octobre.[41] L'épreuve de force de décembre 1962/janvier 1963 fut terminée par l'accord sur l'entrée de l'ONUC à Kolwezi,[42] conclu le 17 janvier 1963 entre l'ONU et le Président du Gouvernement katangais, accord qui représente le règlement politique mettant fin à la sécession katangaise.

1 Première Partie : Le champ D'application du Droit de la Guerre « Ratione Materiae »

1.1 *Les Données Générales du Problème*

Faisons d'abord abstraction des problèmes que pose l'applicabilité du *jus in bello ratione personae*. Les incidents décrits constitueraient-ils des situations où le droit de la guerre serait applicable ratione materiae si des troupes étatiques y étaient engagées? De façon générale: quand se trouve-t-on en présence d'une situation qui donne lieu à l'application du droit de la guerre?

Toute étude concernant l'applicabilité du droit de la guerre dans des situations déterminées rencontre certaines difficultés parce que la notion de « guerre » est très contestée. Jusqu'à la première guerre mondiale, la doctrine du droit international ne connaissait qu'une dichotomie simple: il existait entre Etats ou une relation belliqueuse (état de guerre), régie par le droit de la guerre, ou une relation pacifique, régie par le droit de la paix. La seule difficulté était alors de définir l'état de guerre selon certains critères (p. ex. *animus belligerendi*). Mais depuis la première guerre mondiale, on a réservé plus d'attention au fait qu'il existait certains conflits armés qui n'ont été qualifiés de « guerres » au sens traditionnel ni par les parties au conflit ni par des Etats tiers. Toutefois,

---

39 S/5053 Add. 14 et 15; Valahu, *op. cit.,* p. 296 ss.; Burns-Heathcote, *op. cit.,* p. 193 ss.; Leclerq, *op. cit.,* p. 324 ss.; Gérard-Libois, *op. cit.,* p. 290 ss.

40 S/4940 Add. 7, par. 6.

41 S/4940 Add. 11, Annexe I.

42 S/5053 Add. 15, Annexe IX.

certaines normes du droit de la guerre furent appliquées.[43] Il y a donc des situations où il n'existe pas un état de guerre, mais qui ne sont pas réglées exclusivement par le droit de la paix. Les réactions de la doctrine à l'égard de ce phénomène sont divisées. On peut y discerner trois tendances. Une école relativiste, dont le protagoniste le plus marqué est Grob,[44] soutient qu'une notion unique de la guerre n'existe pas en droit international. Il faut déterminer la signification de la notion de « guerre » séparément pour chaque norme qui s'y réfère. Cette détermination doit se faire d'après une interprétation téléologique,[45] d'après le but de la norme.[46] Une deuxième tendance amplifie la notion de guerre. Elle divise la guerre en guerre au sens formel (traditionnel) et en guerre au sens matériel.[47] Tandis que la guerre au sens formel entraîne, en principe, l'application du droit de la guerre dans sa totalité, la guerre au sens matériel ne rend applicables que les règles visant la conduite des hostilités. Relèvent du domaine exclusif de la guerre au sens formel les règles concernant la guerre économique.[48] En ce qui concerne la neutralité, Guggenheim[49] et Kotzsch[50] adoptent une attitude nuancée.

Une troisième attitude retient, comme le font Guggenheim et Kotzsch, la notion de guerre au sens traditionnel. Mais elle renonce à la notion de « guerre au sens matériel » et admet, d'une façon plus souple, l'applicabilité partielle du droit de la guerre en temps de paix. Cela correspondrait à la fonction ordinatrice que le droit international doit remplir même clans des situations exceptionnelles.[51] Il s'agit donc d'une application du droit de la guerre par voie d'analogie.

En fait, le droit de la guerre doit être, et a été, appliqué sans que l'on tienne compte des finesses juridiques de la définition de la guerre. Des organes appelés à réagir aux questions concrètes du droit de la guerre « seem to have been concerned more with a functional and practical approach than

---

43 Par exemple: le conflit de Mandchourie, 1931–1933, cf. Grob, *The Relativity of War and Peace,* p. 140 ss.; le bombardement de Corfou par l'Italie, 1923, Grob, *ibid.,* p. 244 ss.

44 Voir également McDougal-Feliciano, The Initiation of Coercion: A Multi-Temporal Analysis, AJIL 52 (1958), p. 248 ss., notamment p. 258.

45 Rumpf, *Zur Frage der Relativitiit des Kriegsbegriffs,* Archiv des Viilkerrechts 6 (1956/57), p. 53 ss.

46 Grob, *op. cit.,* p. 189.

47 Guggenheim, Traité, tome II, p. 312; id. RdC 80 (1952 I), p. 173 ss. Kotzsch, The Concept of War in Contemporary History and International Law, p. 55 ss.

48 Guggenheim, *Traité,* tome II, p. 314.

49 *Traité,* tome II, pp. 314 et 494.

50 *Op. cit.,* p. 143.

51 Mosler, Kriegsbeginn, Strupp-Schlochauer, vol. Il, p. 329.

LE DROIT DE LA GUERRE ET LES NATIONS UNIES   245

a theoretical one, paying attention rather to the realities of the situation than to legal niceties ».[52]

Mais quand on pose une question de façon générale et par conséquent théorique, ces « legal niceties » retrouvent leur importance. Cela ne veut pas dire qu'il faille, une fois pour toutes, une définition des états de faits susceptibles d'entraîner l'application du droit de la guerre ou une partie de ce droit (p. ex. les règles visant la conduite des hostilités). Une telle définition satisfait des besoins théoriques. Mais la fonction ordinatrice du droit, qui vient d'être évoquée, n'est pas basée sur des considérations théoriques, elle ne se soumet pas à des définitions scientifiques. Il s'agit là d'une exigence de la raison et de l'humanité: il faut qu'une situation de conflit soit réglée par des normes adéquates, même si elle ne correspond à aucune définition de la guerre (au sens matériel ou formel). Cette attitude est commune à l'école relativiste et à l'opinion qui, renonçant à la notion de guerre au sens matériel, préconise l'application du *jus in bello* en dehors d'un état de guerre. Dans le cadre de la question de savoir si le *jus in bello* est applicable pour des « incidents » le chapitre qui suit s'efforcera de prouver que c'est cette attitude seule qui mène à des résultats valables, qu'il faudra déterminer selon les exigences d'une situation concrète, et non suivant des définitions préconçues, si certaines règles du *jus in bello* doivent être appliquées (si l'on veut: par voie d'analogie) pour résoudre les problèmes juridiques qui se posent.

1.2   *Le Droit de la Guerre et la Notion d' « Incidents »*

1. Le problème de l'applicabilité du droit de la guerre ratione materiae se pose de façon particulièrement délicate pour les hostilités qui se sont déroulées lors de l'action de l'ONU au Congo. Il n'y avait pas un « état de guerre ».[53] La présence des forces armées des Nations Unies ne constituait pas une occupation de guerre ou une occupation assimilée à l'*occupatio bellica* selon l'art. 2 al. 2 des Conventions de Genève. La mission de ces forces: maintenir l'ordre ne fait pas de leur présence une occupation quasi-belliqueuse. Car cette mission, définie par le Conseil de Sécurité, a été acceptée par la République du Congo; le statut des forces des Nations Unies a été déterminé par un accord entre l'ONU et le Congo. Ce consentement de l'Etat-hôte, cet accord entre les parties distingue la présence des forces armées des Nations Unies au Congo de toute occupation belliqueuse ou quasi-belliqueuse, qui est justement

---

52   Green, *Armed Conflict, War and Self-Defense,* Archiv des Völkerrechts 6 (1956/57), p. 394.

53   Voir *infra,* p. 215, note 338.

caractérisée par un défaut d'accord entre les parties.[54] Le droit de la guerre n'étant pas applicable pour la présence de ces forces armées en général, il se pose la question de savoir si le *jus in bello* s'applique pour certains incidents d'espèce, flambées belliqueuses dans une situation essentiellement pacifique.

On pourrait être tenté de chercher le droit applicable pour ces hostilités dans les résolutions du Conseil de Sécurité et dans l'accord concernant le statut de l'ONUC. Ces instruments contiennent des règles relatives au caractère licite du recours à la force. Mais ils sont tacites en ce qui concerne les modalités de ce recours. On ne peut donc que se référer à des règles générales. C'est à cet égard qu'une référence au *jus in bello* s'impose.[55] Dans quelle mesure le droit de la guerre est-il donc applicable pour des incidents armés dans le cadre d'une situation pacifique?

L'application du droit de la guerre n'est guère douteuse quand il s'agit de « large scale international fighting ».[56] Mais pour des escarmouches comme celles décrites ci-dessus,[57] l'applicabilité des règles du *jus in bello* concernant la conduite des hostilités devient question délicate. Le droit de la guerre est-il applicable même pour de petits incidents? Deux problèmes se posent dans ce contexte:

1. Comment peut-on distinguer les situations où il faut encore appliquer le *jus in bello* de celles où ce n'est pas le cas?
2. Comment faut-il évaluer les conséquences juridiques d'hostilités quand on n'applique pas le droit de la guerre?

2. La seconde question n'est, à ma connaissance, pas posée dans la doctrine. La première question est, cependant, très discutée. Voici une revue des thèses avancées:

Strebel[58] considère comme préalable à l'application des Conventions de Genève qu'il existe « une guerre ou un autre conflit armé (qui dépasse le cadre d'un incident) ... ». Strebel n'indique pas de critères matériels selon lesquels on pourrait vérifier si une situation concrète dépasse le cadre d'un « incident ».

---

54   Bowett, United Nations Forces, p. 490, exclut donc à juste titre la notion d'occupation belliqueuse pour ce qu'il appelle « peace-keeping Force ». Il réserve cette notion pour les mesures de coercition des Nations Unies.

55   Bowett, United Nations Forces, p. 503.

56   Kunz, *The Laws of War*, AJIL 50 (1956), p. 317.

57   P. 143 ss.

58   Strebel, Kriegsgefangene, Strupp-Schlochauer, vol. II, p. 343: « ein Krieg oder ein anderer bewaffneter Konflikt (der graduell über einen Zwischenfall hinausreicht) ... ».

LE DROIT DE LA GUERRE ET LES NATIONS UNIES

Siordet[59] exige une interprétation unique de la notion de « conflit » dans les Conventions de Genève, qu'il s'agisse d'un conflit international ou non-international. Il dit:

> L'article 3, même s'il se présente comme une convention en miniature, ne constitue pas en soi une convention séparée, relative aux conflits non internationaux. Il n'est qu'une disposition parmi d'autres, de quatre conventions ayant un objet bien défini: la protection des victimes de la guerre. Les titres mêmes de ces conventions permettent d'éliminer toute équivoque quant aux cas dans lesquels l'une ou l'autre de leurs dispositions – et parmi celles-ci l'article 3 – doivent trouver leur application. Les deux premières visent l'amélioration du sort des blessés et des malades dans les armées en campagne, et du sort des blessés, des malades et des naufragés des forces armées sur mer. La troisième est relative au traitement des prisonniers de guerre. La quatrième enfin est relative à la protection des personnes civiles en temps de guerre. Or, a-t-on jamais considéré que des agents de police à la poursuite de quelques bandits étaient des « forces armées en campagne »?... Nous ne voyons pas pourquoi l'adoption de l'article 3 conférerait une nouvelle valeur aux mots et pourquoi on appellerait dorénavant conflit armé non international des crimes de droit commun comme il s'en produit chaque jour dans tous les pays. L'emplacement même de cet article 3 des événements qui, sans être une guerre internationale, présentent des caractères d'une guerre, et produisent des souffrances du même genre que la guerre.[60]

L'idée sous-jacente de ces lignes parait être que les Conventions de Genève ne sont applicables qu'aux cas de conflits qui présentent le caractère d'une guerre, au sens où ce mot est employé dans le langage quotidien, c'est-à-dire aux cas de conflits d'une certaine importance.

Kotzsch[61] et Siotis[62] arrivent à un résultat semblable. Kotzsch définit la guerre au sens matériel comme suit: « Material war implies a continuous[63] clash of arms conducted by organized armies which engage the responsibility of governments »[64] et plus loin: « A government will be engaged in war upon

---

59 Siordet, *Les Conventions de Genève et la guerre civile,* Rev. Int. Croix-Rouge, 32 (1950), p. 203 ss.
60 Italiques de Siordet.
61 The Concept of War in Contemporary History and International Law.
62 Le droit de la guerre et les conflits armés d'un caractère non international.
63 Italiques de l'auteur.
64 *Op. cit.,* p. 56.

committing acts of military force which are repelled by force and the armed contest qualifies itself as war in the material sense by the presence of the following facts: (1) organized governments as parties to the conflict; (2) capacity for conducting the military operations in conformity with the rules of warfare; a sufficient lapse of time to give evidence of the dual character of hostilities. »[65]

Siotis développe la définition de Kotzsch en considérant comme « caractéristiques essentielles des conflits armés en général »:

a) une lutte prolongée dans l'espace et dans le temps,
b) une lutte intéressant au moins une entité juridique possédant la pleine capacité internationale.[66]

Selon Siotis, les termes « guerre matérielle » et « conflit armé » sont « presque synonymes ».[67] Siotis a apparemment choisi le terme de « conflit » au vu de la terminologie des Conventions de Genève. Kotzsch et Siotis considèrent donc comme préalable à l'application des Conventions de Genève l'existence d'hostilités d'une certaine importance.

Pictet[68] adopte une autre position, réservant aux Conventions de Genève un champ d'application plus large :

> Il suffit qu'il y ait de facto des hostilités ... Tout différend surgissant entre deux Etats et provoquant l'intervention de membres des forces armées est un conflit armé au sens de l'article 2 ... Ni la durée du conflit, ni le caractère plus ou moins meurtrier de ses effets ne jouent de rôle. Le respect dû à la personne humaine ne se mesure pas au nombre des victimes.[69]

Plus loin, l'article 6 al. 1er de la IVe Convention, relative à la protection de la population civile,[70] est commenté de la façon suivante:

> En employant les mots dès le début les auteurs de la Convention ont voulu marquer qu'elle trouvait application dès les premiers actes de violence, même si la lutte armée ne se prolonge pas. Il n'est pas non plus nécessaire

---

65   *Op. cit.,* p. 243 s.
66   *Op. cit.,* p. 21.
67   *Op. cit.,* p. 21.
68   *Les Conventions de Genève du 12 août 1949,* Commentaire publié sous la direction de Jean S. Pictet.
69   Vol. IV, p. 25 s.; voir aussi vol. I, p. 34, vol. II, p. 28, vol. III, p. 29.
70   « La présente Convention s'appliquera dès le début de tout conflit ou occupation mentionnés à l'article 2. » Voir aussi Convention, Art. 5. Ces dispositions ont été introduites dans les Conventions à cause des graves controverses surgies à cet égard lors de la 2e Guerre Mondiale, Pictet, *op. cit.,* vol. I, p. 69.

que les événements aient fait de nombreuses victimes. De simples incidents de frontière peuvent donner lieu à l'application de la Convention, car ils sont peut-être le début d'un conflit plus étendu. La Convention devra s'appliquer dès que des troupes seront en territoire étranger et en contact avec la population civile.[71]

Bien entendu, il y a des normes qui présupposent un contact prolongé:

[Certaines] dispositions supposent une présence assez prolongée des autorités d'occupation, par exemple les articles 52, 55, 56, de même les articles 59 à 62. Mais toutes les dispositions qui ont trait aux droits dont jouissent les personnes protégées et au traitement qui doit leur être réservé s'appliquent sans délai et indépendamment de la durée de l'occupation. [72]

Il y a donc une sorte d'application progressive de la Convention. Cette attitude coïncide, au moins en ce qui concerne le résultat, avec celle de Grob[73]:

The definitions of war required by the various rules of law on war vary greatly in their respective latitudes. Some rules, the laws and customs of war on land or at sea, for instance, spring into life at the slightest provocation.[74] Others are less likely to become applicable ...

In the Hague Convention (II) of 1899 and (IV) of 1907 the contracting powers agreed on such important provisions as the prohibition of the use of poison or poisoned weapons; the prohibition of killing or wounding an enemy who, having laid down his arms or having no longer means of defense, has surrendered at discretion; the prohibition of employing arms, projectiles, or material calculated to cause unnecessary suffering; the prohibition of pillaging a town or place; the treatment of the armed land forces of the enemy, in case of capture, as prisoners of war. The intent and purpose of these provisions is to humanize operations on land. In the preamble of the two Conventions the contracting parties stated that the drafting of the rules was 'inspired by the desire to diminish the evils of war'. 'whether or not military operations are accompanied by naval operations, whether they are geographically limited or not, whether they

---

71   Vol. IV, p. 66.
72   Vol. IV, p. 67.
73   Grob, *The Relativity of War and Peace.*
74   Italiques de l'auteur.

are conducted by large units or merely by minute detachments, whether they extend over a period of years or last a few minutes only, all this cannot possibly make any difference for the application of the above rules of war. Mere border incidents, engagements which in common parlance nobody would call a `war', are thus elevated to the rank of war in relation to the above provisions.[75]

3. Dans la doctrine, on peut donc constater deux tendances. Les unes, prenant comme point de départ la notion de guerre au sens matériel, exigeant des hostilités d'une certaine importance pour qu'il y ait application du *jus in bello*. Les autres, prenant comme point de départ les fonctions des normes particulières, admettent une application du *jus in bello*, dans la mesure où cela est nécessaire, dès le premier coup de fusil.

Pour évaluer ces attitudes différentes, il me paraît utile de recourir à un exemple pour que l'on puisse se rendre compte des conséquences pratiques de l'application ou de la non-application du droit de la guerre dans un cas douteux.

Deux Etats (A et D) sont membres des Nations Unies et parties à la Convention de La Haye concernant les lois et coutumes (de la guerre sur terre et aux Conventions de Genève. Il n'y a pas un état de guerre entre eux. Un détachement de dix hommes (en uniforme), appartenant aux forces armées régulières de l'Etat A, traverse, sur l'ordre du gouvernement de A, la frontière de l'Etat D pour y détruire une installation militaire. L'Etat D, qui avait escompté une telle action, avait donné à ses troupes l'ordre précis de répondre à l'attaque par des armes empoisonnées. Ledit détachement de l'Etat A rencontre une patrouille de la même importance de l'Etat D. Les soldats de A n'obéissent pas à une demande de s'en retourner. Ils poursuivent leur chemin. Les soldats de D tirent. Dans l'escarmouche qui suit, il y a trois morts: un soldat de D, deux soldats de A, l'un tué par un coup de fusil normal, l'autre par une arme empoisonnée. Les soldats qui ont tiré les coups de fusil mortels sont capturés par l'adversaire respectif.

Voilà un incident de frontière qui pourrait arriver tous les jours dans n'importe quelle zone de tension au monde.[76] On ne saurait guère le considérer comme guerre au sens matériel suivant la définition de Kotzsch.

La première question qui se pose est celle de la réparation des dommages. L'obligation de l'Etat A de réparer tout dommage causé par son action n'a rien

---

75   *Op. cit.,* p. 217 s.

76   Voir, pour un cas semblable, le jugement du tribunal de première instance de Manokwari (Nouvelle Guinée néerlandaise) NILR 11 (1964), p. 372.

à faire avec l'application du *jus in bello*. Elle résulte du fait que l'Etat A a violé l'intégrité territoriale de l'Etat D (Art. 2 al. 4 de la Charte des Nations Unies). L'Etat A est donc tenu de verser une indemnité pour la mort d'un soldat de D et de présenter ses excuses, qu'on applique ou non le *jus in bello*.

Selon une conception traditionnelle l'application du *jus in bello* n'entraîne une obligation de réparation que pour la violation du *jus in bello*. Elle repose sur l'idée que le recours à la guerre n'est pas illicite. Cela n'est plus acceptable.[77] Des indemnités sont donc dues aussi bien pour les violations du *jus ad bellum* que pour les violations du *jus in bello*. Mais les deux cas doivent être distingués.

L'Etat D n'a pas violé le *jus ad bellum*. Son action est justifiée comme légitime défense (art. 51 de la Charte). Si, pour cette action, l'on applique le droit de la guerre on peut constater une violation du *jus in bello*, à savoir de l'art. 23 al. 1 er chiffre a du Règlement de La Haye, qui interdit l'emploi d'armes empoisonnées. Il est donc, en vertu de l'art. 3 de la Convention de La Haye, « tenu à indemnité ». La mort de l'autre soldat de l'Etat A n'est pas la conséquence d'une violation du droit de la guerre, mais d'un acte toléré par le *jus in bello*. Il n'y a donc pas de restitution en vertu du droit de la guerre.

Si l'on considère le droit de la guerre comme inapplicable parce qu'il n'y avait pas d'hostilités d'une certaine importance, on est dans l'incertitude. On pourrait peut-être raisonner de la manière suivante: l'action de l'Etat D est en soi justifiée comme légitime défense. Puisque le droit de la paix ne connaît aucune règle pour le cas en question, tout ce qui n'est pas interdit est permis. Le droit de la paix accorderait donc aux Etats une liberté plus grande que le droit de la guerre: un véritable contre-sens. Comme nous verrons ci-dessous,[78] le *jus in bello* constitue un recul du droit à l'égard du jus in pace, mais non vice versa. Il n'y a donc qu'une solution raisonnable pour notre problème: Tuer un soldat par une arme empoisonnée constitue toujours une violation du droit, qui donne lieu à une réparation. D'autre part, il n'est pas douteux que l'Etat D n'est pas tenu à réparation en ce qui concerne la mort du soldat de A qui a été tué par un coup de fusil normal. Autrement le droit de légitime défense n'aurait pas de sens pour l'Etat D.

La seule solution adéquate dans notre cas est donc celle prescrite par la Convention de La Haye. Même si l'on ne veut pas appliquer cette Convention parce qu'il n'y aurait pas une guerre au sens matériel, on ne peut faire autre chose

---

77   Lauterpacht, *Rules of Warfare,* p. 101. Après une véritable « guerre », la responsabilité financière de l'agresseur n'est peut-être pas praticable. Mais c'est là une autre question. Voir également *infra,* p. 172.

78   Voir *infra,* p. 168.

252 PART 4: THE LAW OF ARMED CONFLICT – GENERAL QUESTIONS

qu'orienter les droits et devoirs des Etats en cause d'après les dispositions de ladite Convention. L'honnêteté intellectuelle exige de dire qu'on l'applique.

La deuxième question qui se pose est celle de la responsabilité pénale des soldats capturés. Une règle coutumière du *jus in bello* interdit aux Etats belligérants de punir les soldats de l'adversaire pour des actes qui restent dans le cadre de ce qui est permis par le droit de la guerre.[79] Les soldats de A et de D qui ont tué leurs adversaires par un coup de fusil normal ne sont donc pas susceptibles d'être punis.[80] Ils jouissent des privilèges de prisonniers de guerre et doivent être rapatriés après la fin du conflit.

Il en est autrement pour le soldat de D qui a employé l'arme empoisonnée. On pourrait invoquer, cependant, la doctrine « act of State ». Cette doctrine interdit qu'un Etat punisse l'organe d'un autre Etat pour des actes que ce dernier a accomplis dans l'exercice de ses fonctions officielles, même si ces actes sont contraires au droit international.[81] Puisque le soldat en question a agi sous les ordres de son gouvernement, il ne peut pas être douteux qu'il a accompli un « act of State ». Mais il est généralement reconnu que cette règle (d'ailleurs contestée) souffre une exception en ce qui concerne les violations du droit de la guerre.[82] Celui qui a employé l'arme empoisonnée peut donc être puni. L'ordre supérieur ne l'exculpe pas.[83]

---

79   Dahm, *Zur Problematik des Völkerstrafrechts,* p. 72; Hoffmann, *Strafrechtliehe Verantwortung im Völkerrecht,* p. 73 s.; Mosler, *Die Kriegshandlung im rechtswidrigen Krieg,* JiaiiR 1 (1948), p. 342 s.; Strebel, *Kriegsgefangene,* Strupp-Schlochauer, vol. II, p. 346.

80   Outre les obligations internationales, il se pose ici également un problème de droit pénal, à savoir si des actes permis par le droit de la guerre ne sauraient être punis parce que le droit de la guerre sert comme cause justificative, voir Dahm, *loc. cit.;* Mosler, *toc. 'cit.;* Hoffmann, *op. cit.,* p. 70 ss.; Kotzsch, *op. cit.,* p. 58; Glaser, *Infraction internationale,* p. 89 s.

81   Jennings, *The Caroline and McLeod Cases,* AJIL 32 (1938), p. 94; Manner, *The Legal Nature and Punishment of Criminal Acts of Violence Contrary to the Laies of War,* AJIL 37 (1943), p. 416; Kelsen, *Will the judgement in the Nuremberg Trial Constitute a Precedent in International Law?,* International Law, Quarterly 1 (1947), p. 158 ss.; Barton, *Foreign Armed Forces: Qualified jurisdictional Immunity,* BYIL 31 (1954), p. 358; Verdross, *Vrilkerrecht,* 5° éd., p. 234 ss.; Dahm, *Zur Problematik des Völkerstrafrechts,* p. 40.

    Le terme « act of State doctrine » est également employé pour le principe (contesté) suivant lequel les tribunaux d'un Etat doivent respecter les actes d'un autre "Etat (par exemple des expropriations) que ce dernier a accomplis sur son territoire (voir Bayer, *Die Enteignungen auf Kuba vor den Gerichten der Vereinigten Staaten,* ZaöRV 25 [1965], pp. 30–49). Quoique les deux principes reposent sur l'idée de l'égalité des Etats, le problème est différent, car dans le premier cas, il s'agit de l'immunité de l'acteur, dans le dernier de l'immunité de l'acte (Zander, *The Act of State Doctrine,* AJIL 53 [1959], p. 829)

82   Verdross, *loc. cit.;* Dahm, *op. cit.,* pp. 28,. 45; Balladore Pallieri, *Diritto Bellico,* p. 363. D'un autre avis: Kelsen, *loc. cit.;* Manner, *loc. cit.*

83   Oppenheim-Lauterpacht, *International Law,* vol. II, p. 568 ss.; Glaser, *Infraction internationale,* p. 92 ss.

LE DROIT DE LA GUERRE ET LES NATIONS UNIES

Les règles du *jus in bello* concernant la juridiction pénale des belligérants donnent donc une solution raisonnable pour le cas examiné.

Si l'on n'applique pas le droit de la guerre, le problème de la doctrine « act of State » devient très aigu. Si l'on applique ce principe, aucun des soldats en question ne peut être puni, même pas celui qui a employé l'arme empoisonnée. Si l'on ne l'applique pas, les soldats qui ont tué d'une façon honnête et permise par le droit de la guerre peuvent être punis, de même le soldat de D qui a employé l'arme empoisonnée. Les deux résultats sont aussi peu satisfaisants l'un que l'autre. Il n'est pas nécessaire, aux fins de la présente étude, d'entrer dans la discussion concernant la validité de ladite doctrine en temps de paix.[84] Car il résulte de ce qui vient d'être développé que la seule solution raisonnable de notre problème (application ou non du *jus in bello*) est d'appliquer le droit de la guerre dans notre cas.

4. L'exemple examiné justifie quelques conclusions d'ordre général. Nous avons vu que la non-application du *jus in bello* ne mène qu'à des incertitudes ou même des injustices. Il était indispensable, pour arriver à des résultats clairs et adéquats, de faire des emprunts au droit de la guerre. La raison en est que le droit de la paix ne connaît pas de normes qui règlent une situation exceptionnelle comme le recours à la force. Mais ces situations doivent être réglées de façon adéquate. Si les parties en conflit ne le font pas par voie d'accord, il n'y a qu'une possibilité: recourir aux normes que le droit international a créées pour régler l'emploi de la force armée dans les relations internationales. C'est une procédure que le juriste emploie toujours lorsqu'il se trouve devant une « lacune » ou devant une norme déficiente. Il doit rechercher une solution juste des situations qui lui sont soumises, par voie d'analogie ou d'interprétation extensive ou restrictive des normes en question. En le faisant, il est guidé par les exigences de la situation d'une part, par la *ratio legis*, par le but de la norme à appliquer, d'autre part.

Ces considérations révèlent qu'il ne peut pas être répondu à la question de l'application du *jus in bello* ratione materiae par une définition généralement valable. Une notion comme celle de guerre au sens matériel ou une définition du conflit armé comme « lutte prolongée dans le temps et dans l'espace » ne mènent pas à des résultats satisfaisants.

On doit plutôt se demander, dans chaque cas d'espèce, si une règle du droit de la guerre donne une solution adéquate à la situation 'en question.[85] C'est le

---

84   Voir Dahm, *op. cit.,* p. 39 ss.

85   Cela ne veut pas dire que les notions « état de guerre » et « guerre au sens matériel » n'aient pas d'importance dans d'autres contextes. Pour l'analyse de petits incidents armés. elles n'aident cependant pas.

cas quand le but de la norme et les exigences de la situation concrète coïncident. Les règles relatives à la conduite d'hostilités et à la juridiction pénale des belligérants ont le but de protéger les civils et les militaires à l'occasion d'hostilités qu'un sujet du droit international déclenche contre un autre au moyen de membres de ses forces armées. Il doit donc s'agir d'une action officielle, non d'un fait individuel. L'action doit être entreprise par les membres des forces armées comme tels, c'est-à-dire dans certaines formes qui caractérisent l'action militaire. Ainsi, les participants doivent porter l'uniforme de leur armée. Voilà quelques éléments qui distinguent l'action militaire d'actes qui relèvent de la criminalité pure et simple. Il aurait été juste, dans le cas qui vient d'être examiné, de traiter comme criminelles des personnes civiles ou des militaires en civil qui auraient traversé la frontière avec le même objectif.[86] Dans ce cas, l'action aurait perdu le caractère honnête, je dirais même chevaleresque, qui qualifie l'entreprise militaire. Si l'on est dans le domaine de la criminalité pure et simple, le droit de la paix nous offre des solutions valables (règles relatives à la compétence des Etats de poursuivre et de juger des infractions pénales,[87] traités d'extradition). Dans le cas des opérations militaires proprement dit, les règles du droit de la paix ne correspondent pas aux exigences de la situation.

5. Pour en revenir aux incidents congolais: Les principes élaborés permettent quelques remarques sur l'applicabilité du droit de la guerre ratione materiae[88] lors des incidents décrits ci-dessus.[89] Le droit de la guerre ne saurait être appliqué pour des incidents comme celui de Thysville, où des soldats marocains ont tiré sur une personne privée. Ici, la confrontation de deux corps militaires qui caractérise une situation de conflit susceptible de rendre applicables certaines normes du *jus in bello*, même dans le cadre d'une situation pacifique,[90] fait complètement défaut. La question du dédommagement est réglée par les par. 10 (b) et I de l'accord concernant le statut de l'ONUC:

> If as a result of any act performed by a member of the Force or an official in the course of his official duties, if is alleged that loss or damage that

---

86   Même dans le cadre d'un état de guerre. Ce fut le cas dans l'affaire *ex parte* Quirin (Arrêt de la Supreme Court des Etats-Unis, 317 U.S. 1, 31); voir également la décision du tribunal néerlandais, citée *supra,* p. 154, note 76.

87   Cf. par exemple l'art. VII du Statut des forces de l'OTAN et le projet de la Convention Européenne sur les conflits de compétence en matière répressive, Recommandation 420 (1965) de l'Assemblée Consultative du Conseil de l'Europe, adoptée lors de la 4e partie de la seizième session ordinaire de l'Ass. Cons., 25–29 janvier 1965.

88   L'applicabilité *ratione personae* est supposée; à cet égard voir *infra,* p. 208 ss.

89   P. 143 ss.

90   Voir *supra, p.* 148.

LE DROIT DE LA GUERRE ET LES NATIONS UNIES

> may give rise to civil proceedings bas been caused to a citizen or resident of the Congo, the United Nations shall settle the dispute by negotiation or any other method between the Parties; if it is not Pound possible to arrive at an agreement in this manner, the matter shah be submitted to arbitration at the request of either Party.

Selon le par. 15 dudit accord, aucune action contre l'ONU n'est possible devant les tribunaux congolais. La question de la responsabilité pénale est réglée par le par. 9 dudit accord. Les tribunaux marocains sont compétents pour juger le soldat en question accusé d'avoir commis un délit d'homicide. Cependant, le soldat est probablement justifié parce qu'il a agi dans le cadre des responsabilités pour le maintien de l'ordre public qui lui étaient confiées en vertu du mandat de l'ONUC.

Les autres incidents sont cependant susceptibles d'être régis par certaines règles du droit de la guerre. Ils sont, sous beaucoup d'aspects, comparables à l'incident de frontière qui vient d'être examiné. Les règles du *jus in bello* concernant le choix d'armes (il faut le dire: l'emploi de flèches empoisonnées est interdit![91]), le respect du signe de la Croix-Rouge et le statut des prisonniers de guerre s'y appliquent. La destruction de propriété privée peut être justifiée par les nécessités de la guerre.

En ce qui concerne la réparation de dommages, il faut donc d'abord se demander si le recours à la force de la part de l'ONUC ou des troupes congolaises est justifié, pour l'ONU en particulier, s'il est conforme au mandat. Si cela est le cas, il faut se demander si les moyens du recours à la force ont été licites à la lumière du droit de la guerre. Si cela n'est pas le cas, si par exemple le signe de la Croix-Rouge n'a pas été respecté,[92] l'ONU ou bien la République du Congo sont tenus d'indemniser l'Etat ou l'autorité dont relève la victime.

Cela a été, paraît-il, reconnu dans l'accord entre, la Belgique et l'ONU relatif au règlement des réclamations introduites auprès de l'ONU par des ressortissants belges, qui avaient subi des dommages au Congo.[93] Selon cet accord, l'ONU octroie une indemnisation pour les actes préjudiciables commis par les membres de l'ONUC « ne résultant pas d'une nécessité militaire ». Plus loin, l'ONU déclare « qu'elle ne se soustrait pas à sa responsabilité, s'il était établi

---

91 Voir l'appel lancé par Radio-Katanga le 7 décembre 1961: « Aux armes, Katangais! ... Empoisonnez vos flèches. La bataille se poursuivra jusqu'à ce que le dernier soldat de l'ONU ait quitté le Katanga ou qu'il ait été tué par nos balles ou nos flèches empoisonnées » (Doc. ONU S/4940/Add. 17, par. 13).

92 Pour un tel cas, voir *infra*, p. 223.

93 *Moniteur Belge*, 135e année (1965), p. 9071 s. = Doc. ONU S/6597 Annexe.

que des agents de l'ONU ont effectivement fait subir un préjudice injustifiable à des innocents ... (E)n vertu de ces principes, la responsabilité de l'organisation n'est pas engagée du fait des dommages aux personnes et aux biens qui sont uniquement la conséquence des opérations militaires ... ».

Cette dernière exception en matière de responsabilité de l'ONU va, semble-t-il, plus loin que l'exclusion des dommages résultant d'une nécessité militaire. Que signifie-t-elle? Quoique le texte le suggère, elle ne peut pas signifier que l'ONU n'est pas du tout responsable pour les dommages causés du fait des hostilités au Congo. Car le sens dudit accord est justement d'indemniser ces dommages; cet accord concerne en effet « les dommages aux personnes et aux biens consécutifs aux opérations de la Force des Nations Unies au Congo, en particulier celles qui se sont déroulées au Katanga ». Les documents parlementaires concernant l'accord nous donnent quelques indications pour l'interprétation de la phrase en question. Le rapport de la Commission des affaires extérieures de la Chambre des Représentants dit à cet égard: « L'indemnisation ne pouvait intervenir que si l'ONU était amenée à reconnaître des faits de guerre exceptionnels. »[94] Les réclamants devaient prouver le « caractère anormal du dommage de guerre subi ».[95] Qu'est-ce qui fait le caractère exceptionnel d'un acte de guerre? A mon avis, c'est que cet acte n'est normalement pas commis même en temps de guerre parce qu'il est interdit par le droit de la guerre. La déclaration de l'ONU suivant laquelle elle n'est pas responsable pour des dommages qui sont uniquement la conséquence des opérations militaires, ne peut donc être interprétée que dans le sens suivant: l'ONU ne répond pas des actes prohibés par le droit de la paix, mais permis par le droit de la guerre, mais seulement des actes interdits par le *jus in bello*, résultat qui est en parfaite harmonie avec ce qui vient d'être développé de façon théorique.

Outre les règles concernant le dédommagement, les normes du *jus in bello* relatives à la position des capturés s'appliquent également. Les capturés doivent être traités comme prisonniers de guerre. La puissance détentrice n'est pas autorisée à prendre des mesures judiciaires contre eux en ce qui concerne les actes d'hostilité qu'ils auraient commis lors de ces incidents, dans le cadre de ce qui est permis par le droit de la guerre.[96] Ils doivent être remis (l'expression « rapatriés » n'est pas adéquate dans ce contexte) après la fin des hostilités.[97]

---

94 Documents parlementaires, Chambre, Session 1964/65, Document 1009 n° 2, p. 2. Italiques de l'auteur.

95 *Ibid.*

96 Cette question est d'importance pour les « mercenaires » au Katanga voir *infra*, p. 214 s.

97 Voir par exemple l'incident de Moanda, *supra*, p. 143.

LE DROIT DE LA GUERRE ET LES NATIONS UNIES

2 Deuxième Partie : Le Champ D'application du Droit de la Guerre « Ratione Personae »

2.1 *L'égalité de L'application du Droit de la Guerre lors d'un Conflit Armé*

2.1.1 Les Données Générales du Problème

1. Pour répondre à la question de l'application du *jus in bello* ratione materiae on était conduit, en fin de compte, à entreprendre une analyse de la situation concrète. La question ratione personae requiert surtout des considérations générales.

La première question qui se pose dans ce contexte est de savoir si l'application du droit de la guerre (*jus in bello*) ne doit pas être exclue du fait que les troupes des Nations Unies se trouvent dans une meilleure position en ce qui concerne le droit de recourir à la force (*jus ad bellum*). Le problème se pose aussi pour les incidents armés qui ont eu lieu lors de l'action congolaise. On peut arguer que l'ONUC se trouvait au Congo en vertu d'un mandat qui lui avait été conféré par le Conseil de Sécurité et qui avait été accepté par le Gouvernement central. Les troupes qui agissent dans le cadre de ce mandat ne doivent pas être attaquées; et ceux qui les attaquent illégalement ne sauraient être mis sur un pied d'égalité avec les troupes des Nations Unies en ce qui concerne le droit qui règle la conduite des hostilités.

Dans des termes plus généraux, le problème est le suivant: faut-il introduire dans le domaine du *jus in bello* une discrimination en faveur d'une partie qui se trouve dans une situation juridique supérieure à celle de l'adversaire en ce qui concerne le *jus ad bellum*, par exemple en faveur de la victime d'une agression qui lutte contre son agresseur[98]? Le problème n'est donc pas restreint aux cas où il s'agit de troupes des Nations Unies. Mais il est possible que des considérations particulières s'imposent dans cette dernière hypothèse. Aux fins de la présente étude, il faudra donc d'abord examiner la question de la discrimination entre belligérants en général et se demander ensuite si le résultat ainsi atteint est également valable dans l'hypothèse d'une force armée agissant en vertu d'une décision d'un organe des Nations Unies.[99]

---

98 Le problème est très discuté. Cf. pour la discussion d'avant-guerre: Schmitt, *Die Wendung zum diskriminierenden Kriegsbegriff;* Draft Convention on Rights and Duties of States in Case of Aggression (cité dans Harvard Draft), AJIL 33 (1939) Suppl., pp. 819–909. Pour la discussion récente, voir surtout les travaux de l'Institut de Droit International, Annuaire 47 I (1957), pp. 323–606;48 II (1959), pp. 178–263; 50 I (1963), pp. 5–127; 50 II (1963), pp. 306–356.

99 Cf. François, Annuaire 47 I (1957), p. 331 s.

2. Le droit de la guerre traditionnel était fondé sur le principe de la non-discrimination. Si l'on veut aujourd'hui préconiser le principe de la discrimination, il faudrait prouver, au moins en ce qui concerne des conflits armés entre Etats, une dérogation à ce principe du droit international positif.[100] Une telle dérogation pourrait être survenue parce que certaines raisons d'être de l'égalité des belligérants ont été abolies:

a) Il était généralement reconnu que le droit international n'interdisait pas aux Etats de recourir à la guerre.[101] Sur cette égalité du *jus ad bellum*, on peut facilement fonder l'égalité en ce qui concerne le *jus in bello*.

b) Même ceux qui, comme Vattel, retenaient la possibilité d'un *bellum injustum* étaient amenés à accepter la non-discrimination en ce qui concerne le *jus in bello* parce qu'il n'existait aucune procédure pour déterminer la partie qui menait cette guerre injuste.[102]

La première raison n'est plus valable. Le Pacte de la Société des Nations, le Pacte Briand-Kellogg et, enfin, la Charte des Nations Unies ont successivement développé l'interdiction du recours à la force. Cette interdiction peut maintenant être considérée comme complète, le recours à la force n'étant permis qu'en cas de légitime défense.[103]

La deuxième raison n'a plus qu'une validité restreinte. Il existe une procédure, cependant pas très efficace, pour déterminer l'Etat qui a violé ses obligations en recourant à la force et qui, par conséquent, mène une « guerre injuste »: la décision du Conseil de Sécurité en vertu de l'art. 39 de la Charte.[104] On a même soutenu qu'une telle détermination pourrait être faite par l'Assemblée Générale agissant en vertu de la résolution « Uniting for Peace ».[105]

3. Une question se pose donc: ce développement du droit international implique-t-il une modification de l'ancien principe de la non-discrimination

---

100 Il ne faut donc pas prouver que le principe de la non-discrimination est valable; ceux qui ne veulent pas le reconnaître doivent au contraire prouver qu'il y a été dérogé; Schätzel, *Aggressionskrieg und Haager Kriegsrecht,* Acta scandinavica juris gentium 24 (1954), p. 25.

101 Il est difficile de concevoir cette permission de recourir à la guerre comme un droit subjectif (Oppenheim-Lauterpaçht II, p. 178 s.). Bilfinger (*Vollendete Tatsache und Völkerrecht,* ZaöRV 15 [1953/54], p. 465 parle, à juste titre, d'une indifférence du droit à l'égard du recours à la guerre. Des problèmes semblables se posent en ce qui concerne les permissions du *jus in bello.* Voir *infra,* p. 168.

102 Vattel, *Droit des Gens,* Liv. III, Chap. XII, notamment § 190.

103 Wehberg, *Kriegsverbot,* Strupp-Schlochauer, vol. II, p. 371.

104 Pour les détails, voir *infra,* p. 177 ss.

105 Cf. François, Annuaire 50 I (1963), p. 119.

LE DROIT DE LA GUERRE ET LES NATIONS UNIES   259

en ce qui concerne le *jus in bello*? Pour résoudre cette question, on procédera de la manière suivante: dans la Section 2.1.2 seront d'abord examinées les implications générales de l'interdiction du recours à la force, et ensuite, dans la Section 2.1.3, les conséquences des dispositions de la Charte relatives à la compétence de décision ou de recommandation dont certains organes des Nations Unies sont investis en matière du maintien de la paix.

2.1.2   Les Implications Générales de L'introduction du Recours à la Force

2.1.2.1   *La Question de L'abolition de la Compétence de Guerre*

L'interdiction du recours à la force pourrait d'abord avoir des répercussions sur la naissance ou non d'un « état de guerre ». On a soutenu que, la guerre mise « hors la loi », le recours à la force ne pourrait plus produire un état de guerre.[106] Les Etats auraient perdu la « compétence de guerre ».[107] Si l'on soutient que l'application du droit de la guerre présuppose un état de guerre au sens formel, on arrive, selon ces auteurs, à la conclusion que le droit de la guerre n'est plus applicable. Cette conséquence n'entraîne cependant pas nécessairement la discrimination entre les parties au conflit, parce qu'aucune d'elles ne pourrait alors se prévaloir des avantages du droit de la guerre. Il se peut seulement qu'un nouveau droit se développe dans le vide laissé par la non-applicabilité du droit de la guerre, droit qui pourrait discriminer entre les parties comme par exemple le Harvard Draft le propose.

On a contesté que les Etats aient perdu la « compétence de guerre »[108] parce que la faculté de créer un état de guerre était une émanation de la souveraineté des Etats et que la souveraineté était encore un élément essentiel du droit international actuel. Mais le problème essentiel n'est pas celui de la « compétence de guerre ». Car il faut tenir compte du fait que l'application de la plupart des règles du droit de la guerre ne présuppose pas un état de guerre au sens formel, mais seulement un conflit armé (guerre au sens matériel)[109] ou encore moins. La question de l'application discriminatoire ou non du droit de la guerre se pose donc indépendamment de la qualification d'un conflit déterminé comme guerre au sens formel ou non.

---

106   Cf. les auteurs cités par Mosler, *Die Kriegshandlung im rechtswidrigen Krieg,* JiaSR 1 (1948), p. 348 s.

107   Scelle, Annuaire 47 I (1957), p. 578.

108   Cf. François, Annuaire 47 I (1957), p. 493 s.; cf. aussi Mosler, *loc. cit.,* pp. 345–352. Pour la question de savoir si les Nations Unies possèdent cette compétence voir *infra,* p. 206.

109   Guggenheim, *Les principes de droit international public,* RdC 80 (1952 I), p. 174; pour les détails voir *supra,* p. 145 ss.

2.1.2.2 Le Principe : « Ex Injuria Jus Non Oritur »

1. La question de savoir si un état de guerre est encore juridiquement possible ne nous aide donc pas à trouver une solution du problème de la discrimination. Il faudra examiner d'autres arguments qui pourraient la favoriser. On a soutenu qu'un principe général de droit – « *ex injuria jus non oritur* » – exigerait la discrimination entre belligérants.[110] Le recours à la force étant prohibé, il serait inadmissible qu'un Etat qui aurait commencé des hostilités en ne respectant pas ses obligations internationales pût, du fait de cette violation du droit, acquérir des « droits belligérants ».[111] Le Harvard Draft[112] a clairement développé cette conception. L'art. 3 de ce projet de convention déclare: « ... an aggressor does not have any of the rights which it would have if it were a belligerent ... An aggressor has the duties which it would have if it were a belligerent. »

Cette manière de voir pose deux problèmes: celui de savoir si ce principe « ex injuria ... » est valable sans exceptions, et celui de savoir si l'application égale du droit de la guerre lors d'une guerre illicite viole vraiment ledit principe.

2. De prime abord, il paraît évident que quelqu'un qui a enfreint le droit ne peut pas acquérir des avantages juridiques du fait de cette violation. Mais le principe « *ex injuria jus non oritur* » n'a pas une valeur absolue. Il y a bien des cas où le droit règle une situation donnée sans tenir compte de ce que cette situation a été créée par une violation du droit ou non: *Ex factis jus oritur*.[113] Un exemple significatif en est le droit de la possession en droit romain, suisse et allemand.[114] Pour les actions possessoires, il suffit d'établir la possession (en cas de trouble de la possession) ou la possession préalable (en cas de dépossession). Aucune défense ne peut être fondée sur un droit à la possession.[115] Pour

---

110   Cf. par exemple Yepes, Annuaire 47 I (1957), p. 597.

111   Cf. par exemple Yepes, Annuaire 47 I (1957), p. 597.
       Wright, Annuaire 48 I (1959), p. 192; *id., The Outlawry of War and the Law of War,* APL 47 (1953), p. 370 S.

112   Cf. *supra*, p. 163, note 98.

113   Cette maxime est une application du principe de l'effectivité (Tucker, *The Principle of Effectiveness in International Law,* Law and Politics in The World Community, p. 35). C'est un principe reconnu du droit international public, mais encore mal défini (Cf. De Visscher, *Observations sur l'effectivité du droit international public,* RGDiP 62 [1958], p. 601). Ce principe sert à résoudre des problèmes très divers, niais qui ont en commun « l'idée d'une certaine tension et celle d'une ultime adéquation entre le fait et le droit » (De Visscher, *loc. cit.;* voir également Tucker, *op. cit.,* p. 31 ss.; Kriiger, *Das Prinzip der Effektivität, oder: über die besondere Wirklichkeitsnähe des Völkerrechts,* Festschrift für Spiropoulos, p. 275 ss.).

114   Cf. De Visscher, *loc. cit.*

115   Code civil suisse, Art. 927, 928; Code civil allemand § 863; pour le droit romain cf. Firs-Kunkel-Wenger, *Römisches Rechts,* 3e éd., p. 118. Le droit français connaît également, en matière immobilière, cette séparation entre actions possessoires et pétitoires, cf. Picard,

LE DROIT DE LA GUERRE ET LES NATIONS UNIES 261

décourager tout exercice violent de droits, l'ordre juridique ne tient, provisoirement, pas compte du droit à la possession et protège la situation existante de
possession, même si cette situation ne correspond pas au droit. Il se peut alors,
que « ex injuria jus oritur ».[116] Cet exemple montre que la maxime « ex injuria
jus non oritur » n'est pas appliquée avec une totale rigueur dans les ordres juridiques des Etats civilisés.

Elle ne peut de même pas être appliquée sans réserve dans le domaine du
droit international. Lauterpacht[117] observe à juste titre: « International law, being a weak law, is fully exposed to the impact of the phenomenon to which
jurists have referred as the 'law-creating influence of facts'. But unless law is
to become a convenient code for malefactors, it must steer a middle course
between the law-creating influence of facts and the principle, which is the essence of law, that its validity is impervious to individual acts of lawlessness. »

Il appartient au droit positif d'établir cette « ligne intermédiaire » entre la
maxime « *ex injuria jus non oritur* » et la reconnaissance de faits accomplis.
Aux fins de la présente étude, il sera donc nécessaire de chercher une réponse
à la question de la discrimination dans le droit positif, dans les conventions et
dans la coutume concernant le *jus in bello*.

3. Avant de procéder à un tel examen du droit positif, il faut se poser une
autre question: Est-ce que l'égalité de l'application du *jus in bello* enfreint
vraiment le principe « *ex injuria jus non oritur* »? Cela ne va pas de soi. C'est
seulement quand on se voit en présence d'une telle violation qu'il faut se demander si ce principe a été modifié.

Traité pratique de droit civil français, tome III, Les biens, p. 192 s. Cf. aussi Art. 1168 du Code
civil italien.

116 Wengler (Annuaire 50 I [1963], p. 104) donne un autre exemple pour la non-application du
principe « *ex injuria jus non oritur* »: dans la plupart des législations, les enfants adultérins
ne sont plus, contrairement à l'ancien droit, privés des droits élémentaires des enfants
envers leurs parents. Cf. aussi, pour une discussion dudit principe dans le droit interne
étatique, Schätzel, Annuaire 47 I (1957), p. 459 et Acta scandinavica juris gentium 24
(1954), p. 26 s.
Un autre exemple peut encore être relevé: un criminel ne perd pas, du fait de son
crime, les garanties de procédure; cela a été reconnu par la Cour Européenne des Droits
de l'Homme dans l'affaire « Lawless »: bien que Lawless se livrât à une activité « visant à
la destruction des droits ou libertés reconnus dans la présente Convention » (art. 17 de la
Convention européenne de sauvegarde des Droits de l'Homme et des libertés fondamentales), il ne perdait pas les droits fondamentaux de procédure garantis aux art. 5 et 6 de la
Convention (Publications de la Cour Européenne des Droits de l'Homme, Série A: Arrêts
et Décisions, 1960–61, p. 45). Cette idée est particulièrement valable pour le droit de la
guerre. Le *jus in bello* est une sorte de « code de procédure » pour la réglementation de
conflits armés.

117 *Recognition in International Law,* p. 427.

L'application égale du droit de la guerre ne constitue une violation dudit principe que si le droit de la guerre confère aux belligérants des droits subjectifs qui dépassent ceux possédés par les Etats en temps de paix.[118] Cela est très douteux. Car, dire qu'un certain acte est permis par le droit de la guerre ne signifie pas nécessairement que les parties au conflit possèdent un droit d'accomplir tel acte. Ainsi il est permis par le droit de la guerre de tuer les combattants de l'adversaire, d'occuper le territoire ennemi, de s'emparer des navires de l'autre partie. Mais si l'on considère ces facilités d'un belligérant comme des droits, on arrive à la conclusion qu'il est illicite d'empêcher l'ennemi de procéder à de tels actes, puisqu'il est illicite d'empêcher quelqu'un d'exercer ses droits: résultat dont l'absurdité est évidente. Si les actes mentionnés sont permis par le droit de la guerre, niais interdits par le droit de la paix, cela ne signifie pas que le *jus in bello* accorde plus de droits que le jus in pace. Cette permission signifie seulement que l'adversaire ne doit pas riposter à un tel acte en recourant à des représailles du droit de la guerre, c'est-à-dire à des actes qui dépassent les limites établies par les interdictions du droit de la guerre.[119] Une partie au conflit peut empêcher l'autre d'accomplir des actes permis par le droit de la guerre ou riposter à de tels actes par une mesure également permise par le droit de la guerre, par exemple une contre-attaque, mesure qui, dans le droit de la paix, représenterait un acte de représailles.

Si, par contre, un acte d'un belligérant n'est pas permis par le droit de la guerre, l'autre peut y riposter par une mesure généralement interdite par le droit de la guerre (représaille du droit de la guerre), tout en respectant, cependant, un standard minimum d'humanité.

Le *jus in bello* constitue donc un recul du droit à l'égard du jus in pace. Le champ des actes qui ne sont pas interdits est plus vaste en temps de guerre qu'en temps de paix. Le droit de la guerre traite indifféremment les actes de violence que le droit de la paix a prohibés, mais qu'il n'a pas pu empêcher. Les belligérants jouissent donc, dans le *jus in bello*, d'une plus grande liberté que dans le jus in pace. Mais cette liberté n'est pas protégée par le droit, les belligérants n'acquièrent pas un droit d'accomplir les actes permis. La fonction du droit de la guerre est alors d'empêcher certains excès dans ces actes de violence. Il remplit cette fonction en établissant un certain nombre d'interdictions propres au *jus in bello*. C'est ce qu'on a appelé le caractère prohibitif du droit de la guerre.[120] Non-discrimination (dans ce domaine du droit prohibitif)

---

118   Wright, Annuaire 48 11 (1959), p. 191.
119   Wengler, Annuaire 50 1 (1963), p. 52.
120   United States y. List et al., Trials of War Criminals before the Nuernberg Military Tribunals, vol. XI, p. 1247.

LE DROIT DE LA GUERRE ET LES NATIONS UNIES

ne signifie donc pas que des droits subjectifs sont accordés à un belligérant qui, en recourant à la guerre, a violé ces obligations internationales. Mais il n'est porté atteinte au principe « ex injuria jus non *oritur* » que si l'on conçoit le terme *jus* comme droit subjectif. La non-discrimination exige seulement qu'un belligérant n'ayant pas violé le *jus ad bellum* (par exemple la victime d'une agression) soit soumis aux mêmes interdictions générales du *jus in bello* que le belligérant ayant violé le *jus ad bellum* (par exemple l'agresseur). Le premier ne doit pas dépasser les limites du *jus in bello* en alléguant avoir agi à titre de représaille contre un acte du second qui reste dans le cadre de ce qui est permis par le droit de la guerre. Ainsi le principe de la non-discrimination interdit par exemple à la victime d'agression de détruire la propriété privée de ressortissants de l'Etat agresseur dans une mesure dépassant la nécessité militaire parce que l'agresseur avait occupé une partie du territoire de l'Etat défendeur. Si l'on conçoit la non-discrimination d'une telle manière, il est difficile d'y voir une injustice.

On pourrait objecter à ce raisonnement que le belligérant qui a violé le *jus ad bellum* avait néanmoins le *droit* d'exiger que l'autre partie se conforme aux restrictions du *jus in bello.* Il est vrai que les obligations créées par le droit de la guerre entraînent des droits subjectifs de l'autre partie de demander que ces obligations soient respectées. Mais ces droits ne dépassent pas le cadre de ce qu'un Etat peut demander en temps de paix. Ces droits ne représentent pas, en comparaison avec le droit de la paix, un « *plus* » mais un « *minus* ». En temps de paix, un Etat peut demander qu'un autre s'abstienne de toute attaque contre les forces armées du premier. En temps de guerre, il peut seulement demander que l'autre ne le fasse pas avec des armes qui causent des maux superflus. Si un belligérant qui a violé le *jus ad bellum* peut donc se prévaloir de ces droits que le *jus in bello* confère aux belligérants, il ne s'agit pas d'un *avantage* acquis du fait de la violation du droit, mais, en comparaison avec la situation qui existe en temps de paix, d'un désavantage. Le principe « *ex injuria jus non oritur* » ne se trouverait donc pas violé.

Ce raisonnement n'est cependant valable que dans la mesure où le droit de la guerre est en effet purement « prohibitif ». Il n'est plus valable dans des cas où le droit de la guerre accorde des pouvoirs juridiques qui dépassent ceux que les Etats possèdent en temps de paix. Cela est par exemple contesté en ce qui concerne le « droit » d'un occupant d'exiger l'obéissance de la population du territoire occupé.[121] A part cela, le droit de la guerre connaît des titres

---

121   La plupart de la doctrine est cependant d'avis que ce « droit » ne constitue qu'un pouvoir de fait toléré par le droit de la guerre; cf. Baxter, *The Duty of Obedience to the Belligerent Occupant, BYIL* 27 (1950), p. 235 ss.; Uhler, *Der völkerrechtliche Schutz der Bevölkerung*

d'acquisition de propriété que le droit de la paix ne connaît pas, par exemple la réquisition et le jugement de prise. Il connaît également des droits à l'égard d'Etats tiers au conflit, par exemple le droit de visite des navires d'un neutre.

Il est difficilement contestable que ces pouvoirs des belligérants constituent de véritables « droits ».

4. La question se pose donc en effet de savoir si le principe « *ex injuria jus non oritur* » est modifié par le droit positif. Mais avant d'examiner la pratique. des Etats, quelques considérations de principe sont peut-être utiles à cet égard. Si l'on veut appliquer un principe aussi général que « *ex injuria jus non oritur* », il est justifié de tenir compte d'autres réflexions d'ordre général. Il ne faut pas perdre de vue la fonction fondamentale, les buts élémentaires du droit de la guerre. Ce droit a pour but d'apporter un minimum d'ordre à un état de fait qui est l'expression d'un désordre de la société internationale. Cet ordre est requis par des exigences humanitaires, mais aussi (ou même surtout) par l'intérêt propre des parties belligérantes, qui souffrent moins de dommages étant protégées par le droit de la guerre. Etablir cet ordre est une entreprise délicate. Le *jus in bello* remplit cette tâche en créant un ensemble équilibré de normes.[122] C'est un fait dont il faut tenir compte quand on préconise une discrimination partielle, par exemple une discrimination seulement en ce qui concerne des règles qui établissent de véritables droits des belligérants ou en ce qui concerne des règles qui n'ont pas un caractère « humanitaire ».[123] Ce système d'équilibre est le fruit d'un long développement. Il a résisté – plus ou moins bien – à l'épreuve d'une série de guerres et de conflits armés. Il serait trop dangereux d'enlever des poids d'un côté de la balance. Ce qui resterait du droit de la guerre en serait gravement affecté.

Ledit caractère équilibré du droit de la guerre se manifeste de deux manières: Premièrement, le droit de la guerre établit un équilibre entre actes interdits et actes permis. Certaines permissions ou certains droits constituent les conditions préalables du respect des interdictions. Comment pourrait-on par exemple demander qu'un occupant protégeât la population du territoire occupé, qu'il respectât les droits de cette population, alors que cette même population ne se soumettrait pas à ses ordres et ne s'abstiendrait pas de nuire à

---

eines besetzten Gebiets, p. 39 ss.; Robin, *Des occupations militaires en dehors des occupations de guerre,* p. 15; Charles De Visscher, *L'occupation de guerre,* Law Quarterly Review 34 (1918), p. 74 s.; plus nuancé: Stone, *Legal Controls of Armed Conflict,* p. 724.

122 Scheuner, *Die kollektive Sicherung des Friedens im gegenwärtigen Völkerrecht,* Berichte der Deutschen Gesellschaft für Völkerrecht, vol. 2, p. 12; Kunz, Annuaire. 50 I (1963), p. 94.

123 Cf. pour l'impossibilité de cette dernière distinction Lauterpacht, *Rules of Warfare,* p. 93; Kunz, Annuaire 50 I (1963), p. 44.

l'occupant? La règle qui permet à l'occupant d'exiger l'obéissance de la population du territoire occupé doit donc être vue sous le jour de la fonction du *jus in bello* de protéger la population civile. Sans l'obéissance de la population, cette protection deviendrait impossible. On ne peut donc pas priver un Etat qui a violé le *jus ad bellum* du pouvoir de demander l'obéissance de la population d'un territoire occupé.[124] De manière plus générale, il faut constater qu'on ne peut pas enlever les éléments permissifs du droit de la guerre sans porter préjudice aux éléments restrictifs ou protecteurs.

Deuxièmement, il faut tenir compte du fait qu'un conflit armé international n'est souvent pas restreint à un domaine d'action bien déterminé, par exemple à l'échange de coups de feu dans une région déterminée. Les belligérants tâchent plutôt d'atteindre leurs buts par un ensemble de mesures. Cela est d'une importance primordiale en ce qui concerne les sanctions du droit de la guerre. Le respect du droit de la guerre ne se fonde pas sur des scrupules humanitaires mais surtout sur l'intérêt propre des Etats: ils ont respecté et respectent le droit de la guerre parce qu'ils craignent des représailles et parce qu'ils attendent le même respect de la part de l'adversaire; c'est-à-dire qu'ils respectent le *jus in bello* parce qu'ils pensent réduire le dommage qu'ils subissent eux-mêmes.[125] Une représaille peut être appliquée dans un domaine tout à fait différent de celui de la règle violée. Car la possibilité de représailles dépend du pouvoir des belligérants. Un belligérant disposant par exemple d'une force navale très forte ripostera dans 'ce domaine contre une violation du droit de la guerre sur terre; semblablement le fait que le premier respecte les règles du droit naval sera honoré de la part de l'autre belligérant par le respect des règles concernant la guerre sur terre ou la guerre économique. Le droit de la guerre est donc un ensemble indivisible.[126]

Si l'on prive un belligérant des avantages seulement d'une partie du droit de la guerre, on enlève donc une raison fondamentale du respect du *jus in bello:* l'Etat victime de discrimination n'a plus aucun intérêt à le respecter parce qu'il ne peut pas attendre le même respect. Et puisqu'il faut voir le *jus in bello* comme un ensemble, on ne peut d'aucune manière exclure qu'une violation

---

124   Oppenheim-Lauterpacht, vol. II, p. 218. On pourrait ajouter d'autres exemples de ce type. Ainsi, il est difficile de demander qu'un occupant paye la recompensation prévue par l'art. 52 du Règlement de La Haye si on lui nie le droit d'acquérir propriété du fait d'une réquisition.

125   McDougal–Feliciano, *International Coercion and World Public Order,* Yale Law Journal 67 (1957), p. 812. Cf. aussi le commentaire de l'art. 14 du Harvard Draft (AJIL 33 [1939] Suppl., p. 905. Le commentaire n'emploie ce raisonnement que pour le droit humanitaire, mais il n'indique pas pourquoi ces arguments n'auraient qu'une validité aussi restreinte.

126   Balladore Pallieri, *Diritto Bellico,* p. 146: « ... l'attività bellica constituisce un tutto unico ».

du droit de la guerre provoquée par une discrimination ne se produise dans un domaine où l'on veut en tout cas conserver l'application du droit de la guerre: le droit humanitaire proprement dit.[127] Une discrimination même partielle aura donc comme résultat que « hostilities are to degenerate into a savage contest of physical forces freed from all restraints of compassion, chivalry and respect for the dignity of man ».[128] C'est donc la *pleine réciprocité* dans l'ensemble du droit de la guerre qui garantit le respect du *jus in bello*.[129],[130]

Le principe de la non-discrimination ou de la pleine réciprocité de l'application du droit de la guerre est l'expression d'un réalisme du droit. Le droit international n'est pas capable d'empêcher des conflits armés: il les accepte comme fait accompli. Si le droit tâche de les régler, de réaliser même dans la lutte armée certaines valeurs d'ordre humanitaire, il ne peut le faire qu'en tenant compte de la nature de la chose, c'est-à-dire en respectant dûment les nécessités militaires et l'intérêt propre de toutes les parties au conflit. Le principe de la non-discrimination a donc un sens aussi longtemps qu'une conception réaliste des conflits armés le demande, que les conflits ont besoin de ce système équilibré de normes qui vient d'être décrit. Mais cela ne sera le cas que lorsqu'une organisation internationale détiendra un véritable monopole de la force, et qu'elle pourrait mener une action d'une rapidité et d'une efficacité, telles qu'elle mériterait vraiment d'être considérée comme « action de police ».[131]

5. Une remarque supplémentaire s'impose: nous avons vu que le droit de la guerre accepte l'état de guerre ou les hostilités, qu'il doit régler, comme un fait

---

127   Il n'est pas réaliste de croire, comme Wright (*The Outlawry of War and the Law of War*, AJIL 47 [1953], p. 376), que la discrimination constituerait une dissuasion contre l'agression. Un Etat qui recourt à la force violant ses obligations internationales démontre par ce fait qu'il ne craint pas les sanctions internationales. Il ne se préoccupera pas des restrictions discriminatoires qu'on voudrait lui imposer. La discrimination lui servira comme prétexte pour la violation du droit de la guerre.

128   Lauterpacht, *The Limits of the Operation of the Law of War*, BYIL 30 (1953), p. 212; id., *Rules of Warfare*, p. 92.

129   Kunz, *The Laws of War*, /MIL 50 (1956), p. 320; Mosler, *Die Kriegshandlung im rechtswidrigen Krieg*, JiaöR 1 (1948), p. 356 f.; Brownlie, *International Law and Me Use of Force by States*, p. 407; Baxter, *The Role of Law in Modern War*, ASIL Proceedings 1953, p. 95 f.; id., *Constitutional Forms and Some Legal Problems of International Command*, BYIL 29 (1952), p. 358 s.; Eustathiades, Annuaire 50 I (1963), p. 29 s.; Bindschedler, *ibid.*, p. 80; Andrassy, Annuaire 47 I (1957), p. 397.

130   Ceci est vrai aussi bien pour les relations entre les parties au conflit que pour les rapports entre belligérants et neutres; cf. Lauterpacht, *The Limits of the Operation of the Law of War*, BYIL 30 (1953), p. 238; Komarnicki, *The Place of Neutrality in the Modem System of International Law*, RdC 80 (1952 I), p. 441.

131   A cet égard, voir *infra*, p. 184 ss.

LE DROIT DE LA GUERRE ET LES NATIONS UNIES 267

accompli. Mais cette acceptation n'est que provisoire. L'analogie avec le droit de la possession en droit interne[132] reste ici valable: comme l'action pétitoire peut suivre l'action possessoire après que le droit a atteint son but de rétablir la paix sociale, la question d'une violation du *jus ad bellum* peut de nouveau être posée après la fin des hostilités. Alors il n'y a aucun obstacle à ce que les exigences de la logique juridique soient respectées: un Etat coupable d'une violation du *jus ad bellum* est tenu de réparer tout dommage qui résulte de ce délit international, même si le préjudice en espèces a été causé par un acte permis par le *jus in bello*. A cet égard, la doctrine paraît unanime.[133] Il faut cependant avouer que ces considérations sont quelque peu théoriques car, en fait, la compensation des dommages est en général réglée de façon expresse entre les parties après les hostilités. Cette réglementation dépend alors de beaucoup d'autres facteurs, et non pas seulement de la logique juridique.

6. Ce qui vient d'être développé montre qu'il n'est pas possible de fonder une abrogation du principe de la non-discrimination *durante belle* sur la maxime « *ex injuria jus non oritur* ». Mais dans un domaine comme le droit de la guerre, où le réalisme et les faits priment les réflexions théoriques, il faut contrôler un résultat acquis par des considérations générales à la lumière de la pratique des Etats. A cet égard il existe une pratique abondante dans la jurisprudence concernant les actes de belligérance accomplis par les Puissances de l'axe – considérées comme agresseurs – au cours de la Deuxième Guerre Mondiale.[134] Avec quelques flottements, cette jurisprudence a – explicitement ou implicitement – adopté la thèse de la non-discrimination.

a) Du point de vue de la discrimination, on aurait pu traiter comme illicites tous les actes de belligérance des Puissances agresseurs. Les tribunaux qui avaient à se prononcer sur les crimes de guerre commis par les organes de ces puissances n'ont pas raisonné de cette manière. Ils n'ont condamné un individu que si l'acte dont l'individu était accusé constituait une violation du *jus in bello*. L'individu pouvait donc se prévaloir des permissions du *jus in bello* comme justification.[135] C'est

---

132 Voir *supra*, p. 167.

133 Cf. les résolutions proposées à l'Institut de Droit International par Castrén (Annuaire 50 Il [1963], p. 342) et François (Annuaire 50 I [1963], p. 124); Kunz, Annuaire 50 I (1963), p. 92; Lauterpacht, *Rules of Warfare*, p. 101.

134 Voir pour une analyse de cette jurisprudence Mosler, *Die Kriegshandlung im rechtswidrigen Krieg*, JiaöR 1 (1948), p. 336 s.; Lauterpacht, *Rules of Warfare*, p. 94 ss.; Schätzel, *Aggressionskrieg und Haager Kriegsrecht*, Acta scandinavica juris gentium 24 (1954), pp. 23 ss.; *id*. Annuaire 47 I (1957), p. 455 ss.

135 Cf. le jugement de la Cour de Cassation néerlandaise pour les Crimes de Guerre (Bijzondere Raad van Cassatie) *in re* Zühlke, N.J. 1949 n° 85, p. 133.

ainsi que le Tribunal Militaire des Etats-Unis à Nuremberg fait une distinction très nette entre la violation du *jus ad bellum*, qui n'entraîne la responsabilité pénale que de ceux qui collaborent à la décision politique, et la violation du *jus in bello*, qui constitue une autre sorte de criminalité.[136]

b) Comme indication de l'idée suivant laquelle l'agresseur peut se prévaloir des avantages du droit de la guerre, on peut également citer un jugement du Tribunal Militaire des Etats-Unis qui a admis la nécessité militaire comme justification de destructions[137] « The devastation prohibited by the Hague Rules and the usages of war is that not warranted by military necessity. This rule is clear enough but the factual determination as to what constitutes military necessity is difficult. Defendants in this case were in many instances in retreat under arduous conditions wherein their commands were in serious danger of being cut off. Under such circumstances, a commander must necessarily make quick decision to meet the particular situation of bis command. A great deal of latitude must be accorded to him under such circumstances. What constitutes devastation beyond military necessity in these situations requires detailed proof of an operational and tactical nature. We do not feel that in this case the proof is ample to establish the guilt of any defendant herein on this charge. »[138]

c) Le même tribunal a implicitement admis que l'agresseur pouvait faire respecter ses droits par des représailles.[139] Le Tribunal Militaire International a même admis la licéité de la guerre sous-marine totale menée

---

136 United States *y.* von Leeb et al., Trials of War Criminals before the Nuernberg Military Tribunals, vol. XI, p. 491: « The acts of Commanders and Staff Officers below the policy level, in planning campaigns, preparing means for carrying them out, moving against a country on orders and fighting a war after it has been instituted, do not constitute the planning, preparation, initiation and waging of war or the initiation of invasion that international law denounces as criminal. Under the record we find the defendants were not on the policy level, and are not guilty. under Count I of the Indictment. With crimes charged to have been committed by them in the *manner* in which they behaved in waging the war, we deal in other parts of the judgment. ».

137 Art. 23 al. g du Règlement de La Haye.

138 United States v. von Leeb et al., Trials of War Criminals before the Nuernberg Military Tribunals, vol. XI, p. 541.

139 United States v. von Ohiendorf et al., Trials of War Criminals before the Nuremberg Military Tribunals, vol. IV, p. 493 s. Dans ce cas particulier, le tribunal fut cependant d'avis que les mesures en question n'étaient pas justifiées comme représailles, ou bien parce qu'elles constituaient des contre-représailles illicites, ou bien parce qu'elles ne respectaient pas le principe de la proportionnalité des représailles.

LE DROIT DE LA GUERRE ET LES NATIONS UNIES

par l'Allemagne, attendu que les Puissances Alliées pratiquaient la même chose.[140]

d) Les tribunaux norvégiens ont admis que l'Allemagne avait le droit d'établir des cours martiales pour contraindre la population du territoire occupé à s'abstenir d'actes nuisibles contre la puissance occupante, sous la réserve que ces cours devaient respecter une norme minimale de droit de défense.[141]

e) La question de savoir si l'agresseur pouvait se prévaloir des avantages du droit de la guerre jouait aussi un rôle quand il fallait déterminer la validité de prises ou de réquisitions effectuées par les Puissances de l'axe. Après la fin de la guerre, les tribunaux des Etats occupés n'ont pas déclaré nuls ces actes, ils les ont plutôt jugés selon leur conformité avec le droit de la guerre, sans même poser la question de savoir si ces règles sont aussi valables dans une guerre d'agression.[142] La Cour Maritime et Commerciale de Copenhague a expressément retenu que le caractère illicite d'une guerre n'excluait pas la validité d'une saisie: « La Cour ne peut pas accepter la vue du demandeur que, l'occupation du Danemark par l'Allemagne constituant une violation du droit international, il serait par conséquent exclu de considérer la saisie du bateau (« Adelaide Star ») comme justifiée par le droit international. Une invasion illicite, par analogie avec une guerre illicite – par exemple une guerre commencée en violation

---

140   Il n'apparaît pas très clairement si le tribunal a nié la responsabilité de Dönitz parce que la guerre sous-marine totale était permise comme représaille, ou parce que l'interdiction de cette guerre était, vu la -pratique contraire, tombée en désuétude: « Vu les faits, vu en particulier un ordre de l'Amirauté britannique en date du 8 mai 1940, suivant lequel tous les bateaux naviguant de nuit dans le Skagerrak devaient être coulés, et vu les réponses données par l'amiral Nimitz aux questionnaires qui lui furent adressés et indiquant qu'une guerre sous-marine sans restriction fut menée par les Etats-Unis dans l'Océan Pacifique, dès le premier jour de leur entrée en guerre, Dönitz ne peut être condamné pour violation du droit international en matière de guerre sous-marine » (Procès des grands criminels de guerre devant le Tribunal Militaire International, éd. française, tome I, p. 335).

141   Cf. le jugement du tribunal de première instance d'Oslo *in re* Latza et al., Archiv des Völkerrechts 1 (1948/49), p. 120–125.

142   Des réquisitions et des saisies effectuées par les troupes allemandes ont été considérées comme valables par des cours françaises et néerlandaises: cf. Cour d'Appel d'Orléans, Recueil Sirey 1949 II, p. 141 s.; Arr. Rechtbank Middelburg, N.J. 1948 n° 640. Voir aussi la décision de la Cour d'Appel d'Egée, où le défendeur avait allégué qu'un acte de l'occupant était nul parce qu'émanant d'un « conquérant ». Le tribunal a cependant soutenu que l'occupant avait le droit et l'obligation de prendre les mesures nécessaires pour l'approvisionnement de la population (Annual Digest 15 [1948] n° 186).

d'un pacte de non-agression – peut entraîner les effets juridiques d'une guerre. »[143]

f) D'autres tribunaux ont également constaté expressément que l'application du *jus in bello* était indépendante de la question de savoir si la guerre avait été commencée en violation du *jus ad bellum*. Le Tribunal Militaire des Etats-Unis à Nuremberg constate: « At the outset, we desire to point out that International Law makes no distinction between a lawful and an unlawful occupant in dealing with the respective duties of occupant and population in occupied territory. There is no reciprocal connection between the manner of the military occupation of territory and the rights and duties of the occupant and population to each other after the relationship in fact has been established. Whether the invasion was lawful or criminal is not an important factor in the consideration of this subject. »[144] La Cour Spéciale pour les Crimes de Guerre d'Arnhem déclare: « The rules of international law, in so far as they regulate the methods of warfare and the occupation of enemy territory, make no distinction between wars which have been started legally and Chose which have been started illegally. »[145] Dans le même sens, la Cour d'Appel de Kiel soutient, « que même une guerre qui est contraire au droit des gens reste une guerre dans le sens du droit international et entraîne les conséquences d'une guerre. La guerre est un état de fait qui fait naître certaines conséquences juridiques. En dépit de la violation d'accords internationaux, la guerre qui est contraire au droit des gens est soumise aux règles de la guerre ».[146]

g) D'autres tribunaux paraissent, cependant, plutôt favoriser la thèse de la discrimination. La Cour de Cassation néerlandaise pour les Crimes de Guerre (Bijzondere Raad van Cassatie) soutient par exemple « que les Pays-Bas avaient le droit de répondre au délit international commis par

---

143 « Retten kan ikke give Sagsøgeren Medhold i, at det allerede som Følge af den folkeretmaessige Ulovlighed af den tyske Besaettelse af Danmark skulde vaere udelukket, at Beslaglaeggelsen af MS 'Adelaide Star' var hjemlet ved Folkerettens almindelige Regler. Den ulovlige Invasion findes nemlig, in Lighed med en retsstridig – f.Eks. en i Strid med en Ikke-angrebs-Pagt paabegyndt – Krig, at maatte udløse Krigens Retsvirkeninger » (Blue Starline v. Burmeister & Wain, Jus Gentium vol. 1 [1949], p. 122; Annual Digest 15 [1948] n° 126).

144 *United States v. List et al.,* Trials of War Criminals before the Nuernberg Military Tribunals, vol. XI, p. 1247.

145 *In re* Christiansen, Annual Digest 15 (1948) n° 121.

146 Süddeutsche Juristenzeitung 2 (1947), p. 325: « dass auch der völkerrechtswidrige Krieg ein Krieg im völkerrechtlichen Sinne bleibt und die Rechtsfolgen eines Krieges nach sich zieht. Der Krieg ist eben ein Tatbestand, der Rechtsfolgen auslöst. Der völkerrechtswidrige Krieg unterliegt trotz des Bruches völkerrechtlicher Abmachungen den Kriegsregeln. ».

LE DROIT DE LA GUERRE ET LES NATIONS UNIES   271

l'ancienne Allemagne (le déclenchement d'une guerre d'agression) en employant des représailles qui se référeraient même au fonctionnement du droit normal de la guerre sur terre, sur mer et dans l'air ... ».[147] Cette attitude reviendrait à une certaine discrimination.[148] Le tribunal n'en a cependant pas tiré les conséquences. Il a tout de même toujours examiné la question de savoir si un acte déterminé constituait une violation des lois et coutumes de la guerre. Dans le même jugement, le tribunal dit que l'accusé, un membre de la ss, peut se prévaloir des règles du droit de la guerre comme « justification ».[149]

Dans le jugement *in re* Rauter, le tribunal s'est prononcé d'une façon semblable en ce qui concerne le droit des Pays-Bas de répondre à une violation du *jus ad bellum*. Mais cette prise de position reste également *obiter dictum:* Le tribunal déclare que certains actes de la puissance occupante ne pouvaient pas être justifiés comme représailles parce que les actes auxquels ils ripostaient étaient eux-mêmes justifiés comme représailles; car ces derniers ripostaient déjà à une violation préalable du droit international de la part de l'Allemagne. Le tribunal voit, entre autre, une telle violation dans le fait que l'Allemagne avait déclenché une guerre d'agression, mais il énumère ensuite encore des violations du *jus in bello* pour justifier les représailles néerlandaises.[150] La jurisprudence néerlandaise ne se départ donc pas clairement du principe de la non-discrimination.

La jurisprudence luxembourgeoise paraît, à première vue, également tendre vers la discrimination contre l'agresseur. Mais quoiqu'elle aille très loin dans la négation des droits de l'occupant, elle ne nie pas l'applicabilité du Règlement de La Haye en faveur de l'agresseur. Dans l'affaire Werner, la Cour des crimes de guerre fonde son jugement sur une *violation* du Règlement, à savoir l'exécution d'une mesure qui viole l'art. 52 (contrainte de servir dans l'armée de l'ennemi).[151] Dans l'affaire Hemmerling, le tribunal prétend, peut-être à tort, qu'il y a eu violation des art. 44 et 45 (atteinte au devoir de fidélité de la population à l'égard

---

147   « ... dat Nederland bevoegt zou zijn geweest om de ... volkenrechtlijke onrechtmatige daad van het toenmalige Duitsland te beantwoorden met repressailles, zelfs met betrekking tot de werking van het normale oorlogsrecht te land, ter zee of in de lucht ... » (*in re* Zühlke, N.J. 1949 n° 85, p. 131).

148   Pour cette raison la décision est critiquée par Röling, *ibid.,* p. 137.

149   Le tribunal soutient « dat immers vooreerst in het algemeen het oorlogsrecht niet bepaalde handelingen *rechtvaardigt,* maar integendeel slechts bepaalde handelingen verbiedt » (*ibid.,* p. 133).

150   N. J. 1949 n° 87, p. 155.

151   Archiv des Völkerrechts 2 (1949/50), pp. 233–236.

du souverain du territoire occupé).[152] La jurisprudence luxembourgeoise ne se départ donc pas non plus du principe de la non-discrimination.

En résumant, on peut constater que d'après la jurisprudence des Etats, le principe de la non-discrimination fut encore valable pendant la deuxième guerre mondiale. La pratique confirme donc le résultat atteint par le raisonnement théorique: les règles du *jus in bello* s'appliquent de façon égale à l'agresseur et à sa victime. Le principe « *ex injuria jus non oritur* » ne saurait influencer le fonctionnement du droit de la guerre.

2.1.3 La Charte des Nations Unies et le Droit de La Guerre

La seule interdiction de la guerre ou du recours à la force n'a donc pas affecté le principe de la non-discrimination. La question se pose maintenant de savoir si les dispositions de la Charte des Nations Unies qui établissent un pouvoir de décision ou de recommandation pour certains organes des Nations Unies en matière du maintien de la paix sauraient modifier ce résultat. Dans ce contexte, il est nécessaire d'examiner deux éléments de la Charte:

1. La possibilité de déterminer une violation du *jus ad bellum* par voie d'une décision obligatoire du Conseil de Sécurité (art. 39, 25),
2. la possibilité pour l'organisation d'entreprendre une action coercitive (art. 41 ss., 2 al. 5).

2.1.3.1 *Le Pouvoir du Conseil de Sécurité en Vertu de L'art. 39*

1. Selon l'art. 39 de la Charte, le « Conseil de Sécurité constate l'existence d'une menace contre la paix, d'une rupture de la paix ou d'un acte d'agression ». Il y a donc maintenant un « juge » qui se prononce de façon obligatoire (au moins pour les Etats-membres de l'ONU) sur une violation du *jus ad bellum*. L'argument déjà employé par Vattel[153] pour fonder la non-discrimination n'est donc, de prime abord, plus valable. Dans l'hypothèse d'une telle constatation, il est, théoriquement impossible que des belligérants procèdent réciproquement à des représailles en s'accusant mutuellement d'agression. Mais l'incertitude en ce qui concerne le *jus ad bellum* est un argument qui n'est pas indispensable pour fonder le principe de la non-discrimination. Le raisonnement qui vient d'être développé n'a pas dû l'employer. On ne peut donc pas conclure qu'une constatation faite par le Conseil de Sécurité en vertu de l'article 39 entraîne la discrimination contre la partie qui a violé le *jus ad bellum*.

---

152   *Ibid.,* pp. 494–497.

153   Voir *supra*, p. 164.

LE DROIT DE LA GUERRE ET LES NATIONS UNIES

2. A part cela, il est très douteux que la constatation selon l'article 39 élimine en effet l'incertitude en ce qui concerne le *jus ad bellum*. Le seul cas où une telle constatation a été faite par le Conseil de Sécurité[154] montre bien la raison de ces doutes.

a) La constatation concerne la République de Corée du Nord, qui n'est ni membre des Nations Unies ni reconnue en tant qu'Etat. Il n'est donc pas certain que cette constatation ait un caractère obligatoire pour la Corée du Nord.[155]

b) La décision du Conseil de Sécurité a été prise en l'absence d'un membre permanent. De ce fait, on a déduit l'illégalité ou même la nullité de ladite constatation.[156],[157]

L'exemple de la Corée nous montre donc qu'il est encore possible de contester, avec une certaine raison, le caractère obligatoire ou la validité d'une décision du Conseil de Sécurité prise en vertu de l'art. 39. L'incertitude en ce qui concerne le *jus ad bellum* est donc diminuée, mais non tout-à-fait éliminée. Même l'argument qui fonde l'égalité de l'application du *jus in bello* sur cette incertitude conserve donc une certaine valeur. Le principe de l'égalité de l'application du *jus in bello* ne paraît, en conclusion, pas être affecté par le pouvoir de décision du Conseil de sécurité.

3. Ce résultat est confirmé par la pratique au cours du conflit de Corée. On ne trouve aucune indication que, lors de ce conflit, le droit de la guerre ait été appliqué de façon discriminatoire.[158] Dans les déclarations faites par une série de gouvernements participant aux hostilités, qui avaient placé leurs troupes

---

154 S/1501.

155 Cf. Kelsen, *Recent Trends in the Law of the United Nations*, p. 928 ss. Verdross, *General International Law and the United Nations Charter*, International Affairs 30 (1954), p. 346; Attia, *Les forces armées des Nations Unies*, p. 119 ss.

156 Cf. pour la discussion de cette question Kelsen, *Recent Trends*, p. 940 s.; Attia, *Les forces armées des Nations Unies*, p. 124 ss.; O'Connel, *The Legal Character of the Korean War*, New Zealand Law Journal 27 (1951), p. 362 s. Voir aussi les auteurs cités par Verplaetse, *The* jus in bello *and Military Operations in Korea 1950–1953*, ZaöRV 23 (1963), p. 679 note 1.

157 La validité de la décision du Conseil de Sécurité a également été contestée pour d'autres raisons, par exemple parce que la Corée du Nord n'a pas été invitée aux délibérations (Attia, *op. cit.*, p. 118 s.; O'Connel, *loc. cit.*), parce que la Chine n'était pas correctement représentée (Attia, *op. cit.*, p. 122 ss.; Kelsen, *Recent Trends*, pp. 941 ss.; O'Connel, *loc. cit.*), parce que le Conseil avait méconnu les règles de la Charte concernant l'agression (Attia, *op. fit.*, p. 121; Verplaetse, */oc. cit.*, p. 680 note 1).

158 Baxter, *The Role of Law in Modem War*, ASIL Proceedings 1953, p. 96; Eustathiades, Annuaire 50 I (1963), p. 36; Kunz, Annuaire 50 I (1963), p. 44; Lauterpacht, *Rules of Warfare*, p. 99; Scheuner, *Eine internationale Streitmacht im Dienste der Vereinten Nationen*, ZaöRV 19 (1958), p. 392; Taubenfeld, *International Armed Forces and the Rules of War*, AJIL 45 (1951), p. 678.

sous le « Commandement Unifié », il n'était pas question d'une discrimination. La reconnaissance du droit humanitaire exprimée dans ces déclarations allait parfois même plus loin que la reconnaissance de la part de la Corée du Nord, qui au commencement du conflit n'a expressément reconnu que l'applicabilité de l'art. 3 commun aux quatre Conventions de Genève et des principes de la Convention relative aux prisonniers de guerre.[159] Cette attitude de la Corée du Nord est probablement la raison pour laquelle le Commandement Unifié[160] a adopté une semblable position restrictive, quoique les Etats-Unis aient déclaré appliquer les Conventions de Genève sur une base volontaire[161] et quoique le Commandement Unifié ait donné aux troupes des Nations Unies l'ordre de respecter les quatre Conventions de 1949 ainsi que « les parties de la Convention de La Haye N° IV de 1907 qui s'appliquent en la matière, et ainsi que les autres principes pertinents du droit international ».[162] A part cela, on peut observer qu'il y avait un " tarit *de facto* agreement "[163] entre les parties en ce qui concerne l'applicabilité du droit de la guerre. 11 n'est ici pas question de discrimination.

On arrive donc à la conclusion que le pouvoir du Conseil de Sécurité créé par l'art. 39 de la Charte ne change rien au principe établi de la non-discrimination.

4. L'art. 2 par. 5 ne modifie pas ce résultat, si la constatation faite en vertu de l'art. 39 n'est pas suivie d'une action coercitive. Cet article ne s'applique que dans le cas où le Conseil de Sécurité décide d'entreprendre une action coercitive. Il ne crée pas un devoir d'assistance lorsque le Conseil de Sécurité se borne à faire des recommandations. Car seules des décisions concernant les mesures visées par les articles 41, 42 (et 40) sont obligatoires en vertu de l'art. 25. On priverait le terme « recommandation » de son sens si l'on soutenait qu'une recommandation (du Conseil de Sécurité ou d'un autre organe) entraîne un devoir d'assistance.[164]

---

159   Le Comité international de la Croix-Rouge et le conflit de Corée, t. I, pp. 4–31, 82–88.

160   *Ibid.,* p. 87.

161   Lettre d'Acheson, Le Comité international de la Croix-Rouge et le conflit de Corée, t. I, p. 13 s.

162   Lettre adressée au Secrétaire Général des Nations Unies le 5 juillet 1951 par le représentant des Etats-Unis d'Amérique, Doc. ONU S/2232.

163   Verplaetse, *loc. cit.,* p. 684, aussi p. 722 s.; cf. aussi Attia, *op. cit.,* p. 260 ss.; Greenspan, *The Modern Law of Land Warfare,* p. 26.

164   Cf. Kelsen, *The Law of the United Nations,* p. 91 ss. Voir aussi Goodrich-Hambro, *Charter of the United Nations,* p. 107, Art. 2, par. 5 « imposes no obligations not provided for in other parts of the Charter ». La même interprétation du terme « action » dans l'art. 11, par. 2 *in fine* est soutenue par la C.I.J. dans l'avis consultatif « Certaines dépenses des Nations Unies » Recueil 1962, p. 164 s.); *contra:* Bindschedler, *Die Neutralität im modernen Völkerrecht,* ZaöRV 17 (1956/57), p. 30 s.

LE DROIT DE LA GUERRE ET LES NATIONS UNIES

2.1.3.2 *Les Mesures Coercitives Selon L'art. 42*

La deuxième question qui doit être examinée dans cette section est de savoir si le pouvoir des Nations Unies d'entreprendre des actions coercitives pour le maintien de la paix (art. 42) a modifié le principe de la non-discrimination.

1. Les seules dispositions de la Charte qui se réfèrent expressément au droit applicable au cours d'une action coercitive en vertu des articles 42 ss. sont les articles 2 par. 5 et 49. Le devoir d'assistance prescrit par ces articles modifie essentiellement le devoir d'impartialité que l'institution de la neutralité imposerait autrement aux Etats non directement engagés dans le conflit. Mais cette obligation ne vaut que pour les Etats-membres et même ces derniers peuvent en être libérés par le Conseil de Sécurité (art. 48).[165] En dehors du champ d'application desdits articles de la Charte, l'institution de la neutralité reste en vigueur,[166] bien qu'il soit un peu problématique si une action coercitive des Nations Unies présente les caractéristiques d'un conflit susceptible d'entraîner l'application du droit de la neutralité (surtout si l'on considère que l'applicabilité du droit de la neutralité présuppose un état de guerre au sens formel).[167] Mais il paraît parfaitement concevable que des Etats non-membres ou des Etats libérés de leur devoir d'assistance en vertu de l'article 48 de la Charte puissent avoir les droits et devoirs d'un neutre lors d'une action coercitive des Nations Unies.

2. En ce qui concerne les relations entre les parties au conflit, c'est-à-dire entre les troupes agissant en vertu de l'art. 42 et les troupes de l'Etat qui est l'objet de l'action coercitive, on a soutenu que les Nations Unies auraient le droit de déterminer les règles du droit de la guerre applicables à ce conflit. Les Nations Unies pourraient « select such of the laws of war as may seem to fit its purposes (e.g. prisoners of war, belligerent occupation), adding such others as may be needed, and rejecting those which seem incompatible with its purposes. We think it beyond doubt that the United Nations, representing practically all the nations of the earth, have the right to make such decisions ».[168] Ce pouvoir de déterminer de façon unilatérale les règles applicables à un conflit armé

---

165 Cf. Scheuner, *Neutralität,* in: Strupp-Schlochauer, vol. II, p. 593; Kornarnicki, *The Place of Neutrality in the Modern System of International Law,* RdC 80 (1952 1), p. 467 ss.

166 Scheuner, *ibid.* Cela n'empêche pas les Etats non engagés dans le conflit d'adopter (à leur propre risque) un statut de « non-belligérance ». Mais il ne faut pas oublier que le principe de la non-discrimination a aussi une valeur en ce qui concerne la neutralité (voir *supra,* p. 172 note 130). Cf. aussi Komarnicici, *loc. cit.,* p. 467 ss., 481 ss.

167 Voir *supra,* p. 172.

168 Report of the Committee on Study of Legal Problems of the United Nations, ASIL Proceedings 1952, p. 220.

est évidemment la négation complète du principe de la non-discrimination.[169] Un tel pouvoir ne trouve aucune base expresse dans la Charte. Le Conseil de Sécurité « décide quelles mesures seront prises conformément aux articles 41 et 42 pour maintenir ou rétablir la paix et la sécurité internationales ».[170] En vertu de l'art. 42, il entreprend une action qui « peut comprendre des démonstrations, des mesures de blocus et d'autres opérations exécutées par les forces ... de Membres des Nations Unies ». Tout au moins de façon expresse, ce pouvoir ne se réfère qu'au *jus ad bellum,* au droit des Nations Unies de recourir à la force. Il est intéressant de noter que l'art. 42 contient une notion du droit traditionnel de la guerre: le blocus. C'est là une indication, cependant plutôt faible, qu'en ce qui concerne les modalités de l'emploi de la force par les Nations Unies (*jus in bello*), la Charte renvoie au droit de la guerre traditionnel.

Une limitation importante du pouvoir du Conseil de Sécurité en vertu des art. 39 ss. réside dans le fait que ces mesures n'ont pour but que de « maintenir ou rétablir la paix et la sécurité internationales ».[171] On peut en déduire que les Nations Unies n'ont que les pouvoirs strictement nécessaires à ces fins. Il est difficile de voir pourquoi une application discriminatoire du droit de la guerre en faveur des Nations Unies serait nécessaire pour atteindre ces fins. D'un but restreint doivent résulter des pouvoirs restreints. Jessup[172] opine donc à juste titre que les forces des Nations Unies devraient se soumettre à des restrictions plus sévères que celles du droit de la guerre traditionnel. Il nie par exemple aux troupes des Nations Unies le droit à un butin de guerre.

Dans ce contexte, il faut aussi mentionner que le préambule de la Charte proclame la « foi dans les droits fondamentaux de l'homme, dans la dignité et la valeur de la personne humaine ». « No organization founded on such a basis can properly ignore rules designed to preserve and protect such dignity and worth ... The United Nations Forces must ... behave in a manner consistent with the purposes and ideals of the Organization and, since the rules of war represent a general international attempt to humanize armed conflict, these

---

169   Cf. la critique de Lauterpacht, *The Limits of the Operation of the Law of War,* BYIL 30 (1953), p. 242 s.

170   Art. 39 de la Charte.

171   Eustathiades, Annuaire 50 I (1963), p. 34 s.; Wengler, *ibid.,* p. 106.

172   *A Modern Law of Nations,* p. 217. Brownlie, *International Law and the Use of Force by States,* p. 408 soutient que les Nations Unies pourraient, après la défaite d'un agresseur, jouir de pouvoirs plus étendus que ceux prévus par le droit d'occupation belligérante (dans le même sens: van Asbeck, Annuaire 50 I [1963], p. 79). Ce raisonnement s'inspire du régime établi par les Puissances Alliées en Allemagne après 1945. Mais cette manière de voir n'est guère compatible avec le but restreint d'une action coercitive des Nations Unies (cf. Castberg, Annuaire 50 II [1963], p. 336 s.).

LE DROIT DE LA GUERRE ET LES NATIONS UNIES 277

forces must be subject to the principles embodied in such rifles. »[173] On a argué que même une discrimination partielle peut avoir des conséquences préjudiciables pour ledit droit humanitaire.

Les dispositions de la Charte ne donnent donc aucune indication positive en ce qui concerne la discrimination au cours d'une action coercitive; elles paraissent plutôt préconiser la non-discrimination.

3. Les auteurs qui soutiennent le pouvoir des Nations Unies de déterminer les règles du droit applicable à une action coercitive ou d'autres formes de discrimination ne le fondent, en effet, pas sur des arguments strictement juridiques,[174] mais plutôt sur des considérations d'ordre sociologique: on considère une action entreprise par les Nations Unies comme semblable à une action de police en droit interne et non à une guerre. « As the law in content between police officials and gangsters is on the side of police officials, so is the law on the side of United Nations enforcement action against an aggressor. In an exchange of gun-fire between police officials and gangsters, if a police official is killed by a gangster, the killing is murder, whereas the killing of a gangster by a police officer is excusable homicide committed in the line of duty. Similarity the United Nations has superior rights to those of an aggressor. »[175] Il est permis de répondre à un tel raisonnement par des considérations de caractère semblable: « There is a considerable difference between bringing to book a gang of bandits and collective action against a recalcitrant State. The opportunities for mischief are far greater in the latter connection, which makes it essential that every effort should be made to wage such an action according to the law of warfare. »[176]

---

173   Taubenfeld, *International Armed Forces and the Rates of War,* AJIL 45 (1951), p. 677. Dans le même sens Stone, *Legal Controls of International Conflict,* p. 315 s.: « The very nature of such forces suggests that they should and will have a regard for [the rules of war] even more scrupulous than that of States, this being a proper case of expansion of the technical ambit of law, not merely by analogy, but *a fortiori.* » Cf. aussi Schätzel, Annuaire 47 1 (1957), p. 461.

174   Des arguments d'ordre moral sont également utilisés. Ainsi (selon Rolin, Annuaire 48 II [1959], p. 202) « il serait *inconcevable* que les forces de l'ordre occupant tout ou partie du territoire de l'agresseur soient soumises aux mêmes limitations que l'Etat agresseur se trouvant en position d'occupant » (italiques par l'auteur). Voir aussi le rapport du Comité de l'ASIL cité *supra,* p. 181 note 168. Du point de vue moral, il faut cependant soutenir avec Baxter (*The Role of Law in Modern War,* ASIL Proceedings 1953, p. 98): « If we do not ourselves adhere to the right, we are not better than our enemies. ».

175   Bivens, *Restatement of the Laws of War as Applied to the Armed Forces of Collective Security Arrangements,* AJIL 48 (1954), p. 141. Cf. aussi Wright, *The Outlawry of War and the Laws of War,* AJIL 47 (1953), p. 365 s.

176   Greenspan, *The Modern Law of Land Warfare,* p. 25; cf. aussi Jessup, *A Modem Law of Nations,* p. 188; Kunz, Annuaire 50 I (1963), p. 90.

Certes, on ne peut que spéculer sur le caractère sociologique d'une action coercitive des Nations Unies; car jusqu'à présent l'histoire des Nations Unies ne nous en montre aucun exemple.[177] Mais suivons le raisonnement sociologique. Pour mettre une action internationale sur un pied d'égalité avec une action de police, il faudrait que certaines exigences soient remplies. Il faut, comme nous l'avons vu,[178] que l'organisation internationale dispose d'un véritable monopole de la force: c'est dire qu'une mesure de contrainte de l'organisation internationale doit être la règle et non l'exception et que l'organisation doit disposer d'une force armée si irrésistible qu'elle puisse au moins dans la plupart des cas vaincre toute opposition de façon rapide et efficace (comme c'est la règle pour la police à l'intérieur des Etats).[179] La première exigence n'est pas remplie, et l'on peut douter que la seconde soit remplie lorsque, par un hasard politique quelconque, une action coercitive du Conseil de Sécurité s'avère possible. Les actions militaires qui ont été entreprises en vertu de décisions du Conseil de Sécurité et qui n'étaient pas des actions coercitives: Corée, Congo, Chypre, ont bien prouvé le contraire.[180] Mais outre un pouvoir exécutif efficace, il faut encore deux autres critères pour qu'on puisse traiter de façon analogue l'ordre interne et l'ordre international: l'ordre international devrait disposer de procédures permettant la décision juridique sur tout différend (pouvoir judiciaire) ainsi que le « peaceful change » (pouvoir législatif).[181] l'ONU ne possède ni l'une ni l'autre. La juridiction de la Cour Internationale de Justice n'est obligatoire que dans un nombre limité de cas. Le pouvoir étendu de décision dont est investi le Conseil de Sécurité n'est pas de caractère juridique, mais plutôt politique.[182] D'un autre côté, il ne peut toutefois pas être considéré comme un véritable pouvoir législatif international parce qu'il est restreint au cas où la paix est en danger.

---

177   Dans le cas de la Corée, le Conseil s'est borné à faire des recommandations. Les actions contre le Katanga ne constituaient pas non plus une action coercitive au sens de la Charte; voir *supra,* p. 150.

178   Voir *supra,* p. 172.

179   Lauterpacht, *Rules of Warfare,* p. 99 n'accepte pas l'idée d'action de police « unless the force at the disposai of the international community is so overwheiming as to approach rapid police action permitting no organized resistance ». Cf. id., *The Limits of the Operation of the Law of War,* BYIL 30 (1953), p. 220 s.; Virally, *L'O.N.U. d'hier à demain,* p. 162; François, Annuaire 57 I (1957), p. 391.

180   Virally, *op. cit.,* p. 164; cf. aussi Eustathiades, Annuaire 50 I (1963), p. 30; Ruegger, Annuaire 47 1 (1957), p. 432.

181   Virally, op. cit., p. 158.

182   Virally, op. cit., p. 161; Bindschedler, Annuaire 50 I (1963), p. 25.

LE DROIT DE LA GUERRE ET LES NATIONS UNIES

On arrive donc à la conclusion que la situation sociologique de l'organisation internationale n'est pas encore telle qu'on puisse désigner une action, armée internationale comme « action de police ». Une telle action est -encore trop semblable aux mesures de contrainte utilisées traditionnellement entre Etats. Elle constitue une guerre, au moins au sens matériel du terme.[183] Elle a donc besoin d'être réglée par ce système équilibré de normes que le droit de la guerre a développé sur la base de la non-discrimination.[184] Le principe de la non-discrimination reste donc valable même pour une action coercitive entreprise par le Conseil de Sécurité.[185] Il va sans dire que le même principe reste applicable pour d'autres opérations de troupes qui agissent en vertu d'une décision prononcée par un organe des Nations Unies.

4. Il est peut-être utile de réexaminer le résultat acquis à la lumière de la résolution de l'Institut de Droit International adoptée lors de sa session de Bruxelles le 11 septembre 1963. Le texte de la résolution est le suivant[186] :

> L'Institut de Droit International,
>
> Convaincu que le développement de l'organisation internationale ne permet pas de maintenir intégralement *durante bello* le principe égalitaire des parties dans les conflits armés, en ce qui concerne les relations entre les participants au conflit,
>
> Tenant compte des obligations que les membres de l'ONU ont assumées en vertu de la Charte en ce qui concerne l'action en cas de menace contre la paix, de rupture de la paix et d'acte d'agression,
>
> Considérant qu'il convient de tirer les conséquences juridiques de la prohibition de l'agression en les harmonisant avec les principes humanitaires et les intérêts légitimes de l'Etat victime de l'agression, comme des Etats tiers,

---

183 Greenspan, *The Modern Law of Land Warfare,* p. 25 s.; Jessup, *A Modern Law of Nations,* p. 188; Kotzsch, *The Concept of War in Contemporary History and International Law,* p. 289; · Kunz, *The Chaotic Status of the Law of War,* AJIL 45 (1951), p. 54 s.; Ridder, *La guerra y el derecho de Guerra en el derecho internacional y en la doctrina internacionalista,* Revista de Estudios Politicos 92 (1957), p. 48; Bindschedler, Annuaire 50 1 (1963), p. 25. Ce résultat est contesté par le rapport d'un comité de l'ASIL cité *supra.*

184 Voir *supra,* p. 170.

185 Voir aussi Brandweiner, *Sind die Vereinten Nationen den Kriegsgesetzen unterworfen?,* Neue Justiz 8 (1954), p. 225 ss. qui arrive à ce résultat parce que les Nations Unies seraient soumises au droit international général. Mais il faut tenir compte du fait que la Charte aurait pu modifier le droit international général dans ce contexte (cf. Verdross, *General International Law and the United Nations Charter,* International Affairs 30 [1954], p. 344 ss.).

186 Annuaire 50 II (1963), p. 354 ss.

Accepte les Résolutions suivantes, destinées à constituer une *orienta-tion générale et provisoire pour l'élaboration future* d'une réglementation détaillée en cette matière.[187]

Résolution I.

L'inégalité de traitement des parties *durante bello* est justifiée si le Conseil de Sécurité de l'ONU a désigné l'une des parties comme agresseur et pourvu que cette inégalité de traitement ne dépasse pas les limites in-diquées par les Résolutions suivantes.

Résolution II.

Les obligations ayant pour but de restreindre les horreurs de la guerre et imposées aux belligérants pour des motifs humanitaires par les Con-ventions en vigueur, par les principes généraux du droit ou par les règles du droit coutumier, sont toujours de rigueur pour les parties dans toutes les catégories de conflits armés, y compris l'action coercitive de la part de l'ONU. Il en est de même pour les règles concernant la participation de non-combattants aux opérations de la guerre.

Résolution III.

Outre les mesures que les Etats peuvent prendre légalement en vertu ou par application des décisions ou recommandations des organes com-pétents des Nations Unies, tous les Etats doivent s'abstenir d'aider un Etat agresseur à atteindre les fins de l'agression.

Résolution IV.

Sous réserve des précédentes Résolutions, chaque Etat déterminera dans quelle mesure il peut et doit refuser d'appliquer le principe d'égal-ité dans les relations avec un Etat qui a été désigné par le Conseil de Sécurité dans les conditions précitées comme engagé dans une guerre d'agression. »

Il résulte assez clairement du membre de phrase en italiques que ces réso-lutions constituent des propositions *de lege ferenda*.[188] L'Institut n'est donc, semble-t-il, pas d'avis que le principe de la non-discrimination soit déjà (par-tiellement) l'objet d'une dérogation.

L'Institut retient l'égalité des parties à un conflit armé en tant que princi-pe. Il ne rejette que son application intégrale. On était d'accord qu'il ne faut pas punir les individus (combattants ou non-combattants) ressortissants d'un Etat belligérant illégal pour les fautes de leur gouvernement en les privant de

---

187   Italiques de l'auteur.

188   Cf. François, Annuaire 50 I (1963), p. 113.

la protection des règles du *jus in bello* qui ont été créées pour « diminuer les maux de la guerre ».[189] On s'est rendu compte que tout le droit de la guerre qui concerne la conduite des hostilités a cette fonction protectrice. La résolution n'exclut donc pas l'application égalitaire du droit de La Haye.[190]

Il reste donc, comme l'a constaté Giraud,[191] « fort peu de choses » pour la discrimination. Les différences de vues qui se sont manifestées dans la discussion sont peut-être moins profondes qu'on ne pouvait croire de prime abord.[192] L'Institut devra maintenant discuter de façon détaillée la question de savoir s'il est possible et utile de dissocier certaines parties du droit de la guerre et de les soumettre à un régime discriminatoire sans que le système équilibré du droit de la guerre dans son ensemble en soit ébranlé. Un accord – *de lege ferenda* – pourrait peut-être se réaliser à cet égard en ce qui concerne certains droits de l'agresseur contre des Etats non-engagés dans le conflit, puisque la position de ces Etats est déjà modifiée par l'art. 2 par. 5 de la Charte.[193] De même, on paraît pouvoir s'accorder pour ne pas reconnaître des titres acquis par l'agresseur.[194] Cette question concerne également surtout la position d'Etats tiers ou l'appréciation finale des actes de l'agresseur après la fin des hostilités.[195] Mais il est significatif qu'aucun accord n'a encore été atteint dans la discussion concernant un cas concret où la discrimination serait justifiée. Il n'était peut-être pas très heureux que l'Institut ait mis en question le principe traditionnel de la non-discrimination et ait établi une règle nouvelle sans pouvoir se mettre d'accord sur un seul exemple pour son application. La solution adoptée par la résolution IV – les Etats en question déterminant le champ d'application de la discrimination – n'est pas sans précédent en ce qui concerne la position d'Etats tiers: le statut de non-belligérance qu'un Etat adopte au risque de ne

---

189   Convention concernant les lois et coutumes de la guerre sur terre du 18 octobre 1907, préambule.

190   Kunz, Annuaire 50 I (1963), p. 93 méprend l'auteur de la résolution, François, quand il lui reproche de faire une distinction entre le droit de La Haye et le droit de Genève (voir François, Annuaire 50 I [1963], p. 121).

191   Annuaire 50 II (1963), p. 314.

192   Rolin, Annuaire 50 II (1963), p. 332; cf. aussi François, Annuaire 47 I (1957), p. 330.

193   Cf. pour la discrimination de la part d'Etats non belligérants, déjà « the Budapest Articles of Interpretation », ILA Report of the 38th Conference, Budapest, p. 66 ss. Voir aussi Eustathiades, Annuaire 50 I (1963), p. 39; Wright, *ibid.*, p. 55.

194   Cf. la résolution proposée par Castrén, Annuaire 50 II (1963), p. 342; Jessup, Annuaire 47 I (1957), p. 569.

195   Pour la solution *de lege lata* de cette question, voir la jurisprudence citée *supra,* p. 175. Cf. aussi Lauterpacht, *Rules of Warfare,* p. 105 ss.; Kotzsch, *The Concept of War in Contemporary History and International Law,* p. 295 paraît cependant être d'avis que déjà *de lege lata* l'agresseur ne peut pas acquérir des titres.

282 PART 4: THE LAW OF ARMED CONFLICT – GENERAL QUESTIONS

pas être traité comme neutre. En ce qui concerne la relation entre les parties au conflit, il est extrêmement dangereux de donner un tel pouvoir discrétionnaire concernant le *jus in bello à* une partie au conflit.[196]

De lege tata, il faut retenir qu'il n'y a aucune discrimination entre les parties aux conflits en ce qui concerne l'application du droit de la guerre *durante bello.*

2.2 *La Capacité des Nations Unies d'être Destinataire des Normes du « Jus in bello »*

2.2.1 Les Données Générales du Problème

1. La nécessité d'humaniser et de limiter l'emploi de la force exige, comme nous l'avons vu, que des troupes agissant en vertu d'une décision de l'ONU soient soumises aux restrictions du droit de la guerre. A cet égard, il n'y a pas de difficulté lorsqu'il s'agit de troupes étatiques agissant sous les auspices de l'ONU. Mais pour la force des Nations Unies au Congo ainsi que pour l'UNEF, on a soutenu qu'il s'agit d'une force propre de l'ONU en dépit du fait qu'elle se composa de contingents nationaux.[197] Dans cette hypothèse, l'application du droit de la guerre présente encore d'autres problèmes.

Pour qu'on puisse parler d'une force armée propre des Nations Unies, il faut qu'il existe entre l'Organisation et cette troupe un lien comparable à celui qui existe entre un Etat et ses forces armées. La force armée des Nations Unies devrait donc être un organe de l'Organisation comme les forces armées régulières sont des organes étatiques.[198] Les membres de la force armée des Nations Unies devraient être des agents de l'Organisation, pour les actes desquels les Nations Unies sont responsables comme un Etat répond des actes de ses agents.[199] Les actions de cette force armée organe des Nations Unies, considérées comme actions de l'Organisation, sont donc la source de droits et de devoirs de l'ONU. La conduite de l'organe dans le domaine international est appréciée selon les obligations internationales qui incombent à l'en-lité dont relève l'organe. On devrait en déduire que le droit de la guerre ne saurait être applicable à une force armée organe des Nations Unies que dans la mesure où les Nations Unies comme telles sont liées par ces normes. L'Organisation

---

196 Voir *supra,* p. 181.

197 Bowett, *United Nations Forces,* p. 121; Seyersted, *United Nations Forces,* BYIL 37 (1961), p. 428 s.; pour les détails, voir *infra,* p. 208 ss.

198 Verdross, *Völkerrecht,* 5ᵉ éd., p. 346; Guggenheim, *Traité* I, p. 518 s.

199 Cavaré, *Droit international public positif,* vol. II, p. 410 ss.; Rousseau, *Droit international public,* p. 373; sur les problèmes de la responsabilité pour les actes des membres des forces armées, voir Freeman, *Responsibility of States for Unlawful Acts of Their Armed Forces,* RdC 88 (1955 II), p. 266 ss.

des Nations Unies n'est pas partie aux Conventions relatives au droit de la guerre. Elle ne pourrait donc être liée que par les règles coutumières du droit de la guerre, dont une très grande partie a cependant été codifiée par lesdites Conventions.

Mais il ne va pas de soi que l'ONU soit soumise au droit coutumier en matière de *jus in bello*. Car le droit international général applicable aux Etats ne s'applique pas nécessairement aux Nations Unies. Il n'est plus guère contestable que l'ONU est un sujet du droit international. Elle est donc un membre de la communauté des personnes juridiques coordonnée par le droit international. Mais il n'est pas non plus contestable que certaines règles du droit international, p. ex. les règles concernant la double nationalité, ne sont pas applicables aux. Nations Unies (qui n'ont pas de nationaux). Il faut donc distinguer les règles applicables aux Nations Unies et celles qui ne le sont pas. Cette distinction est étroitement liée à la question de la capacité juridique, ou encore de la personnalité juridique des Nations Unies. On pourrait soutenir que les normes du droit international général sont applicables à l'Organisation des Nations Unies dans la mesure où elle a la capacité d'en être destinataire.

Cependant, le rapport logique entre la capacité juridique des Nations Unies et l'applicabilité d'une règle déterminée doit encore être éclairci. La question de la capacité et de la personnalité juridique fournit néanmoins un bon point de départ pour la solution du problème qui nous intéresse ici.

2. La discussion sur la personnalité juridique des organisations internationales a deux aspects: la première question est de savoir si la personnalité de l'Organisation vaut *erga omnes*,[200] ou seulement vis-à-vis les Etats-membres et les Etats qui l'ont reconnue[201] (aspect personnel); la seconde est de savoir si l'Organisation peut être titulaire de tous les droits et obligations du droit international général, ou seulement de certains d'entre eux (aspect matériel). Les deux questions doivent être distinguées, bien qu'elles soient étroitement

---

200 Dans ce sens, par exemple: Balladore Pallieri, *La personalità delle organizzazioni internazionali,* Diritto internazionale 14 (1960), p. 230 ss.; Quadri, *Diritto internazionale pubblico,* 3' éd., p. 448 ss.; Sereni, *Le organizzazioni internazionali,* p. 77; Seyersted, *Objective International Personality of Intergovernmental Organizations,* p. 45; nuancé: Seidl-Hohenveldern, *Rechtsbeziehungen zwischen Internationalen Organisationen und den einzelnen Staaten,* Archiv des Völkerrechts 4 (1953/54), p. 37.

201 Dans ce sens, par exemple: Mosler, *Die Erweiterung des Kreises der Völkerrechtssubjekte,* ZaöRV 22 (1962), p. 32; R. Bindschedler, *Die Anerkennung im Völkerrecht,* Archiv des Völkerrechts 9 (1961/62), p. 387; v.d. Heydte, *Rechtssubjekt und Rechtsperson im Völkerrecht,* Mélanges Spiropoulos, p. 253; Schwarzenberger, *International Law,* 3' éd., p. 128; Seidl-Hohenveldern, *Die völkerrechtliche Haftung für Handlungen internationaler Organisationen im Verhältnis zu Nichtmitgliedstaaten,* ÖZÖR 11 (1961), p. 502 ss.

liées, *car leur* solution dépend largement de la conception générale de la personnalité juridique des organisations internationales. Dans notre contexte, c'est le second aspect qui est pertinent. A cet égard on peut discerner, dans la doctrine, deux tendances différentes. Certains auteurs prennent comme point de départ le traité international qui institue l'Organisation: ainsi, Bindschedler soutient:

> Les organisations internationales] ne sont pas munies de la pleine personnalité juridique internationale des Etats, mais seulement des droits et devoirs spécifiques qui découlent de leur Statut.[202]

La portée matérielle de la personnalité juridique d'une organisation internationale résulterait donc du traité constitutif.

Une autre conception prend comme point de départ la norme dont l'applicabilité est en question:

> Ainsi, Sereni soutient que les organisations internationales sont soumises à des impossibilités d'agir qui sont liées à leur origine historique et à leur structure. Elles ne peuvent, par exemple, mener une guerre parce qu'elles n'ont ni une population ni un territoire[203] ... Quelques coutumes

---

202　« Es kommt [den internationalen Organisationen] ... nicht die volle Völkerrechtssubjektivität des Staates zu, sondern nur diejenigen Rechte und Pflichten, die sich aus dem Statut ergeben. » R. Bindschedler, *Die Anerkennung im Völkerrecht*, Archiv des Völkerrechts 9 (1961/62), p. 387; dans le même sens: Zemanek, *Internationale Organisationen als Handlungseinheiten in der Völkerrechtsgemeinschaft*, ÖZÖR 7 (1955/56), p. 351; Verdross, *Völkerrecht*, 5e éd., p. 202 s. La C.I.J., dans l'avis consultatif concernant la réparation des dommages subis au service des Nations Unies, se prononce de façon semblable, mais encore nuancée: « les droits et devoirs internationaux d'une entité telle que l'Organisation doivent dépendre des buts et des fonctions de celle-ci, énoncés ou impliqués par son acte constitutif et développés dans la pratique » (C.I.J. Recueil 1949, p. 180; voir également Weissberg, *The International Status of the United Nations*, p. 22). Une disposition expresse conférant la personnalité juridique ne suffit cependant pas. L'organisation n'acquiert la personnalité juridique que dans la mesure où cela est nécessaire pour l'exercice efficace des fonctions qui lui sont imposées ou conférées par la volonté des Etats fondateurs (Mosler, *Die Erweiterung des Kreises der Völkerrechtssubjekte*, ZaöRV 22 [1962], p. 36; Hahn, *Euratom: The Conception of an International Personality*, Harvard Law Review 71 [1957/58], p. 1045 s.).

203　Sereni, *Le organizzazioni internazionali*, p. 82: « a impossibilità di agire che si ricollegano a la loro origine storica e struttura. Essi non possono ad es. muovere guerra, perché non hanno un popolo o un territorio. » Voir également Sereni, *Il concetto di guerra nel diritto internazionale contemporaneo*, Riv. dir. int. 46 (1963), p. 568.

générales n'ont pour destinataires que les Etats et non les sujets à caractère fonctionnel.[204]

Cela signifie que certaines normes qui présupposent des destinataires ayant des structures étatiques ne sont pas applicables aux organisations internationales, mais, comme règle, les normes du droit international général s'y appliquent.[205] On peut bien mettre en doute si cela est une question de capacité juridique[206] ou bien simplement un problème d'applicabilité.

Ces deux manières de concevoir la portée matérielle de la personnalité juridique des organisations internationales ne s'excluent cependant pas nécessairement. Ainsi, Fitzmaurice soutient:

> International organisations only have such capacities and powers as their constitutive instrument gives them ...; together with such powers and capacities as would, under general and universally recognized principles of law, be ascribable to any entity of the class or category created by that instrument.[207]

Ce ne peut être la tâche de la présente étude de résoudre ce problème de façon générale. Aux fins de ce travail, il paraît plus fructueux d'accepter les deux points de départ mentionnés et de se demander, pour chacun d'eux, quelle en est la conséquence pour la capacité des Nations Unies d'être destinataire des règles du droit de la guerre. On doit alors poser deux questions: 1. Est-ce qu'on peut déduire d'une interprétation de la Charte que les fondateurs de l'ONU aient voulu lui conférer cette capacité? 2. Est-ce que les règles du droit de la guerre présupposent des destinataires ayant des structures étatiques, ou est-ce que ces règles peuvent également s'adresser à des entités comme l'ONU?

On verra que ces deux points de départ sont pratiquement inséparables. Car en interprétant la Charte, on doit recourir à la notion des pouvoirs implicites, ou mieux: de la personnalité implicite. Mais en déterminant si un certain

---

204   Sereni, *ibid.,* p. 85 « (A)lcune consuetudini generali hanno per destinatari soltanto gli Stati e non i soggetti a carattere funzionale. ».

205   Sereni, ibid., p. 85. Seyersted, Objective International Personality of. Intergovernmental Organizations, paraît être du même avis, s'il soutient que la différence entre Etats et organisations internationales est une différence de fait (p. 112) et que les normes applicables aux Etats ne sont applicables aux organisations internationales que si les « conditions » (de fait?) sont les mêmes (p. 56).

206   C'est seulement le cas si l'on soutient, comme Morelli, RdC 89 (1956 I), p. 538, que « un sujet qui n'est pas destinataire d'une règle donnée est, par rapport à cette règle, incapable ».

207   Plaidoiries, Réparation des dommages subis au service des Nations Unies, p. 117.

pouvoir est impliqué ou non, on ne peut que tenir compte des exigences de la matière, c'est-à-dire, dans ce contexte, des nécessités du conflit armé. On en revient facilement au droit de la guerre. Mais d'autre part, en analysant les structures que le droit de la guerre présuppose de la part de ses destinataires, on ne saurait faire abstraction de l'acte constitutif de l'Organisation, car c'est cet acte qui est le fondement des structures en question. Les lignes qui suivent traiteront cependant les deux points de départ séparément. Cela rend quelques répétitions inévitables, mais facilitera la mise en relief des problèmes spécifiques aux deux points de vue.

2.2.2 La Capacité des Nations Unies d'être Destinataire des Normes du *jus in bello* Suivant L'interprétation du Droit de la Charte

1. La Charte, nous l'avons vu, ne contient aucune disposition expresse concernant l'applicabilité du droit de la guerre lors d'une action militaire entreprise par les Nations Unies. Il a cependant été exposé que les actions militaires entreprises sous les auspices des Nations Unies doivent être régies par le *jus in bello*.[208] Dans l'hypothèse d'une force relevant des Nations Unies, il n'est guère concevable que les exigences de l'humanisation du conflit ne jouent pas. Si une force armée des Nations Unies est possible d'après la Charte, on doit conclure que les fondateurs des Nations Unies ont voulu doter l'Organisation de la capacité d'être destinataire des normes du droit de la guerre. Cela serait une conséquence de la doctrine des « pouvoirs implicites » développée par la C.I.J.[209] « On doit admettre que [les Membres de l'ONU], en lui assignant certaines fonctions, avec les devoirs et les responsabilités qui les accompagnent, l'ont revêtue de la compétence nécessaire pour lui permettre de s'acquitter effectivement de ces fonctions ».[210] Une action militaire est, suivant le droit international général, « accompagnée » par les devoirs et les responsabilités que le droit de la guerre impose. Une organisation qui, selon la volonté de ses fondateurs, peut entreprendre une action militaire moyennant une force militaire propre, doit donc être revêtue de la compétence et de la capacité nécessaires pour faire face à ces devoirs et responsabilités. S'il résulte d'une interprétation de la Charte qu'une force relevant des Nations Unies est juridiquement possible, la conséquence en est que l'Organisation des Nations Unies a la capacité d'être destinataire des normes du *jus in bello*.[211] La question de savoir si, selon

---

208   *Supra*, p. 184.

209   Avis consultatifs « Réparation des dommages subis au service des Nations Unies », Recueil 1949, p. 174 ss., et « Effet de jugements du tribunal administratif des N.U. accordant indemnité », Recueil 1954, p. 47 ss.

210   C.I.J. Recueil 1949, p. 179.

211   Cf. Strebel, *Kriegsgefangene*, Strupp-Schlochauer, vol. II, p. 344.

la Charte, l'ONU peut être destinataire du droit de la guerre est donc identique avec celle de savoir si les Nations Unies peuvent, d'après la volonté de ses fondateurs, avoir une force armée propre. La réponse à cette question doit d'abord s'orienter vers les dispositions expresses que la Charte contient à cet égard, à savoir le Chap. VII. Ces dispositions envisagent-elles une force armée propre des Nations Unies? Ou bien, les actions militaires entreprises en vertu de ces dispositions doivent-elles être considérées comme actions des Etats-membres? Dans cette dernière hypothèse, le droit de la guerre serait applicable parce que les Etats-membres en sont destinataires, et les Nations Unies n'auraient pas cette capacité.

2. En ce qui concerne la Société des Nations (art. 16 et 17 du Pacte), la doctrine dominante est d'avis que la dernière possibilité a été adoptée[212]: c'étaient les Etats-membres qui – sous la forme d'une guerre de coalition ancien style – menaient l'action militaire destinée « à faire respecter les engagements de la Société ».

Les art. 42 ss. de la Charte des Nations Unies n'envisagent pas une force:-fumée recrutée individuellement par l'Organisation, à la manière du personnel du Secrétariat. Les forces armées visées par ces articles se composent d'unités fournies par les Etats-membres. Cependant, il est généralement reconnu que ces unités ont une relation plus proche avec l'Organisation que les forces établies en vertu de l'art. 16 du Pacte de la SdN. La question se pose donc de savoir si, d'après les art. 42 ss. de la Charte, la relation entre les Nations Unies – représentées par le Conseil de Sécurité – et les unités fournies par les Etats-membres est telle qu'on puisse parler d'une force propre des Nations Unies, qui pourrait être considérée comme organe de l'Organisation. Certaines dispositions amènent à conclure que cela n'est pas le cas. Ainsi, l'art. 42, 2e phrase, parle d'opérations « exécutées par des forces ... *de Membres* des Nations Unies ». L'art. 48, al. 1 er, prescrit que « les mesures nécessaires à l'exécution des décisions du Conseil de Sécurité pour le maintien de la paix ... sont *prises par* tous les *Membres* des Nations Unies ou certains d'entre eux ... ». D'autre part, c'est le Conseil de Sécurité qui, d'après l'art. 42, I re phrase, « peut entreprendre, au moyen de forces aériennes, navales ou terrestres, toute action qu'il juge nécessaire ... ». Les Etats-membres sont, en vertu de l'art. 43, tenus de mettre des forces armées « *à la disposition* du Conseil de Sécurité ». Selon l'art. 45, le Conseil de Sécurité « *fixe* l'importance et le degré de préparation » des contingents

---

212   Goodrich-Hambro, *Charter of the United Nations,* 2° éd., p. 282; Taubenfeld, *International Armed Forces and the Rules of War,* AJIL 45 (1951), p. 672; Seyersted, *United Nations Forces,* BYIL 37 (1961), p. 357; Guggenheim, *Lehrbuch des Völkerrechts,* vol. II, p. 788; contra; Schücking-Wehberg, *Die Satzung des Völkerbundes,* 3e éd., p. 104 s.

de forces aériennes immédiatement utilisables. Le Comité d'Etat-Major assiste le Conseil en ce qui concerne « l'emploi et le *commandement* des forces mises à sa disposition » (art. 47, al. 1er). Le Conseil de Sécurité doit donc être considéré comme compétent pour décider du commandement de ces forces. Cette conclusion est également indiquée par l'art. 47, al. 3: « Le Comité d'Etat-Major est responsable, sous l'autorité du Conseil de Sécurité, de la *direction stratégique* de toutes forces armées mises à la disposition du Conseil. Les questions relatives au *commandement* de ces forces seront réglées ultérieurement. » Cette dernière disposition doit être interprétée de telle sorte qu'il incombe au Conseil de Sécurité de « régler les questions relatives au commandement ».[213]

Les dispositions des art. 42 ss. ne sont donc pas en parfaite harmonie. D'une part, les art. 42 *in fine* et 48 indiquent que les troupes employées en vertu de ces dispositions sont des forces armées des Etats-membres agissant en coalition d'ancien style. D'autre part, les art. 42, 1re phrase, 43, 45, 47 al. 1er et 3 confèrent un pouvoir considérable de contrôle et de direction au Conseil de Sécurité, ce qui indique qu'il s'agit d'une force armée des Nations Unies distincte de celle des Etats-membres. L'interprétation de ces dispositions doit pondérer les deux éléments. Dans la doctrine, on l'a fait avec des résultats divergents. Ross[214] et Ruda[215] attachent plus de poids au premier élément (sans donner des raisons précises), tandis que l'analyse de Kelsen,[216] de Jiménez de Arechaga[217] et de Seyersted[218] parvient au résultat contraire.[219] A cet égard, il est utile de tenir compte des « principes généraux gouvernant l'organisation des forces armées mises à la disposition du Conseil de Sécurité », élaborés par le Comité d'Etat-Major.[220] Ce document a une valeur considérable pour l'interprétation du Chap. VII, en tant que « pratique suivie dans l'application effective du traité ».[221] Les articles qui intéressent dans ce contexte sont libellés comme suit :

---

213 Kelsen, *The Law of the United Nations,* p. 765.

214 *Constitution of the United Nations,* p. 151 s.

215 *El Consejo de Seguridad,* Curso de preparación para la enseñanza sobre Naciones Unidas, p. 125.

216 *The Law of the United Nations,* pp. 762–768.

217 *Derecho Constitucional de las Naciones Unidas,* p. 387 s.

218 United Nations Forces, BYIL 37 (1961), pp. 359–362, 409 s.

219 Dans ce sens également: Weissberg, *The International Status of the United Nations,* p. 202; Carroz-Probst, *Personnalité juridique internationale et capacité de conclure des traités de l'O.N.U. et des institutions spécialisées,* p. 34; Taubenfeld, *International Armed Forces and the Rules of War,* AJIL 45 (1951), p. 674 s.

220 Doc. ONU S/336, S.C.O.R. 2' année, suppl. spécial n° 1.

221 Ch. De Visscher, Problèmes d'interprétation judiciaires, p. 121 ss.

LE DROIT DE LA GUERRE ET LES NATIONS UNIES

Art. 36 :

Les forces armées que les Nations Membres des Nations Unies ont accepté de mettre à la disposition du Conseil de sécurité seront placées sous le *commandement exclusif des nations* qui les ont fournies, *excepté lorsqu'elles opéreront sous l'autorité du Conseil de sécurité.*[222]

Art. 37 :

Lorsqu'il est fait appel à ces forces pour l'exécution des mesures prévues à l'Article 42 de la Charte, *elles passent sous l'autorité du Conseil de sécurité.*[222]

Art. 39 :

Le commandement des contingents nationaux est exercé par des chefs nommés par les Nations Membres respectives. Ces contingents conservent leur caractère national et restent soumis en tout temps à la discipline et aux règlements en vigueur dans leurs propres forces armées nationales.

Art. 40 :

Les commandants des contingents nationaux ont le droit d'être en rapport direct sur toutes les questions avec les autorités de leurs propres pays.

Art. 41 :[223]

Un commandant d'ensemble ou des commandants d'ensemble des forces armées mises à la disposition du Conseil de sécurité peuvent être nommés par ce dernier, sur l'avis du Comité d'état-major, pour la durée de l'utilisation de ces forces par le Conseil de sécurité.

Ces dispositions déterminent une division de compétence entre les Etats fournissant des contingents et les Nations Unies. Tandis que la compétence concernant l'organisation interne des contingents, notamment les questions de discipline, reste du ressort des Etats-membres, les questions concernant l'emploi des troupes, leurs opérations, le choix d'armes etc. relèvent de la compétence du Conseil de Sécurité. Ce pouvoir étendu de commandement dont le Conseil de Sécurité est investi constitue un facteur d'intégration qui permet

---

222 Italiques de l'auteur.

223 Au sujet du texte de l'art. 41, aucun accord n'a pu se réaliser au sein du Comité d'Etat-Major. Ce désaccord ne porte cependant pas sur la partie citée.

de considérer les troupes employées en vertu des art. 42 ss. comme forces armées propres des Nations Unies.[224] C'est l'ONU, non pas les Etats-membres, qui commande les unités et les soldats individuels par la chaîne de commandement.[225] C'est l'ONU qui doit être considérée comme responsable pour des actes accomplis en exécution de ses commandements.[226] Les Etats qui fournissent des contingents sont privés du pouvoir de contrôle en ce qui concerne les opérations des troupes; ils ne sauraient donc en être responsables. Quant au pouvoir disciplinaire que ces Etats retiennent, il va de soi qu'ils doivent l'exercer de bonne foi dans l'intérêt des opérations des Nations Unies. Le pouvoir disciplinaire et pénal est ainsi en quelque sorte le serviteur du pouvoir de commandement dont le Conseil de Sécurité est investi. Il est donc permis de considérer une force armée établie en vertu des art. 42 ss. comme une force armée propre des Nations Unies. Puisqu'il en est ainsi les auteurs de la Charte ont, implicitement, revêtu l'organisation de la capacité d'être destinataire des normes du droit de la guerre.[227] Cette capacité, une fois acquise en vertu de la volonté des fondateurs, doit être conçue comme générale. Elle ne saurait être restreinte aux actions entreprises selon les art. 42 ss., mais elle est également valable dans l'hypothèse d'autres actions militaires des Nations Unies, à condition qu'il s'agisse, en fait> des forces des Nations Unies.[228]

Une autre considération corrobore ce résultat.

On peut se demander si le recours au Chap. VII est vraiment nécessaire pour fonder l'assertion suivant laquelle les Nations Unies peuvent avoir une force armée propre. D'un point de vue théorique, il est préférable de fonder le raisonnement sur des dispositions expresses et détaillées. Mais si l'on tient compte de la pratique, on s'aperçoit que la vie des organisations internationales se déroule de façon quelque peu différente de la lettre des traités constitutifs.[229] En effet, les forces armées des Nations Unies ont été créées en dehors de l'art. 42 de la Charte, et la force de paix de l'OEA à Saint-Domingue entre très difficilement dans le cadre des mesures collectives prévues par les art. 6 et 8 du Pacte de Rio de Janeiro et l'art. 25 de la Charte de Bogota.[230] Mais cette force

---

224 Kelsen, *loc. cit.,* p. 768.

225 Seyersted, loc. cit., p. 409 s.

226 Seyersted, loc. cit., p. 429.

227 Feller, Exposé devant la C.I.J., Réparations des dommages subis au service des Nations Unies, Plaidoiries, p. 76.

228 Seyersted, *loc. cit.,* p. 473 s.

229 Cf. Sereni, *Le organizzazioni internazionali,* p. 175 s.

230 L'art. 6 du Pacte de Rio dispose : « If the inviolability or the integrity of the territory or the sovereignty or political independence of any American State should be affected by an aggression which is not an armed attack or by an extra-continental or infra-continental

interaméricaine est apparemment conçue comme force propre de l'OEA,[231] de même que les forces des Nations Unies en Egypte, au Congo et à Chypre furent considérées comme organes des Nations Unies.[232] Les forces armées des Nations Unies et de l'OEA ne trouvent pas leur fondement juridique dans les dispositions visant l'action contre un agresseur. Elles trouvent (au moins selon la conviction de la majorité des Etats-membres) leur justification dans une tâche plus générale: garantir la paix dans des situations de crise.

Le juriste doit toujours chercher à fonder son opinion sur des règles qui peuvent incontestablement être considérées comme faisant partie du droit positif. A cette fin, l'analyse des art. 42 ss. qui vient d'être faite présente quelque valeur. Mais selon la pratique actuelle, qui est peut-être contestable en droit, le but général d'une organisation, qui est de garantir la paix, suffit comme fondement d'une compétence pour établir une force armée propre. On peut même se demander si cette pratique est assez constante pour qu'il existe déjà une règle coutumière dans le sens de la pratique. Si cela est le cas, on peut conclure, d'une façon générale, que des organisations internationales auxquelles l'acte constitutif confère la tâche de garantir la paix[233] (du monde ou dans une certaine

---

conflict, or by any other fact or situation that might endanger the peace of America, the Organ of Consultation shah' meet immediately in order to agree ... the measures which should be taken ... for the maintenance of the peace and security of the Continent. Est-ce que, l'indépendance politique de la République Dominicaine était menacée? On peut le mettre en doute (sauf en ce qui concerne l'intervention américaine, mais l'action de l'OEA n'est pas dirigée contre cette intervention). C'est donc avec raison que le Secrétaire Général de l'OEA a soutenu (Doc. ONU S/6381, p. 4): « The establishment of the Force demonstrates ... the ability of the Organization of American States to adapt to new conditions and to solve new problems – problems having features which may not have been foreseen when the Charter and the Treaty of Rio were signed. Nevertheless, the objectives for which the Inter-American Force was established clearly come within the broad provisions of the Charter concerning matters affecting the peace and security of the Continent. » Cela doit être compris comme une allusion à l'art. 4 al. a) de la Charte de Bogotá, selon lequel l'objectif de l'OEA est de garantir la paix et la sécurité du continent américain.

231 Voir par. 1 de l'arrangement institutif (Doc. ONU 5/6381, p. 1): « The Inter-American Force is established as a Force of the Organization of American States » (voir également par. 2 de la résolution de la Réunion consultative des ministres des affaires étrangères de l'OEA du 6 mai 1965 – Doc. ONU S/6333). La structure de l'organisation ressemble fortement à celle prévue dans le rapport du Comité d'Etat-Major de l'ONU (cité supra, p. 193) et à celle de l'ONUC. La différence la plus importante est que le commandant ne fut pas nommé par l'Organisation, mais par le gouvernement du Brésil à la demande de l'OEA (résolution de la Réunion consultative des ministres des affaires étrangères de l'OEA du 22 mai 1965 – Doc. ONU S/6377.).

232 Voir infra, p. 208 ss. et supra, p. 187.

233 Outre l'ONU et l'OEA, il faudra compter parmi ces organisations l'Organisation de l'Unité Africaine et peut-être la Ligue arabe.

région) peuvent avoir une force armée propre et doivent par conséquent être considérées comme capables d'être destinataires des règles du *jus in bello*.

2.2.3 La Capacité des Nations Unies d'être Destinataire des Normes du *Jus in Bello*, Suivant les Exigences du Droit de la Guerre

2.2.3.1 *Introduction*

La question de savoir si les normes du droit de la guerre peuvent s'adresser à une entité structurée comme l'ONU ne peut pas être posée de façon globale. Car il paraît douteux qu'une réponse identique puisse être donnée, à cet égard, pour toutes les normes du *jus in bello*.

Certains auteurs soutiennent qu'une action militaire entreprise par les Nations Unies ne saurait être considérée comme guerre au sens formel.[234] Une déclaration de guerre faite contre les Nations Unies serait privée d'effets.[235]

1. D'une telle attitude, on pourrait déduire que les Nations Unies ont seulement une capacité restreinte d'être destinataires des normes du droit de la guerre. Elles ne pourraient pas être destinataires de normes qui présupposent un état de guerre au sens formel.[236][237] Vu cette difficulté, la présente étude procédera de la manière suivante: sera examinée d'abord la question de savoir si l'ONU est susceptible d'être destinataire des règles visant la conduite des hostilités.[238] Si l'on répond à cette question par

---

234 Guggenheim, RdC 80 (1952 I), p. 174; idem, Traité, tome II, p. 312 ss.; Mosler, Kriegsbeginn, Strupp-Schlochauer, vol. II, p. 329; idem, *Die Beendigung des Kriegszustands mit Deutschland und die Entwicklung des Völkerrechtlichen Kriegsbegriffs*: Die Beendigung des Kriegszustands mit Deutschland nach dem zweiten Weltkrieg, éd. par Mosler et Doehring, p. 459; Scheuner, *Die kollektive Sicherung des Friedens im gegenwärtigen Völkerrecht*, Berichte der Deutschen Gesellschaft für Völkerrecht, vol. 2, p. 12; d'autre avis Kunz, *Kriegsbegriff*, Strupp-Schlochauer, vol. II, p. 332.

235 Balladore Pallieri, *Diritto bellico*, p. 37.

236 La position des auteurs cités est cependant, semble-t-il, plus nuancée. Guggenheim, *Traité*, tome II, p. 315 soutient que « des règles particulières sont applicables aux mesures d'exécution forcée des organisations internationales ». I'l admet que le droit de la neutralité, qui présuppose, en général, un état de guerre au tsens formel (*ibid.*, p. 314, mais plus nuancé: p. 494), y est applicable (p. 494). -Mosler, *Kriegsbeginn, loc. cit.*, soutient: « Die völkerrechtlichen Normen des Kriegsrechts sind jedoch insoweit auch auf Sanktionen anzuwenden, als diese zu Massnahmen oder Zuständen führen, für die solche Normen vorgesehen sind. » Cette attitude ne nierait pas nécessairement l'applicabilité de règles présupposant une guerre au sens formel (voir également Mosler, *Die Beendigung des Kriegszustands mit Deutschland, loc. cit.*, p. 459, note 17).

237 Ceux qui soutiennent une conception relativiste de la guerre (voir supra, p. 147) ne peuvent pas éviter une question semblable. Ils doivent même se demander pour chaque norme particulière si les Nations Unies peuvent être destinataire de cette norme.

238 Sous-section II.

LE DROIT DE LA GUERRE ET LES NATIONS UNIES 293

l'affirmative, d'autres règles, qui pourraient présupposer un état de guerre au sens formel, seront examinées.[239][240]

2. Pour des raisons pratiques, on ne procédera pas à l'examen de la première question au moyen d'une analyse du droit coutumier, mais par une analyse de deux textes conventionnels, à savoir le Règlement de La Haye et les Conventions de Genève. Bien que les Nations Unies ne soient pas liées par ces conventions en tant que traités, mais seulement dans la mesure où ces conventions constituent une codification du droit coutumier,[241] l'analyse des dispositions conventionnelles est valable pour la question qui nous intéresse ici, à savoir si les Nation Unies peuvent être destinataire du *jus in bello*. Il n'est cependant pas exclu que le droit coutumier contienne des exigences moins rigoureuses à l'égard de ses destinataires. Mais cette possibilité n'entre en jeu que si l'on nie la capacité de l'ONU d'être destinataire du droit conventionnel.

2.2.3.2 *La Conduite des Hostilités*

1.Il est évident que ces conventions ne visent en principe que des Etats *en* tant que « parties au conflit ».[242] Le Règlement de La Haye ainsi que les Conventions de Genève emploient le terme « Etat ».[243] Cependant, il semble que les auteurs des Conventions de Genève aient préféré les termes « partie au conflit » ou « Puissance » (Puissance en conflit, Puissance détentrice, Puissance occupante). Mais selon certaines indications les termes « Etat » et « Puissance » sont employés comme synonymes: ainsi, l'art. 49 al. 1er de la IVe Convention de Genève parle « de la Puissance occupante ou ... de tout *autre*[244] Etat ».

Les Conventions de Genève et le Règlement de La Haye présupposent que les « Puissances en conflit » réunissent tous les critères de l'Etat. Elles possèdent un territoire. L'art. 2 al. 2 et l'art. 3[245] des Conventions de Genève parlent

---

239 Sous-section III.

240 Cf. pour la nécessité d'une différenciation: Bowett, *United Nations Forces,* p. 488 ss.

241 Le Règlement de La Haye doit être considéré comme droit coutumier: Oppenheim-Lauterpacht, vol. II, p. 229; Verdross, *Völkerrecht,* 5' éd., p. 443. Balladore-Pallieri, *Diritto bellico,* p. 111 ss. exprime cependant certains doutes à cet égard. Pour les Conventions de Genève, il est difficile d'établir dans quelle mesure elles constituent déjà du droit coutumier. En tout cas, la plupart des dispositions de la Convention de 1929 sont devenues du droit coutumier. Pour le statut des prisonniers de guerre, voir Strebel, *Kriegsgefangene,* Strupp-Schlochauer, vol. II, p. 346.

242 Voir une analyse semblable: Bowett, United Nations Forces, p. 511 ss.

243 Règlement de la Haye: Art. 6, 8, 55; I" Convention de Genève: Art. 8; IV' Convention de Genève: Art. 4, 5, 35, 38 ss., 49.

244 Italiques de l'auteur.

245 Articles communs.

du « territoire d'une Haute Partie contractante »,[246] l'art. 47 de la 1re Convention de Genève des « pays » des Parties à la convention. Elles ont une « population »,[247] des « ressortissants ».[248] Elles exercent leur autorité dans ces territoires et sur cette population par les moyens traditionnels propres à l'Etat: elles ont une législation (notamment pénale et militaire)[249] et des tribunaux (notamment militaires).[250] Elles ont des « gouvernements ».[251] Elles peuvent faire valoir un « *intérêt national* »,[252] établir des « Bureaux *nationaux* de renseignements »,[253] doivent accorder aux étrangers, dans certaines circonstances, un traitement *national.*[254]

2. Cette revue des dispositions du Règlement de La Haye et des Conventions de Genève fait surgir de sérieux doutes quant à la question de savoir si ces règles sont applicables aux forces armées des Nations Unies. Les Nations Unies n'ont ni un territoire, ni une population ou des nationaux. Elles ne peuvent pas accorder un traitement national. Elles n'ont pas un gouvernement comme les Etats ni notamment des organes législatifs et judiciaires équivalant à ceux des Etats.[255] Certaines normes des Conventions en question ne pourraient donc pas être appliquées.

Néanmoins, il faut se demander si ce seul fait est susceptible d'exclure l'applicabilité du droit de La Haye ou de Genève. Car pour son applicabilité le défaut de structures et d'institutions étatiques ne constitue pas un obstacle dans trois hypothèses:

a)   La référence à des structures étatiques ne fait pas partie du contenu nécessaire de la norme. Dans ce cas, l'ONU serait également à même de se conformer à cette norme. Elle ne devrait pas posséder les structures étatiques que la norme mentionne.

b)   L'ONU n'est pas en mesure de violer une certaine norme, justement parce qu'elle ne possède pas de structures étatiques. Dans ce cas, la norme n'est

---

246   IIIe Convention: Art. 14, 125; IVe Convention: Art. 5, 6, 35 ss., 48, 49.

247   Ire Convention: Art. 47; IVe Convention: Art. 49.

248   IVe Convention: Art. 4, 38, 48.

249   Règlement de La Haye: Art. 8; Ire Convention: Art. 28 al. 2, art. 49, 54; IIIe Convention: Art. 82, 99.

250   Règlement de La Haye: Art. 30; Ire Convention: Art. 49; IIIe Convention: Art. 5, 82, 87, 102; IVe Convention: Art. 66.

251   Règlement de La Haye: Art. 4; IIIe Convention: Art. 39.

252   Ire Convention: Art. 35.

253   IIIe Convention: Art. 124 ss.

254   IVe Convention: Art. 35 ss.; voir Pictet IV, p. 252 ss.

255   Vu ces difficultés, Draper, *The Legal Limitation upon the Employment of Weapons by the United Nations Force in the Congo,* ICLQ 12 (1963), *p.* 408 ss., conclut que les Nations Unies ne peuvent pas être destinataires du *jus in Bello.*

pas applicable, mais cela ne saurait d'aucune manière être préjudiciable pour l'applicabilité des autres normes des Conventions examinées. C'est notamment le cas pour les normes qui présupposent un territoire et une population.

c) L'ONU peut créer des institutions qui sont semblables aux institutions étatiques exigées par les normes en question; ou bien l'ONU peut faire face à une responsabilité déterminée d'une autre manière compatible avec le but de la norme. Telle est notamment la question en ce qui concerne les normes qui présupposent le troisième élément de la définition de l'Etat, à savoir *l'imperium*, le gouvernement au sens large du terme.

Des exemples éclairciront ces assertions abstraites.

a) L'art. 13 de la IIIe Convention de Genève dispose: « La Puissance détentrice ne pourra limiter l'exercice (de la capacité civile des prisonniers de guerre) soit sur son territoire, soit en dehors, que ... ». La référence au territoire est superflue. On aurait pu dire: « n'importe où ». L'ONU peut donc se conformer à cette norme sans qu'elle doive posséder un territoire.

b) Les art. 35 ss. de la IVe Convention de Genève concernent le traitement des étrangers sur le territoire d'une partie au conflit. L'ONU, faute de territoire, n'est pas en mesure de commettre les actes préjudiciables aux personnes protégées visés par ces articles. Elle ne peut, par exemple, interdire à une personne de quitter son territoire.[256] Les mêmes considérations sont valables pour l'art. 49 al. 6 de la Ir Convention. Les Nations Unies n'ont aucune population à transférer. Il est donc exclu que les Nations Unies puissent violer cette disposition.

> La non-application des dispositions citées n'est donc d'aucune manière préjudiciable. Aucune valeur protégée par le droit de la guerre n'est mise en danger. La non-application de ces normes n'enlève donc pas de poids à l'ensemble équilibré des normes du *jus in bello*.[257]
>
> Quelques remarques générales s'imposent ici qui concernent la question de savoir si les destinataires du *jus in bello* doivent avoir un territoire et une population. Il se peut également dans d'autres cas que des sujets du droit de la guerre n'aient pas de territoire. Il en est ainsi pour les gouvernements en exil, qui représentent en effet des Etats sans autorité effective sur un territoire. Pendant les deux guerres mondiales, des forces relevant de ces gouvernements participèrent tout de même

---

256 IVe Convention: Art. 35.

257 Voir *supra*, p. 170.

aux combats et les Etats représentés par ces gouvernements furent considérés comme destinataires du droit de la guerre.[258]

La règle qu'un destinataire du droit de la guerre doit disposer d'un territoire et d'une population est valable en ce qui concerne la reconnaissance d'insurgés comme partie belligérante.[259] Mais ce critère du territoire et de la population n'est pas fondé sur les nécessités inhérentes au droit de la guerre, mais sur le souci de trouver des éléments distinctifs entre insurgés et une bande de gangsters,[260] problème qui évidemment ne joue aucun rôle en ce qui concerne l'application du droit de la guerre pour des organisations internationales.

De façon générale, on peut conclure: le fait que les Nations Unies n'ont ni territoire ni population n'exclut pas la capacité de l'ONU d'être destinataire des règles du *jus in bello*.

c) Comme nous l'avons vu, les Conventions examinées présupposent que les parties contractantes soient également munies du troisième élément de la définition de l'Etat, à savoir de *l'imperium*. Contrairement aux références au territoire et à la population, cet élément de la structure étatique est, dans beaucoup de cas, nécessaire pour le fonctionnement du droit de la guerre. Cela est dû au fait que le droit de la guerre présuppose que ses destinataires soient en mesure de contraindre les personnes placées sous leur autorité à se comporter de façon compatible avec le *jus in bello*. Les destinataires sont responsables pour les actes des individus qu'ils commandent. Ils doivent être en mesure de garantir que ces individus respectent le droit de la guerre. La question se pose donc de savoir si et comment les Nations Unies peuvent faire face à ces responsabilités.

aa) Si les Conventions parlent de « Gouvernements »[261] qui sont à la tête d'une Puissance en conflit, cela ne veut pas dire qu'un gouvernement étatique au sens technique est indispensable. Ainsi, l'art. 13 de la Ire Convention de Genève parle « d'un gouvernement ou d'une autorité ». Les organes de direction politique et militaire, tels qu'ils sont envisagés par la Charte et développés dans la pratique des Nations Unies, à savoir le Conseil de Sécurité, le Secrétaire Général, le Comité d'Etat-Major et les structures de commandement établies

---

258 Oppenheimer, *Governments and Authorities in Exile*, AJIL 36 (1942), p. 575; Mattern, *Die Exilregierung*, p. 66 ss.

259 Wehberg, *La guerre civile et le droit international*, RdC 63 (1938 I), p. 88; voir aussi Actes de la Conférence de Genève 1949, tome II, Section B, p. 116.

260 Actes de la Conférence de Genève 1949, tome II, Section B, p. 10 ss., 329, 331.

261 Cf. à titre d'exemple: Règlement de La Haye: Art. 4.

LE DROIT DE LA GUERRE ET LES NATIONS UNIES

par ces organes, sont, sous beaucoup d'aspects, comparables aux organes de direction politique étatique et à la hiérarchie militaire étatique. Il paraît cependant douteux qu'ils possèdent le pouvoir (surtout disciplinaire) nécessaire pour contraindre le soldat individuel à conformer son comportement au droit de la guerre.[262] Ce problème doit être traité en relation avec le pouvoir des Nations Unies de légiférer.

bb) En ce qui concerne la faculté des Nations Unies de légiférer, il résulte clairement de la pratique des Nations Unies que les organes institués par la Charte sont en mesure d'édicter des réglementations normatives pour l'ordre interne. Cela vaut également si des forces armées sont incorporées dans cet ordre interne. Les compétences dont le Conseil de Sécurité est investi à cet égard ont déjà été mentionnées.[263] La question du pouvoir réglementaire des Nations Unies est cependant très délicate en ce qui concerne des normes de caractère pénal. Mais les pouvoirs implicites des Nations Unies devraient englober le pouvoir de créer de telles normes si cela correspond aux exigences du droit de la guerre. « L'Organisation doit être considérée comme possédant ces pouvoirs qui, s'ils ne sont pas expressément énoncés dans la Charte, sont, par une conséquence nécessaire, conférés à l'Organisation en tant qu'essentiels à l'exercice des fonctions de celle-ci. »[264]

Les Conventions de Genève et le Règlement de La Haye parlent de deux catégories de sanctions pénales: premièrement, elles permettent aux puissances en conflit d'appliquer leur propre législation pénale pour réprimer des infractions commises par des prisonniers de guerre[265] ou par des personnes privées en territoire occupé.[266] C'est une simple permission qui n'oblige pas les puissances en question à prendre des mesurés pénales pour se défendre.[267] Le défaut d'une législation pénale propre aux Nations Unies n'empêche

---

262 Bowett, *United Nations Forces,* p. 511 ss.

263 Voir *supra,* p. 193.

264 Réparation des dommages subis au service des Nations Unies, Avis consultatif: C.I.J. Recueil 1949, p. 182.

265 IIIᵉ Convention: Art. 82; Règlement de La Haye: Art. 8.

266 IVᵉ Convention: Art. 64.

267 Si l'on admet que les pouvoirs implicites des Nations Unies englobent le pouvoir de créer les institutions nécessaires pour assurer le bon fonctionnement des services des Nations Unies (voir *infra,* p. 203), on peut parfaitement être d'avis que les Nations Unies peuvent prendre ces mesures pénales.

d'ailleurs pas que des mesures pénales et disciplinaires soient prises contre les prisonniers de guerre de l'ONU. Car si les troupes de l'ONU se composent de contingents nationaux qui restent soumis au droit pénal et disciplinaire de leur Etat d'origine,[268] les prisonniers sont également soumis à ce droit, bien que l'ONU soit puissance détentrice. La législation des Etats d'origine constitue les « lois, règlements et ordres en vigueur dans l'armée » de la puissance détentrice.[269] Les tribunaux militaires de l'Etat d'origine seront « les mêmes tribunaux »[270] que ceux compétents pour l'armée de l'ONU comme puissance détentrice. Ainsi, le but des 'dispositions du Règlement de La Haye et de la IIIe Convention de Genève concernant le droit auquel les prisonniers de guerre sont soumis est parfaitement atteint il y a l'assimilation[271] nécessaire entre les prisonniers et les troupes de la puissance détentrice.

La seconde catégorie de dispositions pénales comprend celles qui doivent sanctionner le respect des Conventions de Genève. Celles-ci établissent une obligation de prendre des mesures législatives pour réprimer des infractions graves aux Conventions[272] ainsi que l'abus commercial du signe de la Croix-Rouge.[273] Cette dernière obligation ne joue aucun rôle pour les Nations Unies qui n'ont pas de nationaux susceptibles de se livrer à une activité commerciale où un tel abus serait possible. En ce qui concerne les infractions graves, les Nations Unies devraient, certes, adopter une législation pénale si elles voulaient devenir parties aux Conventions.[274] Le texte des Conventions exclut toute autre solution. Les pouvoirs implicites des Nations Unies devraient permettre une telle législation. Il serait cependant également possible que les Nations Unies fassent une

---

268 Comme c'est le cas pour les troupes envisagées par les art. 42 ss. de la Charte (principes généraux gouvernant l'organisation des forces armées mises à la disposition du Conseil de Sécurité: Art. 39; voir *supra*, p. 193). Il en est de même pour les troupes des Nations Unies au Congo (Accord concernant le statut de l'ONUC: Par. 9, voir *infra*, p. 210).

269 Règlement de La Haye: Art. 8; IIIe Convention de Genève: Art. 82. Pour les difficultés découlant de ces dispositions pour l'action de l'ONU en Corée, voir Verplaetse, *The* jus in bello *and Military Operations in Korea, 1950–1953,* ZaöRV 23 (1963), p. 724.

270 IIIe Convention de Genève: Art. 102.

271 Pictet, *Les Conventions de Genève du 12 août 1949,* Commentaire, vol. p. 430 ss.

272 Ire Convention, art. 49 ss. Les trois autres Conventions contiennent des dispositions identiques.

273 Ie Convention, art. 53.

274 Cf. Bowett, *United Nations Forces,* p. 514.

LE DROIT DE LA GUERRE ET LES NATIONS UNIES

réserve à cet égard. Mais on peut soutenir que lui aussi le droit coutumier contient une norme qui oblige les belligérants à punir des infractions graves au *jus in bello.*

Cependant, l'essentiel de cette obligation n'est pas que les belligérants possèdent une législation dans ce sens, mais que la punition des infracteurs soit en fait assurée. Pour atteindre le but de cette norme, il suffit qu'une répression pénale quelconque des infractions au droit de la guerre soit assurée. Il suffit donc que les infracteurs soient effectivement punis par les Etats qui fournissent des contingents pour une action militaire entreprise par les Nations Unies. Si ces Etats acceptent une telle obligation vis-à-vis des Nations Unies, celles-ci peuvent faire face à la responsabilité de garantir la punition des infracteurs au *jus in bello* et, en particulier, aux Conventions de Genève.[275] Cet engagement remplacera les mesures 'législatives propres des Nations Unies. Si une telle obligation d'un Etat fournissant un contingent n'existe pas ou n'est pas respectée, la responsabilité internationale des Nations Unies est engagée. Mais un tel manquement ne saurait exclure la capacité des Nations Unies d'être destinataire d'une norme exigeant le châtiment des infracteurs au droit de la guerre. Le défaut d'une législation pénale n'empêche donc pas que l'ONU soit destinataire du *jus in bello.*

cc) En ce qui concerne les tribunaux que les Conventions de Genève et le Règlement de La Haye présupposent, les pouvoirs implicites des Nations Unies de créer des tribunaux doivent avoir la même portée que le pouvoir réglementaire. La C.I.J. a d'ailleurs reconnu le pouvoir des Nations Unies de créer les tribunaux essentiels pour assurer le bon fonctionnement des services des Nations Unies.[276] Quant à la répression des infractions graves aux Conventions de Genève, l'art. 49 al. 2 de la 1re Convention permet aux Puissances contractantes

---

275 Un tel engagement a été accepté par les Etats fournissant des contingents pour l'UNEF, tel le par. 7 de l'échange de lettres entre l'ONU et la Finlande (Nations Unies, Recueil des Traités, vol. 271 [1957] n° 3913, p. 137; voir également Debroux, *Le Statut juridictionnel et disciplinaire de la Force d'Urgence des Nations Unies,* Revue de droit pénal militaire et de droit de la guerre 1 [1962], p. 276 s.) qui dispose que le gouvernement finlandais doit « exercer ses pouvoirs de juridiction dans le cas de tout crime ou délit qui viendrait à être commis par un membre dudit contingent national ». Au cas où les Conventions de Genève deviendraient applicables, cela devrait inclure le devoir de punir les infractions graves aux Conventions. Voir également Bowett, *United Nations Forces,* p. 512.

276 Effet de jugement du tribunal administratif des N. U. accordant indemnité, Avis consultatif, C.I.J. Recueil 1954, p. 57.

> de remettre des infracteurs à une autre Partie contractante pour qu'ils soient jugés par cette dernière. Cependant, une telle remise ne libère pas la Puissance remettante de ses responsabilités en vertu des art. 49 ss..[277]

L'analyse qui précède a montré que les structures et compétences de l'ONU sont telles qu'elle puisse faire face aux obligations découlant des Conventions de Genève et du Règlement de La Haye,[278][279] soit parce qu'elle peut créer les institutions exigées par ces Conventions, soit parce qu'on peut atteindre le but visé par certaines dispositions moyennant d'autres procédures. Ces Conventions constituent l'essentiel des règles relatives à la conduite d'hostilités sur terre.

Il est donc permis de conclure, de façon générale, que l'ONU peut être destinataire des normes relatives à la guerre sur terre.

3. En ce qui concerne les normes relatives à la guerre maritime et aérienne, une difficulté de plus surgit. On a soutenu que, si un navire ou un aéronef bat le pavillon des Nations Unies, cela ne saurait avoir les mêmes conséquences que le fait de porter un pavillon étatique.[280] « Qui dit pavillon dit nationalité et qui dit nationalité dit législation »[281] (notion du territoire flottant). L'ONU n'ayant pas une législation civile ou pénale qui saurait être applicable à bord des navires, il est nécessaire que les navires de l'ONU soient immatriculés dans un Etat. Ils devraient battre le pavillon de cet Etat, mais pourraient en même temps battre le pavillon des Nations Unies.[282] Ils auraient donc un statut particulier de double allégeance. Cette double allégeance trouve un parallèle[283] dans le statut des fonctionnaires internationaux qui ont, outre leur nationalité, un lien avec l'organisation internationale qui donne à cette organisation le droit d'exercer la protection diplomatique. Pour les bâtiments de guerre et les aéronefs militaires des contingents nationaux mis à la disposition du Conseil de Sécurité en vertu des art. 42 ss. de la Charte, ce double pavillon est la seule solution raisonnable.

---

277   Ire Convention: Art. 51.

278   L'ONU fut, par exemple, considérée par le C.I.C.R. comme « puissance détentrice »: C.I.C.R., Notes d'information, ne 24 du 16 octobre 1962, p. 3.

279   D'autre avis: Verplaetse, *The* jus in bello *and Military Operations in Korea 1950–1953,* ZaöRV 23 (1963), p. 724; Draper, *The Legal Limitations upon the Employment of Weapons by the United Nations Force in the Congo,* ICLQ 12 (1963), p. 408 s.

280   Commission du droit international, 8' session du 8 mai 1956, Doc. ONU A/CN. 4/103, p. 3; Mosler, *Die Erweiterung des Kreises der Völkerrechtssubjekte,* ZaöRV 22 (1962), p. 29.

281   Sottile, *L'ONU a-t-elle le droit de posséder des navires?* RDIP 34 (1956), p. 281.

282   Sottile, *loc. cit.*; voir également Bowett, *United Nations Forces,* p. 515.

283   Sottile, *loc. cit.*

LE DROIT DE LA GUERRE ET LES NATIONS UNIES 301

Si des bâtiments de guerre ou des aéronefs militaires battant le pavillon des Nations Unies participent à un combat, il n'y a aucun obstacle à ce que les forces navales ou aériennes de l'ONU puissent faire face aux obligations relatives à la conduite des hostilités, par exemple au traitement des naufragés, aux bombardements, aux ruses de guerre, à la procédure de saisie.

2.2.3.3 *Neutralité et Guerre Économique*

1. Il n'est, semble-t-il, plus contesté que les règles concernant la conduite d'hostilités ne présupposent pas un état de guerre au sens formel. La question se pose maintenant de savoir si des règles qui, selon certains auteurs,[284] présupposent un état de guerre au sens formel sont également susceptibles d'être appliquées lors d'une action armée des Nations Unies. Seront examinées dans ce contexte les règles concernant la guerre économique et la neutralité.[285]

2. Quant à la neutralité, son champ d'application est modifié par l'art. 2 al. 5 de la Charte. Dans les cas où elle reste valable (statut de neutralité reconnu par l'ONU, neutralité d'un Etat non-membre) il n'y a aucune raison pour laquelle l'ONU ne pourrait pas avoir les droits et les devoirs d'un belligérant à l'égard des neutres.[286] Les devoirs à l'égard des neutres sont surtout de caractère négatif ou prohibitif, c'est-à-dire que le belligérant doit s'abstenir d'accomplir certains actes incompatibles avec le statut de neutralité (p.e. violation du territoire neutre). En ce qui concerne les *droits*[287] des belligérants dans ce domaine, il s'agit surtout d'un droit de contrôle et de prise. Si l'ONU les exerce – ce qui n'est pas nécessaire –, elle doit respecter la procédure prévue par le droit international, mais rien n'empêche que les Nations Unies le fassent. Les pouvoirs implicites, déjà invoqués plusieurs fois, devraient permettre que les Nations Unies établissent des Cours de prise.

3. Quant à la guerre économique, certaines normes concernant cette matière présupposent des institutions étatiques. C'est notamment le cas pour les règles concernant le traitement de biens et de personnes étrangers (interdiction de confiscation, traitement national). Mais puisque les Nations Unies ne disposent pas d'un territoire national, elles ne sont pas en mesure de confisquer des biens situés sur ce territoire. Ce qui a été dit au sujet du traitement national requis par les Conventions de Genève[288] reste donc valable dans ce contexte.

---

284   Voir *supra,* p. 147, note 47.

285   Il n'est cependant pas certain si l'application du droit de neutralité présuppose un état de guerre au sens formel.

286   Cf. Guggenheim, *Traité,* tome II, p. 494; Scheuner, *Neutralität,* Strupp-Schlochauer, vol. II, p. 593.

287   Voir *supra,* p. 169.

288   Voir *supra,* p. 199.

D'autre part, le droit de la guerre économique n'indique aucune raison pour laquelle les Nations Unies ne pourraient pas prendre des mesures de contrôle du commerce ennemi généralement employées dans la guerre économique et que les Nations Unies sont capables de prendre. Ces mesures de contrôle (système de navicerts, blocus etc.) ne présupposent pas des institutions étatiques.

Cependant, certaines réserves s'imposent ici, eu égard aux fonctions des Nations Unies et à leurs buts.

Le droit de la guerre économique est, sous beaucoup d'aspects, lié au droit de neutralité. La guerre économique comprend trois catégories:

1.   mesures économiques à des fins économiques,
2.   mesures économiques à des fins politiques et militaires,
3.   mesures militaires à des fins économiques.[289]

L'art. 41 de la Charte autorise les Nations Unies à prendre des mesures de la deuxième catégorie. Mais en ce qui concerne des mesures ayant des fins purement économiques, il faut se rappeler que toute action des Nations Unies n'a pour but que de maintenir ou rétablir la paix.[290] Des mesures qui viseraient un enrichissement pur et simple des Nations Unies seraient donc interdites par la Charte. Mais la Charte a laissé aux organes des Nations Unies un champ considérable de liberté en ce qui concerne les moyens de faire face à une rupture de la paix. La Charte n'exclut nullement la possibilité d'affaiblir un agresseur en portant préjudice à sa vie économique. L'interdiction de l'enrichissement n'empêche pas des mesures visant à diminuer la capa cité de résistance économique d'un Etat qui est l'objet d'une opération coercitive des Nations Unies.

Les Nations Unies peuvent donc être destinataires des normes concernant la guerre économique. Si l'on retient que l'application de ces normes présuppose une guerre au sens formel, on arrive donc à la conclusion qu'un état de guerre au sens juridique du terme peut exister entre les Nations Unies et un Etat qui est l'objet d'une action coercitive.

On peut donc conclure, d'un examen détaillé du droit de la guerre que le *jus in bello* ne requiert pas que ses destinataires aient des qualités que les Nations Unies ne pourraient pas posséder.

2.2.4   Conclusion

Les deux méthodes employées pour constater la portée matérielle de la capacité juridique. des Nations Unies amènent alors au même résultat: les Nations

---

289   Held, *Wirtschaftskrieg*, Strupp-Schlochauer, vol. III, p. 857.
290   Voir *supra*, p. 169.

Unies peuvent être destinataire des normes du *jus in bello*.[291] L'analyse du droit de la guerre nous a cependant montré que l'application du droit de la guerre pour des troupes des Nations Unies présente certaines difficultés, surtout parce que les Nations Unies n'ont pas de législation pénale et n'ont guère de pouvoir disciplinaire à l'égard des contingents nationaux mis à leur disposition. On a vu que les Etats fournissant des contingents jouent un rôle important parce que leurs institutions et pouvoirs doivent dans une certaine mesure remplacer ceux que l'ONU devrait avoir, et qui lui font cependant défaut. Mais si l'on accepte l'idée que l'ONU seule est responsable de ces troupes, les Etats qui exercent leur juridiction sur des troupes onusiennes ou sur les prisonniers de celles-ci ne le font pas en vertu d'une obligation propre mais en vertu d'une obligation des Nations Unies à l'égard de l'autre partie au conflit. Ces Etats constituent des « agents » des Nations Unies.[292]

Un mot encore sur les conséquences d'une attitude différente de celle adoptée ici. Si l'on nie la capacité des Nations Unies d'être destinataire du *jus in bello*, il faut se demander si une responsabilité des Etats fournissant des contingents subsiste. Cela ferait surgir une gamme de responsabilités étatiques différentes,[293] situation peu satisfaisante,[294] mais non inconnue en droit international: le problème s'est toujours posé pour des armées de coalition placées sous un commandement unifié.[295] On pourrait même penser à une responsabilité concurrente en ce qui concerne le domaine où l'ONU possède un pouvoir de contrôle effectif.[296] Mais ce système mènerait à des incertitudes

---

291 Même résultat: Seyersted, *United Nations Forces*, BYIL 37 (1961), p. 474; *Idem, Objective International Personality of Intergovernmental Organizations*, p. 56; Guerrero Burgos, *Nociones de derecho de guerra*, p. 28; Cansacchi, *Nozioni di diritto internazionale bellico*, 4ᵉ éd., p. 15; Moreno Quintana, *Tratado de derecho internacional*, tome 2, p. 569 (qui arrive au même résultat pour l'OEA et la SdN); dans ce sens également: Evensen, Folkerettslige problemer forbundet med opprettelse av internasjonale sikkerhetsstyrker for FN (*Problèmes du droit international public relatifs à l'établissement de forces internationales de sécurité par l'ONU*), Internasjonal Politikk 1963, p. 84 s. qui ne considère cependant pas comme opportun que les Nations Unies deviennent partie aux Conventions de Genève; cf. même auteur dans *Peace-Keeping, Experience and Evaluation*, p. 240 s.

292 Bowette, *United Nations Forces*, p. 516; Weissberg, *The International Status of the United Nations*, p. 208 (concerne l'UNEF). Sur quelques aspects pratiques de ce problème voir *infra*, p. 209.

293 Bowett, *op. cit.*, p. 505.

294 Bowett, *loc. cit.*; Taubenfeld, *International Armed Forces and the Laws of War*, AJIL 45 (1951), p. 675.

295 Baxter, *Constitutional Forms and Some Legal Problems of International Military Command*, BYIL 29 (1952), p. 352 ss.

296 Sur les relations entre contrôle et responsabilité, voir Eagleton, *International Organization and the Law of Responsibility*, RdC 76 (1950 I), p. 343.

considérables et à des résultats inégaux injustifiables.[297] La solution proposée
ici, qui accepte la capacité des Nations Unies d'être destinataire du *jus in bello,*
est donc également préférable d'un point de vue pratique.

2.3 *Les Parties en Conflit lors des Hostilités au Congo Comme des Destinataires du « Jus in Bello »*

2.3.1 L'ONUC

1. L'ONU, agissant avec une force armée propre, peut être destinataire du *jus in bello.* Il a déjà été soutenu que lors de la crise congolaise, qui est le point de départ de cette étude, l'ONU s'est en effet servie d'une telle force armée propre.[298] Cette assertion doit encore être examinée de façon plus poussée.

Il est à noter que les forces armées de l'ONU au Congo furent organisées exactement comme l'eussent été les troupes mises à la disposition du Conseil de Sécurité en vertu des art. 42 ss. de la Charte, selon le rapport du Comité d'Etat-Major.[299] Les structures essentielles sont les mêmes: Un commandant et son personnel auxiliaire sont nommés directement par un organe principal des Nations Unies. En outre, la force se compose de contingents qui restent sous la juridiction pénale et disciplinaire de leur Etat d'origine. Les troupes sont sous le commandement exclusif des Nations Unies. Ce qui a été dit au sujet des troupes envisagées par les art. 42 ss. reste donc parfaitement valable pour l'ONUC. En effet, il n'est, à ma connaissance, nulle part contesté qu'il s'agit de troupes propres des Nations Unies.[300]

Il ne paraît donc pas nécessaire d'entrer dans une analyse détaillée du caractère « onusien » des troupes.[301] Il est toutefois utile de relever brièvement les sources et le contenu du lien qui unit les Nations Unies et ses troupes au Congo.

2. Le point de départ de l'analyse doit être un accord entre l'ONU d'une part et l'Etat fournissant un contingent d'autre part. Car ce n'est qu'en vertu de cet accord qu'une unité militaire étatique est privée, dans une mesure limitée, de

---

297 Bowett, *op. cit.,* p. 505.

298 Voir *supra,* pp. 187 et 195.

299 Voir *supra,* p. 193 s.

300 Cf. pour une analyse détaillée du problème Seyersted, *United Nations Forces,* BYIL 37 (1961), pp. 392 ss., 407 ss., 412 ss., 420 s., 424 s., 424 ss., 428 s.

301 Voir à cet égard Seyersted, *loc. cit.* Pour un auteur qui nie la personnalité juridique des Nations Unies et qui, par conséquent, ne considère leurs organes que comme organes communs des Etats-membres (ainsi Kopal, *Otázka ozbrojených sil OSN,* pp. 15 ss., 131 s.), la question se pose de façon semblable. Il doit se demander si une force armée forme un organe commun des Etats-membres des Nations Unies ou si les contingents en question constituent des organes de leur Etat d'origine. En ce qui concerne les forces armées créées en vertu des art. 43 ss. de la Charte, Kopal préconise la seconde solution.

LE DROIT DE LA GUERRE ET LES NATIONS UNIES

son caractère national et placée sous le commandement de l'ONU. Cet accord est la base du transfert du pouvoir de commandement.

Contrairement à la procédure relative à l'UNEF, de tels accords n'ont pas été publiés pour l'ONUC. Mais ces accords, qu'ils existent ou non, en forme écrite, ne peuvent qu'accepter les structures de la force présupposée par les résolutions du Conseil de Sécurité.[302] Ces structures se reflètent d'une part dans l'accord entre l'ONU et la République du Congo concernant le statut juridique de l'ONUC[303] et d'autre part dans les déclarations du Secrétaire Général relatives à la création de la force des Nations Unies au Congo, déclarations qu'a approuvées le Conseil de Sécurité et qui ont, de ce fait, une valeur particulière.[304] Il résulte de ces déclarations que l'ONUC a été organisée selon le modèle de l'UNEF.[305] Les documents relatifs à l'organisation de l'UNEF sont donc également pertinents pour l'ONUC. En outre, ces déclarations soulignent expressément le contrôle exclusif de l'ONU sur les « casques-bleus » au Congo.[306]

3. Les règles concernant l'organisation de l'ONUC telles qu'elles découlent des documents cités et de la pratique des Nations Unies se résument comme suit:

a) « La force est nécessairement placée sous le commandement exclusif de l'Organisation des Nations Unies en la personne du Secrétaire Général, sous le contrôle du Conseil de Sécurité. »[307]

b) Les membres de la force sont assimilés, bien que cela ne soit pas sur fin pied de parfaite égalité, aux fonctionnaires des Nations Unies[308]

Pour tous les membres du personnel des Nations Unies employés dans la présente opération, les règles fondamentales des Nations Unies en matière de service international doivent être considérées comme applicables, notamment en ce qui concerne l'obligation de faire preuve d'une fidélité absolue aux buts de l'Organisation et de s'abstenir d'actes en

---

302 Dans le cas de l'UNEF, les Etats fournissant des contingents ont accepté la structure de cette force en englobant les documents de base de l'organisation de la force dans l'accord entre l'ONU et les Etats participants (voir les accords avec la Finlande, la Suède et la Norvège, NU Rec. des Traités, vol. 271 [1957] n° 3913, 3914, 3917).

303 S/5004.

304 Voir *supra*, p. 141 s.

305 S/PV/873 par. 28.

306 S/4389, pp. 3 et 5.

307 Rapport du Secrétaire Général, Doc. ONU S/4389, p. 3.

308 UNEF, Règlement, art. 6: « Les membres de la Force constituent ... un personnel international placé sous l'autorité des Nations Unies ... ». Ils n'ont cependant pas tout à fait les mêmes privilèges et immunités que les membres du Secrétariat.

PART 4: THE LAW OF ARMED CONFLICT – GENERAL QUESTIONS

rapport avec leurs pays d'origine qui risqueraient d'ôter à l'opération son caractère international et de créer une situation de double allégeance.[309]

c) Les membres de la force demeurent cependant soumis à la loi pénale et aux règlements militaires de leur Etat d'origine « sans préjudice des responsabilités qui leur incombent en tant que membres de la Force [des Nations Unies] ».[310]

d) C'est l'ONU, et non les Etats qui fournissent des contingents, qui représente la force à l'égard des tiers:

   aa) L'ONU conclut les accords qui concernent la force,[311] sur le plan international par exemple l'accord concernant le statut de la force, des accords supplémentaires, des accords de cessez-le-feu[312]; sur le plan du droit national elle signe des contrats d'achat, des baux à loyer[313] etc.

   bb) L'ONU a été tenue responsable pour des actes délictueux que les membres de la force ont commis au service des Nations Unies,[314] autant sur le plan du droit national de l'Etat-hôte[315] que sur le plan du droit international.[316] Aucune demande d'indemnisation n'a été, à ma connaissance, dirigée contre un Etat fournissant un contingent.[317]

---

309 Doc. ONU S/4389, p. 5.

310 UNEF, Règlement, art. 34.

311 UNEF, Règlement, art. 15.

312 Voir *supra*, p. 143 ss.; discussion de détails: Seyersted, *United Nations Forces,* BYIL 37 (1961), p. 412 ss.

313 UNEF, Règlement, art. 20; Accord concernant le statut juridique de l'ONUC, par. 25.

314 Cf. Paul De Visscher, *Observations sur le fondement et la mise en oeuvre du principe de la responsabilité de l'Organisation des Nations Unies,* Annales de droit et de sciences politiques (Louvain) 23 (1963), p. 135.

315 Tel est, semble-t-il, le sens du par. 10 (b) de l'Accord concernant le statut de l'ONUC. En pratique, l'ONUC a établi des Commissions de réclamation qui « jugeaient » sur les réclamations de particuliers.

316 Ainsi, un accord d'indemnisation a été conclu entre l'ONU et la Belgique, qui concerne des dommages subis par des ressortissants belges à la suite d'opérations des forces des Nations Unies au Congo (*Moniteur Belge* du 9 juillet 1965, 135' année, p. 9071 = Doc. ONU S/6597, Annexes; voir également *Le Soir,* 6 août 1965, p. 2 col. 4 et 8/9 août 1965, p. 7 col. 7 ainsi que Doc. ONU S/6589 [protestation de l'URSS]). Dans cet accord, l'ONU déclare « qu'elle ne se soustrait pas à sa responsabilité, s'il était établi que des agents de l'ONU ont effectivement fait subir un préjudice injustifiable à des innocents ».

317 La pratique ne donne en effet aucune indication qu'on ait fait valoir une responsabilité concurrente des Etats participants que De Visscher, *loc. cit.,* p. 136 considère comme possible. Puisque le droit de la guerre connaît des obligations de répression disciplinaire et que le pouvoir de répression disciplinaire demeure auprès des Etats participants, cette responsabilité concurrente est théoriquement possible. Mais si l'on se rallie à la

LE DROIT DE LA GUERRE ET LES NATIONS UNIES

cc)   L'ONU exerce la protection juridique pour les membres de la force dans la même mesure que pour ses agents.[318]

Les forces des Nations Unies au Congo doivent donc être considérées comme organe[319] de l'Organisation, dont les actes créent des droits ou obligations pour les Nations Unies comme le font les actes de troupes nationales pour un Etat. Comme nous l'avons vu dans le cadre des considérations générales,[320] les Etats d'origine exercent les pouvoirs retenus en tant qu'agents des Nations Unies. Lors des actions militaires au Congo, l'ONU était donc sujet de droits et de devoirs du *jus in bello,* dans la même mesure qu'un Etat l'aurait été dans une situation pareille.

2.3.2   Le Katanga

1. Le problème de l'applicabilité du *jus in bello ratione personae* ne se pose pas seulement pour l'ONU, mais également en ce qui concerne ses adversaires. Car l'ONU se vit opposée, plusieurs fois, à des troupes relevant de gouvernements qui se désignaient eux-mêmes comme indépendants. Dans ce cas, il faut se demander si ces troupes relevaient d'entités capables d'être destinataires des règles du droit international et (notamment) du *jus in bello.* Le problème se pose notamment pour les hostilités les plus importantes dans lesquelles l'ONU a été engagée au Congo, celles qui ont eu lieu au Katanga.

2. L'histoire est riche d'exemples où une force armée étrangère qui se trouvait dans un pays déterminé avec le consentement du gouvernement reconnu

---

conception que ces pouvoirs sont exercés par les Etats participants en tant qu'agents des Nations Unies, l'Organisation est responsable, à l'égard d'Etats tiers, d'un manquement des Etats participants dans ce domaine puisqu'elle doit répondre des manquements de ses agents.

318   UNEF, Règlement, art. 30; pour la pratique voir Seyersted, *United Nations Forces,* BYIL 37 (1961), p. 424 S.

319   Il est cependant douteux si la force doit être considérée comme organe subsidiaire du Conseil de Sécurité selon l'art. 29 ou comme partie du Secrétariat chargée d'une tâche spéciale en vertu de l'art. 98. La CIJ laisse cette question ouverte (Certaines dépenses des Nations Unies [article 17 al. 2 de la Charte], Avis consultatif, CI j Recueil 1962, p. 177). Vu le rôle central du Secrétaire Général, il me paraît plutôt adéquat de considérer les forces armées au Congo comme partie du Secrétariat (cf. Gandolfi, *Le rôle du Conseil de Sécurité de l'ONU dans le règlement des conflits internationaux,* Notes et Etudes Documentaires, n° 3115, p. 28); sur la possibilité de forces armées comme partie du Secrétariat voir également: Guérisse-jaquemin-Kellens, *Les forces armées de l'Organisation des Nations Unies face à leur mission sanitaire et humanitaire,* Annales de droit international médical n° 11 (1964), p. 30.

320   Voir *supra,* p. 206.

a été impliquée dans un combat avec des insurgés. Rappelons l'occupation du royaume des Deux-Siciles par l'Autriche (1821I1825) qui avait pour but la liquidation de l'insurrection des « Carbonari », et celle du Mexique par des troupes françaises (1862–1867) qui devaient soutenir l'empereur Maximilien contre le président Juarez. L'exemple le plus récent d'une telle situation est l'action militaire des Etats-Unis au Vietnam.[321]

3. Des doutes planent sur la question de savoir quelles normes du droit international s'appliquent à des conflits semblables. En ce qui concerne les relations entre des insurgés et le gouvernement reconnu, on est, en principe, dans le domaine de l'art. 3 des Conventions de Genève. On a soutenu que les relations entre les parties au conflit interne et les forces étrangères intervenant aux côtés de ces parties ne sont également soumises qu'aux restrictions de l'art. 3.[322] Cela paraît exact si les troupes étrangères sont incorporées aux forces armées des parties en conflit, placées sous le commandement de ces dernières, si les soldats étrangers ont donc un statut semblable à celui des soldats nationaux, plus précisément: du personnel combattant des parties à la guerre civile.

Mais si les forces armées étrangères gardent une position indépendante, l'application de l'art. 3 des Conventions de Genève est une solution peu satisfaisante. Il est difficile de concevoir un conflit avec intervention étrangère comme « conflit armé ne présentant pas un caractère international » au sens de l'art. 3. En outre, les scrupules qui empêchent les Etats de se soumettre, lors d'un conflit interne, aux règles du *jus in bello* dans sa totalité ne sont pas valables pour une intervention étrangère aux côtés du gouvernement légal. Ces scrupules sont dictés par les exigences de la raison d'Etat, par le souci de sauvegarder l'autorité étatique. Cette autorité veut avoir la main libre pour réprimer toute tentative de rébellion. Elle doit avoir la compétence de punir les rebelles comme criminels. Mais, le gouvernement étranger ne représente pas l'autorité étatique qui veut se faire respecter. Il n'a aucun intérêt propre à pouvoir punir les combattants de l'autre partie. Pour l'Etat étranger, des intérêts de caractère international sont en jeu. Il doit les faire valoir avec les moyens prévus par le droit international, à savoir des actes de guerre sanctionnés par le droit de la guerre. Cependant, l'application du *jus in bello* dans sa totalité comporterait, dans les situations envisagées, des difficultés pratiques considérables. Il y aurait, sur le même champ de bataille, applicabilité du *jus in bello* entier et

---

321 Cf. Hooker/Savasten, *The Geneva Convention of 1949: Application in the Vietnamese Conflict,* Virginia Journal of International Law 5 (1965), p. 243 ss.

322 Bartelle, *Counterinsurgency and Civil War,* North Dakota Law Review 40 (1964), p. 286; Kelly, *Legal Aspects of Military Operations in Counterinsurgency,* Military Law Review 21 (1963), p. 118.

de l'art. 3 seul.[323] Vu ces difficultés, il paraît dangereux de développer des solutions généralement valables en ce qui concerne l'application du *jus in bello* lors d'une intervention étrangère dans un conflit interne. Une analyse des circonstances particulières à chaque situation d'espèce est indispensable.

4. Le Katanga avait déclaré son indépendance le 11 juillet 1960.[324] Jusqu'au 14 janvier 1963, fin officielle de la sécession katangaise, le gouvernement central du Congo n'exerça aucun pouvoir effectif dans une grande partie de ce qui était la province du Katanga, mais aucun Etat étranger n'a reconnu le Katanga comme Etat indépendant. L'ONU n'a jamais cessé, en droit de traiter la République du Congo comme une unité. Le Conseil de Sécurité a expressément rejeté « l'allégation selon laquelle le Katanga serait une nation souveraine indépendante » ».[325] Les Nations Unies ont, *de jure,* communiqué avec le gouvernement katangais en tant que gouvernement provincial, non comme gouvernement étatique.[326] Elles considéraient le gouvernement central comme responsable de tous les actes des gouvernements provinciaux, le Katanga inclus.[327] Elles étaient d'avis que ses droits et obligations ne découlaient que de ce qui avait été stipulé avec Léopoldville,[328]

Pour l'application du droit de la guerre, la situation est donc, à première vue, la suivante: le Katanga doit se considérer lié par le *jus in bello* en tant qu'Etat lié par le droit coutumier. Les Nations Unies doivent respecter le droit de la guerre vis-à-vis les troupes katangaises comme à l'égard des troupes du gouvernement central. La difficulté mentionnée ci-dessus, à savoir qu'il y aurait alors deux droits sur le même champ de bataille, ne se pose pas dans ce cas. Il n'y a jamais eu une action militaire concurrente des Nations Unies et du gouvernement

---

323   Hooker/Savasten, *The Geneva Convention of 1949: Application in the Vietnamese Conflict,* Virginia Journal of International Law 5 (1965), p. 257.

324   Pour le développement politique de la sécession, voir surtout Gérard-Libois, *Sécession au Katanga.*

325   Résolution du 24 novembre 1961, S/5002, Considérants.

326   Bowett, *United Nations Forces,* p. 240 s. Voir, par exemple: Lettre en date du 11 décembre 1962 adressée au Ministre des affaires étrangères de la Belgique par le Secrétaire Général, Doc. ONU S/5053/Add. 14 Annexe XIII, p. 2: « Malgré les ambitions et les proclamations de M. Tshombé, le Katanga est simplement une province et non un Etat. » Déclaration du Secrétaire Général, en date du 31 décembre 1962, Doc. ONU S/5053/Add. 14 Annexe XXXI, par. 5: « ... nous ne reconnaissons ni ne reconnaîtrons aucun droit de sécession ou d'indépendance de la province du Katanga; de même, nous ne traitons avec M. Tshombé, ou avec tout autre fonctionnaire du Katanga, qu'en leur seule qualité de fonctionnaire provincial. ».

327   Accord concernant le statut juridique de l'ONUC, par. 47 (Doc. ONU S/5004).

328   Ainsi, l'ONU fit valoir, à l'égard du Katanga, des violations de l'accord concernant le statut de l'onuc (cf. Doc. ONU S/5053/Add. 14 par. 5).

central contre le Katanga. Il n'y a donc, semble-t-il, aucun obstacle à ce que le droit de la guerre soit appliqué.

Les choses ne sont, cependant, pas aussi simples. Puisque, selon l'attitude de l'ONU, les relations entre l'ONU et le Katanga se déterminent d'après les relations entre l'ONU et le gouvernement central, il est donc, théoriquement, possible que l'ONU et le gouvernement central se mettent d'accord sur les modalités des hostilités au Katanga. Si les Nations Unies se prêtent alors, par voie d'accord avec le gouvernement central, à exécuter la législation du gouvernement central qui rendrait punissable la participation aux hostilités en question,[329] si les Nations Unies s'engagent donc à extrader des contrevenants aux autorités judiciaires du gouvernement central, les privilèges des capturés comme prisonniers de guerre en seraient gravement affectés. La règle selon laquelle les prisonniers de guerre ne sauraient être punis pour des actes d'hostilité permis par le droit de la guerre[330] ne jouerait plus. Mais il y aurait, selon l'attitude de l'ONU, un droit d'effectuer de semblables extraditions, et le gouvernement katangais ne saurait s'y opposer.

On ne peut que souligner les conséquences désastreuses qu'une telle conception aurait pour le fonctionnement du *jus in bello*. Elle en enlèverait la condition vitale: la réciprocité.[331] Car en fait, elle reviendrait à ce qu'une partie au conflit puisse, de façon unilatérale, déterminer le droit applicable dans un conflit donné.

Le problème de la position du Katanga en ce qui concerne le *jus in bello* est donc apparenté à celui de la discrimination entre belligérants. L'application de la maxime: « *ex factis jus oritur* » ou bien du principe de l'effectivité[332] s'impose également à cet égard, bien que de façon différente. Il ne s'agit pas de la question de savoir si une entité participant aux hostilités ne peut pas acquérir des

---

329   « L'ordonnance n° 83 (du Président de la République du Congo) du 13 novembre 1961 complétant l'ordonnance n° 70 du 24 août 1961 » (Doc. ONU S/4940/Add. 14 Annexe) disposait: « Tous les officiers et mercenaires non congolais servant dans les forces katangaises qui n'ont pas accepté un engagement contractuel avec le gouvernement central de la République du Congo sont également passibles des peines d'emprisonnement ... » Par une lettre de la même date, le Ministre de l'intérieur de la République du Congo demanda aux Nations Unies de mettre « tous les mercenaires ... à la disposition du Gouvernement de la République du Congo ». Il n'est cependant pas clair si l'ONU s'est engagée à exécuter cette ordonnance comme elle s'était engagée à exécuter l'ordonnance n° 70 qui ne prévoyait que l'expulsion des mercenaires (Doc. ONU S/4940). Selon O'Brien, *Meine Mission in Katanga*, p. 246 s., l'ONU fut également disposée à exécuter des mandats d'amener du Parquet Général de Léopoldville contre les dirigeants politiques du Katanga.

330   Voir *supra,* p. 155.

331   Voir *supra,* p. 171.

332   Voir *supra,* p. 166.

« droits de belligérants » du fait qu'elle a déclenché ces hostilités de façon contraire au droit des gens. Le problème est plutôt de savoir si cette entité peut être destinataire du *jus in bello* encore qu'elle ne soit pas reconnue *de jure*. Mais les raisons qui nous ont induit à préconiser le principe de la non-discrimination restent valables dans ce contexte. Ce principe trouve son fondement dans la fonction du *jus in bello* qui est de mettre un minimum d'ordre dans un conflit, ordre requis aussi bien par les exigences humanitaires que par l'intérêt propre des parties.[333] Le droit de la guerre est le seul moyen que le droit international positif possède pour remplir cette fonction ordinatrice. Il doit donc être appliqué dès qu'il existe un état de fait qui a besoin d'être réglé par ce droit, sans qu'on puisse tenir compte de la légalité de l'origine des hostilités.

C'est le fait d'hostilités de caractère international qui compte pour l'application du *jus in bello*. La non-reconnaissance d'une autorité de fait et les fictions qui en découlent ne doivent pas jouer de rôle pour son application. Dans d'autres domaines, la non-reconnaissance peut avoir des fonctions utiles. Mais le droit de la guerre ne peut que tenir compte des faits.[334] Le droit de la guerre est, par excellence, un domaine où le droit international ne peut qu'accepter que l'effectivité d'un ordre juridique étatique ait été réduit du fait d'une insurrection ou sécession, et qu'un nouvel ordre juridique effectif ait été créé.[335] Les Conventions de Genève l'ont reconnu en disposant que « les membres des forces armées régulières qui se réclament d'un gouvernement ou d'une autorité non reconnue » sont également bénéficiaires des Conventions.[336] Si l'on tient dûment compte des faits, le Katanga remplissait toutes les exigences que le *jus in bello* suppose de la part de ses destinataires. Quoique non reconnu, le Katanga présentait tous les critères d'une organisation étatique.

En fait, les Nations Unies doivent donc, en ce qui concerne l'applicabilité du droit de la guerre, traiter le Katanga comme « Etat ».

Comme nous l'avons vu, les hostilités entre le Katanga et les Nations Unies étaient d'une nature telle que le droit de la guerre devait être appliqué *ratione materiae*.[337] Elles présentent tous les critères d'une épreuve de force

---

333   Voir *supra*, p. 172.

334   Cf. également Seyersted, *United Nations Forces*, BYIL 37 (1961), p. 474.

335   Cf. Guggenheim, *Traité*, tome 1, p. 203 ss.; Chen, *The International Law of Recognition*, p. 350 soutient que la reconnaissance de belligérance a seulement l'effet « of evidence and estoppel ». Autre avis: Morelli, RdC 89 (1956 1), p. 532 s.

336   IIIe Convention: Art. 4 al. A chiffre 3, Ie et IIe Conventions: Art. 13 al. 3; voir également Maresca, *Gli articoli communi delle Convenzioni di Ginevra del 12 agosto 1949*, Riv. dir. int. 36 (1953), p. 110 (déclaration de guerre faite par un gouvernement non reconnu).

337   Voir *supra*, p. 157 ss.

internationale.[338] Si les Nations Unies traitent le Katanga comme Etat en ce qui concerne l'application du *jus in bello,* cela ne saurait être préjudiciable à sa position générale suivant laquelle le Katanga n'est qu'une province du Congo. Le droit international prévoit la possibilité qu'une entité soit considérée comme sujet de droit seulement en ce qui concerne le droit de la guerre. La belligérance reconnue en est un exemple. Le statut des insurgés en vertu de l'art. 3 des Conventions de Genève peut être considéré comme un phénomène semblable.[339]

L'ONU, semble-t-il, s'est inclinée devant les exigences de la situation. Elle n'a pas insisté de façon rigoureuse sur le caractère « provincial » du Katanga. En fait, la position de l'ONU était plus souple.[340] Elle a négocié un cessez-le-feu avec le Katanga malgré les protestations du gouvernement central.[341] Elle s'est bornée à expulser les personnes visées par la législation pénale du gouvernement central, elle a hésité à les extrader.[342]

On arrive donc à la conclusion que le droit coutumier de la guerre était pleinement applicable lors des combats entre les troupes onusiennes et les forces katangaises.[343]

3 Troisième Partie : Aspects Pratiques de L'application du Droit de la Guerre Lors des Incidents au Congo

Une étude théorique comme celle qui précède risque peut-être de perdre de vue les réalités de la pratique. Comment l'application du droit de la guerre

---

338   On peut même se demander si un état de guerre au sens formel existait entre le Katanga et les Nations Unies. Du côté katangais, il y avait, à plusieurs reprises, des déclarations dans ce sens (déjà en février 1961: Doc. ONU S/4750 par. 11; le 25 novembre 1961: Doc. ONU S/4940/ Add. 15 par. 5; le 29 décembre 1962, un « état d'inimitié » fut déclaré; Doc. ONU S/5053/ Add. 14 Annexe XXVIII). Il ne parait cependant pas adéquat de considérer ces déclarations comme « déclaration de guerre » au sens juridique du terme. Au sujet de la déclaration du 25 novembre 1961, Tshombé a lui-même donné des explications atténuantes (Doc. ONU S/ 4940/Add. 16 Annexe III). Les relations entre l'ONU et le Katanga représentaient toujours un mélange très particulier: épreuve de force par voie d'armes et conflit réglé par des moyens diplomatiques. Ces déclarations ne sont que l'expression d'une certaine dégénération de ces relations; l'expression plutôt politique « état d'inimitié » parait plus adéquate. L'ONU a refusé de reconnaître un « état de guerre » (voir Doc. ONU S/5053/ Add. 14 Annexe XII).

339   Siotis, *Le droit de la guerre et les conflits armés d'un caractère non-international,* p. 217 S.

340   Boweft, *United Nations Forces,* p. 240 S.

341   Doc. ONU S/4964.

342   Voir Doc. ONU S/5053/Add. 1 par. 33: « ... on a consulté le Gouvernement central afin de déterminer si des mesures seraient prises en vertu de l'Ordonnance n° 83 ... ».

343   Autre avis: Draper, *The Legal Limitation upon the Employment of Weapons by the United Nations Force in the Congo,* ICLQ 12 (1963), p. 409 s.; Bowett, *United Nations Forces,* p. 223, ne se décide pas.

LE DROIT DE LA GUERRE ET LES NATIONS UNIES

aux troupes de l'ONU, qui présente, comme nous l'avons vu, des difficultés théoriques considérables, peut-elle devenir effective? Comment peut-elle être sanctionnée dans une situation aussi troublée que l'était celle du Congo? Il faut donc, brièvement, examiner les tentatives qui ont été faites pour garantir le respect du droit de la guerre et les résultats qu'elles obtinrent. Cette analyse n'est, d'autre part, pas sans intérêt théorique. Elle mettra en lumière, de façon générale, l'effectivité que le droit de la guerre pourrait avoir lors d'une action militaire entreprise par les Nations Unies.

Des allégations, d'une part ou de l'autre, suivant lesquelles des violations du droit de la guerre auraient été commises lors des incidents du Congo, ne font pas défaut.[344] Vu le caractère limité des conflits ou des incidents, il semble être parfois difficile de distinguer entre allégations concernant des violations du droit de la guerre et allégations visant la criminalité pure et simple. Les remarques qui suivent n'ont pas pour but d'analyser ces allégations de façon détaillée. Elles se borneront à mettre en relief quelques procédures qui sont d'une importance particulière.

3.1 Les Initiatives du CICR

Le Comité International de la Croix-Rouge a le droit de veiller sur le respect des règles humanitaires du *jus in bello*,[345] même si une violation du droit de la guerre repose sur un accord des parties en conflit.[346] Il a exercé ce droit, lors de la crise congolaise,[347] en lançant des appels et en cherchant des assurances, d'une part ou de l'autre, relatives au respect des Conventions de Genève.

1. En ce qui concerne les initiatives de caractère général, des distinctions sont encore indispensables pour éviter des erreurs au sujet de l'attitude du CICR quant au droit applicable lors de ces conflits. Il y a des appels qui ne concernent que les véritables conflits internes congolais où, sans doute, l'art. 3 seul était applicable, et des interventions qui concernent les hostilités auxquelles l'ONUC participait. Ce sont des initiatives de la première catégorie dont fait état le communiqué de presse suivant :[348] [349]

---

344 Voir Bowett, *United Nations Forces*, p. 223 s.

345 Ire, IIe, IIIe Conventions de Genève: Art. 9; IV° Convention: Art. 10; cf. Castrén, *The Present Law of War and Neutrality*, p. 94; voir pour la pratique récente du C.I.C.R. dans ce domaine: Joyce, *Red Cross International*, p. 167 ss.

346 Pictet, *Les Conventions de Genève du 12 août 1949*, vol. IV, p. 79.

347 Cf. Guérisse-Jaquemin-Kellens, *Les forces armées des Nations Unies face à leur mission sanitaire et humanitaire*, Annales de droit international médical n° 11 (1964), p. 41 ss.

348 Publié le 17 novembre 1961, Rev. Int. Croix-Rouge 43 (1961), p. 603.

349 Bowett, *United Nations Forces*, p. 223, qui ne voit pas la différence mentionnée, arrive à la conclusion erronée que le CICR était d'avis que seul l'art. 3 était applicable pour les forces armées des Nations Unies.

314 PART 4: THE LAW OF ARMED CONFLICT – GENERAL QUESTIONS

> Le Comité international a constamment rappelé aux autorités congolais-
> es de droit ou de fait les exigences minima découlant de l'application des
> Conventions de Genève ...

C'est faire assez clairement allusion à l'article 3, mais cette déclaration ne se
réfère qu'aux hostilités entre les autorités congolaises. Comme exemple d'un
appel concernant l'art. 3, citons le suivant :[350]

> A tous ceux qui exercent une autorité sur le territoire du Congo ex-belge.
> Le Comité international de la Croix-Rouge, à Genève, rappelle solen-
> nellement les principes humanitaires reconnus par tous les pays, et selon
> lesquels, notamment, les personnes qui ne participent pas au combat et
> celles qui sont mises hors de combat par maladie, blessure ou captivité
> doivent, en toutes circonstances, être traitées avec humanité.
> Il adjure ces autorités de s'abstenir de toutes prises d'otages, exécutions
> sommaires et mesures de représailles. Le CICR offre ses services égale-
> ment à tous pour aider au soulagement des victimes des événements.

En ce qui concerne l'application des Conventions de Genève aux troupes des
Nations Unies, le CICR ne s'est pas borné à demander le respect des exigences
minima de l'art. 3. Cela résulte clairement des publications y relatives.

Le CICR a sollicité, à des échelons divers, des assurances de l'ONU quant à
l'application des Conventions de Genève. Ainsi, le président du CICR adressa,
au mois de septembre 1961, une lettre à M. Linnér, chargé de l'opération des
Nations Unies au Congo.[351] Cette lettre se réfère à une correspondance entre
le Secrétaire Général des Nations Unies et le président du CICR au sujet de
l'UNEF et à l'assurance donnée, en septembre 1960, par le Quartier général des
Nations Unies à Léopoldville qui déclarait que « les membres de la Force sont
tenus de respecter les principes et l'esprit des Conventions internationales relatives à la conduite du personnel militaire ». M. Linnér répondit, dans une note
en date du 11 octobre 1961[352] que

> the United Nations Organization in the Congo continues to respect
> and adhere to the *principles* of general international Conventions *to*

---

350 Du 22 février 1961, Rev. Int. Croix-Rouge 43 (1961), p. 140.
351 Résumé publié: CICR, Notes d'information n° 2 du 29 septembre 1961, p. 2.
352 United Nations Review, vol. 8, n° 11, p. 45; CICR, Notes d'information, n° 4 du 31 octobre
   1961, p. 2.

LE DROIT DE LA GUERRE ET LES NATIONS UNIES

the extent applicable,[353] particularly when they relate to humanitarian principles.

Le 8 novembre 1961, le Président du CICR envoya au Secrétaire Général une lettre qui concerne le même sujet. Les principaux passages de la réponse du Secrétaire Général ont été publiés[354]:

Je suis entièrement d'accord avec vous pour considérer que les Conventions de Genève de 1949 constituent la codification la plus complète des normes accordant à la personne humaine les garanties indispensables à sa sauvegarde en temps de guerre ou en cas de conflit armé quel qu'il soit. Je tiens aussi à confirmer que l'ONU entend que ses forces armées en campagne appliquent aussi scrupuleusement que possible *les principes* de ces conventions.

A ce propos, vous demandez s'il ne serait pas opportun que l'Organisation des Nations Unies notifie, par une déclaration officielle et publique, qu'elle s'engage à respecter en toutes circonstances les Conventions de Genève. En ce qui concerne la Force d'urgence des Nations Unies, une disposition formelle en ce sens a été inscrite à l'article 44 de son règlement établi par le. Secrétaire général conformément à la résolution 1001 (ES-1) de l'Assemblée générale ; le dit article est ainsi conçu :

« *Respect des conventions.* Les membres de la Force sont tenus de respecter *les principes et l'esprit*[355] des Conventions internationales générales relatives à la conduite du personnel militaire.

Une disposition analogue s'appliquera à la Force des Nations Unies au Congo.

Point n'est besoin, j'en suis sûr, de préciser que toute mesure envisagée par l'ONU ne saurait avoir d'autre objet que de rappeler aux membres de ses Forces les *principes* des Conventions de Genève et de montrer ainsi, sans équivoque possible, que les opérations menées au nom et sous le commandement de l'Organisation doivent être en parfaite harmonie avec *l'esprit*[356] des Conventions. »

Les vues du CICR et de l'ONU telles qu'elles résultent de cet échange de lettres sont en harmonie en ce sens qu'on considère au moins les principes des Conventions de Genève comme applicables. C'est là plus que les exigences minima

---

353 Italiques de l'auteur.
354 Rev. Int. Croix-Rouge 44 (1962), p. 28 s.
355 Italiques de l'auteur.
356 Italiques de l'auteur.

de l'art. 3. Cependant, le degré de l'application des Conventions de Genève demeure vague. Il n'est question que de « principes » et d' « esprit ». Il serait facile de nier une violation dû droit applicable en alléguant que la violation d'une disposition déterminée des Conventions de Genève n'est pas une question de principe. On peut douter si la déclaration donnée par le Secrétaire Général est vraiment celle demandée par le CICR, dans laquelle l'ONU s'engagerait « à respecter *en toutes circonstances* » les Conventions de Genève.

En effet, la Croix-Rouge internationale prit encore d'autres initiatives. A l'occasion du centenaire de la Croix-Rouge, au mois de septembre 1963, le Conseil des Délégués adopta la résolution suivante :[357]

> Le Conseil des Délégués,
>   considérant que les Etats parties aux Conventions de Genève se sont engagés à les respecter et à les faire respecter en toutes circonstances,
>   considérant qu'il est nécessaire que les Forces d'urgence des Nations Unies respectent ces Conventions et soient protégées par elles,
>   marque son appréciation des efforts déjà entrepris à cet effet par les Nations Unies et recommande :
> 1. que les Nations Unies soient invitées à adopter une déclaration solennelle acceptant que les Conventions de Genève s'appliquent à leurs Forces d'urgence *de la même manière qu'elles s'appliquent aux forces armées des Etats Parties à ces Conventions*[358];
> 2. que les Gouvernements des pays qui fournissent des contingents aux Nations Unies veuillent bien, en raison de l'importance primordiale de la question, donner à leurs troupes, avant leur départ de leur pays d'origine, un enseignement adéquat sur les Conventions de Genève, ainsi que l'ordre de se conformer à ces Conventions;
> 3. que les Autorités responsables des contingents acceptent de prendre toutes les mesures nécessaires pour prévenir et réprimer des infractions éventuelles aux dites Conventions.[359]

L'application du droit de la guerre exigée par ce document va beaucoup plus loin que les « principes » acceptés par l'ONU. Aucune prise de position

---

357   Rev. Int. Croix-Rouge 45 (1963), p. 543.

358   Italiques de l'auteur.

359   La XXe Conférence internationale de la Croix-Rouge (tenue au mois d'octobre 1.965 à Vienne) a repris la teneur de cette résolution dans sa résolution XXV (Rev. Int. Croix-Rouge 47 [1965], p. 541 s.).

LE DROIT DE LA GUERRE ET LES NATIONS UNIES

officielle des Nations Unies à l'égard de cette initiative de la Croix-Rouge n'a été publiée.

La résolution met également en jeu la responsabilité des Etats fournissant des contingents. Le CICR l'avait déjà fait dans un mémorandum du 10 novembre 1961, adressé à tous les Etats parties aux Conventions de Genève.[360] On y lit:

> En effet, l'Organisation des Nations Unies n'est pas, comme telle, partie aux Conventions de Genève. En conséquence, chaque Etat reste personnellement responsable de l'application de ces Conventions lorsqu'il fournit un contingent aux Nations Unies.

Comme nous l'avons vu,[361] la responsabilité des Etats participants est très problématique, puisque la troupe est un organe des Nations Unies, placé sous le Commandement exclusif des Nations Unies. La responsabilité des Etats participants telle qu'elle est conçue par le CICR ne correspond pas à la conception juridique de ces troupes. Un autre argument me paraît plus heureux. On lit dans le même mémorandum :[362]

> Enfin, le Comité international se permet de rappeler aux Etats qui pourraient fournir des contingents à une Force d'urgence des Nations Unies qu'aux termes de l'article ter commun aux quatre Conventions de Genève, les Hautes Parties contractantes se sont engagées non seulement à respecter, mais encore à 'faire respecter 'les dispositions de ces Conventions. Il exprime donc l'espoir qu'ils voudront bien, chacun, en cas de besoin, user de leur influence pour que les dispositions du droit humanitaire soient appliquées par l'ensemble des contingents engagés, comme par le commandement unifié.

2. En ce qui concerne les interventions particulières du CICR, il faut de nouveau distinguer entre les interventions en vertu de l'art. 3 des Conventions de Genève et celles relatives à l'ONUC. Les premières concernaient surtout le sort des détenus politiques et militaires des diverses factions congolaises.[363]

---

360   Rev. Int. Croix-Rouge 43 (1961), pp. 592 ss.

361   *Supra*, p. 210.

362   *Ibid*, p. 594.

363   Cf. à titre d'exemple: Rev. Int. Croix-Rouge 42 (1960), p. 574, 43 (1961), pp. 18, 83 s., 140 s.; Doc. ONU S/4976 Annexe 13; CICR, Notes d'information, n° 21 du 31 août 1963, p. 1; *ibid.,* n° 22 du 18 septembre 1962, p. 6.

Les activités du CICR concernant les hostilités dans lesquelles l'ONUC a été engagée se référaient également, dans une large mesure, au destin des prisonniers d'un côté ou de l'autre. Ainsi, le CICR a organisé des échanges de prisonniers.[364] Il a obtenu la libération de militaires étrangers (mercenaires) faits prisonniers par l'ONU.[365] Il s'est également préoccupé du sort de la population civile[366] et, de façon générale, de la conduite des hostilités.[367]

Dans ce contexte, un événement tragique est d'une importance particulière: la mort de M. Olivet, délégué du CICR au Congo. Olivet fut tué lors des combats livrés à Elisabethville au mois de décembre 1961 alors qu'il accomplissait une mission humanitaire, circulant dans une ambulance qui portait l'insigne de la Croix-Rouge.[368] Le CICR demanda qu'une commission impartiale conduisît une enquête pour éclaircir les circonstances du décès de M. Olivet,[369] ce que l'ONU et le Katanga acceptèrent.[370] Le résultat de cette enquête n'a jamais été rendu public ni par l'ONU ni par le CICR. Il ne convient évidemment pas à cette étude de se prononcer sur une culpabilité quelconque. Ce qui intéresse dans ce contexte, c'est l'effectivité de la procédure adoptée. Si l'on peut croire Paul De Visscher,[371] le CICR reçut une indemnité forfaitaire de l'ONU, sans que celle-ci reconnût une obligation juridique ou financière.[372] Si cela est vrai, l'enquête eut des résultats effectifs. La procédure adoptée paraît

---

364   Par exemple, au mois d'octobre 1961, CICR, Notes d'information, n° 4 du 31 octobre 1961, p. 2; *ibid.,* n° 9 du 1" février 1962, pp. 1 et 9.

365   CICR, Notes d'information, n° 32 du 1er avril 1963, p. 3.

366   CICR, Notes d'information, n° 7 du 21 décembre 1961, pp. 2 et 9; *ibid.,* n° 9 du 1er février 1962, p. 3; *ibid.,* n° 29 du 18 janvier 1963, p. 6.

367   CICR, Notes d'information, n° 7 du 21 décembre 1961, p. 9.

368   Doc. ONU S/5053 par. 10.

369   Rev. Int. Croix-Rouge 44 (1962), p. 81.

370   *Ibid.*

371   Paul De Visscher, *Observations sur le fondement et la mise en œuvre du principe de la responsabilité de l'Organisation des Nations Unies,* Annales de Droit et de Sciences Politiques 23 (1963), p. 135.

372   Il y a des raisons de croire que les allégations de De Visscher selon lesquelles Olivet fut tué par des troupes onusiennes, ne sont pas dénuées de fondement. S'il avait été tué par des troupes katangaises, il est très probable que l'ONU, vu ses relations peu amicales avec Tshombé, aurait publié le rapport de la Commission impartiale. L'ONU se trouvait, en ce qui concerne les incidents au Katanga, en face d'attaques de la part de l'opinion publique, surtout en Belgique et en Grande-Bretagne. Elle n'aurait certainement pas omis l'occasion de se défendre dans ce cas particulièrement grave. Bowett, *United Nations Forces,* p. 223, et Draper, *The Legal Limitations upon the Employment of Weapons by the United Nations Force in the Congo,* ICLQ 12 (1963), p. 410 aurait dû écarter ce raisonnement avant de conclure que « no evidence could be obtained to attribute this [killing] to UN Forces ». La manière de voir adoptée ici trouve également un fondement dans des documents publiés par le Gouvernement du Katanga.

LE DROIT DE LA GUERRE ET LES NATIONS UNIES

donc être de valeur pour des cas semblables (espérons cependant qu'ils ne se répéteront pas!).

3. Les activités du CICR décrites ci-dessus, tendant à faire respecter le *jus in bello* par des appels, démarches et demandes d'enquête, devaient être relevées dans cette étude puisqu'elles constituent un élément essentiel de la pratique relative au droit dont l'applicabilité a été analysée de façon théorique dans les chapitres précédents. A l'organisme impartial qu'est le CICR incombe la tâche de contribuer au développement du droit dans un domaine qui, vu sa nouveauté et vu les difficultés juridiques, politiques et administratives qu'il présente, ne peut être développé par les parties en conflit que de façon incertaine et hésitante. On doit reconnaître que ces parties devaient d'abord défendre leurs propres intérêts. Les événements prouvent la valeur du poids moral du pouvoir neutre.

3.2 La Responsabilité des Etats Participants Pour le Respect du Droit de la Guerre : Pratique Suédoise

Les Etats qui fournissaient des contingents pour l'ONUC retenaient la juridiction pénale et le pouvoir disciplinaire à l'égard de ces troupes.[373] Les Etats participants sont cependant tenus d'exercer ces pouvoirs dans l'intérêt des Nations Unies, de façon que les Nations Unies soient en mesure de satisfaire à leurs responsabilités juridiques.

Ce système d'une distribution de pouvoir a été analysé ci-dessus de façon plutôt théorique. Mais pour pouvoir juger la praticabilité du système, il faut se demander comment il a fonctionné en fait.

A cet égard, la pratique des Etats participants ne paraît guère accessible, avec une exception: la Suède.[374] Des tribunaux suédois ont en effet puni des soldats suédois pour des délits commis au Congo.[375] Il semble cependant que l'on se soit heurté à des difficultés pratiques considérables, notamment en ce qui concerne la preuve.[376] Il est impossible, par exemple, d'entendre les témoins éthiopiens, indiens ou indonésiens devant des tribunaux suédois et il paraît extrêmement difficile de les faire entendre dans leurs propres pays.[377] En pratique, beaucoup de poursuites furent annulées pour ces raisons par le

---

373 Voir *supra,* p. 210.

374 Voir les problèmes qui se sont posés à cet égard en vertu de la législation suédoise: Cars, Militär rättskipning vid svenska FN-förband i utiandet (*juridiction militaire relative aux contingents suédois dans les forces des Nations Unies à l'étranger*), Förvaltningsrättslig Tidskrift 27 (1965), p. 157 ss.

375 Cour Suprême de la Suède, arrêt du 25 avril 1963, Nytt Juridiskt Arkiv 90 (1963) Avd. I, n° 44, p. 237 ss.; voir également Cars, *loc. cit.,* p. 164.

376 Cars, */oc. cit.,* p. 173.

377 *Ibid.*

320 PART 4: THE LAW OF ARMED CONFLICT – GENERAL QUESTIONS

chef du contingent suédois sans qu'il y eût une base juridique très certaine.[378]
Ces difficultés pratiques[379] ont conduit la Ligue Belge pour la défense des
droits de l'homme à émettre, dans une résolution,[380] le vœu suivant[381]:

> En ce qui concerne la procédure de constatation des violations des lois
> et coutumes de la guerre et des droits de l'homme ainsi que des princi-
> pes généraux de droit, cette constatation devrait pouvoir se faire dans les
> plus brefs délais par une commission d'observateurs impartiaux choisis
> sur un tableau permanent d'experts désignés à l'avance par les gouverne-
> ments des Etats membres [des Nations Unies].

La commission chargée d'éclaircir les circonstances du décès d'Olivet[382] est un
précédent pour de semblables organismes d'enquête. Mais tant que de tels organismes n'existent pas sur une base permanente, les difficultés décrites subsistent.

Cependant, il faut relever que la Suède possède une institution qui permet
au moins de réduire le danger qu'il soit mis fin à des poursuites pénales de
façon abusive: c'est le *militieombudsman* (commissaire militaire du parlement suédois). L'ombudsman a le droit de mener des enquêtes s'il apprend, de
source quelconque, qu'il y a la possibilité d'un comportement fautif d'un membre de l'armée et il peut enjoindre au parquet d'accuser un soldat d'avoir violé
les obligations de service (*tjänstefel*).[383] Il est vrai que l'ombudsman rencontre
aussi les difficultés pratiques qui viennent d'être relevées. Mais ce qui importe,
c'est qu'il représente un organe de contrôle en plus. Il a l'avantage de ne pas
être lié, pour les enquêtes conduites par lui-même, par les règles de procédure
qui peuvent entraver l'activité de la justice ordinaire. En outre, il peut régler
une affaire par des moyens autres que l'accusation devant la justice ordinaire
(recommander de payer des dommages, par exemple).

---

378 *Ibid.*
379 Il ne s'agit pas seulement de difficulté de preuve: voir United Nations Emergency Force,
  Summary Study of the Experience Derived from the Establishment and Operation of the
  Force, Rapport du Secrétaire Général du 9 octobre 1958, Doc. ONU A/3943 par. 137; déclaration du délégué des Philippines: GAOR 11th session (659th meeting) vol. 11/111, p. 1192;
  Rosner, *The United Nations Emergency Force*, p. 148 ss.
380 Annales de Droit et de Sciences Politiques 23 (1963), p. 144 ss.
381 *Loc. cit.,* p. 145 s.
382 Voir *supra*, p. 223.
383 §§ 96 ss. Regeringsform (Constitution suédoise) du 6 juin 1809, version publiée le 20 septembre 1961: Svensk Författningssamling 1961 (n° 464), p. 1123, modifié par Kungl. Maj'ts
  kungörelse angående beslutade ändringar i regeringsformen och riksdagsordningen du
  26 mars 1965. Selon la version modifiée, il n'y a plus un *militieombudsman* (commissaire
  militaire) et un *justitieombudsman* (commissaire judiciaire), mais deux commissaires qui
  ont les mêmes compétences de contrôle.

En ce qui concerne le comportement des contingents suédois au Congo, le *militieombudsman* a mené une enquête approfondie sur huit incidents où il avait été allégué que des troupes suédoises avaient violé le droit de la guerre.[384] Une lettre d'un professeur de l'Université d'Uppsala et une notice de presse avaient attiré l'attention du *militieombudsman* sur ce sujet. Le rapport du *militieombudsman* constate qu'il n'y avait, en fait, aucune violation du droit applicable. Pour arriver à ce résultat, le rapport examine la question de savoir quelles normes étaient applicables.[385] Il reconnaît que les Conventions internationales relatives au droit de la guerre n'étaient pas applicables puisqu'elles ne lient que les Etats contractants. Il reconnaît donc apparemment qu'il s'agit d'une force armée propre des Nations Unies. Sont applicables le droit coutumier et les principes desdites conventions. Le rapport n'indique pas pourquoi ces principes n'appartiendraient pas au droit coutumier. Il considère comme applicables les règles concernant le traitement humain des prisonniers de guerre, le respect de la vie et de la propriété des particuliers, l'interdiction du pillage, la confiscation du matériel de guerre, l'interdiction de la prise d'otages. Le rapport propose également des mesures pour améliorer l'instruction des troupes suédoises relative aux Conventions de Genève.[386]

L'institution de l'ombudsman méritait d'être mentionnée dans cette étude parce qu'elle a une certaine importance internationale. Il ne s'agit pas d'une particularité du droit suédois. Des commissaires parlementaires chargés de contrôler le bon fonctionnement de l'administration (non seulement militaire) existent également dans d'autres pays, notamment dans tous les pays scandinaves et en Nouvelle-Zélande.[387] Dans d'autres pays, on constate également une tendance à créer une semblable institution.[388] [389] Il fallait donc

---

384 Militieombudsmannens ambetsberättelse avgiven vid Riksdagen, år 1964, p. 240 ss.

385 *Ibid.*, p. 283 ss.

386 *Ibid.*, p. 277 ss.

387 Danemark: § 55 Grundlov (Constitution danoise) du 5 juin 1953; Lov om folketingets ombudsmand nr. 302 du 11 juin 1954. Finlande: § 49 Regeringsform (Constitution finlandaise) du 17 juillet 1919. Norvège: Lov om Stortingets ombudsmann for förvaltningen du 22 juin 1962. Nouvelle-Zélande: Parliamentary Commissioner (Ombudsman) Act 1962, du 7 septembre 1962, New Zealand Statutes 1962 n° 10.

388 En Hollande: Kirchheiner, *Een Ombudsman in Nederland,* Tijdschrift voor Bestuurswetenschappen en Publiek Recht 20 (1965), p. 75 ss.; en Grande-Bretagne: The Parliamentary Commissioner for Administration, White Paper Presented to the Parliament by the Prime Minister and First Lord of the Treasury by Command of Her Majesty, October 1965, Cmnd. 2767; au Canada: Sheppard, *An Ombudsman for Canada,* McGill Law Journal 10 (1964), p. 291 ss. Pour des institutions semblables aux Etats-Unis, voir: Davis, *Ombudsmen in America,* Public Law 1962, p. 34 ss.

389 Les commissaires n'ont cependant pas toujours des compétences dans le domaine militaire. Ce domaine est par exemple exclu dans le projet anglais.

relever l'utilité de cette institution pour un pays qui aurait à encourir des responsabilités du fait qu'il a fourni des contingents aux Nations Unies. Il était, de même, nécessaire de souligner le rôle que l'ombudsman peut jouer en ce qui concerne l'effectivité de l'application du droit de la guerre aux troupes des Nations Unies.

4 Conclusion

Il a été répondu par l'affirmative à toutes les questions que cette étude a posées au sujet du champ d'application du *jus in bello*. Certaines règles du droit de la guerre sont applicables aux incidents les plus bénins; le *jus in bello* s'applique également aux forces armées des Nations Unies. La raison d'être de cette attitude est la nécessité d'avoir un « code de procédure » pour toute épreuve de force militaire à l'échelon international.[390] Cette nécessité ne résulte pas seulement de considérations humanitaires, mais également de l'intérêt propre des parties au conflit: le respect de ce « code de procédure » leur assure une protection. Ce « code de procédure », on ne peut le trouver que dans le droit de la guerre. On ne peut donc que recourir au droit de la guerre, même si le conflit à régler ne correspond pas à la notion traditionnelle de guerre entre Etats. Mais nous avons également pu constater les difficultés théoriques et pratiques qu'un tel recours rencontre. Dans cette étude on a essayé d'indiquer quelques possibilités de surmonter ces obstacles. On s'est efforcé de le faire avec tout le respect possible à l'égard du *jus in bello* traditionnel. Certes, les actions militaires des Nations Unies, celles envisagées par les art. 42 ss. de la Charte et celles entreprises au Congo, présentent des aspects nouveaux et particuliers. Le développement du droit doit en tenir compte. Mais puisque le droit de la guerre est un ensemble équilibré de normes, les réformes nécessaires doivent être faites avec prudence. On ne doit pas amputer le droit de la guerre de ce qui est indispensable à son fonctionnement.[391] Les tendances de réforme doivent donc être réduites à ce qui est vraiment nécessaire. A cet égard, nous devons conclure: il ne faut pas que le droit de la guerre s'adapte aux Nations Unies, il faut que les Nations Unies, dans leur propre intérêt, s'adaptent au droit de la guerre, en créant les institutions convenables pour faire face aux responsabilités qui découlent du *jus in bello*.

---

390 Cf. Kunz, *The Chaotic Status of the Laws of War,* AJIL 45 (1951), p. 59.

391 En ce qui concerne les dangers de réformes irréalistes, voir Pictet, *Les Conventions de Genève du 12 août 1949,* vol. 1, p. 16.

Le Droit de la Guerre et les Nations Unies

Abbréviations

AFDI	Annuaire Français de Droit International.
AJIL	American Journal of International Law (Lancaster, P.A./ Washington, D.C.).
ANC	Armée Nationale Congolaise
Annuaire	Annuaire de l'Institut de Droit International.
Annual Digest	Annual Digest and Reports of Public International Law Cases (London), édité par Lauterpacht.
ASIL	American Society of International Law
BYIL	The British Yearbook of International Law (London)
CICR	Comité International de la Croix-Rouge
CIJ	Cour Internationale de Justice
Doc. ONU	Document official des Nations Unies Cotes : A : Assemblée Générale S : Conseil de Securité S/PV : Conseil de Securité, Procès-verbaux
ERIL	Egyptian Review of International Law/Revue Egyptienne de droit international (Le Caire)
GAOR	General Assembly Official Records
ICLQ	The International and Comparative Law Quarterly (London)
ILA	International Law Association
JiaöR	Jahrbuch für internationales und ausländisches öffentliches Recht (Hamburg)
NILR	Netherlands International Law Review/Nederlands Tijdschrift voor Internationaal Recht (Leiden)
N.J.	Nederlandse Jurisprudentie
OEA	Organisation des États Américains
ÖZÖR	Österreichische Zeitschrift für öffentliches Recht (Wien)
ONU	Organisation des Nations Unies
ONUC	Organisation des Nations Unies au Congo
RdC	Académie de Droit International, Recueil des Cours
RDIP	Revue de Droit International et de Sciences Diplomatiques et Politiques (Genève)
Rev. Int. Croix-Rouge	Revue Internationale de la Croix-Rouge (Genève)
RGDIP	Revue Générale de Droit International Public (Paris)
Riv. dir. int.	Rivista di Diritto Internazionale (Milano)

PART 4: THE LAW OF ARMED CONFLICT – GENERAL QUESTIONS

SCOR	Security Council Official Records
SdN	Société des Nations
Strupp-Schlochauer	Wörterbuch des Völkerrechts, fondé par Strupp, 2ᵉ édition par Schlochauer, 3 vol. Berlin (de Gruyter) 1960, 1961, 1962
Suppl.	Supplement
UNEF	United Nations Emergency Force
ZaöRV	Zeitschrift für ausländisches öffentliches Recht und Völkerrecht (Heidelberg)

Bibliographie

Documents [Etc]

Actes de la Conférence Diplomatique de Genève 1949, 3 vol., Berne 1951.

CIJ: Plaidoiries, Réparation des dommages subis au service des Nations Unies, 1949.

Documents publiés par la Croix-Rouge

1. Documents publiés dans la Rev. Int. Croix-Rouge.
2. CICR, Notes d'information, Bulletin miméographié édité par le service d'information du CICR.
3. Le Comité international de la Croix-Rouge et le conflit de Corée, Recueil de documents, 2 vol., Genève 1952.

Documents des Nations Unies

Documents officiels miméographiés du Conseil de Sécurité et de l'Assemblée Générale.

General Assembly Official Records.

Security Council Official Records.

Documents officiels du Conseil de l'Europe, Assemblée Consultative.

Draft Convention on Rights and Duties of States in Case of Aggression, APL 33 (1939) Suppl. pp. 819–909 (cité Harvard Draft).

Evolution de la crise congolaise de septembre 1960 à avril 1961, Chronique de politique étrangère (Bruxelles) XIV (1961), pp. 557–1133.

La crise congolaise: janvier 1959 août 1960, Chronique de politique étrangère (Bruxelles) XIII (1960), pp. 403–951.

Information contenue dans les journaux suivants

1. Le Soir (Bruxelles).
2. The New York Times, International Edition.
3. Militieombudsmannens ambetsberåttelse avgiven vid Riksdagen, år 1964 (Stockholm).

LE DROIT DE LA GUERRE ET LES NATIONS UNIES

Ouvrages de Caractère Général

Balladore Pallieri, Giorgi(): Diritto bellico, 2° éd., Padova (Cedam) 1954, 463 p.

Cansacchi, Giorgio: Nozioni di diritto internazionale bellico, 4° éd., Torino (Giappichelli) 1963, 176 p.

Castrén, Erik: The Present Law of War and Neutrality, Helsinki (Annales Academiae Scientiarum Fennicae) 1954, 630 p.

Cavaré, Louis: Le droit international public positif, 2' éd., 2 tomes, Paris (Pédone) 1961 et 1962, 716 et 931 p.

Goodrich, Leland M./Hambro, Edvard: Charter of the United Nations, 2' éd., Boston (World Peace Foundation) 1949, 710 p.

Guerrero Burgos, Antonio: Nociones de derecho de guerra, Madrid (Ediciones « JURA ») 1955, 190 p.

Guggenheim, Paul: Lehrbuch des Völkerrechts, 2 tomes, Basel (Verlag fur Recht und Gesellschaft) 1948 et 1951, 1044 p.

Traité de Droit international public, 2 tomes, Genève (Georg) 1953 et 1954, 592 et 592 p. (cité Guggenheim, Traité).

Jessup, Philip C.: A Modem Law of Nations, New York (Macmillan) 195f), 236 p.

Jiménez de Arechaga, Eduardo: Derecho Constitucional de las Naciones Unidas, Madrid (Escuela de Funcionarios Internacionales) 1958, 653 p.

Kelsen, Hans: The Law of the United Nations, London (Stevens) 1950, avec supplément: Recent Trends in the Law of the United Nations, 1951, 994 p.

Moreno Quintana, Lucio M.: Tratado de derecho internacional, 3 tomes, Buenos Aires (Editorial Sudamericana) 1963, 576, 789, 480 p.

Oppenheim, L./Lauterpacht, Sir Hersch: International Law, vol. 2, 7' éd., London/ New York/Toronto (Longmans, Green), 1952, 941 p.; vol. 1, 8e éd., 1955, 1072 p. (cité Oppenheim-Lauterpacht).

Quadri, Rolando: Diritto internazionale pubblico, 3^8 éd., Palermo (Priulla) 1960, 652 p.

Ross, Alf: Constitution of the United Nations, Kobenhavn (Munksgaard) 1950, 236 p.

Rousseau, Charles: Droit international public, Paris (Recueil Sirey) 1953, 752 p. Schiicking, Walther/Wehberg, Hans: Die Satzung des Völkerbundes, 3' éd., vol. 1, Berlin (Vahlen) 1931, 604 p.

Schwarzenberger, Georg: International Law, 3« éd., vol. 1, London (Stevens) 1957, 808 p.

Sereni, Angelo Piero: Le organizzazioni internazionali, Milano (Giuffrè) 1959, 326 p.

Vattel, E. de: Le Droit des Gens, ou Principes de la Loi Naturelle, 2 tomes, Londres 1758, 541 et 376 p.

Verdross, Alfred: Völkerrecht, 5« éd., Wien (Springer) 1964, 690 p.

Virally, Michel: L'O.N.U. d'hier à demain, Paris (Editions du Seuil) 1961, 189 p.

Ouvrages Collectifs

Institut de Droit International, Session d'Amsterdam, Reconsidération des principes du droit de la guerre, Annuaire 47 1 (1957), pp. 323–606.

Institut de Droit International, Session de. Neuchâtel, Reconsidération des principes du droit de la guerre, Annuaire 48 II (1959), pp. 178–263.

Institut de Droit International, Session de Bruxelles, L'égalité d'application des règles du droit de la guerre aux parties à un conflit armé, Annuaire 50, I (1963), pp. 5–127 et 50 II (1963), pp. 306–356.

International Law Association, Report of the 38th Conference, held at Budapest 1934 (1935).

ASIL, Report of Committee on Study of Legal Problems of the United Nations: Should the Law of War apply to United Nations Enforcement Action? Proceedings 46th meeting 1952, pp. 216–220.

Peace-Keeping, Experience and Evaluation – the Oslo Papers, édité par Per Frydenberg, Oslo (Norwegian Institute of International Affairs) 1964, 339 p.

Monographies

Attia, Gamal el Din: Les Forces armées des Nations Unies en Corée et au Moyen-Orient, Genève (Droz) 1963, 467 p.

Beys, Jorge/Gendebien, Paul-Henri/Verhaegen, Benoît: Congo 1963, Bruxelles/ Léopoldville (Centre de Recherche et d'Information Socio-Politiques/ Institut National d'Etudes Politiques), 456 p.

Bowett, D.W.: United Nations Forces, London (Stevens) 1964, 579 p.

Brownlie, Jan: International Law and the Use of. Force by States, Oxford (Clarendon Press) 1963, 532 p.

Burns, Arthur Lee/Heathcote, Nina: Peace-Keeping by U.N. Forces, New York/ London (Praeger) 1963, 256 p.

Carroz, Jean/Probst, Yiirg: Personnalité juridique internationale et capacité de conclure des traités de l'ONU et des institutions spécialisées, Paris (Pédone) 1953, 90 p.

Chen, Ti-Chiang: The International Law of Recognition, London (Stevens) 1951, 461 p.

Dahm, Georg Zur Problematik des Völkerstrafrechts, Göttingen (Vandenhoeck & Ruprecht) 1956, 86 p.

Gandolfi, Alain: Le rôle du Conseil de Sécurité de l'ONU dans le règlement des conflits internationaux, Notes et Etudes Documentaires (Paris) n° 3115, 54 p.

Gérard-Libois, J.: Sécession au Katanga, Bruxelles/Léopoldville (Centre de Recherehe et d'information Socio-Politiques/Institut National d'Etudes Politiqües) 1963, 363 p.

Gérard-Libois, J./Verhaegen, Benoît: Congo 1960, Bruxelles (Centre de Recherche et d'information Socio-Politiques) 2 tomes, 1116 p.

Gérard-Libois, J./Verhaegen, Benoît: Congo 1962, Bruxelles (Centre de Recherche et d'information SocioPolitiques), 453 p.

Glaser, Stefan: Infraction internationale, Paris (Pichon et Durand-Auzias) 1957, 225 p.

Gordon, King: The United Nations in the Congo (Carnegie Endowment for International Peace) 1962, 184 p.

LE DROIT DE LA GUERRE ET LES NATIONS UNIES

Greenspan, Morris: The Modern Law of Land Warfare, Berkeley/Los Angeles (University of California Press) 1959, 724 p.

Grob, Fritz: The Relativity of War and Peace, New Haven (Yale University Press) 1949, 402 p.

Hoffmann, Gerhard: Strafrechtliche Verantwortung im Vôlkerrecht, Frankfurt/ Main-Berlin (Metzner) 1962, 212 p.

Joyce, James Avery: Red Cross International and the Strategy of Peace, London (Hodder & Stoughton) 1959, 270 p.

Kopal, Vladimir: Otàzka ozbrojenl'ch sil OSN (La question de la force armée des Nations Unies), Nakladatelstri êeskoslovenské akademie véd) 1961, 162 p. (résumé en anglais).

Kotzsch, Lothar: The Concept of War in Contemporary History and International Law, Genève (Droz) 1956, 310 p.

Langenhove, Fernand van: Le rôle prééminent du Secrétaire Général dans l'opération des Nations Unies au Congo, Bruxelles/La Haye (Institut Royal des Relations Internationales/Nijhoff 1964, 260 p.

Lauterpacht, Sir Hersch: Recognition in International Law, Cambridge (University Press) 1948, 442 p.

Leclerq, Claude: L'ONU et l'affaire du Congo, Paris (Payot) 1964, 367 p.

Mattern, Karl-Heinz: Die Exilregierung, Tübingen (Mohr) 1953, 78 p.

O'Brien, Conor C.: Meine Mission in Katanga, München (List) 1963, 364 p.

Pictet, Jean S.: Les Conventions de Genève du 12 août 1949, Commentaire, 4 vol,, Genève (C.I.C.R.) 1952, 1959, 1958, 1956; 542, 333, 834 et 728 p.

Robin, Raymond: Des occupations militaires en dehors des occupations de guerre, Paris (Sirey) 1913, 824 p.

Rosner, Gabriella: The United Nations Emergency Force, New York/London (Columbia University Press) 1963, 294 p.

Schmitt, Cari: Die Wendung zum diskriminierenden Kriegsbegriff, München (Duncker 4S: Humblot) 1938, 53 p.

Seyersted, Finn: Objective International Personality of Intergovernmental Organizations, Copenhagen 1963, 112 p.

Siotis, Jean: Le droit de la guerre et les conflits armés d'un caractère non-international, Paris (Pichon et Durand-Auzias) 1958, 248 p.

Stone, Julius: Legal Controls of International Conflict, 2° éd., London (Stevens) 1959, 903 p.

Uhler, Oscar M.: Der vôlkerrechtliche Schutz der Bevôlkerung eines besetzten Gebiets gegen Massnahmen der Okkupationsmacht, Zürich (Polygraphischer Verlag) 1950, 301 p.

Valahu, Mugur: The Katanga Circus, New York (Speller) 1964, 364 p.

Verhaegen, Benoît: Congo 1961, Bruxelles (Centre de Recherche et d'Information Socio-Politiques), 691 p.

328 PART 4: THE LAW OF ARMED CONFLICT – GENERAL QUESTIONS

Weissberg, Guenter: The International Status of the United Nations, New York/London (Oceana Publications/Stevens) 1961, 228 p.

Articles

Balladore Pallieri, Giorgi(): La personalità delle organizzazioni, Diritto internazionale (Milano) 14 (1960), pp. 230–255.

Bartelle, Talmadge L.: Counterinsurgency and Civil War, North Dakota Law Review 40 (1964), pp. 254–291.

Barton, O.P.: Foreign Armed Forces: Qualified Jurisdictional Immunity, BYIL 31 (1954), pp. 341–370.

Baxter, Richard R.: Constitutional Forms and Some Legal Problems of International Command, BYIL 29 (1952), pp. 325–359.

The Dufy of Obedience to the Belligerent Occupant, BYIL 27 (1950), pp. 235–266.

The Rôle of Law in Modern War, ASIL Proceedings, 47th meeting (1953), pp. 90–99.

Bilfinger, Cari: Vollendete Tatsache und Vôlkerrecht, Za6RV 15 (1953/54), pp. 453–481.

Bindschedler, Rudolf: Die Anerkennung im Vôlkerrecht, Archiv des Vôlkerrechts (Tübingen) 9 (1961/62), pp. 377–397.

Bindschedler, Rudolf: Die Neutralitât im modernen Völkerrecht, ZaôRV 17 (1956/57), pp. 1–37.

Bivens, William J.: Restatement of the Laws of War as Applied to the Armed Forces of Collective Security Arrangements, AJIL 48 (1954), pp. 140145.

Brandweiner, Heinrich: Sind die Vereinten Nationen den Kriegsgesetzen unterworfen? Neue Justiz (Berlin-Ost) 8 (1954), pp. 225–227.

Cars, Thorsten: Militâr râttskipning vid svenska FN-fôrband i utlandet, Fôr- valtnings-râttslig Tidskrift (Stockholm 27) (1964), pp. 157–180.

Debroux, François: Le Statut juridictionnel et disciplinaire de la Force d'Urgence des Nations Unies, Revue de droit pénal militaire et de droit de la guerre (Bruxelles) 1 (1962), pp. 269–288.

De Visscher, Charles: Observations sur l'effectivité en droit international public, RGDIP 62 (1958), pp. 601–609.

De Visscher, Charles: L'occupation de guerre, d'après la jurisprudence de la Cour de cassation de Belgique, Law Quarterly, Review (London) 34 (1918), pp. 72–81.

De Visscher, Paul: Observations sur le fondement et la mise en oeuvre du principe de la responsabilité de l'Organisation des Nations Unies, Annales de Droit et de Sciences Politiques (Louvain) 23 (1963), pp. 133–147.

Draper, G.I.A.D.: The Legal Limitation upon the Employment of Weapons by the United Nations Force in the Congo, ICLQ 12 (1963), pp. 387–413.

Eagleton, Clyde: International Organization and the Law of Responsibility, RdC 76 (1950 1), pp. 319–423.

LE DROIT DE LA GUERRE ET LES NATIONS UNIES 329

Evensen, Jens: Folkerettslige problemer forbundet med opprettelse av internasjonale sikkerhetsstyrker for FN, Internasjonal Politikk (Oslo) 1963, pp. 58–89.

Freeman, Alwyn V.: Responsibility of States for Unlawful Acts of their Armed Forces; RdC 88 (1955 II), pp. 263–416.

Green, L.C.: Armed Conflict, War, and Self-Defence, Archiv des Völkerrechts (Tübingen) 6 (1956/57), pp. 387–438.

Guérisse, A. / Jaquemin, Alex / Kellens, Georges: Les forces armées de l'Organisation des Nations Unies face à leur mission sanitaire et humanitaire, Annales de droit international médical (Monte Carlo) n° 11 (1964), pp. 16–45.

Guggenheim, Paul: Les principes du droit international public, RdC 80 (1952 I), pp. 1–188.

Hahn, Hugo J.: Euratom: The Conception of an International Personality, Harvard Law Review 71 (1957/58), pp. 1001–1056.

Held, Hermann: Wirtschaftskrieg, Strupp-Schlochauer, vol. III, pp. 857–862.

Hooker, Wade S. / Savasten, David H.: The Geneva Convention of 1949: Application in the Vietnamese Conflict, Virginia Journal of International Law (Charlottesville, Virginia) 5 (1965), pp. 243–265.

Jennings, B.R.: The Caroline and McLeod Cases, AJIL 32 (1938), pp. 82–99.

Karabus, Alan: United Nations Activities in the Congo, ASIL Proceedings, 55th meeting (1961), pp. 30–38.

Kelly, Joseph B.: Legal Aspects of Military Operations in Counterinsurgency, Military Law Review (U.S. Department of the Army) 21 (1963), pp. 95–122.

Kelsen, Hans: Will the Judgement in the Nuremberg Trial Constitute a Precedent in International Law, The International Law Quarterly (London) 1 (1947), pp. 153–171.

Komarnicki: The Place of Neutrality in the Modern System of International Law, RdC 80 (1952 II), pp. 395–509.

Krüger, Herbert: Das Prinzip der Effektivität, oder: über die besondere Wirklichkeitsnähe des Völkerrechts, Mélanges Jean Spiropoulos, Bonn (Schimmelbusch) 1957, pp. 265–284.

Kunz, Joseph L.: The Chaotic Status of the Law of War, AJIL 45 (1951), pp. 37–61.

Kunz, Joseph L.: Kriegsbegriff, Strupp-Schlochauer, vol. II, pp. 329–332.

Kunz, Joseph L.: The Laws of War, AJIL 50 (1956), pp. 313–337.

Lauterpacht, Sir Hersch: The Limits of the Operation of the Law of War, BYIL 30 (1953), pp. 206–243.

Lauterpacht, Sir Hersch: Rules of Warfare in an Unlawful War, Law and Politics in the World Community, Berkeley/Los Angeles (University of California Press) 1953, pp. 89–113 (cité Lauterpacht, Rules of Warfare).

Manner, George: The Legal Nature and Punishment of Criminal Acts of Violence Contrary to the Laws of War, AJIL 37 (1943), pp. 407–435.

Maresca: Gli articoli comuni delle Convenzioni di Ginevra de 12 agosto 1949, Rivista di diritto internazionale (Roma) 36 (1953), pp. 108–119.

McDougal, Myres S. / Feliciano, Florentino P.: The Initiation of Coercion; A Multi-Temporal Analysis, AJIL 52 (1958), pp. 241–259.

McDougal, Myres S. / Feliciano, Florentino P. International Coercion and World Public Order: the General Principles of the Laws of War, Yale Law Journal (New Haven) 67 (1958), pp. 771–845.

Miller, E.M. (pseudonyme de Schachter, Oscar): Legal Aspects of the Unit2d Nations Action in the Congo, AJIL 55 (1961), pp. 1–28 (une partie de cet article a été publiée en danois sous le nom de Schachter: Nordisk Tidsskrift for International Ret (Kobenhavn) 31 (1961), pp. 149–180 s.

Moneim Riad, Fuad Abdel: The United Nation Action in the Congo and its Legal Basis, ERIL 17 (1961), pp. 1–42.

Morelli, Gaetano: Cours général de droit international public, RdC 89 (1956 1), pp. 437–603.

Mosler, Hermann: Die Beendigung des Kriegszustands mit Deutschland und die Entwicklung des völkerrechtlichen Kriegsbegriffs, dans: Die Beendigung des Kriegszustands mit Deutschland nach dem zweiten Weltkrieg, édité par Mosler et Doehring (Beiträge zum ausländischen öffentlichen Recht und Wilkerrecht. 37), Köln/Berlin (Heymanns) 1963, pp. 454–486.

Mosler, Hermann: Die Erweiterung des Kreises der Völkerrechtssubjekte, ZaöRV 22 (1962), pp. 1–48.

Mosler, Hermann: Kriegsbeginn, Strupp-Schlochauer, vol. II, pp. 326–329.

Mosler, Hermann: Die Kriegshandlung im rechtswidrigen Krieg, JiaöR 1 (1948), pp. 335357.

O'Connel, D.P.: The Legal Character of the Korean War, New Zealand Law Journal (Wellington) 27 (1951), pp. 362–364.

Oppenheimer, F.E.: Governments and Authorities in Exile, AJIL 36 (1942), pp. 568–595.

Ridder, Helmut: La guerra y el derecho de guerra en el derecho internacional y en la doctrina internacionalista, Revista de Estudios Politicos (Madrid) n° 92 (mars-avril 1957), pp. 31–50.

Ruda, José Maria: El Consejo de Seguridad, Curso de preparaciân para la enserianza sobre Naciones Unidas, Rosario (Instituto de Derecho Internacional, Facultad de Ciencias Económicas, Comerciales y Politicas, Universidad Nacional del Litoral) 1961, pp. 109–127.

Rumpf, H.: Zur Frage der Relativitât des Kriegsbegriffs, Archiv des Völkerrechts (Tübingen) 6 (1956/57), pp. 51–55.

Schachter, Oscar: Legal Issues at the United Nations, Annulai Review of United Nations Affairs (New York) 1960–61, pp. 142–161.

Schachter, Oscar: The Relation of Law, Politics and Action in the United Nations, RdC 109 (1963 II), pp. 169–256.

Schätzel, Walter: Aggressionskrieg und Haager Kriegsrecht, Acta scandinavica juris gentium 24 (1954), pp. 17–31.

Scheuner, Ulrich: Eine internationale Streitmacht im Dienste der Vereinten Nationen, ZaöRV 19 (1958), pp. 389–415.

Scheuner, Ulrich: Die kollektive Sicherung des Friedens im gegenwârtigen Wilkerrecht, Berichte der Deutschen Gesellschaft für Vrilkerrecht, vol. 2, pp. 1–25.

Scheuner, Ulrich: Neutralität, Strupp-Schlochauer, vol. Il, pp. 590–596.

Seidl-Hohenveldern, Ignaz: Rechtsbeziehungen zwischen Internationalen Organisationen und den einzelnen Staaten, Archiv des Völkerrechts (Tübingen) 4 (1953/54), pp. 30–58.

Seidl-Hohenveldern, Ignaz: Die vôlkerrechtliche Haftung für Handlungen internationaler Organisationen im Verhältnis zu Nichtmitgliedstaaten, ÖZÖR 11 (1961), pp. 497–506.

Sereni, Angelo Piero:. Il concetto di guerra nel diritto internazionale contemporaneo, Riv. dir. int. 46 (1963), pp. 537–575.

Seyersted, Finn: United Nations Forces, BYIL 37 (1961), pp. 351–475.

Siordet, Frédéric: Les Conventions de Genève et la guerre civile, Rev. Int. Croix-Rouge 32 (1950), pp. 104–122, 187–212.

Sottile, A.: L'ONU a-t-elle le droit de posséder des navires? RDIP 34 (1956), p. 280 s.

Strebel, Helmut: Kriegsgefangene, Strupp-Schlochauer, vol. Il, pp. 343–347.

Taubenfeld, Howard J.: International Armed Forces and the Rules of War, AJIL 45 (1951), pp. 671–679.

Tucker, Robert W.: The Principle of Effectiveness in International Law, Law and Politics in the World Community, Berkeley/Los Angeles (University of California Press) 1953, pp. 31–48.

Verdross, Alfred: General. International Law and the United Nations Charter, International Affairs (London) 30 (1954), pp. 342–348.

Verplaetse, Julian G.: The ius in bello and Military Operations in Korea. 1950–1953, Za6RV 23 (1963), pp. 679–738.

Virally, Michel Les Nations Unies et l'affaire du Congo en 1960, AFDI 1960, pp. 557–597.

von der Heydte, Friedrich August: Rechtssubjekt und Rechtsperson im Völkerrecht, Mélanges Spiropoulos, Bonn (Schimmelbusch) 1957, pp. 237–255.

Wehberg, Hans: La guerre civile et le droit international, RdC 65 (1938 I), pp. 7–126.

Wehberg, Hans: Kriegsverbot, Strupp-Schlochauer, vol. II, pp. 370–373.

Wright, Quincy: The Outlawry of War and the Law of War, AJIL 47 (1953), pp. 365–376.

Wright, Quincy: The United Nations and the Congo Crisis, The Journal of the John Bassett Moore Society of International Law (Charlottesville, Virginia) 2 (1962), pp. 41–55.

332   PART 4: THE LAW OF ARMED CONFLICT – GENERAL QUESTIONS

Zemanek, Karl: Internationale Organisationen als Handlungseinheiten in der Völkerrechtsgemeinschaft, ÖZÖR 7 (1955/56), pp. 335–372.

Articles et Ouvrages Concernant des Questions Marginales

Bayer, Hermann-Wilfried: Die Enteignungen auf Kuba vor den Gerichten der Vereinigten Staaten, ZaôRV 25 (1965), pp. 30–49.

Davis, Kenneth Culp: Ombudsmen in America, Public Law (London) 1962, pp. 34–42.

De Visscher, Charles: Problèmes d'interprétation judiciaire en droit interna-national public, Paris (Pédone) 1963, 269 p.

Jörs, Paul / Kundel, Wolfgang / Wenger, Leopold: Rämisches Recht, 3e éd., Berlin-Gâttingen-Heidelberg (Springer) 1949, 434 p.

Kirchheiner, H.H.: Een Ombudsman in Nederland, Tijdschrift voor Bestuurswetenschappen en Publiek Recht (Elsene-Bruxelles) 20 (1965), pp. 75–81.

Picard, Maurice: Traité pratique du droit civil français, tome III, Les biens, Paris (Pichon et Durand-Auzias) 1952, 1035 p.

Sheppard, Claude-Armand: An Ombudsman for Canada, McGill Law Journal (Montréal) 10 (1964), pp. 291–340.

Zander, Michael: The Act of State Doctrine, AJIL 53 (1959), pp. 826–852.

Décisions Judiciaires
Tribunaux Internationaux

C.I.J.: Réparation des dommages subis au service des Nations Unies, Avis consultatif du 11 avril 1949: Recueil 1949, p. 174.

Effet de jugements du tribunal administratif des NU accordant indemnité, Avis consultatif du 13 juillet 1954: Recueil 1954, p. 47.

Certaines dépenses des Nations Unies (article 17, paragraphe 2, de la Charte), Avis consultatif du 20 juillet 1962: Recueil 1962, p. 151.

Cour Européenne des Droits de l'Homme: Arrêt du 1" juillet 1961: Affaire « Lawless », Publications de la Cour Européenne des Droits de l'Homme, Série A: Arrêts et Décisions, 1960–61, p. 27.

Tribunal Militaire International, Nuremberg: Jugement du 1" octobre 1946: *La République Française, etc. c. Gôring et al.,* Procès des grands criminels de guerre devant le Tribunal Militaire International, tome I, p. 181.

Tribunaux Nationaux

Allemagne: Oberlandesgericht Kiel, arrêt du 26 mars 1947: Süddeutsche Juristenzeitung 2 (1947), p. 325.

Danemark: So og Handelsret, Kobenhavn, arrêt du 24 octobre 1947, *Blue Star Line V. Burmeister & Wain,* Jus Gentium (Kobenhavn) 1 (1949), p. 119 = Annual Digest 15 (1948) n° 126.

Etats-Unis: Supreme Court of the United States, arrêt du 31 juillet 1942: *Ex parte Quirin et al.,* 317 U.S. 1.

United States Military Tribunal, Nuremberg, arrêt du 19 février 1948: *United States v. List et al.,* Trials of War Criminals before the Nuremberg Military Tribunals, vol. XI, p. 1230.

United States Military Tribunal, Nuremberg, arrêts du 8/9 avril 1948: *United States y. von Ohlendorf et al.,* Trials of War Criminals.before the Nuremberg Military Tribunals, vol. IV, p. 411.

United States Military Tribunal, Nuremberg, arrêt du 27 octobre 1948: *United States y. von Leeb et al.,* Trials of War Criminals before the Nuremberg Military Tribunals, vol. XI, p. 462.

France: Cour d'appel d'Orléans, arrêt du 6 avril 1948: Recueil Sirey 1949, Il, p. 141.

Grèce: Cour d'appel d'Egée Annual Digest 15 (1948), n° 186.

Luxembourg: Cour des crimes de guerre, arrêt du 16 juin 1949: affaire « Werner », Archiv des Wilkerrechts 2 (1949/50), p. 233.

Cour des crimes de guerre, arrêt du 28 juillet 1949: affaire « Hemmerling », Archiv des Vôlkerrechts 2 (1949/50), p. 494.

Norvège: Tribunal de première instance d'Oslo, arrêt du 29 janvier 1948: *in re Lat2a et al.,* Archiv des Wilkerrechts 1 (1948/49), p. 120.

Pays-Bas: Arr. Rechtbank Middelburg, arrêt du 18 février 1948: N.J. 1948, no 640, p. 1018.

Bijzondere Raad, Arnhem, arrêt du 12 août 1948: *in re Christiansen,* Annual Digest 15 (1948) n° 121.

Bijzondere Raad van Cassatie, arrêt du 6 décembre 1948: *in re Zühlke,* N.J. 1949, n° 85, p. 129.

Bijzondere Raad van Cassatie, arrêt du 12 janvier 1949: *in re Rauter, N.J.* 1949, n° 87, p. 144.

Landgerecht Manokwari (Nouvelle Guinée Néerlandaise), arrêt du 24 novembre 1961, NILR 9 (1964), p. 372 s.

Suède: Cour suprême de la Suède, arrêt du 25 avril 1963: Nytt Juridiskt Arkiv 19 (1963), no 44, p. 237.

The Historical Evolution of International Humanitarian Law, International Human Rights Law, Refugee Law and International Criminal Law

1   Introduction: The Development of International Law

In order to understand the current relationship between international humanitarian law, human rights law and refugee law, a look back into history is useful. Indeed, this paper tries to show that in order to understand the current shape and functioning of international law, it is necessary to look into its development.

Thus, how does international law develop? International law is a man-made phenomenon. It is shaped by actors who are driven and brought together by the perceived need to solve certain problems existing at the international level, and to do so by creating legal norms addressing the problem. How is it, then, that a problem reaches a sufficient number of these problem solvers? It takes most often special events which trigger such activities. And it takes common ideas, common approaches to what we nowadays call "governance". Finally, it takes opportunities for relevant actors to meet for addressing a problem.

Thus, triggering events, opportunities and ideas are key factors in the development of international law. This fact accounts for the fragmentation of international law into a great number of issue related treaty regimes established on particular occasions, addressing specific problems created by certain events. But as everything depends on everything, these regimes overlap. Then, it turns out that the rules are not necessarily consistent with each other, but that they can also reinforce each other. Thus, the question arises whether there is conflict and tension or synergy between various regimes.

These regimes are, of course, not static. They develop over time. It is a history of making and breaking the law, of applying or not applying the law. In the course of this development, the overlap between these regimes, but sometimes also the empty spaces left between them, become apparent.

It is the purpose of my modest contribution to show this development for four types of regimes, in particular as they overlap in situations of violence. They simultaneously address the questions of rights and duties of the same individual actors, both victims and violators.

2 International Humanitarian Law

"War" is a phenomenon probably as old as the phenomenon of man living together in organised collectivities. These collectivities often fight each other. There have been remarkable changes in the concept of war throughout the ages. These changes have shaped perceptions which have given rise to a concept of war as a relationship between states (and like entities) governed by international law. War as a relationship of military violence between sovereigns (later: sovereign states), yet with limited means against limited targets: this is the result of political practice (cabinet wars) and the philosophical thought of the age of enlightenment in 18th century Europe. Geneva already played an important role at the time. The key ideas were developed by Jean-Jacques Rousseau. This practice ad philosophy is the origin of international humanitarian law. It is the origin of the fundamental distinction between combatants and non-combatants, between persons fighting and those *hors de combat*, between the military effort of a state and the civilian population. This concept inspired a law-making development which found its provisional conclusion with the Hague Peace Conferences.

This law-making started with bilateral treaties, dealing with the fate of prisoners, concluded in the late 18th and early 19th century. The first one was the treaty on friendship and commerce between Prussia and the United States of 1785 (negotiated between King Frederic II and Benjamin Franklin, both strongly under the influence of the French philosophical thought). The next examples are treaties between England and the United States 1813 as well as between Spain and Colombia 1820. A major step in the civilisation or rather nationalisation of warfare was the Paris Peace Treaty 1856.

Later in the 19th and early 20th century, two major treaty regimes develop in parallel fashion. They then begin to merge in 1929. They have been called the Geneva Law and the Hague Law. The distinction has no deeper substantive significance. It is simply due to the fact that a specific triggering event (the Battle of Solferino 1859), the recognition of a problem (the fate of the wounded) by an active mover (Henry Dunant) prompted the development of a treaty regime (the first Geneva Convention of 1864 on the protection of the wounded in the field) concentrating on that particular problem. That treaty regime was progressively adapted to new developments and expanded to new additional issues. Other issues of the laws of war were at the same time dealt with in different for a based on different initiatives (Petersburg Declaration of 1986, Brussels Declaration 1874), a development which, rather due to a caprice of history, found a certain conclusion in the Hague Peace Conferences of 1899 and 1907. These conferences were meant to be what they were called: peace conferences, dealing with peaceful settlement of disputes and limitation of armaments. They were fairly unsuccessful in dealing with their main subject, but they provided a wonderful opportunity to produce a number of treaties on issues of the laws of war which at the time were ripe for codification, the central one being Convention IV, containing as an Annex the Hague Rules on Land Warfare.

Thus, it appeared that two separate regulatory regimes had been established. But it made no sense to keep them apart. The Geneva regime was better organised. The ICRC, the Red Cross movement as a whole, established itself as a moving force, which was supported by the Swiss Federal Council. This institutional back-up provided the opportunity for a continuous adaptation of the "Geneva Law" based on the experience of the respective recent wars: 1929 after the 1st World War, 1949 after the 2nd World War, 1977 during and after Vietnam, the Middle East conflict and the armed conflicts of the decolonisation process. In each of these steps of treaty making, the Geneva conventions took abroad issues which had before been a matter of the Hague Law: prisoners of war in 1929, belligerent oc-cupation in 1949, conduct of war 1977, to mention only the most significant ones.

The constraint on violence established by this combined treaty regime, which is to a large extent also part of customary law, is based on the funda-mental distinction between the military effort of the state and civilian objects, between combatants and the civilian population, between those in a position to fight and those which are not (wounded and sick, prisoners). Why do states accept, and base their behaviour on, this distinction? The moral value if re-specting the well-being and dignity of victims is not be underestimated. It is a body of law to a large extent designed to protect human beings. But the basic conflict of interest which is accommodated by this law is that between states engaged in an armed conflict. These states have the same interest, each in the opposite direction: to do as much damage as possible to the other party and to save one's own assets as far as possible. As an accommodation between these interests results indeed in restraints on violence, this benefits the individual. But is the individual more than a factual beneficiary, is it a holder of rights? A number of newer humanitarian law treaty provisions are formulated in this sense. It is this sharper focus on the individual which leads to the overlap with the law of human rights, the type of regime to which we turn next.

3   International Legal Protection of Human Rights

The development of a legal protection of human rights was, in its beginning, a matter of constitutional law. It started *grosso modo* at the same time as the de-velopment of international humanitarian law, as just described, namely in the

American and in the French Revolution. It is from these two events that a kind of shock wave went around the world, exporting these ideas into the constitutions of many states. But this legal protection was strictly a matter of national law, it was an internal affair of the state. It was, thus, not a matter appropriate for international legal regulation. If international law was concerned with the question of how a state treated human beings, it was only where they belonged to another state, be they aliens doing business in another state, be they prisoners in the hands of an adverse party. The fact that both situations are regulated in one and the same treaty, as was the case in the Prussian-American treaty of 1785, is a telling example of this situation.

The "migration" of human rights law from internal to international law is a result of a number of triggering events of the 20th century.

When international law first became concerned with the question of how a state treated its own citizens, this was due to the fact that there were groups of such citizens towards which the state was in some way hostile for historic reasons. This is the problem raised by the existence of minorities, which became crucial after the 1st World War as the redrawing of the political map of Europe, which took place at the end of this war, created a great number of new minorities. A number of treaties were concluded for their protection.

At the same time, there were also moves to develop a stronger international protection of the individual. But they did not lead very far in the 20ies and 30ies. It is under the shock of an additional triggering event, namely the atrocities which inhumane regimes in the 30ies and 40ies committed against foreigners and their own national alike, that the old concept of a *domaine réservé* ceded to the idea of international concern for human rights. The steps of this development were the following: In the Atlantic Charter of the United Nations, which then prompted a process of formulating programmatic instruments for the international protection of human rights and then of treaty making, both on the universal and the regional level. The programmatic formulations started with the Universal Declaration of 1948. This was the starting point for human rights bodies of the United Nations, but also for regional organisations providing a framework, an institutional backup, an opportunity in the sense I have used the term for developing human rights law. In these decades after 1950, there is, at the universal level, the development of the two UN Covenants, the content of which corresponds to the Universal Declaration, but also a wide array of specialised human rights treaties. In addition, regional regimes were created. The first region to adopt its own treaty regime was Europe with the European Convention on Human Rights signed in 1950 and the European Social Charter of 1961. The Convention is inspired by the text of the Universal Declaration, but the fact that Europe adopted its own treaty regime so soon is rooted in genuine European political currents, in the idea that the Europe to be reconstructed after the War should be based on the values of democracy and human rights. This also explains the progressive character of the Convention.

Human rights treaty regimes differ as to content, but even more so as to enforcement. A common element is the right of the individual to a national remedy. Yet the European Convention, unprecedent and revolutionary at the time, also provided for an international remedy. The scope of this legal protection of the individual still is unparalleled. The communications under the Optional Protocol to the CCPR have developed as a valuable remedy, but its scope is much more restricted than that of the individual complaint under the revised ECHR.

It is mainly in this focus on substantive and procedural rights of the individual that the human rights regimes differ from international humanitarian law. But does that mean that the human rights approach does no longer apply once an armed conflict brakes out? Human rights treaties envisage the problem in the form of state of emergency derogation. The underlying assumption is that their scope of application does not exclude armed conflict.

Quite to the contrary: relevant actors maintain the position that human rights law continues to apply in situation of armed conflict and, thus, can strengthen the legal position of victims and create a synergy between human rights law and international humanitarian law.

As far as law making is concerned, a great deal of the impetus which pushed the development of international humanitarian law in the late 60ies and the 70ies of the 20th century is due to the interest in promoting human rights. This was formulated by the Human Rights Conference in Teheran 1968 and by the General Assembly a few months later in resolutions entitled "human rights in armed conflict". This was soon echoed by a resolution dealing with the same subject adopted by a conference organised by the San Remo Institute, the first great and widely noticed step of the Institute to promote the cause of international humanitarian law and human rights. At the political level, all this paved the way for the confirmation and development of international humanitarian law which was the undertaken by the diplomatic conference held in Geneva from 1974 to 1977. The conference, by the way, paid back part of the debt it owed to human rights by adopting a number of clear cut human rights provisions, in particular by making some rights which are derogable under the Covenant non-derogable as far as the scope of application of international humanitarian law is concerned.

The synergies between international humanitarian law and human rights law, but also their limitations, have also become apparent in the case law of the institutions established by the European Convention on Human Rights.

Already in the 1970ies, the Commission, then the first organ seized with alleged violations of the Convention, held that the Convention applied to, and was violated by, the behaviour of Turkish troupes in Northern Cyprus. Later the Court, in the *Loizidou* case, held that the taking property by Northern Cypriote authorities was attributable to Turkey, and a violation by Turkey. This means, for all practical purposes, that the Hague Regulations and the Fourth Geneva Convention, but also by the European Convention on Human Rights, because the inhabitants of an occupied territory are "within the jurisdiction" of the occupying power according to the terms of Art. 1 of the ECHR, which defines its scope of application.

It turned out that too much hope had been placed in this synergy between the European Convention and international humanitarian law when the victims of a bombardment on Belgrade, which took place during the Kosovo conflict in 1999, claimed to have been violated in their right to life. In the *Bankovic* case, decided in December 2001, the Court held that a bombarded area was not "within the jurisdiction" of the bombarding state, distinguishing this case from *Loizidou*, thus limiting the synergy between international humanitarian law and human rights.

4 International Refugee Law

The development of refugee law, too, is due to a series of triggering events.

The first one was the exodus of great masses of people in the wake of the 1st World War and the ensuing revolutions, The President of the ICRC launched an appeal to the League of Nations, and measures of assistance were taken by the League in 1921. Nansen was appointed as the First "High Commissioner". The emphasis of these measures lay on international assistance and on a regulation of the status of these persons (1928 Arrangement, 1933 Refugee Convention). It was a fear of destabilisation and an interest in burden sharing that prompted states to cooperate in this way.

The next triggering event was the follow of refugees from Germany after 1933. Which, however, did not lead to an effective regime of assistance and protection.

The disasters causing masses of refugees continued: the massive displacement of persons during and after the 2nd World War. The 1951 Geneva Convention dealt with the treatment of *these* refugees. It is specialised human rights treaty concerning the relationship between a state and specific aliens, namely the refugees as defined by the convention. In addition, international measures of assistance and support are undertaken under the auspices of the United

Nations, first by the IRO (until 1952), then by the UNHCR (GA Res. 319(IV) of Dec. 3, 1949).

Yet the problem continues, new situations occur where people have to leave their countries. Thus, the 1951 Convention is extended in a general way to all refugees by the Protocol of 1967.

Thus, international refugee law is a specific treaty regime, administrated and supported by a specialised organ, relating to specific victims of man made disasters (not only armed conflict). It consists of a human rights law component and an assistance component. It does not deal with the armed conflict itself, rather with specific consequences thereof.

5   International Criminal Law

The first event triggering an attempt to establish and administer international criminal law was the suffering caused by 1st World War, which was seen as a matter of personal criminal responsibility of relevant actors, in particular the German Emperor. The Versailles Treaty provided for a criminal prosecution not only for violations of the laws of war, but also for an offence against the sanctity of treaties, thus targeting the violation of the rudimentary limitation of the *ius ad bellum* existing at the time. This attempt did not lead anywhere. Instead, a few prosecutions of war criminal took place before the German supreme court, the *Reichsgericht*.

The next triggering event was the suffering caused during and before the 2nd World War by the regimes in Germany and Japan. They, too, were seen as a matter of criminal responsibility of relevant actors of Germany and Japan. The International Criminal Tribunals were established in Nuremberg and Tokyo. The Nuremberg Tribunal had jurisdiction over three types of crimes: war crimes, crimes against humanity (criminal sanctions for massive violations of human rights) and crimes against peace (criminal sanction for the violation of a customary law prohibiting to use force). International criminal law was, thus, established as a set of secondary norms for three different legal regimes: the law of armed conflict, human rights, prohibition of the use of force.

This new field of international law developed very slowly after the end of the 2nd World War. In 1948, the Genocide Convention was adopted by the UNGA as a development of the concept of crimes against humanity. Apart from that, nothing really happened. Attempts to codify the "Nuremberg Principles" were laid to rest. The grave breaches provisions of the Geneva Conventions of 949 are not a question of *international* criminal law, but they establish a duty to punish violators of the Conventions under *national law*.

THE HISTORICAL EVOLUTION OF INTERNATIONAL HUMANITARIAN LAW 341

The next triggering events giving a new impetus to the development of international criminal law were the conflicts in the former Yugoslavia and in Rwanda. They led to an unprecedent move, namely the creation of two ad hoc criminal tribunals by the Security Council. Their jurisdiction extends to war crimes, crimes against humanity and genocide.

This laid the basis for the creation of a permanent international criminal court by the Rome Statute adopted in 1998, which entered into force in 2002. Its jurisdiction is defined according to Nuremberg triade: war crimes, crimes against humanity/genocide and crimes against peace. But the latter provision is not operational for the time being.

International criminal law, thus, constitutes a body of secondary norms the purpose of which is to enforce an important part of international humanitarian law and fundamental principles of human rights law.

6   Conclusions

Due to the internal necessities of its law-making process, the international legal order, except for a few general rules (the prohibition of the use of force, the law of state responsibility, the law of treaties) is a fragmentated legal order. It is divided into different treaty regimes. But customary law, too, develops in a problem oriented way. It does not change that fragmentation.

Most of these regimes have established their own institutions, which tend to protect the scope of application of the regime.

In concrete situations, these regimes overlap. This is when institutions tend to assert the primacy of *their* respective regime. The technical argument for doing this is *lex specialis*. Quite often it can be heard from both sides, which shows that the problem is somewhat more complicated.

What has to be avoided, indeed, is a situation where an actor bound by the law receives conflicting commands from various parts of the legal order, each claiming precedence over the other. There are various ways of dealing with this problem. A definition of the respective scopes of application which avoid overlap is one way. Parallel or cumulative application is the other solution which may imply certain difficulties. It requires some type of practical concertation between regimes. To come back to the practical example: in the *Bankovic* case, the ECHR defined the scope of application of the European Convention in a way that excludes overlap with international humanitarian law. In the *Loizidou* case, in a situation of belligerent occupation, the Court defined the scope of application in a way which requires parallel application. This means, for example, that such measures as the deprivation of liberty, the taking of persons' lives, the destruction of property by a detaining power or an occupying power must be justified under both regimes, although the criteria for such justification are different.

This is the solution where there can be a synergy between international humanitarian law and human rights. This is important in both directions. Where human rights law is violated, *e.g.* rules relating to the deprivation of freedom, but the victims have no access to an international remedy because the detaining power is not a party to an instrument providing for such remedy, the ICRC, in its function to monitor the respect of international humanitarian law can – and by the way does – step in. On the other hand, the fact that an individual has a remedy under human rights law gives additional strength to the rules of international humanitarian law corresponding to the human rights norm alleged to be violated.

Like many things in the world, the fragmentation of international law involves risks and opportunities.

13

Multiculturalism and the Development of International Humanitarian Law

1 Introduction

Multiculturalism means a social or political system where different cultural groups or individuals belonging to different cultures can live together while preserving and practicing their cultural identity. This contribution tries to elucidate the question whether this concept has any impact on international humanitarian law or, vice versa, whether international humanitarian law has any impact on the functioning of multicultural systems. This possible relationship between multiculturalism and international humanitarian law raises two different questions:

1. Is there a positive or negative impact of culture and, as a consequence, of multiculturalism on international humanitarian law?
2. Does international humanitarian law protect multiculturalism?

2 The Impact of Culture on International Humanitarian Law

The origins of the basic principles of international humanitarian law as we know it today date from the age of the enlightenment in Europe, from the 18th century. Its basic principle of distinction goes back to the thinking of Jean-Jacques Rousseau, formulated in his *Contrat social* of 1762: "Since the aim of war is to subdue a hostile State, a combatant has the right to kill the defenders of that State while they are armed; but as soon as they lay down their arms and surrender, they cease to be enemies or instruments of the enemy; they become simply men once more, and no one has any longer the right to take their lives".[1] Several essential restraints on the conduct of war flow from this sentence: War is a conflict between sovereigns who fight with their military against the military effort of the adversary. Only a limited category of persons are entitled to perform acts of hostility; only a limited category of targets is lawful. This implies both the immunity of those who are *hors de combat* and

---

1 Quoted from the English edition, translated by M. Cranston, 1968, p. 57.

© KONINKLIJKE BRILL NV, LEIDEN, 2021 | DOI:10.1163/9789004380592_015

of the civilian population. It is also the basis of the rule prohibiting "superfluous" injury. This was not only a philosophical postulate; it corresponded
to the reality of the "cabinet wars" of that time (although privateering was
only abolished in 1856).[2] For the purpose of the present article, it must be
noted that this restraint on warfare was not motivated by Christian thinking,
by such ideas as charity or Christian brotherhood. It was a secular philosophy,
based on the rule of reason.[3] In the words of Rousseau: "These principles are
derived from the nature of things; they are based on reason". These ideas had
already been formulated by Vattel and can be found in Diderot's *Encyclopedia*.
Under the influence of these ideas, the first treaty on what we now call international humanitarian law is negotiated between two protagonists of the
age of enlightenment, namely the Prussian King Frederick II (often called
"the Great") and Benjamin Franklin, perhaps a little ahead of their time. In
a chapter of the Treaty of Amity and Commerce between Prussia and the
newly independent United States of 1785, we find provisions on the decent
treatment of prisoners, in the case a war breaks out between the two powers.
There is the rule of reason behind these provisions: it is unreasonable to kill
and mistreat prisoners.

If one looks on the further development of the law of armed conflict through
the Geneva Conventions since 1864, the men who were the driving forces, from
Henry Dunant to Max Huber, certainly acted under a Christian inspiration. But
they took care not to explain the rationale of international humanitarian law
on the basis of the Christian religion, but rather on more general concepts,
such as "humanity", "philanthropy", "civilization" and "progress",[4] for fear that
reliance on specifically Christian values might jeopardize the universality of
the new rules which they intended to achieve. It is a sign of this spirit that the
choice of the red cross as the protective emblem is explained as an homage to
Switzerland.[5]

Like most other rules of traditional international law, international humanitarian law has its roots in the European system of the 18th and 19th century. The
reception of this body of law by the other States of the world constitutes a historic development which has taken place in the 19th and 20th century. During
this process of reception, a debate about the Eurocentrism of international

---

2 W. Grewe, The Epochs on International Law, English edition translated by M. Byers, 2000,
   p. 367 et seq.
3 K.J. Partsch, The Western concept, in: UNESCO/Henry Dunant Institute (eds.), International
   Dimensions of Humanitarian Law, 1988, p. 59 et seq., at 60.
4 Partsch, ibid., p. 61 et seq.
5 Art. 18 of the Geneva Convention of 1906.

law arose. In particular as the result of the codification processes which took place during the 20th century this image of Eurocentrism was overcome. This holds true for international humanitarian law as it does for many other fields of international law. If international law changed in this process, this was due to the change of the political, economic and social problems during that time, not because of an accommodation between cultures. The debate about the universality of human rights or about their uniform application throughout the world is a special case.

Historically speaking, international humanitarian law is, thus, not related to any particular culture, it is, one could say, a-cultural. It applies, and has to apply, regardless of the cultural appurtenance of a person performing acts of war or of a person being the victim thereof. This, however, describes only part of the picture. It neglects the ethical underpinnings which, as already indicated, have also had a bearing on the development of international humanitarian law.

Thus, it is not possible to completely dissociate humanitarian law from ethical commands which also flow from religious commands. In this sense, it is quite telling that in the very moment that the red cross was expressly declared not to constitute a religious symbol, namely at the diplomatic conference of 1906, Egypt and Turkey insisted on the use of the red crescent, and Persia on that of the red lion and sun. The three States made corresponding reservations to Art. 18 of the 1906 Convention.

Thus, the question of the religious foundations of international humanitarian law cannot be avoided as a practical matter. Therefore, those who wanted to promote the idea of international humanitarian law have tried to show that the essentials of international humanitarian law are anchored in the commands of all religions. In this sense, international humanitarian law becomes a multicultural phenomenon. One of the main protagonist of this approach was Jean Pictet. In his introduction to the volume "International Dimensions of Humanitarian Law"[6] he writes:

> [T]he plurality of cultures and the need to take an interest in them and study them in depth is acknowledged. This leads to an awareness that humanitarian principles are common to all human communities wherever they may be. When different customs, ethics and philosophies are gathered for comparison, and when they are melted down, their particularities eliminated and only what is general extracted, one is left with a pure substance which is the heritage of all mankind.

---

6   Above note 3, p. 3.

This is, to say the least, a very special kind of multicultural approach. It tries to disregard different cultural identities in order to integrate or merge all cultures in a limited aspect, namely the respect for humanitarian principles. This is closer to Rousseau's non-religious concept than it appears at a first glance. What mankind has in common, is not so much religious teaching, but reason, hopefully. This was Rousseau's approach.

Even if one considers it possible to extract certain common principles from different religions, this approach, with due respect, is a little too optimistic. It neglects the fact that there is a definite ambivalence in religious teaching about war. The attitude of religions towards war is not necessarily negative, quite to the contrary. The notion of a "just war" has been developed in particular in the monotheistic religions, Judaism, Christianity and Islam,[7] in various forms, although this is by no means the undisputed interpretation of the teachings of these religions. Asian religions (Hinduism and Buddhism) and ancient Chinese philosophies seem to be less inclined to such theories.[8]

As to the means of waging war, the Old Testament is not free from condoning atrocities.[9] The Christian version of the just war concept was at certain times used to justify barbaric treatment of person belonging to the (defeated) enemy.[10] Wars of religion in the Christian world are not known for restraints in warfare, although some of the excesses which occurred were also reason for contemporary critique.[11] In the early days of Islam, the treatment of prisoners (whether to kill or keep them for ransom) was the object of some debate which still is reflected in the Koran.[12]

This ambivalence entails a fundamental danger: Where elements of a culture, be they ethnic, be they religious, induce an attitude of exclusion, the respect for the most fundamental rules of international humanitarian law is in jeopardy. This can be shown for certain wars of colonisation,[13] the German

---

7   Hans Küng, Religion, Violence and "holy wars", 87 IRRC 253 (2005).
8   On Buddhism, see G.I.A.D. Draper, The Contribution of the Emperor Asoka Maurya to the Development of the Humanitarian Ideal in Warfare, in M.M. Meyer/H. McCoubrey (eds.), Reflections on Law and Armed Conflict, 1998, 37. On Chinese philosophy S. Ajibenova, Symbolism of Chinese Philosophy and Nature of Conflict Culture, IICP (Institute for Integrative Conflict Transformation and Peacebuilding) Paper, 2005, p. 4.
9   N. Solomon, Judaism and the ethics of war, 87 IRRC 295 (2005).
10   G.I.A.D. Draper, Christianity and War, in Meyer/McCoubrey, above note 8, p. 5, at 16.
11   A. Holzem, Kriegslehren des Christentums und die Typologie des Religionskrieges, in D. Beyrau/M. Hochgeschwender/D. Langewiesche (eds.), Formen des Krieges, 2007, p. 371, in particular at 379.
12   Y. ben Achour, Islam et droit international humanitaire, RICR 1980, p. 59, at 61 et seq.
13   "Burn their Houses and Cut Down their Corn": Englische Kolonisierungskriege in Virginia und Neu-England 1607–1646, in Beyrau/Hochgeschwender/ Langewiesche, above note 11, p. 243.

warfare in Eastern Europe during the 2nd World War,[14] which systematically and categorically disregarded the human dignity of those populations, for Japanese warfare, for instance in the practice of forced prostitution, for practices of ethnic cleansing in the Balkans conflict in the 1990s – and more examples could be added. Thus, the application of international humanitarian law depends in a very profound way on the respect for other cultures, which is the very essence of multiculturalism.

That being so, it is of course laudable and essential for the actual respect for humanitarian law that writings about that law abound with contributions which try to show, in the sense of Jean Pictet, that international humanitarian law corresponds to the exigencies of a particular culture, religion being a particularly important cultural phenomenon. As to restraints in warfare, it seems to be possible in all major religions to find elements of restraint in warfare, although they may not have been prevalent at all times. The following elements can be singled out:
- the distinction between combatants and non-combatants (civilians);[15]
- the immunity of persons who are *hors de combat*;[16]
- the prohibition to kill innocent vulnerable people (children and the elderly, traditionally also women);[17]
- the prohibition of looting and depriving a population of its means of sustenance (prohibition of "cutting trees");[18]
- a decent treatment of prisoners.[19]

Under current circumstances, emphasizing these religious demands is an important aspect of the measures to induce compliance with the law of armed

---

14 See the documents in Hamburger Institut für Sozialforschung (ed.), Verbrechen der Wehrmacht. Dimensionen des Vernichtungskrieges 1941–1944, 2002, pp. 37 et seq.

15 Islam: Sheikh W. al-Zuhili, Islam and International Law, 87 IRRC 269 (2005); H. Sultan, The Islamic concept, in International Dimensions of Humanitarian Law, above note 3, p. 29 at 37. Hinduism: M.K. Sinha, Hinduism and international humanitarian law, 87 IRRC 285 (2005), at 291 et seq.; N. Singh, Armed conflicts and humanitarian law in ancient India, in C. Swinarski (ed.), Studies and essays on international humanitarian law and Red Cross principles in honour of Jean Pictet, (1984), p. 531, at 532.

16 Islam: Sultan, above note 15, p. 35; Hinduism: Sinha, above note 15, p. 291; Sijngh, above note 15, p. 533. Japan: S. Adachi, The Asian concept, in International Dimensions of Humanitarian Law, above note 3, p. 13, at 16.

17 Islam: M.A. Boisard, De certaines règles concernant la conduite des hostilités et la protection des victimes de conflits armés, in 8 Annales d'études internationales 145 (1977), at 151; Sheikh al-Zuhili, above note 15, at p. 282. Hinduism: Singh, above note 15, at p. 534; African tradition: A.N. Njoya, The African concept, in International dimension of Humanitarian Law, above note 3, p. 5, at 6 et seq.

18 Islam: Boisard, above note 17, at p. 151; Sheikh al-Zuhili, above note 15, at p. 282. Japan: Adachi, above note 16, at p. 16 et seq.

19 Islam: Sultan, above note 3, at p. 33; see already ben Achour, above note 12.

conflict. Where religion is an important social force (as it nowadays is in many societies), in particular where it is interpreted by certain radical forces to call for violence, teaching those religious restraints on warfare becomes particularly relevant, even urgent. As and to the extent that these conflicts have an intercultural character, international humanitarian law has to be multicultural. It depends on the fact that these basic restraints on warfare are required by all religions and that these restraints are not exclusionary, i.e., apply also where the victims belong to another culture, another religion.

If one goes beyond these general considerations and turns to some specific rules, a cultural element can be seen in the fact that some of these rules contain key terms which are culturally loaded. This begins with the famous Martens clause:[20]

> [T]he inhabitants and the belligerents remain under the protection and the rule of the principles of the law of nations, as they result from the usages established among civilized peoples, from the law of humanity, and the dictates of the public conscience.

Notions like "humanity" or "public conscience" are cultural concepts. They must be applied in a cross-cultural way. The same holds true for such notions as "humane treatment", "respect for their person and honour", and the treatment of women "with all consideration due to their sex". Therefore, it is important that comparable concepts are found in religious commands. The Islam, for instance, enjoins those who wage war "never to transgress, let alone exceed, the limits of justice and equity and fall into the ways of tyranny and oppression".[21]

This brings us to the question how international humanitarian law achieves this cross-cultural respect in concrete terms, how it protects, in this sense, multiculturalism.

3 The Protection of Multiculturalism by International Humanitarian Law

International humanitarian law protects elements of culture in various ways. As a matter of principle, it does so in a way which refrains from any value

---

20 Preamble of Hague Convention (IV) Respecting the Laws and Customs of War on Land, 1907.

21 Second Sura, Ayats 109 et seq.; see H. Sultan, The Islamic concept, in International dimensions of Humanitarian Law, above note 3, p. 29 et seq., at 32 et seq.

MULTICULTURALISM AND INTERNATIONAL HUMANITARIAN LAW

349

judgment of the culture in question. It does so in a spirit of respect for other cultures. In this sense, it has a multicultural approach.

The relevant parts of international humanitarian law are the rules on the treatment of persons in the hand of an adverse party (detainees, population of an occupied territory) and the protection of physical manifestations of culture (cultural property).

3.1   *Persons Deprived of Their Liberty*

The basic provisions guaranteeing persons deprived of their liberty a respect for their cultural identity are found in the Third Geneva Convention on the treatment of prisoners of war.

> Art. 14. Prisoners of war are entitled in all circumstances to respect for their persons and honour.
>
> Women shall be treated with all the regard due to their sex ...
>
> Art. 16. ... all prisoners shall be treated alike by the Detaining Power, without any adverse distinction based on race, nationality, religious belief or political opinions, or any other distinction founded on similar criteria.
>
> Art. 34. Prisoners of war shall enjoy complete latitude in the exercise of their religious duties, including attendance at the service of their faith, on condition that they comply with the disciplinary routine prescribed by the military authorities.
>
> Adequate premises shall be provided where religious services may be held.

The latter provision also appears in the Fourth Convention regarding internees.

> Art. 86. The Detaining Power shall place at the disposal of interned persons, of whatever denomination, premises suitable for the holding of their religious services.

Similar principles re-appear in Art. 75 AP I containing fundamental guarantees for persons who are in the power of a party to the conflict and who do not benefit from a more favourable treatment under other provisions:

> [These persons] shall be treated humanely in all circumstances and shall enjoy, as a minimum, the protection provided by this Article without any adverse distinction based upon race, colour, sex, language, religion or belief, political or other opinion, national or social origin, wealth, birth or

other status, or on any other similar criteria. Each party shall respect the person, honour, convictions and religious practices of all such persons ...

The non-discrimination clauses explicitly show that this means a respect for the other culture. A Christian or a Muslim detainee may not be treated better or worse for reason of this religious belief.

The provisions quoted are, first of all, duties of abstention: The detaining power must refrain from any pressure on the detainee not to follow cultural and religious practices, or to follow a different one.[22] The duties of equal treatment, however, go further than a duty of abstention. If a party facilitates the exercise of one religion, it must facilitate the exercise of another religion in the same way.

The Third and the Fourth Convention go a step further. They provide for a positive duty regardless of considerations of equality. A Christian detaining power must provide facilities for a Muslim prayer, and a Muslim detaining power must facilitate holding a Christian service. This is a positive duty, not just a duty of abstention and tolerance.[23] The underlying concept is, as already mentioned, due regard for other cultures, in this sense multiculturalism.

A special case in point is the treatment of women with due regard to the culture to which they belong. Relevant provisions of AP I are:

> Art. 75 (5). Women whose liberty has been restricted ... shall be held in quarters separated from men's quarters. They shall be under the immediate supervision of women.
>
> ...
>
> Art. 76 (1). Women shall be the object of special respect and shall be protected in particular against rape, forced prostitution and any other form of indecent assault.

What is an "indecent" assault is also to be determined by consideration of culture. Also in this respect, due regard for the other culture matters and disregard for the culture of the victims can be, and has been systematically used as a means of warfare, as a means of gaining a victory through the psychological destruction of the population of the adversary. This is the appalling practices perpetrated against Muslim women during the conflict in Bosnia-Herzegovina.[24]

---

22   J. Pictet, The Geneva conventions of 12 august 1949, Commentary, Vol. III, p. 144 et seq., 227 et seq.

23   Pictet, ibid, p. 229.

24   See in particular the case of Kunarac, Kovac and Vukovic, ICTY case no. IT-96-23 and 96-23/1, Trial Chamber, Judgement of 22 February 2001.

MULTICULTURALISM AND INTERNATIONAL HUMANITARIAN LAW

3.2   *Occupied Territory*

The fundamental provision relevant in the present context is Art. 46 of the Hague Regulations of 1907:

> Family honour and rights, the lives of persons, and private property, as well as religious convictions and practice, must be respected.

The section on occupied territories of the Fourth Geneva Convention of 1949 goes into the details of this principle of the respect due to religion:

> Art. 58. The Occupying Power shall permit ministers of religion to give spiritual assistance to the members of their religious communities.
> The Occupying Power shall also accept consignments of books and articles required for religious needs and shall facilitate their distribution in occupied territory.

Be it noted that this is a positive duty, not just a duty of abstention and tolerance.

The duty to respect the cultural identity of *all* inhabitants of the occupied territory may be at odds with, but has primacy over, another principle of the law of occupation, namely the respect of pre-existing local law. An occupying power may not continue to enforce pre-existing local law denying human rights. It must, thus, grant religious freedom to all inhabitants – even if that did not exist before. It must do so, however, with due regard to the religious sensitivities of all inhabitants.

3.3   *Cultural Property*

In the case of occupation, cultural property is already protected by Art. 56 of the Hague Regulations. But the centrepiece of the protection of cultural property is the Hague Convention of 1954 and its two additional protocols (1954 and 1999). The provisions of the Protocols additional to the Geneva Conventions do not add very much to this regime of protection.[25] It imposes on the parties the duty not to use cultural property in a way which would make it a military objective and to refrain from attacks against cultural property (Art. 4 (1) of the Convention). The definition of cultural property in a way hides the problem of the relevance of a multicultural approach. Cultural property is "property of great importance to the cultural heritage of every people". This implies the problem of the evaluation of the relative cultural importance of a

---

25   Art. 53 AP I, Art. 16 AP II, see W. A. Solf, Cultural Property, Protection in Armed Conflict, in R. Bernhardt (ed.), EPIL vol. I, 1992, p. 892, at 895.

certain piece of property. This evaluation is, to begin with, the competence of the State where the property is situated.[26] The external sign of the evaluation is the marking of the property with the distinctive emblem (Art. 17 of the Hague Convention). But is this evaluation the final word, or can it be challenged by another State by putting into question the cultural value of the property? The destruction by the Taliban of the famous Bamiyan valley Buddha statue in Afghanistan in 2001 illustrates the problem.[27] The protection of cultural property also means accepting and respecting the value judgment of a different culture as to the worth of a certain property. Thus, a multicultural approach also underlies the regime of protection established by the Hague Convention of 1954.

4 Conclusion

There is a definite link between the preservation of multiculturalism in times of armed conflict and international humanitarian law. On the one hand, the effective application and implementation of international humanitarian law requires a multicultural approach being taken towards different groups and their activities and achievements. On the other hand, international humanitarian law protects that multicultural approach.

---

26 Solf, above note 25. Only for cultural property "under special protection", there is an international registration process.

27 Whether international humanitarian law applied to that destruction depends on a determination whether there was an armed conflict going on in Afghanistan at the relevant time.

Setting the Scene

New Technologies – New Challenges for IHL?

1 Prelude: The Controversy about the Crossbow

New technologies and warfare are companions. Throughout history, new technology, once developed, has soon been used for purposes of warfare, and a desire for arms superiority over supposed enemies has prompted many a technological development. Over the centuries, this has sometimes been accompanied by legal question marks. A ban on the crossbow as being an inhumane weapon was issued by two popes and one church council (the Second Lateran Council of 1139). The discourse was humanitarian and theological; the reason behind it was the fact that the invention of the crossbow put into question the traditional form of warfare: the knights' armour did not provide protection against crossbow arrows, that new invention thus challenged the belligerent privilege of the knights. That ban on a new technology was, however, never really implemented, new types of weapons and warfare develop unhindered by legal or moral constraints.

Are current attempts to hedge the use of new technologies in warfare something like the fight against the crossbow? The answer to this question lies in the response to a more fundamental question: does the law of armed conflict as it has gained shape over the last two hundred and fifty years protected outdated privileges, or is there a different type of essential value which is challenged by new technologies but which deserves to be preserved?

2 Essentials under Stress: The Principle of Distinction in the Context of Changing Conditions

The fundamental and essential principle governing the law of armed conflict for the last 250 years is the principle of distinction, to which the protection of fighters who are *hors de combat* and the prohibition of causing unnecessary suffering are ancillary. It is based on the concept, developed by Jean-Jacques Rousseau in his *Contrat social* of 1762, that war is a conflict between sovereigns, and limited to engaging their respective military efforts against each other. By thus limiting the group of persons entitled to take actively part in hostilities (combatants) and the scope of persons and things passively affected by them (military objectives), it establishes a far reaching restraint on military violence. Founded by Rousseau as a command of reason, it also had a basis in the reality of the wars taking place in Europe in his time, the so-called cabinet wars.

Contrary to what happened to the ban on the crossbow, this principle survived the disappearance of the military concepts which had surrounded its creation – although these changes in the military context put the principle under serious stress. Just to mention two major challenges to the principle: the development of military aviation and the invention of the atomic bomb. The former allowed extending military action well beyond what used to be called the enemy lines and exposed the civilian population in an unprecedented way to the dangers of hostilities. The latter, by its unprecedented yield of kinetic energy, heat and radiation, facilitates massive attacks where the distinction between civilians and civilian objects on the one hand and military objectives on the other is no longer feasible. Yet the legal principle of distinction has survived these challenges. Soon after the Second World War where this principle had come under such serious stress, a legal and political discourse developed throughout the world maintaining the principle of distinction against this challenge. The judgments of the Military Tribunals established after the war, the so-called Delhi Rules elaborated by the ICRC in 1956, the provisions of the 1977 Additional Protocols on the protection of the civilian population, military manuals nowadays governing the behaviour of many armed forces, and last but not least the Advisory Opinion of the ICJ (International Court of Justice) on the illegality of the use or threat of use of nuclear weapons are the highlights of this discourse which has effectively upheld the principle of distinction.

That resistance of the old principle against the challenges of modern technology may look like a miracle – but it is not. It is firmly grounded in a social and political reality, namely in value convictions prevailing in the international community. These convictions consider the principle as the necessary cornerstone of the protection of the human person even in times of armed conflict, a cornerstone which for the sake of the human person may not be given up.

3   **The Challenges of New Technologies: A Summary**

During the present symposium, the science and science fiction element of modern warfare technology will be explained in greater detail. But in order to elucidate some legal problems, a simplifying summary must be given first. The

NEW TECHNOLOGIES – NEW CHALLENGES FOR IHL?

basic technological innovation we have to deal with is a mixture of computer, space and telecommunication technologies:

- The dependence of both the military and civilian life on computer technology and in particular computer networks does not only create new opportunities, it also leads to a new vulnerability. Putting these computer systems out of action or causing their malfunction can constitute damage as serious as physical destruction, both for the military and for the civilian side. As a consequence, electronic attacks in various forms (e.g. infecting computers with viruses, worms, trojans) constitute a new type of acts harmful to the enemy.
- Computer, space and telecommunications technology provides new opportunities for long distance, tele-guided attacks. They facilitate a high degree of automation of attacks (e.g. the use of robots) which have a great potential to reduce the attackers risk of casualties.
- Computer, space and telecommunications technology provides unprecedented opportunities for collecting, digesting and distributing information. This is an opportunity which can and must be used for taking precautionary measures, making sure that attacks are only directed against military objectives and that excessive civilian damages are avoided. On the other hand, the reliability of the relevant information thus collected and used is often questionable.

4 The Principle of Distinction: Still an Appropriate Yardstick?

The essential question we have now to answer is the following: do the customary legal rules protecting the civilian population, i.e. the essence of the principle of distinction, provide adequate legal guidance for the use and non-use of these technologies? I will try to answer this question by browsing through the major relevant rules.

5 The Action: New Forms of Attacks, So-called Cyber Warfare

The first question arising is that of the object of the rules: AP I speaks of "attacks" which are prohibited or not, and this means, first of all, causing physical destruction of objects or bodily harm to persons. But are the rules limited to this kind of violent action? As to military objectives, energy transmission lines and telecommunication systems have always been considered as such because their use was essential for military action. Is there a difference in military significance between their physical destruction and depriving the military of their use by placing a worm into their computer system?

As to the damage to civilian life, there are clear indications in AP I that the harm to be avoided goes beyond physical destruction or immediate bodily harm. "Starvation" of the civilian population is prohibited. For that reason, the destruction of means essential for the survival of the population is prohibited *"for the purpose of denying them for their sustenance value to the civilian population"*. Similarly, Art. 55 prohibits the use of methods and means of warfare which may endanger *"the health or survival of the population"*. All this points to the rationale underlying the rules on the protection of the civilian population: they are not only concerned with physical destruction, but with preserving a minimum of living conditions for the civilian population. Any action which destroys or seriously damages the living conditions of the civilian population even without involving physical destruction is covered by the prohibitions protecting the civilian population. This is essential for an assessment of so-called cyber attacks.

6   The Actors: Combatants and Hackers

There is a high probability that such "attacks" are not, or at least not only, performed by members of the armed forces, who are combatants, but also by civilians acting with or without a mandate given by a State. It lies in the consequence of the interpretation of "attacks" just developed that the hacker is a civilian taking "a direct part in hostilities", i.e. loses his or her civilian immunity. In the light of the developing technology of targeted killing, this involves a serious risk.

7   The Target: Military Objectives in the Light of Technological Developments

In the light of the military significance of computer networks, many of them are military objectives, be they used by the military only, be they dual use networks. They may be attacks by electronic means, for instance, by infesting them with viruses, but the physical components of the networks, e.g. servers, may also be attacked.

The essential question which remains to be answered is what type of network constitutes a military objective? This qualification certainly applies to networks used by the Ministry of Defence or by an army to transmit relevant information to those actually fighting, for instance, designating targets in air warfare. But what about networks used for financial transactions of the military, in particular where this is a dual use network? Or is even the entire financial transaction system of a State (which could be shut down by a hacker) because of its military significance a military target – including, for instance, the computer centre of the Deutsche Bank in Eschborn near Frankfurt?

8 The Target: The New Vulnerability of a Computer-Dependent Society – New Dimensions of the Principle of Proportionality?

The dependence of life in modern civilization on an infrastructure relying on computer system involves a high degree of vulnerability. That vulnerability must in particular be taken into account when it comes to the application of the principle of proportionality. Shutting down computer systems may yield a high military advantage, but the risk of damage to the essential living conditions of the civilian population is also very high. This must be put on the civilian side on what is called the proportionality equation.

9 Targeting: Precautions in Preparing Attacks

It has been shown that new technologies create new risks for the victims of armed conflicts, but there are also potential benefits. Modern technology provides unprecedented opportunities to collect and transmit information. This is *inter alia* essential for the precautions which have to be taken in the preparation of attacks. Those deciding on an attack "shall do" "everything *feasible* to verify that the objectives to be attacked are neither civilian nor civilian objects". They shall take "all feasible precautions in the choice of methods and means of attack with a view to avoiding ... incidental loss of civilian life ...". The feasibility of such precautions has been greatly increased by modern technology. "*All feasible* precautions" means that a party having these possibilities must use them.

Not only in its own interest, but as a necessary part of obligatory precautionary measures, a party to a conflict must protect its information retrieval systems against outside manipulation and must make every feasible effort to ensure the reliability of relevant information.

These principles apply regardless of the technology which is used for attacking. They are of particular importance in the case of long distance, television-guided or automatically guided attacks. In the latter case, part of the decision-making in conducting an attack is delegated to a computer pro-gramme. The duty to take precautionary measures means in this case that the relevant data concerning target acquisition are fed into the programme to the effect that the principle of distinction is respected.

10 Essentials to Be Preserved

Playing science fiction in warfare involves a high temptation of concentrating on military advantages to be gained and to neglect the basic principle of dis-tinction which preserves the protection of the civilian population. Rousseau, 250 years ago, laid the basis for this principle as a rule of reason. As such, it has withstood serious challenges because of its primordial importance for the pro-tection of the human person. The basic rationale of modern law of armed con-flict must not be forgotten when more modern technologies are introduced into modern warfare. A sound interpretation of existing law can indeed main-tain the principle when we deal with developments of modern warfare which for some of us may be regarded as science fiction. The principle of distinction is not old-fashioned, it must not be modified, it can and must be applied in an appropriate way.

This should be the message of the present symposium.

15

De Facto Control of Land or Sea Areas

Its Relevance under the Law of Armed Conflict, in Particular Air and Missile Warfare

1   The Problem

The law of armed conflict has to take facts into account. Appropriate legal restraints on warfare must be based on the realities of a situation of war. While the law of peace defines the areas where States may act or must refrain from acting by reference to a right of jurisdiction (territorial jurisdiction, jurisdiction over sea areas defined by international law, exemptions from territorial jurisdiction, personal jurisdiction, etc.), the law of armed conflict most often must assign rights and duties on the basis of *de facto* control over areas and persons. The most telling example is the law of occupation: when one party to the conflict invades the territory of another and places that territory under its *de facto* control, the law of armed conflict cannot regard that control as a nullity because, under the law of peace, a State may not exercise any authority on a foreign territory without the consent of the territorial State. The law of armed conflict must take the very fact of control as a given and regulate the situation on the basis of this fact.

De facto control not only matters as far as 'control over areas' is concerned; it may often be decisive in relation to persons. Powers of command and control are, as a rule, established by law, but they may also be created (or set aside) by facts.

How is this control established or terminated in order to be relevant for specific questions arising under the law of armed conflict? In the context of the present article, the question has to be asked in particular whether the control over airspace or aerial superiority matters in this connection. This paper tries to exemplify the control over areas by addressing a few particular problems:
- the beginning and end of occupation,
- blockade,
- the rights and duties of relevant actors concerning humanitarian access,
- the right of medical aviation, and
- the threshold of non-international armed conflict.

© KONINKLIJKE BRILL NV, LEIDEN, 2021 | DOI:10.1163/9789004380592_017

There are few, if any, explicit rules of written law addressing these questions. Rules of treaty or customary law have to be interpreted, taking into account the practice of States.

As to control over persons, this paper addresses two issues, namely
– command responsibility, and
– control over multinational forces.

2   Beginning and End of Occupation

As an occupying power has a number of important rights and duties in relation to the occupied territory, the answer to the question of when that regime of occupation begins to apply and when it ends is crucial.

The relevant provisions dealing with that matter are Art. 42 and 43 of the Hague Regulations.[1] It is necessary to refer to the French text which is the only authoritative one:

> [Art .42 provides:] Un territoire est considéré comme occupé lorsqu'il se trouve place *de fait* sous l'autorité de l'armée ennemie ...
>
> [Art. 43 provides:] L'autorité de pouvoir legal ayant passé *de fait* entre les mains de l'occupant. ...[emphasis added]

It is generally agreed that this still is a valid formulation of the rule of customary law.[2] The relevant question for the beginning of occupation thus is whether an "authority" is *de facto* established. The occupation ends when it has *de facto* ceased to exist.

It is also generally agreed that this authority means effective *de facto* control.[3] The constituent elements of this effective control can be summarized as follows:[4]
– a non-consented physical military presence of the foreign power;
– the ability of the foreign power to exercise governmental functions; and
– the ability of the territorial sovereign to exercise such powers has disappeared.

---

1   Convention IV Respecting the Laws and Customs of War on Land, The Hague 18 October 1907, Annex: Regulations concerning the Laws and Customs of War on Land.

2   *See* T. Ferraro, "Determining the Beginning and End of an Occupation under International Humanitarian Law", Vol. 94, No. 885, *Int'l Rev. Red Cross* 133–163 (2012).

3   *Ibid.,* 139 *et seq.*

4   *Ibid.,* 143 *et seq.*

If, according to these criteria, a belligerent occupation exists, this entails a number of duties and certain rights of the Occupying Power. According to Art. 43 of the Hague Regulations, the Occupying Power is obliged to restore and ensure *"l'ordre et la vie publics".* This is possible only if the foreign presence has reached a certain degree of stability, which allows it to fulfil this responsibility. Thus, there can be an interval between the first military success of an invasion and the beginning of an occupation.[5]

The Hague Regulations formulate this rule as a rule of land warfare. Under the conditions of modern warfare, however, it is difficult to accept that the situation of air warfare is irrelevant in this connection. As the *de facto* control must possess a certain stability, it is more than doubtful whether this type of control is established if the positions of the invading army are still under permanent attack from the air. On the other hand, the necessary physical presence of the foreign force cannot be established through aerial superiority alone.

The criteria for the end of occupation, as a matter of principle, mirror those for the beginning of occupation.[6] Thus, an occupation would generally end with the withdrawal of the foreign forces. But a number of additional factual and legal considerations must be taken into account.

Despite a continued military presence of foreign military forces, the applicability of the law of occupation may cease because of a change in the legal situation. Belligerent occupation is a non-consented foreign military presence.[7] Where the State whose territory is occupied validly agrees to a foreign military presence, the rules concerning that presence are, at least primarily, governed by agreement, not by the law of belligerent occupation.[8] An example is the presence of foreign forces in Iraq since 2003. After the invasion by the U.S. led coalition, a belligerent occupation was established. Later in 2003, the newly established government of Iraq gave its agreement to the continued presence of the allied forces, which had invaded and occupied Iraq. In particular, as the Security Council gave its blessing to the new regime,[9] it should not be doubted that the agreement was valid and therefore capable of changing the legal regime of the foreign presence. It no longer was a belligerent occupation, but an

---

5 *See* M. Zwanenburg, M. Bothe, M. Sassóli, "Is the Law of Occupation Applicable in the Invasion Phase?" Vol. 94, No. 885 *Int'l Rev. Red Cross* 29–50 (2012).

6 *See* Ferraro, *supra* note 2, at 156 *et seq.*

7 *See* Ferraro, *supra* note 2, at 152 *et seq.*; *see also* E. Benvenisti, "Occupation, Belligerent', MN 1", R. Wolfrum, *Max Planck Encyclopedia of Pub. Int'l L.* (2009), online: http://opil.ouplaw.com/view/10.1093/law:epil/9780199231690/law9780199231690?rskey=jPng6v&result=1&prd=EPIL.

8 *See* Ferraro, *supra* note 2.

9 *See* Security Council resolutions 1511, 16 Oct. 2003, and 1546, 8 June 2004.

occupation based on agreement. This does not exclude that in the transition phase depending on the factual situation, certain rules of the law of occupation still apply.

The same effect cannot be attributed to every agreement concluded in respect of an occupied territory. Art. 48 GC IV expressly excludes such effect for an agreement concluded between the occupying power and the "authorities of the occupied territories", *i.e.* any local authority. An example of this situation is the occupation of Northern Cyprus by Turkey since 1974. Under the protection of the Turkish troops, the "Turkish Republic of Northern Cyprus" (TRNC) was proclaimed a State, but it was not recognized by any other State except Turkey. The TRNC consented to the presence of the Turkish troops. But the European Court of Human Rights held that this consent did not change the *de facto* control over the area, and that violations of human rights committed by the agents of the TRNC had to be imputed to Turkey.[10] The holding of the Court is explicitly relevant only for the question whether Turkey exercised in Northern Cyprus "jurisdiction" within the meaning of Art. 1 of the European Convention on Human Rights. But it follows from the reasoning of the Court that Turkey also exercised the kind of *de facto* control which is constitutive for the regime of belligerent occupation. In order to protect those who are subject and exposed to a *de facto* authority, the facts of the situation prevail over legal artefacts like imposed agreements. The population still is under the protection of the law of occupation.

A case of a completely different type, where the end or continuation of an occupation is particularly controversial, is the situation of the Gaze Strip after the Israeli withdrawal on the ground in 2005, the government of Israel considers that it has *de fact* relinquished control over the Gaza Strip and, thus, that the regime of occupation has been terminated as far as this area is concerned.[11] Yet Israel did not completely relinquish the relevant control over the Gaza Strip.[12] There are a number of elements which, taken together, are proof of a continued *de facto* control. First, the Gaza Strip cannot simply be separated

---

10   *See Loizidou v. Turkey (Preliminary Objections)*, no. 15318/89, ECHR (1995), at paras. 52–64; *see also Loizidou v. Turkey (Merits)*, no. 15318/89, ECHR (1996), at paras. 56 *et seq.*

11   Israel Ministry of Foreign Affairs, "The Operation in Gaza, 27 December 2008–18 January 2009: Factual and Legal Analysis" 11 (July 2009), online: www.jewishvirtuallibrary/org/source/.../GazaOpReport0708.pdf.

12   For a detailed analysis, *see* Y. Dinstein, *The International Law of Belligerent Occupation*, 276 (2009); *see also* R. Kolb & S. Vité, *Le droit de l'occupation militaire*, 177 (2009); S. Darcy & J. Reynolds, "An enduring Occupation: the Status of the Gaza Strip from the Perspective of International Humanitarian Law", 15 *J. Conflict Security L.* 211–243 (2010) (and particular at p. 227).

DE FACTO CONTROL OF LAND OR SEA AREAS

from the rest of the occupied territory, namely the West Bank. Under the Oslo Interim Agreement, both Israel and the Palestinian Authority view the West Bank and the Gaza Strip as a single territorial unit.[13] Despite the takeover by Hamas in 2007, this is still the view of the Palestinian Authority. Second, the Gaza Strip is under a kind of constant siege. The airspace is *de facto* and *de jure* controlled by Israel.[14] Maritime activities are also severely restricted and monitored by Israel.[15] The land border with Israel are fenced off and access or exit is only possible through Israeli controlled checkpoints. Over long periods, Egypt had also closed its border with the Gaza Strip. Third, the experience has shown that Israel has the military power to re-enter the territory by military force. All these elements taken together show that Israel has sufficient *de facto* control to justify the conclusion that it still is the occupying power, with the ensuing responsibilities for the welfare of the population. Even the Supreme Court of Israel does not completely share the view of the Israeli Government. It construes a kind of post-occupation responsibility of Israel,[16] a construction qualified as "plainly absurd" by Prof. Dinstein.[17] Therefore, many authors[18] and relevant organs of the United Nations[19] are of the view that the remaining control is enough to fulfill the conditions of The Hague Regulations and that, therefore, Israel still has the responsibilities of an occupying power. One author rightly describes the situation as an occupation *longa manu*.[20]

As to the question that is particularly relevant in the present context, namely whether control over the airspace matter, it must be concluded that this control alone is not enough in order to establish an effective control in the sense of the law of occupation. But, in relation to the particular situation of the Gaza Strip, control over the airspace is an important element of the overall *de facto* control retained by Israel.

---

13 *See* Art. XI (1) of the Israeli-Palestinian Interim Agreement on the West Band and the Gaza Strip, 28 Sept. 1995, 36 *ILM* 551 (1997).

14 *See* Art XIII (4) Annex I to the Interim Agreement.

15 *See* Art. XIV Annex I to the Interim Agreement.

16 *See Bassiouni Ahmed v. Prime Minister of Israel*, HCJ 9132/07 (2008), online: http://elyon1.court.gov.il/files_eng/07/320/091/n25/07091320m25.pdf.

17 *See* Y. Dinstein, *supra* note 12, at 279.

18 For the numerous references *see* S. Darcy & J. Reynolds, *supra* note 12, at 223; *see also* Y. Dinstein and R. Kolb & S. Vité, *supra* note 12; *contra* B. Rubin, "Disengagement from the Gaza Strip and Post-Occupation Duties", 42 *Isr. L. Rev.* 528–563 (2009), (in particular at pp. 534 *et seq.*).

19 *See* Security Council Resolution 1860, 8 January 2009; General Assembly Resolution 63/96, 18 December 2008; Human Rights Council, Resolution S-9/1, 12 January 2009.

20 *See* Kolb & Vité, *supra* note 12, at 179.

3   Blockade

The law of naval or aerial blockade raises issues of *de facto* control which are to a certain degree comparable to those relating to belligerent occupation and are often compared.[21] The blockade is a means of maritime and/or air warfare by which the access to specific enemy ports, airfields or coastal areas is barred for the ships or aircraft of all nations.

A blockade must be effective. The question whether a blockade is effective is a question of fact.[22]

This requires a sufficient degree of *de facto* control of ingress and egress. A blockading force must be "of such a strength or nature that there is a high probability that ingress to and egress from a blockaded area will be detected and prevented by the Blockading Party".[23]

The *San Remo Manual* apparently starts from the assumption that a naval blockade is enforced and maintained by means of a naval fleet. That fleet may however be stations at a distance[24] (long distance blockade) and any means of warfare not otherwise unlawful under the law of armed conflict may be used to enforce it.[25] This includes aircraft also in case of a naval blockade.[26] Whether control by air alone is sufficient is another question. In relation to an aerial blockade, the *HPCR Manual* requires "a sufficient degree of air superiority" for the blockade to be considered as effective.[27]

4   Rights and Duties of Relevant Actors Concerning Humanitarian Access

In relation to the question of humanitarian access to victims of armed conflicts which are in need, the question of factual or physical control matters

---

21   *See* Darcy & Reynolds, *supra* note 12, at 219 *et seq.*

22   *See San Remo Manual on International Law Applicable to Armed Conflicts at Sea,* Art. 93 (L. Doswald-Beck ed., 1995) (the "*San Remo Manual*"). *See also HPCR Manual on International Law Applicable to Air and Missile Warfare,* Art. 151 (Program on Humanitarian Policy and Conflict Research at Harvard University, 2009) (the "*HPCR Manual*").

23   *See Commentary on the HPCR Manual on International Law applicable to Air and Missile Warfare* 291 (Program on Humanity Policy and Conflict Research at Harvard University 2010)(the "*Commentary*").

24   *See San Remo Manual,* at Art. 96; *see also HPCR Manual,* at Art. 152.

25   *See San Remo Manual,* at Art. 97; *see also HPCR Manual,* at Art. 153(a).

26   *See Commentary, supra* note 23, at 287.

27   *See HPCR Manual,* at Art. 154.

concerning the requirement of consent for relief operations. The question which has to be answered in this connection is whether the control of the airspace, or a sufficient degree of air superiority qualify as control in this sense which triggers the consent requirement.

The first provision which has to be analysed in this respect is Art. 23 GC IV which establishes the duty of "Each High Contracting Party" to allow the "free passage" of certain relief consignments. The provision is very open as to the question of which "High Contracting Party" may in particular be so obliged. The key notion is that of "passage". It implies that the consignment passes through an area controlled by a Contracting Party, be it friend or foe. J. Pictet, the authoritative commentator of the Conventions, does not address the issue, but mentions a particular problem which the provision was designed to solve, namely the fate of a population suffering from a "blockade".[28] This implies the control of sea areas is also envisaged by the provision. The concept of "siege" is not mentioned, but after the then (1949) recent experience of the siege of Leningrad, for instance, it must be assumed that this is meant as well, *i.e.* the *de facto* control of a land area around a "besieged" location.

What does *de facto* control mean in this context? To what extent does aerial superiority count? An example to be discussed is the relief for Biafra during the secession was in Nigeria between 1967 and 1970. The status of this armed conflict is controversial. But even the Nigerian government, when it argued about the applicable law, did so on the basis of the rules applicable in international armed conflict.[29] Two phases of the conflict must be distinguished: until May 1968 when Biafra still had access to the sea through its harbour at Port Harcourt, and the time after that date, when Port Harcourt was conquered by the Federal Army and Biafra became completely landlocked. Before May 1968, there was a naval blockade of Port Harcourt. After that date, Biafra was completely surrounded by land area controlled by the Federal Government. The population was starving and desperate attempts were made by humanitarian organizations to provide relief from the outside. The negotiations between the ICRC and the Federal Governments were essentially conducted on the basis of the conditions of relief provided for in Art. 23 GC IV.[30] The problem was that the Biafran Government did not want to accept relief subject to the conditions which the Federal Government was entitled to impose under that provision. It is submitted that requiring supervised day flights (this was

---

28   *See Les Convention de Genève du 12 août 1949, Commentaire,* Vol. IV, 195 (J. Pictet ed., 1956).

29   For an analysis, *see* M. Bothe, "Article 3 and Protocol II: Case Studies of Nigeria and El Salvador", 31 *Am. U. L. Rev.* 899–925 (1982).

30   *Ibid.*

the Nigerian Government's condition) is a "technical arrangement" which the besieging party is allowed to require. The government of Biafra, however, insisted on unsupervised night flights. The ICRC discontinued its flights, while other organizations tried to carry on. A plane chartered by these humanitarian organizations was shot down by the Nigerian air force in 1969. It must be concluded that at any time during the conflict, the Federal Government of Nigeria possessed a degree of *de facto* control, consisting of an effective naval blockade, control over land and aerial supremacy which entitled it to impose the technical conditions mentioned in Art. 23.

The right of access for humanitarian relief was greatly improved by the Additional Protocols of 1977. Concerning international armed conflicts, Art. 70 AP I reads in its essential parts:

If the civilian population of any territory under the control of a Party to the conflict ... is not adequately provided with [essential] supplies, relief actions which are humanitarian and impartial in character ... *shall be undertaken, subject to the agreement* of the Parties concerned in such relief actions. [Emphasis added][31]

The provision does not require the consent of the (*i.e.* all) parties to the conflict, but only that of Parties "concerned in such relief actions". The parties concerned are those providing relief, allowing transit of relief and receiving relief. The latter can only be the party or parties in physical control; as a rule military control of the area of destination. The other party does not have the right to prevent a relief action by refusing an agreement to an action, which does not physically touch its sphere of control.[32] It is not "concerned". The requirement of consent serves the legitimate interests of the parties "concerned". Parties having no physical contact with a relief action have no legitimate interest in the matter.

The notion of control which is essential in this context, means physical control, *i.e.* military domination excluding the other party(ies). It must reflect the realities of a military situation and has nothing to do with any legal claim to control or to exercise jurisdiction. In the context of this paper, it has to be asked whether and to what extent aerial superiority matters? Is control over airspace equivalent to territorial control? The answer can only be "no, but. ...

---

31   *See* Protocol Additional to the Geneva Conventions of 12 August 1949, and Relating to the Protection of Victims of International Armed Conflicts (Protocol I), 1977, 1125 *U.N.T.S.* Art. 70.

32   *See* M. Bothe, *New Rules for Victims of Armed Conflicts,* (2nd ed.) 484 (M. Bothe, K. Josef Partsch & W. A. Solf eds., 2013); *see also* Y. Sandoz, *COmmentaire des Protocoles additionnels,* 841 (Y. Sandoz, C. Swinarksi & B. Zimmermann eds., 1986).

DE FACTO CONTROL OF LAND OR SEA AREAS

" To require the consent of a party to the conflict only because the relief operation takes place within the reach of its bomber planes would overstretch the legal consent requirement. But a relief operation undertaken under these conditions remains risky, yet protected as any civilian (!) activity on hostile territory.

In the case of a non-international armed conflict, the situation is somewhat more complicated. The Diplomatic Conference which negotiated the two Protocols Addition to the Geneva Conventions 1974–77 had in a first phase adopted a provision on relief in a non-international armed conflict similar to the one applicable in the international armed conflicts, just described. The requirement of consent related to the "party or parties concerned".[33] This meant that, as in the case of an international armed conflict, that the agreement was required of any party which physically controlled an area where the relief was distributed or through which it had to pass- whether or not this was a State of a non-State party. Yet, in the final phase, that text became "subject to the agreement of the High Contracting Party concerned". Whether this extends the consent requirement to a situation where relief does not pass through territory controlled by the governmental party is subject to a controversy not to be decided in this paper. Yet the requirement of the consent of the non-State party disappeared, and with that any reference to *de facto* control triggering the consent requirement. But to disregard that consent requirement is unrealistic, even dangerous. It would be an attempt to neglect the basic principle which should be highlighted by this paper, namely that international humanitarian law has to balance the interests at stake on the basis of the factual situation, not on the basis of legal claims not implemented in fact. Yet this development of the text of AP II is typical for the process of redrafting and curtailing the Protocol in the last phase of the Diplomatic Conference.[34] Hollow political claims of State sovereignty were valued higher than a workable protection of the victims of non-international armed conflicts based on a realistic assessment of the requirements of this conflict situation.

International legal doctrine tries to solve this problem by saying that the agreement of the relevant non-State party is necessary at least as a practical requirement.[35] This is certainly correct, but from the point of view of law, it is not satisfactory. The law should respond to the factual necessities of a conflict situation. In light of this deficiency of treaty law, a closer look at customary law is all the more important. The ICRC Customary Law Study indeed clearly states

---

33   For an analysis *see* Bothe, *supra* note 32, at 801.

34   *See* Partsch & Bothe, *supra* note 32, at 695 *et seq.*

35   *See* Bothe, *supra* note 32, at 801.

that the requirement of consent, and the corresponding duty not to refuse it, applies to all parties "concerned", be it in international or non-international armed conflicts.[36]

This triggers a further question of *de facto* control, namely that of the relevant non-State party whose consent must be sought. In situations of multi-party non-international armed conflicts like the ones in Syria, Libya or Lebanon, this may be far from clear. The relevant party is the one which exercises a *de facto* control over areas where a relief goods have to pass or where they are to be distributed. If a party claims to be able to implement international humanitarian law, it must provide some possibility of liaison through which agreement may be asked and granted.

5   The Refime of Medical Aviation

In relation to the regime of medical aviation, the question of factual control matters because different situations of control entail different requirements for the protection of medical flights.

Medical flights over an area "physically controlled" by the party to which the aircraft belongs or by its allies, or over sea areas not controlled by any party, do not require the consent of the opposing party.[37] Flights over areas "physically controlled" by the latter party require its consent,[38] and in the case of flights over the "contact zone", protection of the medical aircraft can only be effective on the basis of an agreement with the other side. This differentiation was chosen in order to adequately balance the various interests at stake in different factual situations.[39] Preference is given to the interest of protecting the medical aircraft if it flies in areas where it cannot really affect the security interest of the other party. The security interest prevails, however, if the aircraft flies over an area controlled by the opposing party. In this situation, protection is therefore dependent on prior agreement. Because the interests to be accommodated really depend on the facts of the situation, "control" can only mean factual control regardless of the legal status of the area in questions.[40] This conclusion is confirmed by a look at the reference to sea areas in AP I. If

---

36   *See* J. M. Henckaerts & L. Doswald-Beck, *Customary International Humanitarian Law*, Vol. I, 197 (2005).

37   *See* HPCR *Manual*, Art. 25 AP I, sec. 77 AMW Manual.

38   *See* HPCR *Manual*, Art. 27 AP I, sec 78(a); *see also San Remo Manual*, Art. 180.

39   *See* Bothe, *supra* note 32, at 170 *et seq.*

40   *See* Sandoz, *supra* note 32, at 288.

sea areas, regardless of the question of whether they are jurisdictional waters or high seas, are "physically controlled" by an adverse party, the protection of medical flights depend on its prior consent.[41]

The notion of control, it is submitted, refers to control over the earth surface (land and sea). Control over the airspace or aerial superiority is a different matter. But the differentiation according to the control on the surface provides a relatively clear criterion. This should not be blurred by a reference to relative air power. However, control over airspace also is a relevant reality. Therefore, Art. 25 AP I *in fine* recommends[42] a notification of flights which might operate within the reach of the other party's surface-to-air weapons systems. It is submitted that the same would apply in a situation where the adverse party has aerial superiority over an area physically controlled on the ground by the party operating the flight.

6 The Threshold of Non-International Armed Conflicts

The notion of control also plays a role concerning the definition of the non-international armed conflict falling within the scope of application of AP II.

Concerning the non-governmental party or parties, Art. 1 para. 1 AP II requires that they "exercise such control over part of [the State's] territory as to enable them to carry out sustained and concerted military operations and to implement [AP II]". What is meant here is *de facto* control over some territory which has a certain extent and stability. For otherwise, the non-State party in question would not be able to implement the Protocol. For example, the non-governmental party must be in a position to care for the wounded and sick and to grant prisoners a decent treatment.[43] As in the case of occupation[44] the degree or intensity of control required to trigger a specific status is a function of the substantive content of that status.

7 Command Responsibility and Multinational Forces

The notion of control also plays a role in relation to persons. That control entails certain responsibilities. And, while control is established by legal acts, *de facto* control also matters.

---

41 *See* Protocol I, *supra* note 31, at Art. 27.
42 *See* Bothe, *supra* note 32, at 173.
43 *See* W.H. Boothby, *Conflict Law*, 30 (2014).
44 *Supra* note 5.

The first example if command responsibility (Art. 87 AP I). *De facto* control determines the scope of that responsibility. The responsibility of commanders not only relates to his or her military subordinates, but also to "other persons under their control". The text does not really specify what type of control is meant. The Commentary[45] suggest that it is, *inter alia*, the *de facto* control which a military commander may possess in an occupied territory. But the core meaning of control pursuant to Art. 87 AP I and the corresponding provision of the ICC Statute (Art. 28 para 1) is that of a power of command over subordinates, which is not necessarily established by law, but is effective due to the facts of a given situation. Command responsibility applies to all persons which *de facto* act under the authority of a certain military commander. Such persons engage the responsibility of the commander and therefore the responsibility of the State of institution to which the commander belongs. It is in this sense that command responsibility has been construed by the ICTY in a number of cases.[46]

The notion of effective control is of particular importance in the case of multinational forces belonging to international organizations, in particular UN peacekeeping forces. These forces are as a rule composed of military contingents retaining a national identity. Whether acts or omissions of these national contingents engage the international responsibility of the organization or that of the participating State depends on the existence of "effective control".[47] The effective control of the organization is as a rule established by a legal act, usually by an agreement between the organization and the participating State. But *de facto* control also matters. In the *Srebrenica* case,[48] for example the Dutch Supreme Court held that as a rule, effective control over the Dutch peacekeeping contingent would be transferred to the United Nations by virtue of the agreement concerning its participation with UNPROFOR. But, the Judgment provided:

---

45 *See* J. de Preux, in Sandoz, Swinarski, & Zimmermann, *supra* note 32, at 1044.

46 *See Prosecutor v. Delalić,* Case IT-96-21-A, Appeals Chamber, 20 Feb. 2001, 40 *ILM* 630 (2001), at 669; *Prosecutor v. Blaskić,* Case IT-95-14-T, Trial Chamber, 3 March 2000, para. 612; *Prosecutor v. Aleksovski,* Case IT-95-14/1-T, Trial Chamber, 25 June 1999, para 106.

47 Art. 7 of the Articles on the responsibility of international organizations for internationally wrongful acts: "The conduct of an organ of a State ... that is placed at the disposal of [an] international organization shall be considered under international law an act of the ... organization if the latter exercises *effective control* over that conduct" (emphasis added); *see also* M. Bothe, "Peacekeeping", MN 19 and 28, *The Charter of the United Nations. A Commentary,* 1171 – 1199 (B. Simma, *et al.* eds., 3rd ed. 2012).

48 Supreme Court of the Netherlands, *Netherlands v. Nuhanović,* Judgment of 6 September 2013, 53 ILM 516 (2014).

the context in which Dutchbat's disputed conduct took place differs in one important respect from the normal situation in which troops made available by a State function under the command of the United Nations. ... During this transitional period not only the United Nations but also the Dutch government in The Hague had control over Dutchbat and also exercised this in practice ... The Court of Appeal's ruling that the State had effective control over the conduct of which Dutchbat and hence the State as well are accused by Nuhanović does not reveal an incorrect interpretation or application of the law on the concept of effective control.[49]

It has to be emphasized that in this case, the circumstance triggering international responsibility was control exercised *de facto*. This was held to prevail over the control transferred by law to the United Nations which, however, could not exercise it in practice. This is a legal construction inspired by the need to protect victims, *i.e.* by considerations of legitimacy.

It was a fundamental error of the European Court of Human Rights that it neglected this simple truth in its decision in the *Behrami/Saramati* case.[50] In relation to KFOR, it assigned to the United Nations a control which it did not possess, neither *de facto* nor *de jure*, and discarded the control which the participating States had both in fact and in law. It thus denied the responsibility of the participating States and left the individual, whose rights had allegedly been infringed by KFOR, without a remedy.[51]

8 Conclusions

It has been shown that under international humanitarian law, the existence of a *de facto* control matters in a number of contexts. Although these contexts differ, there is a kind of red thread leading through these issues: international humanitarian law has to balance the military and civilian protective interests on the basis of the facts of a particular situation. The basic fact on which this paper has focused is physical control over certain areas of land or sea. The law assigns certain rights and duties to the State (or other entity) possessing

---

49   *Supra* note 48, at Sec. 3.12.2 and 3.12.3.

50   *See Behrami v. France,* no. 71412/09 ECHR (2007), and *Saramati v. France, Germany and Norway,* [GC], no. 78166/09, ECHR (2007).

51   For a critique *see, inter alia,* G. Hafner, "The ECHR torn between the United Nations and the States. The Behrami and Saramati Case", *Frieden in Freiheit – Peace in Liberty,* 102–121 (A. Fischer-Lescano *et al.* eds., 2008).

such control: the responsibility of the occupying power, the right to enforce a blockade, the right to control humanitarian relief operations, and the rights and duties of a non-state party to an AP II type conflict. The degree of control required may vary from issue to issue. There can be different answers to the question of how effective is effective. It has also been shown that the facts of control also matter where the issue is control over the conduct of persons. "Effective" control triggers an international responsibility.

In this connection, it is useful to point out that the degree of control required may be a function of the substantive content of the legal regime concerned. An occupying power must in able to fulfil its obligations under Art. 43 of the Hague Regulations. Therefore, the degree of *de facto* control which triggers a regime of belligerent occupation must be as substantial as to allow the party in question to fulfil these obligations. A party to a non-international armed conflict must be able to implement the applicable rules of the law of non-international armed conflict. This determines the scope of control required. In determining whether such *de facto* control exists and entails relevant consequences, air power matters in a number of instances, but it is not exclusively decisive.

This points to a general problem of interpretation of law and facts not only in international humanitarian law. International humanitarian law has to rely on certain broad notions. The most prominent example is proportionality. Procedures allowing a concretization of such notion in specific cases, for instance negotiation or adjudication, are necessary. This also applies where the task is to solve the uncertainties involved in the determination of what is "effective control".

The International Committee of the Red Cross and the Additional Protocols of 1977

1 The History of the Additional Protocols of 1977

It is the traditional role of the International Committee of the Red Cross (ICRC) to prepare draft treaties for the purpose of developing international humanitarian law (IHL), in particular by filling regulatory loopholes.[1] In doing so, it tried in particular to address regulatory insufficiencies which had become apparent in recent conflicts. In this spirit, the four Geneva Conventions of 1949 (GC)[2] were a reaction to the experiences of World War II and conflicts which had happened before that war, in particular the Spanish Civil War. But the four Conventions left aside one crucial area of the law of armed conflict which had been violated during the war – to an extent that one could think it had become obsolete – namely the law relating to the conduct of hostilities[3] and the protection of the civilian population against the harmful effects of hostilities.[4] The ICRC was well aware of this and its efforts did not cease with the end of the 1949 Conference.

At the XIXth International Red Cross Conference held in New Delhi in 1957, the ICRC submitted the *Draft Rules for the Limitation of the Dangers incurred by the Civilian Population in Time of War*, the so-called Delhi Rules.[5] At the

---

1 J. Pictet, 'General Introduction' in Y. Sandoz, C. Swinarski and B. Zimmermann (eds.), *ICRC Commentary on the Additional Protocols of 8 June 1977 to the Geneva Conventions of 12 August 1949* (Geneva: Martinus Nijhoff Publishers, 1987), pp. xxix–xxxv, p. xxix; M. Bothe and K. J. Partsch, 'General Introduction and Guide to Documentation' in M. Bothe, K. J. Partsch and W. A. Solf, *New Rules for Victims of Armed Conflicts, Commentary on the Two 1977 Protocols Additional to the Geneva Conventions of 1949* 2nd ed., reprint revised by M. Bothe (The Hague/Boston/London: Martinus Njihoff Publishers, 2015), pp. 1–16, pp. 1 *et seq.*

2 The four Geneva Conventions of 12August 1949 for the Protection of War Victims, Geneva, 12 August 1949, in force 21 October 1950, 75 UNTS.

3 Pictet, 'General Introduction', note 1, p. xxix.

4 ICRC, Foreword to the Final Act of the Diplomatic Conference of Geneva of 1974–1977, www.icrc.org/applic/ihl/ihl.nsf/Treaty.xsp?documentId=D7D9F26C38F99332C12563CD002D6C-B8&action=openDocument; E. Crawford, 'Geneva Conventions Additional Protocol I (1977)' in R.Wolfrum (ed.), *TheMax Planck Encyclopedia of Public International Law* (Oxford: Oxford University Press, May 2011), www.mpepil.com, MN 3.

5 ICRC, Draft Rules for the Limitation of the Dangers incurred by the Civilian Population in Time of War (Geneva, September 1956), www.icrc.org/ihl/INTRO/420.

374   PART 4: THE LAW OF ARMED CONFLICT – GENERAL QUESTIONS

Conference, they became the object of major controversies, in particular regarding the (il)legality of nuclear weapons.[6] The Delhi Rules *inter alia* encompassed provisions, protecting the civilian population from the destructive force of newly developed weapons, accounting for the rapid technological advance.[7] Article 14 (1) of the Delhi Rules was seen as a reprobation of nuclear weapons, on which agreement at the time was not possible.[8] The conference ultimately did not adopt the Rules, but only took note of them and requested the ICRC to submit them, together with the amendments which had been proposed, to governments. The ICRC did as requested but did not receive a response. Nevertheless, the Delhi Rules had an impact on the ensuing development. Many provisions finally adopted in the 1977 Protocols additional to the Geneva Conventions resemble the corresponding provisions of the Delhi Rules.[9]

The ICRC continued its effort in adopting new resolutions at the XXth and XXIst International Conferences of the Red Cross, held in Vienna in 1965 and Istanbul in 1969. In 1965, Resolution XXVIII was adopted, which contained four principles relating to the 'Protection of the Civilian Populations Against the Dangers of Indiscriminate Warfare' and which urged 'the ICRC to pursue the development of International Humanitarian Law'.[10]

In addition, a number of events made the development of IHL more urgent. It appeared to be especially important to strengthen the protection of victims of non-international armed conflicts (NIAC) beyond the scope of

---

6   Bothe and Partsch, 'General Introduction and Guide to Documentation', note 1, p. 2; Pictet, 'General Introduction', note 1, p. xxix; J. Pokstefl and M. Bothe, 'Bericht über Entwicklungen und Tendenzen des Kriegsrechts seit den Nachkriegskodifikationen', *Zeitschrift für ausländisches öffentliches Recht und Völkerrecht*, 35 (1975), pp. 574–640, p. 575.

7   ICRC, Foreword to the Draft Rules for the Limitation of the Dangers incurred by the Civilian Population in Time of War (Geneva, September 1956), www.icrc.org/ihl/INTRO/420.

8   'Without prejudice to the present or future prohibition of certain specific weapons, the use is prohibited of weapons whose harmful effects – resulting in particular from the dissemination of incendiary, chemical, bacteriological, radioactive or other agents – could spread to an unforeseen degree or escape, either in space or in time, from the control of those who employ them, thus endangering the civilian population'; C. Pilloud and J. Pictet, 'Protocol I – Part IV, Section 1' in Y. Sandoz, C. Swinarski and B. Zimmermann (eds.), *ICRC Commentary on the Additional Protocols of 8 June 1977 to the Geneva Conventions of 12 August 1949* (Geneva: Martinus Nijhoff Publishers, 1987), pp. 585–804, p. 590.

9   M. Bothe, K. Ipsen and K. J. Partsch, 'Die Genfer Konferenz über humanitäres Völkerrecht', *Zeitschrift für ausländisches und öffentliches Recht und Völkerrecht*, 38 (1978), pp. 1–159, p. 40.

10   Bothe and Partsch, 'General Introduction and Guide to Documentation', note 1, p. 2; Pictet, 'General Introduction', p. xxx; ICRC, Final Act of the Diplomatic Conference of Geneva of 1974–1977,www.icrc.org/applic/ihl/ihl.nsf/Treaty.xsp?documentId =D7D9F26C38F99332C12563CD002D6CB8&action=openDocument.

THE RED CROSS AND THE ADDITIONAL PROTOCOLS OF 1977   375

Common Article 3 GC.[11] Coinciding with the rapidly rising number of NIAC was a proportional increase of the civilian participation therein.[12] Moreover, the techniques of these new participants were unconventional, as they utilized guerrilla tactics.[13] Furthermore, the interest in the law of armed conflicts was reinvigorated in the mid-1960s by a number of armed conflicts which split world opinion,[14] such as the conflicts in Vietnam,[15] the Middle East[16] and the struggles against colonial and alien domination and racist regimes, the so-called wars of national liberation.[17] All this provided an impetus for further development of IHL.

An additional driving force came from the concern for human rights.[18] The UN International Conference on Human Rights, convened 1968 in Teheran, marked an important starting point, since it lead to the adoption of Resolution 2444 (1969) by the General Assembly, affirming the need for basic human rights to be applied in all armed conflicts.[19] In the following years, a competition developed between the Red Cross (ICRC and Red Cross Movement) and the UN, relating to leadership in the process of developing the relevant legal rules.[20] The problems of specific political situations mainly sought their forum in the UN. But the ICRC, submitting a wealth of thoughtful material to the international community, with the support of Switzerland as depositary of the Geneva Conventions, managed to retain its leadership role. The ICRC, so to say,

---

11   ICRC, Foreword to Additional Protocol (II) to the Geneva Conventions (1977), www.icrc.org/applic/ihl/ihl.nsf/Treaty.xsp?documentId=AA0C5BCBAB5C4A85C-12563CD002D6D09&action=openDocument (ICRC, Foreword AP II).

12   According to the ICRC about 80 per cent of the victims of armed conflicts since 1945 have been victims of NIAC and NIAC are often fought more cruelly than international conflicts; ICRC, Foreword AP II.

13   Crawford, 'Geneva Conventions Additional Protocol I (1977)', note 4, MN 3.

14   *Ibid.*; Bothe and Partsch, 'General Introduction and Guide to Documentation', note 1, p. 2.

15   The Vietnam Conflict raised in particular questions regarding the rules concerning the conduct of hostilities and the status of 'irregular' fighters.

16   Especially the problem of human rights in occupied territories, e.g. the occupied Palestinian territories, Bothe and Partsch, 'General Introduction and Guide to Documentation', note 1, pp. 2 *et seq.*

17   D.W. Glazier, 'Wars of National Liberation' in MPEPIL, note 4, MN 1.

18   Crawford, 'Geneva Conventions Additional Protocol II (1977)', note 4, MN 5; S. Junod, 'General Introduction to the Commentary on Protocol II' in MPEPIL, note 4, *ICRC Commentary*, note 1, pp. 1319–1336, pp. 1326 *et seq.*

19   *Ibid.*

20   R. R. Baxter, 'Humanitarian Law or Humanitarian Politics? The 1974 Diplomatic Conference on Humanitarian Law', *Harvard International Law Journal* 16 (1975), pp. 1–26, 5 *et seq.*

376 PART 4: THE LAW OF ARMED CONFLICT – GENERAL QUESTIONS

had the better ideas. An essential step was the submission of eight volumes of material submitted to the Red Cross Conference 1969 in Istanbul.[21]

2 The Diplomatic Conference on the Reaffirmation and Development of International Humanitarian Law Applicable in Armed Conflicts in Geneva from 1974 to 1977: Preparation and Main Results

Similar to the procedure before the 1949 conference, the ICRC convened and serviced two *Conferences of Government Experts on the Reaffirmation and Development of International Humanitarian Law Applicable in Armed Conflicts* in Geneva from 24 May to 12 June 1971 and from 3 May to 3 June 1972 to which it presented its proposals and ideas.[22] About forty government delegations attended the first conference.[23] The ICRC did not present a draft to the experts, but a list of the most important problems of humanitarian law.[24] The second session comprised more than 400 experts sent by 77 governments, most of them from Western Countries.[25] The main issues submitted to the Conference were for example methods and means of warfare, especially new forms of warfare like guerrilla warfare and the protection of the civilian population against the dangers of hostilities as well as a better protection of the victims of NIAC.[26] Subsequently, in 1973 the ICRC published two draft Protocols additional to the Geneva Conventions, one relating to international, the other to NIAC and sent them to all governments, accompanied by a commentary.[27]

---

21 XXIe Conférence internationale de la Croix-Rouge, ICRC 'In the Red Cross worldwide', *International Review of the Red Cross*, 51 (1969), 589; Bothe and Partsch, 'General Introduction and Guide to Documentation', p. 3.

22 Bothe and Partsch, 'General Introduction and Guide to Documentation', note 1, p. 3; Pictet, 'General Introduction', note 1, p. xxxi.

23 ICRC, *Draft Protocols additional to the Geneva Conventions of 12 August 1949, Commentary* (Geneva: ICRC, 1973), p. 1.

24 Junod, 'General Introduction to the Commentary on Protocol II', in ICRC Commentary, note 1, p. 1327.

25 Bothe and Partsch, 'General Introduction and Guide to Documentation', note 1, p. 3; Pictet, 'General Introduction', p. xxxi; H. Frick, 'Ein neues Kapitel im humanitären Kriegsvölkerrecht? Zwei Zusatzprotokolle zu den Vier Genfer Rotkreuzkonventionen kurz vor der Verabschiedung', *Vereinte Nationen*, 24 (1976), pp. 178–184, p. 180.

26 Bothe and Partsch, 'General Introduction and Guide to Documentation', note 1, pp. 3 *et seq.*

27 ICRC, *Draft Protocols additional to the Geneva Conventions of 12 August 1949, Commentary*; Bothe and Partsch, 'General Introduction and Guide to Documentation', note 1, p. 4; Pictet, 'General Introduction', note 1, p. xxxi.

THE RED CROSS AND THE ADDITIONAL PROTOCOLS OF 1977

Thus, the ICRC handed the texts over to the States and their decision-making power.[28]

The two draft Protocols constituted the basic working documents for the *Diplomatic Conference on the Reaffirmation and Development of International Humanitarian Law Applicable in Armed Conflicts* (CDDH) from 1974 to 1977 in Geneva.[29] The CDDH was convened and organized by the Swiss government and all States which were parties to the Geneva Conventions or members of the United Nations were invited.[30] All in all 155 nations attended, 11 national liberation movements and 51 intergovernmental or non-governmental organizations participated as observers, so that the total number of delegates ranged around 700.[31] The Conference held four sessions from 1974 to 1977.[32] The first meeting was from 20 February to 29 March 1974, the second from 3 February to 18 April 1975, the third from 21 April to 11 June 1976 and the fourth from 17 March to 10 June 1977.[33] The number of the participating States varied from 107 to 124 in the various sessions.[34] The Conference was subdivided into three *Main Committees*, one *Ad hoc Committee* on 'conventional weapons',[35] all four committees of the whole. In addition, there were a Credentials Committee, a Drafting Committee, and a General Committee as well as numerous working groups.[36]

Although the preparatory conferences just mentioned provided a broad input from all parts of the world, the conceptual work of the ICRC was the decisive foundation for the elaboration of these two treaties. A major conceptual and political point was that the conference was only tasked with the development and confirmation. There could not be any revision or retrogression. The text of the Conventions had to be left intact.[37] This sometimes resulted in difficult drafting problems and makes several elements of the text difficult

---

28   Pictet, 'General Introduction', note 1, p. xxxii.

29   Bothe and Partsch, 'General Introduction and Guide to Documentation', p. 4.

30   Pictet, 'General Introduction', note 1, pp. xxxii *et seq.*

31   *Ibid.*, p. xxxiii.

32   Bothe and Partsch, 'General Introduction andGuide toDocumentation', note 1, p. 4; Pictet, 'General Introduction', note 1, p. xxxii.

33   *Ibid.*

34   *Ibid.*, p. xxxiii.

35   The special designation as 'Ad hoc Committee' reflects the unwillingness of a great number of States to negotiate at the Conference the prohibition of specific weapons. The report adopted by that Committee later was an important basis for the UN Conference on Conventional Weapons in 1980.

36   Bothe and Partsch, 'General Introduction and Guide to Documentation', note 1, pp. 4 *et seq.*

37   Bothe and Partsch, 'General Introduction and Guide to Documentation', note 1, p. 6 *et seq.*

378   PART 4: THE LAW OF ARMED CONFLICT – GENERAL QUESTIONS

to read and understand. The two Protocols were finally adopted by consensus on 8 June 1977.[38] The representatives of 102 States and of 3 National Liberation Movements signed the Final Act on 10 June 1977.[39]

3   ICRC Leadership: The Procedures of the CDDH

The Conference was convened by the Swiss Federal Council.[40] The Head of the Political Department (as it then was) was the President of Conference. Nevertheless, the day-to-day impact of the team of the ICRC was essential. ICRC representatives were involved in the work of the conference as experts and called upon to participate continuously, particularly in presenting orally the articles of the draft Protocols.[41] A representative of the ICRC was on the podium of each of the Conference Commissions and of the plenary.[42] He or she spoke when necessary and participated in the negotiations, also in the informal negotiations. The impact of this participation varied depending on the issues and persons involved. The head of the ICRC delegation was Jean Pictet, then vice-president of the ICRC, the great champion of international humanitarian law, and respected coordinator of the work on the ICRC Commentaries to the four Geneva Conventions. His knowledge and devotion certainly had an impact. Just one example of his personal input: When in the debate there appeared a real threat that the protection of air crews descending in distress might be watered down (now Article 42 AP I) by an attempt to exclude that protection when they were drifting to areas controlled by the party to which they belonged,[43] he launched a fervent

---

38   *Official Records of the Diplomatic Conference on the Reaffirmation and Development of International Humanitarian Law Applicable in Armed Conflicts, Geneva, 1974–1977*, vols. I–XVII (Bern: Federal Political Department, 1978), vol. VII, CDDH/SR. 56, paras 4 and 62 (*Official Records*). Protocol Additional to the Geneva Conventions of 12 August 1949, and relating to the Protection of Victims of International Armed Conflicts (Protocol I), Geneva, 8 June 1977, in force 7 December 1978, 1125 UNTS; Protocol Additional to the Geneva Conventions of 12 August 1949, and relating to the Protection of Victims of Non-International Armed Conflicts (Protocol II), adopted 8 June 1977, in force 7 December 1978, 1125 UNTS; Bothe and Partsch, 'General Introduction and Guide to Documentation', p. 5; Pictet, 'General Introduction', pp. xxxiii *et seq.*

39   Text reproduced in D. Schindler and J. Toman (eds.), *The Laws of Armed Conflicts*, 4th ed. (Leiden/Boston: Nijhoff, 2004), p. 699. Israel did not sign the Final Act.

40   Bothe and Partsch, 'General Introduction and Guide to Documentation', note 1, p. 4; Pictet, 'General Introduction', note 1, p. xxxii.

41   Pictet, 'General Introduction', note 1, p. xxxiii.

42   Bothe and Partsch, 'General Introduction and Guide to Documentation', pp. 10 *et seq.*

43   *Official Records*, vol. VI, pp. 104–110, CDDH/SR. 39.

THE RED CROSS AND THE ADDITIONAL PROTOCOLS OF 1977

appeal to uphold the fundamental principle of international humanitarian law: attacks against persons who are *hors de combat* are prohibited.[44] That view prevailed in the end.[45]

4 Comparison of the 1973 Draft and the Final Text of 1977

The drafts submitted in 1973 took into consideration most of the views given by the experts of the Government Experts Conference.[46] But the ICRC did not include all proposals made at these conferences, as the ICRC could not agree to a number of them or because the proposals brought forward were contradictory.[47]

4.1 *Protocol I: Protection of Victims of International Armed Conflicts*
The proposals of the ICRC concerning Protocol I were largely accepted by the Conference.[48] Several controversial issues had already been abandoned as a result of the previous resistance encountered at the Government Experts Conference. For example, a special distinctive sign for doctors who were not 'medical personnel' in the sense of the Protocol or the general provision on reprisals was abandoned.[49] Most provisions of the 1973 Protocol I draft were adopted without diminishing the protective content. Only in a few cases, the ICRC proposals were seriously modified, for example the provisions on objects indispensable to the survival of the civilian population, works and installations containing dangerous forces, extradition and superior orders.[50] Some rules were significantly developed, for example Article 11 ('Protection of persons'), Article 29 ('Notifications and agreements concerning medical aircrafts') as well as Article 75 ('Fundamental guarantees').[51] Furthermore, a few new elements were added to the ICRC proposals, in particular the provisions on

---

44   *Official Records*, vol. VI, pp. 106–107, CDDH/SR. 39, para. 88 *et seq.*

45   *Cf.* W. A. Solf, 'Article 42 – Occupants of aircraft', *New Rules*, note 1, pp. 258–264, pp. 256 et seq.; J. de Preux, 'Article 42 – Occupants of aircraft' in *ICRC Commentary*, note 1, pp. 493–503, p. 495.

46   Pictet, 'General Introduction', note 1, p. xxxi.

47   *Ibid.*

48   Bothe, 'introduction', in New Rules, note 1, p. 17; Pictet, 'General Introduction', note 1, p. xxxiv.

49   Bothe, note 48, p. 17.

50   See the synoptic table in Bothe and Partsch, New Rules, note 1, p. 19 *et seq.*

51   Further examples: Articles 22, 23, 28, 36, 51, 61–63 AP I; Bothe and Partsch, 'Introduction', note 1, p. 18.

mercenaries, journalists, missing and dead persons and the International Fact-Finding Commission.[52]

4.2 Protocol II: Protection of Victims of Non-International Armed Conflicts

One of the main aims of the Conference of Government Experts in 1971 and 1972 was to offer better protection for the victims of NIAC.[53] In the consultations preceding the Diplomatic Conference, it had even been suggested to adopt a uniform protocol relating to the protection of civilian populations in all armed conflicts, but on the basis of the expert discussions the ICRC decided to draft a separate Additional Protocol containing rules for non-international conflicts.[54]

The 1973 draft contained 47 articles, divided into eight parts and had four main concepts:[55] Firstly, that it should apply to all conflicts which do not take place between States, including wars of national liberation. Secondly, that the definition of the field of application should be similar to that in Common Article 3 of the Geneva Conventions.[56] Thirdly, that a relatively high standard of protection should be guaranteed to the civilian population, persons in the power of another Party to the conflict and also to the members of armed forces or of comparable units on the insurgent side, by limiting the use of methods and means of combat. And finally, that these guarantees should be granted to both sides of the conflicts on the basis of complete equality.[57] In general, the original draft of Protocol II and the version adopted during the Committee

---

52 *Ibid.*

53 M. Bothe and K. J. Partsch, 'Introduction to Protocol II' in M. Bothe, K. J. Partsch and W. Solf, (eds.), *New Rules for Victims of Armed Conflicts, Commentary on the Two 1977 Protocols Additional to the Geneva Conventions of 1949* (The Hague/Boston/London: Martinus Njihoff Publishers, 1982), pp. 604–618, p. 604.

54 Crawford, 'Geneva Conventions Additional Protocol I (1977)', note 4, MN 14; Bothe and Partsch, 'Introduction', p. 693; Junod, 'General Introduction to the Commentary on Protocol II', in ICRC Commentary, note 1, p. 1333. Norway still maintained the proposal of a single Protocol during the Diplomatic Conference.

55 Junod, 'General Introduction to the Commentary on Protocol II', ibid., p. 1333; *Official Records*, vol. I, Part Three, pp. 33 *et seq.*

56 Common Article 3 of the GC and AP II coexist. This is a fundamental change in comparison with the 1972 draft. The ICRC accepted the point of view expressed by numerous experts, that it is desirable that Common Article 3 and Protocol II should coexist autonomously: In fact, to link the Protocol to Common Article 3 would have resulted in restricting the latter's scope of application. Junod, 'General Introduction to the Commentary on Protocol II', in ICRC Commentary, note 1, p. 1328.

57 Bothe and Partsch, 'Introduction', in New Rules, note 1, p. 693.

THE RED CROSS AND THE ADDITIONAL PROTOCOLS OF 1977　　　　381

phase of the Conference were far more comprehensive in scope and detail, similar to AP I, as both were discussed at the same time, than the document that was finally adopted.[58] The reluctance of a number of delegates, which will be discussed in greater detail in the next chapter, lead to a simplified version, containing only the essential rules. A comparison of the Committee draft with the simplified draft shows that in the latter, Part VI on means and methods of combat,[59] Part VI on relief[60] and Part VIII on the execution of the Protocol as well as the terms 'parties to the conflict', the 'adverse Party' or even 'adversary' were deleted.[61] Not everyone was satisfied with the result, but finally the AP II was adopted by consensus too.[62] Those who had favoured a protocol containing a higher level of protection had to concede that it was better to have 'half an egg instead of only an empty shell'.[63]

4.3 *Evaluation*

Despite all the difficulties, especially the inevitable political nature of many debates,[64] it must be emphasised that the result of the conference *grosso modo* corresponds to the ICRC draft as far as AP I is concerned. As to AP II, at least essential elements of the ICRC draft were maintained. It is also noteworthy that almost all of the provisions were adopted by consensus. Indeed, of the 150 articles of the two Protocols, only 14 required a formal vote. Several draft articles and proposals were not put to a vote.[65] Countries from all regions of the world participated in the codification.[66] AP I currently has 174 State Parties and AP II 168 State Parties.[67]

58　Crawford, 'Geneva Conventions Additional Protocol I (1977)', MN 14; Junod, 'General Introduction to the Commentary on Protocol II', p. 1334; Bothe and Partsch, 'Introduction', p. 606.

59　Its basic principles are enshrined in Article 4 AP II ('Fundamental guarantees'), ICRC, Foreword AP II.

60　The provisions concerning impartial humanitarian organizations were adopted in a less binding form than originally foreseen, Articles 33–35 of the ICRC draft, now only Article 18 AP II; ICRC, Foreword AP II.

61　Bothe and Partsch, 'Introduction', in New Rules, note 1, p. 695; Junod, 'General Introduction to the Commentary on Protocol II', ICRC Commentary, note 1, p. 1335.

62　*Ibid.*, p. 1336.

63　Expression used by Bloembergen, Netherlands; see Bothe and Partsch, 'Introduction', p. 607.

64　Pictet, 'General Introduction', note 1, p. xxxiv.

65　*Ibid.*

66　*Ibid.*

67　List of State Parties: www.icrc.org/ihl/%28SPF%29/party_main_treaties/$File/IHL_and_other_related_Treaties.pdf (October 2015).

382   PART 4: THE LAW OF ARMED CONFLICT – GENERAL QUESTIONS

5   Underestimated Problems and Loopholes

While recognizing the overall decisive and positive impact of the ICRC, there is no denying the fact that it underestimated certain difficulties and left a few loopholes. The Conference encountered difficulties of various kinds: some were legal-technical, some concerned military interests and some were based on political considerations.[68] Four problems where the ICRC's initial approach could be questioned will be highlighted.

5.1   *Wars of National Liberation*

The 1973 ICRC draft did not address the issue of wars of national liberation, apparently assuming that this was covered well enough by the Protocol on NIAC (AP II) and attempting to avoid the problem of qualifying special conflicts.[69] The draft was based on the strict distinction between international and non-international conflicts. Only in cases where conflicts crossed national boundaries did the conflict become international.[70] Wars against colonial and racist regimes were covered by Draft Protocol II.[71] Therefore, the Draft Protocol I limited its scope of application to situations referred to in Common Article 2.[72] The ICRC was aware of the desire of numerous States to include wars of national liberation in Protocol I.[73] Yet, in its 1973 Commentary, it indicated that the majority of experts involved in drafting the Protocol did not consider those wars as international.[74]

---

68   Bothe and Partsch, 'General Introduction and Guide to Documentation', in New Rules, note 1, p. 7.

69   B. Zimmermann, 'Article 1 – General principles and scope of application' in *ICRC Commentary*, note 1, pp. 33–57, p. 49.

70   D. P. Forsythe, 'The 1974 Diplomatic Conference on Humanitarian Law: Some Observations', *The American Journal of International Law*, 69 (1993), pp. 77–91, p. 80 uses the term 'geomilitary scale'.

71   K. J. Partsch, 'Article 1 – General principles and scope of application' in New Rules, note 1, pp. 35–51, p. 38.

72   This provision is contained in Article 1 (3) of the Final Act.

73   The majority of experts considered wars of national liberation as being not of an international character, Zimmermann, 'Article 1 – General principles and scope of application', in ICRC Commentary, p. 47.

74   ICRC, *Draft Protocols additional to the Geneva Conventions of 12 August 1949, Commentary*, p. 6; Zimmermann, 'Article 1 – General principles and scope of application', ibid., p. 49; F. Kalshoven, 'Reaffirmation and Development of International Humanitarian Law Applicable in Armed Conflicts: The First Session of the Diplomatic Conference, Geneva, 20 February – 29 March 1974', *Netherlands Yearbook of International Law*, 5 (1974), pp. 2–34, p. 6.

The first problem the conference had to solve regarding wars of national liberation was the participation of liberation movements. This procedural issue blocked the first session of the Conference for a number of weeks. It was only after four weeks of difficult negotiations that the decision was taken to allow liberation movements recognized by regional organizations to participate with a right to speak and to make proposals, but without the right to vote.[75]

Concerning the substance of the controversy, immediately after the opening of the Conference, amendments were presented with the aim of recognizing the international character of wars of national liberation, which led to a highly controversial debate. The amendments' supporters mainly argued that there already existed a legal conviction and international practice recognizing wars of national liberation as international conflicts.[76] The opponents on the other hand considered the expansion of the protocol's scope as an introduction of *jus ad bellum* into *jus in bello*. Furthermore, they argued that the rules contained in Protocol I and the 1949 Convention were unsuitable for situations of wars of national liberation.[77] The main opponents in the debate were, on the one hand, most Western delegations and, on the other, the East European, Asian and African groups. Against the hard-core Western position not to mention wars of national liberation at all, there were different variations of the contrary position, namely to choose as decisive the exercise of the right to self-determination, or the fight against colonial domination, alien occupation and racist regimes or a combination of both. To resolve the controversies, the delegations of Canada and New Zealand suggested the establishment of an inter-sessional Working Group (CDDH/I/78).[78] But the proposal combining the said criteria was put to a vote and the following text was adopted in a roll call vote by a majority of 70 votes to 21 with 13 abstentions:

1. The present Protocol which supplements the Geneva Conventions of 12 August 1949 for the Protection of War Victims, shall apply in the situations referred to in Article 2 common to these Conventions.

---

75 Bothe and Partsch, 'General Introduction and Guide to Documentation', note 1, p. 8.

76 G. Abi-Saab, 'Wars of National Liberation in the Geneva Conventions and Protocols' *Académie de Droit International de la Haye (ed.), Recueil des Cours,* 165 (1979), pp. 353– 445, 376 et seq.; Partsch, 'Article 1 – General principles and scope of application', note 71, p. 40; Baxter, note 20, pp. 13 *et seq.*

77 Abi-Saab, 'Wars of National Liberation in the Geneva Conventions and Protocols', pp. 380 *et seq.;*W.T. Mallison and S. V.Mallison, 'The Juridical Status of Privileged Combatants under the Geneva Protocol of 1977 Concerning International Conflicts', *Law and Contemporary Problems,* 42: 2 (1978), 4–35, 12; Forsythe, note 70, p. 81.

78 Partsch, 'Article 1 – General principles and scope of application', note 71, p. 42; Official Records, vol. VIII, p. 97.

2. The situations referred to in the preceding paragraph include armed conflicts in which peoples are fighting against colonial domination and alien occupation and racist regimes in the exercise of their right of self-determination, as enshrined in the Charter of the United Nations and the Declaration on Principles of International Law concerning Friendly Relations and Cooperation among States in accordance with the Charter of the United Nations.

Between the first and the second session, the United States announced that it was willing to live with the new provision equating wars of national liberation to international armed conflicts (now Article 1 (4) AP I).[79] This solved the diplomatic deadlock in which the conference had been stuck. Political developments which occurred soon after the Conference have made that problem largely obsolescent. Nevertheless, the controversy during the first session gave the impression that the ICRC and the Western States were not well prepared to respond to the needs of the developing countries.[80]

5.2 *The Protection of the Victims of Non-International Armed Conflicts*

Incorporating wars of liberation into the regulatory scope of AP I was a necessary concession to the developing countries, which dramatically reduced their support of AP II. AP II was no longer necessary to give better protection and legal status to liberation movements and their members fighting against colonial powers. Therefore, another interest perceived as primordial by many developing countries gained importance, namely their concern about possible restrictions imposed on their newly gained sovereignty which might result from the high level of protection provided by the new AP II. They were thus against such a protocol, or at least insisted on a lower level of protection.[81] The ICRC and many of the Western and East European delegations had underestimated the resistance which many developing countries would offer against the high level of protection for victims of NIAC.[82] Furthermore, some articles seemed to be too detailed to be realistic or to be applied in internal conflicts.[83] This opposition finally prevailed during the heated final plenary session of the

---

79   Bothe and Partsch, 'General Introduction and Guide to Documentation', note 1, p. 8.

80   Baxter, note 20, 17.

81   C. Lysaght, 'The Scope of Protocol II and its Relation to Common Article 3 of the Geneva Conventions of 1949 and other Human Rights Instruments', *The American University Law Review*, 33 (1983), pp. 9–27, p. 10; C. L. Cantrell, 'Humanitarian Law in Armed Conflict: The Third Diplomatic Conference', *Marquette Law Review*, 61 (1977), pp. 253–278, p. 277.

82   Cf. Junod, 'General Introduction to the Commentary on Protocol II', ICRC Commentary, note 1, pp. 1334 *et seq.*

83   *Ibid.*, p. 1335.

THE RED CROSS AND THE ADDITIONAL PROTOCOLS OF 1977 385

conference,[84] leading to a severe reduction of the content of AP II. A new draft, for which the delegate of Pakistan was the major spokesman,[85], only provided 28 Articles in comparison to the 47 Articles contained in the version adopted during the Committee phase of the Conference. Certain sections (e.g. the rules on methods and means of combat) were almost entirely deleted.[86] Already during the second session, Article 1, which determines the material field of the application of AP II, was significantly reduced in comparison to the ICRC draft by introducing a higher threshold for its application. The ICRC draft had been based on Common Article 3 of the Geneva Convention. It defined the NIAC negatively in two respects, namely excluding, on the one hand, situations that were covered by Common Article 2 of the Conventions, and on the other hand, internal disturbances and tensions as well as isolated and sporadic acts of violence (Art. 1, paragraph 2 of the ICRC draft).[87] In contrast, the provision adopted by the Conference requires that the insurgent groups are under a responsible command and that they control a part of a territory that enables them to implement AP II, which considerably raises the threshold of application.[88]

---

84   *Official Records*, Vol. VII, CDDH/ SR. 49, pp. 59 *et seq.*

85   CDDH/427 and Corr. 1. The head of the delegation of Pakistan, Judge Mushtaq Hussain, took an initiative to save the Protocol; *Official Records*, Vol. IV, pp. 13 *et seq*; Junod, 'General Introduction to the Commentary on Protocol II', note 82, p. 1335; Crawford, 'Geneva Conventions Additional Protocol I (1977)', note 4, MN 14 and 15, Bothe and Partsch, note 53, pp. 695 *et seq.*

86   Cantrell, 'Humanitarian Law in Armed Conflict: The Third Diplomatic Conference', p. 273; See also W. A. Solf, 'Part IV Civilian Population, Introduction' in *New Rules*, note 1, pp. 769–776, 775 (the comparative table).

87   Article 1 of the ICRC Draft 'Material field of application':

    1.   The present Protocol shall apply to all armed conflicts not covered by Article 2 common to the Geneva Conventions of August 12, 1949, taking place between armed forces or other organized armed groups under responsible command.

    2.   The present Protocol shall not apply to situations of internal disturbances and tensions, inter alia riots, isolated and sporadic acts of violence and other acts of a similar nature.

    3.   The foregoing provisions do not modify the conditions governing the application of Article 3 common to the Geneva Conventions of August 12, 1949.

88   Article 1 of AP II. Material field of application:

    1.   This Protocol, which develops and supplements Article 3 common to the Geneva Conventions of 12 August 1949 without modifying its existing conditions of application, shall apply to all armed conflicts which are not covered by Article 1 of the Protocol Additional to the Geneva Conventions of 12 August 1949, and relating to the Protection of Victims of International Armed Conflicts (Protocol I) and which take place in the territory of a High Contracting Party between its armed forces and dissident armed forces or other organized armed groups which, under responsible command, exercise such control over a part of its territory as to enable them to carry out sustained and concerted military operations and to implement this Protocol.

Related to the question of the definition of the NIAC is the problem of the relation of Article 1 AP II to Common Article 3 of the Geneva Convention[89] and whether the existence of a NIAC shall be determined subjectively, by the concerned State, or objectively.[90] The proposals of those opposing the objective determination of a NIAC were rejected. Although a compromise (CDDH/I/GT 56)[91] was adopted unanimously by Committee I,[92] the developing countries, under the leadership of the Columbian representative, attempted to reopen the discussion during the final adoption phase by an oral amendment. After an appeal by the representative of the ICRC, the Columbian representative withdrew this amendment.[93] However, this was only a small success. Seen as a whole, AP II as adopted was considered unsatisfactory by the ICRC and many States. The final version reduced the number of articles to 28 as compared to the original 47 Articles of the ICRC draft and the Committee version. However, it was recognized that this was the only viable compromise.[94]

In light of the fierce debates, which took place during the final weeks of the conference,[95] it is amazing to notice the subsequent development of relevant customary international law towards providing a level of protection which could not be achieved during the conference. The law relating to NIAC has to a large extent been approximated to that of international armed conflicts (IAC). In particular, the ICTY and the ICTR played a decisive role in this development. In 1995 the ICTY stated that:

> [...]in the area of armed conflict the distinction between interstate wars and civil wars is losing its value as far as human beings are concerned. Why protect civilians from belligerent violence, or ban rape, torture or

---

2. This Protocol shall not apply to situations of internal disturbances and tensions, such as riots, isolated and sporadic acts of violence and other acts of a similar nature, as not being armed conflicts.

89 *Official Records*, vol. VIII, CDDH/I/SR. 24, pp. 229 *et seq.*

90 *Official Records*, vol. VIII, CDDH/I/SR. 24, pp. 233 *et seq.*; See as well the Amendment to Article 1 by Romania (CDDH/I/30) in *Official Records*, Vol. IV, p. 7.

91 *Official Records*, vol. X, CDDH/I/238/Rev./1, pp. 93 *et seq.* Only two minor changes have been made: The compromise begins with 'The present Protocol' instead of 'This Protocol' and it refers to 'Protocol I' instead of 'the Protocol Additional to the Geneva Conventions of 12 August 1949, and relating to the Protection of the Victims of International Armed Conflicts (Protocol I)'.

92 *Official Records*, vol. VIII, CDDH/I/SR. 29, p. 287.

93 *Official Records*, vol. VII, CDDH/SR. 49, pp. 66, 68.

94 *Official Records*, vol. VII, CDDH/SR. 49, p. 60.

95 *Official Records*, vol. VII, CDDH/SR. 49, pp. 59 *et seq.*

the wanton destruction of hospitals, churches, museums or private property, as well

as proscribe weapons causing unnecessary suffering when two sovereign States are engaged in war, and yet refrain from enacting the same bans or providing the same protection when armed violence has erupted 'only' within the territory of a sovereign State? If international law, while of course duly safeguarding the legitimate interests of States, must gradually turn to the protection of human beings, it is only natural that the aforementioned dichotomy should gradually lose its weight.[96]

By the beginning of the twenty-first century, that concept had passed into the realm of positive law, as the ICRC observed in its customary law study[97] which convincingly shows the approximation of the rules governing the NIAC to those of the IAC. Thus, thirty years later, the 1973 concept of the ICRC finally prevailed.

5.3 *Nuclear Weapons*

The ICRC was well aware of the fact that including the controversial issue of nuclear weapons had led to the failure of its Delhi Rules,[98] as Article 14 (1) of the Delhi Rules was seen by several governments as a condemnation of nuclear weapons.[99] Therefore, a need to avoid the issue was felt. In the beginning, the ICRC addressed the issue in a declaration, which does not stand out for its clarity. The ICRC further stated in its introduction to the 1973 draft Protocols that '[p]roblems relating to atomic, bacteriological and chemical warfare are subjects of international agreements or negotiations by governments, and in submitting these draft Protocols the ICRC does not intend to broach these problems. It should be borne in mind that the Red Cross as a whole clearly made known its condemnation of weapons of mass destruction at several International Red Cross Conferences and urged governments to reach agreements

---

96 ICTY, *Prosecutor v. Dusko Tadić*, Appeals Chamber Decision on the Defence Motion for Interlocutory Appeal on Jurisdiction, 2 October 1995, para. 97.

97 *Cf.* J.-M. Henckaerts and L. Doswald-Beck, *Customary International Humanitarian Law*, 2 vols. (Cambridge: Cambridge University Press, 2004), vol. I, p. XXIX.

98 C. Pilloud, 'Les Conventions de Genève de 1949 pour la protection des victimes de la guerre, les Protocols additionnels de 1977 et les armes nucléaires', *German Yearbook of International Law*, 21 (1979), pp. 169–179, 171 *et seq.*; W. A. Solf, 'Methods and Means of Warfare Introduction' in *New Rules*, note 1, pp. 217–221, p. 218; Pilloud and Pictet, 'Protocol I – Part IV, Section 1', note 8, p. 590.

99 Pilloud and Pictet, 'Protocol I – Part IV, Section 1', note 8, p. 590.

388 PART 4: THE LAW OF ARMED CONFLICT – GENERAL QUESTIONS

banning their Use'.[100] The ICRC explained its position once more in the introduction to the commentary of the draft articles:

> It should be recalled that, apart from some provisions of a general nature, the ICRC has not included in its drafts any rules governing atomic, bacteriological and chemical weapons. These weapons have either been the subject of international agreements such as the Geneva Protocol of 1925 or of discussions within intergovernmental organizations. This, however, does not imply that the ICRC or the Red Cross as a whole is not interested in a problem whose humanitarian aspects are of a paramount importance. Also the so-called conventional weapons ... are still not covered by these protocols. Yet they are also a matter of concern for the ICRC. ...[101]

The declaration is mostly understood as an indication of the existence of a 'nuclear consensus', a general understanding between the ICRC and the participating States to exclude further discussions on nuclear weapons from the negotiations.[102] During the general debate, some governments were opposed to the Conference dealing with specific weapons at all,[103] especially the nuclear powers which were apparently determined not to address the issue.[104] Early in the diplomatic conference the delegation of the United Kingdom explained that

> they were not intended to broach problems concerned with atomic, bacteriological or chemical warfare, which were the subject of existing international agreements and current delicate negotiations by Governments elsewhere. It was on the assumption that the draft Protocols would not affect those problems that the United Kingdom Government had worked and would continue to work towards final agreement on the Protocols.[105]

---

100 *Official Records*, vol. I, Part 3, p. 2.

101 ICRC, *Draft Protocols additional to the Geneva Conventions of 12 August 1949, Commentary*, p. 2; Pilloud and Pictet, 'Protocol I – Part IV, Section 1', p. 590.

102 S. Oeter, 'II. Means of Combat' in D. Fleck (ed.), *The Handbook of International Humanitarian Law*, 3rd ed. (Oxford: Oxford University Press, 2013), p. 153 *et seq.*; H. Meyrowitz, 'Le statut des armes nucléaires en droit international – 1er part', *German Yearbook of International Law*, 21 (1982), pp. 219–251, 229 *et seq.*

103 *Official Records*, vol. V, CDDH/SR. 9, para. 28 (France); CDDH/SR. 11, para. 64 (Ukrainian Soviet Socialist Republics); CDDH/SR. 11; para. 73 (Hungary); CDDH/SR. 12, para. 24 (Union of Soviet Socialist Republics); CDDH/SR. 17, para. 36 (Argentina).

104 Solf, 'Methods and Means of Warfare Introduction', in New Rules, note 1, p. 219.

105 *Official Records*, vol. V, CDDH/SR. 13, para. 36.

THE RED CROSS AND THE ADDITIONAL PROTOCOLS OF 1977   389

A similar statement was made by the United States.[106] Furthermore, immediately prior to the adoption of draft additional Protocol I, France stressed that in its view the rules of the Protocol did not apply to the use of nuclear weapons.[107]

It is notable that these views were not disputed by other governments, although several delegations had openly attempted to extend the scope of Protocol I to nuclear weapons and had urged to prohibit them.[108] When the Conference defined the mandate that was given to the Ad Hoc Committee to study certain conventional weapons which cause superfluous injury and unnecessary suffering the delegations of Romania[109] and China[110] proposed to delete the word 'conventional', which would have extended the Committee's mandate to nuclear, bacteriological and chemical weapons.[111] The Conference approved the mandate including the word 'conventional' by 68 votes to none, with 10 abstentions.[112]

China especially criticized the 'super powers', accusing them of a mass production of lethal weapons, particularly nuclear weapons, and urged the conference to prohibit the use of nuclear weapons.[113] Nevertheless, no amendments dealing with the subject were proposed for inclusion in Protocol I during the whole conferences.[114] Later in the Conference, the Western Powers addressed the question by declarations interpreting AP I as not applying to weapons of mass destruction.[115] After the consensus adoption of the Protocols, the United States,[116] the United Kingdom[117] and France[118] confirmed their positions interpreting Protocol I: They expressed the understanding that the rules developed in the course of the conferences had been designed with a view to conventional

---

106   *Official Records*, vol. VII, CDDH SR. 58, para. 82, Vol. XIV, CDDH/III/SR. 40, para. 123.
107   *Official Records*, vol. VII, CDDH/SR. 56, p. 193.
108   *Official Records*, vol. V, CDDH/SR.10, para. 36 (Ghana); CDDH/SR.11, para. 13 (Romania); vol. V, CDDH/SR.12, para. 18 (China); vol. V, CDDH/SR.12, para. 32, (Iraq); vol. IX, CDDH/I/SR.60, para. 23, (Philippines); vol. XIV, CDDH/III/SR.8 para. 87, (Albania); Oeter, note 102, pp. 153 *et seq.*
109   *Official Records*, vol. V, CDDH/SR. 9, para. 31.
110   *Official Records*, vol. V, CDDH/SR. 9, para. 40.
111   Pilloud and Pictet, 'Protocol I – Part IV, Section 1', note 8, p. 592.
112   *Official Records*, vol. V, CDDH/SR. 9, para. 50.
113   *Official Records*, vol. V, CDDH/SR.12, para. 18 (China).
114   Solf, 'Methods and Means ofWarfare Introduction', note 104, p. 219.
115   *Official Records*, vol. VII, CDDH/SR. 58, para. 82; vol. VII, CCDH/SR. 58, para. 119 and CDDH/SR. 56, para. 3.
116   *Official Records*, vol. VII, CDDH/SR. 58, para. 82.
117   *Official Records*, vol. VII, CDDH/SR. 58, para. 119.
118   *Official Records*, vol. VII, CDDH/SR. 56, para. 3.

weapons only and that these rules had not been intended to have any effect on and did not regulate or prohibit the use of nuclear weapons.

At the time of signature the United States and Great Britain made declarations similar to their previous statements and confirmed their view interpreting Protocol I as not applying to weapons of mass destruction.[119] On the occasion of ratification several other States affirmed this position.[120] Some commentators say that the declarations of the United Kingdom and the United States were reservations.[121] Others have expressed the opinion that they form a part of the context of Protocol I relevant for its interpretation in accordance with Article 31 (1) Vienna Convention on the Law of Treaties.[122]

The position of the ICRC remained somewhat ambiguous. On the one hand, it found itself constrained to exclude nuclear weapons from the scope of application of the Protocol to facilitate the participation of the Western nuclear powers at the conferences and to ensure the eventual ratification by those powers. On the other hand, it indicated in its introduction to the draft articles commentary that nuclear weapons were at least incorporated in some general provisions.[123] According to the ICRC commentary, 'those are the general rules that already existed in a codified form or as customary law and which were confirmed in the Protocol, namely the provisions of Article 33 of the Draft, the present paragraphs 1 and 2 of Article 35 AP I and the customary rule confirmed by Article 43 of theDraft (present Article 48 AP I)'.[124] Thus, the ICRC repeated its view that the Protocol was without prejudice to the already existing general rules although it declared that it had not included any rules governing atomic weapons in its 1973 drafts. The general rules remain completely valid and continue to apply to nuclear weapons.[125]

India affirmed this view by explaining in an understanding concerning Article 33 that the basic rule contained in Article 35 applied to all categories of weapons, namely nuclear, bacteriological, chemical or conventional

---

119   Printed in: Solf, 'Methods and Means of Warfare Introduction', pp. 219 *et seq.* (United States) and pp. 822 *et seq.* (United Kingdom).

120   Belgium,Canada, France,Germany, Ireland, Italy, theNetherlands and Spain, R. R. Baxter, 'The Evolving Laws of Armed Conflicts', *Military Law Review*, 60 (1973), pp. 99–11, p. 109.

121   Bothe, Ipsen and Partsch, note 9, pp. 43 *et seq.* (individual opinion of Professor Knut Ipsen).

122   Solf, 'Methods and Means of Warfare Introduction', note 104, p. 220; Oeter, note 102, p. 159.

123   ICRC, *Draft Protocols additional to the Geneva Conventions of 12 August 1949, Commentary*, p. 2.

124   Pilloud and Pictet, 'Protocol I – Part IV, Section 1', note 8, p. 590.

125   Pilloud and Pictet, 'Protocol I – Part IV, Section 1', p. 593; Solf, 'Methods and Means of Warfare Introduction', note 104, p. 220; Oeter, 'II. Means of Combat', note 102, p. 157.

THE RED CROSS AND THE ADDITIONAL PROTOCOLS OF 1977

weapons.[126] When ratifying the Protocol in 1999, Ireland made a similar statement in its declaration concerning Article 35, stating 'that nuclear weapons, even if not directly governed by Additional Protocol I, remain subject to existing rules of international law as confirmed in 1996 by the International Court of Justice in its Advisory Opinion on the Legality of the Threat or Use of Nuclear Weapons'.[127]

The controversy about nuclear weapons was one of the reasons for the considerable slowdown of the ratification process in Western Europe. In a way, the question was laid to rest by the 1996 Advisory Opinion of the ICJ on nuclear weapons.[128] The Court considered the controversy as immaterial because customary law rules of the same content as those of AP I applied to nuclear weapons.[129] These rules would, as a matter of principle, rule out the legality of the use of nuclear weapons. But the Court left a possible exception for extreme situations in the form of a *non liquet*: The Court was unable to say whether there were such extreme situations where the use of nuclear weapons would be lawful.[130] The official position of the nuclear powers seems to have comfortably settled in the niche thus left by the Court, if necessary by misinterpreting the Court a little. Thus, the situation is where the first declaration of the ICRC in 1973 put it. It is still ambiguous.

5.4   *Protection of the Natural Environment*

In its draft Additional Protocols, the ICRC made no reference to the protection of the natural environment against the harmful effects of warfare. But this was the decade when the development of international environmental law started with vigour. The first UN Conference on environmental protection was held in 1972.[131] Other fora dealing with military questions addressed the issue of environmental protection while the Diplomatic Conference in Geneva was going on. The United States and the Soviet Union engaged in bilateral negotiations, addressing the ,dangers of the use of environmental modifications for military

---

126   *Official Records*, vol. VI, CDDH/SR. 39, p. 115 (India).

127   ICRC, 'Ratification of the Protocols Additional to the Geneva Conventions of 12 August 1949 by Ireland', *International Review of the Red Cross*, 81 (1999), pp. 418–422, p. 420.

128   ICJ, *Legality of the threat or use of nuclear weapons*, Advisory Opinion of 8 July 1996.

129   ICJ, *Legality of the threat or use of nuclear weapons*, Advisory Opinion of 8 July 1996, para. 64 *et seq.*

130   ICJ, *Legality of the threat or use of nuclear weapons*, Advisory Opinion of 8 July 1996, para. 105.

131   *See* Report of the UN Conference on the Human Environment, www.unep.org/Documents.Multilingual/Default.asp?DocumentID=97.

purposes'[132] in 1974 and the UN General Assembly adopted the *Convention on the Prohibition of Military or any Other Hostile Use of Environmental Modification Techniques* in 1976.[133]

The ICRC was already confronted with respective proposals of delegations at the Second Conference of Government Experts,[134] yet refrained from including them in its draft Protocols.[135] Thus, pleas for environmental protection were reiterated at the Diplomatic Conference.[136] In September 1974 the Delegation of the German Democratic Republic sought a revision of the means and methods of combat, proposing to replace draft Articles 33 and 34 with a text, which *inter alia* prohibited 'means and methods which destroy natural human environmental conditions'.[137] Several months thereafter, the Arab Republic of Egypt, Australia, Czechoslovakia, Finland, the German Democratic Republic (GDR), Hungary, Ireland, Norway, Sudan and Yugoslavia proposed to add a paragraph to Article 33, forbidding the 'use methods and means which disturb or alter the ecological balance of the human environment'.[138] A similar amendment to Article 33 was suggested by the Democratic Republic of Vietnam and Uganda.[139] Environmental protection was then the subject of a new proposal, introduced by Australia, to prohibit both the destruction of the natural environment as a warfare technique and reprisal attacks against the environment.[140] Hungary, Czechoslovakia and the GDR advocated a similar prohibition, emphasizing the importance of a stable environment for the survival of mankind.[141] Eventually, the informal task force *'Group Biotope'* was formed in Committee III and reached the conclusion that the normative approach should be twofold, given that environmental protection is both an end in itself and a means to the end

---

132   Summit meeting between President Nixon and General Secretary Brezhnev, July 1974, www.state.gov/www/global/arms/treaties/environ1.html; *see also* W. A. Solf, 'Article 55 – Protection of the Natural Environment', *New Rules*, note 1, pp. 385–390, p. 386.

133   The Convention was drafted by the UN Conference of the Committee on Disarmament and adopted by the UN General Assembly in December, 1976. Its Art. 1 prohibits *'military or any other hostile use of environmental modification techniques having widespread, long-lasting or severe effects as the means of destruction, damage or injury to any other State Party'*, see United Nations, General Assembly, UN Doc. A/Res/31/72, www.un-documents.net/ a31r72.htm.

134   ICRC, *Report on the Conference of Government Experts on the Use of Certain Conventional Weapons* (Geneva, 1975), p. 76, www.loc.gov/rr/frd/Military_Law/pdf/RC-conf-experts-1974.pdf.

135   *Cf.* Draft Additional Protocols, *Official Records*, vol. I, Part 3.

136   *Cf.* Solf, 'Article 55 – Protection of the Natural Environment', note 132, p. 386.

137   *Official Records*, vol. III, CDDH/III/108, p. 155.

138   *Official Records*, vol. III, CDDH/III/222, p. 156.

139   *Official Records*, vol. III, CDDH/III/238, p. 157.

140   *Official Records*, vol. III, CDDH/III/60, p. 220.

141   *Official Records*, vol. III, CDDH/III/64, p. 221.

THE RED CROSS AND THE ADDITIONAL PROTOCOLS OF 1977 393

of the survival of mankind.[142] This dual approach reflected the variety of the aforementioned proposals and was ultimately implemented in Article 35 AP I (the amended draft Art. 33) and in the new Article 55 AP I.[143] Article 35 (3) AP I elevated the protection of the environment to one of the 'basic rules' of the Protocol and prohibits 'methods or means of warfare which are intended, or may be expected, to cause widespread, long-term and severe damage to the natural environment'. Containing the same prohibition, the new Art. 55 AP I paragraph 1 additionally emphasises the purpose of preventing adverse effects on 'the health or survival of the population'.

Moreover, Article 55 (2) specifically forbids 'attacks against the environment by way of reprisals'.

However, due to the restrictive nature of the three (cumulative!) requirements which define the prohibited damage, the articles are virtually useless. The debate on the legal protection of the environment in times of armed conflict continued.[144] Finally, some 30 years after the adoption of the said articles, the ICRC accurately criticized their inefficacy in a 2011 report, in which it identified the protection of the natural environment as one of the four areas in which humanitarian law had to be strengthened:[145] '[...] each of the three criteria ("widespread, long-term and severe") establishes a high, yet imprecise, threshold [...] Secondly, these criteria apply cumulatively, implying that the norm in question only protects the environment against exceptionally catastrophic events – what may be called "ecocide".[146] On the other hand, the ICRC also affirmed that customary international law 'contains some obligations for [the] protection of the environment', in particular the 'due regard' principle, yet insisted that 'their exact extent and implications would certainly need further clarification or development'.[147]

During the decades following the adoption of the Protocols, armed conflicts have inflicted great harm upon the environment and affected populations. Examples, highlighted by the ICRC in the aforementioned report, include the

---

142   Cf. Official Records, vol. XV, CDDH/III/275, p. 358.

143   Cf. Solf, 'Article 55 – Protection of the Natural Environment', note 132, p. 387.

144   On the development of this discussion, see M. Bothe, 'Military Activities and the Protection of the Environment', Environmental Policy and Law, 37 (2007), pp. 232–238.

145   ICRC, Report for the 31st International Conference of the ICRC, Strengthening Legal Protection for Victims of Armed Conflicts (Geneva, October 2011), Doc.31IC/11/5.1.1, p.5, www. icrc.org/eng/assets/files/red-cross-crescent-movement/31st-internationalconference/ 31-int-conference-strengthening-legal-protection-11–5–1–1-en.pdf.

146   Ibid., p. 15.

147   Ibid., p. 5; Henckaerts and Doswald-Beck, note 97, Rule 43, pp. 143–146, p. 143.

'deliberate destruction of more than 600 oil wells in Kuwait'[148] during the 1991 Gulf War and the bombing of 'the Jiyeh power station [which] led to the release of approximately 10,000 to 15,000 tons of fuel into the Mediterranean Sea'[149] in Lebanon in 2006. In the light of the atrocious effects of such incidents, the ICRC's recent efforts are indeed meritorious.

Yet States did not share the ICRC's concerns and views as to the priority of environmental protection in armed conflict. As the president of ICRC, Dr Jakob Kellenberger, put it: 'With regard to [...] the protection of the natural environment [...] further consultation and research with a view to strengthening the law is not considered a priority by a number of States at this stage'.[150] Nevertheless, the ICRC is not alone: In 2011, the International Law Commission (ILC) included the 'protection of the environment in relation to armed conflicts' in its long-term program of work.[151] In May 2013, the ILC incorporated the topic in its program of work and appointed Ms. Marie G. Jacobsson as the responsible Special Rapporteur, who has delivered three reports which have led to the provisional adoption of a number of principles.[152] Overcoming its initially passive stance, the ICRC has turned into an advocate of environmental protection against the harmful effects of warfare. Its endeavour has gained considerable momentum, yet it remains to be seen whether or not this will translate into actual legal progress.

6 Conclusion

Taken as a whole and despite certain problems which have been described, the preparation and negotiation of the two Additional Protocols of 1977 once more demonstrated the crucial role of the ICRC in the sphere of humanitarian law. The impact of the ICRC was both substantive and procedural. The final

---

148   ICRC, Report for the 31st International Conference of the ICRC, Strengthening Legal Protection for Victims of Armed Conflicts, p. 15.

149   *Ibid.*, p. 14.

150   Statement addressed to the permanent missions in Geneva by Dr Jakob Kellenberger, President of the ICRC, 5 December 2011, www.icrc.org/eng/resources/documents/statement/ihl-development-statement-2011–05–12.htm.

151   M. Bothe, 'Protection of the Environment in Relation to Armed Conflicts', in J. Crawford, A.G. Koroma, A. Pellet, S.Mahmoudi (eds.), *The International Legal Order: Current Needs and Possible Responses. Liber Amicorum Djamchid Momtaz* (Leiden: Nijhoff Publishers 2017), pp. 641–659.

152   *Cf.* Sixty-fifth session of the ILC (6 May – 7 June and 8 July – 9 August 2013), UN Doc. A/68/10, p. 105f.

outcome largely corresponded to the proposals and concerns of the ICRC and meant a major improvement for the protection of civilians in international and non-international conflicts.[153] The content of the Protocols cannot be thought of without the conceptual work of the ICRC. The procedural approach used by the ICRC, its central role in the elaboration of the relevant texts was decisive and seemed to be generally accepted at the time.

Recently, certain States have shown some resistance against the leading role of the ICRC in the development of international humanitarian law, claiming an exclusive (or next to exclusive) role for the 'States', meaning State bureaucracies, in this domain, a kind of *'chasse gardée'* for national ministries. In a polite form, this is reflected in the relevant resolution of the 31st Red Cross/Red Crescent Conference.[154] Yet this short survey of the salutary leading role played by the ICRC in the 1970s has shown, it is submitted, that all those concerned with the suffering of the victims of armed conflicts are well advised to listen to the visions of the ICRC.

153 Pictet, 'General Introduction', note 1, p. xxxiv.
154 31st International Red Cross and Red Crescent Conference, Resolution 1, Strengthening legal protection for victims of armed conflicts, OP 6 ('recognizing the primary role of States in the development of international humanitarian law').

PART 5

Conduct of Hostilities: Protecting the Environment

∵

17

Protection of the Environment in Times of Armed Conflict

1 The Laws of War and the Protection of the Environment – General Considerations

To some people, especially military people, it may still appear to be a strange concept that the protection of the environment as a societal value could impose restraints on the choice of methods and means of warfare. Some would ask: Could the survival of a particular kind of bird prevent me from using all necessary means to defend my country? As a response, one must put the question differently: Is it possible that two States, unable to solve their dispute by peaceful means, can put into jeopardy the survival of mankind by destroying the environment which serves as the basis for the existence of all nations and of future generations?

The two questions clearly show what is at issue. It is, on the one hand, the concept of armed conflict as a situation of regulated and limited violence, limited for the sake of the preservation of certain other societal values. It is on the other hand the global concern for the preservation of the environment, for its own sake or, if one prefers, as a condition for the survival of mankind.

A few comments are required on the concept of regulated or limited violence. It is a major cultural achievement which is always threatened. It is all too easy to ridicule the concept that is lawful to kill people and to destroy property, provided that it is done according to certain rules. But history and recent experience are full of examples which show that armed conflict is bad, but unregulated violence is worse. The concept of regulated violence is in a crucial way linked to the concept that the State is the only legitimate author and object of military violence. Other group violence, experience shows, tends to be unrestrained. It is the fragmentation of States which produces a tendency to unrestrained violence. The disastrous effects of that phenomenon are shown in the conflict taking place in former Yugoslavia, primarily in such abhorrent aberrations of the human mind as ethnic cleansing, but also in relation to something which is very close to environmental concerns, namely the protection of cultural property. This kind of conflict also carries the potential of actions which in a very physical way could put in jeopardy the conditions for the survival of

© KONINKLIJKE BRILL NV, LEIDEN, 2021 | DOI:10.1163/9789004380592_019

mankind, through the use of nuclear weapons or in other ways, if these were at the disposal of those in charge.

The very concept of limited and regulated violence presupposes the idea that there are societal values higher than considerations of military success. The first and foremost of those values is human dignity. Concern for human suffering in warfare is at the very origin of the law of warfare. But the subordination of warfare to certain basic societal values is clearly expressed in a very general way in a norm of the laws of war of a fundamental, crucial character, namely the so-called Martens clause. As formulated in the most recent version, namely in Art. 1 para. 2 of Protocol 1 additional to the Geneva Conventions, it reads: "Civilians and combatants remain under the protection and authority of the principles of international law derived from established custom, from the principles of humanity and from the dictates of public conscience". It is these dictates of public conscience which really reflect the societal concerns of a given time in history. In out days, the dictates of public conscience certainly include environmental concerns. Beyond all the technicalities which remain to be discussed, the Martens clause is the opening through which all the development of the law relating to the protection of the environment which has occurred in the last two or three decades leaves an impact on the laws of armed conflict. Environmental law has witnessed a tremendous development during these decades as the urgency of the environmental problem has become more and more apparent, both on the national and the international level. Environmental concerns have modified many fields of the law. This development cannot stop short of law relating to military activities.

It is on this basis that the question has to be answered whether the law of war as a kind of *lex specialis* prevails over the law of peacetime relations. The concept of the laws of war being a kind of specific body of law which completely replaces or displaces the law of peacetime relations once there is a situation where the law of war is applicable, if it ever was true, no longer corresponds to the modern state of the law. The law of armed conflict serves as a restraint on violence occurring in the relationship between the parties to a conflict. The fact that certain acts of violence are permissible under that body of law as between those parties, is by no means relevant for the different question of what kinds of destruction of values are permissible in respect of the international community as a whole, in relation to global concerns.

In this connection, a word must be said about self defence. It could be argued that self defence may serve as a justification for certain violations of the law relating to the protection of the environment. But this, I submit, would be a complete misconception. Self defence justifies the use of military force against an aggressor, by the victim of an aggression and by those States who

PROTECTION OF THE ENVIRONMENT IN TIMES OF ARMED CONFLICT

decide to defend the victim. The concept of self defence is not designed to legitimize any action which is not in conformity with the laws of armed conflict. Nor is it designed to put into question the fundamental legal values of the international system in which the protection of the environment nowadays figures in a prominent position. There are, however, certain specific, traditional customary rules excluding the unlawfulness of State behaviour, such as the state of necessity, which of course apply also to the rules relating to the preservation of the environment. They must not be confused with the right of self defence and they certainly do no constitute a kind of rule of thumb to justify any departure from those rules.

It is not surprising that the awareness of the environmental problem which can be found in world public opinion is currently reflected in a debate whether and to what extent the traditional law of armed conflict needs revision in order to take sufficient account of the need to preserve the environment. The governments of the world, sitting together in the General Assembly of the United Nations, have provided a rather luke-warm reception to those efforts. The General Assembly buried the relevant discussion in the agenda item of the United Nations Decade of International Law. But it has become difficult nowadays to silence the voice of the environment. The concern for the preservation of the environment in times of armed conflict is reflected in the Rio Declaration of 1992. The pressure for a better legal protection of the environment against military activities in general and the conduct of hostilities in particular will continue. It is one of the purposes of this paper to analyse the legitimacy or otherwise of this pressure.

2 Environment and Land Warfare

Turning now to the more technical rules relating to the protection of the environment in times of armed conflict, a distinction must be made between land warfare and sea warfare, and in relation to land warfare, between the environment situated on the territory of the parties to the conflict and that situated on neutral territory.

In relation to the environment situated on the territory of the parties to a conflict, there are a few fundamental rules restraining methods and means to harm the enemy the effect of which is a certain protection of environmental values. The first of these rules is the prohibition of a destruction of enemy property unless it is "imperatively demanded by the necessities of war".[1] This

---

1   Article 23 (g) of the Hague Rules on Land Warfare.

also protects the environment against wanton destruction. Such wanton destruction is also a grave breach of the Geneva Conventions.

The second, and probably more important, relevant principle is the protection of civilian objects. Many elements of the environment constitute of civilian objects. Consequently, they may not be made the object of attacks. If they suffer from attacks directed against military objectives, there is the fundamental rule of proportionality limiting permissible collateral damage. Damage to civilian objects is not permissible to the extent that it is excessive in relation to the military advantage anticipated from the attack against the military objective.

There are two fundamental problems involved in the application of this rule for the protection of the environment. The first one is the balancing of values involved in the rule of proportionality. Under what circumstances is a damage to the environment excessive in relation to a military advantage? There are difficult value judgements. A military mind's visceral reaction to the problem will be the kind of question put at the outset of out reflections: Could it really be that environmental concerns such as the preservation of certain species could serve as a consideration limiting the possibility of a military action considered useful by a responsible commander? The answer may be obvious to a traditional military mind, and it is thus a very important element of military training to inculcate into the military mind at least some of our modern awareness of the necessity to preserve the environment as a condition of our common survival. But it also seems to be advisable to develop some more concrete treaty rules which reflect in a more precise way the value judgements to be made, in typical situations, between military and environmental concerns (*e.g.* destruction of vegetation).

The second problem is that of the definition of military objectives. Military objectives are limited to those objects which by their nature, location, purpose or use make an effective contribution to military action and whose total or partial destruction, capture or neutralization in the circumstances reigning at the time offers a definite military advantage. This implies that also a piece of land may become a military objective if, for example, it may be used by enemy troops for their passage or as a camp. This means, for practical purposes, that elements of the environment, depending on their use, may become military objectives, regardless of their environmental value. It has thus to be asked whether the protection of the environment as part of the civilian world really is enough. It is submitted that it is not. The idea that certain objects have to be protected even though they are militarily significant is not at all alien to the laws of war. If one takes for example the rules concerning the protection of objects containing dangerous forces, namely nuclear power stations or dykes

PROTECTION OF THE ENVIRONMENT IN TIMES OF ARMED CONFLICT 403

or dams, those objects are, as a rule, protected even when they constitue military objectives because of the contribution they make to the military effort for the State in question. The question has thus to be asked whether and to what extent military objectives, being at the same time valuable elements of the environment which deserve protection for environmental reasons, should enjoy some kind of immunity from military activities. This is a major function (but not the only one) of the provisions of Protocol I additional to the Geneva Conventions concerning the protection of the environment in a specific sense. Those provisions, however, are limited to the prohibition of causing damage which is of a "widespread, long term and severe" character. The meaning of those terms is very controversial. If one looks at the negotiating history of those terms in Protocol I additional to the Geneva Conventions, one has to acknowledge that the threshold of damage which was envisaged by the drafters of those provisions is very high, unacceptably high, it is submitted. Here, we are in a kind of situation where the law urgently needs some kind of development in order to take better account of environmental considerations in a situation of armed conflict.

Even if it may prove difficult to make elements of the environment which are used for military purposes immune from attacks, a protection of the elements of the environment can be achieved by excluding their military use and justifying, by that very limitation, an especially protected status for them. This kind of *quid pro quo* underlies the special protection of non defended or demilitarized zones or localities, of cultural property and, at least in a certain sense, of medical units. Treaty rules allowing for a similar special protection of environmentally valuable areas would be a highly desirable development.

3   Environment on Neutral Territory

As already stated, the relationship between a party to a conflict and a neutral State is essentially governed by the law of peace time. There are, however, a few modifications of this relationship due to the fact that an armed conflict exists. Thus, the neutral State must tolerate certain measures of belligerent parties in relation to neutral shipping, namely the prevention of contraband being delivered to a party to the conflict or even a blockade. The neutral State must prevent its territory from being used by one of the parties to the conflict. There is no rule, however, that the neutral State must tolerate damage to its territory caused by one of the parties to the conflict. Quite to the contrary, Article 1 of the 1907 Hague Convention Respecting the Rights and Duties of Neutral Powers and Persons in Case of War on Land simply states: "The territory of neutral powers is inviolable".

This language appears sufficiently broad to cover all conceivable infringements of a neutral State's territory by warlike activities of belligerent parties. The practice during the Second World War confirms this interpretation. Compensation was paid to Switzerland in cases where collateral damage was caused to Swiss territory from attacks on targets in neighbouring areas of Germany. There is indeed no evidence that a neutral State has to tolerate any damage caused to its territory by belligerent activities of parties to the conflict. The rule of proportionality which applies to collateral civilian damage on the territory of the parties to the conflict does not apply to neutral territory. There is no such kind of reduced integrity of neutral territory. It is true that this rule may render the use of modern weapons of mass destruction in some cases extremely difficult from the legal point of view, which it is anyway. There is certainly no practice of States indicating that this fact has led to a change in the traditional customary rule of neutrality safeguarding the inviolability and immunity of neutral territory.

The fact, however, that the damage to the environment situated on neutral territory is caused through acts of war is, however, not completely irrelevant to the question of State responsibility. Thus, if the damage on the territory of the neutral State C is caused by an explosion occurring on the territory of belligerent B which is due to an attack by belligerent A, it is clear that the damage is attributed to State A, although a material source of that damage is situated on the territory of B. The damage is in this case not caused by State B, nor has State B any duty to prevent it. As to State A, it might plead a state of necessity as a circumstance excluding the wrongfulness of the act. But the existence of an armed conflict does not constitute a state of necessity in this sense. The state of necessity only precludes the wrongfulness if the specific illicit act in question (here: causing damage to the territory of a neutral State) is the only means to preserve a vital State interest against a serious and imminent danger. This, it is submitted, will be the case only in exceptional situations, even in times of war. There is no exclusion of wrongfulness where the norm which is violated is a norm of *ius cogens* or if it is part of a treaty which expressly or explicitly, excludes a state of necessity from being invoked. The latter principle is one of the reasons for a need to clarify, by the development of treaty law, the protection of the neutral environment in times of armed conflict.

The measure of permissible impact on neutral territory is thus established by the normal peacetime rules relating to transfrontier pollution or other harmful transfrontier impact. The basic principle underlying these rules still is the prohibition against causing damage (possibly significant damage) to other States. It is quite clear that the pollution of neutral coasts by oil constitutes a damage in this sense. A negligent or intentional causing of such damage is thus an internationally wrongful act against neutral States.

The legal evaluation of air pollution caused by the burning of oil fields is somewhat more complicated. Whether and to what extent this air pollution has caused any significant damage on the territory of neutral States seems difficult to evaluate. The substances emitted by the fires are not subject to any specific emission control treaty applicable to the parties and in particular to the party causing the fires. In Europe or North America, similar emissions would be relevant under the treaties limiting SO_2 emissions. They could be relevant under a future protocol to the Convention on Climate Change Limiting CO_2 emissions.

4 The Protection of the Environment in Non-International Armed Conflict

Protocol II additional to the Geneva Conventions contains a few regrettable lacunae as far as the rules relating to the conduct of hostilities are concerned. Thus, there is no specific provision protecting "civilian objects against the dangers" nor one protecting the environment. There is only a "general protection of the civilian population arising from military operations". This rule indirectly protects the environment. The same holds true for the rule prohibiting the starvation of the civilian population, which indirectly prohibits attacks on the living base of that population. On the other hand, all international rules concerned with the protection of the environment apply, not between the parties to the conflict, but between the State where the internal conflict takes place and other States. Again, the state of necessity may also be pleaded to limit to a certain extent the international responsibility of that State in case of violations of these rules. Furthermore, the State on whose territory the conflict takes place is not responsible for violations of the law committed by an insurgent party. Also, in this respect, some development or clarification of the law might be advisable, be it only to amend certain environmental law treaties by a state of emergency clause which is found in human rights treaties, and which grants as well as limits a right to suspend certain rights unless the insurgent party finally becomes the government.

5 The Perspective: New Law or Just Better Implementation

It has been shown that the legal protection of the environment in times of armed conflict is not as bad as one might think at first glance. There are rules of the law of armed conflict which provide for some protection of the environment, and the peace time rules concerning the protection of environment apply to a large extent also in times of armed conflict. As a first step, it is certainly necessary to spread this message among military decision makers. Nevertheless, there are some imprecisions and loopholes. The major loophole is that the rules concerning the immunity of civilian objects do not prevent some elements of the environment from becoming military objectives and therefore subject to destruction. The establishment of environmental safe havens in times of war, similar to the protection provided by the rules concerning cultural property, seems to be necessary.

In addition, the rule of proportionality which governs the admissibility of collateral damage on the territory of the parties to the conflict implies difficult value judgements. It might be appropriate to develop some more specific rules in this respect.

Finally, the development of the law of war is somewhat out of step with that of the development of environmental law. The essential purpose of the laws of war is to limit damage. That was also the case in the early development of environmental law as is evidenced by the rule concerning the prohibition of causing transfrontier damage. Nowadays, however, international environmental law, like national environmental law, is more and more governed by the precautionary principle which is recognized by Principle 15 of the Rio Declaration. It seems that action which may have an impact on the environment, even if there is no clear proof of actual harm, must not take place if it can be reasonably avoided. This is difficult to apply to a situation of armed conflict. It is alien to traditional military concepts, and what the recent development of the law of war calls "precautionary measures[2]", is a far cry from the precautionary principle in the sense of environmental law. But for the sake of the survival of our planet, this recent development of the law on environmental protection must not stop short of the law of armed conflict. This is a development, I submit: a desirable one, which cannot take place without the development of new written law. It is in this direction that efforts in law-making should go.

---

2   Articles 57 and 58, Protocol I.

Legal Restraints on Targeting

Protection of Civilian Population and the Changing Faces of Modern Conflict

The international legal rules which determine whether certain targets may or may not be lawfully attacked are based on one of the pillars of the international law applicable in armed conflicts, namely the distinction between the civilian population on the one hand and the military effort of the State on the other. The development of this distinction is a historical and cultural achievement of the age of enlightenment. This fact needs to be emphasized when there is a temptation to consider certain consequences of this distinction as too cumbersome for what is supposed to be a necessary military operation.

1 Distinction

In the centuries before the enlightenment, war was often, and then lawfully so, conducted in a way that made the "civilian" population suffer very drastically.[1] It was in particular the philosopher Jean Jacques Rousseau who, in the second half of the 18th century, developed the idea that war did not constitute a confrontation between peoples, but between States and their rulers ("sovereign's war").[2] This principle limited both the group of persons entitled to perform acts harmful to the enemy (combatants) and the scope of persons and objects which may be the target of such acts (combatants/military objectives).

In the 18th and early 19th century, this distinction corresponded to the reality of the conflicts of those days. It was possible and practicable to keep military activities well apart from the day-to-day life of the citizens, unless such unusual things as a *levée en masse* occurred. It was the technological developments of the late 19th and early 20th century which created the fundamental challenge to this distinction, namely the development of long-range weapons, in particular air warfare. The first rather comprehensive reaction to this challenge was an attempt at international rule making, the so-called Hague Rules of Air Warfare

---

1 Fritz Münch, "War, Laws of, History", in 4 *Encyclopedia of Public International Law* 1386 *et seq.* (Rudolf Bemhardt ed., 2000).

2 Wilhelm Grewe, *The Epochs of International Law* 267 (2000).

of 1923,[3] drafted by a group of experts based on a mandate given by the 1922 Washington Conference on Disarmament. These rules constituted a confirmation of the old distinction and developed its concrete application to the new situation. Rules elaborated by scientific bodies such as the International Law Association were formulated along the same lines.[4]

The great practical challenge to the traditional principle of distinction occurred during the Second World War. There were so many violations of the traditional principle that it was quite appropriate to ask the question whether that rule had survived or whether it had become obsolete.[5] The biggest challenge to the traditional rule of distinction was the development of nuclear weapons. It is, thus, necessary to critically analyze the attitude which States and other relevant actors adopted after the war in relation to that rule. State practice immediately following the Second World War was somewhat puzzled and puzzling. The definition of war crimes in the Statute of the International Military Tribunal is based on the assumption that the rule of distinction was applicable ("wanton destruction of cities, towns or villages, or devastation not justified by military necessity"). But neither the judgment of the International Military Tribunal nor the judgments of the American military courts really address the principle of distinction as a limitation on the choice of targets for bombardments.[6] Furthermore, there was a kind of resounding silence of States in relation to that rule. The Geneva Conventions of 1949, which in many ways clarify and develop the law taking into account the experience of the Second World War, do not address the question, yet most writers were loath to accept that the bombing practices of the war had changed the law.[7]

In 1956, the International Committee of the Red Cross (ICRC) made an attempt to have the question of the validity of the principle of distinction clarified by what was meant to become the Delhi Rules for the Limitation of the Dangers Incurred by the Civilian Population in Time of War.[8] This attempt was based on the assumption that the traditional rule of distinction was still valid,

---

3 *Documents on the Laws of War* 139 (Adam Roberts and Richard Guelff eds., 3d. ed. 2000).

4 Draft Convention for the Protection of the Civilian Population Against New Engines of War, adopted by the 40th Conference of the International Law Association, Amsterdam 1938. *The Law of Armed Conflicts: A Collection of Conventions, Resolutions and Other Documents* 223 (Dietrich Schindler & Jiri Toman eds., 3rd ed. 1988).

5 For a brief analysis of the practice, see Erik Castrén, *The Present Law of War and Neutrality* 402 *et seq.* (1954).

6 *Commentary on the Additional Protocols of 8 June 1977 to the Geneva Conventions of 12 August 1949*, ¶ 1828 (Yves Sandoz et al. eds., 1987).

7 Castrén, *supra* note 5, at 200 *et seq.*

8 *The Law of Armed Conflict, supra* note 4, at 251.

LEGAL RESTRAINTS ON TARGETING 409

but it failed. It became, so to say, the victim of the development of nuclear weapons or, more precisely, of a dispute concerning their legality. The military establishment of the day, it appears, remained completely outside the legal discourse concerning the legality of those nuclear weapons, of which the resolution of the Institut de Droit International of 1969[9] concerning the prohibition of weapons of mass destruction is a lively testimony.

That insulation of the legal discourse disappeared when the issue of the reaffirmation and development of international humanitarian law came on the political agenda as a consequence of the debate about the conduct of the Vietnam War and the issue of "human rights in occupied territory".[10] In 1968, the United Nations General Assembly reaffirmed the traditional principle in its resolution "Respect for Human Rights in Armed Conflicts", which declared: "That it is prohibited to launch attacks against the civilian population as such; That distinction must be made at all times between persons taking part in the hostilities and members of the civilian population. ..."[11]

The negotiations from 1974 to 1977 that led to the Additional Protocol I to the 1949 Geneva Conventions[12] and the reactions of States, including major military powers, after the adoption of the Protocol in 1977 are clearly based on the assumption that the basic content of the rule of distinction is part of customary international law. This is, in particular, reflected in the formulation of the declarations made by the United States and the United Kingdom on the occasion of the signature of the Protocol. In respect of so-called non-conventional weapons, they deny that the "new rules" of the Protocol apply to those weapons, the clear implication being that the "old", i.e., customary law rules do apply. It is made clear that the principle of distinction figures among these old rules.[13]

In addition, a legal discourse developed which now included military lawyers dealing with practical implications of this rule. Military lawyers explained and continued to explain that major bombing campaigns like those during the

---

9 "The Distinction between Military Objectives and Non-Military Objects in General and particularly the Problems Associated with Weapons of Mass Destruction", Resolution adopted by the Institut de Droit International at its session at Edinburg on September 9, 1969. *Id.* at 265.

10 Michael Bothe in Michael Bothe, Karl Partsch and Waldemar Solf, *New Rules for Victims of Armed Conflicts* 2 (1982).

11 G.A. Res. 2444, U.N. GAOR, 23rd Sess., Supp. No. 18, at 50, U.N. Doc. A/7128 (1969).

12 Protocol Additional to the Geneva Conventions of 12 August 1949, and Relating to the Protection of Victims of International Armed Conflict, June 8, 1977, 1125 U.N.T.S. 3, *Documents on the Laws of War, supra* note 3, at 422 [hereinafter Protocol I].

13 See *inter alios* Waldemar Solf, in Bothe, Partsch and Solf, *supra* note 10, at 276, 282.

410 PART 5: CONDUCT OF HOSTILITIES – PROTECTING THE ENVIRONMENT

Vietnam[14] and 1991 Persian Gulf[15] wars were indeed conducted on the basis of these rules. Thus, it can safely be concluded that the rule has survived all major challenges; that it is still part and parcel of customary law. This, however, raises the question of the interpretation of the rule in the light of changing circumstances.

2 The Two-Pronged Test of the Military Objective

As to the selection of targets in general and in air warfare in particular, the basic rule that follows from the distinction between the civilian population and the military effort is the distinction between military objectives and civilian objects. That distinction is to be made on the basis of two interrelated elements, namely the effective contribution the military objective makes to military action and the "definite military advantage" that the total or partial destruction, capture or neutralization of the objective offers. There is no doubt that this is a rule of customary international law and its binding force is, thus, not limited to the parties to Protocol I, which formulates this very principle as follows in Article 52(2): "military objectives are limited to those objects which by their nature, location, purpose or use make an effective contribution to military action and whose total or partial destruction, capture or neutralization, in the circumstances ruling at the time, offers a definite military advantage".[16]

The most recent practical confirmation of the customary law character of these principles is the experts report[17] published by the Chief Prosecutor of the

---

14   Burrus Carnahan, "'Linebacker I' and Protocol I: the Convergence of Law and Professionalism", 31 *American University Law Review* 861 (1982).

15   See Theodor Meron, "The Time Has Come for the United States to Ratify Geneva Protocol I", 88 *American Journal of International Law* 678, 681 (1994).

16   Protocol I, *supra* note 12, at 450.

17   Final Report to the Prosecutor by the Committee Established to Review the NATO Bombing Campaign against the Federal Republic of Yugoslavia, 39 *International Legal Materials* 1257 (2000), *reprinted* herein as Appendix A [hereinafter Report to the Prosecutor]. For an analysis, see, *inter alia, Symposium: The International Legal Fallout from Kosovo,* 12 *European Journal of International Law* 391 (2001), in particular the contributions by William Fenrick, *Targeting and Proportionality during the NATO Bombing Campaign against Yugoslavia,* at 489, Paolo Benvenuti, *The ICTY's Prosecutor and the Review of the NATO Bombing Campaign against the Federal Republic of Yugoslavia,* at 503, and Michael Bothe, *The Protection of the Civilian Population and NATO Bombing on Yugoslavia: Comments on a Report* to *the Prosecutor of the ICTY,* at 531. In addition, see Natalino Ronzitti, "Is the non liquet of the Final Report Established to Review the NATO Bombing Campaign Against the Federal Republic of Yugoslavia Acceptable?" 82 *International Review of the Red Cross* 1017 (2000).

LEGAL RESTRAINTS ON TARGETING

411

Criminal Tribunal for the former Yugoslavia concerning the question whether the NATO bombing campaign against the Federal Republic of Yugoslavia (FRY) involved the commission of crimes which were subject to the jurisdiction of the Tribunal-a report which constitutes an important document if lessons are to be drawn from the Kosovo experience.

The difficulty of the Article 52 (2) definition is its general character. There are, of course, clear cases of "pure" military objectives: military barracks, trenches in a battlefield, etcetera. Where objects are used or usable for different, military and non-military purposes (dual-use objects), their qualification as a military objective or civilian object becomes more difficult. What constitutes an "effective contribution" to military action? What is a "definite" military advantage? What is the difference, if any, between an "indefinite" or a "definite" military advantage? This brings us to the crucial problems of targeting. It must be realized that the application of rules formulated in general terms is a problem lawyers often encounter, not only in the law of war, but also in international law in general-even law in general. Legal rules expressed in general clauses need concretization for their practical application. The question, thus, is how to render the general principle of distinction more concrete in order to have secure standards for targeting.

A standard legislative method of rendering a general rule more concrete is the establishment of a list of cases of application, be it exhaustive or illustrative. This approach has been proposed by Professor Dinstein.[18] It presents a few problems of its own. An illustrative list may be useful for certain purposes, but it cannot terminate the discussion because the qualification of items that are not on the list remains open. The exhaustive list is dangerous, because it can exclude clear cases falling under the general rule, which were just forgotten or not foreseen when the list was drafted. Thus, there is often a tendency to add a catchall clause at the end of a list.[19] At that point one is for all practical purposes back to the illustrative list.

Despite these deficiencies of the list method, the ICRC in 1956 attempted to draft such a list of military objectives.[20] In relation to the difficult or

---

18   See, e.g. Professor Dinstein's paper in this volume.

19   See, e.g., Article 61 (a) (xv) of Protocol I ("complementary activities necessary to carry out any of the tasks mentioned above, including, but not limited to, planning and organization").

20   The list was drafted by the ICRC "as a model" to be annexed to the "Draft Rules for the Limitation of the Dangers Incurred by the Civilian Population in Times of Armed Conflict" (see note 8 *supra*) which the ICRC submitted in 1956 for consideration by the Red Cross Conference of 1957. See ICRC COMMENTARY, *supra* note 6, 2002. These rules became the victim of bitter controversies between governments during that conference (see J. Pokltefl and Michael Bothe, *Bericht über Entwicklungen und* Tendenzen *des*

controversial questions, this list shows all the problems of this method. The list is based on the undisputed fact that there are certain typical military objectives which can indeed be listed, but this is possible only to a limited extent. There are objects that in one context may constitute a military objective, making an effective contribution to military action, while in other circumstances they do not. This is clearly shown in the items on the list that have become quite controversial in the context of the Kosovo campaign, namely lines and means of communication and in particular telecommunication facilities.

As to traffic infrastructure, the formulation of the ICRC list is as follows: "Those of the lines and means of communications (railway lines, roads, bridges, tunnels and canals) which are of fundamental military importance". Thus, a distinction has to be made between those lines and means of communications that are of fundamental military importance and those that are not. Only those lines of communication that are of fundamental military importance are military objectives. This is clearly stated in Article 7, Paragraph 3 of the ICRC Draft Rules to which the list was to be annexed: "However, even if they belong to one of those categories, they cannot be considered as a military objective where their total or partial destruction, in the circumstances ruling at the time, offers no military advantage".

As a consequence, in every instance the question of the military importance of a bridge or railway line is unavoidable. It is submitted that to ask this very question is the only correct application of the rule of distinction. There is no rule saying that railway lines and bridges are always a military objective. Their military importance has to be ascertained in each particular case. This is the crucial problem of dual-use facilities. This problem applies to traffic infrastructure, telecommunication infrastructure and also to energy production and transmission facilities.

In the traditional context of land warfare, the military importance of traffic infrastructure is quite obvious. This traffic infrastructure is needed in order to bring supplies to the front or, as the case may be, to allow a swift retreat of the troops which may then reorganize afterwards. The examples given by Professor Dinstein[21] in order to prove his thesis are all taken from this context. During the so-called Christmas bombing of Hanoi, it was the use of railway lines for logistical support that was put forward as a justification for choosing certain targets (mainly railroads) in the very center of this city.[22] But what

---

Kriegsrechts seit den Nachkriegskodifikationen, 35 Zeitschrift für Ausländisches Öffentliches Recht und Völkerrecht 574, 575, 601 (1975).

21 See Professor Dinstein's paper in the present volume.

22 Carnahan, *supra* note 14, at 864 *et seq.*

was the military importance of the many bridges crossing the Danube River that were destroyed during the Kosovo campaign? There was no front to which supplies could have been moved. It was the declared policy of the NATO States not to create such a front but to renounce to ground operations and to restrict military action to an air campaign. In such a situation, it is very hard to see any military importance of this traffic infrastructure. If there is no such military importance, these means of communication are civilian objects, not military objectives.

With respect to the telecommunication network, the situation may be somewhat different. This network is of military importance even in the context of a conflict where one side uses the strategy of air warfare only, while the other side, by necessity, would have to rely on anti-aircraft defense. This defense certainly depends on telecommunications, but it remains questionable whether each facility using telecommunications equipment that may be found in the country belongs, for that reason, to a network of military significance. Is there a kind of presumption that telecommunication facilities are always, unless the contrary is apparent, related to the military network?

This seems to be the underlying rationale of the Report to the Prosecutor.[23] It brings us to a question of precautionary duties, duties of due diligence in evaluating the military importance of certain objects and more generally the decision-making process to which we will revert below. This was the crucial problem in evaluating the lawfulness of the attack against the television facilities in Belgrade. Could the target selectors just proceed on the basis of the assumption or presumption that the technical equipment of this station was so closely linked to the military network that, although there was an obvious civilian use, its military importance was significant enough that its destruction provided a definite military advantage?

So far, the notion of contribution to the military effort or of military advantage has been discussed in tactical or operational terms. The question then arises whether this notion could also be understood in a broader sense. Can objects that are not related to specific military operations also "contribute to the military effort?" Air attacks have a definite impact on the morale of the entire population and, thus, also on political and military decision-makers. It may well be argued that it was not only the diplomatic efforts by Chernomyrdin and Ahtassari, but also or even mainly the impact of the bombing campaign that finally induced Milosevic to agree to a withdrawal of the Serbian military and

---

23   Report to the Prosecutor, Appendix A, ¶ 72.

police forces from Kosovo. Did the bombing for that reason provide a "definite military advantage"?

As is rightly pointed out by Professor Dinstein and the Report to the Prosecutor,[24] this type of "advantage" is political, not military. The morale of the population and of political decision-makers is not a contribution to "military action". Thus, the advantage of softening the adversary's will to resist is not a "military" one and, thus, cannot be used as a legitimation for any targeting decision. If it were otherwise, it would be all too easy to legitimize military action which uses bombing just as a psychological weapon-and there are other words for this.

The practical importance of this limitation is considerable and not new. It would indeed be impossible to make any meaningful distinction between civilian objects and military objectives as the psychological effect can be produced by an attack on any target, including entirely civilian living quarters. The morale of the civilian population and of political decision-makers was the main target of the nuclear bombs dropped on Hiroshima and Nagasaki-not a legitimate one. During the bombing of North Vietnamese targets, already mentioned, in addition to the military significance of the traffic infrastructure as channels for military supplies, "forcing a change in the negotiating attitudes of the North Vietnamese leadership" was also recognized as a goal of the bombing campaigns against that country.[25] The NATO bombing campaign against the FRY was also designed to induce the Belgrade leadership to accept a settlement of the status of the Kosovo along the lines of NATO terms. Although the psychological impact of a certain attack may be a legitimate consideration in choosing between targets that are for other reasons of a military character, that impact alone is not sufficient to establish the qualification of a certain target as a military objective.

This legal situation introduces a basic ambiguity, or a fictitious character, into targeting decisions to be made within the framework of an armed conflict conducted for humanitarian purposes. As the goal of such a "war" is not the military defeat of an adversary, but the protection of the human rights of the population, the traditional notion of military advantage loses much of its significance. In the Kosovo campaign target selection was made on the basis of the fiction that military advantages and military victory in the traditional sense were sought, although this was not the case. The only real goal was a change of attitude of the Belgrade government. Thus, the question of what

---

24 Professor Dinstein's paper in the present volume and Report to the Prosecutor, *id.,* ¶ 55 ("civilian objects and civilian morale ... are not legitimate military objectives").

25 Carnahan, *supra* note 14, at 867.

really constitutes a military objective within the framework of a humanitarian intervention has to be asked. It would better correspond to the specific character of that particular type of military operation if only "pure" military objectives, in the sense mentioned already above, were considered to be legitimate targets.

3 The Environment – a Military Objective?

An additional comment is necessary concerning the environment as a military objective or civilian object. The rules of Protocol I relating to the protection of the environment, i.e., Articles 35(3) and 55, not only limit the permissible collateral damage to the environment caused by attacks against military objectives, but also limit permissible attacks where the environment itself constitutes a military objective, which is quite possible. Military objectives are not just persons or manmade structures: a piece of land can become a military objective if its neutralization offers a definite military advantage. Interdiction fire is an example. This type of military action is not directly targeted at combatants. The military usefulness consists of the fact that by bringing a certain area under constant fire, the enemy is deterred from entering that area. Cutting down, or defoliating, trees in order to deprive the enemy of cover is another example. The consequences of such actions for the environment may be disastrous. In such cases, for the reasons indicated, the rules of Articles 35(3) and 55 protect the environment when it is a military objective.

An attack against the environment, however, is unlawful only where the damage caused or expected is "widespread, long-term and severe". These three conditions are cumulative. All three must be met for there to be a violation. Therefore, we are back to the problem of general clauses and their concretization. It is true that many of the delegations present at the conference in Geneva that drafted Protocol I favored a very high threshold[26] It appears that the Kosovo campaign has not really given any new impetus to concretize this threshold, as the actual environmental damage remained below that limit. The threshold is still an open question, but the very fact that the Report to the Prosecutor starts its legal assessment of the bombing campaign by analyzing the question of environmental destruction[27] shows that environmental considerations have indeed become an important restraint on military

---

26 Bothe, Partsch and Solf, *supra* note 10, at 346 *et seq.*
27 Report to the Prosecutor, Appendix A, ¶¶ 14–25.

416   PART 5: CONDUCT OF HOSTILITIES – PROTECTING THE ENVIRONMENT

activities, although the legal reasoning of the report in this respect is highly questionable.[28]

In a first approach, the Report to the Prosecutor uses Articles 35(3) and 55 of Protocol I as the basic yardstick to determine the legality of any damage caused to the environment. It does not give a final answer to the question whether these provisions have become a rule of customary international law. The report simply finds that the damage caused by the NATO air campaign does not meet the triple cumulative threshold established by these provisions of being "widespread, long-term and severe".

If one takes the factual findings of the Balkan Task Force established by the United Nations Environment Programme, this conclusion is probably unavoidable. What is interesting, however, is that the assessment made by the committee does not stop at this point. It also analyses environmental damage in the light of the proportionality principle which is the usual test for the admissibility of collateral damage caused by attacks against military targets. This, as a matter of principle, is a valid point. This line of argument could be used as a means to lower the difficult threshold of Articles 35 and 55. Once it was established that collateral environmental damage was excessive in relation to a military advantage anticipated, it would also be unlawful even it was not widespread, long-lasting and severe.

A systematic interpretation of Protocol I would lead to the conclusion that the environment is protected by the combined effect of the general provision limiting admissible collateral damage and the particular provision on environmental damage. It would mean that in a concrete case, the stricter limitation would apply. Unfortunately, the report does not draw this conclusion. Instead, it refers to the formulation of Article 8(2)(b)(iv) of the International Criminal Court (ICC) Statute as "an authoritative indicator of evolving customary international law".[29] This provision, which is quite unfortunate from the point of view of environmental protection, creates a different type of cumulative effect of the rules on the protection of the environment and the proportionality principle. Causing environmental damage is only a war crime if it goes, first, beyond the threshold established by the triple cumulative conditions and, second, beyond what is permissible according to the proportionality principle. In the light of the reservations which the military establishment shows vis-à-vis taking into account environmental concerns as a limitation on military

---

28   Bothe, *supra* note 17, at 532 *et seq.;* Thilo Marauhn, "Environmental damage in times of armed conflict – not 'really' a matter of criminal responsibility?" 82 *International Review of the Red Cross* 1029 (2000).

29   Report to the Prosecutor, Appendix A, ¶ 21.

LEGAL RESTRAINTS ON TARGETING 417

violence, this is probably as far as one could go in the definition of a war crime. It should be stressed, however, that this stance can be accepted only for the definition of the war crime, not as far as the interpretation of the primary rules of behavior relating to the protection of the environment in times of armed conflicts are concerned. The damage caused to the environment is unlawful if it is either excessive or widespread, long-term and severe. Causing the damage, however, is a war crime only if damage fulfils both criteria.

4   Decision-Making: Ascertaining Relevant Facts

As already pointed out, a targeting decision must involve a certain factual evaluation of the actual or potential use of specific objects as to whether they make or do not make a contribution to military action. Protocol I prescribes that efforts have to be made in order to ascertain the military character of an objective.[30] On the other hand, the targeting decision is certainly one which has to be taken in a context of uncertainty. It is unrealistic to require absolute certainty concerning the military importance of a specific object before it can be lawfully attacked, but not requiring absolute certainty is not the same as permitting disregard of the facts.

Whatever the actual standard of due diligence, there is an obligation of due diligence in ascertaining the character of a proposed target. This question arises, in modern decision making, on two different levels, that of target selection at the command level and that of launching the actual attack, which is not the same, as the case of the attack on a bridge which also hit a civilian train (not a selected target) demonstrates.[31] A violation of this duty of due diligence is a violation of the law of armed conflict. In such cases as the attack against the Chinese Embassy in Belgrade, there are reasons to believe that indeed the selection of that particular building as a target was due to a violation of this obligation of due diligence and therefore a negligent violation of the law of armed conflict.

5   Decision-Making: Balancing Processes and Value Judgments

The evaluation of the military advantage to be derived from an attack is not only a matter of the relevant facts, but also a matter of value judgments. What

---

30   Article 57(2)(a)(i).

31   Report to the Prosecutor, Appendix A, ¶¶ 58–62.

constitutes an advantage is a matter of subjective evaluation. This raises the question of "whose values matter?" In a somewhat different context, namely the value judgment involved in the assessment of proportionality, the Report to the Prosecutor states that this must be the judgment of the "reasonable military commander".[32] This statement, plausible as it may appear at a first glance, is problematic. In a democratic system, the value judgment which matters most is that of the majority of the society at large. The military cannot and may not constitute a value system of its own, separated by waterproof walls from that of civil society. Such separation would be to the disadvantage of both the military and civil society. A dialogue between the two, critical and constructive in both directions, is needed.

This is essential for a number of reasons. There is no denying the fact that public opinion in many countries views the military with a critical eye. This is particularly true for certain organizations of civil society engaged in the promotion of human rights. It is certainly in the interest of both the military and civil society organizations to avoid a situation where such critique is based on a lack of understanding and on misconceptions.[33] Furthermore, the practice observed in recent conflicts indeed recognizes that targeting decisions have political implications. This is why certain decisions are reserved to persons that are very high in the governmental hierarchy. Targeting decisions engage the political responsibility to the electorate, i.e., civil society, of those holding high governmental offices. Therefore, these decisions have to be understandable and acceptable to civil society; hence the need for a dialogue.

6 The Problem of Errors

The question of values or value judgments leads to the problem of error or mistake in judgment. Such an error may relate to the facts or to the law. In the case of the Chinese Embassy, it was an error of fact. When the decision was made to attack a particular building, the decision-makers thought, or at least

---

32   *Id.,* ¶ 50.

33   A good example for the problem was the case of a German organization for the preservation of the language which chose "collateral damage" as the "bad expression of the year" for 1999. See the Unwort des Jahres website at http://www.unwortdesjahres.org. The mistake was on both sides. The organization was unaware of the technical character and meaning of the term, and the NATO spokesmen who had used it did not realize that the term transported a wrong message to the public, namely that damage to the civilian population and civilian objects were something which was unimportant and negligible for those who decided on targets in the Kosovo conflict.

this is what we were told, that the building had a military use. The decision-makers did not know that it was the Chinese Embassy, which was obviously not a military objective.

In relation to attacks against railways and bridges, another question arises, namely the error of law. In this case, there was probably no erroneous evaluation of the actual use of those bridges and railway lines as a matter of fact. The essential error, if the view submitted by this paper is correct, consisted in a mistaken view of the law that considered traffic infrastructure as military objectives without asking the question of their military importance in the concrete context. As a matter of principle, an error of law does not exclude responsibility. *Ignorantia iuris* is no excuse or even circumstance excluding the wrongfulness of the behavior.

What are the consequences of these problems of due diligence and error on criminal accountability? The definition of war crimes contained in the statute of the permanent International Criminal Court[34] requires intent.[35] Violations of the laws of war committed by negligence are not subject to the jurisdiction of that court. The situation is, however, different with respect to the ad hoc International Criminal Tribunal for the former Yugoslavia (ICTY). Any violation of the laws and customs of war comes within the jurisdiction of that court according to Article 3 of its statute.[36] Thus, the ICTY would have had jurisdiction to prosecute and punish negligent violations of the laws of war which, as indicated, appear to be quite possible in this case. It is in this context that the question of error becomes most relevant. An error concerning the facts may entail a negligent violation of the respective rule, an error concerning the law, as a rule, does not constitute a valid defense.

7   The Law of War and Humanitarian Intervention-Some General Reflections

It must be stressed that all these considerations concerning lawful means and methods of combat are independent from the question whether the Kosovo air campaign was or was not a violation of the rules of the United Nations Charter prohibiting the use of force. *Jus ad bellum* and *jus in bello* have to be kept separate. This is the essential basis for a realistic approach

---

34   U.N. Doc. A/CONF/183/9, July 17, 1998, *Documents on the Laws of War, supra* note 3, at 667.

35   *Id.,* art. 30, at 690.

36   Statute of the International Tribunal, U.N. Doc. S/25704, May 3, 1993. The text of the Statute is reprinted in 32 *International Legal Materials* 1192 (1993).

to the law of armed conflict that has to treat both parties to a conflict on an equal footing. Questions of the legality or illegality of the use of force in a particular context have to be raised in other contexts, not in that of the application of the *jus in bello*. The equality of the parties in relation to the *jus in bello* is an essential precondition to the effective functioning of this body of law. This is why the Preamble to Protocol I reaffirms this principle in no uncertain terms: "Reaffirming that the provisions of the Geneva Conventions of 12 August 1949 and of this Protocol must be fully applied in all circumstances ... , without any adverse distinction based on the nature or origin of the armed conflict or on the causes espoused by or attributed to the Parties to the conflict".

The principle of the equality of the parties to a conflict does not exclude the need to consider the entire context of a conflict, its intrinsic character, when determining the concept of military objective. Military advantage, as already pointed out, is a contextual notion. Where the declared purpose of a military action is limited from the outset, where the goal pursued is not just victory, but something else, it is difficult to ignore this limitation when it comes to the question what constitutes an advantage in that particular context. Thus, where the exclusive purpose of a military operation is to safeguard the human rights of a certain population, this very context excludes, it is submitted, a legal construction of the notion of military advantage or contribution to the military effort which disregards the life and health of this very population. In other words, in this context, the notion of military objective has to be construed in a much narrower way than in other types of conflict.

This contextual concept of military advantage is, it is submitted, *lex lata*. It must not be confused with proposals *de lege ferenda* demanding special rules for the conduct of so-called humanitarian interventions. If such rules were to be adopted, they could only mean an additional unilateral restraint imposed on those States or organizations which intervene for the sake of safeguarding the human rights of a certain population. Such rules could not and should not affect the rights and duties of the other party to the conflict.

More critical review of the notion of military advantage is needed. If the law were to be developed by a specific legal instrument relating to humanitarian intervention, why not impose on the forces maintaining the rule of law and human rights, obligations that are stricter than the usual rules of targeting valid for any belligerent?

19

The Ethics, Principles and Objectives of Protection of the Environment in Times of Armed Conflict

1 **Introduction: The Question**

Is war the end of ethics or ethical behaviour? Are killing and devastation, as they occur in war, unethical *per se*? If one looks at the ethical discourses over the centuries[1] this is a position which can certainly be found, although if one takes the discourse as a whole, it is an extreme position. Nevertheless, regardless of whether war is or is not unethical *per se*, as the rich literature on war and ethics proves war does not lead to an abdication of ethics.[2] Rather, in relation to war, ethical considerations go in two different, albeit not necessarily mutually exclusive directions. On the one hand there is the virtue of courage in fighting. Courage in fighting for the defence of the soldier's country is also an ethical postulate which can be related to the concept of chivalry. This, on the other hand, brings into play the second direction of ethical considerations, that of ethical demands as a restraint in warfare. Restraint in the ways and means of waging war is a demand of the just war theory which holds that just wars are only those which are, *inter alia*, conducted by just means.[3]

What are the consequences of ethical approaches for the protection of the environment in armed conflict? The just war theory seems to implicate reference to the law of armed conflict in that unlawful warfare is also unethical. While this reasoning may appear to lead to a vicious circle, as will be demonstrated, this is not necessarily the case. In addition, the specific discourse on environmental ethics may also be relevant. The principal demand of environmental ethics is conduct that respects the need to preserve the natural

---

1 *See* A. Biehler, 'Pacifi sm', in particular MN 2 and 4, in R. Wolfrum (ed.), *Max Planck Encyclopedia of Public International Law* (MPEPIL), available at <www.mpepil.com> (last visited 30 September 2013).

2 A. J. Coates, *The ethics of war* (Manchester University Press, Manchester, 1997); R. Sorabji (ed.), *The ethics of war – shared problems in different traditions*, (Ashgate, Aldershot *et al.*, 2006).

3 P. P. Christopher, *Just War Theory: an historical and philosophical analysis* (University of Massachusetts Amherst, 1990).

environment of the planet.[4] Different approaches exist concerning the way in which this goal is to be reached: The ecocentric and the anthropocentric approach.[5] The former demands the preservation of nature for its own sake, while the latter requires this preservation for the benefit of humankind. In the international discourse on environmental policy, the pure ecocentric approach is largely set aside. Rather, an anthropocentric approach which requires the preservation of the environment in order not to jeopardise the living conditions of present and future generations is the prevailing and generally recognised policy principle.[6] In this way, the preservation of the environment is a demand of intergenerational equity.[7]

The purpose of this study is to attempt to clarify the ethical requirements concerning the legal protection of the environment in armed conflict. It takes as its starting point a number of assumptions. The first is that there is an ethical underpinning for the law relating to the protection of the environment in armed conflict. The second assumption is that certain principles can be derived from these underpinnings. Finally, the third assumption is that such principles have inspired and continue to inspire the objectives of designing and applying a legal regime. The point of this study is to demonstrate whether, and if so why, these assumptions are correct.

2 The Ethics of the Laws of War and of Environmental Law

In attempting to answer the question of the protection of the environment in armed conflicts, one immediately encounters the phenomenon of the fragmentation of international law, or the notion that different areas of international law develop in a quasi-autonomous way. The fact of fragmentation can be observed simply by looking at the reality of the international order.[8] Nevertheless,

---

4   The first author to advocate this approach was R. Carson, *Silent Spring* (New York, 1962). For a more recent analysis, *see in particular* H. Rolston, *A New Environmental Ethics: The Next Millenium for Life on Earth* (Routledge, New York/London, 2012).

5   Rolston, *ibid.*, in particular pp. 33 *et seq.*

6   Principle 1 of the Rio Declaration of Environment and Development 1992: "Human beings are at the center of concern for sustainable development".

7   Principle 3 of the Rio Declaration: "The right to development must be fulfilled so as to equitably meet developmental and environmental needs of present and future generations".

8   *See* G. Hafner, 'Pros and Cons Ensuing from Fragmentation of International Law', 25 *Michigan Journal of International Law* (2004) pp. 849–864; A. Fischer-Lescano, 'Regime Collisions: The Vain Search for the Legal Unity in the Fragmentation of Global Law', 25 *Michigan Journal of International Law* (2004) pp. 999–1046.

THE ETHICS OF PROTECTION OF THE ENVIRONMENT

some theorists of international law oppose this view, insisting, instead, on the unity of the legal order[9] as an important consideration in counterbalancing the fact of fragmentation. Indeed, the fragmented areas of international law are not watertight compartments. In the reality of the international system, an addressee of international law is most often subject to various legal regimes in dealing with a single set of facts. This can, but does not necessarily have to, and indeed should not, lead to conflicting legal demands. The international legal order must therefore provide ways and means to accommodate possibly diverging demands coming from different areas of the law.[10]

Two of the areas or fields of the fragmented system of international law are the law of armed conflict and international environmental law.[11] Both these areas owe their very existence to philosophical and ethical considerations, which have already been referred to and are relevant for the present inquiry.

2.1   The Law of Armed Conflict

The essentials of the modern law of armed conflict derive from philosophical concepts developed by Jean-Jacques Rousseau, the great philosopher of the Age of Enlightenment. We owe to him the concept that war is limited to a confrontation between the military organisations of sovereigns, a concept which logically leads to the principle of distinction between civilians and combatants. The ultimate source of the concept is the rule of reason: unnecessary violence is unreasonable and therefore a sin against human nature. The reasoning of Rousseau is still worth quoting:[12]

> War then is a relation, not between man and man, but between State and State, and individuals are enemies only accidentally, not as men, nor even as citizens, but as soldiers, not as members of their country, but as its defenders. Finally, each State can have for enemies only other States, and not men; for between things disparate in nature there can be no real relation.

---

9   P.-M. Dupuy, 'L'unité de l'ordre juridique international', 297 *RdC* (2002) pp. 9–489.

10   Hafner, *supra* note 8, p. 856.

11   M. Tignino, 'Droit international de l'environnment', in R. van Steenberghe (ed.), *Droit international humanitaire: un régime spécial de droit international?* (Bruylant, Brussels, 2013) pp. 267–299; *see also* M. Bothe, 'Conclusion générale', in R. van Steenberghe (ed.), *Droit international humanitaire: un régime spécial de droit international?* pp. 321–331, in particular at pp. 329 *et seq.*

12   J.-J. Rousseau, *The Social Contract*, Book 1 ch. 2, 1762, translated 1782 by G.D.H. Cole, available at <www.constitution.org/jjr/socon.htm> (last visited 24 August 2012).

PART 5: CONDUCT OF HOSTILITIES – PROTECTING THE ENVIRONMENT

> Furthermore, this principle is in conformity with the established rules of all times and constant practice of all civilized peoples. ... The foreigner, whether King, individual, or people, who robs, kills, or detains the subjects, without declaring war on the prince, is not an enemy, but a brigand. Even in real war, a just prince, while laying hands, in the enemy's country, on all that belongs to the public, respects the lives and goods of individuals: he respects rights on which his own are founded. The object of the war being the destruction of the hostile State, the other side has a right to kill its defenders, while they are bearing arms; but as soon as they lay them down and surrender, they cease to be enemies or instruments of the enemy, and become once more merely men, whose life no one has any right to take. Sometimes it is possible to kill the State without killing a single one of its members; and war gives no right which is not necessary to the gaining of its object. These principles are not those of Grotius; they are not based on the authority of poets, but derived from the nature of reality and based on reason.

This philosophical concept is the *fons et origo* of two fundamental principles of the modern law of armed conflict: the principle of distinction and the principle of necessity. The latter principle is often understood or misunderstood as an overbroad justification of the use of military force. But it also constitutes a restraint on the use of force in that only that amount of force is justified which is necessary to achieve a legitimate military purpose.

At the time of Rousseau, this philosophical concept of war corresponded to the realities of warfare, the so-called cabinet wars of the 18th century.[13] That type of warfare soon disappeared, and the wars of our time make the wars of the 18th century look like folklore (although the blood toll of some of them was considerable). Despite this change, however, the rules of the law of war developed pursuant to the philosophical concept of the Enlightenment have withstood the pressure of military facts. The reason lies in the phenomenon of 'public conscience', to use the term of the Martens clause of the Hague Conventions.[14] Public conscience stands in the way of killing innocent civilians and taking their property. To use a term of legal sociology,[15] the resilience of

---

13 S. C. Neff, *War and the Law of Nations* (CUP, Cambridge, 2005) pp. 163 *et seq.*

14 Hague Convention IV, Preamble: "... the inhabitants and the belligerents remain under the protection and the rule of the principles of the law of nations, as they result from the usages established among civilised peoples, from the laws of humanity, and the dictates of the public conscience".

15 N. Luhmann, *Das Recht der Gesellschaft* (Suhrkamp, Frankfurt/Main, 1993) p. 581; A. Fischer-Lescano, *Globalverfassung* (Velbrück, Weilerswist, 2005) pp. 67 *et seq.*

THE ETHICS OF PROTECTION OF THE ENVIRONMENT   425

the principle of distinction and the prohibition of unnecessary suffering can also be explained by the fact of "scandalisation". Related concepts are those of a *colere publique*[16] or indignation.[17] The meaning of these terms is that certain facts are considered to be unacceptable to public conscience and are therefore to be rejected and opposed.

Scandalisation of public opinion is a driving force for maintaining and developing reasonable restraints on military force. The scandalisation of public opinion as a result of the human suffering caused by war thus accounts for both the maintenance of the fundamental principles of the laws of war and for the continuous improvement of this law.[18] The first example of this process was the initiative taken by Henry Dunant who, after being scandalised by the sufferings of the battle of Solferino, appealed to the conscience of European rulers of his time who, in 1864, negotiated the first Geneva Convention.[19] The scandalisation over the use of chemical weapons in the World War I led to their legal prohibition in 1925.[20] This same mechanism led to the adaptations of the Geneva Conventions to new developments after World War I and II by the Geneva Conventions of 1929 and 1949 as well as after the first three decades of post-World War II conflicts by the Additional Protocols of 1977.[21]

The idea that legal restraints on the methods and means of warfare are based on the rule of reason leads to another ethical underpinning of the law of armed conflict. Respect of these rules serves the re-establishment of peace after the war.[22] To put it in more general terms: these legal restraints are needed

---

16 Luhmann, *ibid.*, referring to the expression coined by E. Durkheim, *Über soziale Arbeitsteilung*, 1930, 3rd edition (Frankfurt/Main, 1999), at pp. 118 *et seq.*

17 S. Hessel, *Indignez vous* (Indigènes éditions, Paris, 2010).

18 M. Bothe, 'The Historical Evolution of International Humanitarian Law, International Human Rights Law, Refugee Law and International Criminal Law', in H. Fischer *et al.* (eds.), *Crisis Management and Humanitarian Protection, Festschrift fur Dieter Fleck* (Berliner Wissenschaft sverlag, Berlin, 2004) pp. 37–45, in particular at pp. 38 *et seq.*

19 R. Kolb, *Ius in bello. Le droit international des conflits armés*, 2nd edition (Helbing & Lichtenhahn, Basel, 2009) pp. 39 *et seq.*

20 M. Bothe, *Das völkerrechtliche Verbot des Einsatzes chemischer und bakteriologischer Waffen* (Carl Heymanns, Cologne *et al.*, 1973) pp. 21 *et seq.*, 99 *et seq.*

21 For a brief summary of the history, *see* M. Bothe and K. J. Partsch, in M. Bothe, K. J. Partsch and W. A. Solf, *New Rules for Victims of Armed Conflicts. Commentary on the Two 1977 Protocols Additional to the Geneva Conventions of 1949* (Martinus Nijhoff, The Hague et al., 1982) at pp. 1 *et seq.*

22 Coates, *supra* note 2, p. 273. *See also* B. Orend, '*Jus post bellum*: The Perspective of a Just-War Theorist', 20 *Leiden Journal of International Law* (2007) pp. 571–591, in particular at p. 584.

426   PART 5: CONDUCT OF HOSTILITIES – PROTECTING THE ENVIRONMENT

for the sake of the future existence of the population affected by the war. This is an important point to which we will revert further below.

The rule of reason and the concern for the future have from very early times introduced an element of environmental conservation into ethical rules on the conduct of hostilities:[23] In *Deuteronomy* 20: 19, we find the admonition:

> When you are at war, and lay siege to a city ... do not destroy its trees by taking the axe to them, for they provide you with food ...

A caveat must, however, be added concerning the use of moral arguments relating to the rules of warfare. Generally, ethical principles are not absolute.[24] As general principles, they do not provide easy solutions for every concrete situation. Countervailing principles may limit the scope of one or the other principle. In the context of armed conflict, the will to defend one's country is often considered as an ethical requirement. This approach might give legitimacy to measures which are otherwise problematic from an ethical point of view. The best known example of the resulting tension between various ethical demands is the attempt to justify torture for the sake of a country's security. This is an ethical underpinning of security interests and 'military necessity', in this case not understood as a restraint, but as a circumstance justifying military force. It can be shown, for instance, in the use of ethical language to justify resort to war. As an example, one can quote the National Security Strategy published by President Bush in 2002:

> In the war against global terrorism, we will never forget that we are ultimately fighting *for our democratic values.*[25]

Thus, democratic values are used to give legitimacy to wars which otherwise would be considered as illegal. Seen in this light, legal restraints on the use of military force can be situated in a tension between the ethical requirement of humanity and that of democracy. This tension is in a way related to the perennial question of freedom of opinion and expression on the one hand and the need to defend democracy against internal enemies.

---

23   N. Solomon, 'The ethics of war: Judaism', in Sorabji, *supra* note 2, pp. 108–137, at p. 113.

24   H. Spencer, 'Absolute and Relative Ethics', in *The Principles of Ethics* (1897, new edition, Liberty Classics, Indianapolis, 1978) vol. I, pp. 99 *et seq.*

25   National Security Strategy 2002, p. 7 (emphasis added), available at <http://merln.ndu.edu/whitepapers/USnss2002.pdf> (last visited 30 August 2012).

THE ETHICS OF PROTECTION OF THE ENVIRONMENT 427

In conflicts where a spirit of exclusion based on religious or ethnic criteria reigns, such as conflicts involving ethnic cleansing, the language of morality leads to more bitterness in conflict. Historic experience shows that a spirit of exclusion leads to a disregard of legal restraints[26] and a degeneration of armed conflicts to butchery. In such a situation, the language of morality may even be used to justify war crimes. Thus, extreme caution is necessary where morality is used to justify violence. Otherwise, there can be no adequate balance between "humanity" and "military necessity"[27] which is the basis for a realistic law of armed conflicts, a law which is acceptable and accepted because it adequately takes into account both principles. A duty to conserve nature in warfare may become the victim of such tensions or imbalances.[28]

2.2. Environmental Law

Some elements of what today is called international environmental law have a long history, originating, particularly, in the need to regulate the use of certain shared resources (fisheries, waters).[29] A somewhat more idealistic concern for nature appeared around 1900 as a source of inspiration for law making, both nationally and internationally. However, it is the full awareness of the finite character of the resources of the Earth that has triggered the development of modern environmental law, both national and international, that has taken place since the end of the 1960s.[30] This awareness has led to restraints on human activities, in particular restraints on the exploitation of natural resources, in order to ensure the living conditions of both present and future generations.[31] Care for the next generation is a fundamental principle of human

---

26 M. Bothe 'Multiculturalism and the Development of International Humanitarian Law', in S. Yee and J.-I. Morin (eds.), *Multiculturalism and International Law* (The Hague, 2009) pp. 617–628.

27 H. P. Gasser and N. Melzer, *Humanitäres Völkerrecht*, 2nd edition (Nomos/Schulthess, Zürich *et al.*, 2012) pp. 27 *et seq.*

28 Solomon, *supra* note 23.

29 P. H. Sand, 'The Evolution of International Environmental Law', in D. Bodansky, J. Brunnée, and E. Hey (eds.), *The Oxford Handbook of International Environmental Law* (OUP, Oxford, 2007) pp. 29–43, at pp. 31 *et seq.*; P. Sands and J. Peel, *Principles of International Environmental Law*, 3rd edition (CUP, Cambridge, 2012) pp. 23 *et seq.*; J. Wyatt, 'Lawmaking at the intersection of international environmental, humanitarian and criminal law: the issue of damage to the environment in international armed conflict', 92:879 *International Review of the Red Cross* (2010) pp. 583–646, at pp. 599 *et seq.*

30 M. Bothe, 'Environment, Development, Resources', 318 *RdC* (2005) pp. 333–516, at pp. 410 *et seq.*

31 E. Brown Weiss, *In Fairness to Future Generations: International Law, Common Patrimony, and Intergenerational Equity* (United Nations University, Tokyo/New York, 1988) *passim.*

428   PART 5: CONDUCT OF HOSTILITIES – PROTECTING THE ENVIRONMENT

morality.[32] In the environmental context this concern is now embodied in the principle of intergenerational equity which forms one of the ethical bases of environmental law.[33]

Like the law of armed conflict, the principle of intergenerational equity amounts to respecting a rule of reason: moderation for the sake of human survival. It is simply unreasonable to use resources in a way that nothing is left for users in the future. It should be noted that this is essentially an anthropocentric approach. The purely ecocentric approach, or respect for nature for its own sake, cannot with the same degree of plausibility rely on the rule of reasonable moderation.[34] For this reason, the ecocentric approach remains controversial.

Scientific reflection has certainly played a role in the development of environmental law. The warnings of scientist have triggered political initiatives and as a consequence legal developments as a response to environmental risks and dangers highlighted by the scientific community. The first and probably most influential scientific document was the study by the Club of Rome entitled *The Limits of Growth*, which stirred awareness of the finite character of the Earth's resources[35] and inspired legal developments providing for their more parsimonious use. However, scandalisation, or learning from disasters, has also played a major role. Disasters like oil spills and heavy pollution incidents have been major factors driving the development of environmental law.[36]

Nevertheless, countervailing considerations slowing down or sometimes preventing the development of environmental law also exist. These considerations have mainly been based on economic interests, including, in particular, interests in short term gain. A common method of giving an appearance of legitimacy to such interests has been the invocation of an alleged need to maintain employment.[37] Put in this way, there is a conflict between

---

32   R. Attfield, 'Environmental ethics and global sustainability', in H. A. M. J. Ten Have (ed.), *Environmental Ethics and International Policy* (UNESCO, Paris, 2006) pp. 69–87, at pp. 80 *et seq.*

33   C. D. Stone, 'Ethics and International Environmental Law', in Bodansky *et al.*, *supra* note 29, pp. 292–312, at pp. 304 *et seq.*; T. B. Adams, 'Rawls' Theory of Justice and International Environmental Law', 20 *Global Business and Development Law Journal* (2007) pp. 1–13; E. Agius, 'Environmental ethics: Towards an intergenerational perspective', in Ten Have, *supra* note 32, pp. 89–115.

34   But see H. Rolston, 'Intrinsic values on Earth: nature and nations', in Ten Have (ed.), *supra* note 32, pp. 47–67, at p. 63.

35   D. H. Meadows *et al.*, *The Limits of Growth. A Report to the Club of Rome* (Macmillan, New York, 1972).

36   Sand, *supra* note 29, p. 34.

37   Bothe, *supra* note 30, p. 414.

THE ETHICS OF PROTECTION OF THE ENVIRONMENT

intragenerational equity, in the example expressed as a just concern for the welfare of the workers, and intergenerational equity, expressed as concern for the living conditions of future generations. The notion of "sustainable development" seems to provide a compromise solution for this conflict.[38] As formulated by the Brundtland Report, the principle of sustainable development serves as a guidance for policy and behaviour that "meets the needs of the present generation without compromising the ability of future generations to meet their own needs".[39]

2.3   The Law of Armed Conflict and International Environmental Law

In the beginning of the 1970s, the moral factors driving the development of the law of armed conflict and of environmental law met. When the two Protocols additional to the Geneva Conventions were negotiated, the awareness of the finite character of the Earth's resources could not be left aside.[40] A provision on the protection of the environment in times of armed conflict had to be inserted. The negotiations were in particular driven by a scandalisation which related both to the law of armed conflict and environmental law, namely the use of chemical weapons, in particular the use of herbicides during the Vietnam War with their disastrous environmental and health consequences. However, countervailing military interests proved to be strong. The result has been an ongoing debate of several decades between perceived military requirements and the need to preserve the environment even in times of armed conflict.[41] In this battle, the cause of the environment has gained some ground, but the situation still far from satisfactory. While a compromise formula between long-term environmental interest and short-term economic interest has arguably been found in the notions of sustainable development and more recently in that of a green economy,[42] this compromise has not seemed possible in the case of environmental restraints on warfare. There still is no such notion as sustainable or green warfare.

---

38   Bothe, *supra* note 30, pp. 479 *et seq.*

39   World Commission on Environment and Development, *Our Common Future* (1987) p. 43.

40   Wyatt, *supra* note 29, pp. 610 *et seq.*

41   For an analysis of the historic development *see* M. Bothe, 'Military Activities and the Protection of the Environment', 37 *Environmental Policy and Law* (2007) pp. 232–238.

42   UNEP, *Towards a Green Economy. Pathways to Sustainable Development and Poverty Eradication* (2011) (known as "Green Economy Report"); S. Dröge and N. Simon, 'The Green Economy: An Economic Concepts for Everyone?', in M. Beisheim and Susanne Dröge (eds.), *UNSCD Rio 2012. Twenty Years of Sustainability Policies – Now Put into Practice* (Stiftung Wissenschaft und Politik Research Paper 8, Berlin, 2012) pp. 17–30.

430 PART 5: CONDUCT OF HOSTILITIES – PROTECTING THE ENVIRONMENT

3   Principles

3.1   *The Law of Armed Conflict*

The important principles of the law of armed conflict derived from Rousseau's concept of war are the principle of distinction and the prohibition of 'unnecessary suffering'. The principle of distinction means that attacks may only be directed against military objectives, not against civilian objects or the civilian population.[43] Where attacks against military objectives entail incidental civilian damage, the attack is permissible only if the incidental damage is not excessive in relation to the military advantage anticipated (principle of proportionality).[44] Those who decide on an attack must take 'precautionary measures' to make sure that the attack does not violate these principles.[45] These rules are anchored not only in treaty law, they also constitute customary law.

The prohibition of unnecessary suffering[46] means that acts causing damage to the enemy must be limited to those which are necessary to achieve a military advantage. That prohibition is formulated in a general way in Article 23(e) of the Hague Regulations and in Article 34 of Additional Protocol I (AP I). It is also a leading principle which is the basis for the prohibition of particular weapons as indicated, for example, by the very name of the UN Weapons Convention, formally entitled the Convention on Prohibitions ... of Certain Conventional Weapons Which May be *Deemed to be Excessively Injurious.*[47]

Both principles are important for the protection of the environment in times of armed conflict. Attacks against elements of the environment which are civilian objects are, as such, prohibited. The definition of civilian objects is a negative one, encompassing all those objects which are not military objectives. That definition is therefore formulated by turning the two elements of the definition of the military objective according to Article 52 AP I into a negative phrase. Civilian objects are objects which do not contribute to the military effort of a party to the conflict and whose destruction does not yield a military advantage.[48] The essential weakness of this principle of 'civilian immunity' as a means of environmental protection lies in the fact that it is relatively easy to

---

43   API: Articles 51 and 52. These rules constitute customary law. *See* ICRC, J.-M. Henckaerts, L. Doswald-Beck, *Customary International Humanitarian Law* (ICRC/ CUP, Cambridge, 2005), Rules 1–24, Vol. 1, pp. 3–77.

44   AP I: Article 51.

45   AP I: Article 57.

46   Hague Regulations: Article 23(e); AP I: Article 35(2).

47   Emphasis added.

48   Article 52.

THE ETHICS OF PROTECTION OF THE ENVIRONMENT

turn an element of the environment into a military objective.[49] If a military unit is present, or is about to be present, in a protected area, this area becomes a military objective because the use of the area yields a military advantage.

The proportionality principle relating to incidental or 'collateral' damage entails the question of the respective weight of environmental concerns and military gains in what is called the proportionality equation. The decision whether civilian casualties or damages are 'excessive in relation to the military advantage anticipated' requires a balancing of assets or values. On one side of this 'equation' is the military advantage, on the other the civilian damage. It is generally recognised that this is a rule which, theoretically, is impossible to apply as it requires a quantitative comparison of things which cannot be compared, in particular not quantitatively. Nevertheless, proportionality is a principle which is applied in many fields of the law.[50] This is so because its practical attraction lies in the fact that it establishes reasonable limits for action taken in the furtherance of one particular interest for the sake of safeguarding other interests. Seen in this light, it is a development of Rousseau's idea of reasonable limits of warfare.[51] What is new is the recognition of the need to include environmental damage in the civilian damage to be considered.

This equation determines both the legality and the illegality of attacks and the scope of precautionary measures to be taken. Those who decide upon an attack have to make sure, in particular by seeking appropriate information on the civilian consequences of an attack that the civilian (including environmental) damage is not excessive in relation to the military advantage anticipated. The decider is required to take 'feasible' measures for this purpose. What is feasible in relation to the prognostication, and consequently prevention, of environmental damage is a difficult question which remains to be clarified.

Where an element of the environment is a military objective, attacking, destroying or otherwise damaging it is, as a matter of principle, permissible. It has, however, to be asked whether long-term damage to the environment nevertheless affects the legality of an attack. Articles 35(3) and 55 AP I provide just that restraint.[52] It is submitted, however, that the requirements in these

---

49 M. Bothe, C. Bruch, J. Diamond and D. Jensen, 'International law protecting the environment during armed conflict: gaps and opportunities', 92:879 *International Review of the Red Cross* (2010) pp. 569–592, at pp. 576 *et seq.*

50 E. Crawford, 'Proportionality', in R. Wolfrum (ed.), *Max Planck Encyclopedia of Public International Law*, available at <www.mpepil.com> (last visited 16 October 2012).

51 *See* above text accompanying *supra* note 12.

52 W. A. Solf, in Bothe, Partsch and Solf, *supra* note 21, pp. 344 *et seq.*

432 PART 5: CONDUCT OF HOSTILITIES – PROTECTING THE ENVIRONMENT

provisions are inadequate as the threshold of impermissible damage is both unclear and too high.[53]

The principle forbidding unnecessary suffering renders unlawful any attack which destroys elements of the environment without yielding a significant military advantage. The prohibition of 'wanton destruction' is an expression of the same principle, formulated as the prohibition of destruction not "imperatively demanded by the necessities of war"[54] or of "destruction ... of property not justified by military necessity and carried out unlawfully and wantonly"[55] which constitutes a grave breach. This is also a rule of customary law.[56]

Finally, the guiding principle formulated in the Martens clause[57] that the victims of armed conflicts are protected by the rules based on the "dictates of public conscience" is now also considered to cover environmental concerns.[58]

3.2   International Environmental Law

One of the fundamental principles underlying many rules of international environmental law, as already stated, is intergenerational equity. As articulated in Principles 1 and 2 of the Stockholm Declaration[59] and Principle 3 the Rio Declaration,[60] the principle requires concern for the living conditions of future generations.[61] There is a plethora of rules of environmental law imposing restraints on human behaviour for the sake of preserving the necessary living resources for future generations. Nevertheless, the concrete application of the principle is difficult to determine. The principle provides no hard and fast yardstick for the restraint on the use of resources which the present generation

---

53   Bothe *et al.*, *supra* note 49, pp. 575 *et seq. See* below text accompanying *infra* note 65.

54   Article 22(g) Hague Regulations.

55   Article 147 Geneva Convention IV.

56   *Customary International Humanitarian Law*, *supra* note 43, Rule 50, pp. 175 *et seq.*

57   *See supra* note 14.

58   A. Afriansyah, 'Environmental Protection and State Responsibility in International Humanitarian Law', 7 *Indonesian Journal of International Law* (2010) pp. 242–299, at p. 264.

59   Declaration adopted by the United Nations conference on the Human Environment, 1971:
Principle 1: "Man ... bears a solemn responsibility to protect and improve the environment for present and future generations. ..."
Principle 2: "The natural resource of the earth, including air, water, land, flora and fauna and especially representative samples of natural ecosystems, must be safeguarded for the benefit of present and future generations".

60   Rio Declaration on Environment and Development, 1992:
Principle 3: "The right to development must be fulfilled so as to equitably meet developmental and environmental needs of present and future generations".

61   Bothe, *supra* note 30, pp. 485 *et seq.*

THE ETHICS OF PROTECTION OF THE ENVIRONMENT 433

must accept in order to save them for future generations.[62] The notion of sustainable use or management of specific resources may be helpful, but it does not provide a complete answer to the concrete problems of sustainable development of a whole economy. The latter is much more complex. For instance, the principle of intergenerational equity does not exclude substitution. If a specific resource is exhausted, but others may take its place, intergenerational equity is not (necessarily) jeopardised.[63] If one takes a broader approach through the notion of sustainable development, one is back to the problem of uncertainty of yardstick for what is permissible and what not.

A legal principle which serves to implement the principle of intergenerational equity is the precautionary principle.[64] This principle requires relevant actors to take measures for the preservation of the environment even in the absence of scientific certainty as to the risk of environmental damage. The rationale of the precautionary principle is twofold: it ensures that in case of uncertainty about possible damage the decision-maker errs on the safe side, and it reserves space for a future use of resources. It is mainly this latter aspect which makes the precautionary principle a tool for intergenerational equity.[65]

If interpreted in the light of the preceding reasoning, Articles 35 and 55 AP I have the potential to serve as a tool of intergenerational equity. These two provisions restrain attacks not only on civilian objects, but also on military objectives. They constitute, at least potentially, a comprehensive protection against environmental damage caused by military activities. As the prohibition of attacks is not limited to the traditional immunity of civilian objects, it provides the opportunity to take the needs of environmental conservation into account regardless of the current use, military or not, of that object. In this respect, it provides a better opportunity for environmental preservation than the traditional rule of distinction. However, as the threshold of impermissible damage provided for in these articles is much too high from the point of view of environmental concerns, at least if interpreted according to their negotiating history,[66] they fail to meet this goal. Conventional battlefield damage, for

---

62 *Ibid.*

63 *See* F. Ferrand, 'Le développement soutenable est-il une notion de droit international public?', in M. Bothe and P. H. Sand (eds.), *Environmental Policy. From Regulation to Economic Instruments* (Martinus Nijhoff, The Hague *et al.*, 2003) pp. 245–295, at pp. 260–265.

64 Sand and Peel, *supra* note 29, pp. 219 *et seq.*; Bothe, *supra* note 30, pp. 487 *et seq.*; M. D. Young, 'Intergenerational equity, the precautionary principle and ecologically sustainable development', 31 *Nature & Resources* (1995) pp. 16–27.

65 Bothe, *supra* note 30, at p. 488.

66 *See* above text accompanying *supra* note 53.

instance, is held not to be covered.[67] Nevertheless, if interpreted in a dynamic way, the criteria contained in the two articles could serve as a tool of inter-generational equity in restraining the conduct of warfare. For that purpose, it would be necessary to base the interpretation of the three criteria on an increased knowledge about the long-term character of war damage. This could not happen without a more thorough analysis of the effects of warfare on the environment. A careful analysis of causation chains triggered by hostilities, in particular of their impact on life supporting systems is necessary. This would provide new answers as to whether the effect of an attack is 'widespread' and 'long-lasting'. It would also be necessary to take account of ecological values in determining what is 'severe'.

Another fundamental principle of international environmental law, well enshrined in customary law, is the prohibition of significant transboundary harm.[68] As articulated in Principle 2 of the Rio Declaration and Principle 21 of the Stockholm Declaration, the no harm principle requires states to ensure that "activities within their jurisdiction or control do not cause damage to the environment of other States or of areas beyond the limits of national juris-diction". This includes damage caused by war. This is illustrated, for instance, in the reaction to the long range air pollution caused by the burning oil wells towards the end of the second Gulf War and the long distance maritime oil pollution caused by their destruction.[69] The United Nations Compensation Commission awarded the sum of USD 252 million as compensation for this damage.[70] In terms of the law of armed conflict, the prohibition of causing 'transfrontier' damage is also a part of the law of neutrality, an important rule of which is that the territory of the neutral state is inviolable.[71]

Prevention is, of course, the best means to protect the environment against damage. However, where damage has already occurred, restoration and

---

67   W. A. Solf, in Bothe, Partsch and Solf, *supra* note 21, p. 348.

68   Wyatt, *supra* note 29, pp. 599 *et seq.*; A. Douhan, 'Liability for Environmental Damage', in R. Wolfrum (ed.), *Max Planck Encyclopedia of Public International Law*, available at<www.mpepil.com>; U. Beyerlin and T. Marauhn, *International Environmental Law* (Hart *et al.*, Oxford, 2011) pp. 41 *et seq.*; the leading case still is the *Trail Smelter Arbitration* (1941), 3 *RIAA* 1907.

69   *See* K. Hirschmann, *The Kuwaiti Oil Fires* (Facts on file, New York, 2005) pp. 29 *et seq.*

70   UNCC, Governing Council, *Report and Recommendation made by the Panel of Commissioners concerning the Fifth Installment of "F4" Claims*, UN Doc. S/ AC.26/2005/10, 30 June 2005.

71   *Legality of the Threat or Use of Nuclear Weapons*, ICJ Advisory Opinion of 8 July 1996, paras. 88 *et seq. See also* M. Bothe, 'The Law of Neutrality', in D. Fleck (ed.), *The Handbook of International Humanitarian Law*, 3rd edition (OUP, Oxford, 2013) pp. 549–580, at MN 1108.

THE ETHICS OF PROTECTION OF THE ENVIRONMENT

rehabilitation is necessary. The response of international law to that need is found in the principle of cooperation. Formulated in Principle 7 of the Rio Declaration, it requires states to "cooperate in a spirit of global partnership to conserve, protect and *restore* the health and integrity of the Earth's ecosystem".[72] This cooperation, which includes, for example, technical cooperation, can also be based on the principle of solidarity.[73] In two relevant General Assembly resolutions,[74] solidarity is defined as "a fundamental value, by virtue of which global challenges must be managed in a way that distributes costs and burdens fairly, in accordance with basic principles of equity and social justice, and ensures that those who suffer or [who] benefit the least receive help from those who benefit most". Based on this idea of equity, environmental rehabilitation has become part of post-conflict peace building. It has been an important focus of UNEP's Disasters and Conflicts Programme.[75] There is a vast international practice of bilateral (*e.g.* by such agencies as USAID) and multilateral assistance in post-conflict environmental management. International actors engaged in these eff orts are peacekeeping operations, UNDP, UNEP or the World Bank.[76]

3.3   *The Law of Armed Conflict and International Environmental Law*

The fragmentation of international law entails the problem of a possible conflict between two or more areas of law where both or more areas appear to be relevant for one single situation, for the decision of one actor.[77] In the relationship between the law of armed conflict and environmental law, one aspect of this question is the continued validity of treaties (including environmental agreements) in times of armed conflict. This subject has been dealt with by the ILC.[78] If, as the ILC maintains, environmental agreements continue to be applicable in times of war, both the environmental treaty and IHL

---

72   Emphasis added.

73   D. Campanelli, *Solidarity, Principle of*, MN 6, in R. Wolfrum (ed.), *Max Planck Encyclopedia of Public International Law*, available at<www.mpepil.com>.

74   GA resolution 56/151 of 19 December 2001 and 57/213 of 18 December 2002.

75   *See* <www.unep.org/disastersandconfl icts/> (last visited 31 August 2012). *See From Conflict to Peacebuilding: The Role of Natural Resources and the Environment*, UNEP Policy Paper, 2009.

76   This practice is now extensively documented by a research project undertaken by the Environmental Law Institute (Washington, D.C.), UNEP, the University of Tokyo and McGill University (Montreal), *see* <www.environmentalpeacebuilding.org> (last visited 16 October 2012).

77   *See* above text accompanying *supra* notes 8–11.

78   Draft Articles on the eff ects of armed confl icts on treaties, ILC, *Report on the work of its 63rd session*, 2011, UN Doc. A/66/10.

have to be applied in parallel. This requires a solution of conflicts between the two sets of rules which allows respect for the norms of both areas of law. That principle is already widely recognised and called principle called mutual supportiveness.[79]

As a consequence, the core principles of international environmental law, namely the concern for future generations (intergenerational equity) and the prohibition of causing transboundary damage (intragenerational equity), have to be inserted in the application of the law of armed conflict. This has a number of concrete consequences.

The first consequence is that environmental concerns have to be included to a sufficient degree on the civilian side of the proportionality equation.[80] If and to the extent that elements of the environment constitute civilian objects, damage caused to them by attacks against military objectives has to be balanced against the military advantage anticipated. However, what is the respective weight of that environmental damage in comparison to the military advantage? Can only immediate harmful effects be considered or also long-term and indirect effects? Only if the latter approach is adopted can the protection of elements of the environment, being civilian objects, effectively safeguard the living conditions of future generations.

Second, environmental concerns have to be included in precautionary measures to be taken by persons deciding upon launching attacks, applying where necessary the precautionary principle as it is defined in environmental law.[81] The military commander is not a biologist or a specialist in any other environmental science. Thus it can rightly be asked: how will he be able to weigh the environmental consequences of an attack? The usual instruments of evaluating the environmental consequences of a human activity, such as environmental impact assessments, are not available to the military commander. Nevertheless, ways and means must be found to integrate that knowledge into military decision-making. The recent ICRC Study on customary international humanitarian law suggests that the precautionary principle in the sense of environmental law must indeed be applied in assessing the environmental consequences of an attack which is about to be launched.[82]

---

79 R. Pavoni, 'Mutual Supportiveness as a Principle of Interpretation and Law-Making: a Watershed for the "WTO and Competing Regimes" Debate?', 21 *European Journal of International Law* (2010) pp. 649–679.

80 *See* above text accompanying note 44; Bothe, Bruch, Diamond and Jensen, *supra* note 49, p. 578.

81 *See* Bothe *et al.*, *supra* note 49, p. 578.

82 ICRC, Henckaerts, and Doswald-Beck, *supra* note 43, pp. 150 *et seq.*

THE ETHICS OF PROTECTION OF THE ENVIRONMENT

Third, the interpretation of the triple qualification of environmental damage contained in Articles 35(3) and 55 AP I has to be revisited.[83] If interpreted according to the negotiating history, the two provisions are without real value for environmental protection. However, it is both possible and even necessary to adopt a dynamic interpretation which corresponds to changing attitudes in the international community.

Fourth, the interpretation of the rule prohibiting unnecessary suffering, or of military necessity, has to take account of environmental concerns. There are different degrees of necessity. The judgment that a certain act is necessary implies a judgment that a certain goal must be obtained at the expense of other interests. If environmental concerns are introduced into the notion of military necessity, it means that countervailing environmental interests my render a certain military action 'less necessary'.

Fifth, a rule of customary international law has developed that methods and means of warfare must be employed with 'due regard' for the environment. This rule is now articulated in Article 44 of the *San Remo Manual on Naval Warfare*, Article 89 of the *Manual of Air and Missile Warfare*,[84] and Rule 44 of the *Customary International Law Study*.[85] The interpretation of the 'due regard' principle involves interpretation problems similar to those related to the proportionality principle.

Sixth, hostilities must be conducted in such a way that no significant damage is caused to states not parties to the conflict.[86] This rule derives from two fundamental rules of both environmental law and the law of neutrality, namely the prohibition of transboundary harm enshrined in customary environmental law, on the one hand, and the rule that neutral territory is inviolable, on the other. This rule needs to be reconfirmed.

Seventh, and finally, it is suggested that there is a usage, indeed even an emerging legal duty, to cooperate in post-conflict restoration of elements of the environment that have been damaged by armed conflict.[87] Environmental rehabilitation is certainly becoming (albeit too slowly) an established principle of post conflict peace-building. In this respect, more detailed models for practical procedures need to be elaborated.

---

83 *See* section 3.2.
84 HPCR (Program on Humanitarian Policy and Conflict Research at Harvard University) (ed.), *Manual on International Law Applicable to Air and Missile Warfare* (Bern, 2009).
85 ICRC, Henckaerts, and Doswald-Beck, *supra* note 43.
86 *See* above text accompanying *supra* note 67.
87 *See* above text accompanying *supra* notes 74 and 75.

438   PART 5: CONDUCT OF HOSTILITIES – PROTECTING THE ENVIRONMENT

4   Objectives

Towards the end of the 1960s, awareness of global environmental problems emerged triggering the recognition of the need to address these problems through law. It was also recognised that these developments could not ignore the environmental consequences of war. Thus appeared the meeting, or should one say collision, between the laws of war and environmental law in the 1970s. This encounter has since triggered further developments which have not, however, occurred without setbacks. When attempts have been made to develop IHL in the sense of a better protection of the environment, military interests have several times prevailed over environmental concerns. The legal situation as it stands is not satisfactory.[88] This is why the ICRC, when it launched an initiative to further develop international humanitarian law in particular areas where this was most needed, singled out the protection of the environment in relation to armed conflicts as one of the relevant themes.[89] In the ensuing consultation process states have chosen different problems as priorities. However, the fact that the ILC is planning to work on the problem[90] is encouraging and gives hope for future developments.

The objectives of the further development of the law must be that the ethical and legal principles explained in this paper are clarified and concretised, and that doubt concerning their validity and application is removed. This applies to rules imposing restraints on military operations as well as to obligations to promote and ensure post-conflict rehabilitation. In short, in order to ensure that the living basis for future generations is not jeopardised by warfare, the relevant rules of international law must be strengthened and developed on the basis of the ethical and legal principles.

5   Conclusion

It has been shown that the ethical foundations of international humanitarian law and of environmental law have some points in common. Both regimes are

---

88   Bothe *et al.*, *supra* note 49, in particular pp. 578 *et seq.*

89   *See* the address of the President of the ICRC, 21 September 2010: J. Kellenberger, 'Strengthening Legal Protection for Victims of Armed Conflicts. Th e ICRC Study on the Current State of International Humanitarian Law', 92:879 *International Review of the Red Cross* (2010) pp. 799–804, at pp. 802 *et seq.*

90   International Law Commission, *Report on the work of its 63rd session* (2011), UN Doc. A/66/10, pp. 288 and 347 *et seq.*

THE ETHICS OF PROTECTION OF THE ENVIRONMENT

based on the rule of reason which leads to a concern for the future. Peace is an ultimate goal of legal restraints on methods and means of warfare. Securing peace means safeguarding the possibilities of a decent existence in the future. This is also a major goal of environmental law. The impact that this latter goal has had on the development of positive law is based on the recognition, resulting from scientific analysis of the life supporting systems on Earth, that restraints on human activities are not only necessary to prevent current damage to persons and elements of the environment, but also in order to safeguard the carrying capacity of the Earth. This has led to a new evaluation of legal regulation concerning economic activities, in particular through the growing application of the precautionary principle.

The recognition of the fact that this need of restraint for the sake of future generations must apply to all human activities has been somewhat slower to arrive in military thinking. However, this has happened, albeit still not to a sufficient degree. Nevertheless, various ways and means exist to ensure that concern for future generations or, in a more short-term perspective concern for the life after the war, finds its way into military decision-making. The adoption of two environmental provisions in the first 1977 Protocol additional to the Geneva Conventions was a first step. However, these provisions need new interpretation. Given that customary international law has developed the 'due regard' principle and that environmental rehabilitation has become a general practice in post conflict peace-building, it is clear that environmental values must now be recognised in the balancing of values required by the proportionality principle.

All these developments are certainly laudable from an environmental point of view, particularly in the light of the ethical principles elaborated in this study. Nevertheless, this general recognition of principles still is too abstract. The principles now need concretisation through appropriate procedures. In this process, the epistemic community of international lawyers has a role to play.

20

The ILC Special Rapporteur's Preliminary Report on the Protection of the Environment in Relation to Armed Conflicts

An Important Step in the Right Direction

1   The Protection of the Environment in Relation to Armed Conflicts on the ILC Agenda

In preparation for the sixtieth anniversary of the Geneva Conventions, the International Committee of the Red Cross (hereinafter ICRC) analyzed issues where international humanitarian law was not satisfactory and needed development. It singled out four problem areas:[1] (i) Protection of persons deprived of liberty; (ii) Implementation of humanitarian law and reparation for victims; (iii) Protection of the environment during armed conflicts; (iv) Protection of internally armed conflicts. With a view to taking further action at the 31st International Red Cross and Red Crescent Conference in 2011, consultations with the ICRC followed that announcement. It turned out that a majority of States preferred treating only the first two issues. They did not want to give priority to the latter two issues. This was not the first setback for efforts to promote the international legal protection of the environment during conflicts beyond the unsatisfactory solution of this issue, which is formulated in art. 35 and 55 of Protocol I of 1977 Additional to the Geneva Conventions of 1949. Since the Diplomatic Conference held in Geneva 1974–1977 which adopted the Additional Protocols, many governments and their military establishment have offered a considerable resistance against bringing environmental protection into the law of armed conflict. The fate of the subject matter in the political processes in the UN has been regrettable from an environmental point of view.[2]

---

1   These results have been announced in an address held by the then President of the icrc, Mr. Kellenberger, on 21 September 2010: *See* J. Kellenberger, 'Strengthening Legal Protection for Victims of Armed Conflict', (2010) 92 *International Review of the Red* Cross (hereinafter *IRRC*), pp. 799–804.

2   Michael Bothe, 'Military Activities and the Protection of the Environment', (2007) 37 *Environmental Policy and Law*, pp. 232–238. This is in particular true for the treatment the issue received by the UNGA in 1994, *see* below footnote 22.

© KONINKLIJKE BRILL NV, LEIDEN, 2021 | DOI:10.1163/9789004380592_022

Nevertheless, neither the ICRC[3] nor the environmental community have ever given up on this issue. A number of governments continued their efforts to promote the international legal protection of the environment in times of armed conflict.[4] The United Nations Environmental Program (hereinafter UNEP) has promoted the issue on several occasions and in various ways. It has undertaken an important stocktaking exercise,[5] and its work on post-conflict assessment of damages and assistance to rehabilitation is remarkable.[6] The International Union for the Conservation of Nature and Natural Resources (hereinafter IUCN) has established a Specialist Group which is dealing with the problem. Parallel to these developments, a learning process has taken place in the military. It is no exaggeration to say that in many countries, the armed forces and defense ministries are taking environmental issues seriously.[7]

There can be no denying the fact that the environmental damages caused by war, be they short term and visible or long-term and creeping, are considerable. This has been well documented during the last decades. A few disasters have drawn the attention of a larger public to the problem.[8] There seems to be a general agreement that the rules addressing this problem are not as clear as they should be, and there is a widespread dissatisfaction with the protective content of the existing rules.[9]

Against the backdrop of all this, it is highly laudable that the International Law Commission (hereinafter ILC) decided in 2011 to put the issue "Protection of the environment in relation to armed conflicts" on its long-term program

---

3 *See* below footnote 22 and accompanying text.

4 The most prominent example is the pledge made by the Nordic countries and their national Red Cross societies at the 31st International Red Cross and Red Crescent Conference in 2012 (Pledge P 1290). Fulfilling this pledge, the Nordic countries, together with a number of different institutions, organized a seminar on the premises of the UN in October 2015, which discussed the matter quite thoroughly.

5 UNEP, *Protecting the Environment during Armed conflict. An Inventory and Analysis of International Law,* Nairobi 2009.

6 For references *see* below footnote 16.

7 An important example is the symposium organized by the Naval War College in Newport, R.I., in 1995: *See* R.J. Grunawalt, J.E. King, R.S. McClain (eds), *Protection of the Environment during Armed Conflict,* Naval War College – International Law Studies, vol. 89, Newport, R.I., 1996.

8 Major examples are the use of herbicides by the US in the Vietnam War and massive oil pollution events during the Gulf War 1982–1988.

9 For a stocktaking of the situation, *see* M. Bothe, C. Bruch, J. Diamond, D. Jensen, 'International law protecting the environment during armed conflict: gaps and opportunities', (2010) 92 IRRC, pp. 569–592.

442 PART 5: CONDUCT OF HOSTILITIES – PROTECTING THE ENVIRONMENT

of work.[10] It appointed the proponent of the subject, Marie G. Jacobsson, as Special Rapporteur. She has submitted her first report in 2014.[11] The following contribution tries to comment on some of the issues raised by that report.

2 The Basic Approach of the ILC's Special Rapporteur

As proposed by the Special Rapporteur, the formulation of the subject is broader than the usual controversy about the protection of the environment "during" armed conflicts. The agenda item accepted by the International Law Commission is broader in two respects.

2.1 *The Continued Application of Environmental Law during Armed Conflicts*

First, it is not limited to the rules of the law of armed conflict which explicitly or by implication address the protection of the environment. It also or even mainly covers the application of other norms of international law, in particular environmental law, to the risks and damages which armed conflicts may entail for the environment. Seen in this perspective, as the Report rightly points out, the question of environmental protection in relation to armed conflicts turns out to be part of the broader issue of the fragmentation of international law already addressed by the ILC,[12] albeit in a somewhat different approach.[13] The question to be solved is how rules belonging to the field of the traditional law of armed conflict, or international humanitarian law, relate to the rules pertaining to international environmental law, or to special treaty regimes belonging to this field. Is international humanitarian law a *lex specialis* which displaces environmental law rules? Is a cumulative application of rules belonging

---

10 *Report of the International Law Commission on its 63rd session*, UN Doc. A/66/10, paras. 365–367. *See* M. Jacobsson, 'Foreword. Protection of the Environment in Relation to Armed Conflicts – An Update' in R. Rayfuse (ed.), *War and the Environment*, Brill/Nijhoff, Leiden/Boston, 2014, pp. vii–x.

11 International Law Commission, Sixty-sixth session, *Preliminary report on the protection of the environment in relation to armed conflict*, UN Doc. A/CN.4/674, 30 May 2014. At the time this contribution goes to print, two more reports have been submitted by the Special Rapporteur: 2nd Report, 28 May 2015, A/CN.4/685; 3rd Report, 3 June 2016, A/CN.4/700.

12 International Law Commission, *Report of the Study Group of the International Law Commission on the fragmentation of international law: difficulties arising from the diversification and expansion of international law*, un Doc. A/CN.4/L.682.

13 M. Bothe, 'Conclusion: Le droit international humanitaire, un régime spécial en voie d'autonomisation?' in R. van Steenberghe (ed.), *Droit international humanitaire – un régime spécial de droit international?* Bruylant, Brussels, 2013, pp. 321–331.

THE ILC'S REPORT ON THE PROTECTION OF THE ENVIRONMENT 443

to the two fields of law possible, can there be a relationship of mutual supportiveness? The latter principle deserves particular attention as far as the relationship between environmental law and other legal regimes, including the law of armed conflict is concerned.[14] The report rightly lays these questions on the table. They will have to be answered in the course of the work on this agenda item.

Seen in this perspective, the subject of the protection of the environment in relation to armed conflicts is also part of the broader question, already dealt with by the ILC,[15] of the effect of armed conflicts on treaties. These rules generally favour a continued application of treaties during armed conflicts, and this would in particular cover multilateral environmental agreements.[16] What that means in practice remains to be seen on a case by case basis.

2.2 *Various Phases Relevant for the Protection of the Environment in Relation to Armed Conflicts*

Secondly, the scope of the rules which the Special Rapporteur tries to develop is not limited to behaviour during armed conflicts. It addresses environmentally relevant behaviour taking place before, or rather in preparation of armed conflicts, during armed conflict and after an armed conflict. The discourse concerning the protection of the environment against the risks of war has so far concentrated to a large extent on what happens during armed conflicts. A major concern was the insufficient protection provided for environmental interests by art. 35 and 55 AP I. The preliminary report does not yet discuss the manifold measures States can and must take before an armed conflict occurs to prevent environmental damage which might happen if and when the conflict breaks out. A few examples of this aspect of the subject are suggested below.

The third phase has attracted a lot of attention during the last two decades through relevant work of UNEP.[17] In this perspective, the problem of restoring

---

14   The principle of mutual supportiveness is mainly discussed concerning the relationship between WTO law and other, in particular environmental legal regimes; see *inter alia* L. Boisson de Chazournes, M.M. Mbengue, 'A propos du principe du support mutuel. Les relations entre le Protocol de Cartagena et les Accord de l'OMC', (2007) 111 *RGDIP*, pp. 829–862; R. Pavoni, 'Mutual Supportiveness as a Principle of Interpretation and Law-Making: A Watershed for the "WTO and Competing Regimes" Debate', (2010) 21 ejil, pp. 649–679.

15   *Report of the International Law Commission*, UN Doc. A/66/10, Ch. 6.

16   Bothe *et al. (cit. supra* footnote 9), at pp. 581 *et seq.*, 587 *et seq.*

17   UNEP, *From Conflict to Peacebuilding. Evaluating the role of natural resources in conflicts*, Nairobi 2002; UNEP, *Integrating Environment in Post-Conflict Needs Assessment.* UNEP Guidance Note, 2009.

444 PART 5: CONDUCT OF HOSTILITIES – PROTECTING THE ENVIRONMENT

the environment after an armed conflict has occurred is part of the broader issue of post-conflict peace building.[18]

3 The Continued Validity of Peacetime Customary Law Rules

3.1 *Principles of Environmental Law and Their Application in Relation to Armed Conflict*

If it is taken as seriously as it should be, the part of the report on principles of environmental law is really the core of the subject. It implies a rethinking of the rules concerning the conduct of war which, it is submitted, goes beyond what is expressly stated in the preliminary report. Given the political context, this restraint is probably wise in the perspective of the acceptability of the results of the work in the diplomatic environment of the UN. On the other hand, this is regrettable.

The report first asks what are the relevant principles of environmental law. This is a logical starting point and the core of the subject: Sustainable development, prevention and precaution are key notions. Other principles are also mentioned.

To what extent are these principles parts of positive law? The report provides a thorough stocktaking of this question which is recommended reading for any environmental lawyer. A careful analysis of the practice, which also takes into account some of the resistance which the recognition of the principles has encountered, suggests that these rules have become part of customary law, certainly on some regional levels, but also on the universal level.

But what does their application in relation to armed conflict mean? The report only gives scarce indications on this question. As far as their application during and after an armed conflict is concerned, this can be left to further reports. But as far as the pre-conflict situation is concerned, a few concretizations would have been desirable. A few suggestions in this respect are made below.

The key point which makes the reflections of the report so topical is this: The principles of sustainable development, prevention and precaution impose restraints on decision-makers in respect of manifold human activities. The basic purpose is that the living conditions of future generations and the continued viability of the environmental system of the Earth may not be compromised by present activities. This rule does not only apply to peaceful economic activities.

---

18   United Nations Secretary General, *An Agenda for Peace*, UN Doc. A/47/277 = S/24111, dated 17 June 1992.

THE ILC'S REPORT ON THE PROTECTION OF THE ENVIRONMENT
445

The fundamental message of the report is: it applies comprehensively and also covers military activities in peace and war. Thus, the protection of the environment is a concern which has to be taken into account by States whatever activity they are involved in. This principle is well reflected in art. 13 para. 2 of the Draft International Covenant on Environment and Development (ICED):[19]

> The Parties shall ensure that environmental conservation is treated as an integral part of planning and implementing activities at all stages and at all levels, giving full and equal consideration to environmental, economic, social and cultural factors.

The preparation for armed conflicts, necessary as it unfortunately is, is no exception to that principle. This means that security policy in all its aspects has to integrate environmental concerns. On the other hand, the principle enunciated in the ICED implies a balancing process. Although not expressly mentioned, the factors which have to be taken into account in addition to environmental ones include security concerns.

In addition to the application of peacetime environmental rules in case of armed conflict, the Report rightly stresses the application of international environmental law to UN Peacekeeping Missions.[20]

The devil is then in the detail: What does this general conclusion mean in practical terms? It is clear that the application of those principles has to be adapted to the circumstances of war. The Report[21] gives the example of a duty to cooperate in a case where the usual channels of communication are closed due to the armed conflict. Other ways of transmitting environmentally relevant information must and can be found. As far as the application during armed conflict is concerned, the principle of due regard, which has been recognized in a number of non-binding instruments concerning the law of armed conflict[22] as well as by the ICRC Customary Humanitarian Law Study,[23] is to be regarded as an expression of the continued application of the said principles and has to be interpreted accordingly.

---

19 Commission on Environmental Law of IUCN, *Draft International Covenant on Environment and Development*, 3rd ed., Updated Text, 2004.

20 Report, *cit. supra* footnote 14, para. 47.

21 *Cit. supra* footnote 11, para. 100.

22 San Remo Manual on Naval Warfare, art. 44; Program on Humanitarian Policy and Conflict Research, Harvard University (HPCR), Manual on International Law Applicable to Air and Missile Warfare, 2009, Rule 89.

23 J.M. Henckaerts, L. Doswald-Beck (ICRC), *Customary International Humanitarian Law*, Cambridge University Press, Cambridge 2005, vol. 1, p. 147, Rule 44.

446 PART 5: CONDUCT OF HOSTILITIES – PROTECTING THE ENVIRONMENT

Yet one conclusion has to be retained: considerations of security and defense may not be used as a lock, stock and barrel argument to set aside environmental concerns affected by the conduct of armed conflict.

3.2 *Human Rights, Environmental Protection and Armed Conflict*

The Report[24] also addresses the relationship between human rights and the environment, mainly by an analysis of regional case law. It is important to take into account the human rights dimension of the problem. This follows an important trend of the international discourse. It is too early to find a valid conclusion as to how exactly the trilateral relationship between human rights law, international environmental law and the law of armed conflict might work out. The basic approach should be this: Experience has shown that human rights law has a strong potential to strengthen the protection of the environment. Human rights law has also provided additional support for a better implementation of international humanitarian law. Future reports on the subject could therefore highlight the mutual supportiveness of the three areas of international law.

4 The Principle of Prevention and Precaution in the Pre-Conflict Phase: Some Concretizations

The final document might add some concretizations concerning the application of principles of environmental law relating to military decision-making in peacetime. A few modest suggestions are made here.

4.1 *Weapons*

A problem where the principle just discussed matters in particular is weapons technology. This question is addressed in art. 36 AP I:

> In the study, development, acquisition or adoption of new weapons, means or method of warfare, a High Contracting Party is under an obligation to determine whether its employment would, in some or all circumstances, be prohibited by this Protocol or by other rule of international law applicable to the High Contracting Party.

---

24 *Cit. supra* footnote 11, paras. 157 *et seq.*

THE ILC'S REPORT ON THE PROTECTION OF THE ENVIRONMENT 447

The rules which serve as a standard in the evaluation of new weapons or weapons systems include, as far as the environment is concerned:
- The specific provisions of AP I prohibiting causing damage to the environment which is of a certain severity (art. 35 para. 3, 55 AP I);
- The prohibition of attacks against civilian objects as many, if not most elements of the environment are civilian objects;
- The prohibition of attacking, destroying, removing or rendering useless objects indispensable to the survival of the civilian population (art. 54 para. 2);
- The customary legal principle that "due regard" for the protection of the environment[25] must be observed in relation to all decisions relating to attacks.

Thus, environmental concerns are in many ways relevant for the assessment and evaluation of any new weapon.

4.2 *Rule Making*

The duty of Parties to "ensure respect" for the Protocols and the Geneva Conventions (common art. 1 GC, art. 1 para. 1 AP I) implies, *inter alia*, a duty to establish rules for their application and implementation. Parties are required to communicate such rules to each other (Arts. 48/49/128/145 of the four GC, art. 84 AP I.) The articles of the Conventions also cover non-international armed conflicts (common art. 3.) As to AP II, the same rule may be implied in the general duty of dissemination (art. 19 AP II.)

These rules must of course be established in times of peace. An important element of this rule-making is the adoption of so-called military manuals. Such manuals must duly take into account environmental concerns. For that reason, the ICRC has developed guidelines on the question how military manuals should take environmental concerns into account.[26] These guidelines are currently under revision. They may also serve as a basis for training.

Rules of Engagement are usually issued once a conflict has broken out or is likely to break out soon. They usually are mission specific. But there are rules

---

25 See footnote 24.

26 *Guidelines for Military Manuals and Instructions on the Protection of the Environment in Times of Armed Conflict*, reproduced in Report of the UN Secretary General, UN Doc. A/49/323 (1994), Annex. Without formally approving the text, the UNGA, in its resolution concerning the UN Decade of International Law (GA Resolution 49/50, 9 December 1994), "invited" all States to disseminate these guidelines widely. For a presentation of the Guidelines see H.P. Gasser, 'For Better Protection of the Natural Environment in Armed Conflict: A Proposal for Action', (1995) 89 AJIL, pp. 637–644; for a critique, *see* M. Bothe, (1996) 90 AJIL, p. 76, and a reply by Gasser, *ibid.* at p. 76 *et seq.*

448 PART 5: CONDUCT OF HOSTILITIES – PROTECTING THE ENVIRONMENT

on drafting RoEs. Whenever such rules are drafted, it is important that they take environmental concern duly into account.[27]

4.3 *The Separation of Military Objectives from Environmentally Valuable Areas*

An often neglected aspect of duties designed to minimize harmful effects of warfare which require peacetime measures in order to be effective are "Precautions against the effect of attacks" according to art. 58 AP I. The relevant parts of that provision read as follows:

> The Parties to the conflict shall, to the maximum extent feasible:
> [...]
> (b) avoid locating military objectives within or near densely populated areas;
> (c) take the other necessary precautions to protect the civilian population, individual civilians and civilian objects under their control against the dangers resulting from military operations.

Although this provision is formulated as a wartime obligation, an effective implementation of these obligations is difficult, if not impossible without an adequate preparation in times of peace. Decisions concerning the location of permanent military installation, which according to this provision may not be located in or near densely populated areas, may not be possible in times of war as required because peacetime decisions incompatible with art. 58 AP I have created a *fait accompli.*

The environment cannot be the object of siting decisions. It is simply there, and it cannot be moved away. But it can be affected by siting decisions. The said rule would therefore imply a duty not to locate permanent military installations at places where an attack directed against them would by necessity entail considerable damage to valuable elements of the environment which are civilian objects.

Experience has shown that a typical environmental risk involved in armed conflict is the destruction of environmentally valuable places and spaces. It

---

27   The International Institute of Humanitarian Law (IIHL) has elaborated a kind of guideline for drafting Rules of Engagement: IIHL, *Rules of Engagement Handbook,* San Remo 2009. No. 14 (c) of the Handbook stresses that any Rule of Engagement must reflect the International Law of Armed Conflict.

THE ILC'S REPORT ON THE PROTECTION OF THE ENVIRONMENT 449

was claimed, for instance, that during the Georgia conflict in 2008, a large forest fire in in Borjomi-Kharagauli National Park was caused by the hostilities.[28] To avoid such damages, it is necessary to take protective measures before a conflict occurs.

The ICRC Study on the Current State of International Humanitarian Law (2010) singled out as one of the areas which had to be addressed as being insufficiently developed the protection of the environment in armed conflict. President Kellenberger, in his address presenting the Study, also highlights the need of preventive action:[29]

> for instance, studying the possibility of designating areas of great ecological importance as demilitarized zones before the commencement of armed conflict, or at least at its outset. Such zones may include areas containing unique ecosystems or endangered species.

As already said, this part of the ICRC proposals was not pursued any further in the consultations with States following the ICRC proposals. But the proposal remains relevant and is on the table. Similar proposals have been put forward for many years by the Commission on Environmental Law, now World Commission on Environmental Law, of IUCN.[30] One way to achieve this purpose is to create a procedural framework for establishing such specially protected areas, preferably but not necessarily, by means of a new treaty (protocol additional to the Geneva Conventions). Another way could be the systematic designation of sites protected by the World Heritage Convention (which also include specially valuable nature areas) as sites protected by the Convention of Cultural Property in Times of Armed Conflict, a step which is currently discussed in Germany, but which, as far as natural sites are concerned, would probably require a somewhat broad interpretation of art. 1 of the 1954 Convention. The two approaches would be important steps of implementing the general obligations to protect the environment discussed above.[31]

---

28 This is reflected, in careful words, in Resolution 4.071 of the IUCN World Conservation Congress held in Barcelona in 2008.

29 See Kellenberger, *cit.* footnote 1, at p. 803.

30 See Bothe *et al. cit.* footnote 9, at p. 577.

31 The Nordic pledge (*supra* note 4) might also lead to further developments in this respect. See also 2nd Report, supra note 11, paras. 210–218.

5 Environmental Causes of Armed Conflict: An Important Issue Rightly Excluded by the Special Rapporteur

Disputes concerning natural resources and their use often lead to the violence and to armed conflicts. Such conflictual uses of natural resources all too often entail a serious degradation of the environment. If such conflicts could be avoided by protective measures taken for the environment as well as for the conservation of valuable natural resources, this would be salutary both for peace and for the environment.

The first example which comes to one's mind is water.[32] Adequate rules on sharing water resources are essential both for the preservation of the resource and for avoiding violent conflicts about access or distribution. Another type of problem is posed by mineral resources which are often unlawfully exploited under unacceptable environmental conditions and are prone to become the object of conflict. Competition about these resources is a major source of violent conflict. Strict controls of trade may prevent such consequences.[33] Finally, unlawful exploitation of wildlife (poaching) may also become a source of conflict. Controls performed for the purpose of protecting wildlife may also prevent violent conflict.[34]

The examples show the potential of synergies between the legal prohibition of the use of force and environmental protection. Yet the Special Rapporteur is right in proposing not to deal with these issues. The legal questions which have to be discussed in this context are too different from those which relate to the conduct of armed conflict and its consequences.

6 Conclusions

During the last five decades, we can observe a growing awareness that restraints on manifold human activities are required in order to preserve the viability of

---

32 M. Bothe, 'Wasser – ein Menschenrecht, eine Verteilungsfrage, ein Problem von Frieden und Sicherheit' in S. Breitenmoser *et al.* (eds), *Menschenrechte, Demokratie und Rechtsstaat. Liber amicorum Luzius Wildhaber*, Dike/Nomos, 2007, pp. 103–117, at p. 107 *et seq.*

33 In 2003, governments of many States as well as the EU agreed on the so-called Kimberley Process Certification Scheme to ensure that shipments of rough diamonds are conflict-free. Information available at www.kimberleyprocess.com (last visited 30 December 2014).

34 UNEP, *Democratic Republic of the Congo. Post-Conflict Environmental Assessment*, Nairobi, UNEP 2011, in particular at pp. 24 *et seq.* concerning environmental reasons and consequences of the conflict. *See* also E. de Merode *et al.*, 'The impact of armed conflict on protected-area efficacy in Central Africa, Biology Letters, 22 June 2007, available at www.ncbi.nlm.nih.gov/pmc/articles/PMC2464688/ last visited 30 December 2014.

THE ILC'S REPORT ON THE PROTECTION OF THE ENVIRONMENT 451

the environmental systems of the Earth, which are the basis of all forms of life. However, this general recognition encounters serious difficulties when it is time to draw specific consequences from it. The controversial relationship between environment and economy was the first example of this problem, which has attracted much attention. A recognition of the problematic relationship between the preservation of the environment and military activities followed rather soon,[35] but no real breakthrough has been achieved during decades of debates. In joining the forces which have insisted on the continued application of international environmental law during armed conflict, the Special Rapporteur in the report that is reviewed by the present paper, makes a salutary contribution to rethinking this relationship.

The said report shows that this relationship has many facets. There are two sides of the medal: no preparation for the case of war without duly taking into account environmental concerns – no environmental protection measures without taking into account the eventuality of war.

---

35 An early example is the World Charter for Nature adopted by the UN General Assembly, Resolution 37/7, 28 Oct. 1982. Its OP 5 reads: "Nature shall be secured against degradation caused by warfare or other hostile activities".

21

Protection of the Environment in Relation to Armed Conflicts

A Preliminary Comment on the Work of the International Law Commission

Celebrating the 75th birthday of Djamchid Momtaz, it is appropriate to dedicate to him a contribution dealing with the current work of the International Law Commission, of which he was a member from 2000 to 2006 and Chair in 2005: namely the protection of the environment in relation to armed conflicts. International humanitarian law, which is at the center of the ILC work to be analyzed here, has been one of Momtaz's dearest subjects throughout his academic and diplomatic career. He has also worked on the relationship between international humanitarian law and environmental protection, for instance through his participation in the Expert Seminar on Human Rights and the Environment co-organized by UNEP and the High Commissioner for Human Rights in 2002.

1 The Mandate and the Approach Proposed by the Special Rapporteur

In 2013, the ILC decided to include the topic 'Protection of the environment in relation to armed conflicts' in its program of work. It appointed Maria G. Jacobsson, who had taken the initiative to put this subject before the ILC, as Special Rapporteur. In 2014, she presented her first preliminary report,[1] which was followed by a general debate in the Commission. In 2015, she presented her second report,[2] concentrating on rules applicable during armed conflict and proposed a number of 'Principles'. These were then deliberated by ILC's Drafting Committee which provisionally adopted them in a modified form.[3] The Commission noted them. In 2016, the Special Rapporteur presented her third report,[4] concentrating on, and proposing, principles applicable after a conflict. The Drafting Committee adopted them in modified form[5] and also

---

1   UN Doc. A/CN.4/674, 30 May 2014 and A/CN.4/674/Corr. 1, 11 August 2014.
2   UN Doc. A/CN.4/685, 28 May 2015.
3   UN Doc. A/CN.4/L.870, 22 July 2015.
4   UN Doc. A/CN.4/700, 3 June 2016.
5   UN Doc. A/CN.4/L.876, 3 August 2016; UN Doc. A/CN.4/L.870/Rev.1, 26 July 2016.

© KONINKLIJKE BRILL NV, LEIDEN, 2021 | DOI:10.1163/9789004380592_023

worked on the principles adopted in 2015. Several principles were provisionally adopted by the plenary Commission.[6]

This project has to be seen against the backdrop of a decades-long debate. Since the 1970s, the debate on the law of war and the protection of the environment had centered on rules providing for protection *during* armed conflict.[7] Yet on a closer look, this concentration on obligations applying during conflicts is an inappropriate limitation.[8] Many measures for protecting the environment in relation to armed conflicts can, even must, be taken before a conflict occurs. Further, once the damage has occurred, in violation of applicable international law or not, the question is both what redress is possible, and also whether there are rules on what must be done in the post-conflict phase. This broader view of the problem allows the specific rules of the law applicable *in* armed conflict to be put in the more general perspective of general international law, in particular general environmental law.

2   The Possible Content of the Document: A Preview

After three reports of the Special Rapporteur, three rounds of plenary debate and two deliberations in the Drafting Committee, the shape of the possible outcome appears on the horizon. The rules formulated by the Commission take the form of 'principles', a choice of terminology to be commented on below.[9] The document, as it appears after the deliberations of the Commission in 2016, will be divided into four parts: Introduction (Principles 1 and 2, 3 being reserved; Part I: General principles (Principles 4–8); Part II: Principles applicable during armed conflict (Principles 9–13[10]); Part III: Principles applicable after an armed conflict (Principles 14–18).

There are no specific provisions on the pre-conflict phase. The 'General principles' apply to all three phases: pre-conflict, conflict and post-conflict.

---

6   ILC, Report on the work of the sixty-eighth session (2016), UN Doc. A/71/10, paras. 139 et seq.

7   For a short account see M. Bothe, C. Bruch, J. Diamond & D. Jensen, 'International law protecting the environment during armed conflict: gaps and opportunities', 92 *International Review of the Red Cross,* 2010, pp. 569–592.

8   See M. Bothe, 'The ILC Special Rapporteur's Preliminary Report on the Protection of the Environment in Relation to Armed Conflicts: An Important Step in the Right Direction', in Pia Acconci et al. (eds), *International Law and the Protection of Humanity. Essays in Honor of Flavia Lattanzi,* Brill/Nijhoff 2016, pp. 213–224.

9   Below at 4.3.

10   Supra, note 5.

454 PART 5: CONDUCT OF HOSTILITIES – PROTECTING THE ENVIRONMENT

It is the purpose of the following to try a provisional evaluation of the Principles as they appear at the time of writing (August 2016).

3 Achievements and Problems

3.1 *General Principles (Introduction and Part One)*

It is perhaps regrettable that there are no specific rules on obligations in the pre-conflict phase. One could imagine examples of desirable rules which would be applicable here.[11] One example is the duty to take precautions against attack (Article 58, AP I).[12] These duties are to endeavour to remove civilian objects from the vicinity of military objectives and to avoid locating military objectives within or near densely populated areas. It will be extremely difficult to fulfil these obligations once the conflict has broken out, but it is easier to take these duties into account in a planning and zoning process at any time, whether a conflict is imminent or not. Similarly, the requirements of environmental protection such as the necessity to protect certain habitats can be taken into account when deciding on siting military installations. The development of shooting grounds as refuge for wildlife is a somewhat ambivalent phenomenon in this connection.

The various general principles invite the following comments.[13]

The basic provision on measures to be taken is Principle 2, part of the Introduction:

> Draft Principle 2
> Purpose
>
> The present draft principles are aimed at enhancing the protection of the environment in relation to armed conflict, including preventive measures for minimizing damage to the environment during armed conflict and through remedial measures.

An example of such 'preventive measures' would be the siting decisions just mentioned.

---

11 Bothe, supra, note 8, pp. 219 et seq.

12 Protocol Additional to the Geneva Conventions of 12 August 1949, and Relating to the Protection of the Victims of International Armed Conflicts (Protocol I), of 8 June 1977, 1125 UNTS 3.

13 Italics by the author.

A PRELIMINARY COMMENT ON THE WORK OF THE ILC

Part I then contains a number of generic provisions.

> Draft Principle 4
> Measure to Enhance the Protection of the Environment

1. States shall, pursuant to their obligations under international law, take effective legislative, administrative, judicial and other measures to enhance the protection of the environment in relation to armed conflict.
2. In addition, States should take further measures, as appropriate, to enhance the protection of the environment in relation to armed conflict.

The two paragraphs provide for two different degrees of obligation ('shall' and 'should'). This difference may be explained by the addition of the words 'pursuant to their obligations under international law' in the first paragraph. In other words, States are obliged to do what they are already bound to do by virtue of other rules. Therefore, the strong term 'shall' is appropriate:[14] Perhaps a useful reminder. The weaker paragraph ('should ... as appropriate') is at least a useful exhortation for States to take further measures. Examples would have been welcome.

> Draft Principle 5
> Designation of Protected Zones

> States should designate, by agreement or otherwise, areas of major environmental and cultural importance as protected zones.

This responds to a demand formulated by IUCN many years ago.[15] It was also mentioned in the proposals for a development of international humanitarian law made by the ICRC President in 2011,[16] an element of his proposals which unfortunately did not receive a positive reaction by States. The demand is based on the experience that protection of environmentally valuable sites or areas during armed conflict does not occur so to say automatically during armed conflict. Sites to be protected must be designated as such before hostilities

---

14   ILC, 68th session, Statement of the Chair of the ILC Drafting Committee, Mr. Pavel Šturma, 9 August 2016, p. 3.

15   See Bothe et al., supra, note 7, p. 577.

16   J. Kellenberger, 'Strengthening legal protection for victims of armed conflicts. The ICRC Study on the current state of International Humanitarian Law', 92 International Review of the Red Cross, 2010, pp. 799–804, pp. 802 et seq.

happen. The best way of designation is an agreement between the parties to a conflict. A unilateral designation does not really promise success. Another possibility is a designation by an organ of the United Nations which then can be implemented by the parties.[17]

> Draft Principle 7
> Agreements concerning the presence of military forces in relation to armed conflict

> States and international organizations should, as appropriate, include provisions on environmental protection in agreements concerning the presence of military forces in relation to armed conflict. Such agreements may include preventive measures, impact assessments, restoration and clean-up measures.

This is yet another example of a provision to be implanted by agreement between relevant actors. The exhortation is necessary as this is a neglected aspect of State practice relating to visiting forces.[18] There is, for example, no provision on environmental protection in the UN Model Status of Forces Agreement.[19] The circumstances under which such agreements are concluded vary greatly, hence the addition of the words 'as appropriate'.[20]

> Draft Principle 8
> Peace operations

> States and international organizations involved in peace operations shall consider the impact of such operations on the environment and take appropriate measures to prevent, mitigate and remediate the negative environmental consequences thereof.

Complex peace operations, some of them sizeable undertakings, have a serious influence on the situation of the area where they operate, including the environment. These environmental problems have to be taken into account in

---

17   For details see below concerning Principle 13.

18   On the practice see the 3rd Report of the Special Rapporteur, supra, note 4, para. 161 et seq.

19   A/45/594, 9 October 1990.

20   Statement of the Chair of the Drafting Committee, supra, note 14, p. 6.

A PRELIMINARY COMMENT ON THE WORK OF THE ILC

setting up and conducting a peace operation.[21] It is a strong obligation ('shall'), which is however softened by the word 'consider'.[22]

As to the post-conflict situation, this obligation is strengthened by Principle 14. This aspect has so far been neglected. It is, for example, not mentioned in the 2015 Report of the High-level Independent Panel on Peace Operations.[23]

The first aspect of the problem is the behaviour and attitude of the operation. For instance: what is the impact of their consumptions on local resources? Do such operations consume too much water or produce too much waste? Do peacekeepers go hunting endangered species?

The second aspect is their impact on the functioning of local life. Disarmament or demining activities pose environmental problems which must be taken into account. Peacekeepers may have to restrain unlawful mining activities which pose disastrous environmental problems.

> Draft Principle 6
> Protection of the environment of indigenous peoples
>
> 1. States should take appropriate measures, in the event of armed conflict, to protect the environment of the territories that indigenous peoples inhabit.
> 2. After an armed conflict that has adversely affected the environment of the territories that indigenous peoples inhabit, States should undertake effective consultations and cooperation with the indigenous peoples concerned, through appropriate procedures and in particular through their own representative institutions, for the purpose of taking remedial measures.

Taking into account the specific problems and interests of indigenous peoples is a general *leitmotiv* in current international law.[24] An example is Article 8 (j) of the Convention on Biological Diversity.[25] Fulfilling the duties formulated

---

21 UNEP, 'Greening the Blue Helmets: Environment, Natural Resources and UN Peacekeeping Operations', 2012.

22 Statement of the Chair of the Drafting Committee, supra, note 14, p. 8.

23 UN Doc. A/70/95-S/2015/446.

24 B. Kingbury, 'Indigenous peoples', in R. Wolfrum (ed), *Max Planck Encyclopedia of Public International Law* (MPEPIL), available at www.mpepil.com; 3rd Report of the Special Rapporteur, supra, note 4, para. 121 et seq.

25 1760 UNTS 79.

458   PART 5: CONDUCT OF HOSTILITIES – PROTECTING THE ENVIRONMENT

in paragraph 1 would at the same time mean implementing the purposes of that provision.

The second paragraph belongs to the post-conflict duties. It is a concretization of Principles 15 and 18.[26]

3.2   *Principles Applicable During Armed Conflict (Part Two)*

Concerning the protection of the environment during armed conflict, the controversy concentrated largely on the relevant provisions of AP I, defining the threshold of the prohibition on causing damage to the environment by three qualifications. Only damage which is 'widespread, long-term *and* severe' falls within the prohibition. These three cumulative conditions are generally criticized as inadequate. But it seems that some States still like them. The development, however, has gone beyond these conditions.[27] The principles so far formulated by the Special Rapporteur and the ILC take these developments into account, but in an incomplete manner.

The part on principles applying during armed conflict is introduced by a general rule:

> Draft Principle 9, Paragraph 1
> General protection of the environment during armed conflict
>
> The natural environment shall be respected and protected in accordance with applicable international law and, in particular, the law of armed conflict.

The provision is a kind of reminder, useful as such: there is applicable law requiring the protection of the environment during armed conflict, and that law has to be applied. What is important, in addition, is that the provision expresses an assumption underlying the proposed principles, namely that these rules are not only those of the *ius in bello,* but also other rules. These other rules have to be applied, too. This leads to the question whether and how far the law of armed conflict is a *lex specialis* in relation to these other rules, namely general environmental law and multilateral environmental agreements.[28]

The second paragraph of Principle 9 prescribes a duty of care:

------

26   See below.
27   Bothe et al., supra, note 7, at pp. 684 et seq.
28   See below 4.2.

> Draft Principle 9, Paragraph 2

> Care shall be taken to protect the natural environment against widespread, long-term and severe damage.

It is somewhat regrettable that the three conditions are still there. In this respect, it is useful to compare the proposed principle with other recent formulations of the duty of care, providing for what has become known as the due regard principle:

- ICRC Customary Law Study, Rule 44[29]

  'Methods and means of warfare must be employed with due regard to the protection and preservation of the natural environment. In the conduct of military operations, all feasible precautions must be taken to avoid, and in any event minimise, incidental damage to the environment. ...'

  The duty to take feasible precautions corresponds to a duty of care. It is only in relation to the prohibition *stricto sensu* that the three qualifications also appear in the ICRC Study (Rule 45).

- San Remo Manual on Naval Warfare,[30] Article 44:

  'Methods and means of warfare should be employed with due regard for the natural environment taking into account the relevant rules of international law. Damage to or destruction of the natural environment not justified by military necessity and carried out wantonly is prohibited.'

  It must be emphasized that the three objectionable conditions are not mentioned. They may be hidden in the reference to 'relevant rules of international Law', but the prohibition is much broader and better formulated than the one contained in AP I.

- Manual of Air and Missile Warfare:[31]

  88. The destruction of the natural environment carried out wantonly is prohibited.

  89. When planning and conducting air or missile operations, due regard ought to be given to the natural environment.'

---

29 ICRC, J.-M. Henckaerts, L. Doswald-Beck, *Customary International Humanitarian Law*, vol. 1, Cambridge University Press, 2005, pp. 147 et seq.

30 San Remo Manual on International Law Applicable to Armed Conflicts at Sea, 12 June 1994, document elaborated by a group of experts assembled by the International Institute of Humanitarian Law, San Remo.

31 Manual of International Law Applicable to Air and Missile Warfare, 15 may 2009, Document elaborated by a Group of Experts convened by the Program on Humanitarian Policy and Conflict Research at Harvard University.

PART 5: CONDUCT OF HOSTILITIES – PROTECTING THE ENVIRONMENT

This formulation is obviously inspired by the San Remo Manual and much friendlier to the environment then AP I and the ILC draft principle 9 para. 2.

It is hoped that the final version still to be adopted by the ILC will correct a version which, it is submitted, lags behind the *acquis* concerning the protection of the environment during armed conflict.

Several principles contained in Part Two concerning the protection of the environment during armed conflict relate to the principle of distinction:

> Draft Principle 9, Paragraph 3
>
> No part of the environment may be attacked, unless it has become a military objective.

> Draft Principle 10
> Application of the law of armed conflict to the natural environment
>
> The law of armed conflict, including the principles and rules on distinction, proportionality, military necessity and precautions in attack, shall be applied to the natural environment with a view to its protection

> Draft Principle 11
> Environmental considerations
>
> Environmental considerations shall be taken into account when applying the principle of proportionality and the rules on military necessity.

The three principles 9 para. 3, 10 and 11 apply the rule of distinction, which is the fundamental rule of international humanitarian law, to the protection of the environment. In the debate on the protection of the environment during armed conflict, it has even been maintained that the rules on the immunity of civilian objects are sufficient to protect the environment as elements of the environment are usually civilian in nature.[32] Principle 9(3) is a logical consequence of the rule of Article 52 AP I: anything which is not a military objective is a civilian object and may therefore not be attacked. Incidental damage to the

---

32   For a critique see Bothe et al., supra, note 7, at pp. 576 et seq.

environment caused by attacks on military objectives is limited by the principle of proportionality.

Damage to the (civilian!) elements of the environment may not be excessive in relation to the direct military advantage anticipated. This is also reflected in the rule on precautions to be taken in attacks (Article 57 (2)(a)(iii) AP I). Principle 10 and 11 clarify that environmental concerns are indeed part of this 'proportionality equation', which, it is submitted, constitutes the added value of the two principles. Mentioning 'military necessity' should not be misunderstood as meaning that military necessity is a particular justification of destruction; quite the contrary, the Commission views it as an additional restraint on attacks on military objectives.[33] This should be clarified. Considerations of military 'advantage' are part of the definition of the military objective in Article 52 AP I. Beyond this, what might be considered as military necessity is irrelevant for determining what is a permissible attack and what not.

A special provision (Principle 13) in this Part is related to the General Principle formulated in Part One, namely Principle 5.

> Draft Principle 13
> Protected Zones

> An area of major environmental and cultural importance designated by agreement as a protected zone shall be protected against any attack, as long as it does not constitute a military objective.

It is a question of logic that the designation provided for in Principle 5 must entail some protection during armed conflict. By virtue of Principle 13, this protection is limited to zones designated by agreement. This protection corresponds *grosso modo* to that provided for demilitarized zones pursuant to Article 60 AP I. The scope of the protection will depend on the agreement. The words 'shall be protected against any attack' are not very clear. Article 60 AP I prohibits the parties from extending 'their military operations to [demilitarized] zones' if this is contrary to the agreement designating them. Logically, the prohibition includes any action by the enemy party which has a negative impact on the environment in the zone. The zone, of course, loses its protection if, contrary to the agreement designating it, somehow a military objective

---

33 See the misgivings expressed in the comment by Switzerland, quoted in the 3rd Report of the Special Rapporteur, supra, note 4, para. 88. On the concept envisaged by the ILC, see the Report, supra, note 6, p. 334.

462   PART 5: CONDUCT OF HOSTILITIES – PROTECTING THE ENVIRONMENT

is created in the area, for instance if armed forces enter it. This rule also applies to demilitarized zones according to Article 60 (7) AP I.

In addition to the agreement, Principle 5 provides for forms of designation other than by agreement. It is quite clear that a designation by unilateral declaration cannot have the same protective effect as a designation by agreement. But a prohibition of attacks can be achieved by a unilateral declaration under Article 59 AP I, which provides this protection for 'undefended localities'. Nothing prevents such a declaration being made for environmental reasons.

A designation by the Security Council, an option advocated by IUCN, would lead to the same protection as designation by agreement if that designation is made by a decision binding under Ch. VII in combination with Article 25 of the Charter. If the designation is made in the form of a recommendation, or if it is made by another UN agency, the protection can only be achieved through an implementing agreement between the parties.

3.3   *Principles Applicable after an Armed Conflict*

This part contains a number of useful rules relating to action for the purpose of clarifying how to deal with the detrimental environmental consequences of an armed conflict. This is a problem area where a rich practice has been developed since the 1990s. It is a major field of activity of UNEP.[34]

> Draft Principle 14
> Peace processes
> 1. Parties to an armed conflict should, as part of the peace process, including where appropriate in peace agreements, address matters relating to the restoration and protection of the environment damaged by the armed conflict.
> 2. Relevant international organizations should, where appropriate, play a facilitating role in this regard.

Detrimental effects of warfare are manifold, and this damage affects living conditions in many ways. Water supply and waste water treatment may be halted. Devastated land areas may no longer be usable for agriculture. Therefore, the restoration of the environment is an important element of a return to normal living conditions and hence to lasting peace. Paragraph 1 is a rather soft

---

34   UNEP activities are divided into four areas: post-crisis environmental assessment, post-crisis environmental recovery, environmental cooperation and peacebuilding, disaster risk reduction. Information available at www.unep.org/disasterandconflicts/ UNEPsActivities/tabid/54617/Default.aspx.

A PRELIMINARY COMMENT ON THE WORK OF THE ILC

exhortation ('should address'), but it is difficult to see how the principles could go into more detail. In the Drafting Committee, it was said that the provision did not correspond to a pre-existing obligation, but that it nevertheless had an important normative value,[35] which could mean a strong suggestion *de lege ferenda.*[36]

As to paragraph 2, UNEP has played this role for many years and will hopefully continue to do so.

> Draft Principle 15
> Post-armed-conflict environmental assessment and remedial measures

> Cooperation among relevant actors, including international organizations, is encouraged with respect to post-armed-conflict environmental assessments and remedial measures.

This is a very important principle. 'Relevant actors' include both States and non-State actors.[37] What is required by this provision is exactly what UNEP has been doing since 1999 in relation to a number of conflicts which were taking place and ending during the past two decades.[38] In the light of this practice, it is perhaps regrettable that the obligation to do this is formulated in rather weak terms ('cooperation is encouraged'). It may well be asked whether, in the light of this practice, what has happened and continues to happen no longer is a politically laudable usage, but has grown into a rule of customary law.

A special aspect of the duties formulated in Principle 15 is how to deal with dangerous remnants of war.

> Draft principle 16
> Remnants of war
> 1. *After an armed conflict, parties to the conflict shall seek to remove or render harmless toxic and hazardous remnants of war under their jurisdiction of control that are causing or risk causing damage to the*

---

35   Statement of the Chair of the Drafting Committee, supra, note 14, p. 10.

36   On relevant practice, see 3rd Report of the Special Rapporteur, supra, note 4, para. 154 et seq.

37   Statement of the Chair of the Drafting Committee, supra, note 14, p. 12.

38   Information available at www.unep.org/disastersandconflicts/Introduction/PostCrisis EnvironmentalAssessment/tabid/54351/Default.aspx.

PART 5: CONDUCT OF HOSTILITIES – PROTECTING THE ENVIRONMENT

environment. Such measures shall be taken subject to applicable rules of international law.

2. *The parties shall also endeavour to reach agreement, among themselves and, where appropriate, with other States and with international organizations, on technical and material assistance, including, in appropriate circumstances, the undertaking of joint operations to remove or render harmless such toxic and hazardous remnants of war.*

3. *Paragraphs 1 and 2 are without prejudice to any rights or obligations under international law to clear, remove, destroy or maintain minefields, mined areas, mines, booby-traps, explosive ordnance and other devices.*

Draft Principle 17
Remnants of war at sea

States and relevant international organizations should cooperate to ensure that remnants of war at sea do not constitute a danger to the environment.

Chemical weapons and mines as 'leftovers' of war have at least since the Second World War given rise to considerable controversies, mainly between the countries which had used them and those where they were left.[39] In relation to chemical weapons, a certain progress was achieved by the Convention on the Prohibition of the Development, Production, Stockpiling and Use of Chemical Weapons and on their Destruction.[40] It contains certain obligations relating to old and abandoned chemical weapons, mainly as a duty of the State where they currently are, but also as an obligation of the State which abandoned such weapons elsewhere.[41] As to mines, a controversy between Libya and the former parties to the Second World War concerning mines left on Libyan territory has never really been solved. In recent years, mine-clearing activities have been undertaken not only by the countries where they are, but also as part of assistance programs by other States and international organizations, both governmental and non-governmental. De-mining has become an important part of peacekeeping operations. These activities have not started on the assumption that the relevant actors were bound by international customary law to do what they did. It is arguable, however, that this practice has become the

---

39 On the history of the debate, see 3rd Report of the Special Rapporteur, supra, note 4, p. 244 et seq.

40 1974 UNTS 45.

41 Article II(1)(b) and IV (1) CWC.

object of a rule of customary law. In addition, it has become the object of treaty law by the 2003 Protocol v to the UN Convention on Conventional Weapons,[42] relating to 'Explosive Remnants of War'.[43]

Despite the environmental impact of the use of mines, the concern addressed by this legal development is rather the health and safety of persons. But the environmental consequences of armed conflict have been for more than two decades, as already indicated, a major concern for the international community. UNEP has been at the cutting edge of work in this field.[44] Since the last couple of years, a considerable pressure has been built up by civil society organizations that a treaty be adopted to serve environmental interests, too, providing for a more general duty to remove or render harmless 'toxic remnants of war'.[45] Principle 16 para. 1 expresses the duty which the said civil society movement is advocating, namely a duty (expressed by the strong term 'shall') to seek to remove or render harmless 'toxic and hazardous' remnants of war. This covers any substance having the potential to threaten the life of human beings, animals or plants which are found in land areas as a consequence of war. Para. 2 formulates the obvious: international agreements for cooperation are the best tool for achieving the goal pursued by para. 1. Para. 3 takes into account, in particular, the legal developments concerning explosive remnants just described.

In contradistinction to remnants on land, international practice is not so widespread concerning remnants at sea. Oil spills caused by hostilities and remaining in the respective waters after the end of a conflict have given rise to cooperation concerning clean-up and also to litigation concerning damage caused by them. A duty of cooperation, as formulated in soft terms ('should') in Principle 17, is a solution to the problem.

> Draft Principle 18
> Sharing and granting access to information
> 1. To facilitate remedial measures after an armed conflict, States and relevant international organizations shall share and grant access

---

42   Protocol on Explosive Remnants of War to the Convention on Prohibitions or Restrictions on the Use of Certain Conventional Weapons which may be deemed to be Excessively Injurious or to have Indiscriminate Effects (Protocol v), 2399 UNTS 100.

43   UN Doc. CCW/MSP/2003/2, 27 November 2003.

44   Supra, notes 30 and 31.

45   Toxic Remnants of War Project (TRW), information available at www.toxicremnantsof-war/info. An informative publication is M. Ghalaieny, 'Toxic harm: humanitarian and environmental concerns from military-origin contamination', TRW 2013.

PART 5: CONDUCT OF HOSTILITIES – PROTECTING THE ENVIRONMENT

to relevant information in accordance with their obligations under international law.

2. Nothing in the present draft principle obliges a State or international organization to share or grant access to information vital to its national defence or security. Nevertheless, that State or international organization shall cooperate in good faith with a view to providing as much information as possible under the circumstances.

Remedial measures are not possible without those undertaking them having sufficient information about the factual problem to be solved. Knowledge of the positions of mines is a traditional example. This is why Article 4 of Protocol V to the CCW, just mentioned, provides for the transmission of relevant information. Principle 18 provides for a strong obligation ('shall') to share and grant access to relevant information. 'States' are not only the parties to a conflict, but also third States.[46] Whether the addition 'in accordance with their obligations under international law'[47] is a limitation or a confirmation of this rule is somewhat dubious. The 'shall' would really be meaningless if the provision were to be interpreted as meaning that States are only bound to share information to the extent they are so bound by other rules of international law. The debate in the Drafting Committee does not suggest such a narrow interpretation.[48] It is submitted that in the light of the practice referred to, the better interpretation of the formula is as a hint to the fact that the obligation to share and grant access to information has already become part of customary law.

Paragraph 2 concerning information vital for national defence and security is a necessary exception to the rule of para. 1. It is somewhat difficult to envisage how this particular exception could apply to relevant international organizations. Such organizations will as a rule not possess such information. But military organizations like NATO might possess them, and to this extent it makes sense to have these organizations mentioned in the text.

4 Some General Problems

4.1 *The Scope of Application: What Type of Conflict?*

In the 6th Committee of the General Assembly[49] and in the ILC, it was debated whether the principles apply to both international and non-international

---

46 Statement of the Chair of the Drafting Committee, supra, note 14, p. 17.

47 On existing obligations, see 3rd Report of the Special Rapporteur, supra, note 4, para. 132 et seq.

48 Statement of the Chair of the Drafting Committee, supra, note 13, p. 17.

49 3rd Report of the Special Rapporteur, supra, note 4, para. 40.

A PRELIMINARY COMMENT ON THE WORK OF THE ILC

conflicts. The text of the Principles does not address the question explicitly, but it is generally agreed that the Principles apply in both international and non-international armed conflicts.[50] If one looks at the content of the principles, a differentiated view seems appropriate. There are certain principles clearly addressing States and intergovernmental organizations only. This is the case for the general principles in Part I. On the other hand, the principles contained in Part II, applicable during armed conflict, are formulated in a way which renders them apt for being applied also in a case of non-international armed conflict. In Part III, principles 14 to 16 relate to 'parties to the conflict' or 'relevant Actors'. The content is such that it can be relevant to action taken also by a non-State Party after the end of a non-international armed conflict.

4.2 *The* Lex Specialis *Issue*

In the debate in the 6th Committee of the General Assembly, comments were made to the effect that the law of armed conflict should remain *lex specialis*.[51] The debate stems from that about the relationship between human rights and international humanitarian law and was triggered, in particular, by a somewhat unfortunate formulation used by the ICJ in its Nuclear Weapons Advisory Opinion.[52] In that decision, the Court clearly upheld the concurrent application of both human rights and international humanitarian law. If it said at the same time that international humanitarian law could be *lex specialis*, this would be absolutely contradictory if *lex specialis* meant what it usually means, namely the exclusion of the application of another norm. On the other hand, concurrent application cannot possibly mean that both fields of law apply without change. If both apply concurrently to one and the same situation, they must be somehow adapted if their content is not the same. A closer look shows that this is the true sense of the holding of the Court:[53]

> [T]he protection of the International Covenant of Civil and Political Rights does not cease in times of war ... the right not arbitrarily to be deprived of one's life applies also in hostilities. The test of what is an arbitrary deprivation of life, however, then falls to be determined by the applicable *lex specialis,* namely, the law applicable in armed conflict which is designed to regulate the conduct of hostilities.

---

50   Statement of the Chair of the Drafting Committee, supra, note 14, p. 10; Commentary to draft Principle 1, ILC Report, supra, note 6.

51   3rd Report of the Special Rapporteur, supra, note 4, para. 39; see also ILC Report supra, note 6, p. 329.

52   *Legality of the threat or use of nuclear weapons*, Advisory Opinion, *ICJ Report 1996*, p. 226.

53   Ibid., para. 25.

This means that the application of human rights and in particular of the relevant guarantee of the right to life is not excluded (which would be *lex specialis sensu stricto*), but that it has to be interpreted in context, i.e. in the light of the law of armed conflict.

It is submitted that this rule also applies to the relationship between international environmental law and international humanitarian law which underlies the proposed principles, although the Special Rapporteur states the issue in a somewhat different way.[54] However, the only proposed principle which touches upon the problem is Principle 9 para.1, already discussed, which speaks of 'applicable international law, and, in particular, the law of armed conflict'. This means that it is not only the law of armed conflict which applies to the protection of the environment during armed conflict. Other rules of international law may apply as well. There has to be concurrent application, including the necessary adaptation to the context of armed conflict.

The strongest argument in favour of concurrent application is the work of the ILC concerning the effect of armed conflict on treaties,[55] to which the Special Rapporteur also refers in her Reports.[56] The general principle formulated by the ILC is (Article 3):

> The existence of an armed conflict does not *ipso facto* terminate or suspend the operation of treaties ...

According to Article 7, the ILC provides 'an indicative list of treaties the subject matter of which involves an implication that they continue to apply'. That list includes:

> ...
>
> (c) Multilateral law-making treaties,
>
> ...
>
> (g) Treaties relating to the international protection of the environment,
>
> (h) Treaties relating to international watercourses and related installations and facilities,
>
> (i) Treaties relating to aquifers and related installations and facilities, ...'

---

54   3rd Report of the Special Rapporteur, supra, note 4, para. 10 and 99.

55   Draft articles on the effects of armed conflicts on treaties, in Report of the International Law Commission on the work of its 63rd session, UN Doc. A/66/10, April–August 2011.

56   3rd Report of the Special Rapporteur, supra, note 4, para. 100 et seq.

Thus, treaties concerning various aspects of international environmental law are, at least as a rule, not suspended if an armed conflict breaks out. They continue to apply. There must thus be concurrent application in the sense just described. This is the particular background of Principle 9 para. 1.

4.3 *The Value of the Principles*

Some texts elaborated by the ILC have led to the negotiation and conclusion of international treaties based on them. In all other cases, the value of the ILC texts is a matter of debate: it depends on the concrete case. In some, the Commission's texts are meant to restate customary international law and are received by the international community as an authoritative statement thereof. An example is the articles on the responsibility of States for wrongful acts. Where the Commission does not adopt 'articles', but 'principles', the purpose is to produce an instrument which is less strict, taking into account that a certain aversion against developing international humanitarian law can be discerned among the international community. These options (draft treaty, statement of customary law, statement of general principles) have been in the minds of the members of the ILC when dealing with the topic of the protection of the environment in relation to armed conflict. It has been pointed out above that where the text expresses a strong obligation by using 'shall', there are good reasons to believe that there is a rule of customary law: *lex lata.* Provisions using 'should' must rather be understood as being *de lege ferenda.* The use of wording in this sense is a deliberate choice of the ILC.[57]

5 Conclusions

The project 'principles for the protection of the environment in relation to armed conflicts' is an important document. It deserves a prize for a number of reasons. It has freed the discourse from concentration on the specific obligations of the *ius in bello* and has placed the question where it belongs, namely in the broader context of human activities with an impact on the environment, including but not limited to military activities. It draws attention to relevant activities to be regulated before an armed conflict breaks out, and in particular to the preservation and restoration of the environment after an armed conflict. Useful obligations are formulated for this purpose, and the Commission

---

57 Statement of the Chair of the Drafting Committee, supra, note 14, *passim.*

by using the word 'shall', has not refrained from emphasizing the strength of important obligations relating to the post-conflict phase.

What is regrettable, on the other hand, is that the ILC has not stood up against the reluctance of States to accept any development of the *ius in bello,* a reluctance seen for example regarding the reaction of States to the ICRC proposal to consider developing the law of armed conflict also in relation to environmental protection. The Commission has, at least so far, maintained the three objectionable qualifications of the prohibition stemming from the 1977 Additional Protocol and has refrained from elaborating the 'due regard' principle used in newer instruments to ensure the protection of the environment against the effects of hostilities. 'Due regard ... ', it is submitted, is a better tool to ensure the protection of environmental concerns during armed conflicts.

PART 6

Protected Persons and Human Rights, Relief

∴

Le Sort des Blessés et Malades

Un but Fondamental de la Croix-Rouge

1   Introduction

Les écrits parus jusqu'ici sur la Conférence diplomatique[1] ont, pour la plupart, été consacrés aux problèmes politiques majeurs de la Conférence: la guerre

---

[1]   « Conférence diplomatique sur la réaffirmation et le développement du droit international humanitaire applicable dans les conflits armés », *Revue internationale de la Croix-Rouge,* vol. 57, 1975, pp. 257–261, 385–422 ; R. R. Baxter, « Humanitarian Law or Humanitarian Politics ? The 1974 Diplomatic Conference on Humanitarian Law », *Harvard International Law Journal,* vol. 16, 1975, pp. 1–26 ; D. P. Forsythe, « The 1974 Diplomtaic Conference on Humanitarian Law : Some Observations », *American Journal of International Law,* vol. 69, 1975, pp. 77–91 ; K. Obradovic, « Humanitäres Recht und Politik, Zur Frage der Teilonahme der provisorischen Revolutionsregierung der Republik Südvietnam an der Genfer Konferenz », *Internationale Politik* (Belgrade), vol. 26, 1975, Nº 597, pp. 26–28 ; M. Bothe, « Die Genfer Konferenz über humanitäres Völkerrecht, Bericht über den Stand der Verhandlungen nach der zweiten Sitzungsperiode », *Zeitschrift für ausländisches öffentliches Recht und Völkerrecht,* vol. 35, 1975, pp. 641–655 ; H. Fujita « La guerre de libération nationale et le droit international humanitaire », *Revue de droit international, de sciences diplomatiques et politiques,* vol. 53, 1975, pp. 81–142 ; O. Hugler, « Bemerkungen zu Diplomatenkonferenz über das humanitäre Völkerrrecht », *Neue Justiz,* vol. 29, 1975, pp 617–621 ; K. Ipsen, « Zum Begriff des internationalen bewaffneten Konflikts », *in :* J. Delbrück, K. Ipsen, D. Rauschning (éd.), *Recht im Dienst des Friedens,* Festschrift für Eberhard Menzel, Berlin, Duncker & Humblot, 1975, pp. 405–425 ; M. Bothe, « Krise der Rotkreuz-Idee ?, Grundfragen der Genfer Diplomatische Konferenz über humanitäres Recht », *Europa-Archiv,* vol. 31, 1976, pp. 197–204 ; P. Geouffre de la Pradelle, « Réflexions sur la IIᵉ session de la Conférence diplomatique de Genève sur la réaffirmation et le développement du droit international humanitaire », *Annales de droit international médical,* Nº 26, 1975, pp. 9–44 ; A. Randelzhofer, « Entwicklungstendenzen im humanitären Völkerrecht für bewaffnete Konflikte », *Friedens-Warte,* vol. 58, 1975, pp. 23–54 ; J. Salmon, « Participation du GRP du Sud-Vietnam aux travaux de la conférence diplomatique sur la réaffirmation et le développement du droit international humanitaire applicable dans les conflits armés », *Revue belge de droit international,* vol. 11, 1975, pp. 191–210 ; a. Viñal Casas, « La Conferencia diplomática de Ginebra sobre la reafrimación y el desarollo del derecho international humanitario aplicable en los conflictos armados », *Revista Española de Derecho Internacional,* vol. 19, 1976, pp. 85–90 ; D. E. Graham, « The 1974 Diplomatic Conference on the Law of War : A Victory for Political Causes and a Return to the 'Just War' Concept of the Eleventh Century », *Washington and Lee Law Review,* vol. 32, 1975, pp. 25–63 ; J. E. Bond, « Amended Article 1 of Draft Protocol I to the 1949 Geneva Conventions : The Coming Age of the Guerilla », *Washington and Lee Law Review,* vol. 32, 1975, pp. 65–78 ; H. Meyrowitz,

474 PART 6: PROTECTED PERSONS AND HUMAN RIGHTS, RELIEF

de libération nationale, la guérilla, les armes, etc. Les travaux de la Commission II sont, de ce fait, restés un peu dans l'ombre. La compétence de cette commission concerne le domaine humanitaire put, si l'on veut les questions les plus «Croix-Rouge» : la protection des blessés et malades, les secours à la population civile et la protection civile. Il serait cependant erroné de penser que ce domaine ne soulève aucune question politique. Les problèmes politiques et militaires auxquels cette commission a dû faire face sont peut-être un peu moins évidents, mais quelques-uns sont tout de même fondamentaux. De plus, cette commission a eu à résoudre une série de problèmes juridiques très intéressants. Cet article se propose d'en mettre quelques-uns en relief.

Quelles sont, dans le domaine assigné à la Commission II, les lacunes du droit humanitaire qu'il faut combler? Pour ce qui est du conflit armé de caractère international, la première Convention de Genève de 1949 ne protège que les blessés et malades militaires et quelques catégories très limitées de civils, alors que la quatrième ne contient qu'une disposition de base quant aux personnes civiles qui sont blessées et malades (art. 16). Cette dernière disposition doit être développée.

La première Convention protège le personnel et les unités sanitaires militaires ; la quatrième règle la protection des hôpitaux civils et de leur personnel seulement. Ce qui fait défaut, c'est la protection du personnel et des unités sanitaires civils en général. Il en est de même pour le personnel religieux.

La protection des transports sanitaires militaires terrestres et maritimes prévue par les première et deuxième Conventions est, sauf pour quelques

---

« Les guerres de libération et les Conventions de Genève », *Politique étrangère,* vol. 39, 1974, pp. 607–627 ; K. Hailbronner, « Der Schutz von Sanitätsluftfahrzeugen im Krieg », *in :* M. Bodenschatz, K.-H. Böckstiegel, P. Weides (éd.), *Beiträge zum Luft- und Weltraumrecht,* Festschrift zu Ehren von Alex Meyer, Köln/Berlin/Bonn/München, Heymans, 1975, pp. 127–146 ; M. Mushkat, « Das Kriegvölkerrecht, das Rote Kreuz un die neuen Tendenzen der humanitären Rechtsordnung », *Revue de droit pénal militaire et de droit de la guerre,* vol. 15, 1976, pp. 113–147 ; S. Suckow, « Development of International Humanitarian Law », *The Review,* N° 12, 1974, pp. 50–57 ; K. J. Partsch, « La protection internationale des droits de l'homme et les Conventions de Genève de la Croix-Rouge », *Revue internationale de droit comparé,* vol. 14, 1974, pp. 73–83 ; J. Mirimanoff-Chilikine, « La Conférence diplomatique sur la réaffirmation et le développement du droit international humanitaire applicable dans les conflits armés », *Revue belge de droit international,* vol. 10, 1974, pp. 36–72 ; Ch. Cantrell, « Civilian Protection in Internal Armed Conflicts : The Second Diplomatic Conference », *Texas International Law Journal,* vol. 11, 1976, pp. 305–328 ; K. J. Partsch, « Neue Entwicklungen zum Begriff des internationalen bewaffneten Konfliktes », *Neue Zeitschrift für Wehrrecht,* vol. 17, 1975, pp. 46–52 ; B. Graefrath, « Dritte Sitzung der Genfer Konferenz zur Weiterentwicklung des Humanitären Völkerrecht », *Deutsche Aussenpolitik,* 1976, pp. 1561–1567.

LE SORT DES BLESSÉS ET MALADES

détails, suffisante. Il manque cependant une protection générale des transports sanitaires civils. La protection des transports sanitaires aériens, qui est limitée, en vertu de l'article 36 de la première Convention, au vol « convenu », est cependant absolument insuffisante.

Constitue également un besoin urgent l'adaptation de l'indentification et de la signalisation du personnel et des unités sanitaires aux exigences de la technique moderne.

L'information de la famille des victimes de conflits et l'accès aux tombes de ceux qui sont morts dans un conflit représente une nécessité humanitaire fondamentale.

En ce qui concerne la protection civile, à savoir l'organisation chargée d'assurer la survie de la population civile lors d'un désastre (qu'il soit le fait de la nature ou de l'homme), les Conventions ne contiennent qu'une disposition de base pour les territoires occupés (art. 63, al. 2). Cet article n'est plus adéquat, vu l'importance de la protection civile dans un conflit moderne.

Finalement, la disposition générale des Conventions sur les secours à la population civile (art. 23 de la quatrième Convention) est beaucoup trop restrictive. Les autres dispositions relatives à ce sujet (les articles 55 et suivants de la quatrième Convention) ne concernent que les territoires occupés.

Quant au conflit de caractère non international, les dispositions de l'article 3, commun aux Conventions, relatives aux blessés et malades et aux secours sont aussi laconiques que le reste de cet article. Ici également, un développement du droit humanitaire s'impose.

Qu'a pu faire la Commission II afin de combler ces lacunes ? Alors que les articles sur la protection civile et les secours ont dû être laissés pour la quatrième session, la Commission a pu adopter tous les articles relatifs aux blessés et malades, y compris les questions de l'information et des tombes. L'œuvre qui a pu ainsi être accomplie constitue un progrès très net du droit humanitaire, dont voici quelques éléments essentiels.

2 Le Développement de la Protection des Blessés et Malades

2.1 L'étendue de la Notion « Blessés et Malades » (Art. 8)

L'article 8 contient des définitions. Il est peut-être surprenant que l'on essaie de définir des termes tels que « blessés et malades », « naufragés », etc. Mais, quand on y regarde de plus près, on constate que ces définitions constituent une clarification et parfois une extension importante de la protection accordée par le Protocole. Bien que la portée des définitions soit, selon le texte de l'article 8, limitée au « présent Protocole », et bien qu'elles ne couvrent ainsi pas les mêmes termes quand ils sont employés dans les Conventions, on peut s'attendre à ce que ces définitions jouent aussi, dans la pratique, un rôle important dans l'interprétation des Conventions. Il est difficile de concevoir, par exemple, que la notion de « blessés et malades » soit interprétée de manière plus restrictive dans les Conventions que dans le Protocole.

Cette définition des « blessés et malades » est un bon exemple de la clarification et de l'extension de la protection qui résultent de l'article 8. L'alinéa a) (première phrase) se lit comme suit :

> Les termes « blessés » et « malades » s'entendent des personnes, militaires ou civiles, qui, en raison d'un traumatisme, d'une maladie ou d'autres incapacités ou troubles physiques ou mentaux, ont besoin de soins médicaux et qui s'abstiennent de tout acte d'hostilité.

On ne peut pas protéger un blessé qui continue la lutte. Il s'agit là peut-être d'une condition évidente, mais il est important de le clarifier. La deuxième phrase du même alinéa assimile certaines personnes qui ne sont nu blessées ni malades aux blessés et malades et leur donne donc la même protection :

> Ces termes couvrent aussi les femmes en couche, les nouveau-nés et d'autres personnes qui pourraient avoir besoin de soins médicaux immédiats et qui s'abstiennent de tout acte d'hostilité, tels que les infirmes et les femmes enceintes.

Voilà une extension importante de la protection qui paraît être naturelle, mais que l'on ne trouve guère de façon explicite dans les Conventions.[2]

Il faut pourtant admettre que les définitions adoptées par la Commission II pour les naufragés, les unités et le personnel sanitaires, les transports sanitaires, etc., sont d'une très grande technicité. Elles se distinguent par un amour du détail qui pourrait même paraître exagéré. Il est vrai que toute la richesse de ces détails ne se révèle pas d'emblée au lecteur. Mais on ne doit pas perdre de vue l'idée qui est à la base de ce règlement détaillé : augmenter les possibilités de protéger les blessés et malades, en précisant mieux les dispositions existantes et en excluant de cette façon les limitations de la protection qu'une interprétation restrictive de dispositions plus générales pourrait créer.

---

2 L'article 16 de la quatrième Convention accorde aux femmes enceintes la même protection et le même respect qu'aux blessés et malades.

LE SORT DES BLESSÉS ET MALADES

2.2   *La Protection des Blessés et Malades*

La protection à laquelle les blessés et malades ont droit est définie à l'article 10 correspondant *grosso modo* aux parties de l'article 12 de la première Convention qui ont le même objet. La signification primordiale de l'article 10 réside donc, sans y être limitée, dans la protection des personnes civiles.

Selon l'alinéa 2 de cet article 10, les blessés et malades doivent recevoir, « dans toute la mesure du possible » et dans les délais les plus brefs, les soins médicaux qu'exige leur état. Les mots entre guillemets constituent une addition au texte proposé par le CICR et révèlent un problème fondamental du Protocole. Quel effort peut-on attendre de la part des Parties au conflit si l'on veut être réaliste ? Il existe des pays dont les ressources médicales sont limitées, on ne peut donc pas imposer à ces pays des charges trop onéreuses. *Ultra posse nemo obligatur* est un vieux principe du droit. Les règles du Protocole doivent en tenir compte. Par ailleurs, il est à noter que cette disposition ne limite pas les soins à donner à un « traitement national ». Les parties en question doivent faire tout leur possible pour soigner les blessés et malades, même si le traitement médical accordé aux propres nationaux, en dehors du conflit, n'est peut-être pas très satisfaisant.

3   La Protection de L'intégrité Physique et Mentale (Art. 11)

Vu les brutalités auxquelles les conflits armés donnent souvent lieu, l'article 11, relatif à l'intégrité physique et mentale peut être considéré comme étant un des articles-clés du Protocole. Il développe et complète les dispositions des articles 12 de la première et de la deuxième Convention, 13 et 17 de la troisième et 31 et 32 de la quatrième.

Compte tenu de l'importance de cet article, mais également en vertu des quelques difficultés d'interprétation qu'il présente, il mérite un examen approfondi.

Le paragraphe premier, dans la version adoptée par le Comité de rédaction de la Conférence, se lit comme suit :

> La santé et l'intégrité physiques ou mentales des personnes qui sont tombées au pouvoir de la Partie adverse ou qui sont internées, détenues ou d'une autre manière, privées de liberté en raison d'une situation visée à l'article 1 du présent Protocole ne doivent être compromises par aucun acte ni par aucune omission injustifiés. En conséquence, il est interdit de soumettre les personnes visées au présent article à un acte médical non motivé par leur état de santé ni conforme aux normes médicales

généralement reconnues que la Partie responsable de l'acte appliquerait dans des circonstances médicales analogues à ses propres ressortissants jouissant de leur liberté.

Cette disposition s'applique aux « personnes qui sont tombées au pouvoir de la Partie adverse », donc à tous les prisonniers de guerre et à toutes les personnes civiles protégées par la quatrième Convention, qu'elles se trouvent comme étrangers dans le territoire de la Partie responsable de l'acte ou en territoire occupé, qu'elles soient relativement libres de poursuivre leurs activités normales ou que leur liberté soit restreinte. La disposition couvre également d'autres personnes, y compris les nationaux de la Partie responsable de l'acte, « qui sont internées, détenues ou d'une autre manière privées de liberté » en raison du conflit. Cela est est une formule très globale qui protège toute personne qui, du fait d'être privée de liberté, se trouve particulièrement exposée aux méfaits de la Puissance « détentrice ». La disposition ne couvre cependant pas un criminel ressortissant de la Puissance détentrice qui est en prison pour des faits qui n'ont aucune relation avec le conflit.

L'article 11 s'adresse aux autorités ou aux agents de la Puissance détentrice ou de la Puissance aux mains de laquelle une personne est tombée. Ce sont eux qui pourraient violer ces dispositions. L'article ne se réfère pas aux faits d'un médecin privé ou de l'administration locale sur un territoire occupé (sauf dans le cas où cette administration agit en vertu d'une directive de la Puissance occupante).

Quels sont les actes prohibés par le paragraphe premier ? La notion d'« acte ou omission injustifiés » est générale, mais aussi un peu vague, surtout lorsqu'il ne s'agit pas de la torture pure et simple (qui est évidemment visée par le paragraphe premier), mais d'actes médicaux qui ne sont pas facilement qualifiés de « torture ». La deuxième phrase de ce paragraphe définit donc de façon plus précise l'acte ou l'omission médical qui serait « injustifié ». Cette définition emploie deux critères : premièrement, la motivation de l'acte. Est interdit tout acte qui n'est pas motivé par l'état de santé de la personne en question, mais qui est, par exemple, effectué afin d'obtenir des informations, d'affaiblit un prisonnier, etc. Le deuxième critère est celui d'une certaine norme médicale. On ne se réfère pas aux normes médicales « généralement reconnues ». Il serait trop difficile d'établir ce que cela signifie dans un cas concret. On recourt à la norme « nationale », c'est-à-dire à la norme reconnue par la Partie responsable de l'acte. Mais, pour exclure les normes nationales trop basses qui pourraient exister pour le traitement médical des prisonniers, la disposition se réfère aux normes qui déterminent le traitement des personnes libres. Tout acte médical qui ne correspond pas à ces normes est interdit.

LE SORT DES BLESSÉS ET MALADES

Le paragraphe 2 donne des exemples de l'application du paragraphe premier. Dans la version adoptée par le Comité de rédaction de la Conférence, il se lit comme suit :

> « Il est en particulier interdit de pratiquer sur ces personnes, même avec leur consentement :
> a) des mutilations physiques ;
> b) des expériences médicales ou scientifiques ;
> c) des prélèvements de tissus ou d'organes pour des transplantations, sauf si ces actes sont justifiés dans les conditions prévues au paragraphe 1 du présent article. »

Ces exemples constituent des cas particulièrement horrible – ou dangereux – d'actes médicaux (ou non médicaux) injustifiés. Il y a cependant des cas limités qui sont visés par la clause qui commence par « sauf ... ». Une amputation peut être appelée une « mutilation physique ». Mais elle peut être requise par l'état de santé de la personne en question, elle peut être nécessaire pour sauver sa vie. Une telle intervention chirurgicale est, dans ce cas, conforme aux normes médicales en question. Elle est donc justifiée dans les conditions prévues au paragraphe premier et n'est donc pas défendue comme « mutilation » en vertu du paragraphe 2.

Donner un médicament nouveau qui n'aurait pas encore passé tous les tests requis à un patient qui risquerait autrement de mourir serait peut-être une « expérience médicale ». Mais un tel traitement peut être nécessaire eu égard à l'état de santé du patient et, peut-être, dans le cas exceptionnel et urgent que nous envisageons, conforme aux normes médicales applicables. Le paragraphe 2 ne constitue donc pas un obstacle à ce que la vie d'un patient soit sauvée par un médicament nouveau qui serait son dernier espoir.

En ce qui concerne l'exemple mentionné ci-dessus sous lettre c), des prélèvements de peau pour la transplantation à une autre partie du corps afin de traiter des brûlures sont également justifiés en vertu du paragraphe premier. Le prélèvement de tissus ou d'organes est devenu très important dans la médecine moderne. Des normes médicales y relatives se sont développées ou sont en train de se développer.

Dans les situations visées au paragraphe premier de l'article 11, la tentation est cependant très grande d'abuser des adversaires qu'une Partie a en son pouvoir, en les utilisant comme donneurs, et cela dans une mesure qui ne serait pas compatible avec leur santé. Mais un prisonnier peur être le seul donneur disponible pour sauver la vie d'un coprisonnier. Tout cela montre qu'il s'agit là d'un problème très délicat qui requiert une solution équilibrée.

L'interdiction des prélèvements, prévue au paragraphe 2 cité ci-dessus, est donc soumise à des exceptions, mais des exceptions très limitées et accompagnées de sauvegardes importantes (qui rendent les paragraphes en question très compliqués).

Ne sont permis en tant qu'exception que des dons de sang et de peau puisqu'il s'agit là des deux cas le mieux établis médicalement. Il faut de plus que ces dons soient absolument volontaires, destinés à des fins thérapeutiques, effectués dans des conditions compatibles avec les normes médicales « généralement reconnues » et avec les sauvegardes établies dans l'intérêt tant du donneur que du receveur. La Partie au conflit sous la responsabilité de laquelle ces dons sont effectués doit en tenir un dossier médical (par. 6).

Comme sauvegarde additionnelle, toute violations volontaire des trois premiers paragraphes de l'article 11, donc y compris les dispositions concernant les dons de sang et de peau, constitue une violation grave du Protocole quand elle met gravement en danger la santé ou l'intégrité physiques ou mentales de la personne protégée par ces dispositions.

L'article 11 compte, lui aussi, parmi les dispositions des Protocoles que certains jugent trop compliquées. Il s'agit certes d'un article compliqué. La question de savoir s'il l'est trop pose des problèmes fondamentaux auxquels nous reviendrons dans nos conclusions.

4 Les Besoins Médicaux de la Population Civile en Territoire Occupé

Les articles 55 et 56 de la quatrième Convention sanctionnent déjà le principe selon lequel la Puissance occupante est responsable de ce que les besoins médicaux de la population civile du territoire continuent d'être satisfaits. Puisqu'il s'agit là d'un principe essentiel, il est répété et renforcé au paragraphe premier de l'article 14, Protocole I. Les paragraphes suivants de ce même article étendent les limitations auxquelles est soumise, en vertu des dispositions précitées, la réquisition d'hôpitaux civils à la réquisition des unités sanitaires en général ainsi qu'à celle de leur personnel et rendent ces limitations plus strictes, afin de sauvegarder le traitement médical de la population civile.

5 Les Unités Sanitaires

Les articles 12 et 13 du Protocole règlent la protection (et sa cessation) des unités sanitaires. Ils englobent les unités tant militaires que civiles. Pour ce qui est des unités militaires, ces dispositions n'ajoutent que des détails aux articles

LE SORT DES BLESSÉS ET MALADES

19 et suivants de la première Convention : par exemple, les Parties au conflit sont invitées à se communiquer l'emplacement de leurs unités sanitaires fixes et ne doivent pas utiliser les unités sanitaires pour mettre des objectifs militaires à l'abri d'attaques. La grande innovation de ces dispositions consiste dans l'extension de la protection aux unités civiles autres que les hôpitaux déjà protégés par les articles 18 à 10 de la quatrième Convention.

6   Le Personnel Sanitaire Civil

L'article 15 prévoit la protection du personnel sanitaire civil qui, jusqu'alors, était protégé seulement lorsqu'il s'agissait du personnel d'hôpitaux (art. 20 de la quatrième Convention). Le paragraphe 2 exige que toute assistance possible soit donnée, en cas de besoin, au personnel sanitaire civil aux environs des combats où il est particulièrement difficile pour ce personnel d'accomplir ses fonctions. Des garanties supplémentaires dont données pour les territoires occupés (par. 3) et pour la liberté de mouvement de ce personnel (par. 4).

7   La Protection de la Mission Médicale

L'article 16 spécifie davantage la protection de ceux qui exercent une activité de caractère médical (médecins, infirmiers, etc.). Il est interdit de les punir pour avoir exercé cette activité de façon conforme à la déontologie et de les contraindre à accomplir des actes contraires à la déontologie ou à d'autres règles pertinentes (par. 1 et 2).

Un problème particulièrement délicat est réglé par le paragraphe 3, à savoir les renseignements qu'une personne exerçant une activité de caractère médical doit ou non donner aux autorités des Parties au conflit. Cette question n'est pas tout à fait réglée par les paragraphes protégeant les activités conformes à la déontologie, parce que la déontologie peut varier à cet égard selon les pays et elle est alors subordonnée à la législation nationale. Exception faite des règlements relatifs à la notification des maladies transmissibles, une personne exerçant une activité de caractère médical ne peut être contrainte de donner des renseignements sur ses patients à une partie au conflit qui n'est pas la sienne, quelle que soit la partie à patients à laquelle appartient le patient. D'autre part, une partie au conflit peut toujours contraindre ses propres ressortissants exerçant une activité médicale à fournir des renseignements si la législation nationale le prévoit ainsi. Le but de cette disposition est d'assurer qu'un blessé ou un malade ne renonce pas à consulter un médecin parce qu'il doit craindre que ce dernier donne des renseignements aux autorités, qui pourraient alors poursuivre le patient. Dans cette optique, il eût été peut-être préférable de protéger tout refus de la part d'un médecin de donner des renseignements à la Partie ennemie du patient. Mais la Commission II a choisi autrement, partant de l'idée que cela serait trop demander si l'on privait une Partie au conflit de la possibilité d'obtenir les renseignements voulus de la part de ses propres nationaux.

L'article 16 garantit donc, dans l'intérêt des blessés et malades, la liberté d'exercer la profession médicale sans devoir craindre des inconvénients. Il a une application générale, c'est-à-dire qu'il couvre les militaires et les civils et qu'il s'applique aussi aux relations entre une Partie au conflit et ses propres ressortissants (avec les modifications signalées).

8 Le Rôle de la Population Civile et les Sociétés de Secours

L'article 17 vise le rôle de la population civile et des sociétés de secours en ce qui concerne les blessés et malades. Il reprend, avec quelques changements, le texte de l'article 18 de la première Convention qui ne s'applique qu'aux militaires et à quelques catégories très limitées de civils qui sont blessés ou malades. La fonction principale du nouvel article 17 réside donc, comme dans le cas des articles 10 et 12, dans le fait qu'il étend aux civils en général le champ d'application d'une règle déjà contenue dans les Conventions.

9 Le Personnel Religieux

Quant au personnel religieux, l'article 24 de la première Convention ne protège que « les aumôniers attachés aux forces armées ». En vertu des articles 8 (f) et 15, paragraphe 5, Protocole I, la protection s'étend au personnel religieux attaché aux unités sanitaires civiles.[3]

En vertu des articles 8 (f), 9, paragraphe 2 (a) et (b) du Protocole I et 27 de la première Convention, le personnel religieux attaché à certaines unités et transports sanitaires relevant de pays neutres est également protégé.

---

3 En ce qui concerne le personnel religieux attaché aux moyens de transport sanitaires, il est également protégé dans la plupart des cas, soit parce qu'il s'agit d'une « unité » mobile, soit en vertu des articles 22 (transports terrestres) et 24 (transports maritimes, fluviaux ou lacustres) du Protocole I.

LE SORT DES BLESSÉS ET MALADES

10 Les Transports Sanitaires

10.1 *Généralités*

Comme il a été dit dans l'introduction, la protection des transports sanitaires militaires sur terre et en mer, prévue par les première et deuxième Conventions, peut être considérée comme suffisante.

Quelques précisions utiles ont toutefois été ajoutées. La notion du transport sanitaire a été clarifiée, notamment en précisant que l'affectation à des fonctions sanitaires doit être exclusive. Il peut y avoir des transports sanitaires permanents et temporaires.

Quant aux transports civils sur terre, n'étaient protégés jusqu'alors que des convois de véhicules et des trains-hôpitaux. L'article 22 du Protocole étend la protection aux véhicules particuliers (ce qui constitue également une clarification en ce qui concerne les véhicules militaires).

10.2 *Les Transports Par Voie D'eau*

La deuxième Convention établit un régime très complet de protection des transports sanitaires en mer. Les Protocoles ne veulent pas changer ce régime mais combler seulement quelques lacunes concernant des détails techniques (art. 23). La protection est également assurée si des navires-hôpitaux transportent des blessés, malades et naufragés civils (ce qui n'est pas clair dans la deuxième Convention). Un navire-hôpital peut être prêté non soulement par des sociétés de secours ou des particuliers relevant des pays neutres (art. 25 de la deuxième Convention), mais également par les Etats neutres eux-mêmes et par une organisation humanitaire impartiale, de caractère international. Les embarcations de sauvetage côtières (art. 27 de la deuxième Convention) sont exemptes des conditions de notification prévues pour les navires-hôpitaux par l'article 22 de la Convention.

La grande innovation en ce qui concerne les transports sanitaires par voie d'eau est cependant une disposition qui couvre les cas où la deuxième Convention ne s'applique pas, soit parce que les conditions de la protection établies par la Convention ne sont pas remplies (cas d'un navire-hôpital temporaire, par exemple, qui n ; est pas protégé par la Convention), soit parce que la Convention ne s'applique pas *ratione loci*. L'application de la deuxième Convention *ratione loci* est peu claire. Selon son titre, elle se réfère aux forces armées « sur mer ». L'article 12 parle des « membres des forces armées et (des) autres personnes ... qui se trouveront en mer ». La Convention contient cependant des dispositions relatives aux ports (art. 29) et aux installations côtières (art. 23). Il est donc pour le moins fort douteux qu'elle s'applique à des fleuves ou à des lacs (quelle qu'en soit la délimitation par rapport à la mer).

Le nouvel article 24 du Protocole I prévoit pour tous ces cas de transports par voie d'eau une protection égale à celle des unités sanitaires. Cette protection n'est pas aussi complète que celle des navires-hôpitaux, mais les conditions préalables de la protection sont, par ailleurs, moins restrictives. Quelques dispositions particulières dans cet article tiennent compte de ce que la situation de fait d'un transport par voie d'eau est différente de celle d'un transport terrestre.

10.3   *Les Transports Aériens*[4]

La protection des transports sanitaires aériens, comme il a déjà été mentionné, limitée aux vols convenus par les articles 36 et 37 de la première Convention, est insuffisante. L'évacuation rapide des blessés par voie aérienne est un bienfait que la technique moderne accorde aux victimes des conflits, devenus toujours plus meurtriers du fait de cette même technique. Il est donc particulièrement important que le droit humanitaire facilite cette évacuation. Cependant, l'emploi d'aéronefs, et notamment d'hélicoptères dans les zones de combat, constitue également une méthode de combat très efficace, et la réaction de l'adversaire doit être rapide. Un combattant qui se trouve face à un aéronef inconnu l'attaquera s'il n'est pas immédiatement évident qu'il s'agit d'un aéronef sanitaire.

Ces difficultés de la protection des aéronefs sanitaires (nous n'en avons mentionné que quelques-unes) ont amené la Commission II à prévoir une solution nuancée et équilibrée.[5] On distingue quatre situations différentes dans lesquelles un aéronef sanitaire peut se trouver :

1. Les zones contrôlées par des forces armées amies et les zones maritimes qui ne sont pas matériellement contrôlées ;
2. Les zones contrôlées par une Partie adverse ;
3. Les zones de contact contrôlées par des forces amies ou dont le contrôle n'est pas clairement établi ;
4. Le territoire neutre.

Dans les situations 2 et 4, la protection de l'aéronef dépend de l'accord préalable de la Partie adverse ou de l'Etat neutre (art. 28 et 32). Dans la situation 1, aucun accord n'est requis (art. 26). Dans la situation 3 (art. 27), la protection « ne peut être pleinement efficace que si un accord préalable est intervenu ». A défaut d'un tel accord, les aéronefs sanitaires opéreront à leurs propres

---

4 Pour une analyse des dispositions adoptées par la Commission II, voir Hailbronner, *op. cit.*

5 Voir *ibid.*

LE SORT DES BLESSÉS ET MALADES

risques. Ils doivent néanmoins être respectés lorsqu'ils auront été identifiés en tant qu'aéronefs sanitaires.

Des garanties supplémentaires contre l'abus des aéronefs sanitaires sont prévues à l'article 29. Ces aéronefs ne porteront pas d'armement, pas de matériel destiné à rechercher ou à transmettre des renseignements, etc. Ils ne seront pas utilisés pour des missions de recherche sauf accord préalable de la Partie adverse.

11 La Signalisation

Les problèmes de la protection des aéronefs militaires ont notamment mis en relief l'importance pour le personnel, les transports et les unités sanitaires de pouvoir être reconnus par l'adversaire aussi rapidement que possible et d'une distance suffisamment grande afin d'éviter qu'une attaque ne soit dirigée contre eux. Un petit brassard avec une croix rouge n'est plus suffisant à cet effet. Il faut une combinaison de méthodes techniques modernes pour assurer une meilleure identification.

Tel est le but de l'article 18 et de l'Annexe au Protocole I qui s'y réfère. Cette annexe prévoit d'abord une carte d'identité pour le personnel sanitaire civil et le personnel religieux, qui s'inspire des dispositions des Conventions sur lest cartes d'identité des personnes déjà protégées par les Conventions.

Le chapitre II de l'Annexe contient des dispositions visant à une meilleure visibilité du signe distinctif (croix, croissant, lion-et-soleil rouges sur fond blanc). Le chapitre III prévoit des signaux distinctifs à l'usage exclusif des unités et transports sanitaires : un feu bleu scintillant pour l'aéronef sanitaire, un signal radio ainsi qu'un mode et un code, de radar secondaire de surveillance (SSR). Le chapitre IV contient des règles relatives à la communication. Les détails techniques notamment ceux concernant les signaux radio et l'identification au moyen du SSR doivent être réglés au sein des Organisations internationales compétentes à savoir : UIT, OMCI et OACI. Des mesures ont été prises à cet effet.

Il est à noter que cette annexe technique peut être modifiée par voie d'une procédure simplifiée (art. 18 bis du Protocole I). Des précédents à cette méthode se trouvent déjà dans bon nombre de Conventions contenant des annexes techniques.[6]

---

6 *Cf.* P. Contini, P.H. Sand, « Methods to Expedite Environment Protection: International Eco-standards », American Journal of International Law, vol. 66, 1972, pp. 37–59.

12 Les Représailles

La question de savoir si le Protocole I contiendra une disposition générale sur les représailles n'est pas encore résolue. Cependant, dans la tradition des Conventions, la Commission II a adopté une disposition interdisant les représailles contre les personnes et les biens « protégés aux termes du présent titre », à savoir notamment les blessés, malades et naufragés, les personnes visées à l'article 11, la population civile qui soigne les blessés, malades et naufragés (art. 17), le personnel sanitaire civil, le personnel religieux, les unités et transports sanitaires. On ne peut guère s'imaginer que cette interdiction soit restreinte par une disposition générale sur les représailles.

13 Atténuer les Souffrances des Familles des Victimes d'un Conflit : La Nouvelle Section I bis Sur les Renseignements et les Tombes

13.1 *Les Renseignements Sur les Victimes*

Les Conventions de Genève contiennent déjà un certain nombre de dispositions facilitant l'obtention et l'échange de renseignements sur les victimes d'un conflit. En ce qui concerne les militaires, les Parties au conflit prendront, « en tout temps et notamment après un engagement », toutes les mesures possibles pour rechercher les morts (art. 15 de la première Convention). Elles doivent enregistrer tous les éléments propres à identifier les blessés et les malades et les morts de la Partie adverse tombés en leur pouvoir. Ces renseignements doivent être communiqués à la Partie adverse par l'intermédiaire de la Puissance protectrice et de l'Agence centrale de recherches. Des dispositions semblables se trouvent dans les articles 18 et 19 de la deuxième Convention. Des dispositions détaillées relatives aux renseignements existent pour les prisonniers de guerre (art. 122 et suivants de la troisième Convention) et les personnes protégées en territoire occupés (art. 136 et suivants de la quatrième Convention). Dans ce dernier cas, l'obligation de transmettre des informations au Bureau national de renseignements ne porte cependant que sur les personnes « appréhendée(s) depuis plus de deux semaines, mise(s) en résidence forcée ou internée(s) ». Lorsqu'une personne civile est appréhendée par la Puissance occupante et tuée tout de suite (peut-être parce qu'elle a essayé de d'évader), il n'existe aucune obligation d'enregistrer ce fait ou de donner une information quelconque à qui que ce soit.

Les dispositions existantes, bien que salutaires, ne sont donc pas tout à fait suffisantes. L'obligation de rechercher les victimes est pratiquement limitée à la recherche des militaires blessés ou tombés au champ de bataille. Aucune disposition n'existe statuant une obligation générale de rechercher des personnes

LE SORT DES BLESSÉS ET MALADES

disparues, défaut qui s'est fait sentir cruellement lors de nombreux conflits. L'obligation relative à l'échange de renseignements ne couvre pas toutes les victimes possibles. Outre la limitation déjà mentionnée, elle ne couvre pas les ressortissants d'un Etat non lié par la quatrième Convention ou d'un Etat neutre pendant l'existence de relations diplomatiques (personnes non protégées par la quatrième Convention, article 4, paragraphe 2).

Les articles 20 bis et 20 ter du Protocole I remédient à ces lacunes. L'article 20 bis reflète l'esprit de la nouvelle Section I bis :

> C'est le droit des familles à connaître le sort de leurs parents qui motive au premier chef l'activité des Hautes Parties contractantes, des Parties au conflit et des organismes humanitaires internationaux mentionnés dans les Conventions de Genève et dans le présent Protocole en ce qui concerne les prescriptions de la présente Section.

Cet article constitue une sorte de préambule à la Section I bis. Il ne crée pas un droit subjectif des familles, mais il le présuppose ; il ne se prononce pas sur la question de savoir si ce droit possède un caractère juridique ou moral. Du point de vue juridique, ce qui importe, c'est le fait que toute la Section doit être interprétée à la lumière de ce droit des familles. Quand il y a doute sur l'interprétation, c'est toujours interprétation la plus favorable qui doit l'emporter.

Le paragraphe 1 de l'article 20 ter crée une obligation générale de rechercher les disparus :

> Chaque Partie au conflit doit, dès que les circonstances le permettent et au plus tard dès la fin des hostilités actives, rechercher les personnes qui on été signalées comme disparues par une Partie adverse. Ladite Partie adverse doit communiquer tout renseignement utile concernant ces personnes, afin de faciliter les recherches.

Le paragraphe 2 du même article comble, de façon générale, les lacunes qui résultent du fait que certaines catégories de personnes ne sont pas couvertes par les dispositions des Conventions relatives à l'obtention et à l'échange de renseignements. Elles couvrent toutes les personnes « qui ne pourraient pas être considérées plus favorablement en vertu des Conventions ou du présent Protocole ». L'obligation créée en faveur de ces personnes est double :

1. l'enregistrement des renseignements prévus à l'article 138 de la quatrième Convention en ce qui concerne les personnes détenues pendant plus de deux semaines ou les personnes décédées en captivité, même si la période de détention est de moins de deux semaines ;

2. la recherche er l'enregistrement de renseignements sur des personnes décédées en raison du conflit « dans d'autres conditions », c'est-à-dire en dehors d'une détention.

Le paragraphe 3 de cet article prévoit les détails concernant la transmission des renseignements et les demandes y relatives.

Le paragraphe 4 envisage des accords spéciaux sur les équipes chargées de rechercher, d'identifier et de relever les morts sur les champs de bataille.

13.2 *Les Tombes*

Les dispositions des Conventions concernant le respect des restes des personnes mortes à cause d'un conflit armé et de leurs sépultures (art. 17, par. 3 de la première Convention, art. 120, par. 4 de la troisième Convention et art. 130, par. 1 de la quatrième Convention) ne couvrent pas non plus toutes les victimes possibles. Le premier paragraphe de l'article 20 quater comble cette lacune en statuant l'obligation de respecter ces restes et de respecter, de conserver et de marquer ces sépultures lorsqu'ils « ne pourraient pas être considérés plus favorablement en vertu des Convention et du présent Protocole ».

Les paragraphes suivant de ce même article se réfèrent à des questions qui ne sont pas réglées par les Conventions ou qui, tout au moins, n'y sont pas traitées de façon suffisamment détaillée.

Le paragraphe 2 de l'article prévoit une obligation de conclure des accords (*pactum de contrahendo,* non seulement *pactum de negotiando*) relatifs à l'accès des familles aux sépultures, à l'entretien permanent des sépultures et au rapatriement des restes. Notons que l'accès aux tombes constitue un besoin humanitaire fondamental. Il est essentiel pour atteindre le but de toute la Section 1 bis qui est d'atténuer les souffrances de la famille. Ce *pactum de contrahendo* n'existe cependant pas de façon absolue, mais il est conditionné. Il est obligatoire « dès que les circonstances et les relations entre les Parties adverses le permettent ». Il faut admettre que la tension pendant et après un conflit qu'elle négocie ou conclue un accord sur ces questions. Il est évidemment très difficile de déterminer de façon exacte quand les circonstances[7] permettent la conclusion de ces accords. Le rétablissement des relations diplomatiques ou la conclusion formelle d'un traité de paix ne constituent pas de critères valables. En principe, la disposition doit opérer avant ces événements.

---

7   Au dernier stade des délibérations, on a ajouté les mots « et les relations entre les Parties adverses » après « circonstances », pour tenir compte de certaines objections arabes. A notre avis, l'addition de ces mots ne change pas le sens du paragraphe, car l'état des relations entre les Parties peut être considéré comme une des « circonstances » qui ne permettraient pas la conclusion des accords envisagés. L'addition des mots en question supporte cette interprétation sans être nécessaire pour la fonder.

LE SORT DES BLESSÉS ET MALADES

Mais il se peut, d'autre part, dans des cas extrêmes, que même après le rétablissement des relations diplomatiques les circonstances ne permettent pas la conclusion d'un tel accord. L'interprétation doit s'orienter selon le principe de la bonne foi et de l'esprit de cette Section 1 bis, énoncé à l'article 20 bis. L'application pratique de l'article 20 quater, paragraphe 2 dépendra en tout cas de l'entente des Parties adverses, qui peut être atteinte, le cas échéant, par l'intermédiaire de tiers.

Selon le paragraphe 3 de cet article, les frais d'entretien des sépultures sont, sauf accords contraires à la charge du pays d'origine de la personne décédée. Si ce pays n'est pas disposé à les assumer, l'autre pays peut offrir le rapatriement et, après un délai de cinq ans, il est libre d'appliquer toute sa législation interne en ce qui concerne ces sépultures.

Finalement, le paragraphe 4 règle l'exhumation des restes.

13.3   Le champ D'application de la Section 1 Bis

La Section 1 bis impose des obligations considérables aux Parties au conflit. Elle couvre toutes sortes de victimes d'un conflit. On aurait donc demandé trop si l'on n'avait pas excepté du champ d'application de ces articles les relations entre une Partie contractante et ses propres ressortissants. Une disposition expresse à cet effet a été adoptée par la Commission II, sous réserve cependant de révision par le Comité de rédaction de la Conférence. L'application du Protocole en ce qui concerne les relations entre un Etat et ses propres ressortissants est une question qui pourrait se poser également pour d'autres articles. Certains articles – nous avons déjà mentionné l'article 11 – s'appliquent aussi aux relations entre un Etat et ses propres nationaux. Mais, ce n'est pas le cas pour d'autres articles. Il reste à voir si ce problème peut ou doit être résolu dans un ou plusieurs articles généraux.

En ce qui concerne le champ d'application *ratione temporis,* il est à noter qu'une grande partie des dispositions de la Section 1 bis sont applicables aussi ou même surtout en temps de paix. Il est clair, d'autre part, qu'on ne peut pas appliquer le Protocole de façon rétroactive. Le Protocole ne s'applique donc pas aux conflits de passé. Mais si les conséquences de ces conflits passés sont, de bonne foi, susceptibles d'être réglées par les dispositions de Protocole 1 et notamment la Section 1 bis, ces dispositions s'appliquent dès l'entrée en vigueur de Protocole même si le conflit s'est déroulé avant cette date.

14.1   Les Conflits de Caractère Non International

L'élaboration des dispositions du Protocole II relatives au conflit non international s'est souvent trouvée devant un dilemme : d'une part, on a voulu créer des règles simples et compréhensibles – à cette fin des règles courtes et claires sont nécessaires – et, d'autre part, il se peut que la brièveté ne soit atteinte qu'au prix de la clarté, de la précision ou du niveau de la protection. Il faut donc parfois des règles complexes pour atteindre à la protection voulue.

Nous avons déjà, pour le conflit non international, une règle assez courte, mais jugée trop laconique et trop faible : c'est l'article 3, commun aux quatre Conventions. Ce que l'on a cherché à obtenir en créant un Protocole II additionnel aux Conventions de Genève, c'est une réglementation plus détaillée.

La Commission II a discuté cette question fondamentale en relation avec les dispositions relatives aux blessés et malades le niveau de la protection prévue par le Protocole II ne doit pas, en principe, être plus bas que celui prévue par le Protocole II ne doit pas, en principe, être plus bas que celui prévu par le Protocole I, puisqu'il s'agit ici de questions purement humanitaires qui n'affectent pas le concept de la souveraineté évoqué si souvent dans les débats sur le Protocole II. Les dispositions adoptées par la Commission II pour le Protocole II sont donc, dans la plupart des cas, identiques à celles du Protocole I.

14.2 *Les Principales Différences Entre le Protocole I et le Protocole II*

Ce principe ne vaut cependant qu'avec quelques exceptions, dont nous signalerons les plus importantes. Le Protocole II ne contient pas d'équivalence pour la Section I bis, la Section II sur les transports sanitaires et l'Annexe technique. Il y a cependant une disposition concernant la recherche des blessés, des malades, des naufragés et des morts (art. 13), qui correspond aux articles 15 de la première Convention et 18 de la deuxième. L'article 17 du Protocole II, qui correspond aux dispositions du Protocole I sur les unités sanitaires, couvre aussi bien les unités que les transports sanitaires.

Une autre différence importante se trouve à l'article 16 qui correspond à l'article 16 de Protocole I. L'interdiction de pénaliser le personnel sanitaire pour avoir refusé ou pour s'être abstenu de donner des informations sur les blessés et malades ne vaut que « sous réserve de la législation nationale ». On peut se demander si une interdiction mise de cette manière à la disposition d'une Partie au conflit a encore un sens. Bien que l'on doive admettre que l'interdiction est considérablement affaiblie, elle conserve tout de même une certaine valeur. Elle équivaut à une garantie du *Rule of Law,* du *Gesetzesvorbehalt.* Pour justifier des poursuites contre le personnel sanitaire qui refuse de donner des informations, il faut une loi formelle.

Le Protocole II ne contient pas de disposition correspondant aux paragraphes 3 et suivants de l'article 11, Protocole I, à savoir la réglementation des dons de sang et de peau. La conséquence en est que la possibilité d'obtenir des dons de sang et de peau de la part de personnes tombées aux mains de

LE SORT DES BLESSÉS ET MALADES

491

l'ennemi n'existe pas dans le cas du conflit non international. Tandis que ces dons sont permis sous certaines conditions dans le cadre du conflit international, ils sont absolument interdits, en vertu de l'article 13 bis, paragraphe 2 (c), Protocole II (soit article 11, paragraphe 2 (e), Protocole I), quand il s'agit d'un conflit non international. La Partie au conflit qui veut obtenir des dons de sang de la part des prisonniers n'a d'autre choix que de libérer les prisonniers. Puisqu'il s'agira, dans la plupart des cas, des nationaux de la Partie en question, ce choix paraît néanmoins acceptable.

15   Conclusions

On peut résumer les résultats atteints par la Commission II en cinq points principaux :

a)   l'extension de la protection du droit de Genève, jusqu'alors réservée en grande partie aux militaires, aux civils : blessés et malades civils, unités et personnel sanitaires civils ;

b)   l'adoption d'un article de portée générale concernant l'intégrité physique et mentale de la personne humaine ;

c)   la protection du transport sanitaire aérien devenu si important dans les conflits modernes ;

d)   l'adoption d'un système de signalisation adapté aux conditions d'un conflit conduit avec tous les moyens de la technologie moderne ;

e)   la création de dispositions qui assurent l'obtention de renseignements sur les personnes disparues et un régime plus élaboré pour les tombes de personnes mortes à cause d'un conflit Ces accomplissements ont été réalisés par un système de règles très détaillées, parfois trop détaillées. En dehors de ces résultats principaux, il y a encore un grand nombre de détails qui on été ajoutés aux Conventions de Genève.

Un règlement détaillé implique nécessairement des dispositions complexes et compliquées. On ne peut guère régler une situation complexe par des règles simples. Il faut une certaine complexité du règlement s'il doit être adéquat. Si l'on veut développer la protection des victimes dans une situation aussi complexe que celle d'un conflit armé à notre époque, il faut des solutions nuancées. Ces nuances ne peuvent être obtenues que par un règlement détaillé. Dans beaucoup de cas, la clarté nécessaire ne peut être atteinte par des dispositions simples, parfois trop générales et, par conséquent, trop vagues. Les Conventions de Genève de 1949, qui ne constituent certainement pas un règlement se distinguant par sa simplicité, représentaient déjà un pas dans cette direction. Les Protocoles additionnels ne peuvent que les suivre.

Il est vrai, cependant, que la complication, l'addition de toute sorte de qualificatifs à une règle déterminée, ne sont pas toujours le produit d'un souci de clarté. Mais sont parfois dus à la nécessité d'un compromis qui doit être la dénominateur commun de vues assez différentes. Dans ces cas, le choix qui existait était celui entre une règle compliquée et une renonciation au développement du droit humanitaire.

La Commission II a également dû adopter des clauses qui sont peut-être trop vagues, trop générales, que l'on peut qualifier d'*escape clauses*. Des formules comme « dans toute la mesure du possible » – expression que l'on rencontre à plusieurs reprises – ou « dès que les circonstances le permettent » en sont des exemples. Des dispositions de ce genre, qui affaiblissent l'article, sont parfois nécessaires pour parvenir à un compromis.

Tout cela revient à une question de degré, de mesure. Complexité oui, mais pas trop. Des dispositions vagues sont inévitables, mais il faut les restreindre et ne les appliquer qu'aux cas où elles le sont vraiment en effet. Simplicité oui, mais pas au prix de la clarté.

Il est difficile de juger si les textes adoptés pour la protection des blessés et malades sont le juste milieu entre les dangers auxquels la rédaction de tout texte juridique est exposée, c'est-à-dire entre la complication excessive et la généralité.

23

Relief Actions

The Position of the Recipient State

1   Introduction

As in many other fields, the role of the lawyer is not always easy when it comes to international questions concerning relief actions. Quite often the lawyer is hated or subject to contempt for two mutually exclusive reasons. On the one hand, it is often said that the law is not respected anyway, that nobody listens to the lawyers. He or she thus appears to be superfluous. On the other hand, he is hated because he has to say that the law is not as 'humanitarian' as one would like to think it to be. The lawyer is thus criticized as being too accommodating towards power. To these critiques one has to respond: the professional analysis, interpretation and application of the law does not exclude adherence to ideals. But this professional ethic may not be confused with wishful thinking. Wishful thinking does not serve the lawyer's client, whoever that may be, and it is thus unprofessional. Having this in mind, I shall try to analyse the tricky subject of relief actions.

Not every help is welcome. Even in times of armed conflict, States may be reluctant to accept help which foreign States or organisations are willing to give to the civilian population of a party to the conflict. States may be too proud to admit that they are unable to cope with the problem of supplies for their civilian population. In the case of non-international armed conflicts, relief for the civilian population may also mean relief for a population sympathizing with the rebels. It may enhance the chances of success for the insurgents. Thus, it is by no means a matter of course that help granted to the civilian population in times of armed conflict is welcome to the government which has a responsibility for that population.

2   The 'Recipient' State

In order to clarify the legal position of the recipient State, it is necessary to take into account that there are three different situations in which the question arises. The first situation is that of a relief action for the benefit of the civilian population of a party to an international conflict, or more precisely, to

© KONINKLIJKE BRILL NV, LEIDEN, 2021 | DOI:10.1163/9789004380592_025

PART 6: PROTECTED PERSONS AND HUMAN RIGHTS, RELIEF

that party's own population. That problem is covered by Article 70 Protocol I, which reads as follows:

If the civilian population of any territory under the control of a Party to a conflict ... is not adequately provided with supplies mentioned in Article 69 (food, medical supplies, clothing, bedding, means of shelter and other supplies essential to the survival of the civilian population), relief actions which are humanitarian and impartial in character and conducted without any adverse distinction shall be undertaken, subject to the agreement of the Parties concerned in such relief actions.

The second situation to be envisaged is that of relief for the population of an occupied territory. That situation is covered by Article 59 of the Fourth Convention:

If the whole or part of the population of an occupied territory is inadequately supplied, the Occupying Power shall agree to relief schemes on behalf of the said population and shall facilitate them by all the means at its disposal.

Third, relief actions may go to the population of a country where a non-international armed conflict takes pace. In tis situation, Article 18, para. 2, Protocol II applies:

If the civilian population is suffering undue hardship owing to a lack of the supplies essential for its survival, such as foodstuffs and medical supplies, relief actions for the civilian population which are of an exclusively humanitarian and impartial nature and which are conducted without any adverse distinction shall be undertaken subject to the consent of the High Contracting Party concerned.

3   The Obligation to Accept Relief

According to the correct interpretation, all three provisions provide for an obligation to accept relief. In Article 59 of the Fourth Convention, that obligation is formulated 'the Occupying Power shall agree'. The provisions of Protocol I and II say that 'relief actions shall be undertaken'. This clearly implies an obligation on the effect that these actions shall take place, that is to say that relief has to be accepted. This interpretation is clearly supported by the negotiating record,[1] and by government statements made after the conference, in particular during the ratification process.[2] To put it into the terms of the law of treaties: *Travaux préparatoires* and subsequent practice coincide.

---

1   See Bothe/Partsch/Solf, *New Rules for Victims of Armed Conflicts*, p. 434.
2   Norway, Report by the Ministry of Foreign Affairs, 8 June 1979, St.meld. nr. 102 (1978–79); Switzerland, Message submitted by the Federal Council to the Federal Assembly, 18 February 1981, p. 86.

On the other hand, the fact that there is a duty to accept relief does not mean that everybody is completely free to perform relief actions and to distribute relief supplies as he or she likes. There is the necessity that the High Contracting Party 'concerned' or the Occupying Power grant their consent. Under the provisions of the two Protocols, it is expressly stated that these relief actions shall be undertaken 'subject to the consent of the High Contracting Party concerned'. The situation of an Occupying Power under Article 9 of the Fourth Convention is by no means different. It 'shall agree', meaning that there has indeed to be an agreement before any relief action can take place. This requirement of an agreement, however, does not mean that the High Contracting Party concerned may refuse that agreement at its discretion. Article 59 of the Fourth Convention clearly says '*shall* agree'; the provisions of the two Protocols have to be interpreted accordingly. This was expressly stated in Committee II of the Diplomatic Conference, when Article 70 Protocol I was adopted, by the Delegate of the Federal Republic of Germany and expressly concerned by several other delegates, including those of he United States, The Netherlands, the Soviet Union and the United Kingdom. There is thus a clear negotiating record that the requirement of a consent implies an obligation to give this consent. This consent may only be refused for valid reasons, including imperative considerations of military necessity.[3]

While there should be no doubt about this obligation to accept relief, to admit it, to grant consent to relief actions, this does not solve all practical problems. Four main questions arise:

1. Which is the High Contracting Party 'concerned', especially in the case of a non-international armed conflict?
2. What are 'valid' reasons for refusing consent?
3. What are permissible measures of self-help in cases where consent is illegally withheld?
4. What are permissible counter-actions against relief actions which take place without the consent of the High Contracting Party 'concerned'?

4   The High Contracting Party 'Concerned'

In times of international and non-international armed conflict, the consent of the 'High Contracting Party concerned' is necessary for any relief action. In the case of an international conflict, it is very clear that the Party on whose territory relief is to be distributed is 'concerned' within the meaning of Article

---

3   See Both/Partsch/Solf, op. cit. p. 696.

70 Protocol I. but this rule only applies to non-occupied territory. In the case of occupation, where the *de facto* control of the territory has passed to the Occupying Power, it is that Power whose consent is required.

In the case of a non-international armed conflict (Article 18 Protocol II) it is quite often assumed that the State on whose territory the conflict takes place is in every circumstance to be considered as a High Contracting Party concerned, in other words: the pre-existing government, 'gouvernement sur place', not to use the word 'legitimate' government. That interpretation, however is by no means the only possible one.[4] The ICRC Commentary accepts that interpretation only 'in principle'. It has been shown for the case of an occupation that it is not *de iure* sovereignty over the territory but *de facto* control which forms the basis of the consent requirement and constitutes the 'concern' of a party to the conflict. It follows from that principle that the consent of the established government of a country is required only where a relief action has to pass over territory which is effectively controlled by that government. Thus, where the territory controlled by the insurgents s accessible from the sea or directly from another country, it seems to be a reasonable interpretation of Article 18 not to require the consent of the established government. Looking into State practice, however, I have some doubts whether this interpretation is really going to be accepted.[5] It seems that certain States indeed object to any relief being shipped directly to territories controlled by insurgents.

In the case of Sri Lanka, the majority government also objected to relief being shipped directly to the area controlled by the Tamil rebels. It is important to note, however, that in this case India maintained a right to provide relief.

5 Valid Reasons to Refuse Consent

It has been explained above that the consent of the High Contracting Party Concerned may not be arbitrarily refused, but only for valid reasons. The question then arises what is a 'valid' reason. This has to be determined in the context of the Protocol and the Conventions as a while. There is probably no generally applicable definition of what constitutes a valid reason. Some examples may be given, however. First of all, the desire to weaken the resistance of

---

4   See Both/Partsch/Solf, op. cit. p. 696.

5   See for instance the position of various governments as reflected in the messages submitting the Protocols for parliamentary approval: The Netherlands 'Memorie van Toelichting, Staten-Generaal, Tweede Kamer' 1983–84 18277 nr.3; Switzerland, Message dated 18 Feb. 1981, p. 86; Norway, Report by the Ministry of Foreign Affairs, 8 June 1979, St.meld. nr. 102 (1978–79).

RELIEF ACTIONS: THE POSITION OF THE RECIPIENT STATE

an adversary by depriving the civilian population of its means of subsistence is not a valid reason. This follows from the rules contained in both Protocol I and II that starvation of the civilian population as a means of warfare is prohibited.[6] The freedom to refuse consent is further restricted by human rights considerations, namely, first, the duty of each State party to the UN Covenant on Civil and Political Rights (Art. 2) 'to ensure to all individuals within its territory and subject to its jurisdiction the rights recognized' in this Covenant, such as the right to life (Art. 6); and, secondly, certain rights guaranteed by the UN Covenant of Economic, Social and Cultural Rights, such as the right to an adequate standard of living (Art. 1 para. 2) and the right to the enjoyment of the highest attainable standard of physical and mental health (Art. 12).

On the other hand, reasons of military necessity may be considered as valid. Such is the case where the foreign relief personnel may hamper military operations or can be suspected of unneutral behaviour in favour of the other party to the conflict. In many situations, legitimate military considerations will compete with humanitarian ones. A balancing of different values will then be required which makes it extremely difficult to precisely draw the line between a lawful and an unlawful refusal of consent. The principle of proportionality may also be helpful in this respect, for instance, to outlaw a refusal where the legitimate military considerations are relatively unimportant, but the suffering of the civilian population particularly poignant.

6   Unilateral Action

We must now determine the legal consequences of an unlawful refusal of a High Contracting Party to accept relief and permit supplies to be distributed to the civilian population on its territory. In this case, we must distinguish between relief action undertaken by a private organization, by a State and by another subject of international law, be it an international organization or the ICRC, which is a *sui generis* subject of international law.

In the case of a private organization, the action undertaken without consent cannot constitute a violation of international law because no State is under a duty to prevent such relief actions to be undertaken by its nationals or from its territory. The only international legal question which arises in this context is that of permissible countermeasures of the 'recipient State'. We will revert to this problem.

---

6   Art. 54, Protocol I; Art. 14 Protocol II.

In the case of a relief action undertaken by a State (like that conducted by the Indian armed forces in Sri Lanka), the action constitutes a violation of the territorial integrity of the State in question, the question then arises whether this is a legal or a justified violation or not. International being a decentralized legal order, States depend to a great extent on unilateral action to enforce their rights and other States' obligations. That principle goes beyond the admissibility of reprisals in the technical sense. A unilateral relief action in a case where refusal of consent is illegal may even be considered as an action designed to ensure the respect of the Convention and the Protocol as required by Article 1 common to the Conventions. At least, a relief action undertaken in such a situation without the consent of the State concerned may not be considered to be an illegal intervention.

The general permissibility of unilateral action under current international law is subject to one important limitation, which must be stressed and maintained, that is, the prohibition of the use of force. Any unilateral action which constitutes a use of force and which is not justified under the specific rules justifying military force, such as self-defence, is not permissible. The essential question thus is whether a unilateral relief action constitutes a use of force by the State undertaking it. If a State, by a deliberate action of its armed forces, violates the border of another State and intrudes into the other State's territory, for whatever honourable reason, this constitutes a use of force. There should be no distinction between such uses of force based on the consideration that it was for a good or a bad purpose. Otherwise, we might be back to the old days of humanitarian intervention which was always easy pretext for intervening into the internal affairs of another country.[7] Thus, the laudable motive does not exempt military action from the verdict that it constitutes recourse to force. The only remaining question is whether every action by military personnel, vehicles or aircraft constitutes a 'military' action in this sense. The relevance of that problem may be demonstrated by using another example: Does an aerial intrusion by one single airplane for the purpose of espionage, prohibited as it is under international law, constitute a 'use of force' in the sense of Art. 2 para. 4 of the United Nations Charter? The dominant position seems to be that it does not.[8] It can thus be argued that relief flights by unarmed (although military) transport aircraft do not constitute a use of force, but rather a 'simple'

---

7   See Beyerlin, 'Humanitarian Intervention' in: Bernhardt (ed.) *Encyclopedia of Public International Law,* Instalment 4, p. 212; Brownlie, 'Thoughts on Kind-Hearted Gunmen', in Lilich (ed.), *Humanitarian Intervention and he United Nations,* p. 141 et seq.

8   See Brownlie, *International Law and the Use of Force by States,* p. 364.

RELIEF ACTIONS: THE POSITION OF THE RECIPIENT STATE

border violation, and may thus be justified taking into account the previous illegal conduct of the other State. The same holds true if the action is undertaken by non-military State organs.

For the same reason, a unilateral action undertaken by an international organization or by ICRC in the case of an unlawful refusal of consent may not be considered illegal.

7   Permissible Counter-Measures

Finally, we must examine permissible counter-measures by a State which, legally or illegally, did not grant consent for a relief action undertaken on its territory. Again, we have to distinguish various situations.

In the case of a private relief action passing across a land border, it is obvious that it may be stopped and turned off. Another question is whether the relief supplies may be seized and the relief personnel detained and prosecuted. As a matter of principle, no rule of international law prevents a State from enforcing its rules concerning the crossing of its border, human rights guarantees concerning procedure being respected.

Where a relief action is undertaken by the armed forces of a State, armed counter-measures are permissible even where such action does not constitute a use of force. Due regard has to be paid to the principle of proportionality. This will imply in the case of unarmed and announced relief operations, that the 'recipient' State should use utmost restraint and should try to turn military ships and aircraft off. Art. 27 para. 2 and 31 para. 2 of Protocol I deal with a comparable situation with respect to unauthorized flights of medical aircraft. Although the principle of restraint clearly governs these provision, attacks against the aircraft are not excluded as a last resort. It may, however, be argued that, where a permission was requested and illegally withheld, such an attack would constitute an abuse of right.

In the case of a private relief action undertaken by aircraft, the question of permissible forceful counter-measures is difficult to answer.[9] There is a trend in State practice that the violation of a State's airspace by a private plane is not sufficient ground to justify an attack against that plane. If there are special reasons to assume that the plane constitutes a threat to the State's security, the situation may be different. We are here in a situation where the law is unclear,

---

9   Cfr. Hailbronner, *Der Schutz der Luftgrenzen im Frienden*, p. 41, 67 et seq.

and the rule should be that of restraint for humanitarian reasons. As the International Court of Justice put it in the Corfu Channel case,[10] 'elementary considerations of humanity' limit measures the State may take in order to project its sovereignty.

---

10   ICJ Reports 1949, p. 22.

Human Rights Law and International Humanitarian Law as Limits of Security Council Action

1 The Problem: The Development of Activities of the United Nations beyond the Imagination of the Authors

The activities of the Security Council in the maintaining or restoring of international peace and security have expanded enormously since the end of the Cold War.[1] The breakthrough for Security Council action was the Kuwait crisis – the invasion of Kuwait by Iraq, and the ensuing successful military action to repel it. On this occasion, the Security Council showed considerable creativity in designing measures to cope with the situation, and not all of them corresponded exactly to what could be anticipated by just reading the relevant texts of the UN Charter.[2] This fact and further developments have fomented a debate which existed already during earlier decades, namely a discourse on the legal basis of the powers of the Security Council and their limitations. The question whether and to what extent the norms of international human rights law and international humanitarian law limit the freedom of action, or the creativity of the Security Council in designing action, is a major part of that debate. The political developments and the ensuing legal debate highlight legal uncertainties. Organs of the United Nations exercise public authority in relation to individuals – which raises the question whether they have to apply human rights in doing so, and whether human rights, thus, limits the freedom

---

1 T. Sato, 'The Legitimacy of Security Council Activities under Chapter VII of the UN Charter since the End of the Cold War', in *The Legitimacy of International Organizations*, eds J.-M. Coicaud and V. Heiskanen (Tokyo: United Nations University Press, 2001), 309 *et seq.*

2 S. Lamb, 'Legal Limits to United Nations Security Council Powers', in *The Reality of International Law: Essay in Honour of Ian Brownlie*, eds G.S. Goodwin-Gill and S. Talmon (Oxford: Oxford University Press, 1999), 362. For critical comments on the resolution regarding military action against Iraq 1990, see M. Bothe, 'Die Golfkrise und die Vereinten Nationen – Rückkehr zur Kollektiven Sicherheit?', *Demokratie und Recht* 19 (1991): 2–10; see also the discussion by D. Sarooshi, *The United Nations and the Development of Collective Security: The Delegation by the Security Council of its Chapter VII Powers* (Oxford: Oxford University Press, 1999), 174 *et seq.*; for the armistice regime, see B. Graefrath, 'Iraq Reparations and the Security Couucil', *ZaöRV* 55 (1995): 1–68, in particular at 11 *et seq.*

of action of UN organs, including the Security Council. Armed forces of the United Nations are involved in military hostilities – which raises the question whether the rules of international law relating to such hostilities if conducted by States apply as well to the military operations conducted by the UN. The United Nations are brought into factual situations which were not foreseen by the drafters of the Charter, or were at least not clear in their minds. Whether or not the exercise of public authority by the UN, or the UN becoming a party to an armed conflict, could have been foreseen, it was at least beyond the scope of the imagination of the drafters.

As to the first problem – the application of human rights by the United Nations – there is at least one precedent for the League of Nations exercising public authority in relation to individuals, namely the administration of the Saar. But apparently, no need was felt in 1945 to spell out the law applicable in such a situation. The administration of the Saar had worked smoothly. As to the application of international human rights law, it must however be remembered that this area of international law was only *in statu nascendi* at the time the Charter was negotiated.

As to the application of international humanitarian law, one could have thought that the establishment of a system of military enforcement measures would trigger at least some debate concerning the law applicable to such operations. But the very concept of these operations is not clearly regulated.[3] Sometimes it appears that the troupes engaged in such operations would remain organs of the States placing them at the disposal of the Security Council, sometimes it would seem that they are organs of the United Nations.[4] Both options were used in later practice.

Both questions are different, but on the other hand they belong together in a special way. The question of whether the United Nations are bound by human rights is part of a mega-problem of the current shape of the international order, namely the rules governing the exercise of public power by international institutions, which has become a characteristic aspect of that order.[5] The norms governing the exercise of public power by States are contained in their constitutional and administrative law. Is there a similar body of law for international institutions, in particular the United Nations?

---

3 Already H. Kelnsen, *The Law of the United Nations* (London: The Lawbook Exchange, 1950), 748 *et seq.*, points to a lack of clarity of the provisions on military enforcement measures in many respects.

4 Kelsen, *supra* note 3, at 756, regards both options as being covered by Articles 42 and 48.

5 A. von Bogdandy, R. Wolfrum, J. von Bernstorff, P. Dann and M. Goldmann, eds, *The Exercise of Public Authority by International Institutions: Advancing International Institutional Law* (Heidelberg: Springer, 2010).

HUMANITARIAN LAW AS LIMITS FOR SECURITY COUNCIL ACTION 503

The question of the application of international humanitarian law is of a different nature.[6] That law applies in the relationship between parties to an armed conflict, which is a relationship of legal equality, at least in principle, that is to say the contrary of the exercise of a legally constituted authority. Yet within the body of international humanitarian law, there are many rules for situations where a party exercises some kind of power over protected persons – which is a typical situation for the application of human rights. For this reason, there is, in situations of armed conflict, a parallel application of human rights law and international humanitarian law.[7] To that extent, the questions whether the United Nations are bound by either body of international law belong together.

In regard to both questions, different perspectives have to be distinguished. There are, first, the legal obligations of the United Nations which an organ of the Organization has to respect, and second, the possible powers of the Security Council to set aside or to modify these obligations. This is a problem of the interpretation of the United Nations Charter and of the interplay between the law of the Charter and general international law. But the more extensive the exercise of powers by the UN becomes, the more there is a political problem of the justification or legitimacy of such action. This is a matter of successful policy, or, in its scientific aspect, of political theory.

2 The Basis of Attribution of Security Council Powers

If the Security Council were bound by human rights law and international humanitarian law, this would indeed mean a limitation of its powers. Thus, the *fons et origo* of these powers has to be considered. The UN Charter, this is the basic point of departure, establishes a system of 'enumerated powers' in the sense the term is used in constitutional law. The organs of the United Nations have only those powers which are granted to them by the Charter.[8] These powers are defined in a very general way, yet they are not unlimited.[9]

---

6 R. Provost, *International Human Rights and Humanitarian Law* (Cambridge and New York: Cambridge University Press, 2002), *passim*.

7 *Legal Consequences of the Construction of a Wall in the Occupied Palestinian Territories*, Advisory Opinion, I.C.J. Reports 2004, 136, paragraph 106.

8 M. Bothe, 'Les limites de pouvoirs du Conseil de Sécurité', in *Le développement du rôle du Conseil de Sécurité, Colloque, La Haye, 21–23 juillet 1992*, ed. R.-J. Dupuy (Dordrecht : Martinues Nijhoff Publishers, 1992), 67–81.

9 J. Delbrück, Article 24, margin note 10, in *The Charter of the United Nations: A Commentary*, ed. B. Simma, 2nd edition (Oxford: Oxford University Press, 2002), further discussion *infra* section 3.2.

Since the Advisory Opinion '*Reparation for Injuries*',[10] the ICJ has recognized that these powers have to be interpreted in the sense that they include implied powers, that is, powers that are not expressly mentioned, but are granted by necessary implication for the effective performance of the powers expressly granted.

According to the same logic, there exist implied limitations of these powers. These implied limitations derive from a systematic interpretation of the Charter. The Charter is to be interpreted as a whole. This means in particular that the goals of the Organization, which are formulated in the Preamble, in Art. 1 and in a number of other provisions dealing with specific activities of the Organization, have to be taken into account. The powers of UN organs, including the Security Council, cannot be understood as permitting the violation of principles the protection of which is the very purpose of the UN.

This line of reasoning adopted by the Court clearly indicates that the Security Council is bound at least by the principles of human rights law.

The most fundamental formulation of the UN's adherence to human rights is the 2nd paragraph of the Preamble which expresses the determination of the United Nations 'to reaffirm faith in fundamental human rights, the dignity and worth of the human person, in the equal rights of men and women ...'.

As to the operational parts of the Chamber, both Art. 1 (3) and Art. 55 (c) stipulate a duty of the Organization to further human rights. The UN shall promote 'universal respect for, and observance of, human rights and fundamental freedoms for all without distinction as to race, sex, language, or religion'. Although the drafters of the Charter may not have foreseen that the UN would itself be in a factual position to violate such rights in the relationship between the Organization and an individual, it would be illogical if the UN were entitled not to respect those rights the observance of which it is obligated to promote.

Thus, as a first step in the argument, one can conclude that there is an implied limitation of the powers of the Security Council requiring that the Council, in the exercise of its functions, respects fundamental human rights.

As to the second part of the question, international humanitarian law, one must recall that it has an important human rights aspect. To that extent at least, one must conclude that the Security Council must respect international humanitarian law at least as it contains human rights principles. This is in particular the case for all those provisions which protect persons in the power of a party to the conflict, such as detainees, nationals of a party to the

---

10   *Reparation for injuries suffered in the service of the United Nations*, Advisory Opinion, I.C.J. Reports 1949, 174.

conflict in the territory of the other party, and the population of occupied territory. In relation to other parts of international humanitarian law, in particular the rules on the conduct of hostilities, a similar line of argument has also been used: the rules on the conduct of hostilities, too, enshrine fundamental principles of humanity which the Organization is bound to protect.[11] Yet more generally, one must ask whether and to what extent the United Nations are bound by customary international law, including international humanitarian law.

3 The United Nations and Customary International Law

3.1 *General Considerations*

In order to ascertain whether and to what extent the United Nations and in particular the Security Council are bound by customary law, one has to turn once more to the Advisory Opinion *'Reparation for Injuries Suffered in the Service of the United Nations'*. The question to be answered by the Court was this:

> [H]as the United Nations, as an Organization, the capacity to bring an international claim against the responsible *de jure* or *de facto* government with a view to obtaining the reparation due in respect of the damage caused (*a*) to the United Nations, (*b*) to the victim and to persons entitled through him?[12]

In other words, the General Assembly asked whether the rules of customary international law applicable to States in a comparable situation applied to the United Nations as well, and with what modifications, if any. In its preliminary observations the Court indeed refers to the rules on State responsibility.[13] The Court then asks whether the Organization possesses a competence which a State possesses where the responsibility of another State is at stake, namely the capacity to bring a claim: 'Competence to bring an international claim is, for those possessing it, the capacity to resort to the customary methods recognized by international law for the establishment, the presentation and the settlement of claims ... This capacity certainly belongs to the State ...'.

---

11 T.D. Gill, 'Legal and Some Political Limitations on the Power of the UN Security Council to Exercise its Enforcement Powers under Chapter VII of the Charter', *Netherlands Yearbook of International Law* 26 (1995): 82.

12 *Supra* note 10, at 175.

13 *Supra* note 10, at 177.

But does it also belong to the Organization? The affirmative answer to this question is based on the argument that the parties to the Charter must have endowed the Organization with those capacities which are necessary to enable it to perform its functions:

> Accordingly, the Court has come to the conclusion that the Organization is an international person. That is not the same thing as saying that it is a State ... What it does mean is that it is a subject of international law and capable of possessing international rights and duties, and that it has capacity to maintain its rights by bringing international claims.[14]

A first lesson has to be drawn from the last phrase: the reasoning of the Court does not only relate to rights of the Organization, but also to duties. These duties of the Organization mean limitations of the freedom of action of the Organization.

What are these rights and duties? According to the Court, they are derived from customary international law, but are not necessarily identical with the rights and duties of States:

Whereas a State possesses the totality of international rights and duties recognized by international law [an expression which must be understood as to the totality of rights and duties under *customary* international law], the rights and duties of an entity such as the Organization must depend upon its purposes and functions as specified or implied in its constituent documents and developed in practice.[15]

The question of whether the United Nations has the rights and duties recognized by customary international humanitarian law has thus to be answered by a conditional phrase: yes, if and to the extent that it is necessary for the performance of the functions entrusted to the Organization by the Charter. If that condition is fulfilled, the duties of the Organization under international humanitarian law would have to be respected by all its organs, including the Security Council.

It does not follow from this reasoning that the customary law rights and duties of States and of international organizations must be exactly the same. Quite to the contrary, the reference to the functions entrusted to the organization as the basis for applying international customary law to it may imply some adaptation of the rule which applies to States. This is what the ICJ has

---

14   *Supra* note 10, at 179.

15   *Supra* note 10, at 180.

recognized in the *Reparation for injuries* opinion: it substituted the functional protection which the Organization exercises in favour of its agents for the traditional diplomatic protection exercised by States.

Nevertheless, the essential point of departure for the application of customary international law is the meaning of that law as it applies to States. That kind of transfer of applicable rules from States to organizations corresponds to a fundamental method of legal reasoning: where the lawyer encounters a new problem (e.g. the rule of behaviour of international organizations), he or she will seek advice from rules which are traditionally applied in a similar situation and will then decide whether this similarity justifies the application of the rule (by analogy) to the new problem, *mutatis mutandis* as the case may be. This is essentially what the Court did in the *Reparation for injuries* opinion.

In addressing this problem, the particular characteristic of the area of law in question must also be considered. In this connection, a trend must be noted that international humanitarian law as a whole applies to all kinds of armed conflicts between entities having a status under international law, not only to armed conflicts to which States are parties.[16]

But before addressing the problem as to what these considerations have meant and may mean in practice in relation to human rights and international humanitarian law, two preliminary questions have to be answered: First, are the above considerations also valid for the Security Council in the light of its central position in the system of the Charter? And secondly, could the Security Council set aside these customary law obligations by way of a decision which is binding pursuant to Art. 25 UN Charter?

3.2. *Discretionary Powers of the Security Council?*

The Security Council certainly is a 'political' organ. This means, in practice and in theory, that its activities are rather prompted by political considerations, not by legal ones. But this does not mean that the Council is not bound by international law, that it is not limited by the rule of enumerated powers. The powers may be defined broadly, the Charter may grant the Security Council a very broad discretion, but they are still powers based on, and limited by, the Charter of the United Nations and those rules of international law which bind the United Nations.[17] This principle is expressed by Art. 24 of the Charter.

---

16   J.G. Gardam, 'Legal Restraints on Security Council Military Enforcement Action', *Michigan Journal of International Law* 17 (1996): 318.

17   Lamb, *supra* note 2, at 365.

This principle has been formulate very clearly by the Appeals Chamber of the ICTY in the *Tadić* case:[18]

> It is clear from the [text of Art. 39] that the Security Council plays a pivotal role and exercises a very wide discretion under this Article. But this does not mean that its powers are unlimited. The Security Council is an organ of an international organization. The Security Council is thus subjected to certain constitutional limitations, however broad its powers under the constitution may be. ... [N]either the text nor the spirit of the Charter conceives of the Security Council as *legibus solutus* (unbound by law).

The specific impact of this rule on Security Council activities for the maintenance of international peace and security under Ch. VII is as follows. First, there is a basic condition for the exercise of these powers, namely that there is a situation as described in Art. 39, that is, a 'threat to the peace, breach of the peace, or act of aggression'. As the Security Council 'shall determine the existence of' such a situation, the question arises whether the Security Council may only make this determination where such a situation objectively exists as a matter of law or whether the Council has a discretion or margin of appreciation in making this determination. This is controversial.[19] The Council has shown, to say the least, a great degree of creativity in interpreting Art. 39; For the purpose of the present study, this question is only of indirect relevance, as will be shown.[20]

Once the Security Council has determined that there is a situation as defined in Art. 39, four types of measures may be taken by the Council:
– recommendations;
– provisional measures (Art. 40);
– enforcement measures not involving the use of military force;
– enforcement measures involving the use of military force.

The Council has a discretion whether to take any measure at all (subject to a responsibility to protect),[21] and as to the type of measure it wants to take as

---

18 *Prosecutor v. Tadić*, ICTY, Appeals Chamber, Decision, 2 October 1995 (Case No. IT-94-1-A), para. 28.

19 Lamb, *supra* note 2, at 374 *et seq.* ; E. de Wt, *The Chapter VII powers of the United Nations Security Council* (Oxford and Portland: Hart Publishing, 2004), 133 *et seq.*; A. Stein, *Der Sicherheitsrat der Vereinten Nationen und die Rule of Law* (Baden-Baden: Nomos, 1999), 14 *et seq.*

20 *Infra* section 3.3.

21 *Infra* section 5.3.

well as to the content and shape of the measure. But as to the last mentioned discretion, it is at least limited[22] by two considerations: It must be a measure for the purpose of maintaining or restoring peace and security (which does not mean that it must effectively achieve that purpose),[23] and it must respect any other rule binding the United Nations, subject, however, to the power of the Council to change the applicable rules by a binding decision.

Another legal construction which gives a certain freedom to the Security Council in designing its activities is what in other contexts is called 'margin of appreciation'.[24] It relates to indeterminate legal concepts, giving the body or institution enjoying such a margin the freedom to evaluate facts in relation to the applicable norm. A court would not substitute its own judgement for that of the other decision-making body. That construction is, thus, a question of the relationship between a decision-making and a reviewing body, in constitutional terms a question of separation of powers. Notions like 'necessity' and 'proportionality' lend themselves to such construction.

As a matter of principle, this is a sound construction, but the question has to be asked how far it goes. If this is construed in the sense of an 'authoritative concretization'[25] of its powers by the Security Council which puts its decisions beyond any legal challenge, it would go too far.[26] The borderline, however, is difficult to draw.

3.3   *Customary Law Versus Article 25 of the United Nations' Charter*
The power of the Security Council to take decisions binding the member States mainly relates to measures taken under Ch. VII, that is measures taken for the maintenance or restoration of international peace and security. It lies in the very nature of those that they restrict the freedom of action States would otherwise possess under customary international law. Therefore, rules of international customary law do not necessarily bar Security Council action.[27] The essential limitation of the powers of the Security Council is derived from the principle of attribution:[28] a decision which is not justified by the purpose of maintaining peace and security would be *ultra vires*, and thus, as a matter

---

22   *Tadić, supra* note 18, at para. 32.

23   *Tadić, supra* note 18, at para. 39.

24   B. Martenczuk, *Rechtsbildung und Rechtskontrolle des Weltsicherheitsrats* (Berlin: Duncker Humblot, 1996), 240 *et seq.*

25   M.J. Herdegen, 'The "Constitutionalization" of the UN Security System', *Vanderbilt Journal of Transnational Law* 27 (1994): 152.

26   Martenczuk, *supra* note 24, at 143 *et seq.*, 150.

27   See Gardam, *supra* note 16, at 313; Lamb, *supra* note 2 at 369.

28   Lamb, *supra* note 2, at 366 *et seq.*

of principle, not binding. This entails, however, a difficult problem, namely whether and under what conditions States may pass a judgement on the legality or otherwise of a Security Council decision and may refuse to respect a decision if they consider it to be *ultra vires*.[29]

The question of whether the Security Council could set aside international humanitarian law or human rights law can only be answered in the affirmative if such action were a valid contribution to the maintenance of international peace and security. This is barely conceivable, but not impossible.

There is yet another fundamental limitation to the power of the Security Council to take a binding decision, namely the respect of *ius cogens*.[30] It lies in the very mature of *ius cogens* that it can only be changed by a norm having the same character (Art. 53 VCLoT), which excludes a modification by any other actor.[31] This also bars any modification by the Security Council. This shields the core of human rights law and of international humanitarian law against any infringement by the Security Council.

3.4   *Control of the Legality of Security Council Action*

The somewhat uncertain limits of Security Council powers which have been explained entail the problem of the final arbiter of the issue of legality, or rather of the lack thereof. The procedural variety of the doctrine of self-concretization[32] means that it is the Council itself which is the final judge of its powers. The question was addressed in a somewhat controversial way by the ICJ in the *Certain Expenses* case. The Court said that each organ must, 'in the first place at least', determine its own jurisdiction.[33] The addition of the words 'in the first place' indicates that this determination is not final. It can be challenged.

On the other hand, the judicial review of Security Council action is underdeveloped.[34] The ICJ is not a kind of constitutional court empowered to control the legality of other UN organs. That question may, however, arise as an

---

29   Delbrück, Article 25, margin note 18, in Simma, *supra* note 9. This has been as issue regarding the European Community (now Union), see the Judgements discussed *infra* section 5.2.

30   Herdegen, *supra* note 25, at 156; Lamb, *supra* note 2, at 372 *et seq.*; De Wet, *supra* note 19, at 187 *et seq.*

31   Court of First Instance of the European Communities, *Kadi v. Council and Commission*, Judgement, 21 September 2005 (Case T-315/01), para. 226.

32   *Supra* section 3.2., in particular the next accompanying note 25.

33   *Certain Expenses of the United Nations*, Advisory Opinion, I.C.J. Reports 1962, 168.

34   Martenczuk, *supra* note 24, at 73 *et seq.*; Stein, *supra* note 19, at 347 *et seq.*; Lamb, *supra* note 2, at 363; Gill, *supra* note 11, at 106 *et seq.*

HUMANITARIAN LAW AS LIMITS FOR SECURITY COUNCIL ACTION

incidental question in court proceeding at the national or regional level[35] or even before the ICJ, as it did in the *Lockerbie* case.[36] In that case, the Court did not say that it was bound to respect the determination made by the Council, it only accepted that determination on a *prima facie* basis for the purpose of the indication of provisional measures. A clear and explicit example of incidental control is the decision of the Appeals Chamber of the ICTY in the *Tadić* case,[37] which, in contradistinction to the Trial Chamber, held that it was entitled to review the constitutionality of the Security Council decision to establish the Tribunal.

The relative weakness of judicial control must not be misunderstood as a proof of a lack of legal obligations. There is a legal discourse around the activities of UN organs which is clearly base on the assumption that they are indeed subject to legal obligations.

4 The Debate about the Application of International Humanitarian Law

On the basis of the aforementioned considerations, we can address the question of whether the United Nations, by implication, has rights and duties under international humanitarian law, and duties under international human rights law. What is relevant in this respect is no only the interpretation of the Charter, but also, as the ICJ put it, the development of UN practice. First, the development of the practice relating to international humanitarian law will be considered, as this practice is older than the one concerning human rights.

The question of whether the UN was bound by international humanitarian law came up soon after armed forces which were organs of the UN were established, even before they became involved in armed hostilities. At the centre of this debate was an exchange of views between the ICRC and the United Nations,[38] which, however, somewhat distorted the fundamental issues as it only

---

35 *Infra* section 5.2.

36 *Case concerning questions of interpretation and application of the 1971 Montreal Convention arising from the aerial incident at Lockerbie, Libiya v. united States of America*, Preliminary Objections, I.C.J. Reports 1998, 115; on that case see De Wet, *supra* note 19, at 2 *et seq.*; see also Stein, *supra* note 19, at 347 *et seq.*, in particular at 365 *et seq.* on the *Lockerbie case*.

37 *Tadić*, *supra* note 18, at para. 22.

38 U. Palwankar, 'Applicabilité du droit international humanitaire aux Forces des Nations Unies pour le maintien de la paix', *Revue internationale de la Croix-Rouge* 75 (1993): 245–259; see also D. Schindler, 'United Nations forces and international humanitarian Law', in *Studies and essays on international humanitarian law and Red Cross principles in honour of Jean Pictet* (The Hague: Martinus Nijhoff Publishers, 1984), 521–530.

512 PART 6: PROTECTED PERSONS AND HUMAN RIGHTS, RELIEF

related to the respect of the Geneva Conventions to which the United Nations obviously are not a party and by which they therefore cannot be bound as a matter of treaty law.[39] Since the establishment of the first UN peacekeeping force, UNEF I in 1956, the ICRC emphasized the need that these forces comply with the Geneva Conventions.[40] The United Nations reacted with a compromise formula which is contained in the internal Regulations for UNEF I,[41] and later in those for ONUC[42] and UNFICYP:[43] 'The Force shall observe and respect the principles and spirit of the general international Conventions applicable to the conduct of military personnel.'

This provision is referred to in the Agreement between the United Nations and participating Stated and explained as follows:

> 11. The international Conventions referred to in these Regulations include, *inter alia*, the Geneva (Red Cross) Conventions of 12 August 1949 to which your Government is a party and the UNESCO Convention on the Protection of Cultural Property in the Event of Armed Conflict, signed at The Hague on 14 May 1954. In this connection, and particularly with respect to the humanitarian provisions of these Conventions, it is requested that the Governments of the Participating States ensure that the members of their contingents serving with the Force be fully acquainted with the obligations arising under these Conventions and that appropriate steps be taken to ensure their enforcement.[44]

These texts clearly suggest that the obligations to respect the norms in question are obligations of the United Nations, not of the contributing States. Otherwise, it could not be explained that the text does not differentiate between

---

39 As early as 1971, the Institut de droit international adopted a much broader approach to the question and declared (Conditions of Application of Humanitarian Rules of Armed Conflict to Hostilities in which United Nations Forces May be Engaged, Resolution adopted at the session of Zagreb): 'The humanitarian rules of armed conflict apply to the United Nations as of right, and they must be complied with in all circumstances by United Nations Forces which are engaged in hostilities'.

40 See 'Memorandum of International Committee of the Red Cross, 10 November 1961', *Revue internationale de la Croix-Rouge* 43 (1961): 592.

41 UN Treaty Series 271: 168, Article 44.

42 UN Doc. ST/SGB/ONUC/1: Article 43.

43 UN Treaty Series 555: 132, Article 40.

44 Text as in the Exchange of letters constituting an agreement between the United Nations and Canada concerning the service with the united Nations peace-Keeping Force of the national contingent provided by the Government of Canada, 21 February 1966, UN Treaty Series 555: 120.

parties and non-parties to the Conventions, which is a practical problem regarding the Cultural Property Convention, to which not all contributing States were parties.[45] Consequently, the obligations envisaged by these texts must be obligations under customary law. Then, what is meant by 'spirit and principles' must be the customary law element contained in those Conventions. So far, this is a matter of legal logic. But the texts do not answer the question whether this customary law or armed conflict applicable to the United Nations is the same as that applicable to States in a similar situation. That question is left open, and it remained open for a considerable period.

When the ICRC approached the UN during the Congo crisis concerning the application of the Geneva Conventions, the Secretary-General used the same 'spirit and principles' formula.[46]

Some voices in the doctrinal debate held that the law of armed conflict could not apply to UN Forces because they were 'soldiers without enemies'.[47] This is simply an illusion. From time to time, UN peacekeepers indeed have enemies and they have to fight them like any army fights an enemy army.[48] The thesis is also wrong because it confuses two questions which have to be distinguished: name first, whether the United Nations are generally capable of being a subject of the law of armed conflict; and second, whether it would apply if armed forces of States were in the same situation in which the peacekeepers find themselves.

All these questions were finally clarified by two interrelated instruments, namely by the Convention on the Safety of United Nations and Associated Personnel,[49] on the one hand, and the Secretary-General's 'Bulletin' on 'Observance by United Nations Forces of International Humanitarian Law' of 6 August 1999.[50]

The Bulletin defines its scope of application:

> 1.1 The fundamental principles and rules of international humanitarian law set out in the present bulletin are applicable to United Nations forces when in situations of armed conflict they are actively engaged therein as combatants ... .

---

45   Canada, for instance, ratified the Convention only in 1998.

46   *Revue internationale de la Croix-Rouge* 44 (1962): 28.

47   L.L. Fabian, *Soldiers without Enemies. Preparing the United nations for Peace-keeping* (Washington DC: Brookings Institution, 1971).

48   Palwankar, *supra* note 38, at 247, 254; Schindler, *supra* note 38, at 523; this is also the basis for the Resolution adopted by the Institut de droit international, *supra* note 29.

49   A/RES/49/59, 9 December 1994.

50   UN Doc. ST/SBG/1999/13.

On the other hand:

> 1.2 The promulgation of this bulletin does not affect the protected status of members of peacekeeping operations under the 1994 Convention on the Safety of United Nations and Associated Personnel or their status as non-combatants, as long as they are entitled to the protection given to civilians under the international law of armed conflict.

This mirror indeed the provision on the scope of application contained in the said Convention:[51]

> This convention shall not apply to a United Nations operation authorized by the Security Council as an enforcement action under Chapter VII of the Charter of the United Nations in which any of the personnel are engaged as combatants against organized armed forces and to which the law of international armed conflict applies.

These texts recognize that there are situations during UN military operations which have to be characterized as armed conflict and to which, therefore, the law of armed conflict applies. It is for these situations only that the bulletin formulates a set of rules which indeed reflect the current state of the customary law of armed conflict without going into too many details. If that situation does not exist, then the peacekeepers are indeed soldiers without enemies, and the law of peace, as concretized in the Convention, applies.

Thus, the practice of the United Nations has developed in the sense that the United Nations possesses rights and duties under international humanitarian law similar to those of States in similar situations. This is a legal situation which the Security Council may only modify within the limits explained above. Until now, it has never done so.

5 The United Nations and Human Rights

5.1 *General*

The question of whether the United Nations are bound by international human rights law has a number of different aspects. As has been pointed out above, the question arises in all those situations where the Organization

---

51   Article 2(2).

takes a decision having a direct impact on individuals. Therefore, a major example is the presence of peacekeeping forces in a given territory as those forces by necessity have an impact, *de facto* or *de jure*, on the situation of individuals. The problem of human rights obligations involves a broad range of issues, duties of abstentions, that is, a duty not to interfere with individual rights, and affirmative duties, that is, duties to take positive action to enhance the situation of individuals. Two examples of both aspects will be discussed below.

Before doing so, a general remark must be made: No human right is absolute. Therefore, international human rights treaties provide for limitations of these rights (e.g. Arts 12 para. 3, 19 para. 3 ICCPR, 10 para. 2 ECHR), in particular in the case of emergencies (Arts 4 ICCPR, 15 ECHR). But these possibilities of limitation are themselves subject to limitations. These limitations of limitations may be substantive ('necessary in a democratic society', Art. 19 ICCPR, principle of proportionality), they may be procedural ('prescribed by the law'). An important limitation of deprivation of personal liberty is the requirement that 'anyone arrested or detained on a criminal charge shall be brought promptly before a judge or other officer authorized by law to exercise judicial power' (Art. 9 para. 3 ICCPR). As these limitations of limitations frequently refer to institutions which are typical for States (courts, legislation), their application by international organizations presents a difficulty. The argument that international organizations could not be bound by these human rights because they do not possess the institutions needed to implement these rights or their limitations is not acceptable. It is a countersense to assume that a UN police force could detain a person indefinitely without bringing him or her before a judge because the UN does not have such a judge. On the other hand, it would jeopardize the efficiency of a UN operation to maintain order if it were unable to detain persons for that very reason. The solution of the problem lies in a logical extension of the argument already used by the ICJ in the *Reparation for Injuries* case.[52] Human rights apply to the UN *mutatis mutandis*. If the UN does not possess institutions needed to implement the rights and to administer their limitations, it must create equivalent institutions.

5.2 *A Particular Example: Listing and De-listing Decisions*
A relevant development of international practice which sheds light on the questions treated in this chapter is the debate about so-called targeted sanctions, that is sanctions directly and explicitly subjecting individual persons

---

52   *Supra* section 3.1.

516 PART 6: PROTECTED PERSONS AND HUMAN RIGHTS, RELIEF

or enterprises to restrictions designed to enforce Security Council decisions.[53] This raises the problem as to how the United Nations must respect the individual rights of the persons thus targeted. The list of these resolutions is quite long.[54] One has to distinguish between resolutions obliging States to execute such sanctions against individuals fulfilling certain criteria and decisions explicitly and directly addressing certain individuals. Whether in the latter case the Security Council decisions have direct effect in the law of the Member States is a question which may be answered differently from State to State. But even where there is no such direct effect, the resolution which is binging pursuant to Art. 25 of the UN Charter obliges the Member State to deprive a particular individual of fundamental freedoms, the freedom to enjoy one's property and the freedom of movement. Thus, putting a particular individual on a sanctions list (listing) amount to an exercise of public authority by the Security Council vis-à-vis the individual in question. Whatever measures implementing the lists are taken at the national or EU level, the listing or de-listing decision of the Security Council directly affects fundamental rights of the targeted individuals. Therefore, the question arises whether those individuals could claim if a similar decision were taken by a State authority.

If the decision to freeze assets or to deny access to a country were taken by a State, certain basic procedural human rights would have to be observed: during the administrative procedure, a right to be informed of that procedure and to be heard as well as a right to be informed of the decision would apply. Once the decision is taken, there is a right of judicial review in a procedure which respects procedural justice. In the case of Security Council listing decisions, all these human rights guarantees are absent.

This has led to reactions on the national EU levels in a number of judgements concerning listing decisions. These decisions were implemented by the EC/EU by regulations transposing the listing decisions of the Security Council listing decisions into an EC/EU regulation without giving the persons so listed any additional means of defence. The Court of First Instance held that the EC was bound by the decisions of the Security Council except in decisions

---

53 M Bothe, 'Security Council's Targeted Sanctions against Presumed Terrorists', *Journal of International Criminal Justice* 6 (2008): 541–555 ; C.A. Feinäugle, 'The UN Security Council Al-Qaida and Taliban Sanctions Committee : Emerging Principles of International Institutional Law for the Protection of the Individual?', in von Bogdandy et al., *supra* note 5, at 101–131.

54 The latest examples are S/RES/1973, 17 March 2011, and S/RES/1970, 26 February 2011 concerning Libya.

violating a norm of *ius cogens*.[55] The Court, furthermore, considered the establishment of the 'focal point' as a protection and that the decision respected the *ius cogens* core of the right to judicial protection and that the decision was thus binding.[56] Therefore, it upheld the regulation. The Court of Justice of the European Union, however, reversed that judgement using a completely different reasoning. It held, on the one hand, that the Court was not entitled to review the conformity of Security Council decisions with the Charter or other relevant legal norms.[57] But under EU law the individual was entitled to fundamental human rights, which are part of the EU constitutional order. The constitutional principles of EU law have in the Community (now Union) legal order a rank which is higher than that of an international agreement.[58] They could thus not be set aside by an international treaty, even not by the UN Charter. The restrictions imposed on the plaintiffs in that case amounted to a deprivation of property without due process of law. This was the essential point which led the Court to annul the Regulation.[59] It was immaterial for that result whether the Security Council decision in question was or was not in conformity with UN law. The Court does not indicate whether it would have reached a different result if the Security Council had provided for a fully fledged review of its decision at the UN level, a way of argument which is suggested by the Advocate General in his conclusions.[60]

Whatever the exact legal construction, the practical result is that Security Council decisions disregarding fundamental procedural requirements are not implemented automatically without further scrutiny. In other words, the said procedural human rights requirements constitute a limitation, be it *de facto* or *de iure*, of the powers of the Security Council.

Even before the Court of Justice of the European Communities reached that decision, the cases had not only triggered a considerable doctrinal debate, but

---

55   *Kadi v. Council and Commission, supra* note 31, at para. 226.

56   Ibid., para. 262 *et seq.*

57   Court of Justice of the European union, *Kadi and Al Barakaat International Foundation v. Council and Commission*, Judgement of the Court (Grand Chamber), 3 September 2008 (Cases C-402/05 P and C-415/05 P), para. 287.

58   *Ibid.*, para 289.

59   *Ibid.*, para 369 *et seq.*

60   *Kadi v. Council and Commission*, Case C-402/05 P. Conclusions of Advocate General Maduro, 16 January 2008, para. 54: "Had there been a genuine and effective mechanism of judicial control by an independent tribunal at the level of the United Nations then this might have released the Community from the obligation to provide for judicial control of implementing measures that apply within the Community legal order. However, no such mechanism exists.'

518   PART 6: PROTECTED PERSONS AND HUMAN RIGHTS, RELIEF

also initiatives to improve the Security Council procedure in order to render Security Council decisions less vulnerable against such human rights challenges. Critiques of the Security Council practice came from national governments,[61] NGO position papers[62] and from the Council of Europe.[63] The UN General Assembly dealt with the issue and addressed the Security Council as follows:

> We also call on the Security Council, with the support of the Secretary-General, to ensure that fair and clear procedures exist for placing individuals and entities on sanctions lists and for removing them, as well as granting humanitarian exceptions.[64]

So far, the reactions of the Security Council have not really lived up to the relevant human rights requirements. On an abstract level, the Security Council seems to recognize the problem. In a presidential Statement, it is declared:

The Council is committed to ensuring that fair and clear procedures exist for placing individuals and entities on sanctions lists and for removing them. ... [65]

More concretely, the Security Council adopted a number of resolutions providing for a review of listing decisions and for a de-listing procedure, in particular resolutions 1617 (2005), 1739 (2006), 1735 (2006), 1822 (2008), 1904 (2009), 1988 (2011) and 1989 (2011). Sanctions committees have developed guidelines for this purpose. At a closer look, however, the practical reaction of the Security Council is still far from meeting human rights requirements, although some progress has been made in this direction. Resolution 1730 (2006) requests the Secretary-General to establish within the Secretariat a so-called Focal Point, a kind of revamped letter box where a listed individual can indeed submit a request for de-listing. This triggers a consultation process with the 'designating government(s)', that is the governments which had taken the initiative to have the individual in question listed, and the government(s) of citizenship and residence. If none of those governments recommends a de-listing, the person remains on the list. If one of those governments recommends de-listing,

---

61   Letter dated 19 May 2006 from the Permanent Representatives of Germany, Sweden and Switzerland to the United Nations addressed to the President of the Security Council, UN Doc. A/60/887-S/2006/331.

62   Human Rights Watch, *Un Sanctions Rules must Protect Due Process*, 4 March 2001. Available at: http://www.hrw.org/es/news/2002/02/02/un-sanctions-rules-must-protect-due-process.

63   Council of Europe, Parliamentary Assembly, Resolution 1597 (2008) and Recommendation 1824 (2008), both adopted 23 January 2008.

64   2005 World Summit Outcome, A/RES/60/1, 24 October 2005.

65   UN Doc. S/PRST/2006/28, 22 June 2008.

the Sanctions Committee will take the request on its agenda. The individual is informed about the result. To call this procedure a 'remedy' for the individual would really be an exaggeration. The Advocate General of the Court of Justice of the European Communities comments on this procedure:[66]

> The existence of a de-listing procedure at the level of the United Nations offers no consolation in this regard. That procedure allows petitioners to submit a request to the Sanctions Committee or to their government for removal from the list. Yet the processing of that request is purely a matter of intergovernmental consultation. There is no obligation on the Sanctions Committee actually to take the views of the petitioner into account. Moreover, the delisting procedure does not provide even minimal access to the information on which the decision was based to include the petitioner in the list. In fact, access to such information is denied regardless of any substantiated claims as to the need to protect its confidentiality. One of the crucial reasons for which the right to be heard must be respected is to enable the parties concerned to defend their rights effectively, particularly in legal proceedings which might be brought after the administrative control procedure has come to a close.

Yet further progress has been made in the meantime. The Security Council is aware of the challenges and has asked Member States and 'relevant international organizations' (which certainly alludes to the EU) 'to inform the Committee of any relevant court decisions'.[67] By the same resolution, certain responsibilities for de-listing relating to an important sanctions list, namely the Al Qaida and Taliban list, are entrusted to an Ombudsperson. The positive aspect of the new procedure is that the Ombudsperson has to engage in a dialogue with the listed person.[68] But the information which the Ombudsperson must give to the petitioner still is restricted to procedural questions.[69] As to substance, the Ombudsperson is bound to respect 'the confidentiality of Committee deliberations and confidential communications between the Ombudsperson and Member States'.[70] This still falls shot of the requirement to obtain the information needed for an effective defence. The Ombudsperson reports to the Committee on the information

---

66   *Supra* note 60, at para. 51.
67   S/RES/1904, 17 December 2009, para. 15.
68   S/RES/1904, 17 December 2009, Annex II, paragraphs 5 and 6.
69   S/RES/1904, 17 December 2009, Annex II, para. 1(b) and (c).
70   S/RES/1904, 17 December 2009, Annex II, para. 14.

he or she has collected and on 'the principal arguments concerning the delisting request'. The Committee is obliged to place the request submitted through the Ombudsperson on the agenda, but is otherwise completely free concerning how to deal with it. This is still a far cry from an independent and impartial review of a listing decision. The situation has improved, yet still not decisively, by the recent resolution directing 'the Committee to remove expeditiously individuals and entities on a case-by-case basis that no longer meet the listing criteria'.[71]

Although the respect for human rights by the Security Council, thus, still leaves something to be desired, the following conclusion is important for the present paper: At least on an abstract level, there is a recognition that the Security Council has to abide by fundamental requirements of procedural justice. If the Security Council is reluctant to fully meet these requirements in practice, it has made some concessions to these requirements and it is aware of the consequence of not respecting them – the listing decision in question will not be implemented without an additional procedure at the national or EU level providing the human rights guarantees the Council refuses to grant. The legal logic of this position is somewhat complex: the Security Council seems to recognize that it is obliged to respect human rights, but prefers to forgo the obligatory character of its resolution instead of granting to the persons targeted by it the rights it would be required to grant if it wanted the resolution to be binding and effective.

5.3   *R2P and Human Rights*

Another issue involving human rights obligations of the Security Council is the 'Responsibility to Protect' (R2P).[72] This responsibility is derived from a construction of human rights, especially the right to life, which involves an affirmative duty to protect such rights.[73] This responsibility is understood to impose certain duties on States to act to prevent massive violations of human rights, but the concept must not be misunderstood as legally justifying unilateral action of a State claiming to protect a population by the use of military force against human rights abuses.[74] Where, however, military means to protect a population against human rights violations committed by its own

---

71   S/RES/1988, 17 June 2001, para. 18.

72   International Commission on Intervention and State Sovereignty, *Responsibility to Protect, Report of the International Commission on Intervention and State Sovereignty* (Ottawa: International Development Research Centre, 2001).

73   *Ibid.*, at 14 *et seq.*

74   *Ibid.*, at 54 *et seq.*

HUMANITARIAN LAW AS LIMITS FOR SECURITY COUNCIL ACTION

government are considered necessary, it can only be the Security Council which would legitimize that use of force.

During recent years, a lot of lip service has been paid to the concept of R2P. Two questions have to be distinguished: Has R2P developed into a norm of positive international law? Is the Security Council bound by that rule?

As to the first question, it can be recognized that the alleged rule has some political impact. R2P has been evoked in cases where the Security Council did act. Yet it is difficult to ascertain whether this political trend has really led to the establishment of a rule of positive international law. Too many are the cases of inactivity of States and of the United Nations in cases of human rights violations. To mention only a few: Rwanda, Srebrenica. It is probably more correct to speak of the R2P as an emerging norm or principle.[75] But the recent resolution concerning Libya[76] is interpreted as being an implementation of R2P by the Security Council. The relevant resolution expressly reiterates 'the responsibility of the Libyan authorities to fulfil this responsibility is the basis for Security Council action. This is an element of the UN practice which can be understood as confirming the character of R2P as a norm of positive international law.

What is important for the purposes of the present paper is the fact that it seems to be taken for granted that if R2P were a legal norm, it would not only be addressed to States, but also to the United Nations.[77]

6 Human Rights and Humanitarian Law Combined: Humanitarian Exceptions to Sanctions Regimes

A traditional type of sanction imposed by the Security Council is the embargo, that is, a mandatory interruption of trade relations. This has resulted in serious deprivations of the civilian population, that is of persons who bear no responsibility for the wrongs which triggered the sanction decisions. This has been the object of severe criticism.

In terms of human rights law and international humanitarian law, the question can be formulated as follows. If the embargo relates to an armed conflict, the provisions concerning relief for the civilian apply: Art. 23, 59 GC IV, Art. 69, 70 AP I. The essential content of these norms constitutes customary law and requires that relief actions take place. As a norm of customary law, it could

---

75   *Ibid.*, at 16.
76   S/RES/1973, 17 March 2011.
77   *Ibid.*, at 16.

522 PART 6: PROTECTED PERSONS AND HUMAN RIGHTS, RELIEF

bind the United Nations if they were a Party to a conflict and, as the case may be, an occupying power.

In terms of human rights law, systematically depriving a civilian population of its means of subsistence constitutes a violation of the right to life and the right to the protection of a private sphere of life (Art. 6, 17 ICCPR), of the right to a decent standard of living and the right to health (Art. 11, 12 ICESCR).[78]

Against this legal background, demands have been made, especially by the ICRC, that the Security Council should admit humanitarian exceptions to sanctions regimes.[79] These demands have generally been heeded. The most elaborate example is the 'Oil for Food' programme in the framework of the sanctions against Iraq during the 1990s.[80] Another example is the sanctions regime imposed upon Haiti.[81] It is significant that the recognition of 'humanitarian exceptions' by the Security Council is formulated in resolutions dealing also with another human rights issue, namely listing and de-listing persons on sanctions lists.[82] This practice clearly indicates that the Council considers itself bound by a humanitarian principle according to which economic sanctions may not lead to a massive deprivation of the civilian populations.[83]

7 Towards an International Constitutional and Administrative Law

It was said at the outset that the question as to whether the United Nations, including the Security Council as an organ of the United Nations, is bound by human rights is part of the problem of the increasing exercise of public authority by international institutions. These are new forms of international governance which involve what is called a 'public law approach'.[84] This means that the rules of international governance increasingly resemble similar rules

---

78 De Wet, *supra* note 19, at 219 *et seq.*

79 H.-P. Gasser, 'Collective Economic Sanctions and International Humanitarian Law', *Zeitschrift für ausländisches öffentliches Recht und Völkerrecht* 56 (1996), 880 *et seq.*; De Wet, *supra* note 19, at 226 *et seq.*

80 S/RES/986, 14 April 1995, which provides humanitarian exceptions to the embargo decided by S/RES/661, 6 August 1990.

81 S/RES/841, 16 June 1993, and S/RES/917, 6 May 1994.

82 *Supra* note 54.

83 Herdegen, *supra* note 30, at 156.

84 A. von Bogdandy, P. Dann and M. Goldmann, 'Developing the Publicness of Public International Law: Towards a Legal Framework for Global Governance Activities', In Bogdandy et al., *supra* note 5, at 3–32; S. Kadelbach, 'From Public International law to International Public Law: A Comment on the "Public Authority" and the "Publicness" of their Law', *ibid.*, 33–49.

HUMANITARIAN LAW AS LIMITS FOR SECURITY COUNCIL ACTION   523

applying to State activities, which holds true despite warnings against over-stating these similarities.[85] There is an international constitutional law[86] and an international administrative law.[87] The exercise of public authority by the Security Council is part of the phenomenon. General principles of (State) con-stitutional law are applied to its actions.[88] It entails an obligation to respect human rights.[89]

8   International Organizations and the Rule of Law

International organizations are creations of the international legal system. Therefore, they must be subject to the fundamental rules of that system. Also the United Nations are subject to, not above, international law. Therefore, the question whether the United Nations including the Security Council is bound by human rights and international humanitarian law is part of another re-lated discourse, namely that on the rule of law at both the national and the international level.

The Secretary-General has submitted various reports on the rule of law activ-ities of the United Nations. They essentially address support for the rule of law at the national level, especially in post-conflict situations.[90] Yet the Secretary-General defines the concept of rule of law in very general terms which could well be applied to the United Nations themselves:[91]

> The 'rule of law' is a concept *at the very heart of the Organization's mis-sion.* It refers to a principle of governance in which all persons, insti-tutions and entities, public and private, including the State itself, are accountable to laws that are publicly promulgated, equally enforced

---

85   M. Herdegen, *supra* note 30, at 150 *et seq.*; for a balanced analysis, see Sato, *supra* note 1, at 325 *et seq.*

86   This goes beyond the long-standing debate as to whether the constituent instruments of international organizations can rightly be called 'constitution', see T. Sato, *Evolving Constitutions of International Organizations* (The Hague: martinus Neijhoff Publishers, 1996), 229 *et seq.*; see also P.-M. Dupuy, 'the Constitutional Dimension of the Charter of the United Nations Revisited', *Max Planck Yearbook on United Nations Law* (1997), 1–33, in particular at 19.

87   Kadelbach, *supra* note 84, at 41 *et seq.*

88   Sarooshi, *supra* note 2, at 20 *et seq.*

89   Kadelbach, *supra* note 84, at 41 *et seq.*; se also Feinäugle, *supra* note 53.

90   See, e.g., the SG Report 'The Rule of law and transitional justice in conflict and post-conflict societies', UN Doc. S/2004/616, 23 August 2004.

91   UN Doc. S/2004/616, para. 6 (emphasis added).

and independently adjudicated, and which are consistent with international human rights norms and standards. It requires, as well, measures to ensure adherence to the principles of supremacy of law, equality before the law, accountability to the law, fairness in the application of the law, separation of powers, participation in decision-making, legal certainty, avoidance of arbitrariness and procedural and legal transparency.

The idea that these principles should apply to the United Nations themselves is rarely expressed in United Nations debates. A laudable formulation is found in the statement made by Liechtenstein in the VIth Committee of the General Assembly during the debate on 'The Rule of Law at the National and International Levels' on the 13 October 2008:[92]

> Another disconnect that should be remedied step by step exists between the organization's role as a legislative forum and its own application of relevant rules of international law. We acknowledge that the rule of law at the 'institutional' level is a conceptually challenging notion. It requires United Nations organs to examine the extent to which they are bound not just by the United Nations Charter, but also by applicable rules of customary international law. Given the ever increasing scope of the United Nations' activities, however, improving adherence to international law internally is indispensable to uphold the organization's legitimacy and credibility.

The last sentence takes up an important point which has already been mentioned in the introduction, namely that of the legitimacy of the action of international organizations.[93] The more these activities have a direct or indirect impact on the fate of individuals, the more there is a need for such legitimacy. As a democratic legitimacy is not available to international organizations in the same way as it is for States, respect for the rule of law plays a decisive role for such legitimacy.

Respect for human rights is at the heart of the requirements imposed by the rule of law.

---

92   Available at http://www.regierung.li/index.php?id=387 (accessed 12 February 2012).
93   See the volume edited by Coicaud and Heiskanen, *supra* note 1, on the Security Council in particular, see, Sato, *supra* note 1; see also Dupuy, *supra* note 86, at 32; D.D. Caron, 'The Legitimacy of the Collective Authority of the Security Council', *AJIL* 87)1993): 556 *et seq.*

HUMANITARIAN LAW AS LIMITS FOR SECURITY COUNCIL ACTION 525

Another related discourse leads to the same result, namely the accountability of international organizations,[94] to which the Report of the Secretary-General quoted above refers, too.[95] This discourse has been convincingly formulated by the Committee of the International Law Association on 'Accountability of International Organisations'.[96] This accountability has procedural aspects both as to decision-making (in particular transparency) and as to review mechanisms. It has also a substantive side, namely the requirement that the organization respects human rights and international humanitarian law.[97]

9   Conclusion

This chapter has tried to show that the Security Council in its activities is indeed bound by international law of human rights and international humanitarian law. Various strands of legal reasoning coincide in that result. They are both theoretical and practical. There is no denying the fact, however, that a certain tension exists between the pure legal argument and legal practice. The five permanent members of the Security Council are rather loath to accept legal control of their political action. Yet there are enough political forces at work which prevent this political unwillingness from turning into an obsolescence of the applicable law.

---

94 E. de Wet, 'Holding International Institutions Accountable: The Complementary Role of Non-Judicial Oversight Mechanisms and Judicial Review', in von Bogdandy et al., *supra* note 5, at 855–992. Feinläugle, *supra* note 53, at 130 *et seq.*

95 *Supra* note 91.

96 International Law Association, *Report of the Seventy-First Conference*, Berlin 2004, 164-23.

97 *Ibid.*, Part Two, section four, at 193–196.

PART 7

Occupation

∵

25

Beginning and End of Occupation

1 Introduction

In general terms, a belligerent occupation can be defined as a specific situation where the armed forces of one or more States are for a certain period of time present in the territory of another State without the consent of the latter.

Two situations must, indeed, be distinguished taking into account whether the occupied State has given its consent to the foreign military presence on its territory or not.

Where the territorial ("host") State consents to the presence of foreign States (occupying powers), a contractual relationship exists between the two States. The law of occupation does not apply, with the consequence that the rights and duties of the forces present in the territory flow from the consent.

On the contrary, where consent of the territorial State is lacking, the rights and duties of the occupying forces, and/or the rights and duties of the population of that territory have to be determined by a specific body of international law, *i.e.* the law of belligerent occupation. The matter is specifically regulated by Articles 42 to 56 of the Hague Regulation,[1] and Articles 47 to 68 of the 4th Geneva Convention,[2] which may apply as a matter of treaty law, but also constitute customary law.

It needs to be pointed out that, in addition to these common features, hybrid cases of occupation also exist, where there is consent, but where the agreement in the specific context rather refers to the law of belligerent occupation. This is often the case of an occupation based on an armistice.

Furthermore, the law of occupation also covers the situation where there is "only" an occupation, and no other manifestation of armed conflict. This is clearly implied by Article 2 paragraph 2 which is common to the Geneva Conventions.[3]

---

1 Convention (II) with respect to the Law of and Customs of War on Land, The Hague, 29 July 1899.

2 Convention (IV) relative to the Protection of Civilian Persons in Time of War, Geneva, 12 August 1949.

3 "In addition to the provisions which shall be implemented in peacetime, the present Convention shall apply to all cases of declared war or of any other armed conflict which may

Referring to the above-mentioned definition of belligerent occupation, we must distinguish two essential characteristics: a foreign military presence and the lack of consent of the occupied State.[4] The existence or absence of these two elements will determine the beginning and the end of an occupation.

The question of the conditions under which it is possible to speak of "presence", will be first addressed. This is, for instance, the case of three Dutch soldiers marching through Brussels without the consent of the Belgians authorities; this situation will certainly not be qualified as an occupation of Belgium by the Netherlands. A certain threshold of significance of the foreign military presence must be passed. A primary step will consist in identifying what this threshold is.

The second question concerns the conditions that will determine whether the "consent" is relevant to exclude the qualification of "belligerent occupation". History is full of examples of interventions where the territorial government did no longer, not yet or never did possess any effective governmental power over the territory in question. Does the consent given by such a government really exclude the application of the law of belligerent occupation?

It is necessary to analyse these two sets of questions, in order to ascertain criteria for the beginning and the end of an occupation. These issues will be addressed, in a first approach, assuming that only States are the relevant actors. Thereafter, it will be considered whether the same approach may be valid in case of the presence of forces of international organisations. Special attention will be paid to the consequences of the decisions of the UN Security Council in this respect.

---

arise between two or more of the High Contracting Parties, even if the state of war is not recognized by one of them. The Convention shall also apply to all cases of partial or total occupation of the territory of a High Contracting Party, even if the said occupation meets with no armed resistance. Although one of the Powers in conflict may not be a party to the present Convention, the Powers who are parties thereto shall remain bound by it in their mutual relations. They shall furthermore be bound by the Convention in relation to the said Power, if the latter accepts and applies the provisions thereof".

4 In order to simplify the reasoning, these two issues are dealt by the author assuming that the United Nations do not exist. However, towards the end of the contribution, the author addresses the question of whether his conclusions are affected by UN's decisions.

2 Military Presence

2.1 *The Beginning of Occupation*

According to Articles 42[5] and 43[6] of the Hague Regulation, there is "presence" when the foreign military forces go beyond the situation of fighting.[7] The provisions identify the threshold as characterised by two elements:

- the removal of the effective control of the established government of the territory; and
- the exercise of effective control over the territory by the foreign power.

Therefore, the "authority" has *de facto* passed into the hands of the occupant. This means that the occupying State must be in a position to exercise *de facto* powers similar to that of the government, which has been displaced. This is not yet the case while fighting is still going on. Similarly, there is no occupation where such *de facto* authority is only claimed but cannot actually be exercised.

After the fighting has ceased, and the "hostile army" has gained effective control over part of the entire territory, the situation of occupation begins. This entails important responsibilities to be undertaken by the occupying power; Article 43 expressly provides that the occupant:

> ... Shall take all the measures in his power to restore, and ensure, as far as possible public order and safety[8]

These new responsibilities lie with the occupying State in a very first stage. The Iraqi case showed that the U.S. forces did not realise how fast the threshold from fighting to occupation can be crossed.

---

5 "Territory is considered occupied when it is actually placed under the authority of the hostile army" (*as highlighted by us*).

 The occupation applies only to the territory where such authority is established, and in a position to assert itself".

6 "The authority of the legitimate power having actually passed into the hands of the occupant, the latter shall take all steps in his power to re-establish and insure, as far as possible, public order and safety, while respecting, unless absolutely prevented, the laws in force in the country". (*as highlighted by us*).

7 Article 2 common to the Geneva Conventions does not contain a definition of "occupation", and the relevant provisions of the IV Geneva Convention are "supplementary" to the Hague Regulation (Article 154 of the IV GC) and apply in combination with them.

8 It is worth noting that the French version uses the terms "ordre et vie publics" (*as highlighted by us*).

In that perspective, military powers might need to rethink the rules of engagement. The Iraq war showed indeed that the welfare of the local population was only brought into consideration at quite a later stage.

2.2 *The End of Occupation*

It would seem natural that occupation ends when there is withdrawal of the foreign military forces from the territory, either forced by the local army or voluntary.

It would be the situation of an occupying power actually leaving the occupied area completely, and giving room for the unrestrained exercise of governmental powers by the legitimate government of the territory.

This however is not often the case in reality. The withdrawal could only entail the "thinning out" of the foreign army. Then, it becomes a question of degree whether the effective control has ceased or not.

In case of partial withdrawal, the occupying power cannot relinquish its responsibilities by simply declaring the end of occupation. It has the duty to facilitate the entry of a fully-fledged legitimate government.

The Israeli withdrawal from the Gaza Strip must be assessed in the light of these considerations. It is, however, not clear, whether one can consider that the occupation of the Palestinian territory has been terminated.

3 Belligerent Occupation v. Consented Presence

Occupation is, by definition, an asymmetric relationship: most often, the occupying power possesses a superior force in relation to the government of the occupied State.

In these circumstances, the question of genuine, and freely expressed, consent is delicate.

Article 47 of the IV Geneva Convention provides that consent expressed by the authorities of the occupied territory, after the beginning of occupation, is irrelevant, where it would result in the diminution of the rights of the population guaranteed under the Convention.[9]

---

9   "Protected persons who are in occupied territory shall not be deprived, in any case or in any manner whatsoever, of the benefits of the present Convention by any change introduced, as the result of the occupation of a territory, into the institutions or government of the said territory, nor by any agreement concluded between the authorities of the occupied territories and the Occupying Power, nor by any annexation by the latter of the whole or part of the occupied territory".

BEGINNING AND END OF OCCUPATION

There are, indeed, cases where the former government of a territory had been removed through illegitimate means, and replaced by another government which then gave consent to a foreign military intervention.[10] Consent given in those circumstances is tainted.

The question remains, however, to determine whether the protective regime provided for in The Hague Regulation and the IVth Geneva Convention applies. This assessment needs to be carried out on a case-by-case basis, particularly in situations where the territorial government giving the consent, only controls part of the national territory.[11]

Where it is considered that there is no genuine, freely expressed, consent given by the legitimate and effective government, the foreign military presence must be regarded as belligerent occupation.

It is worth noting that the appraisal of the situation must be based on objective criteria. It cannot depend exclusively on the judgment of the two States involved. The Geneva Conventions therefore provide for an *erga omnes* regime, where the Member States and the International Committee of the Red Cross (ICRC) dispose of a *droit de regard* on the situation.

The next question to be solved is the re-qualification of the evolving situation: consent that did not exist in the beginning of occupation, may occur afterwards, and consequently change the legal regime of the foreign presence. On the contrary, consent initially given may later disappear.

The first situation refers to a "supervening consent": the situation starts as a belligerent occupation until the receiving State consents to the foreign presence on its territory. Article 47 of the IV Geneva Convention does not exclude this possibility, although occupation has already begun: agreement may be found between the occupying power and the government of the occupied State even outside the framework of a common peace treaty.

The Iraqi case gives a good picture: the Interim Government of Iraq has agreed to, and even requested, the continued presence of the Multinational

---

10   For instance, in Hungary in 1956 and Afghanistan in 1980.

11   This is the case of an internationalised armed conflict where the law of international armed conflicts applies, at least to the relationship between the foreign intervening power and the non-governmental party to the conflict. Where the intervening country gains control over an area previously held by insurgents, there are two possibilities: either the authority of the pre-existing government may simply be re-established. In that case, the presence of the forces of the intervening power in this area is based on consent. Or, the authority of the preexisting government is not re-established, at least for the time being. Then, the presence of the foreign intervening power becomes a belligerent occupation if the requirement of Articles 42 and 43 of the Hague Regulation are fulfilled.

Forces (MNF), acting under UN Security Council mandate.[12] The qualification of the current situation raises many questions.

The core issue concerns the independence of the legitimate government giving its consent to the foreign presence. The government expressing such consent must be more than a creation of the occupying power.

In the case of Iraq, the legitimate character of the Interim Government requesting a continued presence, despite the fact that elections have taken place, is at stake. In this respect, it is significant that the UN Security Council has endorsed this arrangement.[13] However, the question remains to determine whether UN's endorsement of such a situation is conclusive.

The second situation refers to a "disappearing consent". This case implies that consent given by the government to foreign military presence may be revoked, may cease to exist or does no longer cover the behaviour of the military forces.

Example of such a situation is the UN General Assembly's Resolution on the definition of aggression.[14] An act of aggression is there defined as:

> The use of the armed forces of one State which are within the territory of another State with the agreement of the receiving State, in contravention of the conditions provided for in the agreement or any extension of their presence in such territory beyond the termination of the agreement.[15]

In such a situation, the continued presence of foreign armed forces is no longer covered by the consent of the receiving State. As soon as the consent ceases to be effective, a belligerent occupation begins. This consideration must be taken into account in the current Iraqi case.

4   Consequences of the UN Security Council

The UN Security Council may take three types of decisions in relation to a situation of foreign military presence in a State:

---

12   Resolution 1511 of 16 October 2003.

13   Resolution 1546 of 8 June 2004.

14   Resolution 3314 of 14 December 1974.

15   An agreement terminates when it is so declared by the receiving State, regardless of the question of whether it was legally entitle to do so. As far as the conditions of applicability of IHL regime are concerned, only the facts are relevant: IHL regime should be applicable where there is a *de facto* situation requiring that application.

- It may address the problem of applicable law to a situation, although such a situation may have developed without any input from the Security Council;
- It may give a mandate for the presence of armed forces of a State or of a group of States;
- It may establish a United Nations presence.

The first possibility has occurred in relation to certain rules applicable to the Israeli occupation of Palestinian territories, as well as in relation to the presence of coalition forces in Iraq. In both cases, the Security Council Resolutions had the sole aim of placing beyond legal doubt the specific legal position regarding the regime of occupation. The Security Council is entitled to use its powers, under Chapter VII of the UN Charter, to facilitate the restoration of peace.

The second possible decision to be taken by the Security Council can be illustrated by the situation in Bosnia-Herzegovina after the Dayton agreement, as well as in Kosovo after the armistice, in East-Timor (first phase) and in Iraq (second phase). The authorised presence of the armed forces of one or a group of States was then qualified then as being UN presence.

It must be stressed that the UN mandate concerns only the *ius ad bellum*. Then, it is a matter of interpretation of the mandate whether it goes beyond the regime of *ius ad bellum* and addresses particular issues of substantive law of occupation. The Security Council has done that, particularly in the case of Iraq and Kosovo.

The last possibility relates to the actual UN presence on the territory of a State, and raises the application of international humanitarian law to the UN troops. In this respect, it is important to stress that the UN troops are bound by customary international law, including the law of belligerent occupation, at least to the extent that the Security Council has not decided otherwise.

In conclusion, it must be emphasised that, in determining the beginning and end of occupation, the necessary case-by-case assessment remains a difficult task. The above-developed analysis tries to point out criteria to define belligerent occupation, *i.e.* significant foreign military presence and absence of consent. The existence and/or non-existence of those criteria will determine the beginning and/or the end of occupation.

The examples given show that there is no definite answer for particular cases. For every situation, a new assessment of the facts according to the objective criteria pointed out, is necessary.

Limits of the Right of Expropriation (Requisition) and of Movement Restrictions in Occupied Territory

(*Expert Opinion*)

1 The Questions

On the occasion of the establishment of the so-called Fire Zone 918 for training purposes of the Israeli Defence Forces (IDF), to be used *inter alia* as a shooting range, the following questions have been put to me:

> Can the expropriation and/or movement restrictions relating to an area of land in occupied territory for the purpose of operating a military training zone be justified under international law?
>
> Does the protection provided by the rules referred to in the first question depend on the persons affected being permanent residents in the area, in particular in cases of forcible evictions or destruction of their property located in the area?

In order to give an answer to these questions, a short overview of the rights and duties of an occupying power (OP) will first be given. These rules will then be applied to the situation of the Fire Zone 918, particularly in the light of the State's reply dated 19 July 2012 to petitions submitted to the Israeli Supreme Court in IHCJ 517/00 and IHCJ 1199/00.[1]

2 The Rights and Duties of an Occupying Power

The powers of an OP are limited by international law. In particular, the OP may take measures only for certain purposes:

---

1 http://www.acri.org.il/en/wp-content/uploads/2012/05/Firing-Zone-918-Govt-Response-19July2012-ENG.pdf.

LIMITS OF THE RIGHT OF EXPROPRIATION

- measures to ensure the security of the OP and to satisfy the needs of the army of occupation,
- measures to ensure the wellbeing and safety of the population of the occupied territory.

The first type of measure is a right of the OP, the latter one also a duty.[2] In any case, the OP must respect certain rights of the population, which are formulated in the Hague Regulations and in the IVth Geneva Convention as well as in Human Rights instruments, which also apply in the relationship between an OP and the population of the occupied territory.[3]

The essential source of these rights and duties is customary international law. It is generally recognized that the relevant provisions of the Hague Regulations indeed constitute customary international law.[4] The same holds true for the IVth Geneva Convention. At least the basic content of the relevant humanitarian rules of the IVth Geneva Convention are generally recognized as forming part of customary international law. This has also been confirmed by the Supreme Court of Israel.[5] The latter rules include certain provisions contained in Part III, Section III on "Occupied Territories" (in particular Articles 55–58), but also of Section I of that Part (in particular Art. 27).[6]

The essential duties of an OP are aptly summarized by the International Court of Justice in the case DRC v. Uganda:[7]

> (The Occupying Power is) under an obligation, according to Article 43 of the Hague Regulations of 1907, to take all measures in its power to restore, and ensure, as far as possible, public order and safety in the occupied area, while respecting, unless absolutely prevented, the laws in force in the (occupied country). This obligation comprise(s) the duty to secure respect for the applicable rules of international human rights law

---

2 See Supreme Court of Israel, *Beit Sourik Village Council v. Government of Israel*, Judgment of 30 June 2004, 43 ILM 1099 (2004), para. 35.

3 International Court of Justice, *Armed Activities on the Territory of the Congo* (*DRC v. Uganda*), Judgment of 19 May 2005, paras. 178 *et seq.*; International Court of Justice, *Legal Consequences of the Construction of a Wall in the Occupied Palestinian Territory*, Advisory Opinion of 9 July 2004, paras. 106, 110, 112 *et seq.*; see also the General Comment No. 31 of the Commission established under the ICCPR, "Nature and General Legal Obligations Imposed on States Parties to the Covenant, 26 May 2004, Doc. CCPR/C/21/Rev.1/Add. 13.

4 International Court of Justice, *Legal Consequences of the Construction of a Wall in the Occupied Palestinian Territory*, above note 3, para. 89.

5 *Beit Sourik*, above note 2, para. 23.

6 *Beit Sourik*, above note 2, para. 35.

7 International Court of Justice, *Armed Activities on the Territory of the Congo* (*DRC v. Uganda*), above note 3 para. 178.

and international humanitarian law, to protect the inhabitants of the occupied territory against acts of violence, and not to tolerate such violence by any third party.

This statement is briefly reiterated in the Wall case.[8]

On the other hand, the Court recognizes that the OP has the right to take measures to ensure its security, or more generally to take measures which are dictated by military exigencies. To determine the permissible scope of these measures, the Court analyses the relevant clauses of the said treaty provisions concerning the law of occupation, in particular articles 49 and 53 GC IV. This leads to a narrow definition of measures taken for reasons of military exigencies. As to human rights guarantees applicable in occupied territory, the Court states that permissible restrictions of those rights are defined by the limitation and derogation clauses of human rights treaties.[9]

The Hague Regulations contain two provisions concerning the protection of private property. Private property must be respected and it cannot be confiscated (Art. 46). Taking of property (requisitions in the terminology of the Hague Regulations) is possible under certain conditions (Art 52):

- They must be "for the needs of the army of occupation";
- They shall be in proportion to the resources of the country;
- They may not be equivalent to a support of the military effort of the OP;
- They must be (adequately) compensated as soon as possible.

The obligation to respect private property in the occupied territory which flows from the Hague Regulations has been expressly recognized by the Supreme Court of Israel.[10] To requisition private property is permissible only if and to the extent that it is "for the needs of the army of occupation". The sense of this provision is to allow an army of occupation to provide for its sustenance out of the resources of the occupied territory. Requisitions typically cover food and lodging. In the words of the UK Military Manual, the OP may requisition commodities and services "for its maintenance".[11] "Only the direct requirements of the army of occupation may be satisfied through them".[12]

As to destruction of property, a specific provision (*lex specialis*) is found in Art. 53 of the IVth Convention. Such destruction is prohibited except where it

---

8   Advisory Opinion, above note 4, para. 124.

9   *Loc.cit.* paras. 135 et seq.

10   *Beit Sourik*, above note 2, para. 35.

11   UK Ministry of Defence, *The Manual of the Law of Armed Conflict*, Rule 11.83.

12   E. Castrén, *The Present Law of War and Neutrality*, Helsinki 1954, p. 238.

LIMITS OF THE RIGHT OF EXPROPRIATION

"is rendered absolutely necessary by military operations". This necessity clearly refers to combat situations. It is to be narrowly construed, which is indicated by the word "absolutely". As a minimum, the destruction needs to be proportional to the potential harm to the affected civilian and their property.[13] A violation of Art. 53 will be as a rule a grave breach according to Art. 147 of the IVth Convention.

Forcible removal of persons from their homes (whether or not relocating them somewhere else) constitutes a "forcible transfer" which is prohibited according to Art. 49 para. 1 of the IVth Convention and according to customary international law. The customary law prohibition applies both to deportations outside the borders of an occupied territory and to "transfers" within that territory. This has been convincingly stated by the ICTY,[14] the proof of the rule being a cumulative view of recent relevant treaty and other instruments.[15] "Forcible" is not to be interpreted restrictively. It is not limited to physical force. It also includes threat of force or coercion, or the use of a coercive environment. The prohibition does not only relate to permanent residents, it covers any person belonging to the population of the occupied territory and being present in the area in question. Exceptionally, evacuations are allowed, namely "if the security of the population or imperative military reasons so demand" (Art. 49 para. 2). That exception clearly refers to combat or similar situations. Therefore, forcible evictions allegedly for the enforcement of planning and construction laws do not fall under this exception and are therefore forbidden, whether or not the persons affected enjoy the status of "permanent residents". As in the case of Art. 53, a violation of Art. 49 will as a rule constitute a grave breach according to Art. 147.

Art. 27 guarantees in a very general way personal rights. Freedom of movement is not mentioned as an absolute right, but it is to a certain extent implied in the rights mentioned in Art. 27.[16] In particular, the use of coercive measures

---

13 J. Pictet (ed.), *The Geneva Conventions of 12 August 1949. Commentary* (Geneva: ICRC), vol IV (1956), Commentary to Art. 53, sec. 3.

14 ICTY, *Prosecutor v. Radovan Krstic*, Case IT-98-33-T, Judgment of the Trial Chamber dated 2 August 2004, paras. 519 *et seq*. The holdings on the question of transfers were not challenged in the appeal.

15 Art. 85 (4)(a) AP I, Art. 17 AP II, Art. 2(g) Statute of the ICTY, Art. 7(1)(d) and 8(2)(b) (viii) ICC Statute, Art. 18(g) ILC Draft Code of Crimes against the Peace and Security of Mankind (1996). In particular the provisions of the ICC Statute must be regarded as a proof of customary law, see M. Bothe, "War Crimes", in A. Cassese/A. Gaeta/J.R.W.D. Jones (eds.), *The Rome Statute of the International Criminal Court: A Commentary*, Oxford 2002, vol. I, at 396.

16 See Pictet (ed.), *op.cit.* note 13, Commentary to Art. 27.

to enforce relocation may constitute the threat of an act of violence against which protected persons must be protected according to Art. 27 para. 1, 2nd sentence. In respect to the freedom of movement, the explicit guarantee lacking in the IVth Convention is granted by Art. 12 of the International Covenant on Civil and Political Rights (ICCPR),[17] which thus fills a lacuna which may be found in the Geneva Convention.

On the other hand, Art. 27 of the IVth Convention allows certain restrictions to be imposed upon protected persons, which includes the population of an occupied territory:

> ... the Parties to the conflict may take such measure of control and security in regard to protected persons as may be necessary as a result of the war.

This provision must not be misunderstood as a kind of catch all justification of measures taken for alleged security reasons. First, it is a general rule over which special rules take precedence. Where the Convention itself regulates the exceptions to the rights it guarantees, these specific definitions and limitations of exceptions cannot be set aside by Art. 27. Furthermore, the term "necessary as a result of the war" is not unlimited, but is restricted to the security reasons of a particular situation in war. As the (American) Military Tribunal in Nuremberg stated:[18]

> General security needs of the occupying army that are not directly related to the current armed conflict and to threats arising from occupied territory cannot be used to justify restrictions on civilians in occupied territory. The balance between military necessity and humanity needs to be done within the local context, where the local civilian population resides.

The rights of the OP and those of the population of the occupied territory have indeed to be seen as a balanced special regime within the law of armed conflict. Neither right is absolute. The rights of the OP cannot be determined without taking the rights of the population duly into account. The yardstick of this balancing process is the principle of proportionality, well recognized by the

---

17   See below.
18   *United States v. List (Hostage Case)*, Case no. 7, 19 Feb. 1948, 11 *Trials of war Criminals before the Nuremberg Military Tribunals under Control Council Law No. 10*, at 1253.

LIMITS OF THE RIGHT OF EXPROPRIATION

Supreme Court of Israel.[19] As shown by the Nuremberg Tribunal, that proportionality argument must not be misunderstood as opening the door wide open to limitless security arguments.

The rights of personal protection are granted to any victim which is affected, in particular to any person prevented from using his or her property or from using his or her freedom of movement. That definition of an entitlement under international law may not be reduced by legislative acts of the OP, such as reserving these rights for permanent residents only. Similar restrictions are irrelevant under international law. International law takes precedence over legislative enactments of the OP.

3 Application to the Present Case

For the purposes of the concrete questions which are the object of this expert opinion, these considerations mean the following:

As it appears from the documentation placed at my disposal, the use of the area in question as a fire zone, including a shooting range for IDF training purposes entails the need that no civilians are present therein. Thus, protected persons, residents of the eight villages in the area, who are present therein, are prevented from using their homes situated in the area and from engaging in their habitual agricultural activities therein (farming and husbandry of sheep and goats). They will be forced to leave and denied access to the area, except for very short periods which do not allow a meaningful use of the land and the homes. The beneficial uses which these persons have enjoyed before since many decades constitute private property in the sense of the Hague Regulations. Thus, denying that use to these persons means a taking of property, a requisition in the sense of the Hague Regulations.

It must be noted that these measures also have an impact on the use of properties outside the area where there will be live firing. The use of property in the entire area, comprising 12 villages, is restricted. These restrictions may well be considered as equivalent to a taking of property.

The OP justifies its measure by the need for training of its armed forces. But the training needs of the armed forces of a State which also happens to be an OP have no connection with the specific needs of an army of occupation. General training needs are not, as such, a "direct requirement" of the army of occupation. This becomes clear from the Statement of the State Attorney in

---

19   *Beit Shourik*, above note 2, paragraphs 36 *et seq.*

the present case. She justifies the "need" for increased training by the lessons learned from the Lebanon conflict in 2006.[20] This perceived general need bears no direct relation with the occupation. The reference to the special topography of the said area, which allows specific training methods, is not able to justify a different view. The added value of the topography of the occupied territory for training purposes is not a lawful consideration for restricting property rights as the military needs in question are of a general nature. The same holds true for the alleged usefulness of being able to train the soldiers in the use of specific weapons. There may be specific training needs for measures to be taken locally in the occupied territory, but no such needs result from the arguments put forward in the State Reply. Thus, the measures taken are unlawful because they are for a purpose not permitted under the Hague Regulations.

Furthermore, the extensive harm caused to the inhabitants of all the twelve villages is out of proportion to the advantage in terms of training conditions. That harm does not only consist of the current loss of the homes and agricultural land. It is the future use of the whole area for the purpose of securing the very existence of the protected population which is in jeopardy. On the other hand, it is stated in the State Reply that at present, as long as there are civilians in the planned Firing Zone, no training involving shooting can take place therein. Thus, alternative solutions for training had to be found and indeed have been found. These solutions have met some military requirements, though not all. For the application of the proportionality principle, it is important that respect of the rights of the affected persons does not mean that the military needs are completely disregarded. There is thus a fair balance of interests, which is the essence of proportionality. The measures are thus unlawful as being disproportionate.

As to the prohibition of destruction of property (Art. 53 of the IVth Convention), this can be justified only "where such destruction is rendered absolutely necessary by military operations". Military training is not a "military operation" in this sense, nor is it, as already explained, "absolutely necessary" to conduct the training at this particular location. The destruction is therefore unlawful.

As to the prohibition of forcible transfers (Art. 49 of the IVth Convention), the only exception permitted by that rule is an evacuation if "the security of the population or imperative military reasons so demand" (Art. 49 para.2). It clearly results from the last phrase of the paragraph that only the risks involved in, and the conditions imposed by hostilities justify or even require an evacuation. After these hostilities have ceased, the persons evacuated have to

---

20   Section 12 of the State Reply.

LIMITS OF THE RIGHT OF EXPROPRIATION

be brought back to the location where they came from. Thus, the permanent training needs of an army of occupation cannot justify forced transfers. These transfers are therefore unlawful.

The measures in question can, for a number of reasons, also not be justified under the general exception clause of Art. 27 of the IVth Convention. As this is a general clause, it could only be applied where there are no applicable special exception clauses, which however is the case here. Second, the exception is limited to measures "necessary as a result of the war". Training is not necessary in this sense. Under the standards developed by the Nuremberg Tribunal,[21] training would not qualify as a justification of measures restricting the rights of protected persons. Third, a measure is also unlawful under Art. 27 para. 4 if it is disproportionate.

The case under review must be distinguished from those cases where the Supreme Court has upheld evictions of Palestinians from their land or homes for security reasons. In those cases, the measures taken were justified by the OP as being protective in nature.[22] It was claimed that they were necessary as a means of defense against terrorist activities. This justification, whatever its merits, is not comparable to the training needs put forward in the present case. Thus, the jurisprudence of the Supreme Court of Israel on the justification of evictions or demolitions for security reasons cannot serve as a basis for the measure taken to facilitate the operation of an IDF shooting range.

Furthermore, the measures under review violate a number of fundamental rights of the affected inhabitants. They violate the guarantee of private property (Art. 46 Hague Regulations). They violate humanitarian guarantees contained in the IVth Geneva Convention (Art. 27). As to Human Rights treaties, they violate the freedom of movement (Art. 12 ICCPR) and the right to an adequate standard of living (Art. 11 of ICESCR).

The violation of the guarantee of private property cannot be justified under the Hague Regulations as it violates the specific provision dealing with a limitation of the right of private property.

Art. 27 of the IVth Convention provides, *inter alia*:

> Protected persons are entitled, in all circumstances, to respect for their persons ... and their manners and customs ...

---

21   See above text accompanying note 18.

22   See, *inter alia, Ayub* et al. *v. Minister of Defence* et al., H.C. 606/78; *Matawa* et al. *v. Minister of Defence* et al., H.C. 610/78, reproduced in M. Sassòli/A.A. Bouvier/A. Quintin (eds), *How Does Law Protect in War?,* 3rd ed. Geneva 2011, vol. II, pp. 1076 *et seq.*

The evictions and denial of access to land prevent the persons affected from pursuing gainful activities in the way they have done for centuries. This forms part of their "manners and customs". Art. 27 is, thus, violated at least in this respect.

Respect for human rights enshrined in a treaty is, as stated by the ICJ,[23] part of "public order and safety" which the OP is obligated to ensure (Art. 43 Hague Regulations). The guarantee of the freedom of movement (Art. 12 ICCPR) has a limitation clause (para. 3). Measures restricting the freedom of movement are permissible if they are, *inter alia*, necessary in a democratic society "to protect national security, public order" etc. But in the context of an occupation, the purposes allowing a restriction pursuant to Art. 12 para. 3 ICCPR) are themselves restricted by the Hague Regulations. Thus, a purpose which is in violation of the Hague Regulations and the Geneva Conventions cannot be a lawful purpose justifying a restriction under art. 12 para. 3 ICCPR. Art. 12 is violated.

Like other rights guaranteed by the International Covenant on Economic, Social and Cultural Rights (ICESCR), Art. 11 constitutes a promotional obligation. States do not guarantee a specific standard of living, but must take measures to promote that standard. But that obligation implies also a prohibition, namely a prohibition of measures preventing the beneficiary of that right to pursue activities for ensuring his or her livelihood. Therefore, Art. 11 ICESCR is violated.

A similar line of argument applies to the duties of the OP to provide for the wellbeing of the population which are implied the IVth Convention (Articles 55 and 56). Preventing inhabitants of an occupied territory to engage in activities for the purpose of producing their food is a violation of Art. 55 of the IVth Convention.

Even if it could be shown that there are specific training needs for measures to be taken under local conditions (*quod non*), the restrictions to be imposed for the purpose of operating the Fire Zone 918 would still be unlawful as they would be disproportionate. They would result in extensive destructions, especially due to the use of live fire without military necessity. They deny a most fundamental right, deeply embedded in the concept of human dignity, namely the right to engage in a meaningful pursuit of one's livelihood. Such a deep cut into the basics of a human existence could be proportionate only in situations of extreme necessity. Such justifying reasons are simply absent in the case under review.

---

23   See above quote accompanying note 7.

4 Conclusion

The measures under review in the present expert opinion constitute violations of
- Art. 46, 52 of the Hague Regulations;
- Art. 27 of Geneva Convention IV;
- Art. 49 para. 1 of Geneva Convention IV;
- Art. 53 of Geneva Convention IV;
- Art. 55 of Geneva Convention IV;
- Art. 12 ICCPR;
- Art. 11 ICESCR.

As forcible transfers and extensive destruction, they also constitute grave breaches according to Art. 147 Geneva Convention IV.

The measures also violate the corresponding rules of customary international law.

27

Cutting off Electricity and Water Supply for the Gaza Strip

Limits under International Law

(*Prelimininary Expert Opinion*)

In the light of reports concerning possible Israeli plans to completely cut off the water and electricity supply delivered from Israel to the Gaza Strip, I have been asked to furnish a legal expert opinion on the legality or illegality of such a measure under international law. In this context, an English translation of highlights from an opinion submitted by Prof. Avi Bell has been communicated to me. That opinion holds that, at least in principle, such a measure would be lawful under international law. With due respect, I come to a different conclusion.

In the meantime, it has been reported that these measures have been executed, at least in part, and that parts of the power distribution system have been put out of function by artillery fire. If and to the extent that these reports are true, these facts may be evaluated in the light of the legal rules developed below. But it cannot be the purpose of the present opinion to express any view on the facts which are developing on the ground, and consequently, the legal reasoning may not be understood as uttering a judgment on any concrete measure taken by Israel.

1 Applicable Law

The answer to the question thus posed is to be found in international humanitarian law and, to the extent applicable in armed conflict, international human rights law. As there is an armed conflict between Israel and the Palestinian side, the rules relating to countermeasures in times of peace are not relevant to the problem at stake.

As to international humanitarian law, relevant rules may be found in the Fourth Geneva Convention. From a technical point of view, its applicability may be controversial. The customary law character of the rules relevant for the question which is the object of this opinion seems, however, to be uncontroversial. As Israel is not a Party to Protocol 1 Additional to the Geneva

CUTTING OFF ELECTRICITY AND WATER SUPPLY

Convention, its rules can only be applied as far as they reflect customary international humanitarian law.

As to countermeasures under international humanitarian law, it must be emphasized that "reprisals" against various types of protected persons are prohibited.

2 The Status of the Gaza Strip under International Humanitarian Law

For the purpose of answering the question posed, the question whether the Gaza Strip will constitutes territory occupied by Israel is decisive. As the Israeli Supreme Court held in *Bassiouni v. the Prime Minister*, the Occupying Power has the duty to provide for the welfare of the population of the occupied territory. If the territory is no longer occupied, the duties of Israel as a party to the armed conflict, according to the Court, are limited to not preventing supplies ensuring a humanitarian minimum of essential supplies for the civilian population. The Court further held that due to the withdrawal of Israel from the Gaza Strip, it had lost the effective control of that territory and, therefore, was no longer an occupying power, and consequently no longer bound by the said duty to provide for the welfare of the population.

With due respect, it is submitted that the Court could and should reconsider that conclusion. It should be taken into account that the withdrawal was not as complete as it should have been in order to terminate Israel's position and ensuing duties as an occupying power. Israel continued to control access to Gaza from land (except for a relatively short border line with Egypt, which however was closed pursuant to an understanding between Israel and Egypt), from the sea and from the air. Israel, thus, remained in full control of the lifelines of the Gaza Strip. It is submitted that this is at least equivalent to a *de facto* control which, according to Art. 42 of the Hague Regulations, is constitutive for an occupation.

If this line of argument is accepted, the cut of electricity and water supply would be a violation of Israel's duty to provide for the welfare of the population. Even if relief actions are undertaken by third parties, this does not relieve the occupying power of that duty (Art. 60 GC IV).

3 The Question of Special Post-Occupation Duties

In addition, it is submitted that there are at least special post-occupation duties if an occupying power withdraws from an occupied territory under conditions such as those of the Israeli withdrawal of 2005.

The law of belligerent occupation, as it is formulated in GC IV and is enshrined customary law, contains safeguards against an occupying power trying to evade its duties by changing the status of the territory (Arts. 47, 54). The case expressly regulated in Art. 47 is so to say the contrary of what happened to the Gaza Strip, namely annexation. But the underlying purpose of Articles 47 and 54 is not limited to the changes specifically mentioned in Art. 47 as not depriving the population of the protections provided by the law of occupation. A withdrawal which does not give back to the territory in question its complete powers of government which would enable the authorities of the territory to provide themselves for the welfare of the population is subject to that broad purpose defining invalid (in the sense of not affecting the protections of the population) status changes. Thus, the change in status which Israel may have tried to achieve by its withdrawal could not deprive the population of the benefits of the law of occupation.

If this line of argument is accepted, the cut of electricity and water supply would be a violation of Israel's duty to provide for the welfare of the population.

The Israeli Supreme Court, in its *Bassiouni* decision, at least seems to allude to a related argument when it stresses "the relationship that was created between Israel and the territory of the Gaza Strip after the years of Israeli military rule in the territory, as a result of which the Gaza Strip is currently almost completely dependent upon the supply of electricity from Israel".

4 The Duty to Maintain Certain Supplies under General Humanitarian Law

Israel's duty to ensure a humanitarian minimum of supplies for the Gaza Strip was recognized by the Israeli Supreme Court in *Bassiouni*. The Court, however, does not really specify the legal basis of this duty. As a consequence, the opinion by Prof. Bell, mentioned above, criticizes the Court (as will be shown erroneously).

A first point of Prof. Bell's critique is derived from an analysis of the provisions of GC IV and AP I on relief. As the ICRC has shown in its Customary Law Study, Art. 70 AP I constitutes customary law. Bell argues that even if the supplies in question constituted relief goods the passage of which had to be allowed under Art. 23 GC IV and the customary law rules corresponding to Art. 70 AP I, these rules only applied to third parties undertaking relief operations, but not to direct supplies furnished by a party to the conflict. Consequently, Bell argues, the said rules do not constitute a basis for an obligation on Israel not to cut supplies. That line of reasoning is flawed as being excessively

CUTTING OFF ELECTRICITY AND WATER SUPPLY

formalistic. The situation of the Gaza Strip is special. At least on the basis of a first search, there are indeed no cases concerning a duty of a party to a conflict to provide electricity and water to the other side. In such a case, the argument that everything is permitted in the absence of a specific practice is incorrect. The solution has to be found in applying general principles which form part of customary law. The principle underlying the customary law rules concerning relief is to ensure that the basic needs of a population continue to be met under the conditions of an armed conflict. The supply cuts discussed here would (subject to the discussion of the specific commodities below) infringe that basic principle.

The same conclusion can be derived from applying a general principle of law. According to Bell's argument, Israel would have to allow the passage if a third party were to furnish those supplies (if that was a practical possibility). Applying the general principle (derived from Roman law) "nemo petit quod statim redditurus est",[1] Israel is prevented from barring supplies it would have to allow under a slightly different organizational setup.

A second argument used by Bell is that electricity generating installations generally are military objectives which can lawfully be destroyed by an adversary. Therefore, the argument continues, it would be illogical if Israel had to provide the supplies it could cut off by destroying the power plant. That argument if flawed by the fact that it disregards a basic condition of the legality of the destruction of dual use military objectives, such as vital infrastructure. Such destruction is subject to the prohibition of causing disproportionate collateral damage. That limitation has been made clear in many analyses of bombings of big cities which put the power grid out of operation (for example the bombing of Baghdad in 1991) which resulted in the inability of hospitals to continue their services thereby causing suffering and death of civilians, in particular the most vulnerable ones. In the situation of Gaza, in view of the malfunctioning of the one and only power plant due to damage or lack of fuel, supply by Israel is the only means to avoid the effects which the prohibition of disproportionate collateral damage is meant to exclude.

As a result of the principle underlying the provisions of humanitarian law relating to relief, it has to be concluded that Israel is prohibited to execute any cuts in supplies which would prevent heeding basic needs of the population of the Gaza Strip. A violation of this obligation cannot be justified as reprisals. As is shown by the ICRC and its Customary Law Study, reprisals against persons

---

1 Nobody may claim anything which he or she must immediately return.

protected by the Geneva Conventions are prohibited. The ICRC concludes that there is at least a trend to the effect that this prohibition includes civilians.

A similar conclusion may be drawn from international human rights law. The basis of its application is the doctrine of extraterritorial application, as it has been developed by courts and international human rights bodies. It not only applies where the beneficiaries are subject to the jurisdiction of a state in a formal sense (detention, occupation), but also where the beneficiary is subject to a decisive influence of the power of a state. This concept would, arguably, make the inhabitants of the Gaza Strip the beneficiaries of human rights norms binding Israel. It is beyond the scope of the present opinion to develop this line of argument in greater detail.

5   The Commodities in Question: Water and Electricity

It is submitted that the definition of relief supplies found in Art. 69 and 70 AP I constitutes customary law. It corresponds to a concept of relief which is required by the circumstances of current living conditions in the world. The key term is "other supplies essential to the survival of the civilian population".

It cannot be controversial that water constitutes a supply in this sense. It is closely related to food, but also to medical supplies as access to clean water is an essential condition for the health of the population.

As to electricity, the decisive point is that living conditions in modern agglomerations depend on the availability of electricity. Gaza is a densely populated area where the energy needed for survival cannot be produced by means other than electricity. This is in particular true for the operation of hospitals and other medical establishments. Thus, sufficient electricity is essential for the survival of the population. Inter alia, the water supply depends on the availability of electricity for pumping stations and other facilities of the water distribution system. Electricity is, thus, a relief commodity the passage of which into a territory in need of it may not be prevented.

6   Conclusion

Under international humanitarian law, Israel is obliged, in the current conditions of armed conflict, to maintain water supplies from Israel to the Gaza Strip at current level and of an electricity supply sufficient to meet the basic needs of the civilian population.

28

The Right to Provide and Receive Humanitarian Assistance in Occupied Territories

(Legal Expert Opinion)

1 Background[1]

A considerable amount of assistance is given to the population of the OPT by international or foreign humanitarian agencies, both governmental (EU, OCHA) and non-governmental. The need for such expert opinion is prompted by certain Israeli practices which impede such assistance in various ways.

These practices consist in particular of the following measures:

- Application of a restrictive and discriminatory planning system to humanitarian projects in Area C,
- Destruction of installations built in the framework of humanitarian assistance, and of relevant equipment,
- Seizure or confiscation of such installations or equipment,
- Restrictions on movement and access of humanitarian workers,
- Harassment, detention or arrest of humanitarian workers.

2 General Legal Framework

Before addressing a number of specific questions to be raised in this respect, a general overview of relevant rules concerning the rights and duties of the Occupying Power must be given.

Belligerent occupation is governed by[2]

---

1 This legal expert opinion (July 17, 2015) is tasked to clarify legal principles governing the provision of assistance by humanitarian agencies in the Occupied Palestinian Territory, in particular in Area C of the West Bank.

2 M. Bothe, 'The Administration of Occupied Territory', in A. Clapham et al. (eds.), The 1949 Geneva Conventions: A Commentary, 2015, pp. 1455–1484, at MN 3–5; E. Benvenisti, 'Occupation, Belligerent', paras. 12–16, in R. Wolfrum (ed.), Max Planck Encyclopedia of Public International Law, www.mpepil.com (last visited 4 July 2015) (hereinafter MPEPIL); Y. Dinstein,

---

© KONINKLIJKE BRILL NV, LEIDEN, 2021 | DOI:10.1163/9789004380592_030

- Customary international humanitarian law, to a large extent codified by the Hague Regulations;[3]
- Geneva Convention IV on the protection of civilian in armed conflict;[4]
- International human rights law, including the ICCPR[5] and the ICESCR.[6]

Israel admits the applicability of the relevant rules of customary humanitarian law. It denies the *de iure* application of the IVth Convention. That question, however, must be regarded as settled in the light of the Advisory Opinion of the International Court of Justice on the construction of a wall in the OPT[7] and of various instruments adopted by UN organs. The IVth Geneva Convention applies.

Israel also denies the applicability of international human rights norms in the OPT (so-called extra-territorial application). On the basis of several holdings of the ICJ,[8] that question, too, must be regarded as settled in the sense that relevant human rights law applies.

3   The General Duties of the Occupying Power

The powers exercised by an occupying power are defined in the Hague Regulation as a *de facto* authority, as distinguished from the legal authority exercised by a State on its territory. This is reflected in the text, French being the only authoritative one:

> Art. 42 : "Un territoire est considéré comme occupé lorsqu'il se trouve placé *de fait* sous l'autorité de l'armée ennemie".
> Art. 43 : "L'autorité de pouvoir légal ayant passé *de fait* entre les mains de l'occupant ... "[9]

     The International Law of Belligerent Occupation, CUP 2009, at 4 *et seq.*, on human rights at 69 *et seq.*

3   Convention (IV) Respecting the Laws and Customs of War on Land, 18 October 1907, and its Annex: Regulations Concerning the Laws and Customs of War on Land.

4   Convention (IV) Relative to the Protection of Civilian Persons in Time of War, 12 August 1949, 75 U.N.T.S. 287. The Protocol Additional to the Geneva Conventions of 12 August 1949, and Relating to the Protection of Victims of International Armed Conflicts (Protocol I), 8 June 1977, 1125 U.N.T.S. 3, only adds a few details regarding the law of belligerent occupation.

5   International Covenant on Civil and Political Rights, 16 December 1966.

6   International Covenant on Economic, Social and Cultural Rights, 16 December 1966.

7   ICJ, *Legal Consequences of the Construction of a Wall in the Occupied Palestinian Territory*, Advisory Opinion of 9 July 2004, para. 101.

8   ICJ, *Legality of the Threat or Use of Nuclear Weapons*, Advisory Opinion of 8 July 1996, para. 24; *Construction of a Wall* (note 6), para. 106.

9   Emphasis by the author.

HUMANITARIAN ASSISTANCE IN OCCUPIED TERRITORIES

The *de facto* character of this power of the occupant has been clearly explained, already in 1950, by R. Baxter, one of the world's leading specialists on the law of armed conflicts of the last century:[10]

> "The source of the inhabitants' duty of obedience can only be the power of the occupant to demand it. The law must take as its starting point the fact of military supremacy and then set forth to place limits of reasonableness on the occupant's *factual capacity* to control those who within the area he holds."

The same principle is formulated by the UK Manual on the Law of Armed Conflict:[11]

> "The law of armed conflict does not confer power on an occupant. Rather it regulates the occupant's use of power. The occupant's powers arise from the actual control of the area."

This *de facto* power is shaped and limited by international law. The law permits the occupying power to exercise certain specific competences[12] and enjoins it to refrain from certain acts. The power is, in particular, subject to a number of duties.

The general duties of an Occupying Power are formulated in a general way in Art. 43 of the Hague Regulations. The only authoritative version of the Regulations is French, and as the English text in general use does not accurately render the French original, the latter must be quoted as the starting point of the analysis:

> "[L'occupant] prendra toutes les mesures qui dépendent de lui en vue de rétablir et d'assurer, autant qu'il est possible, *l'ordre et la vie publics* en respectant, sauf empêchement absolu, les lois en vigueur dans le pays.[13]"

---

10 R.R. Baxter, 'The Duty of Obedience to the Belligerent Occupant', 27 BYIL 235–266 (1950), at 261, emphasis by the author.

11 UK Ministry of Defence, The Manual of the Law of Armed Conflict, 2004, para. 11.9. See also Dinstein, *op.cit.* note 1, at 46, 49 *et seq.*

12 Dinstein, *op.cit.* note 1, at 46 speaks of "jurisdictional rights".

13 The English text in general use is "public order and safety", which is less far reaching then "ordre et vie publics", Benvenisti, *loc.cit.* note 1, para. 22.

554 PART 7: OCCUPATION

This obligation to ensure public order and public life means a general duty to ensure the wellbeing of the population, as far as possible under the circumstances. It is, in modern parlance, a duty of good governance.[14]

This implies a number of specific duties to provide for the wellbeing of the population. An important aspect of this duty are specific rights accorded to the population by further provisions of the HR and GC IV. Of particular importance is Art. 46 HR:

> "Family honour and rights, the lives of persons, and private property, as well as religious convictions and practice, must be respected.
> Private property cannot be confiscated.."

GC IV also contains a general guarantee of personal rights (Art. 27):[15]

> "Protected persons are entitled, in all circumstances, to respect for their persons, their honour, their family rights, their religious conviction and practices, and their manners and customs. They shall at all times be humanely treated, and shall be protected against all acts of violence ..."

There is no guarantee of private property as in the HR, but according to Art. 53 GC IV, the

> "... destruction of real or personal property ... is prohibited, except where such destruction is rendered absolutely necessary by military operations."

This is a very narrow permission for destructions which does not cover demolitions as practiced by Israel. It will be discussed below whether other aspects of the law of occupation could nevertheless justify such practices.

GC IV adds specific duties concerning particular aspects of the wellbeing of the population:
– education (Art. 50),
– health services (Art. 56),
– provision of food and medical supplies (basic needs, Art. 55).

In parallel to these norms of international humanitarian law, human rights law applies and guarantees a number of relevant rights to the members of the population of occupied territories. These are in particular:

---

14   Bothe, *loc.cit.* note 1, MN 8 and 33.
15   This provision is not limited to occupied territories.

HUMANITARIAN ASSISTANCE IN OCCUPIED TERRITORIES

- the right to liberty and security of person (Art. 9 ICCPR),
- freedom from interference with privacy, family or home (Art. 17 ICCPR),
- protection of the family (Art. 23 ICCPR, Art. 10 ICESCR),
- right to an adequate standard of living (Art. 11 ICESCR), "including food, clothing and housing",
- right to health (Art. 12 ICESCR),
- right to education (Art. 13 ICESCR).

4 Rules Relating to Relief Actions

Art. 43 HR does not specify the means through which the occupying power would fulfil its general duty to provide for the wellbeing of the population. If it is unable to do so with its own resources, relief actions undertaken by third actors may be a way. Thus, the general duty of the Occupying Power enshrined in the customary law of belligerent occupation is a basis for duty to accept and facilitate relief. As will be shown, the general duties of the Occupying Power are relevant for a number of important details of humanitarian assistance.

Yet international humanitarian law also contains a number of specific rules concerning relief operations. Art. 59 GC IV is of particular importance for the questions covered by the present opinion, namely a duty of the occupying power to allow and facilitate relief actions:

> "If whole or part of the population of an occupied territory is inadequately supplied, the Occupying Power shall agree to relief schemes on behalf of the said population, and shall facilitate them by all means at its disposal.
>
> Such schemes, which may be undertaken by either by States or by impartial humanitarian organizations such as the International Committee of the Red Cross, shall consist, in particular, of the provision of consignments of foodstuffs, medical supplies and clothing."

Accepting and facilitating relief is a secondary obligation of the Occupying Power. Art. 60 expressly states that such relief actions shall not free the Occupying Power from its primary obligations in relation to the wellbeing of the population, in particular the obligation to ensure the food and medical supplies (Art. 55 GC IV) and the functioning of the health care system (Art. 56 GC IV).

Art. 69 AP I of 1977 adds a few items to the basic needs formulated in Art. 55 GC IV. Relief actions for occupied territories "shall be implemented without delay".

As Israel has not ratified AP I, the latter provision is not binding as a matter of treaty law, but it may be considered as constituting customary law, which *ipso facto* applies to all States. In order to create more certainty as to which particular rules constitute customary law, the ICRC has published an expert study restating the relevant rules of customary humanitarian law, including the necessary references of State practice,[16] which confirms the customary law character of the provisions regarding relief.

The obligation imposed on the occupying power is twofold: an obligation to agree and an obligation to facilitate, the latter going beyond the obligation to agree. As formulated, these obligations are absolute, not subject to any conditions.[17] The only condition clearly implied in the very text of Art. 59 GC IV is that there must be an "agreement". This requirement safeguards the control interest of the occupying power which enables the occupying power to fulfill its responsibilities, already mentioned.

The provision does not specify how this agreement is to be concluded. As a rule, it will first be requested by the organization planning to undertake a relief action. The provision does not provide for any refusal to conclude such an agreement for whatever reason. However, there are few if any absolute duties. Concerning the occupying power's possibility to refuse an agreement, a rule which has been developed in the interpretation of the provision on relief for non-occupied territory (Art. 70 AP I) might be applied as well for relief action destined for occupied territories, namely that the necessary agreement may only be refused for valid reasons, not for arbitrary or capricious ones. This seems to be a reasonable interpretation although the powers of control which the occupying power possesses are of a nature different from that of territorial control possessed by a State on its own territory, as already explained above. Regarding Art. 70 AP I, this interpretation is firmly established by the negotiating history.[18]

---

16   ICRC/J.-M. Henckaerts/L. Doswald-Beck, Customary International Humanitarian Law, Cambridge 2005; on the duty to facilitate relief actions: vol. 1, p. 194.

17   J. Pictet (dir. publ.), Les Conventions de Genève du 12 août 1949. Commentaire, vol. IV, Geneva 1956, p. 344.

18   M. Bothe, in M. Bothe/K.J. Partsch/W.A. Solf, New Rules for Victims of Armed Conflicts. Commentary on the Two Protocols Additional to the Geneva Conventions of 1949, 2nd ed. Leiden/Boston 2013, p. 485.

This raises the question what is a valid and what an arbitrary reason. Details concerning this problem and the ensuing practical questions will be addressed below.

In addition to the specific provisions of international humanitarian law relating to relief, the provisions of human rights law mentioned above are also relevant for relief actions. In particular the provisions of the ICESCR imply a positive duty of the occupying power to take measures for the purpose of enabling the inhabitants of the occupied territory to enjoy the respective rights, and to do so also through international cooperation (Art. 2 ICESCR). An appropriate form of this cooperation is allowing and facilitating relief actions. This legal situation must be taken into account in the determination of what constitutes an arbitrary withholding of consent.

5 The Application of the General Rules of the Law of Occupation to Practices Impeding Relief

5.1 *Withholding Consent*

Arbitrary withholding consent is a contextual question. This opinion tries to highlight certain important examples of arbitrary refusals.

Inter alia, withholding consent is arbitrary if it, or the purpose behind it, violates other obligations of the occupying power.

Humanitarian projects which suffer from refusals often tend to establish some kind of building or fixed installation (schools, health centers, water works). The reasons for refusal are often said to be based on the necessity of enforcing the law, namely applicable building law. At a first glance, the enforcement of building laws can be considered as being derived from the duty of the occupying power to ensure public order and life (Art. 43 HR). But as a matter of legal logic, the occupying power cannot be allowed to enforce building laws if these building laws themselves contravene the international law of occupation. There is indeed a basic flaw in the planning law relating to Area C. It is applied, and the pre-existing law has been amended in a way which makes any meaningful and reasonable land use planning, including the necessary participation of the Palestinian population in the planning process, impossible.[19] Land use planning which allows building exclusively works for the benefit of

---

19   See UN Office for the Coordination of Humanitarian Affairs: Restricting Space: The Planning Regime Applied by Israel in Area C of the West Bank, December 2009; Human Rights Committee, International Covenant on Civil and Political Rights, Concluding observations on the fourth periodic report of Israel, Doc. CCPR/C/ISR/CO/4, 21 Nov. 2014, para. 9; T. Boutruche/M. Sassòli, Expert Opinion on International Humanitarian Law Requiring the Occupying Power to Transfer Back Planning Authority to Protected Persons

558   PART 7: OCCUPATION

the settlements.[20] It is therefore discriminatory. It makes it impossible for Palestinian landowners to make a reasonable use of their real property. The *de facto* prevention of legitimate uses of real property violates the guarantee of private property enshrined in Art. 46 HR. Enforcement of such law is a violation of the international law of occupation. Withholding consent as a means to enforce these unlawful building laws is therefore "arbitrary".

Denying consent for building schools or medical facilities where these are needed by the population will also be a violation of the rights to health and education (Art. 12 and 13 ICESCR). For this reason too, such refusal is arbitrary in the sense just described.

The real reason for refusing consent to humanitarian relief operations is often designed to implement an overall land use concept for Area C which tries to concentrate the Palestinian population in certain urban areas and leave or create free space for Israeli settlements and military activities. This is an unlawful purpose, as it furthers the settlement policy which violates Art. 49 GC IV, prevents the freedom of movement of the Palestinian population and violates the Palestinian right to self-determination because it creates (and is meant to create) conditions which jeopardize the viability of the Palestinian State.[21] Refusal of consent based on these considerations is "arbitrary".

As the refusal of consent also means a denial, or at least a restriction, of human rights, refusal is subject to the principles of necessity and proportionality, which mark a general limit of all limitations of human rights. A refusal violating the principles of necessity and proportionality is therefore "arbitrary".

5.2   *Demolitions*

The only provision allowing the destruction of property in occupied territories is Art. 53 GC IV quoted above. Its conditions are by no means fulfilled in the cases of demolitions under review in the present context. As far as can been seen, Israel does not rely on Art. 53 or a corresponding provision of customary law.

Instead, it is argued that house demolitions are measure to enforce building laws and as such justified by Art. 43 HR. Demolitions of unlawfully erected buildings were lawful under the law in force in the occupied territory when the occupation began, in this case Jordanian law. However, that enforcement measure is unlawful because, as already stated in relation to withholding of

---

      Regarding Area C of the West Bank, pp. 24 et seq., available at http://rhr.org.il/heb/wp-content/uploads/62394311-Expert-Opinion--FINAL-1-February-2011.pdf. (last visited 4 June 2015).

20   Human Rights Committee, *loc.cit.* note 18, para. 9.

21   See ICJ, *Construction of a Wall, loc.cit.* note 6, in particular para. 122.

consent, the building law in question itself constitutes a violation of the law of occupation. This law, as applied and modified by the Israeli administration, makes it virtually impossible for a Palestinian to erect any new building in Area C. This is a violation of the right to the protection of private property (Art. 46 HR) and of fundamental social rights. The enforcement of a law which violates international law cannot be internationally lawful.

These measures at least constitute a limitation of the right to the respect of property enshrined in Art. 46 HR. As any limitation of fundamental rights, such limitation is itself limited by the rule of necessity and proportionality. Proportionality requires a balancing of the pros and cons of a measure. In this context, the needs of the population, its social rights (rights to an appropriate standard of ling, to health and to education) put a heavy weight on the scales on the side of the cons.

Any form of "confiscation" is prohibited by Art. 46 HR.

The demolitions are also a violation of Art. 17 ICCPR (freedom from arbitrary or unlawful interference with one's home). As this interference is unlawful under the law of armed conflict which primes any otherwise applicable local law, it must also be considered as "unlawful" in the meaning of Art. 17 para. 1 ICCPR.[22]

5.3   *Relief Actions without Consent*

Where consent is lawfully withheld, the consequences for the persons or institutions undertaking relief actions differ depending on the legal status of the relief organization. If the action is undertaken by a State or by an intergovernmental organization, undertaking a relief action without (lawfully withheld) consent is an internationally wrongful act. But if the operation is undertaken by an entity which is not acting on behalf of a State or an intergovernmental organization, conducting the operation does not constitute an internationally wrongful act as there is no subject of international law to which the activity in question can be imputed. But it is a risky act as it is internationally lawful if the occupying power prevents such activity. The measures preventing such unauthorized relief are governed by the law of the occupying power.

As most relief actions are financed or otherwise sponsored by States or intergovernmental organizations, it has to be asked whether it is also an internationally wrongful act for a State or intergovernmental organization to finance or otherwise promote relief actions undertaken by non-governmental

---

22   See already Human Rights Committee, International Covenant on Civil and Political Rights, Concluding observations on the second periodic report of Israel, 5 August 2003, Doc. CCPR/CO/78/ISR, para. 16.

organization without the (lawfully withheld) consent of the occupying power. As a matter of legal logic, a State should not be entitled to finance or promote activities which, if undertaken by the State itself, would be unlawful.

In this connection, it must be emphasized that relief actions undertaken without consent are not completely unprotected. Measures taken by the occupying power to prevent or stop such operations have to respect certain limits which will be discussed below.

If consent is unlawfully withheld, the situation is different. If a relief operation undertaken by a State or intergovernmental organization is conducted in the absence of a consent which had to be granted, a first question to be considered is whether conducting such operation constitutes a lawful countermeasure against the illegal act of withholding consent (Art. 22, 49 *et seq.* ILC Articles on the Responsibility of States – ARS). Yet according to Art. 49 (1) ARS, a countermeasure may only be taken "in order to induce (the State having committed an internationally wrongful act) to comply with its obligations ..." This possibility will be discussed in section 6 below. First, the legal status of a relief operation has to be considered even where it does not constitute a "countermeasure" in the sense described.

If the relief operation is undertaken by a non-governmental actor, the justification as countermeasure is not possible anyway. But if the occupying power takes a measure to prevent the operation, that measure is internationally unlawful despite the fact that the necessary consent had not been granted. For in order to justify the measure, the occupying power would have to rely on an act, namely withholding consent, which itself is unlawful. Under these circumstances, preventing the operation would be equivalent to enforcing an illegal act, which is unlawful. No right can be derived from an illegal act. Such preventive measure would at least constitute an abuse of rights. The measure would constitute the exercise of a right given for a legitimate purpose for a purpose which is not legitimate. This is an arbitrary and therefore "abusive exercise" of the right.[23] The old Roman law adage has become a general principle of law: *nemo auditur allegans turpitudinem suam* (no one is heard relying on his own turpitude). This principle is well established in international arbitral jurisprudence.[24]

Although non-governmental organizations undertaking relief actions are not the direct addressees of these international legal rules, they are the

---

23   A. Kiss, 'Abuse of Rights', MN 6 and 12, MPEPIL (note 1).

24   C. Binder/C. Schreuer, 'Unjust Enrichment', paras. 36 and 37, MPEPIL (note 1). For the application of the principle in the field of human rights, see C. Tomuschat, 'International Covenant on Civil and Political Rights (1966)', para. 25, MPEPIL (note 1).

HUMANITARIAN ASSISTANCE IN OCCUPIED TERRITORIES

beneficiaries thereof. In particular, the States where such organizations are incorporated or which otherwise sponsor such relief actions, and in addition all States which are entitled and obliged to ensure respect for the Geneva Conventions[25] may claim on their behalf and for their benefit that the occupying power respect these rules.

In addition, it must be taken into account that refusing a consent which the State is under an obligation to grant amounts to an unjustified denial of certain human rights, as explained above. Consequently, preventing a relief operation which the State was under an obligation to allow and facilitate also constitutes such a denial.

5.4   *Treatment of Relief Workers*

The provisions of GC IV concerning relief are formulated in a way which relates to the consignment of goods only. But relief in this sense is not limited to such consignments, as is indicated by the words "in particular" in Art. 59 (2) GC IV. It has become a widespread practice, which amounts to the formation of a rule of customary international law, that relief operations are conducted by relief personnel, be it foreign or local. In the case of foreign relief operations, a duty of admission and working permission is reasonably implied in the duty to facilitate relief. The same duty also comprises a right to employ local personnel. This also applies to the protection of both foreign and local relief personnel. As to foreign relief personnel,[26] this rule is recognized and concretized by Art. 71 AP I, which contains details balancing the interests of relief operations on the one hand and the interests of the occupying power (or of the State where the relief operation takes place) on the other. This rule is not binding on Israel as a matter of treaty law. But the rule can be considered as customary law[27] and also as a reasonable interpretation of Art. 59 GC IV.

The rule that it is essential for relief operations to be operated or accompanied by relief personnel has also been formulated by the UN General Assembly:[28]

> "The General Assembly ...
> Calls upon all governments and parties in complex humanitarian emergencies, in particular in armed conflict and post-conflict situations,

---

25   See below 6.2.

26   Although the text of the provision does not expressly distinguish between foreign and local personnel, the focus of its content is on foreign personnel.

27   ICRC/Henckaerts/Doswald-Beck, *op.cit.* note 15, p. 200 *et seq.*

28   Resolution 58/114, 17 Dec. 2003, OP 10, emphasis by the author.

in countries where humanitarian personnel are operating, in conformity with the relevant provisions in international law and national laws, to cooperate fully with the United Nations and other humanitarian agencies and organizations to ensure *the safe and unhindered access of humanitarian personnel as well as supplies and equipment* in order to *allow them to perform efficiently their task* of assisting the affected civilian population ..."

This means in particular: Admission formalities including visa may be required. But they must be handled in a way which does not compromise the viability of relief actions. This is implied in the duty to "facilitate" relief schemes (Art. 59 GC IV). In particular, visa requests must be handled swiftly. Visa may not be denied on arbitrary grounds.[29] Abusive controls at entry and checkpoints are prohibited.

According to Art. 71 AP I and the corresponding rule of customary law, relief personnel must be "respect and protected". This means, on the one hand, that such personnel must not be attacked or otherwise harassed or intimidated. On the other hand, it also means that the occupying power must allow them to fulfil their tasks and may not unnecessarily prevent them from discharging their functions.[30] This includes freedom of movement.[31] Only in cases of "imperative military necessity" may their movement be temporarily restricted. The mission of relief workers may, however, be terminated if they engage in activities outside their humanitarian mandate. The protection of local personnel is at least implied in the occupying power's duty to facilitate the operation.

Certain general rules also have to be respected in relation to relief personnel. They may not be attacked as they are civilians. This applies also in case of unauthorized relief operations or in the case of an operation whose mandate was terminated.

Personnel belonging to intergovernmental organizations may also enjoy immunities if they fall into the relevant categories of applicable treaties.[32]

---

29   ICRC/Henckaerts/Doswald-Beck, *op.cit.* note 15, p. 202.

30   Bothe, in Bothe/Partsch/Solf, *op.cit.* note 17, p. 490.

31   ICRC/Henckaerts/Doswald-Beck, *op.cit.* note 15, p. 200.

32   In particular the Convention on the Privileges and Immunities of the United Nations, 13 Feb.1946, to which Israel is a party. Israel is not a party to the Convention on the Privileges and Immunities of Specialized Agencies, 21 Nov. 1947, nor to the Convention on the Safety of United Nations and Associated Personnel, 9 Dec. 1994. This question cannot be dealt with in detail in the framework of the present Opinion.

HUMANITARIAN ASSISTANCE IN OCCUPIED TERRITORIES

Human rights law also applies relating to the treatment of relief workers by the occupying power. This applies to both foreign and local personnel. It is of particular relevance for the question of detention. Art. 9 and 10 ICCPR have to be observed. "Arbitrary" arrest and detention are prohibited, subject to a derogation according to Art. 4 ICCPR.[33] The question of "arbitrariness" may be answered differently where a relief action takes place without consent, but any measure taken against personnel of unauthorized relief operations must respect the principles of necessity and proportionality which govern any limitation of human rights.

5.5   *Request of Consent and Forms Thereof*

According to Art. 59 GC IV, the duty to grant consent relates to "relief schemes". This may include, as the case may be, individual consignment or operations. But the term "schemes" is broader than that. It also covers a broader plan of relief operations which can be submitted to the occupying power, requesting the consent thereto. This includes the possibility that several relief organizations together submit such a scheme. A good example of such a "scheme" is the "Strategic Response Plan" published by UNOCHA, and shared with the competent authorities of the occupying power, which contains an assessment of relief needs, a systematic concept of action to be taken to respond to those needs and a list of concrete projects, including information on the organizations undertaking them.[34] As a matter of principle, it is not, at least not necessarily, a violation of the occupying power's duty to facilitate a relief scheme if it asks for more details concerning the plan. Whether or not a refusal is arbitrary or not if these details are not given depends on the circumstances of the situation. But given the degree of detail given in the said project list, it would be difficult for the occupying power to argue that this is an insufficient basis for a decision to accept the relief projects so listed. Furthermore, the occupying power must exercise restraint in asking for information which the relief organization may or even must legitimately withhold to safeguard fundamental rights of the beneficiaries. Asking for such information may amount to an unlawful impediment of humanitarian relief actions.

The form of consent is not specified in GC IV nor in AP I. Therefore, it can be express (which is of course the preferred form), but also implicit. As in any case of declarations construed by implication, this involves questions of

---

33   On the question of the state of emergency, see Human Rights Committee, *loc.cit.* note 18, para. 10.

34   http://www.ochaopt.org/documents/srp_2015.pdf. The list is included in the document http://fts.unocha.org/reports/daily/ocha_R3_A1067__1_April_2015_(03_03).pdf.

interpretation concerning the relevant behaviour, including the interpretation of silence. The application of the old Roman law adage *"qui tacet consentire videtur, si loqui potuit ac debuit"* (who is silent appears to consent if he could have and should have spoken) is uncertain. Yet there are situation where silence must be interpreted in good faith as consent. A special circumstance supporting such conclusion in the present case is the fact that the proposal comes from a United Nations agency. All States are under a general duty to cooperate with the United Nations (Art. 2 nos. 2 and 5 of the Charter). It would be contrary to this general obligation if a State just remained silent although it had objections against a proposal submitted to it in the exercise of the functions of the UN in conformity with the Charter.

5.6 *Cooperation with the Occupying Power*

The whole situation of relief operations, and in particular the consent requirement, implies that there must be some intercourse between the organizations providing relief and the occupying power. Relief operations are not subversive or clandestine actions. In particular, the obligation to agree does not mean that consent must be given without questions being asked. There may be negotiations between the organizations providing relief and the occupying power. Such negotiations must be conducted in good faith by both sides. Whether and to what extent one or the other side may make concessions on questions of principle is first of all a question of evaluating chances of success in these negotiations. It is not the task of the present legal opinion to speculate about relevant circumstances in this context.

Yet there is also the legal question whether such concessions may mean foregoing a legal position which an organization has so far taken by refusing to accept certain Israeli practices as legal. In this respect, too, a distinction must be made between positions taken or declaration made by States or intergovernmental organizations on the one hand and attitudes of non-governmental organizations, on the other. Only subjects of international law (i.e. States or intergovernmental organizations) are legally empowered to modify, through their behaviour, an international legal relationship. It is only them whose attitudes could possibly be understood as amounting to acquiescence and to recognizing the legality of certain Israeli practices and thus prevent the negotiating party from treating these practices as illegal in the future.

However, the fact alone that negotiations are conducted and that some concessions are made in these negotiations cannot be understood as such recognition. Such recognition should not be assumed easily. The purpose of such negotiations or even cooperation is to facilitate humanitarian relief. It would be contrary to the purpose and spirit of the treaty provisions designed to promote relief operations if the intercourse between the giving organizations and the receiving State were construed as legal impediments for such relief because it would be interpreted as involving a recognition which the negotiating party is unwilling or unable to give. The application of humanitarian rules shall not affect any status questions. This is a principle of humanitarian law which is best expressed in the final paragraph of Art. 3 common to the GC:

> "The application of the preceding provisions shall not affect the legal status of the Parties to the conflict."

The same rule underlies Art. 70(1) 2nd sentence:

> "Offers of such relief shall not be regarded as interference in the armed conflict ..."

The holding of the ICJ in the *Namibia* case points in the same direction: An obligation not to recognize as lawful an unlawful situation

> "should not result in depriving the people of Namibia of any advantages derived from international cooperation."[35]

The conclusion to be drawn is clear: humanitarian action in favor of the victims of armed conflict or belligerent occupation may not be hindered by status considerations, in particular by the fear that such action could be (mis)understood as amounting to a recognition of, or acquiescence with, an unlawful act or situation.

In the case of negotiations between non-governmental organizations and the occupying power, there is no such question of recognition having international legal effects.

6   The Position of Third States

Regarding the possible role of third States in respect of Israeli practices preventing or restraining relief, two questions have to be distinguished:

---

35   ICJ, *Legal Consequences for States of the Continued Presence of South Africa in Namibia (South West Africa)*, Advisory Opinion of 20 June 1971, para. 125.

566 PART 7: OCCUPATION

– first, States may be affected because Israeli measures, in particular demolitions, affect their property or, in the case of measures against relief workers, their nationals;
– second, the general role of third States, i.e. States not parties to a conflict, in ensuring respect for international humanitarian law.

6.1 States Affected in Their Individual Rights

Where objects, in particular buildings, are unlawfully demolished, which are the property of a State having provided the construction as humanitarian assistance, or the property of its nationals, this demolition constitutes an internationally wrongful act committed by Israel vis-à-vis the State in question and entails the corresponding consequences.

If relief workers are treated in a way incompatible with the rules explained above, this constitutes an internationally wrongful act committed by the Occupying Power against the State of which the relief workers are nationals.

In both cases, the general rules on the consequences of internationally wrongful acts apply.

6.2 Ensuring Compliance with International Humanitarian Law

In its Advisory Opinion concerning the Construction of a Wall in the Occupied Palestinian Territory, the ICJ clearly formulated the basic principles which have to guide the action by third States to ensure and promote compliance by Israel with the basic legal rules governing the situation of occupation, including the rules on access for humanitarian relief (Reply D to the question put by the General Assembly):

> "All States are under an obligation not to recognize the illegal situation resulting from the construction of the wall and not to render aid or assistance in maintaining the situation created by such construction; all States parties to the Fourth Geneva Convention relative to the Protection of Civilian Persons in Time of War of 12 August 1949 have in addition the obligation, while respecting the United Nations Charter and international law, to ensure compliance by Israel with international humanitarian law as embodied in that Convention."

According to the Court, the basis for these obligations of *all* States, i.e. States which are not parties to the Palestinian conflict, is twofold:

1. The majority of the relevant norms create obligations *erga omnes*.
2. Art. 1 common to the Geneva Conventions enjoins all Sates to respect and to ensure respect for the Conventions.

As practically all States are parties to the Geneva Conventions, the scope of application of the two principles is practically equal.

In its opinion, the Court does not elaborate on the question what measures States could take in order to fulfill this obligation. It only says that they must respect the Charter and international law. This excludes at least the use of force. But positively speaking, what kind of measures are to be envisaged? On an abstract level, the measures to be envisaged are those which have the potential of inducing Israel (and where necessary the Palestinian Authority) to comply with the applicable rules. The following lines are a kind of catalogue of such measures which States must consider in fulfilling their duty to ensure respect of the Geneva Conventions, in particular by reacting against the establishment of unlawful impediments for humanitarian relief:[36]

- Political dialogue,
- Public statements,
- Non-public demarches,
- Unilateral restriction, countermeasures,
- Conditionality of trade and assistance
- Evocation of State responsibility,
- International dispute settlements,
- International cooperation.

Political dialogue: In the reality of the international system, both development and application of international law are determined by a political discourse between relevant actors, and only to a limited extent on high handed enforcement. This is the basis of the functioning of the UN system. A responsible use of this discourse is necessary. The duty to ensure the respect of the Conventions implies a duty to use the potential of such discourse. Especially those States which, for historic or political reasons, have the chance of being listened to by parties to a conflict are called upon to use this opportunity, be it bilaterally or in appropriate fora.

The discourse will not always take the form of a dialogue. Some other forms are described below.

Public statements: Political dialogue, i.e. a discourse between parties listening and talking to each other, is not always possible. The conflict in and around Palestine frequently is an example of this phenomenon. In such situation, violations of IHL must trigger public statements by third States. It is a violation of the said duty to ensure respect to remain silent in front of significant breaches

---

36   The list is to a certain extent inspired by the European Union Guidelines on promoting compliance with international humanitarian law (IHL), OJEU 2005/C 327/04.

of the Conventions. This is an obligation which is honored in practice by many States, perhaps not by enough States.

Non-public demarches: A verbal reaction to violations must not necessarily be public. There are situations where non public demarches may be more effective. Public demarches may stiffen the reaction by the addressee, which non public demarches will not or rarely do. But due to a certain lack of transparency which is necessarily involved in this instrument to ensure compliance, its effectiveness is somewhat speculative.

Unilateral restrictions, countermeasures: Deprivation of certain advantages is a classical reaction to violations of the law, in modern terminology "countermeasures". Such measures include restraints on financial transactions performed by the target State or by persons acting for the target State, travel restrictions for such persons, import or export restrictions. Such restrictions do not pose legal questions where the target State or person has no legal claim to the advantage it/he or she is deprived of (retorsion in traditional terminology). Where there is a legal entitlement to that advantage, the countermeasure constitutes the violation of an international obligation unless rendered lawful by the relevant rules of the law of State responsibility. Accordingly, countermeasures may only be taken by the injured State under the conditions set out in Arts. 49 et seq. ILC ARS. Common Art. 1 of the GC does not exempt third States wishing to react to violations of the GC from this limitation. This is also implied in the holding of the ICJ, quoted above, that measures taken by States pursuant to Art. 1 common to the GC must respect international law.

Thus, countermeasures involving the non-performance of an obligation binding the State taking the measure are lawful only in the case of *erga omnes* obligations in the sense of Art. 48 para. 1 ARS being violated. They are limited to measures defined in Art. 48 para. 2. Generally speaking, the GC contain *erga omnes* obligations. Thus, this type of counter-measure taken by third States is as a matter of principle lawful.

Conditionality of trade and assistance: A related form of measures reacting to, or trying to prevent, IHL violations is the conditionality of trade or assistance: A particular item may not be traded if it can be anticipated that it will/might be used for IHL violations. A certain aid is only granted if it is associated with measures taken to ensure respect of IHL. This is of particular relevance for arms exports or military aid, but not limited to it.

As to arms exports, an important new treaty prescribing this type of conditionality is the Arms Trade Treaty of 2 April 2013. Its Art. 6 para. 3 reads:

> "A State shall not authorize any transfer of conventional arms ... , if it has knowledge at the time of authorization that the arms ... would be used in the commission of genocide, crimes against humanity, grave breaches of

the Geneva Conventions of 1949, attacks directed against civilian objects or civilians protected as such, or other war crimes as defined by international agreements to which it is a Party."

A similar principle is formulated by the EU in the Council Common Position 2008/944/CSFP of 8 December 2008 defining common rules governing control of exports of military technology and equipment. The Common Position establishes eight criteria for export controls, among them

> "Criterion Six: Behaviour of the buyer country with regard to the international community, as regards in particular its ... respect for international law.
> Member States shall take into account, *inter alia*, the record of the buyer country with regard to:
> ...
> (b) its compliance with ... international humanitarian law."

Evocation of State responsibility: State responsibility may be invoked, as a matter of principle, by the injured State. It may be invoked by a State which is not injured only in the case of the violation of an *erga omnes* obligation, and only as regards particular consequences of the wrongful act. In the case of a violation of the law of armed conflict, the injured State is as a rule the party to the conflict to the detriment of which that violation is committed. This means that the claim of third States is limited to the consequences of the unlawful act which are enumerated in Art. 48 para. 2 ARS: cessation of the illegal acts, assurances and guarantees of non-repetition and reparation in favor of the injured State and/or the beneficiaries of the obligation breached. Accordingly, all States have the right to demand compensation for victims of violations which occurred in the OPT, for instance persons whose houses have unlawfully been destroyed or who have been unlawfully evicted from their land. By virtue of common Art. 1 GC, there is an obligation to exercise this right.

International dispute settlement, institutions: The examples of possible measures to be taken by third States suffice to show that there is a potential for controversy between third States and the occupying power. What institutions can be used to solve these controversies? The usual procedure used in international practice, namely negotiations, is of course the first option. There are other voluntary procedures which may be used.

Israel has not recognized the obligatory jurisdiction of the ICJ under the optional clause of Art. 36 ICJ Statute. Its *ad hoc* acceptance of the ICJ in a concrete case is highly improbable. If there can be a judicial settlement of a dispute between Israel and a third State, resort to arbitration would probably be a solution, if any, because this can be tailor made for the interests which parties to the litigation would like to protect and preserve.

Fact-finding or inquiry is an established element of international dispute settlement. As Israel is not a party to AP I, the obligatory competence of the International Humanitarian Fact-finding Commission established pursuant to Art. 90 AP I does not apply. But its jurisdiction can be recognized *ad hoc* by any party to a conflict, and its rules provide for sufficient flexibility to design a procedure fitting the interests of all parties.

Inquiry is also a dispute settlement procedure provided for by the GC (Arts. 132 GC III, 149 GC IV). But the inquiry commission has to be established in each particular case, which is the disadvantage of this procedure in comparison with Art. 90 AP I, where there is a commission already in existence.

International cooperation: Various procedures have been shown which have the potential to induce parties to a conflict, in particular an occupying power or a detaining power, to comply with IHL. These procedures or tools are options for each specific "third" State. But they will be more effective if they are not just used by one State alone, but by many States together. This is the case for international cooperation in devising or using the tools described.

Conclusion: There is a great variety of measures which third States can take in order to induce the Occupying Power to comply with international humanitarian law, including the law relating to humanitarian assistance which is the object of the present expert opinion. Some of these tools to ensure compliance with IHL are formal procedures, others are informal. What matters is the appropriate mix of their use. Their effectiveness deserves to be made the object of further research. Their use, although – as has been shown – to a large extent obligatory, still depends on political will.

7 Conclusion

International law provides a solid basis for humanitarian assistance. The core of the legal issues is the general obligation of the Occupying Power to provide for the wellbeing of the population of the occupied territory. This rule is also the rationale for the basic obligation of the Occupying Power to accept and facilitate relief operations. Admittedly, the Occupying power has security interests which it may safeguard by appropriate measures. But it may not do so in a way which compromises the said basic duty to accept and facilitate relief actions. Doubts about the legal situation must be solved taking this fundamental principle into account. Third States have various possibilities to induce the Occupying Power to comply with its obligations – which is an important humanitarian asset.

PART 8

Other Issues Concerning the Law of Armed Conflict

∵

29

Neutrality in Naval Warfare

What is Left of Traditional International Law?

1   Introduction: The Basic Question

Traditionally, the sea is an important theatre of war and it has remained so, albeit to a limited extent, in the conflicts which have taken place after World War II.[1] The major case of a naval war was the Falklands/Malvinas conflict. Naval operations were important during the Gulf War between Iraq and Iran; they were so to a lesser extent during the recent Gulf War. Naval warfare also took place during the conflicts between Israel and Egypt, India and Pakistan and in Vietnam. It is obvious that naval war operations affect the navigational activities of third States. But these activities may in many respects also have an impact on the position of the belligerent powers. Over the centuries, international rules regarding the respective rights and duties of neutrals and belligerents have developed, which strike a difficult balance between the interests of both sides.[2] The basic rationale underlying this part of the law can be reduced to two basic principles: the neutral State should not be impaired in its normal situation; on the other hand, it should not tip the balance in favour of one of the belligerents. From these basic principles, a number of concrete rules are derived which form part of customary international law, but are in part also codified by international treaties.[3]

There are certain limitations on the sojourn of warships of the belligerent States in neutral waters. On the other hand, belligerent States have the right to prevent the transportation of goods relevant to the enemy war effort by neutral

---

1   For a concise summary on naval warfare operations which have taken place during conflicts after World War II, see N. Ronzitti, *The Crisis of Traditional Law Regulating International Armed Conflicts at Sea and the Need for its Revision,* in N. Ronzitti, ed., The Law of Naval Warfare 1, 4 *et seq.* (1988).

2   R.L. Bindschedler, *Neutrality, Concept and General Rules,* in R. Bernhardt, ed., 4 Encyclopaedia of Public International Law 9 *et seq.*; Y. Dinsteain, *Neutrality in Sea Warfare,* in Bernhardt, ed., *ibid.,* at 19 *et seq.*; E. Castrén, The Present Law of War and Neutrality 241 *et seq.* (1954).

3   Dinstein, loc. cit. n. 2, at 19 *et seq.*; see also N. Ronzitti, in ASIL Proc. 604 (1988). The most important relevant Treaties are the 1907 Hague Convention XI Relative to Certain Restrictions with Regard to the Exercise of the Right of Capture in Naval War and Convention XIII Concerning the Rights and Duties of Neutral Powers in Naval War.

© KONINKLIJKE BRILL NV, LEIDEN, 2021 | DOI:10.1163/9789004380592_031

574   PART 8: OTHER ISSUES

ships (contraband). They have thus a right to visit and search neutral merchant
ships and may, if contraband is carries, seize ship and cargo through a prize
procedure. A specific means of interdicting intercourse between the enemy
and the outside world, which affects both enemy and neutral shipping, is the
blockade.

In contradistinction to the rules of land warfare, there has been no update
of neutrality law since the Hague Conference of 1907. It is thus necessary and
legitimate to ask what the rules of neutrality in naval warfare have become
since. There are three particular reasons for asking this question. The first one
concerns the basic status of neutrality, what can be called the double dichotomy. Under traditional international law, there is a dichotomy between war
and peace and between neutrality and belligerency. This double dichotomy
has come under pressure in State practice for the last five decades at least.[4] The
second reason for asking the question is the effect of the UN Charter on the law
of neutrality.[5] Has the UN Charter in any way superseded the tradition law of
neutrality? Have the rules of neutrality been modified by those on the legality
of the use of force? The third reason is that specific practices have developed in
the field of naval warfare and new technological options have come up which
may or may not have modified the traditional law of naval warfare.[6] It has to
be asked whether the concept of blockade is still valid. New concepts have
evolved, such as 'quarantine', 'interdiction', 'exclusion zone'. Modern technology has developed and caused new problems, in particular through the development of long-range means of detection and the effect of modern weapons
and attacks. The developments of modern warfare may also have an impact on
traditional notions of permissible (military) targets.

2   **The Problem of the Double Dichotomy: War and Peace – Neutrality
        and Belligerency**

There has been a long debate in doctrine and practice on the question whether an intermediate status exists between neutrality and belligerency. During
World War II, certain States described their position as one of non-belligerency,[7]
which meant that they supported one of the belligerents, probably in violation

---

4   Bindschedler, loc. cit. n. 2.
5   Bindschedler, *ibid.,* at 13; Castrén, op. cit. n. 2, at 433, *et seq.*
6   Y. Dinstein, Sea Warfare, in Bernhardt, ed., loc. cit. n. 2, at 201 *et seq.*; Ronzitti, loc. cit. n. 1, at
    10; Y. Dinstein, in ASIL Proc. 607 (1988).
7   Bindschedler, loc. cit. n. 2, at 13; Castrén, op. cit. n. 2, at 251, *et seq.*

of the laws on neutrality, but did not want to become parties to the ongoing armed conflict. A closer analysis shows that the question of non-participation in an armed conflict which is not neutrality *stricto sensu* arises in two different contexts.

Firstly, the question of the legal status of non-participation in an armed conflict relates to the dichotomy of war and peace. The essential question in this respect is the definition of the scope of application of the law of war, the *ius in bello, ratione materiae*. Does the law of war apply only in case of a formal state of war, or also in case of an armed conflict of an international character, where for one reason or another, a formal state of war does not exist? In a development of several decades, the notion of armed conflict has to a great extent replaced that of war in order to define situations where the law of war applies.[8] The notion of armed conflict is expressly used by the Geneva Conventions of 1949 and Protocol I Additional thereto of 1977, in order to define their scope of application. But it is submitted that these provisions of the Geneva Conventions do not constitute exceptions, but rather reflect a rule which has developed under customary international law, at least as far as the conduct of hostilities and the protection of war victims is concerned.

Whether this development has also affected the law of neutrality is, however, doubtful. Important authors still hold the view that the application of the law of neutrality indeed requires the existence of a state of war.[9] In State practice after World War II, there are cases where States protested against certain measures taken by belligerent States against merchant ships of States which were not parties to the conflict on the ground that no formal state of war existed. Consequently, the belligerent did not have the powers of control over neutral shipping as they would have had against neutrals in the case of a formal state of war. That view, however, seems to be too formalistic and does not correspond to the requirements of situations of armed conflict. If there is actual fighting, it seems to be both unrealistic and inappropriate to deny belligerents a power of control over the flow of contraband. It seems that during the Iran-Iraq War, 'neutral' States indeed accepted a power of visit for

---

8 See K.J. Partsch, *Armed Conflict*, in R. Bernhardt, ed., 3 Encyclopaedia of Public International Law 27 (1982); also W. Meng, *War*, in Bernhardt, ed., op. cit. n. 2, at 290 *et seq*. His view is much too restrictive as to the applicability of the 'law of war' in situations where no formal state of war exists.

9 Bindschedler, loc. cit. n. 2, at 10; E. Kussbach, *L'évolution de la notion de neutralité dans les conflits armés actuels*, 17 Military Law and Law of War Review 26 (1979).

the belligerent States and no longer raised the question of the existence of a formal state of war.[10]

The consequences of this controversy for the existence of an intermediate status between belligerency and neutrality are quite clear. If the status of neutrality only exists in the case of a formal state of war, then there must be a different kind of non-party status. These considerations seem to underlie the formula used in Protocol I Additional to the Geneva Conventions, where the State not participating in an armed conflict is described as 'neutral or other State not party to the conflict'.[11] Although these provisions remove any doubt as to the application of certain provisions of the Protocol, there is still considerable uncertainty as to the law governing non-participation in armed conflicts in general. This is a situation which should certainly be remedied in any future revision of the law of neutrality and of naval warfare.

The use of the notion of non-belligerency mentioned above has, however, a different background. It was originally used to describe a situation where a State supported a belligerent party, probably in violation of he law of neutrality, without actually becoming a party to that conflict. This kind of involvement in the armed conflict, however, does not lead, as a matter of law, to a kind of intermediate status between neutrality and belligerency. The rendering of unneutral services is indeed a violation of the law of neutrality and may give rise to an appropriate reaction by the belligerent party which is the victim of that violation, in particular to reprisals or a declaration of war. But such a violation does not by itself lead to the cessation or exclusion of the status of neutrality.[12] That status only ends if and when the 'non-belligerent' State, as a consequence of a reaction by a belligerent State, is drawn into the armed conflict.

This last-mentioned situation raises the more general questions of the effect which acts of violence occurring between a belligerent and a neutral State may have on the latter's neutral status. There may indeed be a number of situations where such acts occur or even must occur.[13] A neutral State must defend its territory where a belligerent uses it for military purposes. Such actions to defend the neutral status may lead to actual fighting. If such fighting is limited to small-scale operations to repel certain intrusions, this does not change the status of a neutral State. Only if such limited fighting degenerates into a

---

10   Bindschedler, loc. cit. n. 2, at 10; Partsch, loc. cit. n. 8, at 27; see also the practice reported by Ronzitti, op. cit. n. 1, at 7 *et seq.*

11   Articles 2(c), 9(2), 19, 31, 39, 64 of Protocol I. *Cf.*, M. Bother, K.J. Partsch, W.A. Solf, eds., New Rules for Victims of Armed Conflicts 106 (1982).

12   Bindschedler, loc. cit. n. 2, at 13.

13   Castrén, op. cit. n. 2, at 259 *et seq.*

larger-scale operation, then the (former) neutral State becomes as a matter of fact a party to the conflict. It may well be that this describes the situation of the United State during certain times of the Iran-Iraq War, but this appears to be highly doubtful.

3   The Law of Neutrality and the Prohibition of the Use of Force

At first glance, it may indeed appear as if the UN Charter excludes the possibility of neutrality. All States must join against an aggressor and assist the victim. Ideally, there are just two sides, that of the aggressor and that of the victim. This system, however, has not worked in this way because of the inability of the Security Council to fulfil its functions.[14] Only recently has it appeared that, quite surprisingly after more than forty years, the system might work as originally conceived. But until now, the more traditional situation has prevailed: there have been armed conflicts with parties and non-parties. Thus, the traditional situation of neutrality has remained unchanged. The rules of neutrality were indeed relied upon and applied in practice. States exercised a right of visit and search and other States acquiesced in it. Prize courts were instituted.[15] Thus, the traditional conflict pattern where a status of neutrality is legally and factually possible continues to exist.[16]

But this does not necessarily mean that the UN Charter and in particular the prohibition of the use of force contained therein has no bearing on the law of neutrality. Indeed the law of neutrality developed at time when resort to war was not prohibited. Thus, measures of coercion permissible under the traditional law of neutrality are not necessarily legal under current conditions. But this question forms part of a more general one, namely that of the relation between the law of war, the *ius in bello* and the prohibition of the use of force, the *ius contra bellum* (the traditional term *ius ad bellum* being really the wrong expression under modern international law).

The rules of the *ius in bello* and the *ius contra bellum* constitute two different levels of legal restraint on violence. The law of war comes into operation where the law of peace has been broken, no matter by whom. The law of war does not know or recognize the distinction between aggressor and victim, it applies in

---

14   Castrén, op. cit. n. 2, at 433, *et seq.* ; Bindschedler, loc. cit. n. 2, at 13.

15   Ronzitti, loc. cit. n. 1, at 7.

16   M. Jenkins, *Air Attacks on Neutral Shipping in the Persian Gulf: Legality of the Iraqi Exclusion Zone and Iranian Reprisals,* 8 Boston College International & Comparative Law Review 517, 525 (1985).

an equal manner to both sides.[17] The laws of war apply independently of any legal justification of a party's participation in a conflict under the *ius contra bellum*. The *ius ad bellum* does not justify any violations of the laws of war. But the reverse is also true. The laws of war do not justify any violations of the *ius contra bellum*. In this sense, no belligerent right exists which would justify an action illegal under the normal rule of the law of peace. An aggression fought by legal means is still an aggression, and that aggression engages the responsibility of the aggressor for the armed action as a whole, even if there is no violation of the laws of war.

It must be stressed in this respect, that the legal yardstick under the *ius contra bellum* indeed is the action as a whole, not the individual act of violence occurring within the framework of an armed conflict. Once an armed conflict has started because aggression has occurred, it is not possible to ask the question, whether there is an armed attack or a situation of self-defence, for each individual shot fired. Within the framework of an armed conflict, the legal yardstick for the individual act of violence is the law of war only, not the *ius contra bellum*. If no armed conflict exists, it is the individual action which needs to be evaluated in the light of the *ius contra bellum*. There exists, thus, a principle of double scrutiny. Violence between States has to be submitted to both the legal yardstick of the *ius contra bellum* and that of the *ius in bello*. Where there is an armed conflict, however, the scrutiny under the *ius contra bellum* applies only to the armed conflict as a whole, not to the individual act of violence. Where there is an individual act of violence in a generally peaceful situation (what is often called an incident), that action has to be evaluated both under the *ius contra bellum* and the *ius in bello* (to the extent that the *ius in bello* is at all applicable in relation to an 'incident').[18]

What are the consequences of this legal situation for the law of neutrality? Where there are acts of coercion under the law of neutrality, the double scrutiny principle must also apply. The admissibility of such acts must be evaluated both under the law of neutrality and under the *ius contra bellum*. In other words, the law of neutrality, as a matter of principle, cannot justify violations of the prohibition of the use of force. But in contradistinction to the relation between belligerents, there exists no overall violent situation between a neutral and a belligerent State. Thus, the double scrutiny principle applies not to the situation as a whole, but to the individual act of violence or coercion.

---

17   Bothe, Partsch, Solf, eds., op. cit. n. 11, at 33; for a more detailed analysis see M. Bothe, *Le droit de la guerre et les Nationa Unies*, in 5 Etudes et travaux de l'institut universitaire des hautes études internationales 163 *et seq.* (1967).

18   On the latter problem, see Bothe, op. cit. n. 17, at 149 *et seq.*

NEUTRALITY IN NAVAL WARFARE

In order to test and illustrate this principle, certain acts of coercion relevant under the law of neutrality may be analysed more closely. The first case in point is the right of search and visit in relation to neutral commercial shipping. If a neutral merchant ship is ordered or even forced to stop in order to facilitate a visit, this does not constitute a use of force against the flag State which would be prohibited under the Charter. Under the definition of aggression, adopted by the General Assembly[19] the attack on the 'marine merchant fleet' is mentioned as an example of aggression thus excluding an attack on an individual merchant ship. The right to visit and search has indeed remained unchallenged in postwar naval conflicts.[20] Whether a use of force against a merchant ship going beyond what is necessary for enforcing a right to visit and search constitutes an 'armed attack' (and thus triggers a right of self-defence) is, however, a difficult question. On the other hand, an attack on a warship certainly constitutes a forbidden attack of the 'sea forces' of a State within the meaning of Article 3(b) of the Declaration on Aggression. If neutral merchant ships are assembled as a convoy and protected by warships, an attack on them might also constitute an attack on the 'marine fleets' within the meaning of the said provision. This would buttress the traditional, but controversial view according to which the right of visit and search does not exist in relation to merchant ships travelling in convoy under the protection of neutral warships.[21] It appears that the United States relied on this rule in organizing the passage of 'neutral' tankers under the protection of United States warships through the Gulf during the Iran-Iraq War.[22]

Another traditional institution of the law of naval warfare is the blockade. A blockade aims to prevent both neutral and enemy shipping from entering or leaving a blockaded port or coast.[23] Interesting in our context is the interdiction of neutral shipping. To the extent that neutral merchant ships are prevented from going to or from the blockaded port, such action is not a violation of the prohibition of the use of force for the reasons just stated. If, however, a neutral warship is stopped, this also constitutes, for the reason just stated, a prohibited attack. There remains, however, the question whether there is an

---

19   GA Res. 3314 (XXIX) of 14 December 1974. See M. Bothe, *Die Erklärung der Generalversammlung der Vereinten Nationen über die Definition der Aggression* (The Declaration of the General Assembly of the United Nations on the Definition of Aggression), 18 GYIL 127 (1975).

20   Ronzitti, loc. cit. n. 1, at 7 *et seq.*

21   On this controversy, see, on the other hand, Dinstein, op. cit. n. 2, at 24 *et seq.,* also R. Stödter, *Convoy*, in Bernhardt, ed., loc. cit. n. 8, at 128 *et seq.*

22   Ronzitti, op. cit. n. 1, at 9.

23   L. Weber, *Blockade*, in R. Bernhardt, ed., op. cit. N. 8, at 47.

independent justification of such action under the *ius contra bellum*. If the blockading State is the aggressor, there is certainly none. But what about the case where the blockading State is acting in self-defence against the blockaded State? That use of force is certainly justified as between the blockading and blockaded State. But the neutral State is not an aggressor. Its legal position is in no way impaired by the fact that another State has committed an aggression. Self-defence justifies the use of force against the aggressor. But it is at least difficult to construe self-defence as also having a kind of collateral effect against non-aggressors. The situation would, however, be legally different if the actions of the warship itself constitutes an act of aggression. But the mere fact that a neutral warship tries to approach a blockaded port does not constitute an act of aggression. A clear justification of a blockade enforced against a neutral warship could only be found where such action is authorized by the UN Security Council. Such authorization would render legal any action taken against neutral warships trying to break a blockade.[24]

The situation just described raises a more general issue, that is, the right of self-defence of the neutral State. The rights and duties of a neural State imply to a certain extent self-defence action. As the neutral State may not allow the use of its territory by a belligerent, it is its duty to defend that territory against intrusion by belligerent forces.[25] In addition, the neutral State also possesses a right of self-defence where its warships are attacked. As is well known, this question played an important role during the Gulf War, although most of the publicity was generated by two erroneous decisions: the decision of the responsible officer of USS *Start* not to attack an aircraft which was in reality attacking the ship, and that of the commander of USS *Vincennes* to attack an airplane which was a civilian one and not attacking the ship. The principle underlying the United States attitude is quite clear. United States ships were demonstrating their right of passage through the Gulf. According to the rule established by the International Court of Justice in the *Corfu Channel Case*, a ship which is (not unexpectedly) attacked while demonstrating and using its right of passage has the right to respond by force.[26] This general statement, however, does not solve the real problem. Self-defence in this connection also presupposes an attack by the other side. Thus, force in self-defence may only be used if it is reasonably certain that there is indeed an attack. As the examples have shown, this requires a very difficult factual judgment in conflict conditions such as those prevailing in the Gulf. Had there been an armed conflict

---

24   See also infra text accompanying note 46.

25   See B.-O. Bryde, *Self-defence,* in Bernhardt, ed., loc. cit. n. 2, at 212 *et seq.*

26   ICJ Reports 1949, at 4, in particular at 30 *et seq.*

NEUTRALITY IN NAVAL WARFARE

between Iran and the United States, the situation would have been much simpler in legal terms. Under the laws of war, shooting down a military aircraft would have been legal, no matter what the mission of that aircraft was at the time of the shooting. The only thing the ship commander had to make sure was whether it was a military aircraft or not. In the framework of an armed conflict, the question of the legality of the individual action under the *ius contra bellum* does not arise. But as pointed out above, the relationship between a neutral and a belligerent is a peaceful one, not a situation of armed conflict.

The legal characterization of actions taken by a neutral State against the armed forces of a belligerent may of course vary according to the legal status of the place where they take place. Military action of the neutral State against warships belonging to a belligerent party may serve as an example. The right of sojourn of warships in neutral waters is limited. They have the right of passage and they have a limited right to stay in neutral ports (so-called 24-hours-rule).[27] If a warship does not leave a neutral port where it is not entitled to remain, the neutral power may take such action as to render the ship incapable of taking part in the war.[28] This may involve the use of force against the ship. It is a use of force authorized under the law of neutrality, and not a use of force prohibited under the *ius contra bellum*, although there may be no attack against the neutral State. But the belligerent ship, in this case, is in an area which is subject to the territorial jurisdiction of the neutral State. The exercise of such jurisdiction against the warship is not an armed attack under international law. Warding off a foreign intrusion by using force is legal even where this intrusion can not be characterized as an armed attack.[29] It is not an illegal use of force under the *ius contra bellum* if a neutral State prevents belligerent warships from using neutral waters in a manner inconsistent with their neutral status.

Having analysed situation where a neutral State may use force, certain situations involving the use of force against the neutral State may also be considered. The main problem in this respect is that of permissible reactions against violations of the law of neutrality committed by the neutral State. If a State violates the law of neutrality by rendering assistance to one of the belligerents (unneutral services), reprisals against that State are certainly permissible. Under traditional international law, it would have been legal to disregard the neutral status completely and to attack the neutral State. Hence, the *ius contra bellum*, excludes a reaction which would be legal under the traditional law of

---

27   Article 12 of the Hague Convention XIII.

28   Article 24 of the Hague Convention XIII.

29   AS to the cases of aerial intrusion, see K. Hailbronner, Der Schutz der Luftgrenzen im Frieden (the Protection of Aerial Boundaries in Peacetime) 13 *et seq.* (1972).

582   PART 8: OTHER ISSUES

neutrality. Even if an unneutral service amounts to an armed attack, which is possible where, for instance, a neutral State lends its territory to one of the belligerents and permits its use as a basis of hostile action, the legality of a response by the use of force, depends on the status of the whole conflict under the *ius contra bellum*. If the belligerent party affected by that unneutral service is acting in self-defence, then it may also react in self-defence against the neutral State. If the affected party, on the other hand, is the aggressor, it does not enjoy a right of self-defence against the State which supports a self-defence action by the victim of aggression.

To sum up, the *ius contra bellum* and the law of neutrality constitute different levels of restraint concerning the use of force. As a practical matter, there are a few cases where the *ius contra bellum* prohibits actions which would be legal under traditional rules of the law of neutrality. To that very limited extent, the modern law relating to the use of force has indeed modified the traditional law of neutrality.

4   Specific Types of Measures in Modern Naval Warfare

4.1   *Naval Blockade*
As already mentioned, blockade means a complete interdiction of all sea traffic to and from a particular harbour or coast. It thus affects neutral and enemy shipping alike. A traditional blockade is the so-called close blockade, which is enforced by ships in a position in the vicinity of the blockade port, but also by aircraft, mines and submarines. In modern times, the notion of long-distance blockade has been introduced. This became controversial because it was doubtful whether it could be an effective bar to access to the blockaded port, effectiveness being an essential element in the legality of a traditional blockade.[30]

The fundamental question in relation to the law of blockade, however, is not that of long-distance blockade, but the question whether the blockade is still a valid legal concept at all. First, Sate practice in relation to blockade makes it doubtful whether it is still used as a means of warfare. Although there have been no formal declarations of blockade since World War II,[31] in a number of cases, access to certain coasts or ports was indeed barred by belligerents.[32] The

---

30   *Cf.,* W.O. Miller, *Law of Naval Warfare,* 62 US Naval War College International Law Studies 265 (1980); J. Mc Nulty, *Blockade: Evolution and Expectation, ibid.,* at 184.

31   Ronzitti, loc. cit. n. 1, at 9.

32   For example, see B.A. Harlow, *The Law of Neutrality at Sea for the 80's and Beyond,* 3 Pacific Basin Law Journal 44 (1984).

NEUTRALITY IN NAVAL WARFARE

lack of formal reliance on this legal concept does not necessarily mean that the concept has fallen into desuetude. Such a kind of negative practice must be accompanied by a corresponding *opinio juris*, for the traditional customary law of blockade to be changed.[33] The concept of blockade, however, seems to be very much alive. It is mentioned in the UN General Assembly's definition of aggression as a measure of warfare which may constitute an illegal aggression.[34] It is enumerated among the measures which might be considered as enforcement action under Article 42 of the UN Charter. A blockade was instituted against Iraq in the recent Gulf crisis.

The essential question, however, is whether the concept of blockade has undergone certain modifications in view of recent developments of treaty law, in particular, to what extent has it been modified by Article 23 of the Fourth Geneva Convention on the Protection of War victims and by Article 54 and 70 of Protocol I Additional to the Geneva Conventions. Article 23 of the Fourth Convention provides for the free passage of certain relief consignments, although under very restrictive conditions. If that provision modified the traditional law of blockade, it did so only to a very limited extent. Article 54 of Protocol I prohibits starvation as a means of warfare. Article 70 provides for the passage of relief consignments, and the obligations to grant such passage go much further than those provided for in Article 23 of the Fourth Convention.[35] There are some indications that Article 54 was not meant to change the traditional law of blockade, but Article 70 certainly constitutes a serious limitation on the right of the blockading State to bar access to a blockaded port or coast. Food, medical and other supplies essential to the survival of the civilian population must be allowed to pass a blockade. The recent UN practice in relation to Iraq seems to be inspired by the respect for that principle.

It must be stressed that the means of enforcing the blockade is to stop and seize a 'blockade runner'. The essential difference between the normal control of neutral shipping and a blockade consists in the fact that a blockade runner can be seized for the mere breach of a blockade, even if I does not carry contraband. The use of force against a blockade runner is permissible to the extent necessary to stop and seize it. A blockade does not give any right to destroy neutral ships where no attempt is made to stop and seize them. If a belligerent State enforcing a blockade just by attacking from a distance (which was the

---

33   Ronzitti, op. cit. n. 1, at 9 *et seq.*

34   GA Res. 3314 (XXIX) of 14 December 1974. *Cf.*, Bothe, loc. cit. n. 19, at 127.

35   On this question, see Bothe, Partsch, Solf, eds., op. cit. n. 11, at 336 *et seq.*; Ronzitti, op. cit. n. 1, at 35.

584   PART 8: OTHER ISSUES

case during the Gulf War), this amounts to the establishment of an exclusion zone which, as will be shown, is unlawful.[36]

4.2 Quarantine or Interdiction

The notion of quarantine[37] was invented by the United States during the Cuban missile crisis.[38] The notion is different from that of a blockade because the so-called quarantine did not bar shipping in general from going to and from Cuba. The 'interdiction' was limited to specific shipments.[39] In term of the law of war, such interdiction causes no problem whatsoever. In the context of an armed conflict, the shipment of materials to those affected by the quarantine could certainly be stopped by any belligerent as being war material destined for the adverse party. It is, thus, certainly inappropriate to consider quarantine as a new notion in the field of the laws of naval warfare.

The real legal problems posed by the quarantine relate to the *ius contra bellum*. To the extent that the enforcement of the quarantine constituted a use of force within the meaning of Article 2(4) of the UN Charter, it could only be justified if it was a reaction to an armed attack or if it was justified by the authorization of a competent international organisation, a question which cannot be dealt with in this connection in greater detail.

4.3 Laying Mines

The practice of laying mines[40] has been quite common during conflicts since World War II. They were used in order to block access to certain ports or sea areas. Like a blockade, it is a measure which affects belligerents and neutrals alike. Laying mines is certainly and act of force against the State whose territory is affected thereby. Under the law of armed conflict, laying mines must conform to the requirements of Hague Convention XIII of 1907. This was stressed by the International Court of Justice in the *Nicaragua Case* in relation to the mining of certain Nicaraguan harbours by the United States,[41] and also by the United States in relation to the laying of mines by Iran in the Persian Gulf.[42]

---

36   See *infra* § 4.4.
37   L. Weber, *Cuban Quarantine,* in Bernhards, ed., op. cit. n. 8, at 126.
38   See L.C. Meeker, *defensive Quarantine and the Law,* 57 AJIL 515 (1963); C.Q. Christol, C.A. Davis, *Maritime Quarantine: The Naval Interdiction of Offensive Weapons and Associated Material to Cuba* 525 (1962).
39   W.O. Miller, *Belligerency and Limited War,* 62 United States Naval War College International Law Studies 170 (1980).
40   Ronzitti, loc. cit. n. 1, at 5 *et seq.*
41   ICJ Reports 1986, at 112.
42   See the references quoted by Ronzitti, loc. cit. n. 1, at 5.

NEUTRALITY IN NAVAL WARFARE

The essential content of the said Convention is that it is forbidden to use contact mines in a way which may render them indiscriminate weapons. Thus, it is forbidden to lay unanchored automatic contact mins or anchored automatic contact mines which do not become harmless as soon as they have broken loose, or to use torpedoes which do not become harmless when they have missed their mark. In addition, it is forbidden to lay automatic contact mines with the sole object of intercepting commercial shipping. It must be noted in this respect that these obligations apply not only to belligerent parties, but also to neutral power using mines to protect their territorial waters.

4.4   *Special Zones*

What became known as the 'exclusion zone' during the Falklands/Malvinas conflict[43] resembles quite closely the notion of 'war zones' instituted by Germany around the British Isles during World War II.[44] It was a zone where any ship, neutral or belligerent, could be sunk without warning. Admiral Dönitz was not condemned for war crimes on that account, but only because the United States practised the same in the Pacific. The rule as such remained unaffected.

During the Falklands/Malvinas conflict there were really two versions of the exclusion zone. The first one was a sort of limitation of the theatre of war. It was directed only against Argentine naval forces. If this kind of declaration poses any problem under international law, it is the question whether such a declaration creates a situation of confidence that no attack is to be expected outside that zone. A further declaration, however, extended the meaning of the exclusion zone so as to include neutral shipping, which would be considered as hostile if found in the zone and thus liable to attack. Against this extension of the exclusion zone, there were some neutral protests. In order to consider the legality of such zones, one has to stick to the old rule that neutral shipping is subject to visit and search and to be taken as a prize where contraband is found, but not to more sweeping acts of violence. It is in this sense that the sentence of the Nuremberg Tribunal has to be understood. The question thus arises whether this exclusion zone has become accepted under a new development of customary law. The answer must clearly be negative. There was enough protest against the declaration

---

43   Ronzitti, loc. cit. n. 1, at 40; Jenkins, loc. cit. n. 16, at 526 *et seq.* A good general overview on the subject-matter of exclusion zones is given by W.J. Fenrick, *The Exclusion Zone Device in the Law of Naval Warfare,* 24 Can. Yb. Of International Law 91 (1986).

44   See j. Schmitt, Die Zulässigkeit von Sperrgebieten im Seekrieg (The Admissibility of Exclusion Zones in Naval Warfare) 66 *et seq.* (1966).

586   PART 8: OTHER ISSUES

to prevent British practice becoming an element of the formation of new law, at least for the time being.

The forgoing analysis of the legal situation is confirmed by the practice of the United Nations in relation to the Gulf War. When Iraq instituted a fifty-mile war zone around Kharg Island and attacked neutral ships, the practice of indiscriminate attacks on such shipping[45] was condemned several times by the UN Security Council. In this connection, it is also necessary to oppose views which are found in legal literature according to which a tanker, even a tanker flying a neutral flag, carrying oil exported from a belligerent oil-producing State, would constitute a military objective because the revenue derived from such exports is so essential to the war effort of the belligerent. Such indirect advantage can never be the basis of the military character of an objective. This view is also in contradiction to the fundamental principle of the law of neutrality that a neutral may not be impaired by the armed conflict. Again, this situation may be changed on the basis of a binding SC Resolution authorizing forceful measures against exports which would foster the war effort of an aggressor.[46] Measures against neutral shipping going beyond the traditional rights of visit and search, and of seizing contraband, would require a special enabling resolution by the Security Council.

It has thus to be concluded that so-called exclusion zones have not become a new element of the positive law of neutrality in naval warfare. Practice shows, however, a certain inclination of States to establish zones from which they want to bar all traffic. These tendencies must be viewed very critically and must be carefully restricted in any future codification.

5   **The Impact of the New Law of the Sea**

Article 88 of the 1982 LOSC reads: 'The high seas shall be reserved for peaceful purposes'.

There is general agreement, however, that this Article does not really mean what it says, if taken literally. It is not meant to exclude all military activities on the high seas, it only prohibits the use of the high seas for committing acts of

---

45   On the illegality of these actions, see also Jenkins, loc. cit. n. 16, at 534 *et seq.*

46   It as to be noted that at the time of writing, the measures against Iraq authorized by the Security Council did not include the use of force against ships navigating or aircraft flying over, the high seas or international straits. *Cf.,* SC Res. 661 of 6 August 1990 and 670 of 25 September 1990.

NEUTRALITY IN NAVAL WARFARE

aggression.[47] Thus, naval warfare is not outlawed by the 1982 LOSC. However, the new Convention may have a restraining effect on naval operations which are also relevant for the law of neutrality.

The recent development of the law of the sea is characterized by a substantial expansion of the rights of a coastal State, a phenomenon which has rightly been called 'territorialization' or 'terranization'[48] of the sea. Three developments are of particular importance for the law of naval warfare, namely the status of international straits, the rights of coastal States relating to the continental shelf and the regime of the exclusive economic zone (EEZ).[49]

The regime of international straits has not only become more important because more international passages have become territorial waters due to the extension of those waters under recent developments of the law of the sea, but also because the regime of passages has been developed or at least clarified to a certain extent by the 1982 LOSC in particular, due to the distinction between innocent passage and transit passage. As is well-known, the question of the right of passage through straits presented a particular problem during the Gulf War. Generally speaking, one has to distinguish two situations: the coastal State may be neutral or may be at war. Where the coastal State is neutral, the rules of the 1982 LOSC and those relating to neutrality can be applied concurrently.[50] Transit rights under the law of the sea do not go beyond rights of transit under neutrality law. Thus, the 24-hours-rule would also apply and the waters of an international strait may not be used as a basis for maritime hostilities by the belligerent States. On the other hand, the existence of an armed conflict would not justify a neutral coastal State's barring or severely limiting military traffic through a strait if that traffic is compatible with the law of neutrality.[51]

Where the coastal State is a party to the conflict, the existence of transit rights would certainly not affect the right of control which the belligerent State

---

47 B.O. Byrde, *Militärische und sicherheitspolitische Implikationen der neuen Seerechtskonvention* (Military and Security Policy Implications of the new Law of the Sea Convention), in J. Delbrück, ed., Das neue Seerecht. Internationale und nationale Perspektiven (The new Law of the Sea. International and National Perspectives) 162 (1984).

48 Graf Vitzthum, *Einleitung*, in Graf Vitzthum, ed., Die Plünderung der Meere (Looting the Seas) 13 (1981); Ronzitti, loc. cit. n. 1, at 28.

49 D.H.N. Johnson, *Straits*, in R. Bernhardt, ed., 11 Encyclopaedia of Public International Law 323 *et seq.* (1989); *Innocent Passage, Transit Passage*, in Bernhardt, ed., *ibid.*, at 120 *et seq.*; C.L. Rozakis, *Continental Shelf*, in Bernhardt, ed., *ibid.*, at 82 *et seq.*; L. Gündling, *Die 200 Seemeilen-Wirtschaftszone* (The 200 Miles Economic Zone) (1983).

50 On this question, see Bryde, loc. cit. n. 47, at 174 *et seq.*

51 Harlow, loc. cit. n. 32, at 50.

possesses over neutral shipping. These rights exist as to neutral shipping on the high seas; they would *a fortiori* exist where the neutral ship is in the territorial waters of a belligerent. The essential question, however, is to what extent the belligerent coastal State has the right to exclude neutral shipping from its territorial waters forming part of an international strait. The practice during the Gulf War in this respect seem to be somewhat contradictory. In this respect, there seems to be a need for clarifications *de lege ferenda*.

As to the continental shelf, it is clear that it cannot be equated with territorial waters. The rights of a coastal State in relation to the continental shelf are not comprehensive sovereign rights, but limited to the exploration and exploitation of the natural resources of the shelf. Third States are excluded from building structures on the continental shelf, but apart from economic activities, the continental shelf has to be treated like the seabed of the high seas. Thus, a neutral State has no right or duty to prevent military activities on the continental shelf, a right or duty it would have if these activities took place in its territorial waters.[52] It is an open question, however, how far the duty not to hinder economic activities being carried out by the coastal State on its continental shelf would limit the possibility of military activities.[53] A reverse question may also be put: to what extent could a belligerent State control economic activities on the continental shelf of a neutral State? Could it, for example, prohibit the production and transportation of oil from continental shelf sources where such oil is destined for export to another belligerent State? If such oil was transported on the high seas by a neutral ship, it could certainly be seized.

It is also quite clear that the EEZ cannot be equated with territorial waters. Thus, a neutral coastal State has no right or duty to exclude military activities of belligerent States in this zone. As in relation to the continental shelf, the question is how far the economic rights enjoyed by the coastal State in relation to the EEZ may limit the right of the belligerent States to conduct military activities, including fighting. Military activities will certainly quite often constitute a considerable risk or impediment for economic activities of the coastal State, in particular fishing. This is a question, which, it is submitted, requires some clarification *de lege ferenda*. On the other hand, the question of control of neutral economic activities just discussed in relation to the continental shelf also arises in respect of certain activities of a coastal State in the EEZ.

---

52   *Ibid.*, at 52.

53   Byrde, loc. cit. n. 47, at 169, 173.

NEUTRALITY IN NAVAL WARFARE

6 New Technology and the Protection of the Environment: The Question of Collateral Damage

Naval war activities under modern conditions of warfare may in many respects not only affect economic activities of a neutral coastal State in the waters near to its coast, but also, more generally speaking, the marine environment of these waters and the coastal areas of the neutral States themselves. The question thus arises whether and to what extent such collateral damage to the environment and the property of the neutral State and its nationals is legally acceptable.

The fundamental principle which must underlie the answer to this question is the rule that the neutral State must not be impaired by the armed conflict. This is, in turn, the basis of the provision of Article 1 of the Fifth Hague Convention respecting the rights and duties of neutral powers and persons in case of war: the territory of neutral powers is 'inviolable'. It follows that the belligerent may not cause any damage to neutral territory as a result of hostilities. During World War II, damages were indeed paid where collateral damage had been caused to Switzerland by an attack which hit a German town.[54] The principle of proportionality which governs the admissibility of collateral damage caused to civilians or civilian objects does not apply to collateral damage caused to neutral States. It is submitted that the same holds true for damage caused to the neutral territory by military operations carried out at sea. Thus, the attack on a tanker navigating off the coast of a neutral State which leads to pollution of the coastal waters and coastal areas of that State would be an illegal act in relation to the neutral State and give rise to a claim for compensation.

Whether this principle holds true where legitimate neutral activities were impaired in the EEZ or if collateral damage was caused to neutral ships navigating on the high seas in the vicinity of military activities is, however, doubtful. It would seem that at least on the high seas, neutral ships, although they may not be attacked, operate at their risk and peril when they move close to military operations.[55]

---

54 G. Jaccard, *Über Neutralitätsverletzungsschäden in der Schweiz während des Zweiten Weltkriegs* (On Damages Caused by Violations of Swiss Neutrality During the Second World War), 87 Zeitschrift des Bernischen Juristenverbandes 225 *et seq.* (1951). These question were the object of a study by a group in which both F. Kalshoven and this author took part. Unfortunately, the institution which commissioned the report has so far not given the permission to publish it.

55 See *e.g.* the note of the 'Service juridique' of the French Ministry of Foreign Affairs concerning French ships which may be hit by accident during the Japanese attacks 21 January 1938, A. Kiss, VI Repertoire de la pratique française en matière de droit international public, no. 1086.

7   Conclusions

It appears from the foregoing that the fundamental rules concerning neutrality in relation to warfare at sea which were codified in 1907 have to a large extent remained unchanged.[56] State practice is still based on, and invokes, those codifications. Certain modern development, however, have modified these traditional rules in significant details. The main elements of these changes are the development of the concept of war and armed conflict, the prohibition of the use of force in the Charter of the United Nations; international humanitarian law codified and developed in the 1949 Geneva Conventions and the 1977 Protocols Additional thereto, the new rules of the law of the sea, and changing technological and economic environment.

Generally speaking, legal restraints on warfare have become tougher while war becomes more and more dreadful. It is, however, difficult to ascertain clearly the development of customary law in relation to maritime neutrality. The relationship between the new rules and the traditional rules of maritime neutrality is by no means always clear. The law of maritime neutrality is certainly one of the fields which deserves much thought *de lege ferenda*.

56   Milles, loc. cit. n. 30, at 265.

Conflits Armés Internes et Droit International Humanitaire

1 Introduction

Le maintien de l'ordre à l'intérieur d'un pays n'est, en principe, pas régi par le droit international public, mais par le droit interne. Le droit international traditionnel ne limite donc guère la liberté des Etats de façonner ce droit interne selon leur discrétion. Des tendances récentes du droit international public restreignent cependant le libre choix des moyens pour maintenir l'ordre interne, et cela surtout à deux points de vue : celui de la protection des droits de l'homme et celui de la protection des victimes de conflits armés en vertu des règles du droit de la guerre. Les deux points de vue (droits de l'homme et droit humanitaire) sont liés entre eux, mais ils ne sont pas identiques.[1]

2 Le Droit Traditionnel

Pour l'application des règles du droit de la guerre dans les conflits internes, le droit traditionnel prévoyait un seuil bien net et clair : la reconnaissance des insurgés comme belligérants. Cette reconnaissance conduisait à l'application intégrale du droit de guerre, avant cette reconnaissance le conflit n'étant régi que par le droit interne.[2] L'application des règles du droit de la guerre est cependant soumise à des nécessités propres. La réciprocité, ou plus exactement la possibilité de représailles que possèdent les deux Parties, contraignent les adversaires a s'imposer certaines restrictions indépendamment du statut juridique du conflit. Le défaut d'une telle auto-limitation conduit à une escalade de la cruauté, le conflit dégénère et devient de plus en plus

---

1 Voir H. Meyrowitz, « Le droit de la guerre et les droits de l'homme », *Revue du droit public,* 1972, pp. 1059 et ss ; K.J. Partsch, « Menschenrechte und überliefertes Kriegsrecht », *NZWehrr,* 1974, pp. 1 et ss.

2 H. Wehberg, « La guerre civile et le droit international », *R.D.C.,* 63, 1938, 1, pp. 39 et ss. ; E. Castrén, *Civil War,* 1966, pp. 97 et ss.

inhumain et cruel. L'histoire du XIXe siècle nous offre des exemples des deux alternatives, aussi bien ceux, de l'auto-limitation des Parties que ceux de la dégradation du conflit .[3] Après ces expériences, des voix se levèrent, dans la doctrine déjà vers la fin de siècle dernier,[4] dans le cadre de la Croix-Rouge internationale depuis le début de ce siècle,[5] qui postulèrent l'application du droit de la guerre aussi dans le cadre de conflits armés internes, même s'il n'y avait pas reconnaissance de belligérance. Depuis, ces voix ne se sont pas tues. Mais bien qu'on ait pu observer l'application *de facto* de certaines règles du droit de la guerre dans des conflits internes de ce siècle,[6] on ne peut pas conclure que ces précédants avaient conduit, avant 1949, à une modification de la règle traditionnelle.

3   Les Conventions de Genève de 1949

Le pas décisif dans le développement de la protection des victimes de conflits internes fut l'article 3, commun aux quatre conventions de Genève de 1949, qui prévoit l'application de certaines règles humanitaires aux conflits armés non internationaux. Ce pas, important mais modeste, constitue cependant un recul vis-à-vis des projets adoptés par la Conférence de la Croix-Rouge de 1948 à Stockholm. Ces projets prévoyaient l'application intégrale de conventions aux conflits non internationaux.[7] Déjà en 1949, on voit la difficulté décisive qui s'oppose a une réglementation internationale du conflit interne : les Etats ne sont pas prêts à renoncer à leur « souveraineté », c'est-à-dire, dans ce contexte, à leur liberté de choix des moyens utilisés dans la lutte contre une insurrection. Ainsi, il ne reste du grand dessein de Stockholm d'une réglementation complète du conflit interne que quelques règles minimales sur la protection des victimes.

---

3 Un exemple de la première alternative est la guerre de sécession américaine, bien que la question de la reconnaissance des Confédérés n'ait pas été tout à fait claire, cfr. J. Siotis, *Le droit de la guerre et lest conflits armés d'un caractère non international*, 1958, pp. 78 et ss. Comme exemple de l'autre extrême on peut citer les rébellions cubaines de 1868 à 1895, Siotis, *loc. cit.*, pp. 89 et ss.

4 Sous le forme de la reconnaissance obligatoire de la belligérance, Siotis, *loc. cit.,* pp. 128 et ss.

5 Siotis, *loc. cit.,* pp. 136 et ss.

6 Siotis, *loc. cit.,* pp. 146 et ss.

7 Cfr. le texte de l'article 2, par. commun aux projets de convention, *Actes de la Conférence diplomatique de Genève de 1949,* vol. 1, pp. 47, 61, 72, 111. Voir également Siotis, *loc. cit.,* pp. 187 et ss.

CONFLITS ARMÉS INTERNES ET DROIT INTERNATIONAL HUMANITAIRE

4 Les Dèveloppements D'après 1949

L'article 3 n'est cependant pas la fin d'un développement, mais plutôt un pas sur la voie vers une protection plus complète des victimes des conflits internes. Les développements que l'on peut observer depuis 1949 se caractérisent par la mise en question des limites de l'article 3. D'abord, la distinction entre conflit interne et conflit international tend à s'effacer. La plupart des conflits ont des éléments internationaux aussi bien que non internationaux.[8] En plus, notamment les Etats du Tiers-Monde insistent sur ce que les guerres de libération anticoloniale doivent être considérées comme des conflits internationaux au sens des conventions de Genève.[9] D'autre part, l'application de l'article 3 se heurte à des difficultés. Certains Etats se refusent à reconnaître que certains événements qui se déroulent sur leur territoire constituent des conflits armés au sens de l'article 3.[10] Mais le C.I.C.R. peut entreprendre des activités en faveur des détenus politiques même dans des cas qui se situent en dehors du champ d'application de l'article 3 (Grèce, Chili).[11] De temps en temps, le C.I.C.R. peut obtenir que les Etats appliquent, au moins de fait, certaines parties des Conventions de Genève bien qu'il s'agisse d'un conflit non-international. Lors du conflit du Biafra, le Nigéria a par exemple mené des négociations avec le C.I.C.R. sur les actions de secours entreprises par ce dernier, comme si l'Article 23 de la IVᵉ convention était applicable[12]

5 Une Nouvelle Etape : Le Protocol II Additionnel Aux Conventions de Genève

A la lumière de ces tendances et problèmes, la protection des victimes des conflits armés non internationaux prit nécessairement une place primordiale dans les efforts en vue de développer le droit de Genève. Les étapes de ces

---

8   Cfr. D. Schindler, « Die Anwendung der Genfer Rotkreuzabkommen seit 1949 », *Schweizerische Jahrbuch für internationales Recht,* 1965, pp. 75 et ss.

9   N. Ronzitti, *Le guerre di liberazione nazionale e il diritto internazionale,* 1974, pp. 15 et ss., qui donne des références détaillées.

10   Ainsi la France dans le premier stade du conflit algérien, voir Siotis, *loc. cit,* pp. 210 et ss.

11   Voit J. Moreillon, *Le Comité international de la Croix-Rouge et la protection es détenus politiques,* 1973, *passim.* Voir également l'étude de l'institut Henry Dunant, reproduite à l'annexe du message du Conseil fédéral suisse, en date du 19 juin 1977, *Bundesblatt,* 1977, II, p.1155.

12   Cf. P. Mertens, « Les modalités de l'intervention du Comité international de la Croix-Rouge ans le conflit du Nigéria », *A.F.D.J.,* 1969, pp. 197 et ss.

efforts sont bien connus. Sur la base des décisions prises à la Conférence de la Croix-Rouge tenue à Istanbul en 1969, le c.i.c.r. convoqua deux Conférences d'experts gouvernementaux. Se fondant sur ces délibérations, il élabora les deux projets de Protocoles additionnels aux Conventions de Genève, le premier pour les conflits internationaux, le deuxième pour les conflits non internationaux. Dans le projet de Protocole II soumis à la Conférence, le c.i.c.r. renonçait à certains éléments de ses propositions initiales, qui s'étaient heurtées à la résistance de certains experts gouvernementaux.[13] La Conférence diplomatique traite de ces projets en deux lectures. Lors de la « première lecture » – l'adoption des textes dans les trois Commissions de la Conférence – l'essentiel du projet de Protocole II établi par le c.i.c.r. fut maintenu, sauf deux ou trois exceptions.[14] Certains éléments furent même ajoutés au texte. Mais, lors de la « deuxième lecture » – l'adoption des articles du Protocole II en séance plénière – la délégation du Pakistan proposa une « version simplifiée ». Des négociations parfois dramatiques menèrent à une réduction essentielle du contenu du Protocole II. Ce texte réduit fut finalement adopté dans son ensemble, par consensus, le 10 juin 1977.

6   Les Données Politiques du Problème

Pour évaluer et comprendre les résultats de la Conférence, il faut se rendre compte du fait que le développement de la protection des victimes de conflits armés s'est situé dans le cadre des antagonismes qui existent à l'échelon mondial. Le caractère humanitaire du but de la Conférence a peut-être parfois atténué l'acuité de ces antagonismes, mais il ne les a certainement pas éliminés. Ceci vaut pout l'antagonisme Nord-Sud aussi bien que pour l'antagonisme Est-Ouest.

Les pays du Tiers-Monde tenaient d'abord et surtout à la réévaluation des guerres de libération anticoloniales. Quant aux conflits internes en dehors de ce contexte anticolonial, ils soulignaient la souveraineté de l'Etat : selon au moins la plupart de ces pays du Tiers-Monde, la liberté de l'Etat dans la lutte contre des insurgés ne doit pas être restreinte, le règlement international du conflit interne ne droit donner aucune base juridique a une immixtion étrangère.[15]

---

13   Voir *infra*.

14   Notamment les articles 1 (seuil d'application) et 39 (concours du c.i.c.r. à l'observation du Protocole).

15   Cf. les déclarations des représentants du Nigéria, cddh/sr. 49, p. 8 et du Cameroun, *ibid.*

CONFLITS ARMÉS INTERNES ET DROIT INTERNATIONAL HUMANITAIRE 595

L'attitude des pays de l'Ouest, en ce qui concerne le Protocole II, a été déterminée surtout par des considérations humanitaires. Il faut cependant admettre que certains de ces pays ne perdirent pas de vue le fait qu'ils avaient leurs problèmes internes propres : la Grande-Bretagne le problème de l'Irlande du Nord, le Canada celui du Québec, etc.

Les pays socialistes se sont alliés au Tiers-Monde en ce qui concerne la question des guerres de libération. Mais, sur le Protocole II, ils n'ont pas partagé les réticences du Tiers-Monde quant aux effets que ce Protocole pourrait avoir sur la souveraineté nationale. En ce qui concerne cette question, la position socialiste était très proche de celle des pays de l'Ouest.[16]

7 La Question des Guerres de Libération Nationale

La question des guerres de libération nationale fut abordée déjà lors de la première session de la Conférence dans le sens voulu par le Tiers-Monde. Contre la résistance des pays occidentaux, la Conférence vota l'adoption d'un nouveau paragraphe de l'article 1er du Protocole I qui donne à la guerre de libération nationale et anticoloniale le statut d'un conflit international.[17] Avec cette décision, le Tiers-Monde avait perdu tout intérêt dans le développement de la protection de victimes dans le cadre du Protocole II, puisqu'il était clair que les victimes de conflits anticoloniaux étaient protégées par le Protocole I. Les forces au sein du Tiers-Monde qui lutaient contre le Protocole II en utilisant l'argument de la sauvegarde de la souveraineté nationale étaient donc libérées et purent déterminer la position de beaucoup des pays de ce groupe.

8 Le Contenu du Protocole II

Le cadre général étant ainsi établi, nous pouvons procéder à un examen plus détaillé du contenu du Protocole II.

8.1 *Le champ D'application et le Niveau de Protection*
Le premier problème, qui s'était déjà posé aux Conférences d'experts gouvernementaux, était celui du champ d'application. Le C.I.C.R. avait dès le début prévu deux Protocoles, un Protocole pour le conflit international et un autre

---

16   Cf. la déclaration du représentant de l'Union soviétique, CDDH/ SR. 49, pp. 6 et ss.
17   CDDH/48, para. 1–14. Cf. G. Abi-Saab, « Les guerres de libération nationale et la Conférence diplomatique sur le droit humanitaire », *Annales d'études internationales,* 1977, pp. 63 et ss.

Protocol pout le conflit non international. Il n'avait donc pas repris la grande idée de la Conférence de Stockholm de 1948, c'est-à-dire l'application intégrale du droit humanitaire aux conflits de caractère non international. Déjà dans les propositions faites à la première Conférence d'experts gouvernementaux, le C.I.C.R. suggéra un Protocole spécial pour les conflits non internationaux.[18] Cette conception fut notamment contestée par la Norvège. Mais le concept norvégien d'une seul Protocole pour les deux catégories de conflit n'a jamais pu rassembler beaucoup de soutien au sein des Conférences d'experts gouvernementaux ou à la Conférence diplomatique.[19] Le C.I.C.R., d'autre part voulait développer le droit dans deux domaines dont l'importance s'était fait sentir dans la pratique. Il a par conséquent proposé une réglementation spéciale pour la zone grise entre le conflit interne et le conflit international et une autre pour la situation de tensions et troubles intérieurs.[20] Ces deux projets furent les premières victimes de résistances des Etats. Les projets d'une déclaration des droits fondamentaux de la personne humaine en période de troubles intérieurs ou de dangers publics et d'un règlement particulier relatif aux cas de l'aide extérieure dans un conflit non international et de la situation où la Parie qui s'oppose aux autorités au pouvoir remplit les critères d'un Etat ne furent plus présentés à la Conférence diplomatique.

Le problème du champ d'application du Protocole II demeura difficile. Se posa notamment le problème de la relation entre le seuil d'application du Protocole et le niveau de la protection prévue. Si le seuil d'application est bas c'est-à-dire si la définition du conflit comprend aussi des conflits d'une importance mineure, les Etats ne sont pas enclins à accepter un niveau élevé de protection des victimes. Si le seuil d'application est élevé, c'est-à-dire si la définition du conflit non international ne comprend que des conflits d'une intensité majeure, les Etats sont davantage enclins a accepter un niveau élevé de protection. Mais il y a aussi des Etats qui préfèrent la combinaison entre un seuil élevé et un niveau de protection bas. Cette relation entre le seuil d'application et le niveau de la protection est clairement reflétée dans l'article 1er du Protocole II : « Le présent Protocole ... s'applique à tous les conflits armés ... qui se déroulent sur le territoire d'une Haute Partie contractante entre ses forces armées et des forces armées dissidentes ... qui ... exercent sur une partie de son territoire un contrôle tel qu'il leur permette de mener des opérations militaires

---

18   Conférence d'experts gouvernementaux, 24 mai – 12 juin 1971, Documentation, vol. I, p. 25.

19   Conférences d'experts gouvernementaux, 24 mai – 12 juin 1971, Rapport sur les travaux de la Conférence, pp. 42, 70.

20   Conférence d'experts gouvernementaux, 3 mai – 3 juin 1972, Rapport sur les travaux de la Conférence, vol. I, pp. 98 et ss. 12 ; vol. II, p.22.

CONFLITS ARMÉS INTERNES ET DROIT INTERNATIONAL HUMANITAIRE 597

continues et concertées et d'appliquer le présent Protocole ». Ce texte lie le niveau de protection avec le seuil d'application de façon peut-être désastreuse. Plus détaillées sont les dispositions du Protocole, plus élevé est le niveau de la protection, et plus difficile devient l'application du Protocole. Mais si une Partie au conflit ne peut pas appliquer le Protocole, le conflit ne tombe pas dans le champ d'application du Protocole II. Ce texte fut adopté lors de la deuxième session de la Conférence, et il pesa sur la suite des travaux, parce que chaque disposition devait être évaluée à la lumière de l'effet qu'elle aurait pu avoir sur le seuil d'application. A cet égard, la rédaction finale du texte a peut-être eu un effet salutaire, parce qu'elle a baissé le seuil d'application. Le lien entre la possibilité d'appliquer le Protocole et son seuil d'application reste une question difficile parce qu'il implique un contre-sens, au moins du point de vue humanitaire : si les insurgés ne sont pas en mesure de traiter leurs prisonniers comme il le faut, ils ne sont plus tenus de le faire, pour cette même raison, et le gouvernement établi ne l'est pas non plus.[21]

Ce lien aussi bien que la condition que les insurgés doivent contrôler une partie du territoire sont le résultat des travaux de la Conférence. Le C.I.C.R. avait proposé comme seule condition de l'applicabilité du Protocole la direction par un commandement responsable. Certaines délégations voulaient aller plus loin dans la restriction du champ d'application : elles voulaient le faire dépendre d'une décision du gouvernement en place. Ces propositions ne furent cependant pas acceptés, et un amendement colombien proposé en plénière, qui aurait eu le même effet, ne fut pas mis aux voix. Certaines délégations ont essayé de réintroduire, sous une forme modifiée, cette condition d'une reconnaissance de la part du gouvernement en place par voie de déclaration interprétative.[22] Mais un très grand nombre d'Etats a clairement refusé d'accepter cette interprétation.[23]

Ces restrictions du champ d'application de la nouvelle réglementation pour le conflit non international ont provoqué des craintes quant aux effets que la nouvelle définition pourrait avoir sur le champ d'application de l'article 3 commun aux quatre conventions. Si le nouveau Protocole a un champ d'application restreint, il est absolument nécessaire que l'article 3 ne soit pas compromis par ces restrictions. Pour éviter cet effet, le C.I.C.R. dans le projet soumis à la Conférence et la Conférence elle-même ont clairement disjoints le champ d'application de l'article 3 d'une part et celui du Protocole II de l'autre.

---

21 Cf. M. Bothe, « Die Genfer Konferenz über humanitäres Völkerrecht, Berich über den Stand der Verhandlungen nach der zweiten Sitzungsperiode », *ZaöRV*, 1975, pp. 644 et ss.
22 Cf. les déclarations du Brésil et de la Tanzanie, CDDH/SR. 49, Annexe, pp. 4 et 13.
23 Cf. les déclarations de la déléguée du C.I.C.R., CDDH/SR. 49, pp. 13 et ss.

Ceci est le sens de la formule utilisée à l'article 1er, paragraphe 1, qui dit que le présent Protocole « développe et complète l'article 3 aux conventions de Genève du 12 août 1949 sans modifier ses conditions d'application actuelles ». Cette disjonction n'est pas non plus compromise par le paragraphe 2 du même article qui dit : « Le présent Protocole ne s'applique pas aux situations de tensions internes, de troubles intérieurs, comme les émeutes, les actes isolés et sporadiques de violence et autres actes analogues, qui ne sont pas considérées comme des conflits armés ». Puisque le Protocole II ne modifie pas les conditions actuelles de l'application de l'article 3 commun aux conventions, la définition négative du conflit armé contenu au paragraphe 2 de l'article 1er ne peut concerner que le Protocole II et non pas l'article 3. La question du champ d'application de l'article 3 reste donc ouverte.

En somme, l'article 1er de Protocole II est le résultat d'un compromis entre les protagonistes de la souveraineté étatique et ceux qui, dans l'intérêt des victimes du conflit, tenaient une application plus vaste des dispositions de Protocole II. Ce compromis fut très difficile à obtenir, tellement difficile que personne n'a finalement osé, lors de l'adoption finale en plénière, perturber l'équilibre acquis,[24] ce qui a empêché, entre autre, que l'on ait pu remédier à un défaut sérieux de l'article 1er. Cet article n'est applicable qu'aux conflits « qui se déroulent sur le territoire d'une Haute Partie contractante entre *ses* forces armées (c'est-à-dire les forces armées du gouvernement établi) et des forces armées dissidentes ou des groupes organisés ... ». Les luttes entre les groupes dissidents eux-mêmes ne sont pas couvertes par la définition. Des situations comme celle de la guerre civile au Liban et en Angola ne tombent donc pas sous le champ d'application du Protocole II. Ceci est au moins le résultat d'une interprétation litérale du texte. On ne peut qu'espérer qu'une pratique s'établira qui corrigera ce défaut du texte.

8.2   *La Question de la Force Obligatoire du Protocole II*

Le Protocole II est, selon l'article 1er, applicable à un conflit armé entre le gouvernement établi et des groupes dissidents. Mais le Protocole se tait quant à la question de savoir à quel titre le Protocole est obligatoire pour les Parties au conflit. La force obligatoire va de soi pour les Parties contractantes représentées par leurs gouvernements établis. Mais *quid* des insurgés ? Cette question a été discutée dès le début des Conférences gouvernementales. Lors de la première Conférence, le C.I.C.R. a souligné que

---

24   Comme on l'a vu, un amendement oral présenté par la Colombie tendant à donner au gouvernement établi le pouvoir de décider s'il existe ou non un conflit au sens de l'article premier n'a pas été mis aux voix, CDDH/SR.49.

CONFLITS ARMÉS INTERNES ET DROIT INTERNATIONAL HUMANITAIRE

l'article 3 ne lie pas uniquement le gouvernement de l'Etat contractant, mais qu'il s'impose à l'ensemble de la population et que, par conséquent, les rebelles sont inclus parmi ceux qui doivent en respecter les termes. L'obligation date de 1949. Il en irait de même si l'article 3 devait être développé par les voies d'un Protocole additionnel.[25]

Le fondement juridique de cette thèse, d'ailleurs toujours soutenue par le C.I.C.R.,[26] laisse place au doute. Peut-on vraiment dire que les insurgés sont liés par les actes du gouvernement établi contre lequel ils se sont dressés ? La pratique des Etats ne confirme pas la thèse du C.I.C.R. en tant que concept généralement valable en droit international public. Il n'existe pas de règle générale selon laquelle les insurgés seraient liés par tous les traités conclus antérieurement par le gouvernement de l'Etat en cause. La pratique des Etats varie à cet égard. Mais d'autre part, il a toujours été reconnu que l'article 3 des conventions de Genève est un cas spécial.[27] Quoique les auteurs qui en parlent reconnaissent les difficultés de la construction juridique, ils n'en concluent pas que la validité obligatoire de l'article 3 pour les insurgés serait impossible en droit.[28] La meilleure explication de ce résultat est probablement l'existence d'une règle coutumière qui étend la validité d'une ratification donnée par un Etat à un nouveau sujet du droit qui s'établit, ne serait-ce que provisoirement, sur le territoire de cet Etat. Le même problème s'est posé pour l'article 19 de la convention de La Haye de 1954 sur la protection des biens culturels, et de nouveau certains doutes furent exprimés quant à la possibilité de lier des insurgés par un traité conclu par le gouvernement établi.[29] La convention est de toute évidence basée sur le concept que cette possibilité existe au moins pour les règles sur le respect des biens culturels envisagées en ce qui concerne un certain minimum du droit humanitaire.

La question se pose de savoir si cette thèse vaut aussi pour le Protocole II. L'article 5 adopté par la Commission I de la Conférence donnait une indication

---

25 Conférence d'experts gouvernementaux, 24 mai – 12 juin 1971, Rapport sur les travaux de la Conférence, p. 50.

26 J. Pictet, *Commentaire*, vol. II, « La convention de Genève pour l'amélioration du sort des blessés, des malades et des naufragés des forces armées sur mer », 1959, p. 34.

27 J.A. Frowein, *Das de facto-Régime im Völkerrecht*, 1968, pp. 154 et ss. ; P. de La Pradelle, *La Conférence diplomatique et les nouvelles conventions de Genève*, 1951, p. 217.

28 Certains délégués à la Conférence diplomatique de 1949, tirèrent en effet cette conclusion, cf. *Actes de la Conférence diplomatique de Genève de 1949*, tome II, section B, pp. 89, 95.

29 E. Lattmann, *Schutz der Kulturgüter bei bewaffneten Konflikten*, 1974, pp. 96 et ss.; K. Unverhau, *Der Schitz von Kulturgut bei bewaffneten Konflikten*, thèse, Göttingen, 1935, p. 97.

très nette que c'était en effet l'avis de la Conférence : « Les droits et devoirs qui découlent du présent Protocole valent de manière égale pour toutes les Parties au conflit ». Mais cet article est une des victimes e la rédaction en deuxième lecture. C'était un des principes du processus de rédaction d'éviter, chaque fois que ces mos se trouvaient dans le texte, l'expression « parties au conflit ». Le but de cet exercice linguistique était d'éviter l'impression que le gouvernement établi et les insurgés pourraient se situer sur un pied d'égalité puridique, quant à l'application du Protocole II au moins. Est-ce qu'il s'agit donc d'obligations unilatérales du gouvernement établi ? Une telle interprétation irait radicalement à l'encontre des intentions de la grande majorité des Etats représentés à la Conférence. Ceci a été confirmé avec vigueur par des explications de vote soumis par les Pays-Bas et la Belgique.[30] Les obligations découlant du Protocole II doivent valoir pour toutes les Parties au conflit. La suppression de l'article 5 et la suppression des mots « parties au conflit » n'était en effet qu'un exercice linguistique, qui a changé l'apparence du texte, mais non pas son contenu juridique.

Quoique le droit humanitaire ne repose pas sur un principe strict de réciprocité, un certain degré de réciprocité est néanmoins indispensable pour son bon fonctionnement. Ce degré de réciprocité ne peut être atteint que par les obligations réciproques. Une interprétation selon le principe de l'effet utile requiert donc que les Protocoles valent de manière égale pour toutes les Parties au conflit. Cette extension exceptionnelle de la validité d'un traité, qui est acceptée par la pratique générale en ce qui concerne l'article 3 commun aux conventions, doit s'appliquer également au Protocole II.

8.3   *La Non Intervention*

Pour apaiser les craintes des pays du Tiers-Monde que le Protocole ne puisse affecter défavorablement la souveraineté interne ou externe de l'Etat, le C.I.C.R. avait déjà inclus dans son projet un article intitulé « non intervention » : « Aucune disposition du présent Protocole ne doit être interprétée comme portant atteinte à la souveraineté des Etats, ni comme autorisant les Etats tiers à intervenir dans le conflit armé ». La version finale de cet article est beaucoup plus explicite dans le sens voulu par les pays du Tiers-Monde :

Aucune disposition du présent Protocole ne sera invoquée en vue de porter atteinte à la souveraineté d'un Etat ou à la responsabilité du gouvernement de maintenir ou de rétablir l'ordre public dans l'Etat ou de défendre

---

30   Pays-Bas : CDDH/SR.50, Annexe, p. 7 ; Belgique : CDDH/SR.49, Annexe, p. 3 ; cf. également la déclaration italienne, CDDH/SR.50, Annexe, p. 5.

CONFLITS ARMÉS INTERNES ET DROIT INTERNATIONAL HUMANITAIRE 601

l'unité nationale et l'intégrité territoriale de l'Etat par tous les moyens légitimes.

Aucune disposition du présent Protocole ne sera invoquée comme une justification d'une intervention directe ou indirecte, pour quelque raison que ce soit, dans le conflit armé ou dans les affaires intérieures ou extérieures de la Haute Partie contractante sur le territoire de laquelle ce conflit se produit.

A vrai dire, les deux paragraphes ne disent que ce qui est évident. Le Protocole ne restreint la liberté des Etats en ce qui concerne le maintien de l'ordre que dans la mesure qui résulte du texte du Protocole. Le Protocole ne doit pas servir de prétexte à une immixtion étrangère. Certes, ces dispositions peuvent être un certain obstacle à une argumentation juridique abusive qui essayerait de justifier une intervention étrangère. D'autre part, ces dispositions peuvent elles-mêmes servir de base à une argumentation abusive dans un autre sens. Il existe un certain danger que cet article soit utilisé comme clause 'évasion pour justifier des violations du Protocole. Il est à noter, dans le contexte, que le paragraphe 1er ne parle que des *moyens légitimes* pour le maintien ou le rétablissement de l'ordre. Les moyens qui violeraient le Protocole ne seraient plus des moyens légitimes au sens de l'article 3.

Les craintes des pays du Tiers-Monde que le Protocole II puisse servir de justification à une intervention étrangère se sont également reflétées dans la discussion sur d'autres dispositions. Les sauvegardes prévues par l'article 3 n'ont pas été jugé suffisantes. La première Commission de la Conférence a donc réduit presqu'à néant l'article 39 du projet du C.I.C.R. qui prévoit le concours du C.I.C.R. à l'observation des dispositions du Protocole. Le peu qui resta a cet article fut finalement une autre victime fut la disposition de l'article 33, paragraphe 2 (ancienne numérotation) statuant que les actions de secours, ne seront pas considérées comme une ingérence dans le conflit armé.[31]

8.4   *Les Garanties Fondamentales*

Sous le titre II « Traitement humain », le Protocole II prévoit une série de garanties fondamentales. L'article 4, paragraphe *a*), reconnaît un droit à un traitement humain de façon assez générale. Le paragraphe 2 garantit le droit à la vie et à l'intégrité physique et mentale. Le paragraphe 3 concerne la protection des enfants. L'article 5 prévoit des garanties particulières pour les personnes privées de liberté. Il est à noter que dans le cadre d'un conflit non international, il n'y a pas de statut de prisonnier de guerre. Des propositions tendant à

---

31   CDDH/SR. 53.

introduire cette notion aussi dans le cadre du Protocole II n'ont pas abouti.[32] Comme remplacement des garanties générales qu'en découlent du statut du prisonnier de guerre, l'article 5 prévoit quelques droits fondamentaux pour les personnes privées de liberté et même les personnes dont la liberté est limitée. Il est à noter que les deux premiers paragraphes de l'article 5 prévoient des obligations d'un degré différent. Tandis que les droits prévus au paragraphe 1 doivent être respectés sans qualification, les droits mentionnés au paragraphe 2 ne doivent être respectés que « dans toute la mesure des moyens » des responsables. L'article 6 prévoit finalement des garanties procédurales pour les poursuites pénales.

Les articles sur les garanties fondamentales n'ont pas subi de réduction essentielle lors de l'adoption finale des textes. La plupart des modifications proposées et adoptées ne concernent que des questions de rédaction et de véritable simplification. Deux exceptions à ce résultat satisfaisant doivent cependant être mentionnées. L'article 8, paragraphe 4 (ancienne numérotation), (visites aux personnes détenues par des représentants d'une organisation humanitaire impartiale) a été supprimée. Il en est de même du paragraphe 5 de l'article 10, qui interdisait l'exécution de la peine de mort avant la fin du conflit armé. La suppression de ce paragraphe est particulièrement regrettable. Le C.I.C.R., dans ses premières propositions, avait essayé de créer un statut semblable à celui d'une prisonnier de guerre aussi dans le cadre du conflit non international.[33] Mais ces propositions se sont heurtées à une résistance considérable et le C.I.C.R ne les a pas retenues dans le projet qu'il a soumis à la Conférence diplomatique. Les Parties au conflit peuvent donc toujours traiter tous ceux qui prennent part aux hostilités comme de simples criminels. Dans ce contexte, le sursis de la peine de mort prévue à l'ancien article 10, paragraphe 5, acquiert une valeur particulière comme la seule protection du « combattant »contre l'extermination.

Un autre problème posé par les dispositions sur les garanties fondamentales est celui de la relation entre ces garanties et les dispositions du Pacte sur les droits civils et politiques. Les dispositions de Protocole II correspondent dans une large mesure à certains articles du Pacte : l'article 4, Protocole II a certains éléments des articles 6, 7 et 8 du Pacte, l'article 5 a certains éléments

---

32   Cf. Conférence d'experts gouvernementaux, 24 mai – 12 juin 1971, Rapport sur les travaux de la Conférence, pp. 502 et ss. ; *idem*, seconde session, 3 mai – 3 juin 1972, Rapport sur les travaux de la Conférence, vol. I, pp. 79 et ss.

33   Conférence d'experts gouvernementaux, 24 mai – 12 juin 1971, Rapport sur les travaux de la Conférence, pp. 50 et ss. ; *idem*, seconde session, 3 mai – 3 juin 1972, Rapport sur les travaux de la Conférence, vol. I, pp. 79 et ss.

CONFLITS ARMÉS INTERNES ET DROIT INTERNATIONAL HUMANITAIRE 603

de l'article 10 et à l'article 14 du Pacte. Cela ne veut pas dire que les Pactes contiennent déjà tout ce qui est dans le Protocole. L'article 5 du Protocole II est beaucoup plus détaillé que l'article 10 de Pacte. La différence réside dans le fait qu'il peut être dérogé à certaines dispositions des Pactes en cas de danger public exceptionnel, notamment aux articles 10 et 14 du Pacte. Dans cette situation, les dispositions du Protocole ont pour effet de maintenir la garantie des droits de l'homme aussi en cas d'état d'urgence. Une dérogation faite en vertu de l'article 4 du Pacte ne vaut pas pour les dispositions du Protocole. D'autre part, l'application du Protocole II ne dispense pas de l'observation des dispositions du Pacte si ces dernières ont une portée plus vaste que celle du Protocole. En d'autres mots, la disposition applicable qui prévoit un niveau plus élevé de protection des droits de l'homme doit être appliquée. L'application de Protocole II et celle des Pactes ne s'excluent pas mutuellement, les deux traités se complètent réciproquement.

8.5   *La Protection des Blessés et Malades*

Les dispositions sur les blessés et malades, le personnel et les unités sanitaires sont ceux où les similarités entre les Protocoles I et II sont les plus grandes. Pour beaucoup d'articles, la Commission II de la Conférence avait adopté un langage identique pour les deux Protocoles. Dans ce domaine aussi, quelques réductions ont été faites los de l'adoption finale en plénière.[34] La perte de substance n'est cependant pas grande.

8.6   *La Conduite des Hostilités et la Protection de la Population Civile*

Les dispositions concernant la conduite des hostilités et la protection de la population civile furent celles que la rédaction finale affecta le plus. Furent supprimés notamment les articles concernant la règle fondamentale sur les méthodes et moyens de combat, l'interdiction de la perfidie, la règle de base sur la protection de la population civile, la définition de la population civile, la protection générale d'objets civils. Certains éléments essentiels des articles de cette partie du Protocole II ont cependant été retenus ailleurs, par exemple les idées de l'article 22 (quartier) à l'article 4, paragraphe 1 nouveau. Il faut également souligner que l'idée de base de la protection de la population civile n'est pas touchée, puisque les trois premiers paragraphes de l'ancien article 26 (nouvel article 13) ont été adoptés sans changement. Restent également interdits la destruction des biens indispensables à la survie de la population civile

---

34   Suppression des définitions (article 11) , transfert de l'article 12*bis* dans les garanties fondamentales, suppression de l'article 12*bis* para. 2, suppression de quelques éléments des articles 13, 14, 17 et 18.

604 PART 8: OTHER ISSUES

et, en principe au moins, le déplacement forcé de la population civile. On peut en conclure que les efforts en vue d'introduire certains éléments du droit de La Haye dans le cadre de la réglementation relative aux conflits non internationaux n'ont échoués que partiellement. Certains éléments essentiels du droit de La Haye ont été introduits dans cette réglementation, notamment le principe de l'immunité de la population civile contre toute attaque dirigée contre elle. Il s'agit là d'un pas décisif dans le développement de droit humanitaire.

8.7   *Protection Civile et Actions de Secours*

Le développement d'une sorte de statut pour la protection civile est une des grandes innovations du Protocole I. Mais la Commission compétente de la Conférence n'avait déjà adopté qu'une disposition très sommaire sur la protection civile pour le Protocole II. Ce bref article fut supprimé lors de l'adoption finale.

Pour un grand nombre de délégations, les articles sur les actions de secours en faveur de la population civile constituaient le cœur même du Protocole II. Ces actions de secours sont peut-être le moyen le plus efficace pour réduire les souffrances de la population civile lors d'un conflit interne. D'autre part, il s'agit là d'un domaine où es craintes du Tiers-Monde concernant des interventions étrangères sont les plus vives, et cela se justifie certainement à la lumière de certaines expériences historiques récentes. La Commission II avait cependant adopté une disposition sur les actions de secours dans le cadre d'un conflit non international, qui contenait une bonne part des éléments de la réglementation relative aux conflits internationaux, notamment des règles sur le transit des envois de secours et la protection du personnel participant à une action de secours. Lors de l'adoption finale il ne demeura de ce règlement qu'un principe de base : « ... des actions de secours en faveur de la population civile, de caractère exclusivement humanitaire et impartial et conduites sans aucune distinction de caractère défavorable, seront entreprises avec le consentement de la Haute Partie contractante concernée ». Cette disposition retient le caractère obligatoire des actions de secours. Celles-ci doivent donc être entreprises par les Etats ou organisations qui sont en mesure de le faire, elles doivent être acceptées, leur passage doit être autorisé. La pierre de touche du compromis finalement acquis est cependant la condition du consentement de la « Haute Partie contractante concernée ». Deux remarques sont nécessaires à cet égard. Le caractère obligatoire de l'action implique que ce consentement ne peut pas être refusé de façon arbitraire.[35] Deuxièmement,

---

35   Voir les explications de vote soumises par la Belgique et la République fédérale d'Allemagne, CDDG/SR.53, Annexe, pp. I et ss.

CONFLITS ARMÉS INTERNES ET DROIT INTERNATIONAL HUMANITAIRE   605

rien ne spécifie quand la Haute Partie contractante est « concernée ». Est-ce qu'elle est concernée par toute action de secours entreprise sur son territoire ou est-elle concernée seulement si les envois passent par un territoire effectivement contrôlé par le gouvernement établi ? Il va de soi que les pays du Tiers-Monde soucieux de sauvegarder leur « souveraineté » préféreront l'interprétation dans le sens de la première partie de l'alternative. Mais ce texte fut proposé par une délégation dont les efforts en vue de promouvoir la cause des actions de secours lors de la Conférence diplomatique sont particulièrement notoires et méritoires : la délégation de la Finlande. Une interprétation selon le deuxième terme de l'alternative rendrait donc certainement justice à l'intention de celui qui a proposé le texte. Mais il faut probablement admettre que le texte constitue un compromis de forme qui cache l'absence d'une interprétation généralement acceptée. Dans cette situation, il appartient à la pratique, et notamment au C.I.C.R. dans ses négociations, de développer cet article dans son application et d'arriver, d'un cas à l'autre, à une interprétation acceptée.

8.8   *Les Institution de la Croix-Rouge*

Les articles adoptés par les Commission contenaient des dispositions sur les activités des sociétés de secours et notamment des institutions de la Croix-Rouge (les articles 14, 33 § 1, 34 et 19 déjà mentionnés). Notions ici encore l'article 34 sur la collecte et la transmission de renseignement sur les victimes du conflit. De tout cela, il ne reste, après la rédaction finale, qu'une constatation sommaire. Les sociétés de secours locales pourront « offrir leurs services en vue de s'acquitter de leurs tâches traditionnelles à l'égard des victimes du conflit armé ». Il est à noter que derrière la notion de « tâches traditionnelles » se cache une vaste gamme d'activités qui sont, de cette façon, autorisées par le Protocole II. Il est d'autre part nécessaire de relever que l'article 18 nouveau n'autorise que l'offre des services de ces sociétés et ne concerne que les sociétés locales, il ne dit rien des sociétés étrangères, ni de la Ligue, ni du C.I.C.R.

8.9   *L'exécution du Protocole*

La version adoptée par les Commission contenaient aussi une série d'articles sur l'exécution du Protocole (article 37 – Diffusion ; 38 – Accords spéciaux ; 39 – Concours à l'observation du présent Protocole). De tout cela, il ne reste qu'une disposition sommaire sur la diffusion. Ici également, la perte de substance n'est cependant pas trop grande. Les questions réglées par les articles 38 et 39 (ancienne numérotation) sont largement couvertes par les dispositions de l'article 3 commun aux quatre conventions, qui prévoient déjà que le Comité international de la Croix-Rouge pourra offrir ses services aux Partis au conflit, et que les Parties au conflit pourront mettre en vigueur par voie d'accords spéciaux, tout ou partie des conventions. Il paraît tout à fait justifié d'interpréter cette dernière disposition comme comprenant aussi des documents additionnels aux conventions, c'est-à-dire comme invitant les Parties à mettre en vigueur non seulement les conventions, mais aussi le Protocole additionnelle II.

9 Appréciation D'ensemble

L'appréciation d'ensemble du Protocole II ne doit pas prendre comme point de départ ce qui est souhaitable, mais la situation juridique existante. Quel progrès ce Protocole représente-t-il à l'égard de la situation actuelle ? La réponse est simple. Le Protocole II constitue un progrès très net par rapport à l'article 3 commun aux quatre Conventions et au Pacte sur les doits civils et politiques. Les garanties fondamentales d'un traitement humain ont été renforcées. La protection des blessés et malades est beaucoup mieux assurée, principe de l'immunité de la population civile est établie, les actions de secours en faveur de la population civile ont une meilleure base juridique.

Mais il est tout à fait légitime de se demander si un meilleur progrès aurait été possible. Dans notre présentation du Protocole II, nous avons relevé à plusieurs reprises certains défauts sérieux. Ces défauts auraient-ils pu ou dû être évités ? S'est-on assez battu pour les éliminer ? Etait-il justifié d'accepter, lors de l'adoption finale des textes, la rédaction effectuée par une version simplifiée ? Il ne faut pas exagérer l'effet négatif de la version simplifiée. Des omissions critiquables ont été commises beaucoup plus tôt. A cet égard, on peut se demander si l'omission d'un règlement sur des situations de troubles ou de tensions intérieurs, qui équivaudrait à des dispositions sur les détenus politiques, doit être vraiment regrettée.[36] Il est fort douteux que le temps soit vraiment mûr pour une réglementation expresse de la question des détenus politiques.[37] Il y avait un danger réel à ce qu'un texte adopté ait été plus restrictif que la pratique actuelle. Ce qui est regrettable est le fait que la zone grise entre le conflit interne et le conflit international n'est pas rendue plus claire et que la lutte entre plusieurs groupes dissidents n'est pas couverte par le Protocole II. En ce qui concerne le seuil élevé de l'application du Protocole II, il serait au moins imprudent de vouloir soutenir qu'un meilleur résultat des négociations aurait pu être obtenu. La position de ceux qui tenaient à un seuil élevé était trop forte. Le déroulement du débat final et le vote final sur l'article 1er le prouvent

---

36 Cf. J. Freymond, *Guerres, Révolutions, Croix-Rouge*, 1976, p. 132.

37 Cf. le message du Conseil fédéral suisse, cité *supra* note 11, et les conclusions de l'Institut Henry-Dunant, *ibid.,* pp. 118 et ss.

CONFLITS ARMÉS INTERNES ET DROIT INTERNATIONAL HUMANITAIRE 607

en fin de compte. En ce qui concerne, enfin, la version simplifiée, l'effet le plus regrettable en est la suppression du sursis de la peine de mort. En revanche, la version contient des simplifications méritoires. Dans d'autres domaines, les pertes subies par le texte ne sont pas trop grandes.

Beaucoup de délégations ont évidemment accepté cette version sur la base de la présomption que le Protocole tel qu'il avait été établi par les Commissions risquait de ne pas obtenir les deux tiers requis dans le vote final sur le Protocole dans son ensemble. L'acceptation de certaines rédactions ne se justifie que par le souci de sauver le Protocole dans son ensemble. Mais la base de l'argumentation, c'est-à-dire le danger d'un rejet du Protocole II à défaut de la majorité requise existait-elle ? On ne peut que spéculer à cet égard. Mais nombreuses sont les délégations qui dans leur déclaration finale ont constaté qu'elles avaient toujours des objections fondamentales à l'égard de l'idée même d'un Protocole II. Un nombre considérable de délégations a souligné que c'est seulement l'initiative prise par le Pakistan de présenter un projet simplifié qui leur a permis de passer de l'opposition au moins à une attitude de non oppositions. Citons encore à titre d'exemple l'intervention du délégué du Zaïre[38] :

> Plusieurs dispositions de ce projet de Protocole II empiètent sur les règles de droit interne des Etats et par là même compromettent dangereusement la souveraineté et les compétences territoriales de ces Etats qui, conformément au § 7 de l'article 2 de la Charte des Nations Unis, relèvent du domaine réservé. L'erreur de ce projet de Protocole II, du moins dans certaines de ces dispositions, a été de traiter sur un pied d'égalité un Etat souverain et un groupe de ces ressortissants insurgés, un gouvernement légal et un groupe de hors-la-loi, un sujet de droit international et un sujet de droit interne ... A cet égard, la délégation zaïroise remercie la délégation du Pakistan et, à travers elle, le autres délégations qui ont contribué à l'élaboration du projet simplifié, dont le grand mérite est d'avoir estompé la personnalité juridique que le projet de Protocole II adopté en Commission conférait à la rébellion.

Il n'est plus possible de compter les voix, mais il est fort probable que les pays adhérant à une telle attitude auraient au moins rassemblé un tiers des voix. Un rejet du Protocole II dans le vote final aurait été plus désastreux que les défauts et insuffisances du Protocole II adopté.

---

38   CDDH/SR. 56, pp. 44 et ss.

PART 9

Implementation and Enforcement of IHL

∴

Fact-finding as a Means of Ensuring Respect for International Humanitarian Law

1   Fact-finding: A General Introduction

Fact-finding plays a major role in today's international relations, but not only in international relations. In many contexts, it is an important element of procedures serving to secure compliance and/or to settle disputes. For uncertainty about facts, diverging claims about what "really happened" often constitutes a substantial part of a dispute. Certainty about actual facts often is a first step in ensuring compliance with an obligation. This is true for many types of disputes, be they of a social, political or legal character. But as the contexts differ, the function of ascertaining facts (commonly called "fact-finding") varies, and so do the rules governing the process of ascertaining facts.

This paper tries to elaborate some specific characteristics of ascertaining facts in international relations and in particular in the framework of procedures designed to ensure a better implementation and respect of international humanitarian law. In order to do this and to put some order into the multiplicity of procedures which can be observed, an abstract framework of analysis is proposed.

On a relatively high level of abstraction, it is possible to describe the course of fact-finding procedures by a common scheme:[1]

Initiation (suspicion/unilateral claim, routine)
↓
Determination of a mandate
↓
Taking evidence (problem of access and reliability)
↓
Evaluating evidence
↓
Statement of facts (report, judgment)
↓
Reaction

---

[1] See also the various steps of the procedure described by *Sylvian Vité*, Les procédures internationals d'établissment des faits dans la mise en œuvre du droit international humanitaire, 1999, pp. 187 et seq.

© KONINKLIJKE BRILL NV, LEIDEN, 2021 | DOI:10.1163/9789004380592_033

This general scheme is helpful as a framework of comparative analysis. As already indicated, procedures for ascertaining facts serve different purposes. This can be seen in each of these procedural steps. Both the actors and the rules governing the process vary according to the context.

What matters most is, of course, the last phase, or the end result. It is directly related to the ultimate purpose or function of the procedure. Why fact-finding? Any fact-finding procedure is undertaken with a view to measures which might be taken as a result of it, or with a view to a certain effect produced by it. It sets the agenda of various actors. Furthermore, the intended result also determines the design of the various phases of the procedure.

This applies to very different procedural forms of "fact-finding" in a narrow sense, also called "inquiry", may constitute a specific separate or self-contained procedure. But it serves nevertheless a purpose beyond that procedure, mostly the settlement of a dispute or the creation of trust in another actor's behaviour (confidence-building). Where fact-finding is used within the context of measures taken to monitor and ensure compliance with a treaty regime (so-called "verification", in particular within the framework of arms control and disarmament regimes) its purpose is to detect violations, deter violations and to create confidence. The structures of the relevant procedures are geared to that purpose.

It is with this general perspective in mind that our analysis deals with different actors in this field.

2 Fact-finding: Actors, Institutions and Functions

There are essentially four different types of institutions or bodies engaged in ascertaining facts: States, organs established in common by two or more States, inter-governmental organisations (or specific organs of these organisations) and non-governmental organisations. In some cases, individuals may also undertake fact-finding without being an organ of one of these four types of entities. Fact finding by intergovernmental institutions may include permanent international organisations (e.g. United Nations) and treaty-based organs (e.g. the IHFFC[2]). The ICRC is a particular institution having inter alia fact-finding functions.

---

2 For details see below III.2.

ENSURING RESPECT FOR INTERNATIONAL HUMANITARIAN LAW

Before or within these bodies or institutions, fact-finding procedures relating to facts which are of international legal relevance may be initiated by various actors and may be pursued in various ways.

2.1 Fact-finding by the State Concerned

There is, first, unilateral fact-finding by the State concerned, i.e. the State where relevant facts happened or are still happening. It has its own agenda for clarifying facts. It may just engage in a "lessons learned" process. A more fundamental example are "truth and reconciliation commissions" or the like. This type of fact-finding often occurs in a post conflict situation as part of a process of re-establishing normalcy in a conflict-torn society. Establishing the truth may be part of a normalisation process. In recent years, it has become an important element of post-conflict peace building.[3]

In these cases, usually the government and/or the parliament of the country in questions sets up a commission for the purpose of inquiring into violations of human rights and international humanitarian law with a view to put an end to impunity and to create, by clarifying the past, a basis for future peaceful living together of different groups in the society. Whether this clarification then leads to any criminal prosecution is a question which varies from case to case.

A decisive question is whether the result achieved is really accepted as the truth and can serve as a basis of reconciliation. This depends on the political context and the personalities chosen for the purpose of fact-finding. Foreign participation in such an exercise may add to its credibility. This was, for instance, the case of the truth commissions in Sierra Leone and Guatemala. In the case of the former, the Commission was appointed by the President of Sierra Leone, but the United Nations High Commissioner for Human Rights was involved in the selection of non-citizens.[4] The chair of the latter was a person appointed by the UN Secretary-General.[5] The foreign participation gave additional may in other cases be considered an unwelcome infringement on the State's sovereignty.

Where such international input is welcome or even considered essential, the State concerned may even seize international bodies for the purpose of

---

3   The rule of law and transitional justice in conflict and post-conflict societies. Report of the Secretary-General, UN Doc. S/2004/616; see also the statement of the Secretary-General before the Security Council on September 24, 2003, S/PV 4833, p. 3.

4   Sierra Leone Truth and Reconciliation Commission Act, 2000, sec. 3.

5   The German professor *Christian Tomuschat*, see *Christian Tomuschat*, Friedenssicherung durch Wahrheitsfindung. Die Kommission zur Aufklärung der Vergangenheit in Guatemala, Vereinte Nationen 47(1999), p. 192.

establishing relevant facts. An example is the Commission on the Truth in El Salvador, created on the basis of the peace agreements between the parties to the internal conflict, which consisted exclusively of foreign nationals.[6]

2.2 Fact-finding as a Means of Interstate Dispute Settlement

The second major function of fact-finding is its use as a means of dispute settlement between States, be it by bodies created *ad hoc* for a particular controversy or by referring this task to an existing institution. States create enquiry commissions or the like to clarify facts which are the object of, or relevant for, disputes existing between them.

In these cases, a procedure for ascertaining facts is created, or seized, on the basis of an agreement between the parties to a dispute. There may be a preceding agreement in a general form providing for such a procedure. Then, it is possible that one party unilaterally triggers the process. If there is no provision for such unilateral initiation of the procedure, there must be an *ad hoc* agreement between the parties. The result of the procedure usually is a statement of the facts. But it is assumed that the clarification of the facts will facilitate the solution of a dispute.

Under the name of "inquiry", procedures of this type are a traditional means of dispute settlement. This is witnessed by the treaties adopted by the Hague Peace Conferences, the First Hague Convention of 1899 and Second Hague Convention of 1907.[7] Commissions of inquiry were a major feature of the so-called Bryan Treaties, a series of bilateral dispute settlement agreements concluded by the United States 1913 and 1914.[8] As a means of dispute settlement, inquiry is mentioned in Art. 33 of the United Nations Charter and in the "Principles for Dispute Settlement" adopted by the Conference for Security and Co-operation in Europe.[9]

Under the Hague Convention of 1907, the fact-finding body is created *ad hoc* according to procedures established by this treaty. But States may also create permanent bodies to ascertain relevant facts. A body of this type is the

---

6 See the report "From Madness to Hope": The Twelve-Year War in El Salvador, UN Doc. S/25500, Annex.

7 Hague Convention for the Pacific Settlement of Disputes, 29 July 1899; 18 October 1907 (Second Hague Convention), Art. 9 et seq.; published in *Karin Oellers-Frahm/Andreas Zimmermann*, Dispute Settlement in Public International Law, 2nd ed. 2001, p. 6; Report of the Secretary-General on methods of fact-finding, 1 May 1964, UN Doc. A/5694, paras. 11 et seq.

8 *Hans-Jürgen Schlochauer*, Bryan Treaties (1913/1914) in: EPIL vol. I, pp. 509 et seq.

9 Report of the CSCE Meeting of Experts on Peaceful Settlement of Disputes Adopted at La Valetta, February 8, 1991, *Oellers-Frahm/Zimmermann*, supra n. 7, p. 163.

ENSURING RESPECT FOR INTERNATIONAL HUMANITARIAN LAW
615

International Humanitarian Fact-Finding Commission (IHFFC) established pursuant to Art. 90 of Protocol I Additional to the Geneva Conventions. It is competent to ascertain the relevant facts where there are allegations of grave breaches or other serious violation of the Conventions and the Additional Protocols.[10] But it may also offer its good offices.

In these cases, the procedure is triggered by one party to the dispute or by both of them if they agree beforehand on using it. The latter is the only possibility under the Second Hague Convention,[11] the former is possible under Art. 90 AP I.

The result is a statement of facts. Art. 35 of the Second Hague Convention reads:

> The report of the commission is limited to a statement of facts, and has in no way the character of an award. It leaves to the parties entire freedom as to the effect to be given to the statement.

It is apparently this openness which, in the view of the drafters of the Second Hague Convention, constitutes the appeal of this type of procedure. Similar considerations may have prompted the drafters of the provision of the Geneva Conventions on enquiry[12] and of Art. 90 AP I.[13] But there is bound to be a purpose behind an inquiry. Inquiry procedures considered as successful have indeed served as a basis for solving a conflict.[14] The Geneva Conventions and Art. 90 make it clear that there is a definite purpose behind the fact-finding procedure, namely to ensure respect for international humanitarian law. This was made explicit already in the First Convention of 1929 (Art. 30):

> On the request of a belligerent, an enquiry shall be instituted, in a manner to be decided between the interested parties, concerning any alleged violation of the Convention; *when such violation has been established the belligerents shall put an end to and repress it as promptly as possible.*[15]

---

10 Although the text of Art. 90 only relates to AP I, the Commission is of the view that it can also accept the task of enquiry in violations of AP II.

11 Art. 10.

12 First Convention of 1929, art. 30; Conventions of 1949, common article 52/53/132/149.

13 See *Karl Josef Partsch*, in; Bothe, Michael/Karl Josef Partsch/Waldemar A. Solf, New Rules for Victims of Armed Conflicts, 1982, p. 544.

14 See for instance the *Dogger Bank* and *Red Crusader* cases, below notes 18 and 20.

15 Emphasis added.

The Commission shall submit to the Parties a report of the findings of fact of the Chamber, *with such recommendations as it may deem appropriate*.[16]

While other fact-finding procedure are booming (as will be shown), there has only been scarce use of fact-finding or inquiry as a means of interstate dispute settlement in the first half of the 20th century and even less so after the 2nd World War.[17] The case most often cited is that of the *Dogger Bank* of 1904 between Great Britain and Russia. That dispute was resolved on the basis of an enquiry by experts, leading to compensation being paid by Russia.[18] Two cases of application of the 1907 Hague Convention are reported, none of them having led to any kind of result.[19] As to the time after the 2nd World War, two cases are reported, one of them, the *Red Crusader Incident* between the United Kingdom and Denmark, was indeed resolved on the basis of the report of the commission enquiry.[20] Neither the inquiry procedure established by the Geneva Conventions nor the IHFFC have ever been used. In the light of allegations made in the aftermath of the hostilities between Israel and Arab States of October 1993, the ICRC indeed proposed an inquiry on the basis of common article 52/53/132/149, but no agreement on it could be achieved.[21]

The reasons for this apparent lack of interest in fact-finding or inquiry as an independent means of international dispute settlement remains to be discussed after a presentation of other types of fact-finding.[22]

Fact-finding as an independent, so to say self-contained procedure has to be distinguished from procedures for ascertaining facts which are a part of other dispute settlement procedures, in particular international conciliation or judicial proceedings.

2.3   *Fact-finding and International Conciliation*

Conciliation or mediation is not so much concerned with what happened in the past, but more directly with the solution of a controversy for the future for the future. However, clarification of facts, still existing or having occurred in

---

16   Emphasis added.

17   For an elaborated analysis, see *Vité*, supra n. 1, pp. 15 et seq.

18   *Peter Schneider*, Digger Bank Incident, in EPIL vol. I, p. 1090.

19   Report of the Secretary-General on methods of fact-finding, supra n. 7, paras. 42 et seq.; Permanent Court of Arbitration, Annual Report 2004, p. 49.

20   *Jörg Polakiewicz*, Red Crusader Incident, in EPIL vol. IV, p. 63.

21   *François Bugnion*, Le Comité international de la Croix-Rouge et la protection des vicitmes de la guerre, 1994, pp. 1099 et seq.

22   See below III.1.

ENSURING RESPECT FOR INTERNATIONAL HUMANITARIAN LAW 617

the past, may indeed contribute to solutions for the future. This is why fact-finding is indeed a possible element of conciliation procedures.

Thus, the so-called Geneva General Act of 1928[23] refers to inquiry as a possible part of a conciliation procedure (Art. 15 para. 1):

> The task of the Conciliation Commission shall be to elucidate the questions in dispute, to collect with that object all necessary information by means of enquiry or otherwise, and to endeavour to bring the parties to an agreement.

That concept of inquiry as a part of conciliation procedures is well developed by the American Treaty on Pacific Settlement (Pact of Bogotá) of April 13, 1948.[24] It creates, inter alia, a "procedure of investigation and conciliation" (Articles XV et seq.). As to the role of fact-finding in the conciliation procedure, Art. XXII states:

> ... The Commission shall institute such investigation of the acts involved in the controversy as it may deem necessary for the purpose of proposing acceptable bases of settlement.

This shows quite clearly the subordinate character of fact-finding in relation to conciliation. In this context, its only function is achieving a settlement. This being so, the conciliation procedure can nevertheless be limited to fact-finding (Art. XXVI) if the circumstances so require:

> If, in the opinion of the parties, the controversy relates exclusively to questions of fact, the Commission shall limit itself to investigating such questions, and shall conclude its activities with an appropriate report.

Conciliation procedures have been included in the dispute settlement clauses of a considerable number of international treaties.[25] They are a major element in the dispute settlement system created by the CSCE/OSCE.[26] They were introduced in the Geneva Conventions in 1929[27] and maintained and expanded in 1949.[28] Conciliation has fared a little better than inquiry as a means of

---

23 LNTS 93, 343; *Oellers-Frahm/Zimmermann*, supra n. 7, p. 93.
24 *Oellers-Frahm/Zimmermann*, id., p. 231.
25 *Rudolf Bindschedler*, Conciliation and Mediation, in: EPIL vol. I, pp. 721 et seq.
26 Supra n. 9.
27 Art. 87 of the Prisoners of War Convention.
28 Common article 11/11/11/12.

618 PART 9: IMPLEMENTATION AND ENFORCEMENT OF IHL

international dispute settlement, but not very much.[29] There is at least one *cause célèbre* in recent years, namely the mediation by the Holy See between Argentina and Chile concerning the Beagle Channel.[30] But on the other hand, neither the OSCE procedures nor those established by the Geneva Conventions have been used so far.

2.4   *Fact-finding and International Adjudication*

Ascertaining facts, i.e. taking evidence constitutes a major component of the judicial settlement of disputes.[31] It is beyond the scope of the present paper to analyse this in greater detail. What matters in the present context is the comparison with other procedures for ascertaining facts. For that purpose, it has to be recalled that international adjudication is performed by a great variety of institutions having very different structures.[32] There are permanent international tribunals competent for interstate dispute (ICJ, ITLOS), quasi-judicial bodies for the same purpose (WTO Panels and the Appellate Body), and arbitral tribunals. In the field of the protection of human rights, there are regional courts and a number of other bodies also dealing with specific cases in a manner which at least resembles adjudication, such as the procedure governed by the Optional Protocol to the ICCPR. There are interstate procedures before human rights bodies, but mostly the procedures relate to claims put forward by victims of human rights violations against a State allegedly having violated these rights. The structure of this type of procedure varies from that of the interstate processes. A further and differently structured type of international adjudication are international criminal tribunals.

In contradistinction to the procedures of inquiry and conciliation, the use of international adjudication in all its forms has tremendously developed during the last decades. In 1972, the President of the ICJ, in an address on the occasion of the fiftieth anniversary of the creation of the international judicial system stated: "There is an observable decline in the number of cases submitted not only to this Court, but to international arbitration in any form". And he

---

29   For a review of the earlier practice, see *Hans von Mangoldt*, Arbitration and Conciliation, in: Hermann Mosler/ Rudolf Bernhardt (eds.), Judicial Settlement International Disputes, 1974, pp. 417 et seq., at 484 et seq.

30   *Karin Oellers-Frahm*, Beagle Channel Arbitration, in EPIL vol. I, p. 363 et seq., at 366.

31   *Vité*, supra n. 1, pp. 18 et seq.

32   See *Pemmaraju Sreenivasa Rao*, Multiple International Judicial Forums: A Reflection of the Growing Strength of International Law or Its Fragmentation, Michigan Journal of International Law 25 (2005), pp. 929 et seq.

ENSURING RESPECT FOR INTERNATIONAL HUMANITARIAN LAW

explained: "All States have the sovereign power to use or to bypass the Court".[33] The idea to perpetuate the example of the tribunals of Nuremberg and Tokyo and to establish an international criminal jurisdiction had at that time become the victim of the political circumstances of the Cold War.

These negative trends have definitely been reserved, both as to the ICJ and as to other institutions of international adjudication. The ICJ has become a very busy court. WTO dispute settlement is booming. International arbitration has regained momentum.[34] The European Court of Human Rights is in danger of cracking down under its heavy case load. The 1990ies have seen the re-establishment of international and "hybrid" criminal jurisdictions, culminating in the establishment of the International Criminal Court. On the other hand, not all institutions which exist are actually used. The OSCE Court has yet to receive its first case. In the field of human rights, the interstate procedures which do exist under various treaty regimes only play a marginal role, if any. The affected individuals, supported by organisations of the civil society, are those who create the heavy case load of the courts and institutions. But in general, one can state that reliance on adjudication has greatly increased in the international system. This may be one explanation for the relatively scarce use of non-judicial procedures, including procedures for ascertaining facts.

It is the common element of the judicial procedures that they result in a legally binding statement on what the law is in a given situation. Taking evidence is geared towards that result and limited to what is necessary for that purpose. In contradistinction to the other procedures just described, the result is not open. The judgment declares how the parties are expected to behave as a matter of law.

The procedural structure of interstate judicial settlement, of human rights courts and of criminal tribunals is of course different, and so are there rules on taking evidence. It presents different problems depending on the type of proceedings. There are essentially three different types of international judicial proceedings:

- interstate proceedings, before the ICJ or arbitration tribunals;
- proceedings instituted by individuals against a State before human rights courts or quasi-judicial human rights bodies;

---

33 See *Hermann Mosler*, Introduction, in: Mosler/Bernhardt, supra n. 29, p. 3. For an analysis of this decrease, see *Helmut Steinberger*, The International Court Justice, id., pp. 193 et seq., at pp. 211 et seq.

34 See for example the statistics of the Permanente Court of Arbitration. There were no intestate cases before that arbitral institution between the end of the 2nd World War and 1988; since then, 12 interstate cases have been submitted for arbitration.

620 PART 9: IMPLEMENTATION AND ENFORCEMENT OF IHL

– proceedings instituted against individuals before international criminal courts.

The interstate proceedings, as a matter of principle, are of the adversarial type. This means that the tribunal in question has to rely on the evidence put forward by the parties. The ICJ, however, is not strictly bound in this way. It may ask the parties to supply specific evidence or to give explanations (Art. 49 of the Statute) and it may *motu proprio* entrust an individual or an organisation to make an enquiry (Art. 50). This is without prejudice to the rule that any party must prove the facts on which it relies to found its legal claim. If it does not succeed in doing so, the burden of proof becomes relevant, which has indeed played a major role in cases before the ICJ. Examples are, in particular, cases relating to the circumstances of the use of armed force, beginning with the *Corfu Channel* case,[35] continuing with *Nicaragua*,[36] *Oil Platforms*[37] and the *Congo*.[38]

Proceedings before human rights courts are also to a large extent of the adversarial type.[39] It is up to the complaining victim to furnish the relevant facts to the satisfaction of the court in question. But the European Court of Human Rights may in addition take evidence, also *motu proprio*, "which it considers capable of providing clarification of the facts of the case".[40] There is also a duty of the defendant State to cooperate with the Court which to some degree mitigates the deficiencies of the adversarial system.[41] Another element is the role of NGOs which may assist victims in presenting the evidence or which may themselves present such evidence in the form of *amicus curiae* briefs.

The process before the ad hoc international criminal tribunals, too, is at least to a large extent of the adversarial type, one of the parties being the public prosecutor. What has been said for the human rights courts applies *mutatis mutandis* here. A major problem of taking evidence before international

---

35 ICJ Reports 1949, p. 4.

36 Military and Paramilitary Activities in and against Nicaragua (Nicaragua v. United States of America), ICJ Reports 1986, p. 14.

37 Case Concerning Oil Platforms (Islamic Republic of Iran v. United States of America), Judgment of 6 November 2003, paras. 57 et seq.

38 Case Concerning Armed Activities in ten Territory of the Congo (Democratic Republic of the Congo v. Uganda), Judgment of 19 December 2005, paras. 57 et seq.

39 *W.J. Ganshof van der Meersch*, European Court of Human Rights, in EPIL vol. II, p. 201 et seq., at 209.

40 Rule 42 of the Rules of the European Court of Human Rights, November 4, 1998, *Oellers-Frahm/Zimmermann*, supra n. 7, p. 456.

41 See also *Jörg Nowak*, Staatliche Mitwirkung in Tatsachenfeststellungsverfahren zum Schutz vor Folter, 1997.

ENSURING RESPECT FOR INTERNATIONAL HUMANITARIAN LAW   621

criminal tribunals is the fact that this occurs quite often a long time after the facts, and far away from the place of the crime.

2.5   *Fact-finding by Intergovernmental Organisations*

Ascertaining facts also plays important role in the activities of intergovernmental organisations.[42] International organisations frequently use fact-finding as a genuine means to perform their various tasks. First the League of Nations, and then the United Nations have used fact-finding in various contexts as part of their activities for the maintenance of international peace and security. This is also the case with the OAS[43] and the OAU/AU. Usually, the purpose is to find a reliable factual basis for further measures to be taken by the Organisation. Since the very beginning of the United Nations, both the General Assembly and the Security Council have used inquiry commissions for that purpose. A few recent examples may suffice to state the case.

In 1992, the Security Council created a fact-finding mission for Yugoslavia to enquire into the allegations of massive violations of international humanitarian law.[44] After its chairman, the commission became known as Kalshoven Commission. The result of its appalling findings was the creation of the ICTY by the Security Council.[45]

In 2002, there were allegations of violations of human rights and international humanitarian law when Israeli troupes has forcefully entered the Palestinian city of Jenin. The Secretary-General established a fact finding mission, which was welcomed by the Security Council.[46] Unfortunately, that commission, although it has become operational, was finally not admitted on site.

In 2004, when there were horrible reports about massive human rights violation in the Darfur region of Sudan, the Security Council requested the Secretary-General to established a fact-finding mission, which then was to be

---

42   *Vité*, supra n. 1, pp. 55 et seq.; Report of the Secretary-General, supra n. 7, paras. 22 et seq., 149 set seq.

43   Report of the Secretary-General, supra n. 7, paras. 330 et seq.

44   Resolution 780 of 6 October 1992. The relevant part of the resolution reads: "The Security Council ... requests the Secretary-General to establish, as a matter of urgency, an impartial Commission of Experts to examine and analyse the information submitted ... together with such other information as the Commission of Experts may obtain through its own investigations or efforts, ..., with a view to providing the Secretary-General with its conclusions on the evidence of grave breaches of the Geneva Conventions and other violations of international humanitarian law committed in the territory of the former Yugoslavia".

45   Resolution 827 of 25 May 1993.

46   Resolution 1405 of 19 April 2002.

622   PART 9: IMPLEMENTATION AND ENFORCEMENT OF IHL

headed by Professor *Antonio Cassese*, former President of the ICTY, to enquire into the violations of human rights and international humanitarian law and also into the nature of the crimes allegedly committed in the area.[47] The result of its report was that the Security Council referred the case to the Prosecutor of the International Criminal Court.[48]

The examples show that a prominent function of fact-finding is to provide a basis for further measures to be taken by the organisation. This means that the results must be given into the hands of the organ which has instituted the fact-finding process. Certain limitations in this regard, however, are to be observed. The Darfur fact-finding mission, right from the beginning, was undertaken with a view to criminal prosecutions to be instituted later. This meant that part of the information has to be treated as confidential in order not to compromise the later criminal proceedings.

While these examples taken from the practice of the United Nations took place *ad hoc* and were related to a specific controversy, fact-finding is also undertaken by international organisation as a part of their routine monitoring or supervisory activities. In the field of human rights, the thematic and country rapporteurs of the Human Rights Commission[49] have to be mentioned. In this case, fact-finding is part of a political process of building a scenario of pressure designed to promote better respect for human rights. The process is triggered by the Commission, according to its usual procedures. It does not depend on the consent of the State concerned, only on site activities of the rapporteurs do.

Other examples are the routine verification processes of the OPCW[50] and monitoring by the IAEA on the basis of the safeguards system.[51] Both are treaty based and have a specific structure tailor-made for the specific purposes of the procedures. In these cases, the function of fact-finding is transparency, in particular transparency about compliance, detection of violations and confidence building. In this context, already the mere existence of fact-finding procedures is a means to ensure compliance. Transparency means that the State in question has to justify before a relevant public what it does or does not do. This also means that transparency, under certain conditions, must be limited. This is, for example, the case of verification measures in the field of disarmament. The

---

47   Resolution 1564 of 18 September 2004.

48   Resolution 1593 of 31 March 2005.

49   See *Henry J. Steiner/Philip Alston*, International Human Rights in Context, 2nd ed. 2000, pp. 641 et seq.

50   Convention on the Prohibition and Development, Production, Stockpiling and Use of Chemical Weapons and on their Destruction, 13 January 1993, Art. VI.

51   Non-Proliferation Treaty, Art. III.

ENSURING RESPECT FOR INTERNATIONAL HUMANITARIAN LAW

information obtained, as a rule, remains in the hand of the Secretariat of the organisation in charge. This is as a rule enough to build confidence.

2.6 Fact-finding by the ICRC

An important actor in fact-finding relating to international humanitarian law is the ICRC. Technically, it is not an intergovernmental organisation. But it resembles IGOs in that it derives its functions from the Geneva Conventions and the Protocols additional thereto, i.e. from international treaties. An important aspect of its activities in favour of the victims of armed conflicts consists indeed of fact-finding. It serves two different purposes. First, fact-finding is needed to assess the needs of different kinds of victims. In this respect, kit is an important preliminary measure for relief operations.

Secondly, it is part of the activities of the ICRC to ensure compliance with international humanitarian Law. The purpose of that fact-finding, too, is a limited transparency, i.e. limited to the ICRC, as the results are generally treated as confidential. It is only where access is consistently denied or where violations observed by the ICRC are not stopped that the ICRC goes public and uses the general transparency as a means to induce compliance.

For both purposes, the ICRC's rights of access to victims, in particular to prisoners of war is very important. This right is treaty based, in the case of prisoners of war on explicit provisions of the Third Convention,[52] generally in the "right of initiative".[53]

All this is a core element of the implementation of international humanitarian law.

2.7 Fact-finding by Non-Governmental Organisations

Last but not least, non-governmental organisations play a major role in international fact-finding, in particular in the fields of environmental protection (Greenpeace) and of human rights (Amnesty International, Human Rights Watch). Amnesty International has published numerous reports concerning alleged violations of international humanitarian law.[54] Human Rights Watch recently published the well researched report "Off Target" concerning the respect for international humanitarian law by both sides during the American and British intervention in Iraq.

---

52 Art. 126 of the IIIrd Convention.

53 Common article 9/9/9/10 of the Conventions, art. 81 (1) AP I, see the ICRC Commentary to the Additional Protocols, Art. 81, marg. notes 3309 et seq.

54 Examples are recent reports concerning the detainees at Guantanamo Bay.

624 PART 9: IMPLEMENTATION AND ENFORCEMENT OF IHL

3   Fact-finding as a Means to Implement and Enforce International
     Humanitarian Law

3.1   *Overview and Development*

On the basis of these reflections, the role of the different fact-finding procedures for a better implementation and enforcement of international humanitarian law can be clarified.

The role of international courts and quasi-judicial bodies varies greatly, and so does the fact-finding undertaken by these bodies. There is, first of all, the International Court of Justice whose role has greatly increased in recent years. Its function is to state in a legally binding way violations of international law and (if so requested) to award damages for these violations. This also applies to international humanitarian law. The Court has fulfilled these functions in the Nicaragua[55] and the recent Congo case.[56] These judgments were the result of extensive fact-finding by the Court. The two cases show the potential of the Court in this field.

Arbitration similarly plays the increasing role. A recent example is the Eritrea-Ethiopia Claims Commission dealing with violations of international humanitarian law during the conflict between these two States.[57] In the basis of extensive fact-finding, it has rendered a number of awards, stating either that violations of international humanitarian law has happened or could not be proved, and that one of the States was liable to pay compensation for a particular case of damage.

Whether and to what extent human rights bodies play a role in enforcing international humanitarian law, which applies in parallel to human rights law, still is a matter of some controversy, but it has been recognised as a matter of principle by the International Court of Justice.[58] This means that a violation of a human right can at the same time constitute a violation of international humanitarian law, and that the human rights remedy (a complaint by the individual victim before a human rights tribunal) also covers the violation of international humanitarian law.[59] Thus, taking evidence, i.e. fact-finding

---

55   Case Concerning Military and Paramilitary Activities in and against Nicaragua, Nicaragua v. United States of America, Judgment of 27 June 1986.

56   Case Concerning Armed Activities in ten Territory of the Congo, Democratic Republic of the Congo v. Uganda, Judgment of 19 December 2005.

57   See for example the award rendered 28 April 2004, 43 ILM 1249 (2004).

58   Legal Consequences of the Construction of a Wall in the Occupied Palestinian Territory, Advisory Opinion, 9 July 2004, paras. 102 et seq.

59   As to the inter-American practice, see the *Tablada* case decided by the Inter-American Commission of Human Rights, IACHR Report No. 55/97.

done by and for international human rights tribunals may also be relevant for international humanitarian law. This has become increasingly important in recent years.

Another important development is that of international criminal courts. The establishment of the two *ad hoc* tribunals for the former Yugoslavia and for Rwanda have opened a new chapter as to the ways and means of ensuring respect of international humanitarian law. The ICC has its own procedure of investigation which is in the hands of the Office of the Prosecutor.

As the Security Council has stated on several occasions that systematic violations of international humanitarian law constitute a threat to the peace,[60] the entire array of measures within the power of the Security Council can be triggered by fact-finding relating to violations of international humanitarian law. Examples are the creation of the International Criminal Tribunal for the Former Yugoslavia and that for Rwanda, both preceded by a fact-finding mission. A recent example of this practice is the case of Darfur. Other UN organs or bodies play different roles in the field, in particular the rapporteurs of the Human Rights Commission and the High Commissioner for Human Rights.

The role of fact-finding by the ICRC and by NGO s has already been explained.

Fact-finding is indeed a major tool for a better implementation and enforcement of international humanitarian law, yet it has become multifaceted and complex.

This development of these various institutions involved in ascertaining fact in international relations generally and in respect of international humanitarian law in particular was bound to have an impact on fact-finding as a means of interstate dispute settlement and on the procedures created for that purpose by the Geneva Conventions and the Additional Protocols. In order to understand that phenomenon of non-use of certain dispute settlement procedures, it is necessary to recall it is not limited to fact-finding. It also applies, albeit to a lesser extent, to conciliation and also to certain judicial and quasi-judicial institutions. Examples are the non-use of OSCE dispute settlement and of the interstate complaints in the filed of human rights. Interstate cases before the institutions of the European Convention on Human Rights have only played a marginal role.[61] The same holds true

---

60   Resolutions 827 (1993) (former Yugoslavia); 955 (1994) (Rwanda); 1564 (2004) (Darfur).

61   In the 55 years of the existence of the European Convention, there have been, technically speaking, 18 cases, in reality only 6: Greece v. U.K. (Cyprus, 1956, 1957), Greece v. Turkey (Cyprus, 1974, 1975, 1977), Austria v. Italy (South Tyrol, 1960), Ireland v. U.K. (Northern Ireland, 1978), [several States] v. Greece (internal situation in Greece, 1968, 1970), [several States] v. Turkey (internal situation in Turkey, 1982).

for the intestate procedure art. 26 of the ILO Constitution.[62] The interstate procedures existing under other treaties (ICCPR, ACHR, CERD, CAT) have not been used at all.[63] One of the reasons of the non-use of those procedures may be that the decision to seize an interstate dispute settlement body means overcoming a threshold. As a rule, the necessary effort is not made where the issue is essentially an altruistic one as in the case of human rights and international humanitarian law. States have been extremely reluctant to lodge complaints as a kind of *action popularis* in the "public", in the common interest. Generally speaking, the booming of international judicial dispute settlement relates to other matters. Where issues of human rights and/or international humanitarian law are submitted to an interstate dispute settlement body, the "plaintiff" State must have a rather strong political motivation to do so. In most of the interstate cases before the institutions of the European Convention, there was a serious political conflict between the plaintiff and the defendant State (Cyprus v. U.K.; Austria v. Italy; Ireland v. U.K.; Greece v. Turkey).[64] If this political motivation exists, (as in the cases of Nicaragua and Iran v. the United States, Congo v. Uganda, Rwanda and Burundi, or the cases concerning the application of the Genocide Convention against Yugoslavia/Serbia-Montenegro), States have apparently preferred to use judicial procedures instead just fact-finding or conciliation. This accounts for the increasing role of the ICJ in this field. It is not really at odds with the traditional wisdom that fact-finding is more acceptable to States because it is less offensive to State sovereignty. This is seen from the perspective of the potential defendant. If a plaintiff thinks that it has a good case, it will use the stronger judicial forum.

Where fact-finding is initiated by third parties, in particular IGOs and NGOs, which have an agenda of their own, these actors usually have that sufficient impetus to engage in such procedures which is lacking where the States just decide ln their own. This accounts for the widespread use of fact-finding by international organisations and NGOs. The costs involved in a bilateral fact-finding procedure also constitute a restraining factor.

---

62 See *Manfred Nowak*, U.N. Covenant on Civil and Political Rights, 2nd ed. 2005, Art. 41 marg. note 2.

63 *Nowak*, id.; *Christian Tomuschat*, International Covenant on Civil and Political Rights, Human Rights Committee, in EPIL vol. II, pp. 1115 et seq.

64 *Nowak*, id.

3.2 Fact-finding as a Means of Implementing and Enforcing International Humanitarian Law: Current Situation and the Role of the IHFFC

On the basis of these reflections, it will now be attempted to specify the possible role of the IHFFC as a means of ensuring a better respect for international humanitarian law. At the outset, the particular context in which the relevant text, i.e. art. 90 AP I, was negotiated has to be recalled. Apart from dissemination, the attention of the negotiators of the Protocols, as far as ensuring respect for international humanitarian law is concerned, concentrated on two traditional instruments already found in the Conventions: the Protecting Powers and inquiry.

As to inquiry, this traditional instrument was considered as useful by many States despite the fact that it had not been used. The negotiators wanted to improve the situation by eliminating the need to establish the inquiry body *ad hoc* by a special compromise, a need which might account for the non-use of the inquiry procedure found in the Conventions since 1929. Thus, it was proposed to create a standing commission. The proposals which were made, however, went far beyond what is now in Art. 90. It was proposed to create a body with obligatory monitoring functions which it could even trigger on its own initiative.[65] This was bitterly opposed by a number of delegations.[66] Even a general obligation to accept an inquiry initiated at the request of a State party was not acceptable. The compromise was to adopt a copy of the optional clause of Art. 36 of the Statute of the International Court of Justice.[67]

As has just been shown, the possibilities and practices of fact-finding in the field of international humanitarian law have since then considerably developed. What is, in this complex new content, the role of the IHFFC as an institution specifically created for the purpose of ascertaining facts where there are allegations of violations of international humanitarian law? When the Commission was created by the Diplomatic Conference 1974–77, the multiplicity of procedures just described was not imagined. The functions of the Security Council were hampered by the phenomenon of the so-called automatic veto. Resort to the International Court of Justice was rather rare. No international criminal tribunal existed, and those who advocated its establishment were regarded as utopians. The enforcement of international humanitarian law by human rights tribunals was certainly not a perspective which came to mind of

---

65 See *Partsch*, supra n. 13, pp. 539 et seq.

66 See also *Vité*, supra n. 1, p. 203.

67 *Partsch*, supra n. 13, p. 240.

the negotiators. It was assumed and hoped that the maximum acceptable for States in terms of a third party dispute settlement procedure was that Commission with a limited jurisdiction.

Does the fact that the circumstances have changed mean that the IHFFC has become superfluous, in particular in the light of the fact that it has so far not been seized by any State and that there are so many "competing" institutions? An answer to this question, which this author thinks is negative, has to single out what are the specific traits the IHFFC presents for the States to take advantage of, which the other procedures do not have. These specific characteristics are

- that it is an interstate procedure which is very much influenced and even shaped by the States concerned;
- that the procedure is confidential;
- that its result stops short of a statement of the law.

All three elements are important, in particular in the light of the situation described above.

State influence on the procedure: The parties to the procedure, not a fact-finding body coming with the authority of the Security Council or that of the Prosecutor of the ICC, determine the scope of the case. This is obvious where the Commission offers its good offices (Art. 90 par. 2 (c)(ii)). But although the scope of an enquiry will be determined by the allegation (Art. 90 par. 2 (c)(i)), the procedure possesses a cooperative character. It is up to the parties, both parties (!), to decide whether the report is rendered public.

Confidentiality: This element is related to the first one. It is important for States that there is no naming and shaming involved as is the case with many other procedures.

No statement of the law: This remains important in relation to the various judicial procedures. Once the facts are stated, the parties can agree on what follows. If the ICJ has jurisdiction in the case, one party can still go to the ICJ for a declaration of the law and an award of damages. But this is highly improbable. The facts being ascertained will as a rule facilitate an agreement among the parties on the question of just compensation. The Commission may even offer its good offices to arrive at such an agreement. This may be less expensive and less time consuming than going to the ICJ or to arbitration. Thus, although the Commission can and will deal with questions of law, it can do so in a more flexible way than any court.

In relation to the ICC, an early functioning of the Commission may render superfluous the need to call upon the Prosecutor of the ICC. The stated facts may facilitate a party's decision itself to prosecute, which would exclude the jurisdiction of the ICC.

ENSURING RESPECT FOR INTERNATIONAL HUMANITARIAN LAW 629

The IHFFC is not the only institution charged with fact-finding for the purpose of a better implementation of international humanitarian law. There remains, however, a considerable potential for it, in particular in cases where the States concerned want to retain a control of the procedure which either the Security Council or the ICC Prosecutor might take from them.

There remains the question whether and how the Commission could overcome its independence on States deciding to use it. The answer depends on the concept of "good offices". On the one hand, as has been explained, the Commission has no right to initiate a fact-finding mission *motu proprio*. On the other hand, it may "facilitate, through its good offices, the restoration of an attitude of respect for the Conventions and this Protocol" (Art. 90 (2)(b)(ii)). Art. 90 does not say that it can do so only within the framework of an ongoing procedure initiated by a State against another State. In other words, the Commission is able to offer its good offices without being asked to do so, while the State to whom they are offered is of course free to refuse them. The good offices clause, thus, is the key which opens the door for a proactive role of the Commission.[68]

3.3 Perspectives: The Relationship between Different Bodies Involved in Ascertaining Facts

Having elaborated the specific role the IHFFC in the overall complex of ascertaining facts in current international relations, a few comments must be added concerning its relationship to other bodies tasked with ascertaining facts relevant for their functions which have been mentioned.

The first question is that of the relationship between the Commission and the United Nations. Assuming that the Security Council requests the assistance of the Commission, the situation presents particular problems. When the Security Council acts under Ch. VII of the Charter, it may adopt decisions which are binding on the member States and probably also on intergovernmental organisations. It may create fact-finding bodies as its subsidiary organs or oblige the Secretary-General to establish such bodies as part of the Secretariat, but it may also task existing bodies, including the IHFFC. In doing so, the Council is bound by the Charter and also, according to a prevailing view, by customary norms relating to the protection of human rights,[69] but arguably

---

68   *Vité*, supra n. 1, p. 214, set seq.

69   The exact scope of the obligation of the Security Council to respect human rights is controversial. The Court of First Instance of the European Communities limits this obligation to the core guarantees which constitute *ius cogens*: Kadi v. Council and Commission, Judgment of 21 September 2005, Case T-315/01, paras. 226 et seq.; Yusuf et al. v. Council and Commission, Judgment of 21 September 2005, Case 306/01, paras. 277 et seq. For a

not by the details of the AP I concerning the confidentiality of the work of the Commission. As a matter of expediency, however, there is no reason why the Council should disregard these rules. If the Council wants to establish a fact-finding procedure of a different nature, it can do so, and it has done so, without having recourse to the services of the Commission. If the Council wants to mandate the Commission to undertake a fact-finding mission, it will, as a rule, do so because it wants to use the particular advantages the Commission has to offer, which have been described above.

As to the ICC, it has already been pointed out that findings of the Commission may be used in subsequent criminal proceedings. This can cause a problem even where the State concerned itself institutes criminal proceedings. In the course of public proceedings, that State may use the findings which the Commission submits if all the parties to the Commission proceedings agree on them being made public (article 90 (5)(c) APERI). If that agreement is lacking, the findings may not be used.

Where there is necessary agreement, the question of how the findings are used in those proceedings is a matter of the law of criminal procedure of the State in question. From the point of view of the law governing the work of the Commission, there is no objection against members of the Commission or experts or investigators engaged by the Commission testifying before the national court. From the point of view of the procedural rights of an alleged perpetrator, it is, however, important that the findings of the Commission do not deprive that person of his or her right to challenge any evidence used against him or her.

These considerations apply *mutatis mutandis* to the ICC. The ICC is an institution tasked to ensure the application of international humanitarian law. This means that the UCC has to accept international humanitarian law las it is as a whole – which includes the rules concerning to confidentiality of the investigations of the Commission. Thus, unless there is an agreement by all parties to a Commission proceeding, its findings may not be used by the ICC, nor may members or investigators of the Commission be obliged to testify before the ICC. This limitation is implied in article 87 (6) of the ICC Statute which deals with assistance by intergovernmental organisations. On the other hand, if the use of this information is permissible from the point of view of the confidentiality of the Commission's proceedings, the rights of the defence have to be respected, as indicated.

---

somewhat broader view, see *Hans-Peter Gasser*, Collective Economic Sanctions and International Humanitarian Law, Heidelberg Journal of International Law 56 (1996), pp. 871, at 880 et seq.

4 Conclusions

The ways and means to ensure respect of international humanitarian law are diverse. Various actors play various roles on this scene. There are various actors representing the "public" interest, the international community. First, there is ICRC, impartial, experienced, of high moral standing, mostly using a diplomatic approach. There are public prosecutors, albeit not in all cases, depending on details of the rules concerning jurisdiction. There is the Security Council, powerful, sometimes high-handed, and sometimes inefficient. There are the victims, having more and more access to remedies. However, a decentralised procedure being to a larger extent in the hands of the States directly concerned has a necessary function in this complex mix of procedures. This, it is submitted, is provided by the International Humanitarian Fact-Finding Commission.

Remedies of Victims of War Crimes and Crimes against Humanities

Some Critical Remarks on the ICJ's Judgment on the Jurisdictional Immunity of States

Dans son "Faust", Goethe confère le rôle de conseiller un étudiant au diable, à Méphistophèlés. Quant aux études de droit, M. les déconseille en forts termes:[1]

> Es erben sich Gesetz und Rechte
> Wie eine ew'ge Krankheit fort ...
> Vernunft wird Unsinn, Wohltat Plage;
> Weh dir, dass du ein Enkel bist!
> Vom Rechte, das mit uns geboren ist,
> von dem ist leider nie die Frage.

Dénigrement injuste, venu de la plume d'un juriste médiocre comme Goethe? Ou est-ce que le jugement de la Cour internationale de Justice que nous discutons est une preuve de ce que Goethe avait raison?

A vrai dire, Goethe nous pose une question qui est aujourd'hui plus pertinente que jamais: celle de la légitimité de l'ordre juridique. Cette question devient d'autant plus importante pour l'ordre international que cet ordre a un impact direct pour les individus. Quelles sont donc les circonstances qui fondent la légitimité de cet ordre juridique? Et est-ce le jugement de la Cour satisfait aux exigences qui en découlent? Le raisonnement qui suit donne à cette question une réponse plutôt négative.

---

1 Johann W. von Goethe, *Faust. Der Tragödie erster Teil, Studierzimmer*: \\ Les lois et les droits se succèdent \\ Comme une éternelle maladie ... \\ Raison devient folie, bienfait devient tourment; \\ Malheur à toi, fils de tes pères, malheur à toi! \\ Car du droit né avec nous, hélas, \\ Il n'en est jamais question.
Traduction française, accessed 30 October 2013, www.archive.org/details/lefaustdegoethe toogoet.

1 The Fundamental Question of Legitimacy

The central thesis of this chapter is that the International Court of Justice (ICJ) has in its judgment on the *Jurisdictional Immunities of the State*[2] neglected fundamental requirements of the legitimacy of the international legal order. It will try to prove this point in three steps:

First, on a more technical level, it will show that the reasoning of the Court is not as compelling and elegant as it admittedly appears at a first glance, and that therefore the Court could *lege artis* have decided differently, and second, that there are more profound reasons why the Court should have held in favour of Italy or at least limited the scope of its holding. Third, that by not doing so, the Court has damaged the legitimacy of international adjudication.

2 The Case: Some Facts and Contradictions

The events which are at the origin of the case before the ICJ are well known. Two different types of gross violations of the law of armed conflict are at issue: on the one hand, two horrible massacres, committed by German forces in Italy (Civitella) and in Greece (Distomo), and on the other hand the treatment of Italians deported to Germany as forced labour. Neither the events nor their qualification as gross violations of international law are in dispute. In contradistinction to other groups of victims of war crimes and crimes against humanity committed by Germany before or during World War II, the victims of these violations have not received any compensation. When they claimed compensation by suing Germany before the Italian and Greek courts, Germany raised the defence of state immunity, and the governments of these countries supported the German claim. Thus, the three governments were in agreement on the issue of immunity. But not all courts abided by that agreement. In one case, the Greek Supreme Court,[3] and in others, the Italian *Corte di Cassazione* denied immunity.[4] Be it mentioned by the way that the latter court did so

---

2 ICJ, *Jurisdictional Immunities of the State (Germany v. Italy: Greece Intervening)*, Judgment of 3 February 2012, ICJ Reports 2012, 99.

3 Hellenic Supreme Court, *Prefecture of Voiotia v. Federal Republic of Germany*, Judgment of 4 May 2000, Case No. 11/2000.

4 Italian Supreme Court, *Ferrini v. Federal Republic of Germany*, Judgment of 11 March 2004, Decision No. 5044/2004, reprinted in: *Rivista diritto internazionale* 87 (2004): 539 et seq. (Italian) and *International Law Reports* 128 (2006): 658 et seq. (English); Italian Supreme Court, *Criminal Proceedings against Josef Max Milde*, Judgment of 13 January 2009, Decision No. 1072/2009, reprinted in: *Italian Yearbook of International Law* 18 (2008): 325 et seq.

despite the fact that in cases involving Italy, it had denied the justiciability of claims arising out of acts of warfare.[5] When Germany brought the case against Italy before the ICJ, the Italian government was in a somewhat awkward position: it had to defend the position of its courts despite the fact that it had and probably still espoused a different view and had said so before its own courts. On the other hand, one of the true parties in interest, namely the victims, was not before the Court to defend its position. These were "missing voices".[6] This constituted a somewhat awkward procedural situation – despite the fact that the academic agents did a very good job in defending the positions of the Italian courts and thereby of the victims. This procedural dilemma makes it a bad case, and bad cases make bad law. The legitimacy of the legal order is in jeopardy.

3   The Fundamental Approach

If one takes as a point of the departure the rule of immunity and tries to find exceptions to that immunity by counting cases which have so far, in deviation from the alleged rule, denied immunity concerning war crimes and gross violations of human rights, one cannot come to a result which is different from that reached by the Court. There are not enough cases having denied immunity. But was it the right way to put the question, even on level of legal technique?

The first fundamental flaw in the approach of the Court (and of many authors) is to treat state immunity as an absolute structural principle of the international order. This is not true, neither conceptually nor historically. State immunity is an exception to territorial sovereignty which indeed is a principle at least as fundamental as state immunity. Sovereign equality also means equal territorial sovereignty. Historically, the US Supreme Court case *Schooner Exchange v. McFaddon*[7] is generally seen as the point of departure of the judicial recognition of state immunity. The essential argument of that case, however, does not rely on sovereign immunity as a structural principle

---

5   Italian Supreme Court, *Markovic et al.*, Order of 5 June 2002, Order No. 8157/2002.

6   Markus Krajewski and Christopher Singer, "Should Judges Be Front-Runners? The ICJ, State Immunity and the Protection of Fundamental Human Rights", *Max Planck Yearbook of United Nations Law* 16 (2012): 1–34, 31 et seq.

7   US Supreme Court, *The Schooner Exchange v. McFaddon*, Judgment of 24 February 1812, 11 US 116.

REMEDIES OF VICTIMS OF WAR CRIMES

of international law, but on implied consent. In the words of Chief Justice Marshall: "All exceptions (...) to the full and complete power of a nation within its own territories must be traced up to the consent of the nation itself. They can flow from no other legitimate source. This consent might be either express or implied".[8]

The *Schooner Exchange* had entered US waters in distress. Chief Justice Marshall considered this to be an entry by consent. He argued: "The implied license therefore under which such vessel enters a friendly port, may reasonably be construed, and, it seems to the Court, ought to be construed, as containing an exemption from the jurisdiction of the sovereign, within whose territory she claims the rites of hospitality".[9]

This reasoning is a far cry from recognising a structural principle of international law requiring the jurisdictional immunity of foreign states. At least historically, the thesis of the Court that state immunity forms part of the principle of sovereign equality[10] is thus not true. According to Marshall's reasoning, state immunity is neither absolute nor comprehensive, it depends on the circumstances of the case. It is contextual. Therefore, a recent analysis of the *Schooner Exchange* case rightly called the doctrine of absolute immunity a "myth".[11] But during the nineteenth and early twentieth century, it became customary to follow the *Schooner Exchange* precedent. However, the rule of state immunity has regularly been adapted to changing circumstances in international relations.[12] New developments in international relations triggered new types of cases. Courts and legislators took a fresh look on state immunity. The rule of state immunity was adapted accordingly. State immunity was denied when the cases no longer corresponded to the *Schooner Exchange* rationale. The most important developments in this respect were the denial of immunity for *acta iure gestionis*[13] since the end of the nineteenth century and for so-called local torts. The latest development of this kind is the US legislation excluding immunity in cases where the defendant state sponsors terrorism.[14]

---

8   Ibid., 136.

9   Ibid., 144.

10   Ibid.,, para. 57.

11   Lee M. Caplan, 'State Immunity, Human Rights and *Jus Cogens*', *American Journal of International Law* 97 (2003): 741–81, 753.

12   Krajewski and Singer, "Should Judges Be Front-Runners?" (n. 6), 8 et seq.

13   Peter-Tobis Stoll, "State Immunity", in Rudiger Wolfrum, ed., *Max Planck Encyclopedia of Public International Law* (Oxford: oup, online edition), accessed 30 October 2013, MN 6.

14   Public Law 104–132 and 110–181; 28 USC § 1605(a).

636 PART 9: IMPLEMENTATION AND ENFORCEMENT OF IHL

4 The Local Torts Rule

The acts for which the plaintiffs before the Italian and Greek courts claimed compensation were no doubt acts *iure imperii*. Thus, the first mentioned reason for denying immunity did not apply. But the massacres of Civitella and Distomo could fall under the local torts rule. That rule is formulated by the UN Convention on State Immunity[15] (article 12) in the following terms: "(...) a State cannot invoke immunity from jurisdiction before the court of another State (...) in a proceeding which relates to pecuniary compensation for death or injury to the person, or damage to or loss of tangible property, caused by an act or omission which is alleged to be attributable to the State, if the act or omission occurred in whole or in part in the territory of that other State and if the author of the act or omission was present in that territory at the time of the act or omission".

Read in the light of Marshall's reasoning, that provision confirms the principle of territorial sovereignty and limits the construction of implied consent accordingly. Its scope of application is not restricted to particular activities (such as traffic accidents caused by service vehicles of a foreign state). It is broad and general. US courts have applied the local torts rule in cases of murder allegedly committed by foreign secret service agents.[16] The Court deals with this rule,[17] but leaves the question whether it constitutes customary law open. It maintains, instead, that even if it were a customary law rule, it would not be applicable in case of military activities, and that therefore the general rule of immunity applied to military activities.[18] This is an oversimplification. The Court's analysis of the relevant state legislative practice[19] is, with due respect, somewhat surprising.[20] The Court notes that the overwhelming majority of states having a local tort clause in their state immunity legislation has no exception clause for military activities. But it

---

15 United Nations Convention on Jurisdictional Immunities of States and their Property, 2 December 2004, A/RES/59/38, annex.

16 US District Court for the District of Columbia, *Letelier v. Republic of Chile*, Judgment of 11 March 1980, 488 F.Supp. 665, Judgment of 5 November 1980, 502 F.Supp; US Court of Appeals for the 9th Circuit, *Liu v. Republic of China*, Judgment of 29 December 1989, 892 F.2d 1419.

17 ICJ, *Jurisdictional Immunities* (n. 2), paras. 62 et seq.

18 Ibid., para. 69.

19 E.g. US, Foreign Sovereign Immunities Act, 21 October 1976, Public Law 94–583; UK, State Immunity Act 1978, 20 July 1978, 1978 ch. 33; Australia, Foreign States Immunities Act 1985, Act No. 196 of 1985; Canada, State Immunity Act 1980, R.S.C., 1985, c. S-18, as amended.

20 ICJ, *Jurisdictional Immunities* (n. 2), paras. 70 et seq.

REMEDIES OF VICTIMS OF WAR CRIMES

seems to be more important for the Court that two states have such a military exception clause.

The Court also relies on the drafting history of the UN Convention of State Immunity in the ILC. Its local tort rule, quoted above, does not contain an exception for military activities. But to prove its point, the Court relies on a half sentence in the ILC's Commentary to show that it must nevertheless be understood as containing such exception.[21] But this is an over-emphasis on one sentence in a commentary. The non-application of the local tort rule to military activities is not as self-evident as the Court seems to think. The European Convention on State Immunity,[22] not applicable in the present case, indeed contains an exception clause for military activities. But it has a specific purpose which is important for European states, namely that of preserving the primacy of status of forces agreements. This is also the explicit purpose of limited military exception clauses contained in some national legislation quoted by the Court[23] and of national court decisions referred to by the Court as well.[24] Although the explicit provision of the European Convention is formulated in a general way, this is not really a compelling proof that the local torts rule has developed with a kind of tacit exception for military activities. In this connection, it must be emphasised that the status of forces agreements which the clause of the European Convention is intended to preserve do not deprive the victims of unlawful acts of foreign forces of their judicial remedies: they open the way for a different type of remedy, namely action against the victim's own state.[25]

5   The Case Law

Beyond the local torts rule, the Court relies on an extensive analysis of the case law concerning the question whether there is an exception to the rule of state immunity in cases of war crimes, crimes against humanity and other grave violations of human rights.[26] At a first glance, the reasoning of the Court is clear and convincing: only the Italian and Greek cases which in the case before the

---

21   Ibid., para. 69.

22   European Convention on State Immunity, 16 May 1972, ETS No. 074.

23   Canada, Australia and Israel, see ICJ, *Jurisdictional Immunities* (n. 2), para. 71.

24   Ibid., para. 72.

25   NATO Status of Forces Agreement, 19 June 1951, accessed 5 December 2013, http://www.nato.int/cps/en/natolive/official_texts_17265.htm, art. VIII(5).

26   In particular ICJ, *Jurisdictional Immunities* (n. 2), para. 85.

PART 9: IMPLEMENTATION AND ENFORCEMENT OF IHL

Court are alleged to be a violation of the rule of immunity have denied immunity. This, goes the argument, is not enough to establish a new customary rule providing for an exception to the old rule of immunity. But at a closer look, the true legal situation is not that easy to ascertain.

First, in the light of what has been said concerning the true scope of the traditional rule of immunity, this approach means asking the question the wrong way around. The question is not whether there is a new exception to an otherwise absolute rule of immunity. In the logic of the historic origin of the rule, it must rather be asked whether the rule of immunity also applies to new types of cases which so far had not been before national courts. Furthermore, seen with a critical eye, the picture of the case law is much more differentiated than the approach of the Court might make it appear. At a closer analysis, there are five types of cases:

– cases not directly relevant for the question of customary law as they rather relate to the interpretation of national legislation concerning sovereign immunity,
– cases not directly relevant because of their narrower scope,
– courts granting immunity without internal dissent,
– courts split on the question of immunity, but granting it by a narrow majority decision,
– courts denying immunity.

The British and Canadian[27] cases quoted by the Court[28] fall into the "not relevant" category. In particular the cases of *Al-Adsani v. Kuwait*[29] and *Jones v. Saudi Arabia*[30] emphasised by the ICJ relate to questions of the interpretation of the UK State Immunity Act 1978. In the latter case, only one Judge, Lord Hoffmann,[31] is of the view that customary international law requires the UK to grant immunity. If the majority is of the view that the national legislation entitles the foreign state to immunity, it expresses no view as to whether customary law does so as well.

The case of *McElhinney v. Ireland*,[32] relied upon by the Court,[33] is relevant for the conclusion that the local tort rule does not constitute customary law, but it

---

27   Canada, Court of Appeal for Ontario, *Bouzari v. Iran*, Judgment of 30 June 2004, No. C38295.

28   ICJ, *Jurisdictional Immunities* (n. 2), paras. 72 et seq.

29   UK, High Court, Queen's Bench Division, *Al-Adsani v. Government of Kuwait*, Judgment of 15 March 1995, 103 ILR 420 (qb 1995); 107 ILR 536 (ca 1996).

30   UK, House of Lords, *Jones v. Saudi Arabia*, Judgment of 14 June 2006, [2006] UKHL 26.

31   ICJ, *Jurisdictional Immunities* (n. 2), para. 101.

32   ECtHR, *McElhinney v. Ireland*, Grand Chamber Judgment of 21 November 2001, Application No. 31253/96.

33   ICJ, *Jurisdictional Immunities* (n. 2), para. 72.

is not relevant for the immunity for war crimes and crimes against humanity. It related to a rather small border incident, not to torture or similar violations of fundamental values. The decision of the Slovenian Constitutional Court[34] on which the ICJ relied, too, is also not really relevant because its holding is rather limited. In the first part, the yardstick of the decision on the constitutional complaint was whether the judgment of the ordinary court was "arbitrary" in rejecting the applicant's claim because of the defendant's immunity. This is not equivalent to a Constitutional Court's holding that there is immunity. In the second part of the judgment, the Slovenian Constitutional Court considered immunity as a proportional limitation of the right to a judicial remedy, but that proportionality judgment was based on the erroneous premise that the plaintiff could claim compensation before German courts.[35] The value of the Slovenian decision as an expression of customary law is therefore limited.

In the most recent case in question, the judgment of the Polish Supreme Court in *Natoniewski v. Federal Republic of Germany*,[36] there is an elaborate argument for maintaining immunity, and no report of a dissent. It is the only one which really falls into the second category.[37]

In the other cases quoted by the ICJ in favour of the doctrine of immunity, the courts were narrowly split: the US Court of Appeal in *Princz* (2 to 1),[38] the Special Supreme Court of Greece in *Margellos* (6 to 5)[39] and the European Court of Human Rights in *Al-Adsani* (9 to 8).[40]

This is the jurisprudence to which one has to add the Greek and Italian cases denying immunity (*Voiotia*,[41] *Ferrini*,[42] *Milde*[43]). Thus, the true overall

---

34   Slovenian Constitutional Court, *AA v. Germany*, Judgment of 8 March 2001, Case Up-13/99–24.

35   German courts, with the approval of the German Federal Constitutional Court, have consistently held that no individual rights arise out of violations of the laws of war which occurred during World War II, BVerfGE (Decisions of the Federal Constitutional Court) vol. 94, 318.

36   "The Supreme Court Decision of 29 October 2010, Ref. No. IV CSK 465/09 in the Case Brought by Winicjusz N. against the Federal Republic of Germany and the Federal Chancellery for Payment", *Polish Yearbook of International Law* 30 (2010): 299–303.

37   The French cases are too laconic to classify them.

38   US Court of Appeals, *Princz v. Federal Republic of Germany*, Decision of 1 July 1994, 26 F.3d 1166 (DC Cir. 1994).

39   Greek Special Supreme Court, *Margellos v. Federal Republic of Germany*, Judgment of 17 September 2002, 129 ILR 525.

40   ECtHR, *Al-Adsani v. United Kingdom*, Grand Chamber Judgment of 21 November 2001, Application No. 35763/97.

41   See above (n. 3).

42   See above (n. 4).

43   See above (n. 4).

picture of the case law is much more open than would appear from reading the ICJ's analysis. Especially the fact of split courts indicates the existence of a tension, of new developments. This should have invited the ICJ to be at least more careful in its analysis and not to simply disregard the fact that there is law making in progress.

The reasoning of the Court not being compelling on a technical level, we have to turn our attention to the fundamental issues, i.e. fundamental reasons for denying immunity.

6 Fundamental Reasons for Denying Immunity

The fundamental reason for denying immunity is the value orientation which currently characterises the international legal order. The characterisation of certain norms as *ius cogens* is an expression of this development, but not the only one. This is the essential point of what has been coined as constitution-alization.[44] Constitutionalization implies the need to implement fundamental values of the international order, *inter alia* by increasing and strengthening the remedies available for that purpose. Implementation of fundamental values is a crucial element of the current international order. State immunity for war crimes and gross violations of human rights is incompatible with that idea. State immunity is no more accepted in the international legal order as, and to the extent that, it would shield gross violations of fundamental values of that order.

Objections are raised against that kind of legal logic, and the Court accepts some of them. These objections, as they are developed in the reasoning of the ICJ,[45] rely on two distinctions which, with due respect, are irrelevant:

The first, it is submitted: irrelevant, distinction is that between primary, substantive norms on the one hand, and secondary, procedural norms on the other.[46] That distinction is used by the Court to reject the *ius cogens* argument often put forward as a basis for denying immunity in cases of gross violations of fundamental international norms: only the substantive, primary norms are *ius cogens*, but not the secondary, procedural norms necessary for the implementation and enforcement of those primary norms. Therefore, goes the argument, these secondary norms cannot override the traditional norm of state

---

44 Jan Klabbers, Anne Peters and Geir Ulfstein, *The Constitutionalization of International Law* (Oxford: OUP, 2011); Martti Koskenniemi, "International Legal Theory and Doctrine", in Wolfrum, ed., *Max Planck Encyclopedia* (n. 13), MN 29.

45 ICJ, *Jurisdictional Immunities* (n. 2), paras. 92 et seq.

46 See ibid., para. 95.

REMEDIES OF VICTIMS OF WAR CRIMES

immunity. But does this type of logic which deprives fundamental norms of an effective remedy really correspond to the importance of these imperative primary norms?

The second distinction, which is a question of the internal logic of the international legal order, plays a role in the doctrinal debate about immunity. It is not even discussed by the Court, but was argued by Germany:[47] while it is recognised that the personal immunity of perpetrators who are state organs no longer exists in cases of war crimes and gross violations of human rights, the immunity of the state is held to subsist.[48] True, both types of immunity have to be distinguished – but why should the wrong-doer state be obliged to leave its agents to the criminal jurisdiction of other states while that state's pecuniary interests are preserved because the state still enjoys immunity? It would be an unacceptable contradiction of values if that distinction were to shield the state in contradistinction to the perpetrator. As far as immunity is concerned, that distinction must be considered as irrelevant.

Quite to the contrary: denial of the immunity of state organs for official acts constituting war crimes and crimes against humanity, starting with the trials of Nuremberg and Tokyo, was the first step by which the international legal order accorded a higher rank to the implementation of basic values than to the regard for foreign sovereignty. This denial is now firmly established in international law. It is a matter of the internal consistency of that legal order not to exempt pecuniary claims against the state itself from this reliance on basic values.

Both distinctions are rather formalistic. If they are used to hinder the enforcement of fundamental values of the international system, this puts the legitimacy of the legal order into jeopardy. This is so obvious that one has to ask why the Court is willing to derive such consequences from the said distinctions. Are there additional reasons behind these arguments?

7 The Real Pros and Cons of National Courts Dealing with Compensation of War Damages

The Court does not discuss an argument which is often found in the legal literature, namely that courts were unable to deal with mass claims after a war.

---

47   ICJ, *Jurisdictional Immunities of the State (Germany v. Italy: Greece Intervening)*, Public Sitting of 15 September 2011, cr 2011/20, 26, Christian Tomuschat.

48   Christian Tomuschat, "L'immunite des États en cas de violations graves des droits de l'homme", *Revue Générale de Droit International Public* 109 (2005): 51–74, 56.

It would result in chaos. This contention is not true: Courts nowadays are accustomed to dealing with mass claims. The practice of the UN Compensation Commission adjudicating war damages of the Second Gulf War on a massive scale is a proof.[49] In the United States in particular, the class action procedure has been developed to deal with mass claims.[50] Had Germany won the case before the ICJ, no chaos would have resulted – especially in the light of the fact that most justified claims are indeed settled.

But even if courts can do it – is it desirable that they have a role in this field? This raises the question whether state immunity is salutary because it reserves the possibility to settle the question of compensation for war damages, including compensation for gross violations of the law of armed conflict, to intergovernmental dealings which preferably result in treaties. There can be no doubt that after a war having caused massive damages, treaty making is useful to bring some order in a complex situation. The *ius cogens* argument must not, and does not, stand in the way of reasonable treaty making on the consequences of war, including the question of compensation for victims. A good regulation by treaty is the preferred solution. But this does not mean that this solution is exclusive of others. Solution by treaty means an arrangement between the state bureaucracies negotiating the treaties. The question must be asked, both in terms of efficiency and of legitimacy, whether it is appropriate to leave this question to the bureaucracies alone.

The history of post-war treaty making has not been a general success story. A large part of the intergovernmental dealings after the World War I, in particular the reparations question, account for the disaster which followed.[51] The record after the World War II is better, but the regulation of compensation has been fragmented and disparate. This leads to the crux of the case before the ICJ. In its pleadings, Germany heavily relied on the fact that compensation was paid to many victims.[52] But there is no or, in the case of forced labour, at least no good[53] explanation of the reason why the

---

49 UNSC, Resolution 687 (1991), S/RES/687(1991), 3 April 1991, paras. 16 et seq.; Provisional Rules for Claims Procedure, 26 June 1992, S/AC.26/1992/10, annex.

50 For a concise and critical review of the phenomenon of class action see Burkhard Hess, „Kriegsentschädigungen aus kollisionsrechtlicher und rechtsvergleichender Sicht", in Wolff Heintschel von Heinegg et al., eds., *Entschädigung nach bewaffneten Konflikten: Die Konstitutionalisierung der Welthandelsordnung* (Heidelberg: C.F. Mueller, 2003), 107–212, 193 et seq.

51 Ignaz Seidl-Hohenveldern, "Reparations", in Rudolf Bernhardt, ed., *Encyclopedia of Public International Law*, vol. 4 (Amsterdam: North-Holland, 2000), 178–80.

52 ICJ, *Jurisdictional Immunities of the State (Germany v. Italy: Greece Intervening)*, Public Sitting of 15 September 2011, CR 2011/20, 12 et seq., Susanne Wasum-Rainer.

53 See below text accompanying n. 72.

particular plaintiffs before the Italian and Greek courts had not received any compensation. There is a loophole in the compensation schemes which has remained unexplained. This has rightly been called a *"Gerechtigkeitslücke"*[54] (justice gap). The Italian and Greek cases are an indication of this justice gap which the relevant intergovernmental dealings have neither filled nor explained.

The problem solving capacity of the united bureaucracies having thus proven questionable, national courts can and must step in. The role of national courts in securing the enforcement and implementation of international law has become crucial in many fields of international law.[55] At least to fill these loopholes, a role for national courts is necessary. It can correct errors and inequities resulting from intergovernmental dealings and provide legitimacy for the entire system. The compensation for forced labour awarded by Germany during the World War II, which is now granted through the Foundation "Remembrance, Responsibility and Future", would not have been possible without the widespread litigation in the US. The existence of individual remedies finally forced governments to see to it that justice was done to the victims. In that particular case, it was rendered technically possible by the fact that there were numerous relevant defendants who could not claim state immunity. But should this coincidence make all the difference? That does not seem to be appropriate. State immunity as conceived by the ICJ prevents national courts from playing their necessary and salutary role.

8 Beyond Technicalities: The Value Orientation of Today's International Order

This role of national courts advocated in this chapter corresponds to the value orientation of the international order which has become an important characteristic of that order. This is what is transported by the notion of "constitutionalization".[56] It requires the implementation of its fundamental values. This implementation is based on a divers system of remedies.[57] Access to justice is a crucial part thereof.

---

54 Hess, "Kriegsentschädigungen" (n. 50), 198.

55 Francesco Francioni, "International Law as a Common Language for National Courts", *Texas International Law Journal* 36 (2001): 587–98.

56 See above (n. 44).

57 Andreas Fischer-Lescano, *Globalverfassung: Die Geltungsbegründung der Menschenrechte* (Weilerswist: Velbrueck, 2005), 129 et seq.

It is sometimes said that state immunity is a necessary condition for the good functioning of international relations. This argument was heavily relied upon by Germany.[58] Yet how important must that good functioning be if it is accepted as preventing the implementation of the most important and fundamental values of the international community?[59]

9 The Appropriate Role of the ICJ

Had the Court recognised these developments it would have meant a certain amount of creativity. The Court would have contributed to the development of the law by promoting a norm which may still be *in statu nascendi*. Was it entitled to do so? Could the Court be a promoter, even a forerunner of legal developments? Yes it can![60]

To develop international law is not the exclusive prerogative of the states in the sense of state bureaucracies. These bureaucracies, internationally linked as they are, can no longer be regarded as the incorporation of "the state" in the manner of Louis XIV: "L'Etat, c'est moi!" That very concept was challenged by the Italian courts. Yet the bureaucracies stood together in defending their exclusive grip on the development of international law. But the reality of today's international relations is much more diverse.[61] Civil society plays a role. The impact of non-state actors in the development of international law (private norm entrepreneurs) is a reality. The increasing role of non-state actors in this field is a major element in the constitutionalization of international law.[62] Courts, both national and international ones, actively

---

58   ICJ, *Jurisdictional Immunities of the State (Germany v. Italy: Greece Intervening)*, Public Sitting of 12 September 2011, CR 2011/17, 55 et seq., Robert Kolb. He recognises the justice problem and takes refuge in stating that there can be no perfect justice!

59   On the notion of international community see Bardo Fassbender, *The United Nations Charter as the Constitution of the International Community* (Leiden: Nijhoff, 2009); Georges Abi-Saab, "Cours general de droit international public", *Recueil des Cours* 207 (1987): 9–463, 51 et seq.

60   Krajewski and Singer, "Should Judges Be Front-Runners?" (n. 6), 30.

61   Ingo Venzke, *How Interpretation Makes International Law* (Oxford: OUP, 2012), in particular at 64 et seq.; Michael Bothe, "Private Normunternehmer im Volkerrecht: Gedanken zur Fortentwicklung des Volkerrechts durch nicht-staatliche Institutionen", in Holger P. Hestermeyer et al., eds., *Coexistence, Cooperation and Solidarity, Liber Amicorum Rüdiger Wolfrum*, vol. 2 (Leiden: Nijhoff, 2012), 1399–1422.

62   Anne Peters, "Membership in the Global Constitutional Community", in Klabbers, Peters and Ulfstein, *Constitutionalization* (n. 44), 153–262, 157 et seq.

REMEDIES OF VICTIMS OF WAR CRIMES

contribute to the continuous formation and reformation of international law. In doing so, courts yield at least as much legitimacy as the United States bureaucracies.

Therefore, it is a role of the Court to give creative answers to current fundamental issues of the international order. This is a legitimate function of international courts and tribunals.[63] This function characterises their practice.[64] The history of the Court is full of examples for this function. It started with the bold decision to recognise the objective international personality of the United Nations and the right of "functional protection" of its agents.[65] Further examples are the role of equity emphasised in the *North Sea Continental Shelf* case[66] and the development of the notion of *erga omnes* obligations in *Barcelona Traction*.[67] In these three cases, the Court developed the law by interpreting it on the basis of certain values: good functioning of the United Nations, equity, implementation of fundamental principles of the international order, e.g. the prohibition of aggression and of genocide as well as the protection of basic human rights. On the other hand, the inclination of the Court to fulfil this lawmaking function has varied.[68] Regrettably, the Court refused to play this role in the present case, too.

It would at least have been appropriate for the Court not to bar the development of an emerging norm.[69] In the past, the Court has indeed played its role

---

63   For a deeper analysis, see Armin von Bogdandy and Ingo Venzke, "International Courts as Lawmakers", in Rudiger Wolfrum and Ina Gatschmann, eds., *International Dispute Settlement: Room for Innovations?* (Heidelberg: Springer, 2013), 161–214; contra Abdul G. Koroma, "An Investigation of International Courts, Public Authority and its Democratic Justification", ibidem 215–220; a more elaborate version is published in the Special Issue: "Beyond Dispute: International Judicial Institutions as Lawmakers", *German Law Journal* 12 (2011), in particular Armin von Bogdandy and Ingo Venzke, "Beyond Dispute: International Judicial Institutions as Lawmakers", *German Law Journal* 12 (2011): 979– 1004, and Armin von Bogdandy and Ingo Venzke, "On the Democratic Legitimation of International Judicial Lawmaking", *German Law Journal* 12 (2011): 1341–70.

64   For some newer examples see Bogdandy and Venzke, "International Courts as Lawmakers" (n. 63), 165 et seq.

65   ICJ, *Reparations for Injuries Suffered in the Service of the United Nations*, Advisory Opinion of 11 April 1949, icj Reports 1949, 174, 183 et seq.

66   ICJ, *North Sea Continental Shelf*, Judgment of 20 February 1969, icj Report 1969, 3, 45 et seq. (paras. 83 et seq.).

67   ICJ, *Barcelona Traction Light and Power Company, Limited (Belgium v. Spain)*, Judgment of 5 February 1970, icj Reports 1970, 3, paras. 33 et seq.; see Jochen A. Frowein, "Obligations erga omnes", in Wolfrum, ed., *Max Planck Encyclopedia* (n. 13).

68   Bogdandy and Venzke, "International Courts as Lawmakers" (n. 63), 165 et seq. with further references.

69   Krajewski and Singer, "Should Judges Be Front-Runners?" (n. 6), 31.

in this sense. In the *German-Icelandic Fisheries dispute*,[70] for example, it found a way to decide in favour of Germany without compromising the development of new rules which at the time of that judgment were about to see the light – and have become the new law of the sea only a few years later. But in the present case, the Court has refused to play its role in this salutary way. By closing the door to the necessary role of national courts in the re-establishment of a just order after conflicts, the International Court of Justice has damaged the legitimacy of the international system.

10   Conclusion and Perspectives

The problem of the justice gap or legitimacy gap has apparently been felt by representatives of Germany in that case. To dispel these doubts concerning the legitimacy of the procedure and the result, high ranking German officials repeatedly declared that this case was not a case against the victims, but dealt with an entirely different issue.[71] From a formal point of view, this is absolutely correct. But seen in the perspective of the victims, it meant that they were deprived of what they considered to be their last hope to obtain a compensation for their and their relatives' suffering. For them it is hard to accept that the case did not really concern them.

The ICJ itself recognises this justice gap. At two places in the judgment, the Court expresses doubts concerning the German policy of non-payment. Regarding the Italian forced labour cases, the Court addresses the reasons for the German refusal to pay compensation. It "considers that it is a matter of

---

70   ICJ, *Fisheries Jurisdiction Case (Federal Republic of Germany v. Iceland), Merits*, Judgment of 25 July 1974, icj Reports 1974, 175, paras. 42 et seq. The Court based its finding in favour of Germany in particular on an exchange of notes which had taken place between the parties, recognised the dynamic character of the applicable rules and invited the parties to settle their future relations by negotiations based on equitable principles.

71   ICJ, *Jurisdictional Immunities of the State (Germany v. Italy: Greece Intervening)*, Public Sitting of 12 September 2011, cr 2011/17, 18 et seq. Susanne Wasum-Rainer. In a declaration issued after the judgment of the ICJ, the German Foreign Minister Westerwelle said: "Das Verfahren war nicht gegen die Opfer des Nationalsozialismus gerichtet. Ihr Leid hat die Bundesregierung stets voll anerkannt. Naturlich geht es auch nicht darum, die deutsche Verantwortung fur die Verbrechen des zweiten Weltkrieges in Frage zu stellen oder zu relativieren" (available on the website of the German Embassy in Greece, "IGH-Urteil zur Klärung des Grundsatzes der Staatenimmunitat", accessed 4 November 2013, www.griechenland.diplo.de/Vertretung/griechenland/de/o8/Aussenminister__Westerwelle_zum__igh__Urteil.html.

REMEDIES OF VICTIMS OF WAR CRIMES

surprise – and regret – that Germany decided to deny compensation to a group of victims on the ground that they had been entitled to a status which, at the relevant time, Germany had refused to recognise, particularly since those victims had thereby been denied the legal protection to which that status entitled them".[72]

This is as far as a critique of one of the parties to the litigation could go in an *obiter dictum*. What the Court had in mind was the German argument that no compensation was given to prisoners of war (as this is lawful detention) and that the persons subjected to forced labour were entitled to prisoner of war status. Thus, it was argued, they were not entitled to compensation although they were not treated as prisoners of war by Germany. That argument is difficult to understand, but apparently the Italian government was unable (or unwilling?) to achieve, in its dealings with Germany, the result required by justice.

Further on, in an apparent effort to close the justice gap which the decision of the Court had maintained, the Court invites the parties to remedy the situation in which it had left the victims: "In coming to this conclusion, the Court is not unaware that the immunity from jurisdiction of Germany in accordance with international law may preclude judicial redress for the Italian nationals concerned. It considers however that the claims arising from the treatment of Italian military internees referred to in paragraph 99, together with other claims of Italian nationals which have allegedly not been settled – and which formed the basis of the Italian proceedings – could be subject of further negotiation involving the two States concerned, with a view to resolving the issue".[73] Is this a declaration of bankruptcy by the Court, recognising the justice gap, not being able to close it and handing it back to the bureaucracies? For the victims, it is a weak consolation, and, as far as one knows from public sources, this suggestion by the Court has not produced any consequence.

To come back to the beginning: what about the "the rights we are born with"? For the sake of the legitimacy of the international legal order, they deserve more respect than the Court has been willing to pay to them, despite some allusion to regrets.

---

72   ICJ, *Jurisdictional Immunities* (n. 2), para. 99.

73   Ibid., para. 104.

33

Prevention and Repression of Breaches of International Humanitarian Law

1 Introduction

This article is concerned with a very specific and limited part of the overall subject «national means of implementation of international humanitarian law». It will deal with a number of problems related to criminal or disciplinary sanctions for the violation of international humanitarian law. It is this aspect of national implementation on which so far most attention has been focused.

1.1 A Look Back into History

The idea that serious violation of the laws of war must be punished is probably as old as the notion of the laws of war itself. However, in former times an amnesty was usually granted after the war was over, very often on the basis of peace treaties[1]. That situation radically changed with the First World War. The peace treaties concluded after that war contained some provisions on the punishment of war criminals, and some trials of war criminals indeed took place. The major step forward in the criminal repression of breaches of the laws of war, however, was prompted by the Second World War. As often in human history, a catastrophe was needed to induce real progress. The two significant steps in the development of criminal sanctions for violations of the laws of war were on the one hand the Nuremberg and Tokyo trials of major war criminals and other trials of war criminals by the national courts of the Allied Powers, and on the other hand the conclusion in the Geneva Conventions of 1949 of provisions requiring criminal sanctions to repress grave breaches of these Conventions by effective penal legislation.[2] These provisions are further developed by articles 85 to 87 of Protocol I of 1977. Article 85 adds new elements to the list of grave breaches contained in the Conventions. Article 87 states a rule which

---

1 Jeschek, War Crimes, in: Bernhardt (ed.), Encyclopedia of Public International Law, Instalment 4, p. 295. On the history of criminal sanctions for violations of international law, see Green, The Law of Armed Conflict and the Enforcement of International Criminal Law, 22 Canadian Yearbook of International Law 3 et seq. (1984).

2 See art. 49 First Convention, art. 50 Second Convention, art. 149 Third Convention, art. 146 Fourth Convention.

PREVENTION AND REPRESSION OF BREACHES

was probably already implied in the Conventions, but not expressly spelled out, namely that there is a general obligation to prevent and suppress breaches, be they grave or not. That need not be necessarily done by penal legislation, it can be done by other means, in particular by disciplinary measures.

1.2   *Institutional Aspects*

A fundamental question involved in the repression of breaches is that of the competent authority, that is to say, the competent prosecution agency and the court competent to condemn the alleged offender. In the present circumstances, this can only be a national court, be it the court of the party to which the offender belongs, or that of the enemy or of a neutral country.[3] This is true for the trials after the First and the Second World Wars, it is submitted, space not permitting analysis in greater detail of the true character of the two «international» tribunals.[4] The efforts to create an international criminal court have so far remained a matter of private idealistic lobbying, have not taken any significant roots in diplomatic practice. Taking into account the difficulties encountered by much less ambitious means to deal with violations of international humanitarian law through impartial third party procedures,[5] it is highly improbable that the idea of an international criminal court will develop as a matter of state practice. This being so, any relevant reflections on repressions of breaches of international humanitarian law must concentrate on repression by national authorities. This leads us to the two major problems with which this article is concerned.

1.3   *The Fundamental Questions*

Procedural and substantive law applied by national courts is first of all national law. But as it is a violation of international law which has to be repressed, the question arises as to the relationship between the violation of international law and of national criminal law.

The second problem is that of the effectiveness of national repression of international wrongs. The relative scarcity of cases in this field is certainly not due to the absence of violations, but to a reluctance of states to honour their relevant obligations under the Geneva Conventions. That question will be dealt with in the last part of this article.

---

3   Jeschek, loc. cit., p. 295; Green loc. cit., pp. 11 et seq.

4   Jeschek, Nuremberg Trial, in: Bernhardt (ed.), Encyclopedia of Public International Law, Instalment 4, pp. 50 et seq.; Röling, Tokyo Trial, ibid, pp. 242 et seq.

5   Abi-Saab, The Implementation of Humanitarian Law, in: Cassese (ed.), The New Humanitarian Law of Armed Conflict, pp. 310 et seq.

650   PART 9: IMPLEMENTATION AND ENFORCEMENT OF IHL

2 The Relationship between the International Law of Armed Conflicts and National Criminal Law: Basic Problems

2.1 *National and International Law*

It is well-known that the application of international law within national legal systems is determined by the national constitution.[6] There are various ways in which states achieve the conformity of the behaviour of national actors with international law. But the internal application of international law is not only a function of the constitutional system, it is also a question of the content of the international norm itself. There are many norms which by their very content are not capable of internal application because they are not self-executing. This is the case with the provisions of the Geneva Conventions and Protocol I concerning grave breaches. They provide for an obligation of the state to enact and apply a criminal legislation. But they do not themselves constitute this criminal legislation. In particular, they do not provide for any specific criminal sanction. Thus, national legislation is necessary to implement the provisions on grave breaches.[7]

The same holds rue for other treaties and for international customary law of armed conflicts. There are no provisions or customary rules providing for specific punishment. All that is left to national legislation. If offenses are to be punished, they are so only on the basis of national implementing legislation. Any speculation as to whether this situation might change is beyond the scope of the present article.

2.2 *Implementation of International Humanitarian Law by National Criminal Law: Basic Options*

The question now arises as to how the punishable act is defined by national criminal legislation. To solve this problem, three basic options are available:

a) the application of general criminal law;

b) a reference by national legislation to international law;

c) the autonomous national definition of particular criminal acts related to armed conflicts.

These three basic options can be noted in state practice concerning the Geneva Conventions or other norms of the international law relating to armed conflicts, a combination of the three approaches being of course possible. It is thus appropriate to look into the problems presented by each of these approaches.

---

6 For a general discussion on the relationship between international law and municipal law, see D.P. O'Connell, International Law, vol. I, London 1965, pp. 37–88.

7 Jeschek, loc. cit. (note 1), p. 295.

PREVENTION AND REPRESSION OF BREACHES

3   Application of General Criminal Law: Opportunities and Fallacies

There are many states which have not adopted any legislation for the repression of grave breaches of the Conventions or Protocol I.[8] Many of them have simply kept silent on the matter. But where explanations are given, be it by official statements of the government, or by unofficial means, the general trend of such pronouncements is to say that the general criminal law of the state in question is sufficient in order to fulfill that state's obligations under the Geneva Conventions.[9] Two basic questions are involved in this approach. The first is whether indeed it is true that any offence which constitutes a grave breach of the Conventions and Protocol I is covered by national criminal law, i.e. constitutes also an offence as defined by national criminal law.

Even where this is so, the question arises as to whether this system provides for adequate sanctions and an adequate distinction between legal and illegal conduct in the particular circumstances of an armed conflict.

3.1   *Breaches of the Law of Armed Conflict Punishable under International Criminal Law*

It has to be conceded to those favouring the general criminal law approach that practically all countries have legislation providing for the punishment of the following acts: homicide, infliction of bodily injury, destruction and damaging of property, unlawful taking of property, unlawful depravation of liberty, offenses against the honour of another person, miscarriage of justice. All the breaches defined by the Conventions and Protocol I amount to one of these acts, subject, however, to the definition of particular crimes in national law. It is not possible in the context of this article to give an overall comparative view of national criminal law concerning the question whether indeed everything which has to be punished under the Geneva Conventions and Protocol I is covered, taking into account the details of national definition of crimes.

---

8   For a survey of this legislation, see Respect of the Geneva Conventions, Measures Taken to Repress Violations, Reports submitted by the International Committee of the Red Cross to the XXth and XXIst International Conferences of the Red Cross, 2 vols., 1971. See also Levasseur/Merle, L'état des législations internes au regard de l'application des obligations contenues dans les conventions de droit humanitaire, in: Droit humanitaire et conflits armés, Université Libre de Bruxelles. Colloque des 28, 29 et 30 janvier 1970, 1976, pp. 219 et seq. On the question of the non self-executing character of the provisions concerning grave breaches, see Rolin, ibid, 254 et seq.

9   Jeschek, loc. cit. (note 1), p. 296. Respect of the Geneva Conventions, Measures Taken to Repress Violations, Reports, loc. cit. This stance is often challenged. For a critical review of the former Spanish situation, see Pastor Ridruejo, Los Delitos contra el Derecho de gentes en el Codigo de Justicia Militar, in: Revista Española de Derecho Militar, No. 10, 1960, pp. 9–20.

It must suffice to indicate some areas where problems might be found. In the case of outrages against personal dignity which do not constitute bodily injury, for example Art. 85 (4) (c) Protocol I, it may well be doubtful whether the general provisions protecting personal honour are sufficient. It may also be asked whether a delay in the repatriation of prisoner, Art. 85 (4) (c), always constitutes an unlawful deprivation of liberty under national law. Deprivation of the right to fair trial, Art. 85 (4) (e) will not necessarily constitute miscarriage of justice in the sense of a national definition.[10]

But even where the national definitions of criminal acts cover any grave breach of the Conventions, the question remains whether the penal sanctions provided for peace time acts really correspond to the special circumstances of armed conflict. In addition, there are certain crimes not constituting grave breaches of the Conventions but requiring criminal repression which are not regularly found in national criminal legislation, such as attacks against a parliamentaire, breach of armistice, degrading treatment of dead persons (not involving thefts). As to the misuse of the red cross this is, as a rule, not covered by general criminal law, but this is a question on which most specific legislation exists at the national level.[11]

3.2 The Distinction between Legal and Illegal Combat Activity: International Law and Justification under National Criminal Law

The problem which confronts us when we try to distinguish between legal and illegal conduct in relation to an armed conflict may be illustrated by a simple example.[12] Killing the enemy constitutes intentional homicide. Why is it not punishable if done in regular combat during an armed conflict? This is not only a moral question on which conscientious objection may be based, it is also a legal one. To what extent is killing not punishable in armed conflict? To what extent is it punishable?

The general justifications of national criminal law (self-defence, state of necessity and others) do not provide an adequate answer for these questions.

---

10   This is true for the Belgian draft statute (Chambre des Représentants, 1962–1963, 577 No. 1, pp. 12–15) relating to the repression of grave breaches of the Geneva Conventions, see Levasseur/Merle, L'état des législations internes au regard de l'application des obligations contenues dans les conventions de droit humanitaire, in Droit humanitaire et conflits armés, Université Libre de Bruxelles. Colloque des 28, 29 et 30 janvier 1970, 1976, pp. 219 et seq., 237.

11   Good examples for such national legislative measures are the Red Cross Acts of Austria in 1962 (BGBl., 1962, No. 196) and Ireland in 1954 (No. 28 of 1954).

12   For a general discussion of this problem see Oehler, Internationales Strafrecht, 1973, p. 564.

PREVENTION AND REPRESSION OF BREACHES

Although national approaches to this problem vary, it is safe to say that there exist specific legal reasons which reduce the scope of relevant criminal law provisions in a way which prevents combat activity from being considered a criminal act or which otherwise excludes the illegality of, or punishment for, acts of war under national law. But what are these reasons? Is any combat activity justified? Only that which is directed by a combatant against a military target? Only that which is legal under international law? To what extent are detention or acts against detainees justified? Is there some kind of implied reference to international law in order to give an answer to the national justification problems? Certainly, satisfactory answers can be found to these questions. But there is a lot of legal insecurity involved. It is this insecurity which poses constitutional problems in many countries on the basis of guarantees of due process and the rule of law, but which also raises questions under international law such as the rule «*nullum crimen sine lege*» which is also enshrined in international instruments such as article 7 of the European Convention of Human Rights and article 15 of the UN Convenant on Civil and Political Rights.

We can thus conclude that what has been called the general criminal law approach is not sufficient as a means of implementing the grave breaches provisions of the Geneva Conventions and Protocol I and may lead to unconstitutional or even internationally unlawful insecurity as to the definition of crimes and justification causes.

4   National Legislation Referring to International Law

The necessary definition of the criminal act under national law may be formulated by a simple reference to international law, a national law providing that a certain violation of international law constitutes a crime, is punishable under national law. There are, and this is clear from state practice, several ways of achieving this, in particular global or specific references, the latter with various degrees of specificity. A very global and comprehensive reference to international law is the definition of war crimes to be found in section 93 of the Criminal Code of the German Democratic Republic: «A persons who, in connection with an armed conflict, violates generally recognized international norms, in particular ... (follows an illustrative list).» The notion of «generally recognized international norms» is meant to cover both customary law and any treaty binding upon the German Democratic Republic.[13] Thus, not only

---

13   See Commentary to the Penal Code (Kommentar zum Strafgesetzbuch) of the German Democratic Republic, East Berlin 1981, p. 278.

grave breaches are repressed as war crimes, but any breach. This definition of the criminal act is of course very broad. It covers acts of various degrees of gravity. This raises the question of whether there is a possibility of differentiating punishment according to gravity. The general punishment provided is imprisonment of not less that one year. In connection with an aggression, it is not less than five years, in case of «particularly grave consequences» it is life imprisonment or death.

A very general reference to international humanitarian law is also contained in Sec. 11 of the Swedish Penal Code. It provides for punishment of a person who, «in the conduct of war», acts contrary to «existing treaties», or who «in a case other than in warfare» violates rules concerning certain protected persons. References to the laws of war may also be found in article 8 of the Dutch Act of 1952 on military criminal law.[14] According to this provision, any violation of the laws and customs of war is punishable by imprisonment of up to ten years, but the provisions on aggravating circumstances are much more precise than in the case the Criminal Code of the German Democratic Republic, and, of course, aggression is not mentioned. Switzerland (article 109 of the Code of Military Justice)[15] follows a similar approach, but the violation of international treaties and of the laws and customs of war are placed into separate subparagraphs. In both the Dutch and the Swiss legislation, there are some specific provisions besides this general reference to international law.

This leads us to the second subcategory of this approach, to what could be called the specific reference approach. This approach has been, in particular, adopted by the United Kingdom and many Commonwealth countries in the form of the Geneva Conventions Acts.[16] Grave breaches of the Geneva Conventions are made a crime by a specific reference to those provisions of the Four Conventions (and article 85 of Protocol I, as the case may be) which define grave breaches. The Conventions are published as a schedule to the Act. The punishment varies according to the gravity of consequences.

This incorporation by reference approach assures complete conformity between national and international law, subject to the risk, which cannot be avoided, that national interpretation of the same provisions of international law lead to different results. But apart from the difficulty, it is certainly a valuable system of assuring that every act or omission which violates international

---

14 Stb. 1952 No. 408 (Wet Oorlogsstrafrecht).

15 Swiss Code of Military Justice (SR. 321.0, Militärstrafgesetz) of June 13, 1979.

16 For the United Kingdom: Geneva Conventions Act, Ch. 52 of 1957; Australia: Geneva Conventions Act of 1957; Canada: Geneva Conventions Act 1964–65, R.S.C. 1970, Ch. G-3.

PREVENTION AND REPRESSION OF BREACHES

humanitarian law is indeed subject to criminal repression. On the other hand, this approach causes some problems, too.

The first problem is that of the relationship between the specific offense and general criminal law. It has to be asked whether the fact that a certain offense is punishable under the specific provision referring to international law excludes, on the basis of the *lex specialis* rule, the application of general criminal law. This problem is often not solved by the legislation in question. On the other hand, the situation in Switzerland is very clear. The application of more severe norms of general criminal law is reserved. Thus, the reference to international law really constitutes a residual clause to cover those cases where general criminal law is not adequate. Thus, some of the problems discussed above concerning the application of general criminal law still remain. In particular, the question of punishable and non-punishable conduct in the particular circumstances of an armed conflict remains, so far as the application of general criminal law is concerned.

In respect of the definition of a criminal act by reference, problems vary according to the degree of specificity. Where the reference is very broad and dynamic (that is to say the law referred to is not necessarily that existing at the time of the adoption of a criminal law statute, but that applicable at the time of the punishable act), the problem of *nullum crimen sine lege* may still be raised. On the other hand, a specific reference like that contained in the Geneva Convention Acts, may be rather cumbersome. A static reference to a text which is annexed to the criminal law statute (this is the case with the Geneva Convention Acts) also poses a problems of conformity between national law and international law if the treaty is amended without a corresponding change in the national implementation legislation.

5   Autonomous Definition of Criminal Acts in Relation to Armed Conflicts

A different approach is to define textually certain violations of international law in the criminal provision itself. This approach was chosen by Belgium in a draft statute submitted to Parliament in 1963 providing for the repression of grave breaches of the Geneva Conventions.[17] This bill (number 577) repeats the formulation of the provisions of the Geneva Conventions on grave breaches. The bill is, however, not entirely autonomous. A reference to the Convention is

---

17   Art. of the Belgian Draft Code, loc. cit. (note 10).

still included as acts are punishable only if committed against persons protected by the Conventions.

Still more, but not completely, autonomous is a German draft statute for the repression of grave breaches, which, however was never published or submitted to the Parliament, but was given a wide distribution to interested circles.[18] It distinguishes two areas of criminal repression, the application of general criminal law and the application of the specific statute. «Belligerent acts» are only punishable according to the special statute. This solves of course the difficult question of justifications in relation to an armed conflict. The draft statute then mentions a number of other specific acts punishable under its provisions.

The German and Belgian drafts were not pushed further when it became apparent that the Geneva Conventions might be amended or supplemented. Recently, the Belgian Government has made it clear that the project will be brought up to date and resubmitted to Parliament in a new version, taking into account the requirements of Protocol I.[19]

Statutes like the two drafts just described can of course also contain criminal provisions additional to the grave breaches of the Geneva Conventions, in particular causing damage to cultural property. They can also include breaches of the Geneva Conventions which are not «grave» as defined in the relevant articles, for instance causing obstacles to the fulfilment of humanitarian functions.

The problems posed by this approach are related to the conformity of national and international law. An autonomous definition of the crime could theoretically be construed in a manner incompatible with the international obligation. This risk should, however, not be overestimated. In the legal system of many countries, the rule is established that statutes have to be interpreted in the light of the international obligations of the country. On the other hand, even a textual reference to an international treaty does not exclude varying national interpretations. In addition, the autonomous definition will as a rule not be completely «pure», some supplementary references to international law, as the Belgian case show, remaining necessary. The advantage of this autonomous approach is the clarity of the definition of the crime. A certain independence from the international norm may also be advantageous, in particular in two cases: the national norm can also be applied before or in the absence of ratification by the prosecuting State and can also be applied in an armed conflict where the other party is not bound by the Geneva Conventions and Protocol I.

---

18   Levasseur/Merle, loc. cit., pp. 219 et seq., 236.

19   A. Andries, La Mise en Œuvre des Protocoles additionnels en Belgique, in : Revue Internationale de la Croix-Rouge 69 (1987), p. 281 et seq.

PREVENTION AND REPRESSION OF BREACHES

6   Disciplinary Sanctions

The problems just discussed concerning the criminal law repression of breaches are to a certain extent repeated on a lower level as far as disciplinary sanctions are concerned. As it has already been stated, article 87 of Protocol I requires States to repress any violation. But for breaches which are not «grave», the States remain free as to the mode of repression. It can very well be effected by disciplinary sanctions.

Disciplinary measures constitute a reaction to the violation of service obligations. Then, the question is that of the definition of service obligations, and here we encounter the same or similar problems as those just discussed relation to the definition of criminal acts. What is necessary is making the respect of international law part of the service obligations. Disciplinary regulations in many countries are completely silent on that matter. On the other hand, a good example of making respect of international law part of the service obligations is the French Règlement Générale de discipline,[20] which contains a kind of summary of the most important rules of international humanitarian law. Also in Switzerland,[21] the respect of international law is made part of the service obligations by including it in the articles which are read before an oath is taken.

7   Some Further Problems

Some general problems of criminal and disciplinary repression of breaches remain to be dealt with which are posed regardless of the specific approach concerning the relationship between national and international law.

7.1   *Superior Orders*
One of these problems is that of superior orders, or, to put it in other words, the question whether and to what extent the fact that a violation was ordered by a superior excludes or attenuates the criminal or disciplinary responsibility of the obeying subordinate. The Geneva Conventions and Protocol I are completely silent on this question. There is a strong tendency in legal literature and also a certain tendency in state practice to disregard superior orders as

---

20   Decret No. 66–749 du 1er octobre 1966 portant sur le règlement de discipline générale dans les armées, art. 34.

21   Service regulations (DR 80) of the Swiss Army (51: 2d) 1980, art. 202 para. V.

658   PART 9: IMPLEMENTATION AND ENFORCEMENT OF IHL

a means of excluding illegality or guilt.[22] In this sense, article 19 of the Swiss Code of Military Justice, 95 of the Criminal Code of the German Democratic Republic and 9 of the Belgian Code point in the same direction, but differ in important details.

7.2 *Jurisdiction* Ratione Loci

The definition of the territorial scope of application of national criminal law varies from country to country. Many countries provide for the application of their criminal law where the actor or victim are their nationals. But many countries rely essentially on a territoriality principle, making their criminal law applicable only to acts committed within their territory or on board their ships and aircraft. In relation to grave breaches of the Geneva Conventions, however, the universality principle is imposed upon the member states. The duty to prosecute exists without regard to the place where an act is committed, and without regard to the nationality of the offender or the victim. Each «High Contracting Party has to provide for effective penal sanctions» (article 146 of the Fourth Convention). In those countries where the universality principle is not the rule concerning the application of criminal law, legislation is thus necessary in order to ensure the application of national criminal law on this basis.[23]

Related to this problem, there is the further question of extradition.[24] If a State-Party to the Geneva Conventions does not want to prosecute, it has to extradite the offender if so requested by a State establishing probable cause. *Aut dedere aut judicare* is the rule established by the Conventions. Politically speaking, this may be an awkward situation for a neutral State, especially where the offender has a high official position. From the legal point of view, implementing legislation will be necessary in many States, as extradition, in the absence of a bilateral extradition treaty, is, according to national law, a matter of the discretion of the executive branch of government. It may well be necessary, or at least appropriate, to reduce this discretion by specific implementing legislation.

---

22   Green, Superior orders in national and international law, 1976; Jeschek, loc. cit. (note 1), p. 297.

23   This problem is in particular addressed by the provisions of the Geneva Convention Acts dealing with their scope of applications («Any person ... whether inside or outside of the State ...») or jurisdiction (see e.g. sec. 3 para. 2 of the Canadian Geneva Convention Act. R.S.C. 1970, Ch. G-3).

24   Jeschek, loc. cit. (note 1). p. 297.

PREVENTION AND REPRESSION OF BREACHES

8   The Effectiveness of Criminal and Disciplinary Repression

The international means of implementation of the Geneva Conventions and Protocol I are, generally speaking, not in a satisfactory shape.[25] The difficulties encountered with the designation of protecting powers and the slow progress made in the acceptance of the Fact Finding-Commission (article 90 Protocol I) are the best known examples of this weakness.[26] It follows that national means of implementation are indispensable to ensure the respect of international humanitarian law. Criminal and disciplinary repression are an important part of these national implementation procedures. International humanitarian law certainly cannot do without them. It is thus necessary to evaluate how effective they are and how their effectiveness can be improved.

If one looks into the practice of States under the Geneva Conventions, one cannot say that the experience is really encouraging. Legislative reaction to the Geneva Conventions has been largely inadequate. Reliance on general criminal law may often have been an excuse for legislative or bureaucratic inertia rather than a valid explanation of the legal situation. In the case of Belgium and Germany, there might have been an excessive zeal for perfect solutions. The ongoing negotiations on the Protocols have also served as an excuse (and perhaps a good one) for more than twenty years of legislative inactivity. But the inadequacy of national legislation is only one side of the coin. There have been prosecutions in countries where there was no specific legislation, but as far as comparative materials exist, one can say that only a small portion of the tremendous mass of violations which have occurred after the entry into force of the Geneva Conventions have been prosecuted. Where the offender was in the hand of the enemy party, this may have been due to consideration of reciprocity and fear about the treatment of the parties' own prisoners which might have been the result. As far as the offenders were in the hands of the party to which they belonged, that party was often reluctant to discredit its own conduct by publicly admitting violations. It is certainly worthwhile to analyse the prosecutions which indeed took place in order to find out whether any specific motivation for this particular state behaviour can be found. Apparently, the legal obligation existing under the Geneva Conventions is not enough to ensure

---

25   See supra note 5.

26   At the time of this writing, 69 states are parties to Protocol I. Only 10 parties have made a declaration provided for under Art. 90 of Protocol I. These States are the following: Sweden, Finland, Norway, Switzerland, Denmark, Austria, Italy, Belgium, Iceland, the Netherlands.

repression. On the basis of a better knowledge of the cases, more could probably be done in order to induce States to honour their obligation to prosecute.

9 Some Conclusions

It appears that some implementing legislation is necessary. The exclusive reliance on general criminal law for the repression of grave breaches of the Conventions will as a rule not be adequate. A comparative analysis of State criminal law might be helpful in order to show more exactly where specific problems involved in this approach may be found.

States should learn from each other in order to make sure of satisfactory national implementing legislation. A single model act which could just be adopted by all countries will not certainly be a good solution. National means of implementation must fit into the national legal order and the national legal culture. If on the international legal, for instance in the Red Cross organisation, some drafting suggestions were formulated, it should rather be a checklist of problems with a collection of possible solutions, which may be found in practice or developed in theory.

All this should contribute to making criminal repression of grave breaches of the international law of armed conflicts a natural part of a military justice system.

10 A Postscript: Criminal Repression of Breaches of the Law Relating to Internal Armed Conflicts

It is well-known that non-international armed conflicts are often more cruel than international ones. However, neither article 3 common to the Geneva Conventions nor Protocol II additional thereto provide for the repression of breaches by national criminal law. The role of criminal law in the context of an internal armed conflict is very different from that in relation to international armed conflicts. While in the latter case, the function of criminal law is the repression of breaches of applicable international norms, of the *ius in bello*, criminal law in the context of an internal conflict is also used to repress the participation in the conflict, to sanction rebellion and to penalize violations of the prohibition of the use of force, of what in the internal legal order may be equivalent to a *ius ad bellum*.

One of the consequences of this fact is that, in an internal armed conflict, something like a prisoner of war status, with the ensuing protections for acts

PREVENTION AND REPRESSION OF BREACHES

which are in conformity with the laws of war does not exist. To put it in other words: if one party to an internal conflict captures members of the armed forces of the other, it may try them as traitors whether or not they behaved in accordance with the applicable rules of article 3 common to the Geneva Conventions, or of Protocol II. Whether a State is quite often forced not to do this, to refrain from prosecuting prisoners, for reasons of reciprocity, is another question, political, not legal. But this may only be a first basic approach. If the conflict is of a nature that considerations of reciprocity play a certain role, then there is also a necessity to distinguish, as far a criminal prosecution is concerned, between orderly conduct in an armed conflict, which may not be punished, and conduct which is a violation of the applicable rules of humanitarian law. In absence of treaty obligations in this field, however, it is probably customary law that we have to rely on for that purpose. The answer of Protocol II to this question is a rather timid one, namely article 6 paragraph 5. It invites the parties to the conflict to «grant the broadest possible amnesty to persons who have participated in the armed conflict» after the end of the hostilities. This copies in certain way the amnesty approach used in former times also for international conflicts. It benefits those who, during the conflict respected the rules as well as those who did not. This may not be always satisfactory.

If here is an obligation to punish, it could only be deduced from rules concerning the protection of human rights. Article 2 paragraph 2 of the UN Convenant on Civil and Political Rights imposes of each State party the duty to adopt such legislative measures as may be necessary to give effect to the rights recognized by the Convenant. This implies a kind of duty to protect human rights, including, one could argue, a duty to protect them by criminal legislation repressing serious violations of these rights.

34

Complementarity

Ensuring Compliance with International Law through Criminal Prosecutions – Whose Responsibility?

1   Historic Overview

The idea to use criminal law as a sanction of the violation of the laws of war, and of rules prohibiting war (in this case the treaty guaranty of Belgian neutrality), came up during World War I.[1] It was reflected in the provision of the Versailles Treaty[2] concerning the punishment of the German Emperor and other persons alleged to have committed serious violations of the laws of war. Since that time, a controversy goes on about who should prosecute such persons. The international option envisaged by the Versailles Treaty proved not to be workable, due to adamant German resistance.[3] A national substitute was then established with the consent of the victorious alliance, namely the prosecution of a number of German officers before the highest German court, the *Reichsgericht*, which, however, also did not work convincingly.[4]

Nevertheless, the idea of criminal sanctions for violation of fundamental norms of the international community was maintained. At the end of World War II, the punishment by the States of the perpetrators could not be envisaged. The first solution was a kind of double-track approach: Two international tribunals were created as common organs of the victor/victim States, the military tribunals of Nuremberg and Tokyo. They were established to prosecute only the major war criminals.[5] In addition, the victorious States prosecuted "minor" (if this is the right word) perpetrators before their own national courts, in particular those established in occupied Germany on the basis of legislation adopted by the Allied Control Council.[6] In addition, a number of victim States conducted prosecutions against German nationals outside Germany. The wave

---

1   For a brief historic review, see Cassese 2003, p. 327 et seq.; Heilmann 2006, p. 30 et seq.
2   Art. 227.
3   Hankel 2003, p. 45 et seq.
4   Hankel 2003, *passim*, conclusions at p. 518 et seq.
5   Kleffner 2008, p. 63; Cassese 2003, p. 353 et seq.
6   Jescheck 1997, p. 750 et seq.; Jescheck 1961, p. 373 et seq.

© KONINKLIJKE BRILL NV, LEIDEN, 2021 | DOI:10.1163/9789004380592_036

ENSURING COMPLIANCE THROUGH CRIMINAL PROSECUTIONS

of these prosecutions ebbed by the beginning of the 1950ies, although there are still recent cases, in particular in Italy. Another victim State conducted selected prosecutions, namely Israel.[7] During the occupation regime, Germany was only entitled to prosecute crimes by Germans against Germans. It was only after the end of the occupation regime in 1955, more precisely after the formal revocation of the relevant Allied legislation in 1956, that Germany comprehensively started to prosecute its own war criminals, a crucial case being the Auschwitz case in Frankfurt in the 1960ies.[8]

The first relevant treaty adopted in the aftermath of World War II was the Genocide Convention of 1948.[9] Its solution of the problem was national prosecution with an international option. Art. 6 provides for punishment by the courts of the "State of the territory in which the crime was committed" or by an international tribunal, which, however, was not established by that treaty.

The Geneva Conventions of 1949 exclusively rely on national jurisdictions to prosecute and punish "grave breaches",[10] with two important innovations which in a certain way lay to rest the question of victor's justice. Prosecution and punishment of these crimes is the right and the duty of *all* States. Thus, the principle of universal jurisdiction is clearly established by this treaty,[11] but it is supplemented by a duty to prosecute or to extradite. It is many years later that the Genocide Convention was also interpreted as to allow universal jurisdiction and a duty to prevent genocide.[12]

An international treaty establishing an international court similar to the tribunals of Nuremberg and Tokyo proved to be impossible in the aftermath of World War II and the beginning of the Cold War. The substantive law of the Statutes applied by the two tribunals was formulated by the International Law Commission pursuant to a mandate by the UN General Assembly. But these "Nuremberg Principles"[13] were not adopted by the General Assembly, nor was an international criminal tribunal created. Furthermore, the relevant provisions of the Geneva Conventions and the Genocide Convention remained a

---

7   The Demjanjuk and Eichmann cases, see *inter alia* Große 1995.

8   For a summary see http://de.wikipedia.org/wiki/NS-Prozesse.

9   Convention on the Prevention and Punishment of Genocide, adopted by General Assembly Resolution 260 (III) of 9 December 1948.

10   Arts. 49, 50 GC I, 50, 51 GC II, 129, 130 GC III, 146, 147 GC IV.

11   See Henckaerts / Doswald-Beck / ICRC 2005, p. 604 et seq.

12   See the references in Henckaerts / Doswald-Beck / ICRC 2005, p. 605.

13   Principles of International Law Recognized in the Charter of the Nuremberg Tribunal and the Judgment of the Tribunal, adopted by the International Law Commission July 1950, Report of the International Law Commission covering its Second Session, 5–29 July 1950, Doc. A/1316, pp. 11–14.

dead letter. For more than 40 years after the adoption of these treaties, there are no examples of cases prosecuted or punished pursuant to those rules.[14]

This situation changed dramatically in the early 1990ies, with respect to both national and international criminal prosecution. The Security Council established international tribunals for the prosecution and punishment of violations of international humanitarian law in the former Yugoslavia[15] and in Rwanda[16] as part of UN enforcement measures.[17] The two tribunals thus created did not have exclusive jurisdiction over the crimes which fell within their jurisdiction. There was concurrent jurisdiction with a primacy of international jurisdiction:[18]

1. The International Tribunal and national courts shall have concurrent jurisdiction to prosecute persons for serious violations of international humanitarian law committed in the territory of the former Yugoslavia since 1 January 1991.

2. The International Tribunal shall have primacy over national courts. At any stage of the procedure, the International Tribunal may formally request national courts to defer to the competence of the International Tribunal

   [...].

It is noteworthy that in defining concurrent jurisdiction and primacy, the Statute does not specifically mention the courts in the former Yugoslavia, it simply refers to "courts", meaning the courts of any State. This is particularly important as at the time of the creation of the ICTY and later the ICTR, a revival of the concept of universal jurisdiction can be observed in relation to war crimes, crimes against humanity, genocide, and other violations of fundamental human rights, in particular torture. Indeed, the first case before the ICTY, Tadić, was not a deferral from a court in the former Yugoslavia, but from a prosecution pending in Germany. Thus, the question of concurrent jurisdiction does not only arise in the relation between the international tribunal and the country of the perpetrator, but also in that between the international court and

---

14   If one looks at the cases concerning individual responsibility quoted by Henckaerts / Doswald-Beck / ICRC (2005, p. 3651 et seq.), they either date from the late 1940ies or are decided after 1990.

15   Resolution 827 (1993), referring to the Annex of the Report of the Secretary-General (S/25274) which contains the Statute of the ICTY.

16   Annex to Resolution 955 (1994).

17   This qualification of the measure taken by the Security Council has been confirmed by the very first decision of the Appeals Chamber of the ICTY in the Tadić case, Case no. IT-94-1-AR72, Decision of the Appeals Chamber dated 2 October 1995, pars. 32–40.

18   Art. 9 of the Statute of the ICTY. See Kleffner 2008, p. 64 et seq.

ENSURING COMPLIANCE THROUGH CRIMINAL PROSECUTIONS

the courts of any other country having jurisdiction, be it only on the basis of universal jurisdiction.

The resurgence of universal jurisdiction has also triggered a problem of concurrent jurisdiction in a horizontal perspective: is there a primacy for the jurisdiction of certain States, in particular the State to which the perpetrator belongs or that to which the victim belongs? It is often said, and to a certain extent confirmed by practice, that there is a rule of "subsidiarity", that is that universal jurisdiction only applies where the State having primary jurisdiction does not exercise it. We will revert to this problem below.[19]

The developments just described paved the way for the creation of the International

Criminal Court (ICC). The first step on this way were texts elaborated by the International Law Commission (ILC): the old Code of Offences against the Peace and Security of Mankind, adopted by the ILC in 1954, was reviewed, new versions were adopted in 1991 and 1996,[20] none of which gained much approval from States. For the purpose of the present paper, it is important to note that the Code enshrines the principle of universal jurisdiction, with an obligation to prosecute or extradite, however "without prejudice to the jurisdiction of an international criminal court" (Art. 8 and 9). Thus, there is a primacy of an international criminal court. The work on the Code, however, has not been pursued.

But parallel to the work on the Code of Offences, the ILC submitted in 1994[21] the draft of a Statute of an International Criminal Court. This later became the basis for the Statute of the International Criminal Court adopted in Rome 1998.

It was clear that the new Statute also had to address the issue of concurrent jurisdiction. While it was inherent in the very concept of the *ad hoc* tribunals being enforcement measures decided by the Security Council that they must have primacy over national courts, the question was different for a court to be established voluntarily by treaty. In the latter case, the national interest to be protected against intrusive criminal prosecution had a much bigger bargaining power. In other words: a concession had to be made to what is often called the sovereignty interest of States in order to make the international court acceptable at all.[22] Therefore, already the ILC draft was based on the concept

---

19   See below sec. 4.

20   Report of the International Law Commission on the Work of its Forty-Eighth Session, Yearbook 1996 II, pp. 2, 17 et seq.

21   Report of the International Law Commission on the Work of its Forty-Sixth Session, UN Doc. A/49/355, pp. 3–31. See Kleffner 2008, p. 70 et seq.

22   Kleffner 2008, p. 96; Solera 2002, p. 149 et seq.

of primacy of national procedures. The way in which this principle was expressed, however, was somewhat unclear. The principle of primacy of national prosecutions is more alluded to than clearly spelt out in the Preamble:

> *Emphasizing further* that such a court is intended to be complementary to national criminal justice in cases where such trial procedures may not be available or may be ineffective;

In the operative part of the Draft, that idea is reflected in the provisions on admissibility:

> Art. 35
> The Court may [...] decide, having regard to the purposes of this Statute set out in the preamble, that a case before it is inadmissible on the ground that the crime in question:
> (a) has been duly investigated by a State with jurisdiction over it, and the decision of that State not to proceed to a prosecution is apparently well-founded;
> (b) is under investigation by a State which has jurisdiction over it, and there is no reason for the Court to take any further action for the time being with respect to the crime; [...]

This appears as a variation and a limitation of the *ne bis in idem* principle. A case may be, but is not necessarily, inadmissible where a State has acted, and has done so in a reasonable way. The principle of primacy of national jurisdiction is implied in these formulations. The international jurisdiction should intervene where the national jurisdiction over most serious crimes has not worked properly, that is as it is expected from the point of view of international law, but only in this case.

These ideas are more clearly expressed in the Rome Statute. Both the preamble and Art. 1 emphasize the "complementarity" of the jurisdiction of the Court:

> *Emphasizing* that the International Criminal Court established under this Statute shall be complementary to national criminal jurisdictions;
> [...]
> Art. 1
> [...] [The Court] shall be complementary to national criminal jurisdictions
> [...]

ENSURING COMPLIANCE THROUGH CRIMINAL PROSECUTIONS

A case is inadmissible where this principle of complementarity is not respected (Art. 17). In addition, the principle of *ne bis in idem* is formulated in a way similar to the text of the ILC. The principle of complementarity has proved to be one of the most important arguments in the efforts to promote the acceptance of the Court. In order to render a case inadmissible, States must "only" prosecute the relevant crimes themselves. Then, it is said, they have "nothing to fear" from the Court.

These conditions of admissibility are spelt out in detail. Here lie the major differences with the ILC text. It is to these formulations that we must now turn our attention.

2 The Criteria of Complementarity

As already indicated, the principle of complementarity is the reverse side of the coin of primacy of national jurisdiction. Normally, it is the State having jurisdiction over a crime, be it only on the basis of universal jurisdiction, which prosecutes and punishes the perpetrator. In addition, normally, the principle of *ne bis in idem* applies also in the relationship between the international and national jurisdictions. Thus, the trial before the international court would be inadmissible. Only in exceptional circumstances[23] is this not the case. The condition which triggers the exception is that the State having jurisdiction is unable or unwilling to "genuinely" carry out an investigation or prosecution (Art. 17 (1). The essential point thus is the distinction between a prosecution or investigation which is "genuine" and another one which is not. Consequently, a national prosecution does not trigger the *ne bis in idem* rule where the national procedures show such unwillingness or inability (Art. 20 (3)). Thus, the principle of complementarity really finds its expression in two different provisions: in Art. 17 where there has not been any action by the national authorities, and Art. 20 where there has been such action, but not in a proper way.

The dividing line between situations which fall under the principle of complementarity and those which do not urgently needs concretisation. The qualification that there must be an unwillingness of inability "*genuinely* to carry out the investigation or prosecution" is a compromise formula reached in the negotiations,[24] which raises more questions then it solves. A further step towards this concretisation is found in Art. 17 itself. Paragraph 2 of this provision provides three tests of unwillingness:

---

23   Solera 2002, pp. 149 et seq., 157.
24   Holmes 2002, p. 674.

668 PART 9: IMPLEMENTATION AND ENFORCEMENT OF IHL

- national procedures are used to shield the perpetrator, a case of abuse of national jurisdiction;
- unjustified delay in the procedure;
- violations of fundamental principles of the rule of law.

Useful as these indicators may be, the criteria are difficult to handle. An intention to shield the perpetrator will always be denied by the State in question and will be hard to prove. One can argue that it will nevertheless be possible.[25] Examples, old as well as recent ones, shed some doubt on this possibility: The lenient prosecution of German war criminals after World War I[26] probably is a case of such an unwillingness. But would it have been obvious enough for a court like the ICC to conclude that it was indeed? More recently, it was argued before German courts and elsewhere that the United States justice system was indeed unwilling to genuinely carry out an investigation concerning command responsibility in respect of the events in Abu Ghraib. But could that be proven with the necessary certainty?

In the only case where this has so far become a practical issue before the ICC, the Darfur case, the Pre-Trial Chamber so to say played it safe. It held that at least where there was no indication whatsoever that the specific alleged crimes were investigated by national authorities, this was a sufficient proof of the unwillingness to prosecute.[27]

The criteria for inability are somewhat easier to apply:[28] a total or substantial breakdown of the national judicial system which leads in particular to an inability to take the relevant evidence.

These concretizations are certainly helpful, but some of the criteria are open to different interpretation in different cases. Therefore, there is a need for further concretisation *ad hoc*.

This brings us to the concretization of the criteria by the Court itself. This is a function of the procedural decision in which the principle of complementarity is to be applied.

3 The Procedural Position of Complementarity

The jurisdiction of the court as well as the admissibility of a case are preliminary procedural questions which have to be assessed and decided at an early

---

25 Holmes 2002, pp. 674, 675.

26 See above note 3.

27 Pre-Trial Chamber 1, Decision of 27 April 2007, ICC-02/05-01/07, pars. 21, 23, 24.

28 Kleffner 2008, p. 160.

ENSURING COMPLIANCE THROUGH CRIMINAL PROSECUTIONS

stage of the proceedings, at least as a matter of principle. This assessment is somewhat different for different "trigger mechanisms" of the Court procedure and for different phases of the procedure.

There are three types of trigger mechanisms (Art. 13):
- referral by a State;
- referral by the Security Council under Ch. VII of the Charter;
- initiation of an investigation or prosecution by the Prosecutor *proprio motu*.

The court procedure always starts with the Prosecutor. Referrals made by a State or by the Security Council are submitted to the Prosecutor who then conducts the proceedings. Under Art. 13 (a) and (b), "situations" are "referred to the Prosecutor". It is important that the Prosecutor is aware of objections to admissibility at this early stage. Accordingly, in the case of a State referral or *proprio motu* proceedings, there is a notification procedure allowing States to raise objections to the investigation (Art. 18 (1)). Where there are such objections, the Prosecutor must defer to the jurisdiction of a State or request an authorization to proceed from the Pre-Trial Chamber. This also makes sure that the Court can concretize the vague criteria of complementarity at an early stage of the proceedings. An appeal lies against the decision of the Pre-trial Chamber. Thus, at a very early stage of the procedure, the correct application of the principle of complementarity is in the hands of a judge. The Prosecutor cannot decide on his own that there is a situation where the principle of complementarity does not apply.

In the later phases of the proceedings, the Court has to decide on jurisdiction and admissibility *motu proprio* and *ex officio*. Jurisdiction and admissibility may then also be challenged:
- by the accused;
- by a State having jurisdiction;
- by a State the consent of which is required for the Court being able to exercise its jurisdiction.

The challenge is brought before the Pre-Trial Chamber or the Trial Chamber depending on the stage of the proceedings. Their decision can be appealed. Thus, there is a comprehensive judicial control of the respect of the principle of complementarity.

The early assessment of admissibility does not apply in the case of a Security Council referral. The procedure established under Art. 18 does not apply to Security Council referrals. This raises the question of whether the principle of complementarity is at all applicable in this case. One could argue that a referral decision under Ch. VII of the Charter is binding on States and that all States are therefore legally prevented from challenging this decision by relying on a principle which is not contained in the Charter, but "only" in a normal treaty, namely in the ICC Statute. On the other hand, Art. 25 of the UN Charter only entitles the Security Council to bind Member States. It does not imply a power of the Council to modify the powers of international institutions established by treaties which are separate from the Charter.[29] This is confirmed by the text of the ICC Statute.[30] Art. 13 enables the Court to exercise its jurisdiction "in accordance with the provisions of this Statute". This formula applies equally to all three trigger mechanisms. In addition, Art. 17 on admissibility and Art. 19 on challenges to jurisdiction and admissibility apply to all three trigger mechanisms and do not make any distinction between them. This means that the question of complementarity must also be assessed in the case of a Security Council referral. The practice of the Prosecutor, of the Pre-Trial Chamber, and of the Security Council in the Darfur case, so far the only referral by the Security Council, indeed follows this approach.[31] In his reports to the Security Council, the Prosecutor keeps analyzing the question of complementarity.[32] So does the Pre-Trial Chamber in its decision concerning the opening of the proceedings.[33] Finally, in reacting to the report of the Prosecutor, the Security Council itself confirms the relevance of the principle of complementarity.[34]

4 Vertical and Horizontal Concurrence of Jurisdiction: Complementarity and Subsidiarity

It has already been pointed out that most, if not all crimes coming under the jurisdiction of the ICC are also subject to universal jurisdiction. Thus, as a matter of principle, the issue of complementarity arises with respect to all States, not only in relation to certain States possessing a closer link to the crime under consideration, such as the State where the crime is alleged to have been committed or of which the alleged perpetrator is a national. The question which has thus to be answered is this: does the willingness and ability of any "third"

---

29   Condorelli / Villalpando 2002, p. 578.

30   Heilmann 2006, p.153 et seq.

31   See Heilmann 2006, p. 157.

32   See Eighth Report of the Prosecutor of the International Criminal Court to the UN Security Council pursuant to UNSCR 1593 (2005), in particular p. 11 et seq.

33   Pre-Trial Chamber 1, Decision of 27 April 2007, ICC-02/05-01/07, pars. 19–24.

34   See the Statement of the President of the Security Council of 16 June 2008, S/ PRST/2008/ 21: "The Security Council recalls its decision [...] that the Government of Sudan [...] shall cooperate with and provide any necessary assistance to the International Criminal Court and the Prosecutor [...] *while stressing the principle of complementarity of the International Criminal Court"* (emphasis added).

ENSURING COMPLIANCE THROUGH CRIMINAL PROSECUTIONS 671

State to prosecute and punish an alleged perpetrator render the case before the ICC inadmissible? That question has to be considered from different angles.

As a practical matter, the issue of complementarity can only arise in relation to a State where the alleged perpetrator is actually present or about to be present, for example because of an extradition procedure. Any other State may have jurisdiction, but it will be unable to exercise it if the alleged perpetrator is not within its reach.

The issue of "concurring complementarity" really arises where the State of which the perpetrator is a national does not act and another State is able and willing to prosecute on the basis of universal jurisdiction.

This brings us, as a first step, to the question of concurrent jurisdiction under the rule of universal jurisdiction. It is often said that universal jurisdiction may only be exercised if the State having a closer link to the case (in this sense primary jurisdiction) fails to exercise its jurisdiction. This is called the principle of subsidiarity of universal jurisdiction. Whether this principle is part of positive international law and, if so, to what extent it limits universal jurisdiction is highly controversial. The principle is sometimes used erroneously by governments to escape their duty to exercise jurisdiction to prosecute grave breaches of the Geneva Conventions.[35] A case in point is the refusal of the German Federal Advocate General to prosecute U.S. officials allegedly involved as responsible commanders in the torture events of Abu Ghraib. The reasons for this refusal were formulated as follows:[36]

> It is true that the principle of universal jurisdiction (§ 1 CCAIL[37]) is applicable to the crimes subjected to the threat of punishment in the CCAIL. According to this principle, the application of the CCAIL does not require any relation to domestic issues whatsoever. However, the principle of universal jurisdiction does not automatically legitimize unlimited criminal prosecution. The aim of the CCAIL is to avoid impunity and ensure criminal prosecution. This must, however, occur in the framework of non-interference in the affairs of foreign countries. This also follows from Article 17 of the Statute of the International Criminal Court (ICC), which has to be read in context with the provisions of the CCAIL. According to the ICC Statute, the jurisdiction of the ICC is subsidiary to that of the State of the perpetrator or of the perpetrated act; the ICC can only take

---

35   For the German example, see Bothe 2007.

36   An English translation of the decision of the Advocate General appears in International Legal Materials (ILM) 45/1 (2006), p. 119.

37   Code of Crimes against International Law.

action if the nation-states first called upon to adjudicate are unwilling or unable to prosecute. It is for the same reason that a third state cannot examine the legal practice of foreign states according to its own standards, or correct or replace it in specific cases.

The national legislation of the Federal Republic of Germany allows for subsidiarity in the CCAIL [...]

This statement is, at least for two reasons, legally flawed.

First, it is a misunderstanding of the relationship between universal jurisdiction and the principle of non-interference in the internal affairs of another country. It is the very purpose of the principle of universal jurisdiction to overcome the prohibition of interference. A State may not use its sovereignty to shield the commission of the most serious crimes.

Secondly, it is a misconception of the significance of Art. 17 ICC Statute. Art. 17 deals with the relationship between an international institution and member States, the principle of subsidiarity deals with the relation between States enjoying equal rights. The interests at stake in both situations are totally different. Thus, it is not possible to deduce from the principle of subsidiarity consequences for the principle of complementarity.

The flaws of the legal argument point to the fact that the statement is a clear case of politically motivated unwillingness to prosecute.

Nevertheless, there remains the question whether there is, as a limitation of the principle of universal jurisdiction, a kind of primary jurisdiction of the State having the closest link with the alleged criminal act. In this sense, the principle of subsidiarity has been formulated by the Spanish Supreme Court:[38]

[...] it has to be admitted that the necessity of judicial intervention pursuant to the principle of universal jurisdiction remains excluded when territorial jurisdiction is effectively prosecuting the crime of universal character in its own country. In this way one can speak about a principle of necessity of jurisdiction, which is derived from the very nature and from the finality of universal jurisdiction.

The application of this principle determines the scope of territorial jurisdiction, whenever there is concurrence between this one and that based on universal jurisdiction.

This criterion does not allow the exclusion of the application of Art. 23.4 of the Law on Judicial Power establishing as a requirement that

---

38   Spanish Supreme Court 2003, p. 1205 et seq., revised by the author.

ENSURING COMPLIANCE THROUGH CRIMINAL PROSECUTIONS 673

there is proof that there is inactivity or ineffective prosecution on the part of the territorial courts. This requirement would render meaningless the principle behind universal prosecution, given that such requirement would prove practically impossible and would be an extremely delicate type of evaluation at this early point in the procedure.

[...] it is necessary that the acts constitute a universal crime. The showing of serious and reasonable indication that the serious crimes denounced have not so far been prosecuted effectively by the territorial courts, whatever the reason may be, without implying any pejorative judgment as to the political, social or economic conditions that have *de facto* determined such impunity".

Thus, the Spanish court gives a certain primacy to the "territorial court", but only if the latter proceeds in a proper way to avoid impunity. But is important to note that the Spanish court, in contradistinction to the quote from the German Federal Advocate, emphasizes as the essential point that justice is done, not that sovereignty is preserved. It is in this way that the principle of necessity of jurisdiction is established.

What does this line of argument mean for the complementarity of the proceedings before the ICC in relation to national courts exercising their universal jurisdiction?

The Spanish Court briefly deals with the question by referring to an argument used by the court below, namely that universal jurisdiction should not be exercised where there is an international court competent to deal with the crime in question. Such reasoning would be in line with the principle of necessity of jurisdiction put forward by the Supreme Court. That conclusion would be confirmed if the Draft Code of Offences against the Peace and Security of Mankind[39] was taken as a precedent. It provides for the primacy of the jurisdiction of an international criminal court over universal jurisdiction. As to the Rome Statute, the drafters were aware of the fact that there could be several States having jurisdiction in a particular case, on the basis of universal jurisdiction or for other reasons. But they did not address or even solve the question of how to decide between competing jurisdictions requesting a deferral from the Court.[40] For the time being, the question is open.

---

39   Above note 20.
40   Kleffner 2008, p. 175 et seq.

5   Conclusions

The principle of complementarity is a central piece of the compromise which facilitated the adoption of the Rome Statute. It strikes a balance between the common weal, that is the interest of the international community to have violations of its fundamental values prosecuted and punished, and the sovereignty interest of States not to become the object of intrusive interventions by that community. The dividing line between the situations where one or the other interest prevails is difficult to draw. The Rome Statute does not only provide for a differentiated solution of this problem. One can criticize the line drawn by the Statute that it is too favourable to the sovereignty interests of States, in particular the States of the perpetrators. But it makes it at least difficult for a State to get way with inaction. The fact that the dividing line is strictly controlled by the ICC serves the interests of both the State of the perpetrator and those of the victims and the international community.

Bibliography

Bothe, Michael (2007): La juridiction universelle en matière de crimes de guerre – menace sérieuse contre les criminels? Un point d'interrogation sur l'Allemagne. In: Droit du pouvoir – pouvoir du droit. Mélanges offerts à Jean Salmon. Brussels: Bruylant, p. 833 et seq.

Cassese, Antonio (2003): International Criminal Law. Oxford: Oxford University Press.

Condorelli, Luigi / Santiago Villalpando (2002): Can the Security Council Extend the ICC's Jurisdiction? In: Antonio Cassese / Paola Gaeta / John R.W.D. Jones (eds.): The Rome Statute of the International Criminal Court. Oxford: Oxford University Press, p. 571 et seq.

Große, Christina (1995): Der Eichmann-Prozess zwischen Recht und Politik. Frankfurt/Main: Peter Lang.

Hankel, Gerd (2003): Die Leipziger Prozesse. Hamburg: Hamburger Edition.

Heilmann, Daniel (2006): Die Effektivität des Internationalen Strafgerichtshofes. Baden-Baden: Nomos.

Henckaerts, Jean-Marie / Louise Doswald-Beck / ICRC (eds.) (2005): Customary International Humanitarian Law, vol. I. Cambridge: Cambridge University Press.

Holmes, John T. (2002): Complementarity: National Courts versus the ICC. In: Antonio Cassese / Paola Gaeta / John R.W.D. Jones (eds.): The Rome Statute of the International Criminal Court. Oxford: Oxford University Press, p. 667 et seq.

ENSURING COMPLIANCE THROUGH CRIMINAL PROSECUTIONS

Jescheck, Hans-Heinrich (1961): Kriegsverbrechen. In: Karl Strupp / Hans-Jürgen Schlochauer (eds.): Wörterbuch des Völkerrechts, vol. 2. Berlin: de Gruyter 1961, p. 373 et seq.

Jescheck, Hans-Heinrich (1997): Nuremberg Trials. In: Rudolf Bernhardt (ed.): Encyclopedia of Public International Law, vol. III. Amsterdam: North-Holland Publishing, p. 747 et seq.

Kleffner, Jann (2008): Complementarity in the Rome Statute and National Criminal Jurisdictions, Oxford: Oxford University Press.

Solera, Oscar (2002): Complementary jurisdiction and international criminal justice. In: International Review of the Red Cross, No. 845, IRRC 2002, p. 145 et seq.

Spanish Supreme Court (2003): Peruvian Genocide case. Decision no. 712/2003, 20 May 2003. Translation in: International Legal Materials (ILM) 42/5, p. 1200 et seq.

The Role of National Law in the Implementation of International Humanitarian Law

Jean Pictet's concern for the victims of armed conflict has always led him to advocate a realistic approach to the development of international humanitarian law. The law must not only comply with high moral, humanitarian standards, it must take into account the realities of armed conflict, it must be a law which reasonable military men can accept and apply. It is thus most fitting at this occasion to reflect on some of the basic conditions of the practical application of international humanitarian law.

1   Introduction: The Problems

The application of the *Geneva Conventions* and the *Protocols additional* thereto is a highly complex question.[1] Repeated violations of international humanitarian law have dramatically shown us that its respect and implementation are far from being a matter of course. Thus, the ways and means of implementing this body of law, of making it work in practice, of ensuring its respect wherever it has to be applied has been a matter of constant concern. This was the case in the Geneva Diplomatic Conference 1974 through 1977, it has remained true in practice since.

The first problem we have to face in this connection is the fact that humanitarian law has to be applied in an extreme situation of the life of a State, where the survival of the State may be at stake. Compliance with the law may not always rank high in priority when the life of the State is in danger. There will be interests of self-preservation which might, at least on a superficial analysis by some relevant actors, militate against abiding by the law. How can the law be made to be respected despite these pressures? The *Conventions* and the *Protocols* provide for a number of international procedures and institutions to secure compliance therewith: the system of Protecting Powers and their

---

1   *Cf. inter alia Ch. Dominicé Patrnogic*, Les Protocoles additionnels aux Conventions de Genève et le système des puissances protectrices, Annales de droit international médical, No. 28 (juillet 1979), pp. 24–50.

THE ROLE OF NATIONAL LAW

677

substitute,[2] the role of the ICRC,[3] the International Fact Finding Commission.[4] All this is laudable, but far from being perfect. Certainly, no watertight system to ensure compliance is provided.[5] States are loath to accept international controls, third-party supervision or dispute settlement procedures even in times of peace – and quite naturally more so in times of war. There is yet another traditional means of securing compliance with the law: the reprisal. But this institution has fallen in disrepute even in times of peace. Being based on a unilateral serious risk of mutual accusations and escalation of illegal conduct.[6] It involves a serious risk of hurting innocent people. Thus, the *Conventions* and *Protocol I* rightly try to restrict the use of reprisals.

The relative inefficiency of these international means to secure compliance with law thus leads to the necessity that enforcement of the law must be based on national measures. The situation is comparable to that of the law of arms control, where national means of ensuring compliance and national means of verification and control are also indispensable.[7]

The second problem is that of the complexity of the law. The *Conventions* and the *Protocols* are drafted by diplomats and lawyers in the language of diplomats and lawyers – despite some laudable efforts to produce texts which are understandable for a broader public. What can a simple soldier do with a text like Art. 44 *Protocol I* (including the reservations accompanying it and all its relevant negotiating history)? In order to be capable of practical application these texts have to be transposed into a language which will be understood at the relevant level of action, which means *inter alia* that we will need different texts for different levels.

Our third problem is what could be called the incompleteness of the law. The *Conventions* and the *Protocols* are incomplete in a double sense. First, there are number of provisions which are not self-executing, *i.e.* they cannot be applied in the internal sphere of the States without some measure of

---

2   *Ch. Dominicé, J. Patrnogic*, loc. *cit; K.J. Partsch, in Bothe/Partsch/Solf*. New rules for Victims of Armed Conflicts, pp. 64 ff.

3   *Y. Sandoz*, Le droit d'initiative du Comité international de la Croix-Rouge, 22 German Yearbook of International Law 352 (1979).

4   *K.J. Partsch, loc. cit.,* (*cf. supra* note 2), pp. 535 ff.

5   See generally on this subject *M. Bothe*, International obligations, means to secure performance, *in* Bernhardt (ed.), Encyclopedia of Public International Law, Instalment 1 (1981), pp. 101 ff.

6   *M. Bothe, loc. cit.* (*cf. supra* note 5); *S. Nahlik*, Le problème des représailles à la limière des travaux de la Conferénce diplomatique sur le droit humanitaire, 82 RGDIP 130–169 (1978).

7   Art. IV Biological Weapons Convention; Art. XII ABM Treaty (SALT I); Art. II Partial Underground Test Ban Treaty, Art. XV Salt II Treaty; generally on the subject of national means the secure compliance with international law, *M. Bothe, loc. cit.* (*cf. supra* note 5), p. 103.

678 PART 9: IMPLEMENTATION AND ENFORCEMENT OF IHL

implementation by the State, in particular implementing legislation. The best example are the provisions concerning the repression of breaches. States are under a duty to punish certain acts (grave breaches), but these provisions are not in itself capable of being the basis of a criminal judgement, they need to be supplemented by some kind of criminal statute.[8] Secondly, there are cases where the application of certain provisions depends on the existence of some kind of national act. Protection of voluntary aid societies, for instance, is not granted on the basis of their function alone. In order to be protected, they must be duly recognized or authorized by a State.[9] Thus, no protection is granted unless the State intervenes and recognizes or authorizes the society.

The operation of international humanitarian law thus depends to a large extent on domestic action. As it is not a matter of course that this action is taken at all and is taken in an adequate way, this paper proposes to look a little closer into the following problems: What kind of action has to be taken by States? Are they any obstacles against this action being taken or being taken in an adequate way? What can be done on the international level to ensure that adequate action is taken?

2 The National Measures Required

2.1 *Dissemination and Rule-making*

International law is to great extent unenforceable in the way national law can be enforced: by a sheriff, a policeman, a public prosecutor, a supervisory agency. Its respect is to a large extent based on voluntary compliance by the relevant actors which, by the way, is to a great extent also true for national law. This voluntary compliance presupposes that the relevant actor knows the law, that he accepts it as a yardstick of his action, that compliance with the law becomes part of his working routine. This is called the internalization of norms.[10] How

---

8 For a survey of this legislation, see Respect of the Geneva Conventions, Measures Taken to Repress Violations, Reports submitted by the International Committee of the Red Cross to the XXth and XXIst International Conferences of the Red Cross, 2 vols, 1971. See also *G. Levasseur, R. Merle*, L'état des legislations internes au regard de l'application des obligations contenues dans les conventions internationales, *in* Droit humanitaire et conflicts armés, Université Libre de Bruxelles, Colloque des 28, 29 et 30 janvier 1970, 1976, pp. 217 ff. On the question of the non self-executing character of the provisions concerning grave breaches, see *H. Rolin, ibid.*, pp. 254 ff.

9 *Cf.* Art. 26 First Geneva Convention; Art. 8 (c) Protocol I.

10 *M. Bothe, loc. cit.* (*cf. supra* note 5), p. 102 ff.; *E. Blenk-Knocke*, Zu den soziologischen Bedingungen völkerrechtlicher Normenbefolgung, 1979, pp. 90 ff.

THE ROLE OF NATIONAL LAW

can this internalization be achieved? The first and indispensable method is dissemination, teaching. Their importance has not only been stressed by the relevant provisions of the *Conventions* and the *Protocols*, but also by a resolution of the Diplomatic Conference of 1977.[11] Those who will be called upon to apply the law must be taught – and if necessary retaught – what it is. Initiatives for teaching humanitarian law have been taken at the international level. They have been a major concern of the ICRC, in particular during the last years. The International Institute of Humanitarian Law in San Remo, in co-operation with the ICRC, has also played a prominent part in these activities.[12] The main responsibility, however, for teaching humanitarian law to the troops rests with the States. It is only them which will reach each and every soldier with teaching and instruction. For this purpose, law teachers must be educated, education material is needed. This also, despite the efforts made by international institutions, is a responsibility of the States. It is through appropriate teaching and teaching materials that the texts of the *Conventions* and the *Protocols* can be transposed into something understandable for, and understood by, any soldier, of whatever rank, who will have to apply them.[13]

The second problem of internalization of the *Protocols* resided in the fact that the troops (and also civilian personnel who must apply the *Protocols*, such as civilian personnel of the Occupying Power or civilian civil servants having to deal with medical services) are part of the administrative apparatus of the State. The *Conventions* and the *Protocols* are not the kind of text on the basis of which this apparatus is accustomed to function. It usually functions pursuant to national administrative rules (which in turn may require, according to the national administrative and constitutional systems, enabling legislation). These administrative rules also serve the purpose of translating the text of the relevant international treaties into something understandable for the members of the administrative apparatus.[14]

Related to the problem of internalization is that of availability of legal expertise. Even where the troops have received good legal education, questions

---

11   Resolution 21 (IV).

12   *Cf.* 1er Cours international sur le droit de la guerre pour officiers, 16 Th Military Law and Law of War Review, pp. 1–157 (1977).

13   In the Federal Republic of Germany, most of the teaching material (Leitfaden für den Unterricht – guidelines for teaching) takes the form of administrative regulations (zentrale Dienstvorschriften), see *e. g.* Zentrale Dienstvorschrift 15/5, Allgemeine Bestimmungen des Humanitätsrechts.

14   It has to be noted to the first and very influential codification of the law of war, the Lieber Code of 1863, is a document belonging into the category of internal executive regulation: it was promulgated as General Orders Nr. 100 by President Lincoln.

680   PART 9: IMPLEMENTATION AND ENFORCEMENT OF IHL

as to the lawful course of action will arise which are not easy to solve. There
may be, for instance, many borderline cases as to the application of such difficult articles as Art. 44 para. 3 or the principle of proportionality. Here, it is
important that legal expertise is available where the decision is taken. Art. 82
Protocol I stipulates a duty of the States to ensure this. It is an important organisational problem to be solved by States.[15]

2.2   *Implementing Legislation or Regulation*

Another kind of national measures is legislation implementing non-self-
executing provisions of the *Conventions* and the *Protocols*. The most important
kind of provisions in this connection is criminal legislation. Both the *Conventions* and the *Protocols* provide for a duty of the States to repress grave breaches.
Many of those breaches constitute punishable offenses by any standard of criminal legislation,[16] namely homicide and infliction of bodily harm. Insofar as this
is the case, no further legislation is needed to make the said duty operative in the
domestic sphere. But there are a number of provisions where the consistency between national criminal law and the international obligation to punish certain
acts is not a matter of course, in particular with respect to acts mentioned in Art.
85 para. 4 *Protocol I*. States must – and this is a duty implied in the obligation to
repress grave breaches – scrutinize their criminal law in order to ascertain that
it allows criminal prosecution and punishment for any grave breach States are
supposed to sanction. This implies to substantive law as well as to procedural
law (e.g. jurisdiction over foreign offenders where the act has been committed
outside national territory). Where there is no applicable provision of national
law, new legislation must be enacted. In addition, it will be desirable anyway
that States enact special criminal legislation for the law of war in general, as this
is a complex involving special problems where the "normal" provisions of state
criminal law and criminal procedure are not necessarily appropriate.

In order to ensure the respect of the *Conventions* and the *Protocols*, criminal
repression of grave breaches is not the only duty of the States. They are also required to sanction other breaches by appropriate penal or disciplinary action
(Art. 87 *Protocol I*). This duty must also be implemented by appropriate legislation. Here again, an obligation of States exists to check existing and adopt new
legislation, if necessary.

There are other provisions of the Protocols which presuppose the existence
of domestic legislation by referring to it. Examples are Arts. 16 para. 3, 34 para.

---

15   *K.J. Partsch, loc. cit.,* (note 2), pp. 499 ff. (with further references).
16   See *H. Jescheck,* Der strafrechtliche Schutz der internationalen humanitären Abkommen,
      65 Zeitschrift für die gesamte Strafrechtswissenschaft 458–478 (1953), at pp. 459 ff.

THE ROLE OF NATIONAL LAW

4 *Protocol I.* For other provisions, national implementing legislation is at least appropriate. An example is Art. 76 para. 3, the duty to "endeavour to avoid the pronouncement of the death penalty on pregnant women or mothers having dependent infants". This provision, as any "endeavour" clause, is not self-executing. In cases where the death penalty is mandatory for certain offences, for instance murder, special legislation is needed to implement this duty. It is also questionable whether the power of pardon generally granted to the executive is sufficient to prevent the execution of death penalty where this execution is prohibited under *Protocol I* (Art. 76 para 6, 77 para. 5).

A last group of provisions, which have to be considered in our context, are those which require certain acts of national authority as a condition of protection. They relate to the protection of medical services and civil defence. Medical personnel are persons *assigned*, by a Party to the conflict, to specific medical purposes; medical units must either "belong" to the State or be *recognized* or *authorized* by the competent authority thereof; medical transports must be *under the control* of a competent authority; the marking of medical personnel, units, or transports can only be made *with the assent* of the competent authority; the use of distinctive signals may *be authorized* by the competent authority. Civil defence organizations are those which are *organized or authorized* by the defence personnel is *assigned* by a Party to the conflict to the performance of those functions.

This assignment, authorization, recognition or control is an act of the State, which must be governed by some kind of legal regulation, be they statutory or administrative. Thus, it seems necessary or at least highly desirable for the purpose of a meaningful implementation of the *Protocols* that some rules are adopted by States for this purpose.

In all these cases, it must be made sure that the necessary authorizations are issued, the required directions are given. Under certain constitutional systems, enabling legislation is necessary or at least appropriate for this purpose. It is, as a minimum, desirable that administrative regulations are issued to this end.

There are also a number of practical and organisational measures required in order to render protection effective. The necessary identity cards for protected personnel must be issued or prepared, the means for marking (if marking is not already done in times of peace, which as a rule is not done for civilian establishments) must be held in store, etc. National parliaments will be involved in all this at least through the adoption of the budget, as all this requires financial resources.[17]

---

17 See the Message of the Swiss Federal Council, dated 18 Feb. 1981, submitting the Protocols Additional to the Geneva Conventions for approval of the Swiss Federal Assembly, pp. 90

682   PART 9: IMPLEMENTATION AND ENFORCEMENT OF IHL

3   Problems and Obstacles

The process of national implementation of international humanitarian law has so far not been given much attention[18] by lawyers,[19] political scientists or sociologists.[20] We thus know relatively little about it. More research is certainly needed on this question.

So far, there is no publication collecting current texts in national means of implementation, although some efforts to gather this information have been undertaken by Red Cross institutions.[21] There are some rather well known examples of national implementing criminal legislation and of administrative regulations or codes of conduct for the troops.

It seems, however, that the overall record of implementing rule- and law-making in respect of the *Geneva Conventions* has so far been rather mediocre. This submission remains to be verified by empirical research, but supposing it is true, what could be the reasons? Again, for lack of relevant empirical research, it is only possible to submit some hypothesis, which remain to be tested. This is the modest purpose of the following considerations.

3.1   *Awareness*

The first obstacle to the adoption of all measures just described may be a lack of awareness. The dependence of international humanitarian law on national measures of implementation is a fact which so far has only been partly recognized. This author knows from his own experience that negotiators at Geneva

---

ff. For the point of view of developing countries, see the remarks by the representative of Mongolia at the Geneva Diplomatic Conference, CDDH/II/SR.30 = OR IX. P. 310. Unfortunately, the summary record does not reflect the vividness of the actual remarks and the concern voiced by them.

18   A notable exception is criminal law. The provisions of the Geneva Conventions and the Protocols Additional thereto concerning repression of breaches have been largely commented upon in legal literature, see *K.J. Partsch, loc. cit.,* (note 2), pp. 507 ff.; *W. Solf, E.R. Cummings*, A Survey of Penal Sanctions under Protocol I to the Geneva Conventions, 9 Case Western Reserve Journal of International Law, pp. 205–251 (1977).

19   But see *W. Schwenck*, Gesetzgeberische Konsequenzen aus den Verboten der Zusatzprotokolle, 20 Neue Zeitschrift für Wehrrecht 199–212 (1978).

20   A notable exception is the work by *E. Blenk-Knocke, supra* note 10.

21   See in particular the surveys prepared by the ICRC, supra note 8. The ICRC has published a collection of texts implementing the 1929 Conventions: Recueil de textes relatifs à l'application de la Convention de Genève et à l'action des sociétés nationales dans les états parties à cette convention, 1934; also very useful are the references provided in Bibliography of International Humanitarian Law, 1980, pp. 276 *et seq.*

THE ROLE OF NATIONAL LAW

were not fully aware of the whole complexity of the process of national implementation required by the *Conventions* and the *Protocols*, although a number of problems were recognized and have been discussed.[22] There are thus reasons for doubt that State administrations which have to draft the necessary bills or to adopt the relevant administrative rules are in all cases aware of the problems they are now facing. Attention has been given to teaching,[23] also to criminal law,[24] but it has been demonstrated that the task of law- and rule-making goes far beyond that.

A good example of awareness is the message of the Swiss Federal Council submitting the *Protocols* for approval of the Swiss Federal Assembly,[25] which expressly refers to the need of updating the existing regulations and also considers the costs of doing so.

On the other hand, some of the reports submitted to the ICRC by National Red Cross Societies concerning the repression of breaches[26] show a shocking lack of problem conscience. One Society, for instance, just mentions the fact that the *Conventions* had been ratified by the country and, for that purpose, been submitted for parliamentary approval. Certain Societies submitted that existing legislation responded to the need to repress breaches, while the text accompanying such statement clearly showed that there were loopholes and deficiencies.[27] One could even find national provisions which, in the view of this author, clearly contravene the *Conventions*.[28]

3.2 *Knowhow*

It has also been shown that the whole problem of national implementation is highly complex and complicated. It constitutes a challenge to national rule-markers. It requires a high degree of expertise both in legislative draftsmanship and knowledge if the international legal problems involved. This expertise is a scare resource. It may not be available in every administration where it is needed.

---

22   *Supra* note 17.
23   *Supra* notes 12 and 13.
24   *Supra* notes 8 and 16.
25   *Supra* note 17.
26   *Supra* note 8.
27   See also *G. Levasseur, R. Merle, loc. cit. (supra* note 8), pp. 227 ff., 250.
28   Art. 280 of the Spanish Código de Justiciar Militar which implies that pillage is not illegal if done on express order; Art. 281 of the same implying that "necessity" might justify a direct attack against hospitals and medical establishments or transports (*loc. cit. supra note* 8, Vol. II, p. 44).

684   PART 9: IMPLEMENTATION AND ENFORCEMENT OF IHL

3.3   *Inertia*

Bureaucracies are not always and everywhere kwown for their swiftness. The process of preparation of laws and of drafting rules is cumbersome and slow, especially when a problem is as difficult as the one we are facing here. A process of concentration between various ministries of a government (defence, justice, interior, foreign affairs at least) or even between branches of the armed forces is necessary. It is submitted that this fact accounts for much of the slowness in the implementing process of the *Geneva Conventions*.

This may explain the fact that in the Federal Republic of Germany a draft statute for the repression of breaches of the *Geneva Convention*, which existed already in the early 6oies or even before, has so far not been adopted by the Federal Government to be submitted to the Federal Diet.[29]

It also explains that rules are often issued very quickly where an urgent need is felt (Code of Conduct for the Nigerian Armed Forces at the occasion of the Biafra conflict) or where at least a special interest provides for the acceleration of the process, be it only that an administration (or a specific part) considers it as a question of prestige to have a good implementing record.[30]

3.4   *Countervailing Interests*

The last and perhaps most difficult problem in relation to our problem is the existence of certain interest which militate against, or against faithful, implementation. It is common knowledge that objections have been raised against a number of provisions of the new Protocols for a variety of reasons, mainly what was called state sovereignty, and military security. The *Protocols* being a difficult compromise, not every government is entirely pleased with them. Within many governments, the views on these questions are far from being uniform.

As to the implementing process, this hinders effective implementation in two ways.

Where a certain part of the administration or the military establishment entirely dislike important elements of the new *Protocols* (this question apparently does not arise any more with the *Conventions* themselves) it may pressure not only against ratification, but also against implementation. It may also exert pressure for a certain (restrictive) interpretation when implementing rules are

---

29   For a text of the drafts bill, see ICRC, *loc. cit.* (*supra* note 8), Vol. I, p. 15.

30   The perhaps best known examples of internal rules transforming the international law of war into administrative regulations are the US Army Field Manual and the British Manual of Military Law, Part III (The Law of War on Land). A codification of the law of war by parliamentary legislation is the Italian Legge di guerra of 1938.

THE ROLE OF NATIONAL LAW

adopted. Where different views on the questions within governments, this in itself slows down the implementation process.

3.5 *Implementation and Interpretation*

The last point raises another fundamental issue with regard to implementation: the consistency between the implemented international norms and the national implementing devices.

In view of the difficulties of the problems involved, errors may occur anyways. This may, *inter alia*, be a problem with a special implementation document, the official national translation to be used where the national language is not one of the languages in which the *Protocols* are authentic. But, and this is probably more important, implementation (in this connection also: translation!) means interpretation. The text of the *Protocols* will have to be transformed into the elements which will be used as guidelines for concrete decisions. This transformation thus unfolds, clarifies, develops the original text. Where this original text is unclear, open to differing interpretation, it is quite possible to "solve" these uncertainties in the process of this transformation and give *Protocols* the meaning one wants them to have. Necessary as this clarification through transformation may be, there is a grave danger involved in it: that essential protective elements are act in good faith. A small illustration of the difficulties which may be encountered in this process of transformation is the fact that the concentration of the German text between the German speaking countries took place without the participation of the GDR – it is probably a good guess that the reason was a reluctance to make a linguistic enterprise a battlefield for fights about interpretation.

4   Some Suggested Solutions

Tentative as the hypothesis on problems and obstacles of national means of implementation are any solutions which might be suggested. But the hypothesis put forward imply some logical answers: dissemination, assistance, pressure or motivation, control.

The lack of awareness can and must be remedied by spreading this awareness among those whose task it would be to take the relevant steps for implementation. This is an aspect of dissemination. Dissemination will not just mean spreading the knowledge of the text, it means, in its more sophisticated form, drawing the attention of specific target groups to "their" specific task. The ICRC, in its dissemination activities, should make national means of implementation a focus of its activities.

686   PART 9: IMPLEMENTATION AND ENFORCEMENT OF IHL

4.1 *Assistance*

The lack of knowhow, of legal expertise can be overcome by adequate means of assistance, both in terms of financial and intellectual resources.[31] Art. 6 *Protocol I* (qualified persons) may be used for this purpose. Legal experts able to give advice on national means of implementation would be personnel having a task "to facilitate the application of the Conventions and the Protocol" within the meaning of this article. Another idea might be to draft at least certain elements of model statutes or regulations which could be used by States.

With respect to both suggestions, a *caveat* is necessary. As these national means of implementation have to fit into existing domestic legal and organizational structures, models tested in one country are not necessarily good for another, foreign advice based on the advisor's own national experience has to be given and accepted with a high degree a scepticism. The same is of course true for model rules which might be invented without reference to a particular national legal order. The transplantation of legal regulations from one legal system to another is like an organ transplantation: the transplanted element may be rejected by the new environment and not work well.

4.2 *Pressure or Motivation*

Inertia of bureaucracies may be overcome by providing some kind of motivation for activity. The diplomatic efforts of the ICRC to persuade relevant actors to do something are necessary also for the specific task discussed here.

But there is more: competition and prestige may be used as incentives. If there were some comparative publication of or on national means of implementation, States might consider it as a question of prestige to have a good implementation record. Measures to promote this will be discussed under the heading of control.

4.3 *Control*

Non-implementation or bad implementation through bad interpretation could be prevented or at least rendered more difficult through some kind of scrutiny.

So far, neither the *Conventions* nor the *Protocols* provide for any mechanism for this purpose. Such procedures could thus only be voluntary. There are, however, precedents for the creation of such voluntary controls through a

---

31   A good example for this is the work of an eminent Swiss criminal lawyer, J. Graven, on the Ethiopian Penal Code, *cf. G. Levasseur, R. Merle, loc. cit.* (*supra* note 8), p. 224.

reporting system established by resolutions which are not legally binding.[32] It thus seems possible and appropriate that a resolution of the International Red Cross Conference and/or of the United Nations General Assembly calls upon States to report biannually

a) if they are not yet Parties to the Protocols, on the progress of the ratification process,

b) on national measures taken for the implementation of the *Conventions* and the *Protocols*

These reports should be examined by a committee of experts to be established by the ICRC. The committee should report to the ICRC, and its report should be published. Its rules of procedure should make sure that the committee is not used as a forum to consider complaints against specific violations, because this would make the whole procedure unacceptable.

The creation of a reporting system for the second purpose just mentioned could also be considered by a meeting pursuant to Art. 7 *Protocol I*. The disadvantage of this procedure would be that it is restricted to the High Contracting Parties of *Protocol I*, and that it would thus not be possible to provide any mechanism of pressure for ratification. If a reporting system in a way makes life more difficult for the States Parties to the *Protocols*, it should at the same time do so for States not Parties.

---

32 An example are certain reporting procedures in the field of human rights, *cf.* United Nations Action in the Field of Human Rights, 1980, pp. 317 ff., in particular the system of periodic reports on human rights established by ECOSOC Resolution 624 B (XII) of 1 August 1956.

Printed in the United States
By Bookmasters